PEARSON

mymarketinglab™

Learn to think like a marketer using:

- **Study Plan:** The Study Plan helps ensure that students have a basic understanding of course material *before* coming to class by guiding them directly to the pages they need to review.
- **Mini-Simulations:** Move beyond the basics with interactive simulations that place students in a realistic marketing situation and require them to make decisions based on marketing concepts.
- **Applied Theories:** Get involved with detailed videos, interactive cases, and critical-thinking exercises.
- **Critical Thinking:** Experience real marketing situations that might not always have a right answer but will have a best answer. This allows for great discussion and debate with classmates.

And More:

- **Self-Assessments**
- **Videos**
- **Pearson eText**
- **Flash Cards**

Go to www.mypearsonmarketinglab.com

"Marketing: Defined, Explained, Applied by Michael Levens brings crisp clarity to each chapter's content. The text weaves concepts around examples in a direct way, not seen before. I receive great student reviews on this text and that really helps with engagement all semester long."

Arlene Peltola
Cedar Crest College

"Levens' Marketing: Defined, Explained, Applied is a concise yet complete introduction to marketing concepts. I use it for sections of marketing concepts for both business majors and non-business majors. With its engaging format and timely, relevant examples this is a text that our students actually read!"

Susan Carder
Northern Arizona University

"Short examples at the end of every few paragraphs or every section help students understand the material better. Students no longer have the time to sit down, read long chapters, and remember every detail in every chapter. This is a real marketing book, yet accommodating to the fast-paced lives of American students. It's perfect . . . I love it!"

Bridget Jones, Student
Virginia Commonwealth University

Marketing: Defined, Explained, Applied

Second Edition

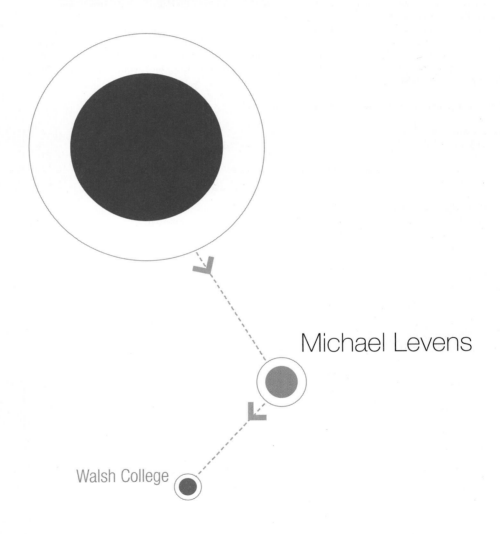

Michael Levens

Walsh College

Prentice Hall

Boston Columbus Indianapolis New York San Francisco Upper Saddle River
Amsterdam Cape Town Dubai London Madrid Milan Munich Paris Montréal Toronto
Delhi Mexico City São Paulo Sydney Hong Kong Seoul Singapore Taipei Tokyo

Editorial Director: Sally Yagan
Editor in Chief: Eric Svendsen
Executive Editor: Melissa Sabella
Editorial Project Manager: Kierra Bloom
Development Editor: Laura Town
Director of Editorial Services: Ashley Santora
Editorial Assistant: Elisabeth Scarpa
Director of Marketing: Patrice Lumumba Jones
Senior Marketing Manager: Anne Fahlgren
Marketing Assistant: Melinda Jensen
Senior Managing Editor: Judy Leale
Sr. Production Project Manager/Supervisor: Lynn Savino Wendel
Senior Operations Supervisor: Arnold Vila
Operations Specialist: Cathleen Petersen
Sr. Art Director/Design Supervisor: Janet Slowik
Art Director: Steven Frim
Text and Cover Designer: Michael Fruhbeis
Cover Art: Shutterstock
Manager, Rights and Permissions: Hessa Albader
Editorial Media Project Manager: Denise Vaughn
MyLab Product Manager: Joan Waxman
Media Project Manager: Lisa Rinaldi
Full-Service Project Management: Bookmasters, Inc.
Composition: Integra Software Services, Ltd.
Printer/Binder: Courier/Kendallville
Cover Printer: Lehigh-Phoenix Color/Hagerstown
Text Font: 10/12 Minion

Credits and acknowledgments borrowed from other sources and reproduced, with permission, in this textbook appear on appropriate page within text.

Library of Congress Cataloging-in-Publication Data

Levens, Michael.
Marketing : defined, explained, applied / Michael Levens.—2nd ed.
p. cm.
Includes bibliographical references and index.
ISBN 978-0-13-217715-3 (pbk. : alk. paper)
1. Marketing. I. Title.
HF5415.L47568 2011
658.8—dc22 2010039067

Prentice Hall
is an imprint of

PEARSON

www.pearsonhighered.com

10 9 8 7 6 5 4 3 2 1
ISBN 10: 0-13-217715-3
ISBN 13: 978-0-13-217715-3

Brief Contents

Contents

About the Author

Michael Levens is Chair of Business Administration and Marketing at Walsh College. Dr. Levens has previously served as the Head of Consumer Research and Innovation at OnStar, Brand Manager at SAAB, and has held a variety of marketing leadership positions at General Motors. Dr. Levens has extensive global experience working in 25 countries on five continents and also has award-winning entrepreneurial experience with a business start-up, receiving Global 1st Runner-up honors in the 1995 International Entrepreneurial Challenge (MOOT CORP®).

Educated in the United States and Australia, Dr. Levens holds a Postdoctoral Qualification in Marketing and Management from the A.B. Freeman School of Business at Tulane University, Ph.D. in Organization and Management (Marketing) from Capella University, M.B.A. from Bond University, and B.S. in Management Systems (Marketing) from Kettering University. His research is focused on affluent consumer behavior and non-traditional bundling strategies. Dr. Levens has conducted more than 100 research projects throughout the world and has presented his research at conferences hosted by the Advertising Research Foundation, American Marketing Association, Association of Marketing Theory and Practice, Automotive Market Research Council, and the Canadian Marketing Association. He regularly provides consulting services to Fortune 100 companies and consults pro bono for major not-for-profits. Dr. Levens is a Fellow of the Chartered Institute of Marketing and has been named to the Fulbright Specialist Roster. He is also active in the American Marketing Association, Detroit Economic Club, and MENSA. Dr. Levens has been appointed to three different boards of directors and presently serves as a Director and Marketing Chair of the Eisenhower Dance Ensemble.

Marketing: Defined, Explained, Applied

Michael Levens

The Meaning of **Marketing**

Chapter Overview Everyone has some experience with marketing. Whether or not you have worked in a marketing position in an organization, you have certainly been exposed to advertising, evaluated sales offers, made purchase decisions, and promoted yourself in some capacity, such as applying to a college or university. These, and many other aspects of everyday life, place you in marketing situations.

Of course, understanding marketing requires much more than simply recalling and becoming aware of everyday experiences. Understanding marketing requires a familiarity with the strategies that businesses use to create awareness and interest in their products and services. Understanding marketing also requires a familiarity with the processes that consumers knowingly and unknowingly follow when evaluating and making purchase decisions. In addition, understanding marketing requires that you have knowledge of the various activities that marketing comprises, including those tasks that promote and enable transfer of ownership, enable flow of goods from manufacturer to consumer, and help facilitate completion of the first two categories of tasks. Understanding marketing also requires familiarity with disciplines, such as economics and psychology, that have provided context to what is currently known as marketing. This chapter is designed to provide a foundation for your study of marketing by explaining the meaning of marketing.

Chapter Outline

Marketing pp. 3–4

Objective 1. What is marketing?

Marketing Concept pp. 5–8

- **Evolution of Marketing: Early Years Until 1950** p. 6
- **Evolution of Marketing: 1950–Present** pp. 6–7
- **Evolution of Marketing: Social Responsibility** pp. 7–8

Objective 2. What is the marketing concept? How has marketing changed?

Marketing Functions pp. 9–10

- **Internal Marketing Participants** p. 9
- **External Marketing Participants** pp. 9–10

Objective 3. What are marketing functions? Who performs them?

MARKETING (pp. 3–4)

DEFINED **Marketing** *is an organizational function and a collection of processes designed to plan for, create, communicate, and deliver value to customers and to build effective customer relationships in ways that benefit the organization and its stakeholders.*[1]

EXPLAINED

Marketing

Marketing is a distinct activity within an organization, generally referred to as the marketing department. Marketing is also a set of tasks, such as assembling, pricing, and promoting, which may or may not be performed by the marketing department, that result in products, services, ideas, and other tangible and intangible items. Those items, in turn, produce profits or achieve some other stated goals for an organization and its stakeholders, including shareholders, employees, or donors. Profits or other organizational goals are achieved by creating value for consumers. The creation of **value** is the realization of benefits that are at parity or that exceed the cost of products, services, or other items. Customers, such as students, parents, professors, and the rest of society, search for value on a daily basis when making purchase decisions.

Marketing has grown from roots in economics, psychology, sociology, and statistics. One important concept that marketing has borrowed from the study of economics is the idea of utility. **Utility** is the satisfaction received from owning or consuming a product or service. Utility, in a marketing sense, is the value that consumers attach to that marketer's products or services. Supply and demand for products and services influence price, production costs influence supply, and utility influences demand. The utility that consumers attached to BMW products, and the subsequent increase in demand, influenced the German automaker to add U.S.-based production in Spartanburg, South Carolina, in 1994 and to greatly expand the manufacturing facility in 2006. Over 1.5 million BMWs have been produced in the automaker's first plant outside of Germany. Consumers are the ultimate adjudicators of utility. If consumers perceive that a particular product or service has utility, then they are inclined to consider purchasing that product or service.

A **need** is a necessity to meet an urgent requirement. A **want** is a desire for something that is not essential. For instance, a person has a need for food, but a person simply wants ice cream. There are strict definitions for wants and needs. However, businesses often use marketing to transform a want into a *perceived* need for a particular product or service. Businesses can increase **demand**, the financial capacity to buy what a person wants, for that business's brand of products or services through marketing activities such as advertising. A **brand** is a promise to deliver to consumers specific benefits associated with products or services. The brand can contrast the products or services of one company with the products or services of another company and, through effective marketing, command a perception of greater value that can lead to higher sales revenue and profits.

APPLIED

Marketing

In practice, marketing is much more than simply selling or advertising. Marketing influences you as a consumer through your current and future career choices, and through the economy. Businesses create value through their offerings, communicate that value to consumers, and then deliver value in exchange for money from consumers. Marketing applies to more than just products or services, however. Marketing extends to a variety of tangible and intangible items, including the following:

- Products
- Services
- People
- Places
- Causes
- Events
- Ideas

Facebook is a social networking utility created in 2004. Currently, Facebook has about 500 million users around the world and allows contacts with friends and colleagues to communicate and share photos, videos, and other links. People register with an e-mail address and join one or more networks based on companies, schools, or regions. In addition to allowing people to connect with each other, the site also has evolved as a marketing tool for individuals and businesses. The Facebook platform allows the hosting of events, such as the 2008 Presidential debates in partnership with ABC News, and also allows advertisements to be placed on networks. Target enjoyed considerable success through its involvement with Facebook. Target took its hip image to Facebook by sponsoring a page identified as the "Dorm Survival Guide." Target made considerable preparation for the page, including an effort to understand how users interact on Facebook. Based on that insight, discussion groups, decorating tips, and pictures of dorm rooms complemented the product information.

Target's initial campaign registered over 27,000 users and helped increase sales over 6% from the previous year. Target has continued to partner with Facebook in social media activities. The Target Rounders program uses college-age students to promote the company on Facebook in return for discounts and incentives.[2]

PHOTO: Lenscap/Alamy Image.

EXAMPLE MARKETING

The Corvette ZHZ, offered exclusively by Hertz as part of its "Fun Collection" vehicle rental portfolio in the United States, has both product and service characteristics. The vehicle is a product, but the rental is a service. The Hertz Corporation, the world's largest general-use car rental brand with 8,100 locations in 147 countries, creates value for its customers in a variety of ways. Some of those methods include working with General Motors, manufacturer of the Chevrolet Corvette, to offer a product that Hertz's competitors do not. Few people might rent the 436-horsepower Corvette ZHZ, but the Hertz vehicle rental portfolio also includes subcompacts to minivans to luxury cars, and those choices are presented to consumers as innovative and contemporary.[3]

PHOTO: © 2010 Hertz System, Inc. Hertz is a registered service mark and trademark of Hertz System, Inc.

>> END EXAMPLE

Products include items often used or consumed for personal use, such as shavers or ice cream, and items that are consumed by businesses or used to produce items that are resold, such as raw materials or components. Services include items that are used and not retained by the consumer, for example, a massage or a haircut, and items that are used and not retained by businesses, such as repair or maintenance services.

Beyond products and services, many other items can also be marketed. People such as celebrities, athletes, and politicians are engaged in marketing themselves and building their own brands. Similarly, as you build your career, you will constantly be marketing yourself to others. Places, from London to New York, can also be marketed. Place marketing can be designed to accomplish one of a wide variety of objectives, such as introducing potential visitors to a place with which they may not be familiar, reinventing a location to stand for something different from what it is currently known as, or encouraging more frequent visits. Causes, including many not-for-profit organizations such as the Humane Society, museums, and art institutes, are also marketed to potential donors and to those who may use the services of the not-for-profit. Events, such as the Olympics, the Super Bowl, and the World Cup, market themselves, but also serve as marketing platforms for other businesses. Ideas, such as anti-littering campaigns and political views, as well as concepts and messages, are also marketed.

MARKETING Concept (pp. 5–8)

DEFINED *The **marketing concept** is an organizational philosophy dedicated to understanding and fulfilling consumer needs through the creation of value.*

EXPLAINED

Marketing Concept

Marketing, as stated earlier, involves the creation of value that results in effective customer relationships. **Customer relationships** are created when businesses and consumers interact through a sales transaction of a product or service and continue that relationship based on ongoing interaction between the business and the customer. The management of customer relationships, commonly referred to as **customer relationship management (CRM)**, involves those elements of business strategy that enable meaningful, personalized communication between businesses and customers. CRM is composed of activities that are used to establish, develop, and maintain customer relationships. For example, customer-generated reviews can create a feedback mechanism and reinforce a strong relationship between businesses and customers. The understanding and interaction with customers becomes increasingly important as customers have greater access to information about different choices. By implementing CRM, a business is committing to understanding customer lifetime value. **Customer lifetime value** includes the projected sales revenue and profitability that a customer could provide to a firm. If customer relationships serve as the foundation for marketing activities, then a business is practicing the marketing concept. CRM and associated concepts are discussed in greater detail in Chapter 6.

APPLIED

Marketing Concept

Although generally considered a contemporary idea, the marketing concept has been used for many years, in practice, if not in name, by businesses trying to distinguish themselves from their competition by focusing on the customer. L.L.Bean founded its business in 1912 by referring to the customer as " . . . the most important person ever in this office—in person or by mail." L.L.Bean developed a marketing philosophy based on customer service and marketed a guarantee to provide " . . . perfect satisfaction in every way."[4] Currently, many businesses, as well as churches, schools, and state and local tourism entities, practice the marketing concept by focusing on fulfilling the expectations of their customers.

EXAMPLE MARKETING CONCEPT

Missouri began an advertising campaign in 2008 with its central message: "Close to home. Far from ordinary." This message is designed to attract visitors from nearby states. The idea is that visitors will drive to Missouri and experience the wide range of activities available. The message concentrates on the actual experience of travel, and not simply the destination. Practicing the marketing concept, this advertising has targeted specific groups of individuals, including families, young women, and baby boomers. By targeting certain groups, Missouri can create tailored messages that in turn create additional value that surpasses the value that might be obtained by communicating a broader message to the entire population.

Contrast Missouri's advertising campaign to the Las Vegas advertising campaign. Look at the two ads, and you can see that they appeal to different groups. After Las Vegas moved away from previous advertising as a family destination, the "what happens here, stays here" advertising campaign clearly establishes Las Vegas as an adults-only playground. The campaign focuses on the core benefit of a wide range of adult activities and targets those who place value on those activities. Las Vegas's advertising campaign even inspired the 2008 movie *What Happens in Vegas*.[5]

PHOTO: Missouri Tourism Commission.

>> END EXAMPLE

Evolution of Marketing: Early Years Until 1950

Sales and marketing activities have existed in varying forms throughout time, from ancient civilizations through the modern era. Traditionally, the marketing emphasis was placed on the production of crafts, agricultural products, and other goods for sale through local markets. Over time, distinctive marks and designs such as cattle brands were associated with these products to distinguish one seller from another.

The early years of American marketing included advertisements that were placed in newly created media, such as newspapers and magazines, as well as the formation of the first advertising agency in the United States. In 1704, the *Boston News-Letter* published the first newspaper advertisement offering items for sale. The advertisement was for real estate on Oyster Bay, Long Island.[6] The first American magazine ads were published in Benjamin Franklin's *General Magazine* in 1742.[7] The first advertising agency was opened in Philadelphia in 1843.[8]

Sales opportunities in the United States expanded rapidly after the Revolutionary War as individuals moved across the country selling products such as clocks and books.[9] These sales roles evolved to salespeople managing orders for newly formed manufacturing companies of the nineteenth century.[10]

Through the early part of the twentieth century, both marketing and sales activities were designed to support production. Products were often created, and then customers were sought. The **production orientation** reflects a business focus on efficient production and distribution with little emphasis on any marketing strategy. This period existed roughly from the mid-1800s until the 1920s. With the advent of the Great Depression in the late 1920s and early 1930s, and the resulting increase in product inventory, the sales function became a primary activity and was considered synonymous with marketing. A **sales orientation** reflects a business focus on advertising and personal selling to create demand and move product inventory. This period lasted from the 1930s into the 1950s.

Evolution of Marketing: 1950–Present

From the 1950s into the 1980s, companies generally focused on the needs and wants of consumers more than they did in prior years. A **consumer orientation** reflects a business focus on satisfying unmet consumer needs and wants. Also in the 1980s, businesses began to consider not only consumers but also suppliers as sources of value-based relationships. A **relationship orientation** reflects a business focus on creating value-added relationships with both suppliers and consumers. A value-added relationship is much more than buying and selling. The idea of value-added relationships involves business practices that support long-term relationships. These relationships may incur short-term costs, such as additional customer support and enhanced after-sales service, but are intended to reinforce the value of the product or service, relative to the competition.

EXAMPLE **EVOLUTION OF MARKETING: 1950–PRESENT**

Work to Live
not live to Work
KELLY
Talent at work

Kelly Services, operating in 37 countries and territories and providing employment to over 750,000 employees annually, provides business services, such as temporary staffing services and outsourcing solutions, and consumer services, such as temporary and full-time job placement. Kelly's marketing efforts are targeted both to employers and to workers who are unemployed or looking to change careers. Kelly's "work to live, not live to work" advertising is targeted primarily toward workers and creates value for them by identifying with an individual's desire to balance work and home life. Kelly's communication to employers is designed to address specific needs in automotive, contact center, education, electronic assembly, engineering, finance and accounting, health care, information technology, legal, light industrial, marketing, office, scientific, and security clearance. Kelly's consulting and outsourcing activity uses the advertising message "If it's outside your scope, it's probably within ours." Value is created for business clients by offering expertise in specific employment fields.

PHOTO: © 2008 Kelly Services, Inc.

>> END EXAMPLE

Evolution of Marketing: Social Responsibility

During the last decade, there has been an increased focus on social responsibility, ethics, and accountability in business. The overriding idea is that a person (or business) can make money by focusing on socially responsible marketing activities and abiding by high ethical standards. Social responsibility is the idea that businesses consider society as a whole as one of their stakeholders and that businesses make decisions that take into account the well-being of society. For example, organizations such as the American Marketing Association (AMA) developed standards of ethical behavior for marketers.

A major issue that organizations must consider when practicing socially responsible marketing involves how products affect the global environment. Everything from the pollution generated by producing the products, forms of packaging used and their potential for recycling, and the amount of energy used to consume products must be considered. Some organizations adopt operating standards that govern their socially responsible marketing practices, while others choose to financially support causes that benefit society. Many accomplish both by developing green marketing products and supporting cause-marketing activities. Socially responsible marketing can be both altruistic and profitable. A recent study by Cone LLC found that two-thirds of Americans claim that they consider a company's business practices when making purchase decisions.[11] Social responsibility and related concepts are discussed in greater detail in Chapter 4.

EXAMPLE **EVOLUTION OF MARKETING: SOCIAL RESPONSIBILITY**

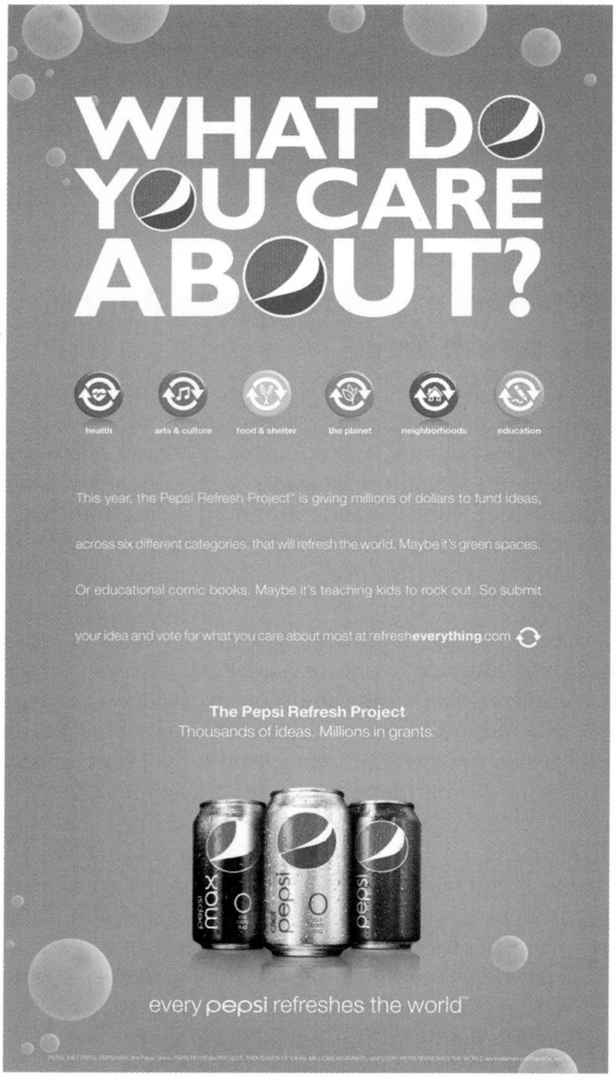

Pepsi, a PepsiCo brand sold in 200 countries, made a major decision in 2010 by electing not to run its traditional Super Bowl advertisement and, instead, launched a $20 million social responsibility campaign. The Pepsi Refresh Project was designed to provide millions of dollars to fund ideas that will "refresh" the world. Pepsi launched an advertising campaign using television; online sources including Facebook, Twitter, and YouTube; radio; print; and outdoor billboards inviting people, businesses, and nonprofits to submit ideas that would have a positive impact on the world; these ideas were eligible within six categories: Health, Arts & Culture, Food & Shelter, The Planet, Neighborhoods, and Education. Each month, visitors to its Web site voted on the ideas. At the end of the month, finalists were selected to receive grant money—up to $1.3 million. Pepsi's objective was to create more two-way communication and to establish deeper relationships with its customers than can typically be achieved through more traditional advertising campaigns.[12]

PHOTO: PepsiCo Inc.

>> **END EXAMPLE**

MARKETING Functions (pp. 9–10)

DEFINED **Marketing functions** *are activities performed within organizations that create value for specific products or services.*

EXPLAINED

Marketing Functions

Noted management guru Peter Drucker identified the critical role that marketing performs for business: "Because the purpose of business is to create a customer, the business enterprise has two—and only two—basic functions: marketing and innovation. Marketing and innovation produce results; all the rest are costs. Marketing is the distinguishing, unique function of the business."[13] The process of creating value through uniqueness occurs well before and well after the selling process. Marketing functions can be grouped into three general categories with functions from each category occurring throughout the marketing process. The three categories are the following:

- Exchange functions
- Physical functions
- Facilitating functions

Exchange functions are activities that promote and enable transfer of ownership. Examples of exchange functions include buying, selling, and pricing, as well as advertising, sales promotion, and public relations. **Physical functions** are activities that enable the flow of goods from manufacturer to consumer. Examples of physical functions include assembling, transporting and handling, warehousing, processing and packaging, standardizing, and grading. **Facilitating functions** are activities that assist in the execution of exchange and physical functions. Examples of facilitating functions include financing and risk-taking, marketing information and research, as well as the promise of servicing.

Internal Marketing Participants

There are many different marketing stakeholders. Those stakeholders within a business or with direct oversight include the following:

- Marketing department
- Other business departments
- Business leadership/board of directors

The marketing department performs a primary role in managing marketing functions, including activities such as establishing a product or service portfolio, determining pricing, establishing distribution channels, and creating promotions. These elements compose the most common representation of the marketing mix, referred to as the **4 Ps** (Product, Price, Place, and Promotion). The marketing mix is a collection of marketing variables that are managed to achieve the desired sales performance in a target market. In addition, functions such as defining the brand and creating a CRM process are all activities performed by the marketing department.

Other business departments, such as finance, use marketing information and contribute to marketing activities in a variety of ways, including securing financing for expanded manufacturing or by providing cost information to marketing to assist in understanding the profitability of marketing decisions. Persons in positions of business leadership, such as the president or chief operating officer, and the board of directors also consume marketing information and make decisions to support or limit marketing activities through resource allocation.

External Marketing Participants

There are a number of marketing stakeholders that operate outside a business, yet have tremendous influence on marketing activities. They include the following:

- Investors
- Consumers/customers
- Advertising/PR agency
- Information providers/marketing research companies
- Government
- Partners
- Competitors

Investors can influence marketing ideas through letters to management and through attending shareholder meetings. Recent investor actions have included proposals to practice more socially responsible marketing.

Consumers and customers influence marketing through purchase decisions and feedback on survey questions. Advertising and public relations companies assist businesses in understanding consumers and customers, as well as in presenting products and services in the most favorable perspective through the creation of media content. Information providers and marketing research companies collect a wide range of consumer and market information for marketing departments. Whether studying the success of advertising or the product desires of consumers, the collection of information is critical to marketing decisions.

The government primarily influences marketing through legislation or regulation. Partners, other businesses or organizations that already work with or may work with a particular business, influence marketing choices by presenting opportunities to reach more consumers or to share in the cost of marketing activities. Competitors also influence marketing actions by their advertising investment and product launches. Thus, there are many marketing stakeholders, and their collective efforts will ultimately define the level of success a business will realize in their marketing practices.

EXAMPLE **EXTERNAL MARKETING PARTICIPANTS**

At Gongos Research,
we understand the big picture.
We get that you need
that "aha" moment.
In fact, we'll discover
plenty of them for you.
Not only do we find the
story behind the data,
we provide the insights
you need to create
products and services
consumers will love.
gon
gos
research
Gongos: the step between guessing and knowing

When people think of marketing research, they tend to think of receiving phone calls during dinner and being stopped at shopping malls to complete surveys. In fact, the marketing research field is far more complex. Gongos Research is a custom marketing research company that has enjoyed rapid growth through the use of technology and innovation such as i°Communities and metaCommunities. These are private online communities of individuals who have chosen to become active in the communities' social aspects (such as creating their own discussion groups) and business aspects (such as completing surveys), and are compensated for their involvement. Gongos Research assists a wide range of businesses in many different business sectors, including financial services, automotive, powersports, and consumer products.

PHOTO: Courtesy of Gongos Research, Inc.

>> **END EXAMPLE**

APPLIED

Marketing Functions

In practice, some businesses view marketing from a limited perspective by considering it synonymous to sales or advertising. Other businesses understand that marketing performs a broad range of functions, ranging from securing products to servicing products after a sale, and that the marketing activity is connected to all other business functions. Successful businesses generally consider marketing departments as the link between customers and businesses. Marketing departments are in a unique position to identify and communicate customer requirements to other departments within an organization, such as finance, accounting, manufacturing, and business planning.

Visual Summary

Part 1 **Explaining (Chapters 1, 2, 3, 4, 5)**
Part 2 Creating (Chapters 6, 7, 8, 9)
Part 3 Strategizing (Chapters 10, 11)
Part 4 Managing (Chapters 12, 13, 14, 15, 16, 17)
Part 5 Integrating (Chapters 18, 19, 20)

Chapter 1 Summary

Building on the idea that everyone has some experience with marketing, the concept of marketing and marketing functions was developed and expanded. Marketing involves the creation of value that results in effective customer relationships. Marketing is used for a variety of tangible and intangible items, including the following:

- Products
- Services
- People
- Places
- Causes
- Events
- Ideas

Marketing functions are the tasks that are applied to the various items that can be marketed. Marketing functions can be grouped into three general categories:

- Exchange functions
- Physical functions
- Facilitating functions

A variety of marketing stakeholders either utilize or contribute to marketing activities:

- Marketing department
- Other business departments
- Business leadership/board of directors
- Investors
- Consumers/customers
- Advertising/PR agency
- Information providers/marketing research companies
- Government
- Partners
- Competitors

Marketing pp. 3–4
value
Marketing is about creating value that leads to effective customer relationships.
Marketing Concept pp. 5–8
philosophy
The marketing concept is an organizational philosophy built on customer lifetime value.
Marketing Functions pp. 9–10
activities
Marketing functions are activities that facilitate, promote, or enable transfer of ownership and flow of goods from manufacturer to consumer.
Capstone Exercise p. 13

Chapter Key Terms

Marketing (pp. 3–4)

Marketing *is an organizational function and a collection of processes designed to plan for, create, communicate, and deliver value to customers and to build effective customer relationships in ways that benefit the organization and its stakeholders. (p. 3)* **Opening Example (pp. 3–4) Example: Marketing (p. 4)**

Key Terms (p. 3)

Brand is a promise to deliver specific benefits associated with products or services to consumers. **(p. 3)**
Demand is the financial capacity to buy what one wants. **(p. 3)**
Need is a necessity to meet an urgent requirement. **(p. 3)**
Utility is the satisfaction received from owning or consuming a product or service. **(p. 3)**
Value is the benefits that exceed the cost of products, services, or other items. **(p. 3)**
Want is a desire for something that is not essential. **(p. 3)**

Marketing Concept (pp. 5–8)

Marketing concept *is an organizational philosophy dedicated to understanding and fulfilling consumer needs through the creation of value. (p. 5)* **Example: Marketing Concept (pp. 5–6) Example: Social Responsibility (p. 8)**

Key Terms (pp. 5–7)

Consumer orientation reflects a business focus on satisfying unmet consumer needs and wants. **(p. 6)**
Customer lifetime value is the present value of all profits expected to be earned from a customer over the lifetime of the customer's relationship with a company. **(p. 5)**
Customer relationship management (CRM) is the activities that are used to establish, develop, and maintain customer relationships. **(p. 5)**
Customer relationships are created when businesses and consumers interact through a sales transaction of a product or service and continue based on ongoing interaction between the business and the consumer. **(p. 5)**
Production orientation reflects a business focus on efficient production and distribution with little emphasis on any marketing strategy. **(p. 6)**
Relationship orientation reflects a business focus on creating value-added relationships with suppliers and consumers. **(p. 6) Example: Evolution of Marketing 1950–Present (p. 7)**
Sales orientation reflects a business focus on advertising and personal selling to create demand and move product inventory. **(p. 6)**

Marketing Functions (pp. 9–10)

Marketing functions *are activities performed both by consumers and by businesses involved in value creation for specific products or services. (p. 9)* **Example: External Market Participants (p. 10)**

Key Terms (p. 9)

4 Ps are the most common classification of a marketing mix and consist of product, price, place, and promotion. **(p. 9)**
Exchange functions are activities that promote and enable transfer of ownership. **(p. 9)**
Facilitating functions are activities that assist in the execution of exchange and physical functions. **(p. 9)**
Physical functions are activities that enable the flow of goods from manufacturer to consumer. **(p. 9)**

Capstone Exercise

One aspect of marketing is the art of making people want something that they may not need. Of course, as a socially responsible marketer, we are not advocating that you mislead people with your promotions or advertising.

The key is to understand what people want versus what they need. Your personal wants and needs change, depending on your economic position, your age, your gender, and where you live.

1. Write one sentence describing a need, and write one sentence describing a want.
2. Make a list of 10 items that you want and 10 items that you need.
3. Compare your list with the list of someone of the opposite gender. Can you explain the differences?
4. Ask someone who is at least 10 years older or younger than you to make the same list, and then compare the two lists. What are the differences? What are the reasons for those differences? If you had more or less money, would your list change?
5. Think about what would be on your list if you lived in another country. What about if you lived in the Sudan in Africa, versus if you lived in France in Europe?
6. The key to this exercise is try to understand why some of the things you think you need are really things you want. Why are things that are really wants on your needs list?

Application Exercise

Use the following marketing concepts in this chapter to tackle and solve a marketing problem: value, utility, the marketing concept, want, and need.

First, start by thinking about health care products. Health care, in general terms, is the treatment and prevention of illness. There are many products available in grocery stores, drug stores, discount stores, etc., within this category for us to consider purchasing.

The Marketing Problem

Choose a product in the health care category after considering the following situation.

> You feel you may be catching a cold and stop by your local store to check out the products in their heath care section.

The Problem

Describe a product that helps relieve cold symptoms in the health care category. What is the product's value? Utility? What prompted you to buy it, a want or a need?

The Solution

Complete the following Problem/Solution brief using your product in the health care category, chapter concepts, and college resources.

1. From the Marketing Manager's Point of View
   a. Problem Definition
   b. Analysis
   c. Product's Value
   d. Target Market
   e. Solution
2. From the Consumer's Point of View
   a. Problem Definition
   b. Analysis
   c. Product's Value
   d. Is Product a Want or Need?
   e. Solution

Resources:

Marketing Defined, Explained, Applied 2e, Michael Levens
The College Library
Retail or Online Field Trip
Assigned Reading—*Brand Week, Advertising Age, WSJ,* scholarly publications, category trade journals
Blog your problem from either point of view, gather responses/posts (www.blogger.com/start)

The **Market** in **Marketing**

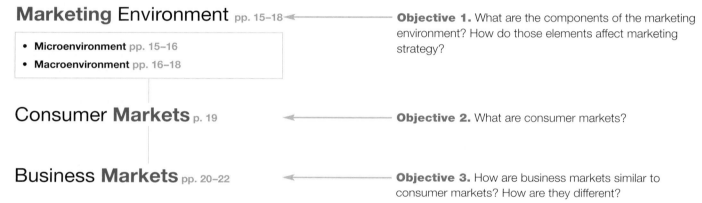

Chapter Overview In the previous chapter the concepts of marketing and marketing functions were presented and developed, based on the idea that everyone has at least some experience with marketing. This chapter expands those comments by considering the elements of the marketing environment. In addition, consumer markets are discussed as well as business markets.

Chapter Outline

MARKETING Environment (pp. 15–18)

DEFINED *The* **marketing environment** *is a set of forces, some controllable and some uncontrollable, that influence the ability of a business to create value and attract and serve customers.*

EXPLAINED

Marketing Environment

Businesses strive to create value that leads to productive customer relationships. Many factors influence value creation and the nature of customer relationships, including factors that are internal to the business and factors that are external to the business. The **internal environment** of a business involves all those activities, including marketing, that occur within the organizational functions in a business. **Internal marketing** is the implementation of marketing practices within an organization to communicate organizational policies and practices to employees and internal stakeholders. The topics of internal marketing efforts are the business's resources, including human and financial capital, as well as intangible assets, such as brands or patents. These factors represent many of the elements that can influence changes within a business.

The **external environment** of a business involves all activities, such as supplier and customer actions, that occur outside the organizational functions of a business. **External marketing** is the implementation of marketing practices directed outside the business to create value and to form productive customer relationships. External marketing influences the external environment in distinct areas, including the microenvironment and the macroenvironment, which can either enhance or diminish the ability of a business to create value for its customers.

APPLIED

Marketing Environment

In practice, businesses typically concentrate their efforts on developing strategies that assist in managing the microenvironment. The increasing sophistication of methods to gather marketing research information, from checkout scanner data to purchase transaction databases, allows for quicker responses to changes in the microenvironment. More companies are realizing the importance of internal marketing to employees and internal stakeholders. Such internal marketing communicates the values and expectations of the business and creates business proponents in the marketplace when the employees interact with others. Many companies are also engaged in lobbying the U.S. government and governments of other countries to influence the macroenvironment. Businesses, however, typically do not directly influence the macroenvironment.

Microenvironment

The **microenvironment** includes those forces close to a company, yet outside its internal environment, that influence the ability of a business to serve its customers.[1] The microenvironment comprises entities such as customers, suppliers, competitors, and other businesses that assist or influence a business's ability to sell, distribute, promote, and develop products or services.

A tool that helps determine where power exists in the microenvironment of a business is Porter's Five Forces of Competitive Position Model.[2] The Porter analysis can assist a business with understanding the potential for new product development, the attractiveness of a particular market segment, or the potential to reduce costs of supply or distribution, among many other applications.

The central concept of the Five Forces of Competitive Position Model is that five forces determine the power in a business's microenvironment. Those forces are the following:

- Threat of new entrants
- Bargaining power of suppliers
- Bargaining power of customers
- Threat of substitute products
- Competitive rivalry within an industry

The Health Care and Education Reconciliation Act was signed into law by President Barack Obama on March 30, 2010. Building on its predecessor, the Patient Protection and Affordable Care Act, the health care initiative affected both consumers and businesses in a variety of ways. Coverage is expanded over several years to 32 million Americans who were uninsured at the time of the bill signing. Some other elements of the law include the creation of state-based health care exchanges for the uninsured and self-employed, families with income under a particular level are subsidized, Medicare prescription drug assistance is provided, Medicaid coverage is expanded, insurance companies are forbidden from denying coverage to certain groups of individuals such as children and individuals with pre-existing conditions, and most individuals are mandated to purchase insurance. The implications are extensive. Demand for medical services and hospitals will most likely increase. The HMO industry will most likely be negatively impacted through increased competition and governmental mandates. Individuals may also have new or different choices as the law is implemented. There will be a variety of exchanges of information, and marketing activities, among the government, individuals, insurance companies, health care providers, and many other entities impacted by this law.[3]

PHOTO: Pincasso/Shutterstock.

The threat of new entrants can influence a business's level of power in an industry by the existing barriers to entry. Strong barriers to entry, such as intellectual property or economies of scale, provide a company power to resist new entrants.

Suppliers can assert power if they are the only one or one of a few businesses that can provide a particular product or service. Buyers (or customers) can also exert power on a business through the number and nature of buyers. The more buyers that are available, the less important an individual buyer is to a business. The fewer buyers that are available, the more power they can project. In some cases, one buyer, such as Walmart, is so large that it constitutes a significant percentage of total purchases from a business.

The threat of substitutes can reduce the power of a business if many substitutes exist for a particular product or service. If a product exists that is tied to another product, such as certain technical computer software, there is less threat from substitutes.

The nature of the rivalry among existing industry competitors influences the balance of power in the industry. Any change in status, whether it be the quantity and size of competing businesses, their portfolio, or their financial position, will influence the power any one business can exert on the industry.

EXAMPLE MICROENVIRONMENT

OnStar, a subsidiary of General Motors (GM) that provides subscription-based communication, tracking, diagnostic, navigation, emergency response, and other convenience services, is available on most GM vehicles and a few non-GM models. The product, referred to as telematics, is a combination of telecommunications and informatics/computer science. It consists of a mobile phone, onboard computer, sensors, and a Global Positioning System beacon. The product is available at no charge for a specific duration when an eligible new vehicle is purchased. After an initial period the service is subscription-based priced at approximately $200 annually. While unique to certain vehicles, many of the OnStar services have substitute products available. A mobile telephone could be considered a substitute for the OnStar hands-free calling service, a roadside service such as the American Automobile Association could be considered a substitute for OnStar's roadside assistance, and a portable navigation system could be considered a substitute for OnStar's Turn-by-Turn Navigation. The value that customers attribute to substitute products, including considerations such as switching costs, ease of use, and capability, influences the value that the customers attribute to the bundle of OnStar services.[4]

PHOTO: dundanim/Shutterstock

>> END EXAMPLE

Macroenvironment

The **macroenvironment** includes societal forces that are essentially uncontrollable and influence the microenvironment of a business. Part of the external environment of a business, the macroenvironment contains the following variety of sub-environments:

- Economic
- Social and cultural
- Competitive
- Legal
- Political
- Technological

EXAMPLE MACROENVIRONMENT

A legislative change can create challenges for some businesses, and opportunities for others. As a result of a 2010 law requiring newly manufactured diesel-fueled trucks to meet new environmental emission standards, a New Jersey–based motor oil and fluid manufacturer and supplier, Prime Lube, looked to Europe, which has been dealing with similar standards since early 2000, for potential partners. Prime Lube became one of the first U.S. distributors of the German product BlueSky Diesel Exhaust Fluid, and began manufacturing it in the United States in July 2010. BlueSky is injected into the catalytic converter of a truck in a mist form where it interacts with nitrous oxide, the black soot that is released from most diesel exhaust systems, and converts it to water and carbon dioxide. The result is close to zero emissions. Prime Lube took advantage of a change in the macroenvironment to secure a new product that solves challenges for its customers before its competitors could do so.[5]

PHOTO: Jack Cronkhite/Shutterstock.

>> END EXAMPLE

Economic Environment

As mentioned, one of the components of the macroenvironment is the economic environment. The **economic environment** includes factors that influence consumer purchase ability and buying behavior. Inflation rates, income levels, and unemployment levels all contribute to the economic environment. **Inflation** is an increase in the price of a collection of goods that represents the overall economy. As inflation increases, prices of items such as gasoline, food, and health services generally rise, and, if average income does not keep pace, products and services can become too expensive for consumers. The result is that demand generally decreases either voluntarily or involuntarily. **Income levels** are average consumer earnings used to approximate national earnings. Changes in income inversely relate to changes in demand. **Unemployment levels** are the number of unemployed persons divided by the aggregate labor force. Increases in unemployment reduce the ability of individuals to purchase products and services.

Social and Cultural Environment

The **social and cultural environment** includes factors that relate marketing to the needs and wants of society and culture. Changes in various types of demographics contribute to the social and cultural environment. **Demographics** are characteristics of human population that are used to identify markets. These characteristics include elements such as age, race, and household structure. As consumers age, levels of income generally increase and life stages change. The result is differing product and service demands. Businesses must carefully track changes such as age to make sure their portfolio continues to provide value to a market of relevant size. The United States is becoming an increasingly diverse market. As population segments such as Hispanics, Asian Americans, and African Americans increase, product and service requirements and different advertising methods change to reach diverse audiences. Household structure is also changing. There are more single-family households because people wait to marry later in life or not at all. The quantities and types of products and services produced need to reflect these realities.

EXAMPLE **ECONOMIC ENVIRONMENT**

The American Recovery and Reinvestment Act (ARRA) of 2009 included a number of either new or expanded tax benefits on expenditures to reduce energy use or create new energy sources. ARRA provided for a uniform credit of 30% of the cost of qualifying improvements up to $1,500. Expiring on December 31, 2010, the law sharply increased demand, during a very difficult economic time, for a wide range of products such as insulation, energy-efficient exterior windows and doors, and energy-efficient heating and air conditioning systems as well as contractor services.[6]

PHOTO: Christina Richards/Shutterstock.

>> END EXAMPLE

Competitive Environment

The **competitive environment** includes factors that relate to the nature, quantity, and potential actions of current and potential competitors. Changes in the context of competitors contribute to the competitive environment. If a business operates with a small number of competitors, there are fewer requirements to react to a competitive action and more time to make strategic decisions. In a competitive market, however, many more factors can impede a business from taking the actions that it wants to take. For example, if maintaining margins on products is important to generate money to fund important new product development, then a competitor's aggressive move to reduce price could hurt that business strategy. Maintaining margins would take second place to a need to respond to maintain market position.

EXAMPLE **COMPETITIVE ENVIRONMENT**

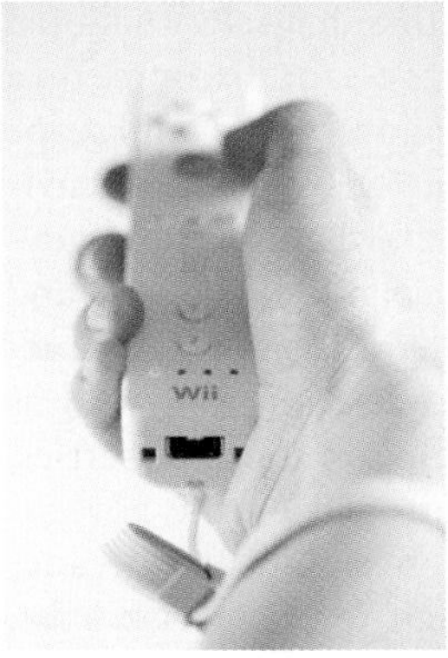

The 1972 launch of Pong, a video game that looked like video table tennis, is credited as greatly expanding the video game market. Pong first appeared in arcades, but Atari launched a home version in 1974. Atari's home version was a console-based game system that used cartridges and was wildly successful. In the early 1980s, competition from PC manufacturers and other video game manufacturers began eroding Atari's market share. A lack of product investment and oversupply of inventory, among other factors, caused a dramatic decline in Atari's fortunes. Atari struggles to this day.

In contrast, Nintendo entered the U.S. market in the early 1980s with its proprietary console, the Nintendo Entertainment System. Nintendo had to convince resellers to stock its product in light of Atari's problems. Nintendo reduced the risks of resellers by agreeing to take back products that did not sell. Nintendo carefully controlled its inventory and focused on building quality products. It built a strong market presence and used that presence to influence resellers to stock a higher share of its products than those of competitors. Nintendo enjoyed great success with this strategy and continues that success today with its Wii system, among other products.

PHOTO: ST Images/Alamy Images.

>> END EXAMPLE

Legal Environment

The **legal environment** includes factors that provide rules and penalties for violations, and is designed to protect society and consumers from unfair business practices and to protect businesses from unfair competitive practices. Changes in legislation and regulations contribute to the legal environment. There are many different categories of legislation, including trade practices (fair trade), business competition, product safety, environmental protection, consumer privacy, fair pricing, packaging, and advertising disclosure and restrictions. Regulatory agencies include the Federal Communications Commission (FCC), an agency responsible for regulating interstate and international communications by television, satellite, cable, radio, and wire; the U.S. Consumer Product Safety Commission (USCPSC), an agency responsible for protecting consumers from unreasonable risks of serious injury from over 15,000 types of consumer products; and the Food and Drug Administration (FDA), an agency within the Department of Health and Human Services that has nine different centers, ranging from radiological health to food safety. In addition to national governmental legislation and regulations, there are also state and local legal requirements. The legal environment can become even more complicated as businesses increase global activities and must deal with foreign governments' legal environments that are different from those within the United States.

Political Environment

The **political environment** includes factors that select national leadership, create laws, and provide a process for discourse on a wide range of issues. Changes in form of government and scope and type of social movements contribute to the political environment. A federal system of government, where a central government performs specific duties such as national defense and state and local governments have limited autonomy, is practiced in the United States. However, some countries, such as North Korea, are dictatorships. Everything in those countries, including commercial practices, is controlled by the government. The implications for businesses are significant, because investment may be restricted when high levels of risk exist. Social movements, either a new political party or cause, can also create trends such as interest in "green" or "fair trade" products. Whether protesting in cities or funding advocacy advertisements, these causes can have tremendous influence on consumer attitudes and interest in products or services.

Technological Environment

The **technological environment** includes factors that influence marketing based on scientific actions and innovation. Changes in consumer perspectives on scientific activities and new discoveries contribute to the technological environment. Policies on cloning, stem cell research, or other controversial topics influence marketing opportunities. Funding is either made available or is restricted based on consumer perspectives that are often translated into legal framework. New discoveries, such as fiber-optic cable and hybrid vehicle propulsion systems, create marketing opportunities where businesses can take advantage of creating value in a way that competitors cannot. Consumption patterns could change based on the significance of the product or service.

EXAMPLE TECHNOLOGICAL ENVIRONMENT

Even existing technology, when utilized in a different context, can create unique customer value. Domino's Pizza Tracker allows customers to follow the progress of their pizza from order through delivery via a Web interface. The interactive tool uses a customer phone number to identify status as the pizza passes through five distinct stages: Order Placed, Prep, Bake, Quality Check, and Out for Delivery. Advancing mobile technology will create further opportunities for Domino's and other pizza companies as well as companies involved with manufacturing and suppliers of other products and services.[7]

PHOTO: Rena Schild/Shutterstock.

>> END EXAMPLE

Consumer **MARKETS** (p. 19)

DEFINED **Consumer markets** *are the end user of the product or service and include individuals and households that are potential or actual buyers of products and services.*[8]

EXPLAINED

Consumer Markets

Both macroenvironments and microenvironments influence, through factors such as demand and supply, consumers and businesses as they make purchase decisions. U.S. consumer buying power exceeds $10 trillion.[9] Over one-third of that buying power comes from the California, Texas, New York, and Florida consumer markets.[10] Consumer markets exist with respect to the product or service being marketed and can be considered as broad as the population of an entire country for certain food products, or as small as the limited number of people who can afford to be space tourists. **Consumer products** are products that directly fulfill the desires of consumers and are not intended to assist in the manufacture of other products.[11] Consumers make purchase decisions in consumer markets by assessing the utility of the products and services offered. A **consumer's surplus** occurs when a consumer purchases a product or service at a price less than the utility of the product or service.[12] This surplus reflects a marketer's missed opportunity to charge more for products or services and reflects an advantage to consumers. However, a significant disparity between purchase price and perceived utility may cause consumers to question what might be wrong with the product or service to warrant such a discount. Ultimately, marketing links production and consumption in the consumer market.

APPLIED

Consumer Markets

In practice, purchase decisions in consumer markets are influenced heavily by the marketing and promotion of brands. Brands are used to convey value to consumers and conveying this value is accomplished through a wide range of marketing activities, including advertising and sales promotion. Marketing can be used to influence perceptions of utility and present one brand of product or service as different from another. Certain consumer markets, such as the market for shampoo and other personal care products, are saturated with brands, while others, such as the market for ultra luxury yachts, are served by few brands. Regardless of the number of competitors, each brand strives to be unique, as opposed to its competition, while remaining relevant to its consumer market.

Business MARKETS (pp. 20–22)

DEFINED **Business markets** *include individuals and organizations that are potential or actual buyers of goods and services that are used in, or in support of, the production of other products or services that are supplied to others.*[13]

EXPLAINED

Business Markets

Similar to consumers, businesses purchase many products and services to fulfill needs. Products and services are used to create other products and services. Products and services also are consumed by the business through the course of its normal operations. Participants in the business market include manufacturers, some of which may also sell directly to consumers, intermediaries, and entities that wholesale products. Participants also include business customers, for example, other businesses, institutions such as churches and universities, and governments, both United States and foreign. Businesses can be classified by several systems, including the **North American Industrial Classification System (NAICS)**, which classifies businesses operating in the United States, Canada, and Mexico into groups based on their activities. For example, paging services are classified as 513321. The first two numbers represent the sector, in this case information. The third digit represents the subsector of broadcasting and telecommunications. The fourth digit represents the industry group of telecommunications. The fifth digit represents the industry of wireless communication carriers, except satellite, and the sixth digit represents the U.S. paging industry.

Business-to-business, also referred to as **B2B**, involves the sale of products and services from one business to another. Businesses involved in B2B sales range in size from one-person small businesses to large multinational companies. Although different in size, firms operating in business markets face market characteristics that are similar to those businesses that operate in consumer markets. Compared to consumer markets, business markets generally are organized by similar geographic locations, such as automotive parts manufacturers clustering in southeastern Michigan.

B2B marketers tend to work with fewer but considerably larger customers than do consumer marketers. The consumer market does influence demand in the B2B market. **Derived demand** is the demand for a product or service that results from the demand for another product or service. Consider the situation of a dress where the raw material, cotton, is spun, weaved, tailored, shipped, and sold to consumers. The demand for dresses and other cotton products increases the demand for cotton.

Demand for business products and services can be created from a variety of circumstances, including the demand for a complementary product or service, shortages in inventory stock for manufacturing, or dramatic changes in market economic conditions. Just as with consumer products, demand for business products can be responsive to price changes or may experience few effects from price changes, based on the nature of the product, such as price range and number of competitors.

Demand can also be influenced by the circumstances of the buying situation. There are three major classifications, or **buyclasses**, of business buying situations.[14] These include the following:

- **New tasks**—A first-time or unique purchase decision that requires extensive effort. An example of this is when ACME publishing company buys a printing press to print its own books rather than work through its vendor.
- **Modified rebuy**—A buyer decides to consider alternative sources for the company's purchasing requirements. For example, ACME publishing company asks for bids from other print vendors rather than stay with its current vendor.
- **Straight rebuy**—A buyer decides to continue the existing procurement relationship and does not see any reason to search for additional information to assist in the purchase process. For example, ACME publishing company continues to print its books with the same vendor that it has used for the past five years.

Compared to consumer marketing, B2B markets tend to have more individuals in the buying process, the process tends to be formal, and business relationships tend to be longer-term. A **buying center** is the collection of individuals who perform specific roles in the procurement process. There are six specific roles performed by individuals in the buying center:[15]

- The INITIATOR is the first to identify the need to buy a particular product or service to solve an organizational problem.
- INFLUENCERS are those who assist in developing evaluation criteria and whose views influence the buying center's buyers and deciders.
- The BUYER holds the formal authority to choose the supplier and to arrange terms of condition.

- The DECIDER ultimately approves all or any part of the entire buying decision—whether to buy, what to buy, how to buy, and where to buy (in routine purchasing situations the buyer is often the decider).
- USERS consume or utilize the product or service.
- The GATEKEEPER controls the flow of information to decision makers and influencers.

Depending on the type of buying situation, some or all of the steps in the buyer purchase process are conducted. There are eight distinct steps, or phases, in the buyer purchase process (see Figure 2.1).[16]

A decision a business must make when determining how to fulfill a purchasing need is whether to make, buy, or lease the product. A business may choose to produce a product if the company has the capability and capacity to do so. There may also be a strategic reason to manufacture certain items instead of externally sourcing them. Examples could include a government not wanting to externally source critical military components for security reasons or an automaker not wanting to externally source its powertrain components so as to retain a competitive uniqueness. A business may also decide to purchase the product from a supplier. Reasons for sourcing a product from a supplier could include cost advantages or a lack of technical expertise for that specific product. A business could also lease a product. If a particular product is exposed to rapid technological change or requires regular servicing or other support, a leasing option might be most appropriate.

FIGURE 2.1 **Steps in the Buyer Purchase Process**

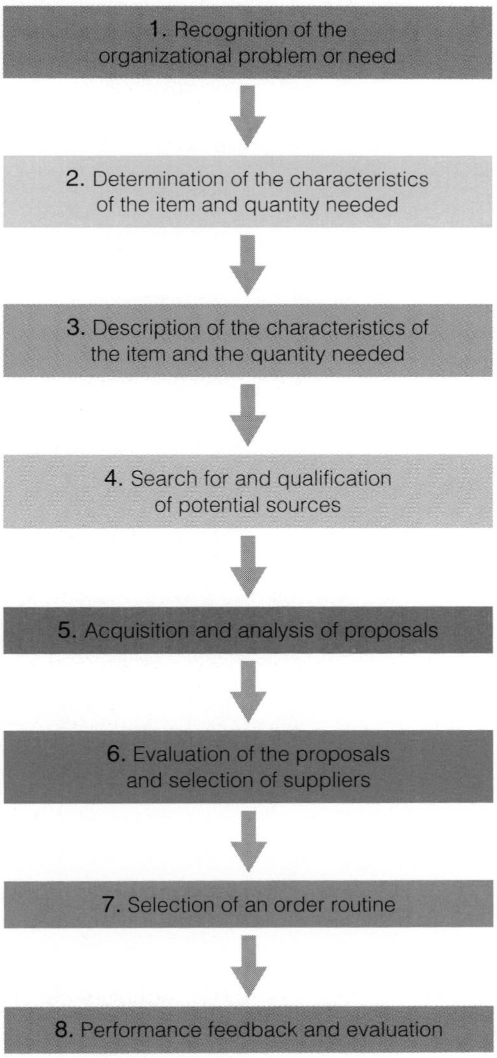
1. Recognition of the organizational problem or need
2. Determination of the characteristics of the item and quantity needed
3. Description of the characteristics of the item and the quantity needed
4. Search for and qualification of potential sources
5. Acquisition and analysis of proposals
6. Evaluation of the proposals and selection of suppliers
7. Selection of an order routine
8. Performance feedback and evaluation

APPLIED

Business Markets

Successful marketing to either business or consumer markets requires an understanding of customers and what creates value for those customers. Business uniqueness is important for businesses selling to either consumer or business markets. While branding is important in business and consumer markets, the nature of the purchasing process in B2B requires particular attention to the buying process. Structured processes, such as those required to secure government or institutional business, require a level of sophistication in the processes of particular entities. Personal relationships are another critical factor in B2B because far fewer customers account for a greater percentage of total sales. Most personal relationships would be cost prohibitive in business-to-consumer (B2C) markets.

Some businesses, such as private equity groups, are purchasing a wide range of related businesses, including suppliers and manufacturers. Different elements of the operations of these businesses are being combined and managed to extract greater profitability from the value chain. Other businesses are forming partnerships with their suppliers to manage cost exposure and to keep suppliers financially viable. This is because many companies have single sources of supply due to economies of scale and business conditions could dramatically change, which would cause incredible financial pressure on suppliers and their customers.

EXAMPLE **BUSINESS MARKETS**

Since being founded over 80 years ago, Caterpillar has grown to be the world's largest maker of construction and mining equipment, diesel and natural gas engines, and industrial gas turbines. Caterpillar manufactures more than 300 products in 23 countries and serves customers in 200 countries. Caterpillar considers itself a leader in building the world's infrastructure with three primary business lines: machinery, engines, and financial products. Selling directly to other businesses involved in building infrastructure, Caterpillar creates value for its customers through its primary business lines but also offers equipment rental, remanufacturing, and logistics services. Having a wide range of products and services is critical to Caterpillar's success with its business customers.[17]

PHOTO: Dmitry Kalinovsky/Shutterstock.

>> END EXAMPLE

Visual Summary

Chapter 2 Summary

Building on the concept of marketing and the marketing function, the marketing environment was introduced, as were consumer and business markets. The marketing environment is a set of forces, some controllable and some uncontrollable, that influence a business's ability to create value and attract and serve customers. Many factors influence value creation and the nature of customer relationships in the marketing environment. Some of those influential factors are internal to the business, while others are external. The internal environment of a business involves all activities, including marketing, that occur within the organizational functions in a business. The external environment of a business involves all activities that occur outside the organizational functions of a business. The external environment can be divided into the microenvironment and the macroenvironment. The central concept of the Five Forces of Competitive Position Model is that five forces determine the power in a business's microenvironment. The macroenvironment includes societal forces that are essentially uncontrollable and influence the microenvironment of a business.

Consumer markets include individuals and households that are potential or actual buyers of products and services that assist in further production only indirectly or incidentally, if at all. Business markets include individuals or organizations that are potential or actual buyers of goods and services that are used in, or in support of, the production of other products or services that are supplied to others. Business markets generally are organized by similar geographic locations, are influenced by consumer market demand, exist in fewer numbers, involve more individuals in the buying process, and are subject to a more formal buying process than are consumer markets.

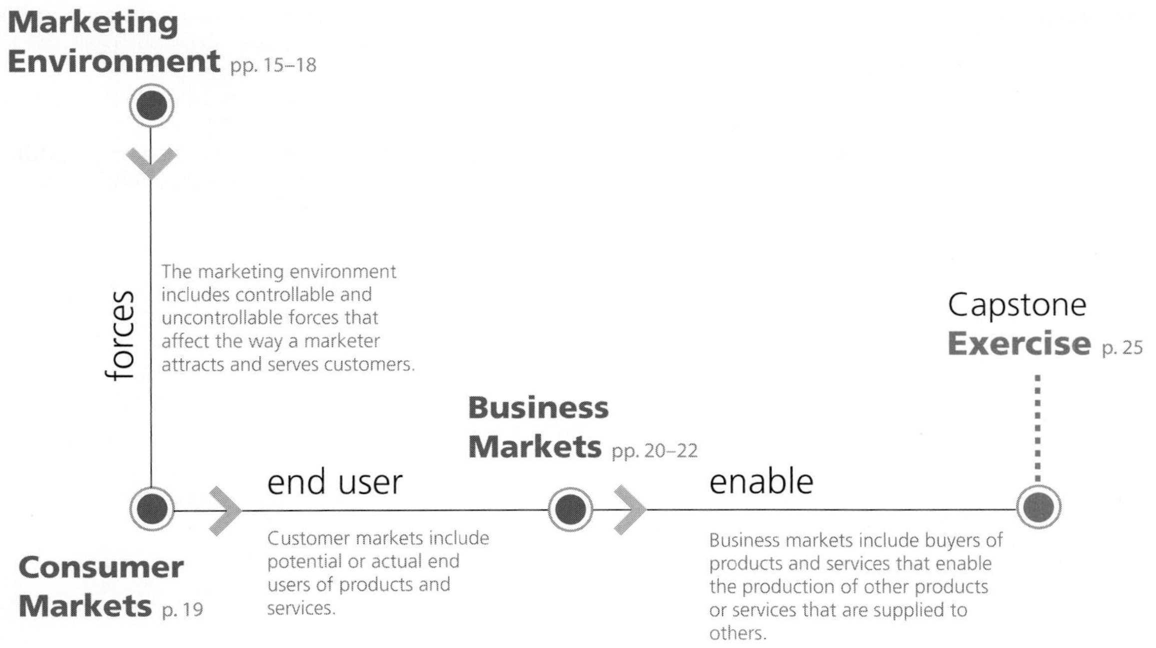

Marketing Environment pp. 15–18
forces
The marketing environment includes controllable and uncontrollable forces that affect the way a marketer attracts and serves customers.
Consumer Markets p. 19
end user
Customer markets include potential or actual end users of products and services.
Business Markets pp. 20–22
enable
Business markets include buyers of products and services that enable the production of other products or services that are supplied to others.
Capstone Exercise p. 25

Chapter Key Terms

Marketing Environment (pp. 15–18)

Marketing environment *is a set of forces, some controllable and some uncontrollable, that influence the ability of a business to create value and attract and serve customers. (p. 15)* **Opening Example (pp. 15–16)**

Key Terms (pp. 15–18)

Competitive environment includes those factors that relate to the nature, quantity, and potential actions of competitors. **(p. 17) Example: Competitive Environment (pp. 17–18)**

Demographics are characteristics of human population used to identify markets **(p. 17)**

Economic environment includes those factors that influence consumer purchase ability and buying behavior **(p. 17)**

External environment of a business involves all those activities that occur outside the organizational functions of a business **(p. 15)**

External marketing is the implementation of marketing practices directed outside the business to create value and to form productive customer relationships. **(p. 15)**

Income levels are average consumer earnings used to approximate national earnings. **(p. 17)**

Inflation is an increase in the price of a collection of goods that represent the overall economy. **(p. 17)**

Internal environment of a business involves all those activities that occur within the organizational functions in a business. **(p. 15)**

Internal marketing is the implementation of marketing practices within an organization to communicate organizational policies and practices to employees and internal stakeholders. **(p. 15)**

Legal environment includes those factors that provide rules, and penalties for violations, designed to protect society and consumers from unfair business practices and to protect businesses from unfair competitive practices. **(p. 18)**

Macroenvironment includes societal forces that are essentially uncontrollable and influence the microenvironment of a business. **(p. 16)** **Example: Macroenvironment (pp. 16–17)**

Microenvironment includes those forces close to a company, yet outside its internal environment, that influence the ability of a business to serve its customers. **(p. 15)**

Political environment includes factors that select national leadership, create laws, and provide a process for discourse on a wide range of issues. **(p. 18)**

Social and cultural environment includes factors that relate marketing to the needs and wants of society and culture. **(p. 17)**

Technological environment includes factors that influence marketing, based on scientific actions and innovation. **(p. 18)**

Unemployment levels are the number of unemployed persons divided by the aggregate labor force. **(p. 17)**

Consumer Markets (p. 19)

Consumer markets *include individuals and households that are potential or actual buyers of goods and services that assist in further production only indirectly or incidentally, if at all. (p. 19)*

Key Terms (p. 19)

Consumer products are products that directly fulfill the desires of consumers and are not intended to assist in the manufacture of other products. **(p. 19)**

Consumer's surplus occurs when a consumer purchases a product or service at a price less than the utility of the product or service. **(p. 19)**

Business Markets (pp. 20–22)

Business markets *include individuals and organizations that are potential or actual buyers of goods and services that are used in, or in support of, the production of other products or services that are supplied to others. (p. 20)* **Example: Business Markets (pp. 21–22)**

Key Terms (p. 20)

Business-to-business, also referred to as B2B, involves the sales of products and services from one business to another. **(p. 20)** **Example: Business Markets (pp. 21–22)**

Buyclasses are major classifications of business buying situations. **(p. 20)**

Buying center is the collection of individuals that perform specific roles in the procurement process. **(p. 20)**

Derived demand is the demand for a product or service that results from the demand for another product or service. **(p. 20)**

North American Industrial Classification System (NAICS) classifies businesses operating in the United States, Canada, and Mexico into groups based on their activities. **(p. 20)**

Capstone Exercise

This chapter's exercise is based on a model that allows you to assess the structure of any industry. The methodology was developed by Michael Porter and is called the Five Forces of Competitive Position. The Five Forces include the following:

- Bargaining power of suppliers
- Bargaining power of buyers
- Threat of new entrants
- Threat of substitutes
- Rivalry among competitors

The Five Forces provide a way to understand the business models of industries. How competitive is the industry? What does it take to succeed? How easy is it to get into the business? How does the industry make money? Taken together, these answers give you a way to understand the likelihood of success and the potential for profit in this industry. It is important to understand the key factors to be successful. Those key factors also help determine whether or not a certain industry could be successful.

To fully understand this process, take a look at the home improvement industry. Two big competitors, Home Depot and Lowe's, dominate this industry. Each has a large piece of the market. Other smaller stores have joined forces in horizontal channels like True Value and Ace Hardware. The do-it-yourself market has driven demand in recent years, but will growth be maintained? Take a look at Home Depot Inc. Do some research. Investigate its retail organization (Home Depot), its wholesale distribution organization (HD Supply), and its catalog sales channel (Home Decorator). Using Porter's Five Forces of Competitive Position summarize the business structure of the home improvement industry, in general, and Home Depot Inc., specifically. Explain how you think Home Depot Inc. uses these three major business units (separately and in combination) to improve its competitive advantage.

Application Exercise

Use the following marketing concepts in this chapter to tackle and solve a marketing problem: marketing environment, macroenvironment, social and cultural environment, value.

First, start by thinking about a category of produce that is organic and locally grown. In general terms, organic foods are made in a way that limits or excludes the use of synthetic materials during production, and local connotes within close distribution from farm to store. We are beginning to see many products available in grocery stores, farm stands, and large mass merchandisers within this category for us to consider purchasing.

The Marketing Problem

Choose a product in the organic or local produce category, and then choose a brand in that category after considering the following situation.

> You are new to the category and can't decide if you believe in the macroenvironmental food trends regarding the positive benefits of buying and consuming organic, local produce.

The Problem

Describe produce that clearly says it is organic or locally grown on its packaging or signage. What is the product's value? What are the controllable and uncontrollable forces that influence value? What is the social or cultural environment that supports or disrupts purchasing this produce?

The Solution

Complete the following two Problem/Solution briefs using your product and brand in the organic local produce category, chapter concepts, and college resources.

1. From the Marketing Manager's Point of View
   a. The Problem Definition
   b. Analysis
   c. The Product's Value
   d. Solution
2. From the Consumer's Point of View
   a. The Problem Definition
   b. Analysis
   c. The Product's Value
   d. Determine If This Is a Want or a Need
   e. Solution

Resources:

Marketing Defined, Explained, Applied 2e, Michael Levens
The College Library
Retail or Online Field Trip
Assigned Reading—*Brand Week*, *Advertising Age*, *WSJ*, scholarly publications, category trade journals
Blog your problem from either point of view, gather responses/posts (www.blogger.com/start)

Planning and Marketing in an Organization

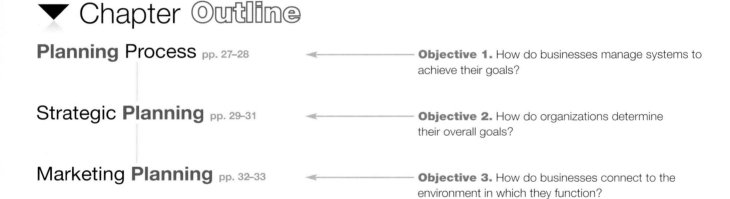

Chapter Overview In the initial chapters, you considered marketing, marketing functions, and the marketing environment. This chapter expands those concepts by considering the marketing functions within an organization. The marketing activity plays a pivotal role in connecting consumers to businesses by developing an understanding of customer requirements. Marketing also performs a critical function within businesses to concentrate every business activity on generating desired financial results based on fulfilling consumer requirements. The concept of marketing in an organization is considered through exploring the planning process and how businesses manage marketing planning.

Chapter Outline

PLANNING Process (pp. 27–28)

DEFINED *The **planning process** is the series of steps businesses take to determine how they will achieve their goals.*

EXPLAINED

Planning Process

Businesses consist of many functions, such as marketing, finance, and operations. These business functions can be considered **systems**, a group of interacting related parts that perform a specific function.

Business planning is a decision process for people and businesses to manage systems to achieve an objective. By understanding the systems that influence a business and making decisions based on that understanding, businesses increase the likelihood of a desired outcome, such as increased market share or higher profits. All businesses, from a one-person shop to a large multinational conglomerate, should engage in the planning process. The complexity of the process can depend on the size of the business and the number of different products and services offered. Large businesses may have multiple committees to initiate, review, and approve plans, yet a single individual may handle that function at a small business. The length of time addressed by business planning also differs, based on the nature of competition in the specific business market and the characteristics of the products or services the business offers. However, business planning is an ongoing effort and typically addresses some specific short-term objectives as well as some longer-term objectives. A short term may be weeks or months for some high-tech products, but it may also be a year or more for major capital goods such as large appliances or automobiles. The aim of business planning is the creation of a business plan.

A **business plan** is a written document that defines the operational and financial objectives of a business over a particular time. A marketer contributes a variety of inputs to the business plan, including the following:

- A comprehensive review and assessment of a business's marketing environment
- An explanation of what the marketing function is attempting to achieve in support of the business plan
- A discussion of how a business intends to achieve its marketing objectives
- A process to allocate resources and monitor results

Although marketers provide critical inputs to the business plan, the marketing function also must work with other business functions, such as finance, manufacturing, and human resources. These other areas may support or resist marketing initiatives due to different strategic visions for the business or the desire to control resources. As a marketer, remember the importance of your position and advocate that you perform an essential activity of injecting customer requirements into the many systems within an organization. That customer connection is fundamental in linking businesses to consumers.

APPLIED

Planning Process

"Good fortune is what happens when opportunity meets with planning." Thomas Edison's quote identifies the potential that businesses can realize by choosing to plan. The opposite is also a possibility; by failing to plan, a business risks the potential for bad fortune in the future. That is not to say that planning guarantees success or that failing to plan guarantees failure. Businesses practice varying forms of planning and have varying levels of success. Some businesses have elaborate planning processes with entire staffs dedicated to developing business plans, while others have little or no resources dedicated to planning. Many resources can

Whole Foods Market, the world's largest natural and organic foods retailer with 289 locations in the United States, Canada, and the United Kingdom, articulates its business mission through the following motto: Whole Foods, Whole People, Whole Planet. The company's stated core values elaborate on this motto:

- Selling the Highest Quality Natural and Organic Products Available
- Satisfying and Delighting Our Customers
- We Support Team Member Happiness and Excellence
- Creating Wealth Through Profits & Growth

- Caring About Our Communities & Our Environment
- Creating Ongoing Win-Win Partnerships with Our Suppliers

Whole Foods Market's business vision includes leadership in the quality food business. The vision also includes being a mission-driven company that aims to set standards of excellence for food retailers. Whole Foods sets objectives, develops its portfolio, and manages its business based on its mission and vision. The company has enjoyed success with annual sales exceeding $8 billion.[1]

PHOTO: Hannamariah/Shutterstock.

be devoted to the planning process. However, it is the level of involvement of the various activities within a business in developing and implementing the business plan that most influences the potential for success.

An organization may need to communicate its business plan in a variety of situations. This typically necessitates different versions of the business plan. A formal, detailed, written plan as outlined earlier in this section is often used when communicating with external stakeholders or for planning within an organization. An oral version of the business plan, based on essential elements of the written plan, is used for business negotiations or funding requests in advanced stages. An **elevator pitch**, a brief description of a product or service designed to gain attention of desired parties and to generate interest in achieving a desired outcome, is generally used at initial stages of business negotiations or funding requests. The pitch is generally between 30 seconds and 3 minutes in duration and is common in requests by new businesses for venture capital.

Strategic **PLANNING** (pp. 29–31)

DEFINED **Strategic planning** *determines the overall goals of the business and the steps it will take to achieve them.*[2]

EXPLAINED

Strategic Planning

Business planning can be categorized into two different levels:

- Strategic planning is typically completed by the top management of a business, as opposed to tactical planning that is typically done within the various functions within a business. Nike is engaged in strategic planning when it evaluates growth potential in different athletic shoe segments, such as cross-training, running, and basketball, and decides that an opportunity exists for a new entry in the basketball segment.
- **Tactical planning** is the process of developing actions for various functions within a business to support implementing a business's strategic plan. Tactical planning occurs when the Nike marketing department decides to introduce Nike Hyperdunk Basketball Shoes and determines the characteristics of the product, the price of the product, the method of distribution, and the types of promotion to support the launch.

The strategic planning process includes the following four critical elements:

- Establish the business mission.
- Identify the business vision.
- Define the business objectives.
- Develop the business portfolio.

A **business mission** is a statement that identifies the purpose of a business and what makes that business different from others. The mission statement should be neither trite nor verbose. The scope of the mission should not be so broad that any strategy could be developed within that scope. It should also not be so specific that flexibility to take advantage of market opportunities is restricted. The mission should at least reflect the compelling benefit that a business offers to consumers. Starbuck's business mission is the following: "Establish Starbucks as the premier purveyor of the finest coffee in the world while maintaining our uncompromising principles while we grow."

A **business vision** is a statement in a strategic plan that identifies an idealized picture of a future state a business is aiming to achieve. A business vision complements a mission statement by providing a description of the end state if the strategic plan is implemented successfully. A business vision is generally targeted for use within a business, as opposed to the mission statement, which is directed at all stakeholders. Microsoft co-founders Bill Gates and Paul Allen had a vision of "A computer on every desk and in every home." General Electric's vision is "To become #1 or #2 in every market we serve and revolutionize this company to have the speed and agility of a small enterprise." Avon Products, Inc., the world's largest direct seller of beauty and beauty-related products, has the following vision: "To be the company that best understands and satisfies the product, service and self-fulfillment needs of women—globally."

After establishing a business mission and business vision, to translate the mission and vision throughout a business, objectives must be developed. A **business objective** is something a business is attempting to achieve in support of an overarching strategy. Successful objectives can be expressed by the mnemonic S.M.A.R.T. and include the following:[3]

- **Specific**—Does the objective refer to a unique event?
- **Measurable**—Can the objective's achievement be determined using established metrics?
- **Achievable**—Is the objective possible, given business constraints?
- **Relevant**—Will the objective support a desired business strategy?
- **Time-bound**—Is there a duration for attaining the objective?

Objectives can be established to address many different requirements, including financial requirements such as sales revenue and profitability, operational requirements such as productivity and efficiency, and marketing requirements such as market share and brand awareness. Examples of some objectives include "to increase sales by 25%" and "to expand retail locations to every country in Europe."

The products or services that a business presents to consumers must reflect the business's mission, values, and objectives. A business portfolio, also known as a product portfolio, is a collection of products, services, and their corresponding brands that a business manages to achieve stated goals. A business portfolio that reflects the strengths of a business and limits its weaknesses provides the best opportunity for a business to realize success. The more products and services a business offers, the more opportunities there are to serve different consumers. However, there are also higher costs to manage all the products and services. **Portfolio analysis** is the process that a business uses to evaluate the different combinations of products and services that the business offers, based on business objectives.

APPLIED

Strategic Planning

A variety of tools is available that can assist businesses in their strategic planning processes. These range from traditional to contemporary models. A classic model for conducting a portfolio analysis is the Boston Consulting Group (BCG) growth-market matrix. The BCG matrix (see Figure 3.1) assists in identifying which products or services should receive more or less investment, and which market sectors could benefit from more or fewer product or service offerings. The BCG matrix includes two variables: market share on the x-axis and market growth rate on the y-axis. The ranges, typically referred to as high and low, should be set relative to economic realities, such as the rate of inflation, as well as the characteristics of the market sectors, such as the number of competitors and leading market share, being analyzed.

FIGURE 3.1 BCG Growth-Market Matrix

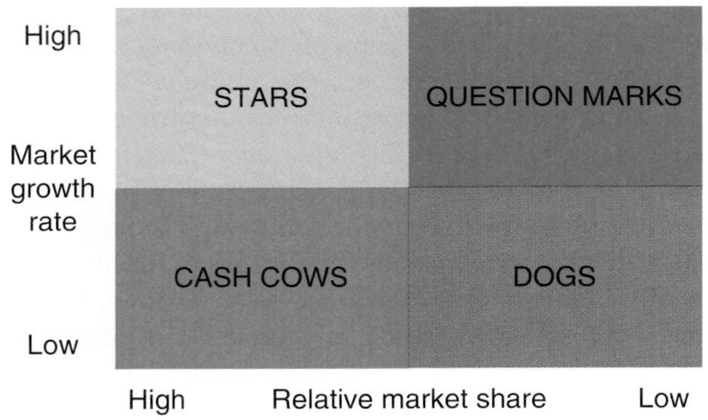

Stars represent products or services with high growth and high market share. Placement in this category indicates tremendous strategic value to a business. The number of consumers and the potential for significant profits in this sector require strong consideration for investment of resources. Money generated from this sector can support products or services in other sectors. An important strategy for Stars is to ensure that the products or services remain relevant to consumers.

Cash Cows are products or services with high market share and low growth opportunities. Stars often become Cash Cows when competitors enter their market and growth slows. Cash Cows do not require the level of investment that Stars require because there is limited potential to grow. Instead, the current position is managed to generate money to support other aspects of a business.

Question Marks are products or services with low relative market share in a sector with high growth. Although there is potential in this sector, a significant financial investment is required to take advantage of that potential. Question Marks could evolve into Stars, but they could also drain resources from other potential investments within the portfolio.

Dogs are products or services with low relative market share in a low-growth sector. Although there is limited potential, there is an opportunity for a product or service to maintain its position. Little or no additional investment is warranted unless products or services in this sector are connected to products or services in a higher-potential sector. Strategies for offerings in this sector often include selling this part of the portfolio or reducing financial support while removing cash and then divesting.

The BCG matrix has limitations, including the consideration of only two dimensions: market share and market growth rate. High market share does not guarantee financial profits, and limited market share does not guarantee poor financial results. Growth is not the only indicator of market attractiveness, and investment or divestment decisions made solely using the BCG matrix may be shortsighted.

EXAMPLE STRATEGIC PLANNING, BCG MATRIX

Deckers Outdoor Company entered into an agreement in 1985 with Teva founder Mark Thatcher to produce and distribute Teva sandals. Teva's portfolio has grown from its iconic sport sandal to include a wide range of products, including trail-running shoes, adventure shoes, casual shoes, casual sandals, and water shoes.[4] As Teva considers a new product or a new market segment, the growth rate and market potential of that product are charted to determine how each will serve the overall goals and objectives of the company. A hypothetical classification of Teva's portfolio using the BCG matrix is presented graphically in Figure 3.2 and discussed individually within each element of the BCG matrix.

FIGURE 3.2 Sample BCG Growth-Market Matrix for Teva Products

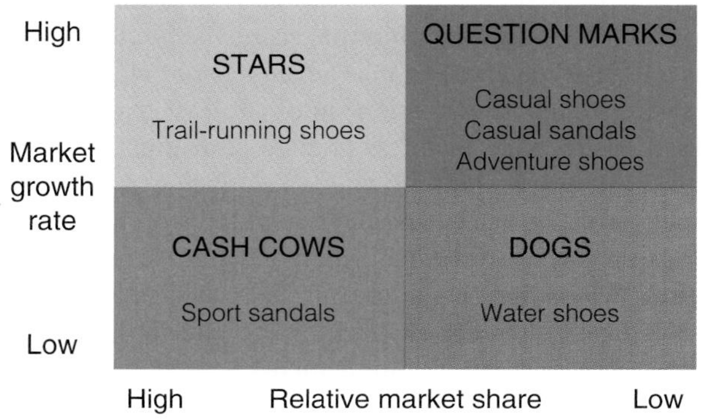

Stars: Although the trail-running shoes entered the market segment facing strong competition, Teva's reputation for outdoor performance has extended to the trail-running shoe. The market share and the growth rate have exceeded goals and Teva's product is a Star.

Cash Cows: The Teva sport sandal continues to be the Cash Cow for the business.

Question Marks: The introduction of Teva's casual shoe has been less impressive. The competition in this category is significant and quality control has proved challenging. The casual shoe is a Question Mark. Casual sandals and adventure shoes are also in this category because of a low market share in growing markets.

Dogs: The Teva water shoe is struggling. Consumers do not seem to differentiate between the traditional sport sandal and the water shoe. The water shoe has relatively high production costs and a higher retail price than the sport sandal. Management is considering exiting this category.

PHOTO: Dick Stada/Shutterstock.

>>END EXAMPLE

A contemporary model assisting strategic planning efforts is the **balanced scorecard**, developed in the early 1990s by Robert Kaplan and David Norton as a management system to relate business vision and mission to individual business activities.[5] The balanced scorecard considers a business from four different perspectives, including financial and nonfinancial measures:

- **Customer perspective**—How do customers view us?
- **Internal business perspective**—What must we do well?
- **Innovation and learning perspective**—Can we continue to grow and generate value?
- **Financial perspective**—How do shareholders view us?

The scorecard identifies the relationships between the different perspectives and business vision and strategy. Each is influenced by the business vision and strategy, and each perspective influences all the other perspectives.

EXAMPLE STRATEGIC PLANNING, TEVA BALANCED SCORECARD

A hypothetical example for the Teva portfolio is illustrated in Figure 3.3. For each perspective, a list of objectives derived from the strategic plan is identified. Measures of success and a list of initiatives to achieve the objectives also are identified.[6]

FIGURE 3.3 Teva Scorecard

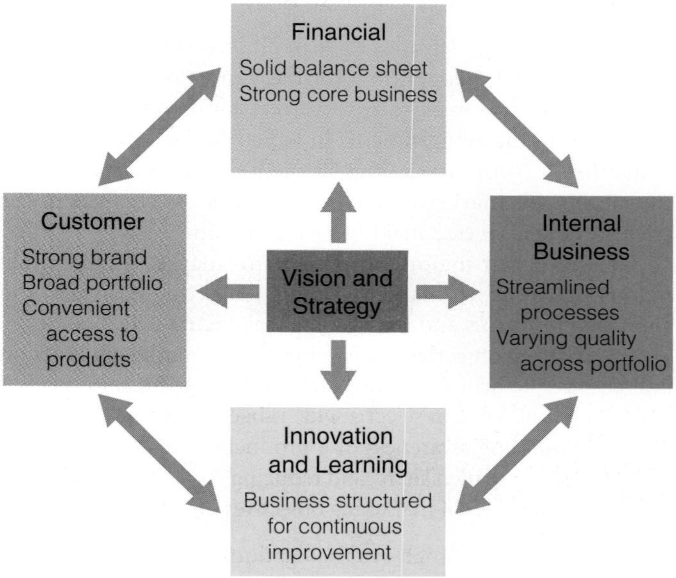

>>END EXAMPLE

Marketing PLANNING (pp. 32–33)

DEFINED **Marketing planning** *includes those activities devoted to accomplishing marketing objectives.*

EXPLAINED

Marketing Planning

Strategic planning identifies the overall direction of a business. Individual functions within a business must develop plans to support the business strategy. Marketing planning connects businesses to the environments in which they function, in particular to the consumers of the business's products and services. The ability for marketing planning to address changes in the environment is an essential business function.

There are four major components of marketing planning: marketing objectives, marketing audit, marketing strategies, and allocating resources and monitoring (see Figure 3.4).

A **marketing objective** is something that a marketing function is attempting to achieve in support of a strategic business plan. A marketing function can select a wide range of possible objectives, including building awareness of a product or service, increasing sales, increasing market share, and reducing resistance to a product or service. Examples of marketing objectives include the following:

- Increase sales of high-end navigation systems among owners of European luxury cars by 10% in one year. This can be measured through analyzing annual sales data.
- Increase market share of a specific brand of office furniture within the business market by 5% in six months. This can be measured through industry data published by an office furniture trade association.
- Create awareness of a new wetsuit line among high school swimmers. This can be measured through a questionnaire given to high school swimmers.

FIGURE 3.4 Four Major Components of Marketing Planning

EXAMPLE **MARKETING PLANNING**

Speedo launched the LZR Racer swimsuit, a full-body suit, in 2008, several months in advance of the Beijing Olympics. After 25 world records were broken at the 2008 Olympics, second only to 30 world records in the 1976 Olympics when goggles were first allowed, initial demand for the new swimsuit by athletes of all levels skyrocketed. Speedo's marketing objective was to use the Olympics to launch the new product. Speedo collaborated with NASA to help design the suit that dramatically reduces drag in the water. Even though the suit noticeably improved swimming times, some swimming organizations have banned full-body suits for competitions because the suits are considered unfair performance-enhancing gear. Speedo responded to concerns by launching the LZR Racer Elite in 2010, in compliance with all FINA (International Swimming Federation) requirements and rules governing collegiate, high school, and club swimming in the United States.[7]

PHOTO: Schmid Christophe/Shutterstock.

>>END EXAMPLE

After marketing objectives are established, the next step is the marketing audit. A **marketing audit** is the comprehensive review and assessment of a business's marketing environment. An important part of the marketing process is that a business understands the external and internal forces that can influence its success.

Once the marketing audit has been completed, the marketing function is responsible for developing marketing strategies. A **marketing strategy** is a statement of how a business intends to achieve its marketing objectives.[8] A marketing strategy includes two critical functions:

- Select a target market.
- Create an appropriate marketing mix for the target market.

A **target market** is a group of consumers that a business determines is the most viable for its products or services. Consumer wants, needs, and business resources and strategies all contribute to the selection of a target market. In some cases, several targets are selected. A **marketing mix** is a group of marketing variables that a business controls with the intent of implementing a marketing strategy directed at a specific target market. As discussed in Chapter 1, the most common variables of the marketing mix include product, place, pricing, and promotion.

A **product strategy** identifies the product and service portfolio, including packaging, branding, and warranty for its target market. An automobile manufacturer creates a product strategy when it decides to offer consumers a choice of a diesel or hybrid engine in a new vehicle. This strategy helps meet growing consumer demands for a wider choice of engine types. A **place strategy** identifies where, how, and when products and services are made available to target consumers. A newspaper publisher develops a place strategy when it decides to offer customers newspapers in newsprint and online. A **pricing strategy** identifies what a business will charge for its products or services. A company creates a pricing strategy with its clothing brand when that company decides to charge more for products sold in its retail stores than for the same products sold through the company Web site. A **promotion strategy** identifies how a business communicates product or service benefits and value to its target market. A perfume manufacturer develops a promotion strategy when that manufacturer decides to advertise a new brand of perfume both in-store and on television.

Following the development of marketing strategies, the next step is allocating resources and monitoring performance. People and money both must be assigned to support implementation of marketing strategies. The monitoring process is essential to determine if the target market is responding to marketing strategies. Proper monitoring requires identifying performance measures so that actual performance can be compared to expected performance. Performance measures can include different variables, for example, customer satisfaction, average value of customer orders, and level of advertising recall.

The result of marketing planning is the creation of a marketing plan. A **marketing plan** is a document that includes an assessment of the marketing situation, marketing objectives, marketing strategy, and marketing initiatives. The marketing plan can be an independent document or it can be contained within a business plan; it indicates the necessary actions to achieve specific marketing objectives. The marketing plan is discussed in detail in Chapter 11 and a comprehensive marketing plan is included in that chapter's appendix.

APPLIED

Marketing Planning

In practice, marketing planning is subject to the same challenges as business planning, including a potential lack of focus on business objectives, a lack of involvement of all aspects of the marketing activity in the planning process, and the failure to track performance against objectives. The structure and culture of a marketing activity has much to do with managing these potential challenges. Clear roles and responsibilities regarding planning responsibility and the level of understanding of a business's environment contribute significantly to successful marketing planning.

SWOT analysis is a tool that helps identify business strengths, weaknesses, opportunities, and threats. A SWOT analysis can assist in the marketing planning process, particularly with the marketing audit.

Strengths and weaknesses are based on internal characteristics, and opportunities and threats are external. Strengths and opportunities can be considered potential advantages, but weaknesses and threats are problems to be addressed. Strategically, weaknesses must be examined to search for opportunities. Strengths should be managed against potential threats. The Five Forces of Competitive Position Model, discussed in the previous chapter, can also assist in completing a marketing audit.

Marketing performance must be evaluated relative to objectives, as well as against the overall financial investment in the marketing activity. Increasingly, marketing is being asked to justify its contribution to business performance through identifying a return on marketing investment. Marketing planning should be designed to identify the relative contributions of each aspect of the marketing activity, including advertising and promotions, toward achieving overall objectives. **Return on marketing investment (ROMI)** is the impact on business performance resulting from executing specific marketing activities. Funding can then be allocated to the most efficient investment option. ROMI is discussed in detail in Chapter 19.

EXAMPLE **MARKETING PLANNING, SWOT**

Studying the Jeep SWOT analysis leads to questions about the appropriateness of the portfolio and the potential for new market segments that might be viable. Price sensitivity among consumers, as well as shopping patterns and promotional opportunities that leverage brand strength, should also be considered.

PHOTO: Andresr/Shutterstock.

>>END EXAMPLE

Visual Summary

Part 1 Explaining (Chapters 1, 2, 3, 4, 5)
Part 2 Creating (Chapters 6, 7, 8, 9)
Part 3 Strategizing (Chapters 10, 11)
Part 4 Managing (Chapters 12, 13, 14, 15, 16, 17)
Part 5 Integrating (Chapters 18, 19, 20)

Chapter 3 Summary

Building on the concepts of marketing, marketing functions, and the marketing environment, this chapter expanded those concepts by considering the marketing function within an organization, and particularly its role in planning. The planning process includes specific actions undertaken and methods used to determine the best way to accomplish an objective. The strategic planning process includes four critical elements:

- Establish the business mission
- Identify the business vision
- Define the business objectives
- Develop the business portfolio

Marketing planning includes activities devoted to accomplishing marketing objectives. There are four major components of marketing planning:

- Marketing objectives
- Marketing audit
- Marketing strategies
- Allocating resources and monitoring

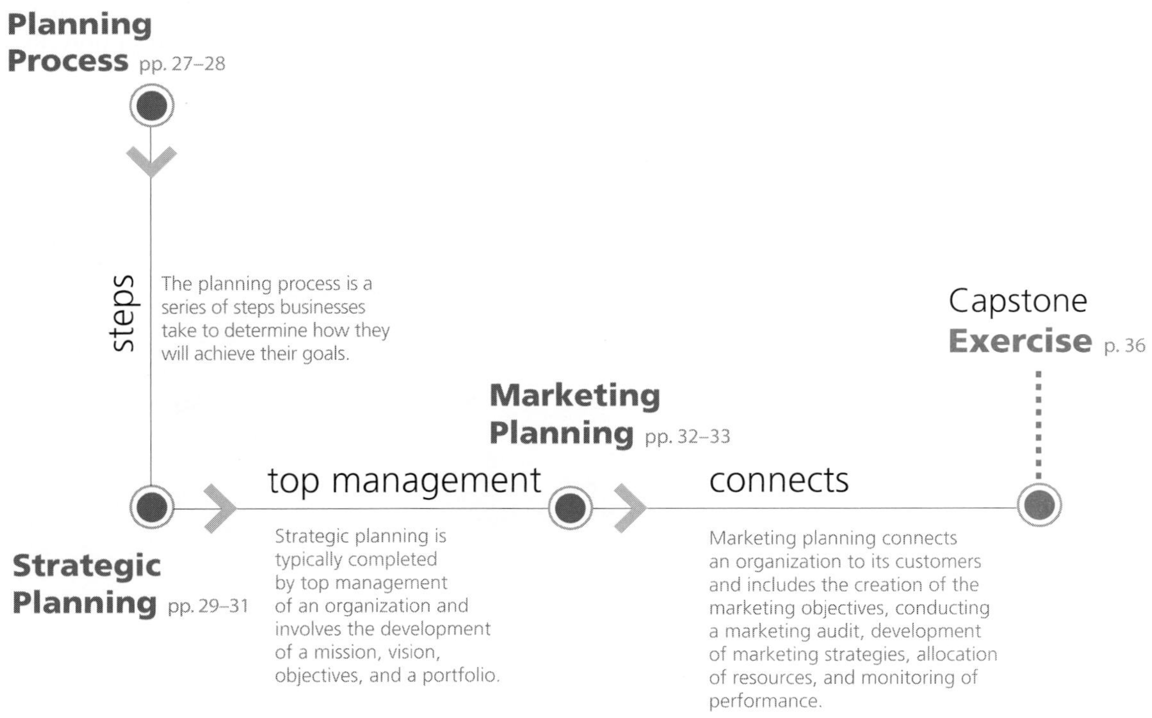

Planning Process pp. 27–28
steps
The planning process is a series of steps businesses take to determine how they will achieve their goals.
Strategic Planning pp. 29–31
top management
Strategic planning is typically completed by top management of an organization and involves the development of a mission, vision, objectives, and a portfolio.
Marketing Planning pp. 32–33
connects
Marketing planning connects an organization to its customers and includes the creation of the marketing objectives, conducting a marketing audit, development of marketing strategies, allocation of resources, and monitoring of performance.
Capstone Exercise p. 36

Chapter Key Terms

Planning Process (pp. 27–28)

***Planning process** is the series of steps businesses take to determine how they will achieve their goals. (p. 27)* **Opening Example (pp. 27–28)**

Key Terms (pp. 27–28)

Business plan is a written document that defines the operational and financial objectives of a business over a particular time and how the business plans to accomplish those objectives. **(p. 27)**

Business planning is a decision process for people and businesses to manage systems to achieve an objective. **(p. 27)**

Elevator pitch is a brief description of a product or service designed to gain attention of desired parties and to generate interest in achieving a desired outcome. **p. 28)**

Systems are groups of interacting related parts that perform a specific function. **(p. 27)**

Strategic Planning (pp. 29–31)

***Strategic planning** determines the overall goals of the business and the steps the business will take to achieve those goals. (p. 29)*
Example: Strategic Planning, BCG Matrix (pp. 30–31)
Example: Strategic Planning, Teva Balanced Scorecard (p. 31)

Key Terms (pp. 29–31)

Balanced scorecard is a management system that relates a business's vision and mission to individual business activities. **(p. 31) Example: Strategic Planning, Teva Balanced Scorecard (p. 31)**

Business mission is a statement that identifies the purpose of a business and what makes that business different from others. **(p. 29)**

Business objective is something that a business attempts to achieve in support of an overarching strategy. **(p. 29)**

Business vision is a statement in a strategic plan that identifies an idealized picture of a future state a business is aiming to achieve. **(p. 29)**

Cash Cows are products or services with high market share and low growth opportunities. **(p. 30) Example: Strategic Planning, BCG Matrix (pp. 30–31)**

Dogs are products or services with low relative market share in a low growth sector. **(p. 30) Example: Strategic Planning, BCG Matrix (pp. 30–31)**

Portfolio analysis is the process a business uses to evaluate the different combinations of products and services that the business offers based on its objectives. **(p. 29)**

Question Marks are products or services with low relative market share in a sector with high growth. **(p. 30) Example: Strategic Planning, BCG Matrix (pp. 30–31)**

Stars represent products or services with high growth and high market share. **(p. 30) Example: Strategic Planning, BCG Matrix (pp. 30–31)**

Tactical planning is the process of developing actions for various functions within a business to support implementing a business's strategic plan. **(p. 29)**

Marketing Planning (pp. 32–33)

***Marketing planning** is the part of business planning devoted to connecting a business to the environments in which that business functions in order to accomplish the business's goals. (p. 32)* **Example: Marketing Planning (p. 32)**

Key Terms (pp. 32–33)

Marketing audit is the comprehensive review and assessment of a business's marketing environment. **(p. 32)**

Marketing mix is a group of marketing variables that a business controls with the intent of implementing a marketing strategy directed at a specific target market. **(p. 33)**

Marketing objective is something that a marketing function is attempting to achieve in support of a strategic business plan. **(p. 32)**

Marketing plan is a document that includes an assessment of the marketing situation, marketing objectives, marketing strategy, and marketing initiatives. **(p. 33)**

Marketing strategy is a statement of how a business intends to achieve its marketing objectives. **(p. 32)**

Place strategy identifies where, how, and when products and services are made available to target consumers. **(p. 33)**

Pricing strategy identifies what a business will charge for its products or services. **(p. 33)**

Product strategy identifies the product and service portfolio, including packaging, branding, and warranty for its target market. **(p. 33) Example: Marketing Planning (p. 32)**

Promotion strategy identifies how a business communicates product or service benefits and value to its target market. **(p. 33)**

Return on marketing investment (ROMI) is the impact on business performance resulting from executing specific marketing activities. **(p. 33)**

SWOT analysis is a tool that helps identify business strengths, weaknesses, opportunities, and threats. **(p. 33) Example: Marketing Planning, SWOT (p. 33)**

Target market is a group of consumers that a business determines to be the most viable for its products or services. **(p. 33)**

Capstone Exercise

This chapter introduces several tools for marketing planning. The BCG matrix (p. 30) typically reflects market share and market growth on the two axes. However, you can also use a BCG matrix to reflect other measures.

Easy Rider Car Rental is a single-location operation in Smalltown, USA. A new marketing manager has been hired to analyze business and propose areas for further marketing focus and growth potential. The manager identified the following six business units:

Gross revenues per year	$2M	
Leisure car rentals	$900,000	45%
Corporate car rentals	$540,000	27%
Refueling/Fuel packages	$100,000	5%
Insurance add-ons	$300,000	15%
Misc. accessories (baby seats, GPS, etc.)	$160,000	8%

Here are some facts the manager has to consider:

- A new Intel plant has been built and will open within the next six months
- Insurance and miscellaneous income has very little related expense
- Very little profit is derived from refueling. This is viewed as a customer service.

Based on the information the manager has collected, place each of the five business units on a BCG matrix with growth potential (low to high) and revenues generated (high to low) as the two axes.

- Explain your placement choices.
- What to do think the marketing manager should do with this analysis?

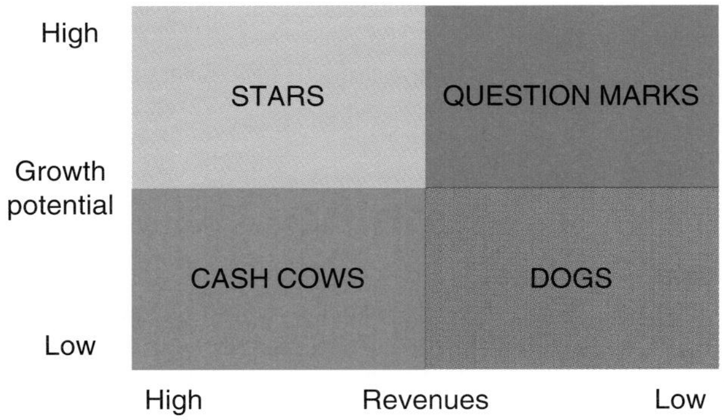

Application Exercise

Use the following marketing concepts in this chapter to tackle and solve a marketing problem: planning, SWOT, mission, target market.

First, start by thinking about a category of products in the higher education market. In general terms, higher education refers to academies, universities, colleges, vocational universities, community colleges, liberal arts colleges, institutes of technology, and certain other collegiate-level institutions, such as vocational schools.

The Marketing Problem

Choose a product in the higher education category, and then choose a brand in that category after considering the following situation.

> You plan to attend college and graduate school before working in your field.

The Problem

Describe a planning approach to finding a higher education institution that will provide you what you need to succeed in your career. Conduct a SWOT on two colleges. What is the target market of each of these schools?

The Solution

Complete the following Problem/Solution brief using your product and brand in the higher education category, chapter concepts, and college resources.

1. From the Marketing Manager's Point of View
   a. The Problem Definition
   b. SWOT Analysis
   c. The Product's Value
   d. The Target Market
   e. Solution
2. From the Consumer's Point of View
   a. The Problem Definition
   b. SWOT Analysis
   c. The Product's Value
   d. Solution

Resources:

Marketing Defined, Explained, Applied 2e, Michael Levens
The College Library
Retail or Online Field Trip
Assigned Reading—*Brand Week, Advertising Age, WSJ,* scholarly publications, category trade journals
Blog your problem from either point of view, gather responses/posts (www.blogger.com/start)

A Broader Perspective on **Marketing**

Chapter Overview The previous chapters examined the purpose of marketing in commerce, including marketing's business functions, its application to consumer and business markets, and its role within an organization. This chapter discusses marketing from a broader perspective by examining its social, legal, and ethical aspects. Additionally, this chapter considers marketing's relationship to society as well as how laws are used to regulate marketing.

Chapter Outline

MARKETING and Society (p. 39)

DEFINED *A* **society** *is a community, nation, or group that shares common traditions, institutions, activities, and interests.*

EXPLAINED

Marketing and Society

Perhaps you enjoy a cup of coffee in the morning, brewed at home or in your local coffee shop. If you stop to think about it, you might realize that the coffee you are savoring is the result of an interconnected series of marketing actions. A coffee grower (probably in a faraway country) cultivated, harvested, and shipped the beans to a manufacturer. The manufacturer then roasted, packaged, and passed along the coffee to its retailers and distributors. Grocers stocked the shelves of their stores with attractive packages of the beans, and then consumers transformed the beans into cups of piping hot coffee.

Except for products and services provided by governments or institutions, everything in our modern consumer society is the result of marketing. Products must be developed, manufactured, distributed, advertised, and priced. Based on statistics from the Organization for Economic Cooperation and Development (OECD) for 2007, the United States is the largest single economy, with a **Gross Domestic Product (GDP)** of almost $14 trillion. Global GDP, including U.S. data, was over $70 trillion, reflecting part of the worldwide nature of commerce.[1]

Given marketing's economic importance, the interests of society are complex. On the one hand, a competitive marketplace and creative marketing can improve customer satisfaction. On the other, governments and institutions take a keen interest in consumer safety, public safety, and anticompetitive or unethical business practices.

APPLIED

Marketing and Society

The United States is described as a "consumer society" because much of it is organized around commerce and consumer satisfaction. Modern society binds together a variety of groups and individuals in a web of interrelated activity:

- Consumers enjoy benefits from the variety of product choices brought to them through marketing. They also determine the success or failure of businesses by deciding which products to buy.
- Businesses market products and services for consumption by consumers and other businesses. Their livelihood depends on these purchases, and boundaries are set on their actions by governments and other organizations.
- Governments collect taxes from consumers and businesses and attempt to promote the welfare of the economic system by regulating any anticompetitive behavior by marketers.
- **Nongovernmental organizations (NGOs)**, like Consumers Union (CU) or People for the Ethical Treatment of Animals (PETA), are groups of private individuals that monitor the behavior of marketers or governments. They use their influence to achieve social goals such as product safety or animal rights.

With marketing so intertwined with society, it makes sense to pause and view the subject from a broader perspective. Three aspects of marketing and society worth exploring in more detail are culture, consumerism, and environmentalism.

It is important to balance the characteristics of environmentally sustainable products with market requirements and to understand the consumer value of any market offering. Philips, a $26 billion company active in 100 countries, is active in consumer products, health care, and lighting. Its stated mission is to "Improve the quality of people's lives through timely introduction of meaningful innovations." In 1994, Philips introduced "Earthlight," an energy-efficient compact fluorescent bulb. Despite the unique performance characteristics of the product, the product was expensive ($15) and was incompatible with most conventional lamps. Philips learned from this and reintroduced the product in 2000 branded as Marathon to emphasize the bulb's five-year lifespan. The product was designed to work with existing lamps, repriced with a promise to save $20 over the life of the bulb, and the packaging contained the Energy Star seal, the U.S. Environmental Protection Agency and U.S. Department of Energy program to identify energy-efficient products. Upon relaunch of the product, sales increased 12% in what had been a flat market. The product has been a consistently strong performer for Philips, helping sales of green products increase from 20% of total company sales in 2007 to 31% of total company sales in 2009.[2]

PHOTO: Artlomp/Shutterstock.

MARKETING and Culture (pp. 40–43)

DEFINED **Culture** *is the shared values, beliefs, and preferences of a particular society.*

EXPLAINED

Marketing and Culture

Although each of us is an individual, with our own clear likes and dislikes, we are also members of larger groups (or societies). Being together and interacting with other people is a normal part of life. Psychological research into social conformity tells us that individual views and behavior can be strongly influenced by other people. As market researcher Mark Earls said, "We are a 'we' species, laboring under the illusion of 'I.'"[3]

APPLIED

Marketing and Culture

Culture can be discussed at the national level (for example, the United States), regional level (for example, the Midwest), local level (for example, Chicago), or in terms of subcultures (for example, skateboarders). Some defining aspects of American culture include the following:[4]

- The right to choose your own destiny
- Taking control of yourself and your environment
- Egalitarianism ("All people are created equal.")
- Change equals progress
- "Time is money"
- Charity and "giving back"
- Strength in diversity

Companies craft products and services to fit nicely into this cultural landscape. State and private universities in the United States market their services as a way for students to take control of their personal destinies. Whenever a product is advertised as "new and improved," it addresses cultural beliefs that change and progress are good things. Overnight delivery services and online banking are built upon a "need for speed" among Americans, who believe that wasted time means lost opportunities.

Marketing is both a reflection of a culture and a powerful influence upon it. Clever marketers tune into what is happening within a culture (sometimes called the *zeitgeist*) and transform their insights into profitable marketing opportunities.

Certainly the most visible form of marketing is advertising. On any given day, you are exposed to hundreds of advertising messages through mediums such as TV, the Internet, cell phones, billboards, transit (for example, buses, airport boards), magazines, and newspapers. Not all of these messages are noticed or remembered, but every so often an advertisement is successful at more than just selling a product. Its content taps into a shared feeling among members of a society, and its catchphrases are repeated in situations having almost nothing to do with the original ad.

EXAMPLE CULTURE

In 2006 Dos Equis, a Mexican beer brand imported, marketed, and sold in the United States by Heineken USA, Inc., introduced the so-called Most Interesting Man in the World to represent its brand. The tanned, silver-bearded gentleman with an adventurous lifestyle personifies American cultural elements of individualism and achievement. The desire to be interesting and to share unique experiences is the central theme of the brand's advertising message. Humor is injected into the larger-than-life stories through a series of quotes to describe the Most Interesting Man in the World. "The police often question him just because they find him interesting," "His reputation is expanding faster than the universe," and "He once had an awkward moment, just to see how it feels" are just some of the folklore attached to this larger-than-life character. Engagement between the brand and consumers extends into social media with Dos Equis' Most Interesting Man–focused Facebook page boasting almost 200,000 fans. The Most Interesting Man in the World helped Dos Equis to realize a 22% sales increase between 2008 and 2009.[5]

PHOTO: Monkey Business Images/Shutterstock.

>> END EXAMPLE

Fashion is another way that marketing influences culture. Designers like Zara or Juicy Couture introduce new fashion styles on a regular basis, and their ideas affect what consumers feel is new, fresh, and exciting. Fashion brands are built upon image, and this foundation must be continually reinforced or it becomes stale.

eMarketer estimates that by 2014 there will be more than 250 million Americans on the Web.[6] The Internet and World Wide Web have taken the globe by storm, with marketing playing a major role in their lightning-fast adoption by consumers. E-mail has replaced traditional letter writing and phone calls. Customers sit on their couches and shop e-retailers such as Amazon.com, QVC.com, or BestBuy.com instead of driving to their local mall. Each of these demonstrates marketing introducing products based on new technology that eventually becomes a daily part of our shared culture.

Not everyone thinks that the interaction between marketing and culture is beneficial. Marketing is seen by many people as encouraging consumption, which can become excessive or even addictive. Product packaging is sometimes wasteful and harmful to the environment. Advertising to children may exploit those members of society who are unable to make fully informed decisions. If marketers do not consider the impact of their actions on society, then, in some cases, society may decide to regulate marketing behavior. Two parts of our culture are interconnected: consumerism and environmentalism.

Consumerism

Consumerism describes the organized efforts on the part of consumer groups or governments to improve the rights and power of buyers in relation to sellers.[7] Consumerism does not need to be coordinated in any formal manner. One example of consumerism is when consumers decide, each on his or her own, to stop buying a company's products due to its business practices. In some instances, organized collective actions (called **boycotts**) can be very effective in correcting what consumers believe to be unethical or harmful marketing behavior. Boycotts work because they result in lowered sales and profitability, directly attacking something very precious to businesses: their pocketbooks. Another way boycotts influence corporate behavior is through any negative publicity they may generate. Firms that ignored or resisted boycotts have been depicted as insensitive bullies in the news media. Due to their harmful impact on financial situations and brand image, companies tend to avoid boycotts if possible.

Although consumerism in the United States has roots as far back as the early 1900s, the latest period of consumer activism began in the mid-1960s. Rising inflation led many consumers to question the real value of their purchases. More and more, they sought protection from false advertising, poor-quality products, and deceptive pricing practices.[8] At the forefront of this movement were authors like Ralph Nader, whose 1965 book *Unsafe at Any Speed* argued that owners should be protected from potentially dangerous automobiles like General Motors' Chevrolet Corvair. Upset by the negative publicity, the automaker hired private detectives to follow the author. GM's president later publicly apologized to Nader for its actions, but many observers attribute the passage of tougher automotive safety legislation to this incident.[9]

Recognizing this rising wave of consumerism, governments tried to codify the rights of individual consumers. The Consumer Bill of Rights (identified in Table 4.1) was outlined in President John F. Kennedy's 1961 inaugural speech. The bill was intended to explicitly define the four basic rights to which each and every consumer is entitled, including the right to be *safe*, to be *informed*, to be *heard*, and to *choose freely*. Many federal organizations and laws, such as the Consumer Product Safety Commission and the Truth in Lending Act, came into existence as a result of these four tenets. In 1985, the concept of consumer rights was endorsed by the United Nations and expanded to eight basic rights.[10]

Advocacy groups such as Consumers International, Consumers Union, and the Better Business Bureau act on behalf

Table 4.1 Consumer Bill of Rights

The right to safety	To be protected against products, production processes, and services that are hazardous to health or life
The right to be informed	To be given facts needed to make an informed choice, and to be protected against dishonest or misleading advertising and labeling
The right to choose	To be able to select from a range of products and services, offered at competitive prices with an assurance of satisfactory quality
The right to be heard	To have consumer interests represented in the making and execution of government policy, and in the development of products and services
The right to satisfaction of basic needs	To have access to basic essential goods and services, adequate food, clothing, shelter, health care, education, and sanitation
The right to redress	To receive a fair settlement of just claims, including compensation for misrepresentation, shoddy goods, or unsatisfactory services
The right to consumer education	To acquire knowledge and skills needed to make informed, confident choices about goods and services while being aware of basic consumer rights and responsibilities and how to act on them
The right to a healthy environment	To live and work in an environment that is nonthreatening to the well-being of present and future generations

of consumers to promote their rights in the marketplace. Although they lack the legal authority of government bodies, these groups can bring substantial pressure on marketers through the media, by political lobbying, or by organizing consumer boycotts. At its core, consumerism is a signal that customers are not all happy, docile, and satisfied. Militant customers are quite willing to take aggressive action, and wise marketers attempt to be prepared for the results.[11]

EXAMPLE CONSUMERISM

Since 1988, over 200 companies and 1,000 products have been boycotted in the United States. Boycott targets cover a wide range of industries and issues, such as the following:

- **Environmental safety** Since 1999, boycotts by groups such as the Rainforest Action Network have influenced over 400 large retailers and users of timber to phase out all products using wood from old-growth forests.
- **Genetically modified foods** Greenpeace and other organizations threatened boycotts of food marketers, including Heinz, Gerber, Frito-Lay, McDonald's, and Burger King, to ensure that their products are free of genetically modified ingredients.
- **Animal rights** Boycotts by PETA persuaded McDonald's, Burger King, and Wendy's to require humane production practices from their suppliers of chickens, eggs, and other meats.
- **Facebook** Inspired by changes to Facebook privacy policy, some Facebook users staged a boycott of the site while others closed their accounts. Some protesters used another form of social media, Twitter, to communicate with boycotting individuals.

Research by Davidson, Worrell, and El-Jelly found evidence that boycotts can be effective in changing corporate behavior. Boycotts send a strong signal to marketers' wallets, resulting in a type of "stakeholder capitalism" where consumers discover empowerment in their wallets.[12]

PHOTO: Selena/Shutterstock.

>> END EXAMPLE

Environmentalism

Each year, about 130 million people are born, placing even greater demands on our planet's resources. Societal concerns over climate change, diminishing natural resources, and pollution are causing a growing number of consumers to question their consumption habits.

Environmentalism is an organized movement of citizens, businesses, and government agencies to protect and improve our living environment. As a social movement, environmentalism is expressed in a variety of ways, from consumer boycotts of environmentally unfriendly products to formal government legislation. While consumerism is concentrated on enhancing the rights and power of buyers in relation to sellers, environmentalism considers the costs of meeting consumer requirements and advocates care for the environment. Some businesses choose to respond to environmentalism by implementing environmental sustainability practices. **Environmental sustainability** is achieving financial objectives while promoting the long-term well-being of the earth. Other businesses make decisions based on potential consumer responses or to meet minimum legal requirements.

Green marketing is a catchall phrase describing how marketing has responded to the environmental movement by offering more ecologically responsible products and services. Being "green" can mean many things, from ensuring that your product is free of harmful chemicals to arranging a means to recycle or reclaim some of your product's ingredients at the end of its useful life. Environmentally responsible questions for marketers include the following:

- What chemicals or processes will be used to create this product?
- How much energy will be consumed in its creation?
- Can the product be used safely and with minimal impact on the environment?
- Can the product be disposed of or recycled in a manner that poses minimal or no risk to the environment?
- Is there a more environmentally sound alternative to this product?

The terms "green" and "marketing" are contradictory concepts when considered separately. The traditional role of marketing is to support and enhance consumption of goods and services while green, synonymous with sustainability, refers to reducing the effects of consumption.[13]

Through the principles of environmental sustainability, some businesses are working to find a balance between financial requirements and environmental responsibilities. Businesses can look to differentiate themselves from their competitors through efforts in green marketing. However, fundamental marketing concepts still apply and it becomes critical not to arbitrarily create and overemphasize a green product at the expense of customer satisfaction elements such as convenience, quality, and value.[14] Businesses can "green" themselves in any of three ways:[15]

- Value-added processes (such as new technology in a manufacturing tool)
- Management systems (such as environmental, health, and safety objectives)
- Products or services (such as redesigning a product using materials that can be recycled)

EXAMPLE ENVIRONMENTALISM

A growing number of consumers will only use cleaning products made from environmentally friendly ingredients. This "green cleaning" movement is expected to achieve a 30% share of the household cleaning market by 2013, up from just 3% in 2008.

Method is a company that sells biodegradable cleaning products, including laundry detergent, dish soap, spray cleaners, and scented plug-ins. Combining thoughtful design with "green" ingredients at an affordable price, Method's slogan is "people against dirty." The company's watchwords are *environment, safety, efficacy, design*, and *fragrance*.

Products come in appealing packages with fresh scents like lavender or ylang-ylang. One of Method's most innovative products is the omop, which is a nontoxic, microfiber floor cleaner. In keeping with the growing importance of "green" products, Method can be found at 160 retailers such as Target, Lowes, and Costco in the United States, Canada, United Kingdom, Australia, France, and Japan as well as on Amazon.com and on its own Web site.

According to market research firm Kline & Company, Method was one of the fastest-growing companies of its type in 2009, with sales of $200 million (up 135% from 2006).[16]

PHOTO: Michal Bednarek/Shutterstock.

>> END EXAMPLE

The market for environmentally and socially responsible products can be divided into distinct customer segments. A segmentation study conducted by the Natural Marketing Institute in 2007 identified the following five core groups in the United States based on lifestyles of health and sustainability in Figure 4.1 (LOHAS):[17]

FIGURE 4.1 Five Core Groups

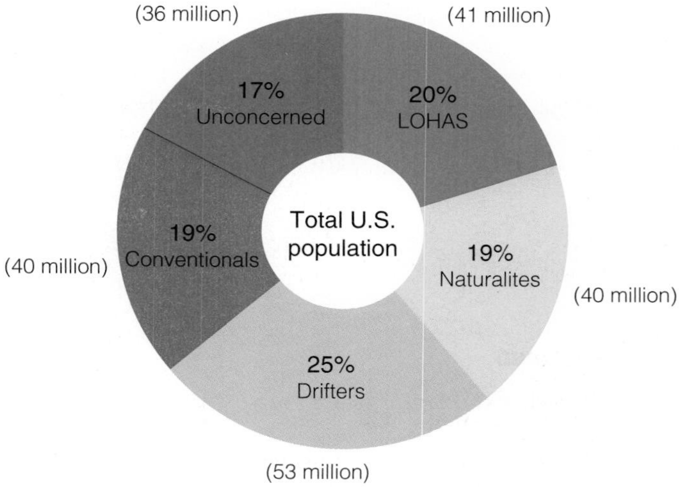

- **LOHAS** are dedicated to the health of themselves and the planet. They purchase environmentally friendly products and are active in related causes.
- **Naturalites** focus on natural and organic products, especially food and beverages.
- **Drifters** mean well, but they are price sensitive and trendy regarding their purchases. They have several rationalizations for not buying environmentally friendly products.
- **Conventionals** are practical and do not have overtly "green" attitudes, but they will recycle, conserve energy, and engage in other mainstream eco-behaviors.
- **Unconcerned** do not make protecting the environment or improving society a priority. They demonstrate no environmentally responsible behavior.

In 2008, about 30% of Americans could be classified as members of a LOHAS segment.[18] They spent 10% more in warehouse clubs and bought more cereal, jelly, pasta, produce, and soup than "non-green" consumers. The economic impact of consumers who have adopted an environmental mindset can be tremendous. According to research by Mambo Sprouts Marketing, 7 in 10 consumers are willing to spend up to 20% more for "green" sustainable products.[19]

Organic foods are those grown without the use of pesticides or synthetic fertilizers. These products are considered better for the environment because they reduce pollution and conserve water and soil. The market for organic foods was $4.4 billion in 2008, and is expected to increase to $6.8 billion by 2012.[20] Smart marketers are paying attention to the social risks, and the economic rewards, presented by the environmental movement.

MARKETING and the Law (pp. 44–45)

DEFINED **Laws** *are rules of conduct or action prescribed by an authority, or the binding customs or practices of a community.*

EXPLAINED

Marketing and the Law

Although the vast majority of businesspeople conduct themselves in a responsible and ethical manner, the risks are too great to assume that everyone will do so. To protect consumers and maintain economic stability, the U.S. government periodically institutes laws and regulations to deter harmful marketing behavior. Areas of marketing that are of particular interest to legislators include the following:

- False advertising
- Deceptive pricing practices
- Tobacco advertising
- Children's advertising
- Product safety
- Nutritional labeling
- Consumer privacy
- Fairness in lending practices

A broader definition of "law" also includes social practices or customs. Whether as individuals or in organized groups, from time to time consumers themselves attempt to limit some business activities and encourage others. As of 2006, there were approximately 20,000 NGOs outside the United States and about 2 million in the United States.[21] Although these actions lack the official rule of law, they can be equally (or more) effective in governing marketing behavior if a business is truly consumer-oriented.

APPLIED

Marketing and the Law

The federal government has created several official agencies to protect the interests of consumers and the general public. These agencies are taken very seriously, because businesspeople who violate the agencies' standards can be affected professionally and personally and face fines or imprisonment. Each of the following regulatory bodies has influence over areas of policy related to marketing:[22]

- **Consumer Product Safety Commission (CPSC)**—This agency monitors product safety and issues recalls for unsafe products. It also establishes standards for product safety.
- **Environmental Protection Agency (EPA)**—The EPA develops and enforces regulations to protect the environment, some of which affect the materials and processes used to manufacture products.
- **Federal Communications Commission (FCC)**—Any firm that uses broadcast media (telephone, radio, or television) for marketing is affected by FCC rules.
- **Federal Trade Commission (FTC)**—The FTC enforces laws against deceptive advertising and product labeling regulations.
- **Food and Drug Administration (FDA)**—This agency enforces laws and regulations on foods, drugs, cosmetics, and veterinary products. Before introducing new drugs and other products into the marketplace manufacturers must first obtain FDA approval.
- **Interstate Commerce Commission (ICC)**—The ICC regulates all interstate bus, truck, rail, and water operations. ICC regulations and policies can impact the efficiency of marketing distribution channels.

Regulations are rules or orders issued by an official government agency that has proper authority and which carry the force of law. Marketers must learn to successfully operate within constraints imposed by these requirements. Table 4.2 contains some major federal laws that have fostered regulations on marketing activity.[23]

From a consumer perspective, the most visible areas of government regulation on marketing are advertising, pricing, and product safety. The FTC is responsible for ensuring compliance with a wide range of regulations on pricing and promotion. Examples of federal regulation in these areas include the following:[24]

- Advertisers must have documented proof of any claims made in an advertisement before the ad runs—letters from satisfied customers are usually not sufficient.
- It is illegal to say that a product has a "retail value of $15.00, your price: $7.50," if $15.00 is not the prevailing price for the product in the retailer's geographic area.
- It is illegal to advertise any product when a company has no plans to sell it, but instead plans to switch customers to another item at a higher price (called bait-and-switch).

The FTC looks at advertising from the point of view of a reasonable consumer and asks, "Would a typical person looking at this ad be fooled or harmed by this?" If the answer is yes, the FTC may issue a cease and desist order, forcing the marketers to stop running the deceptive ad. It may also invoke civil penalties (which can range from thousands to millions of dollars) and might even force the company to create new ads to correct any misinformation.

Table 4.2 Major Federal Laws and Regulations

Law	Area of Marketing Regulated by Law
Sherman Antitrust Act (1890)	Distribution (for example, exclusive territories) Pricing (for example, price fixing, predatory pricing)
Food and Drug Act (1906)	Product safety (for example, food and drugs)
Clayton Act (1914)	Distribution (for example, tying contracts and exclusive dealing)
Federal Trade Commission (FTC) Act (1914)	All areas of marketing that result in unfair business practices
Robinson-Patman Act (1936)	Pricing (for example, price discrimination)
Wheeler-Lea Amendment to FTC Act (1938)	Promotion (for example, deceptive or misleading advertising)
Lanham Trademark Act (1946)	Branding (for example, brand names and trademarks)
Fair Packaging and Labeling Act (1966)	Packaging (for example, truth in labeling)
National Traffic and Motor Vehicle Safety Act (1966)	Product safety (for example, automobile and tire safety)
Cigarette Labeling Act (1966)	Product (for example, cigarette package warnings)
Child Protection Act (1966)	Product safety (for example, children's product safety)
Child Protection and Toy Safety Act (1966)	Packaging (for example, child-resistant packages)
Consumer Credit Protection Act (1968)	Promotion (for example, credit terms, loan terms)
Fair Credit Reporting Act (1970)	Information sharing (for example, credit reporting)
Consumer Products Safety Commission Act (1972)	Product safety (for example, safety monitoring, recalls, safety standards)
Magnuson-Moss Consumer Product Warranty Act (1975)	Product (for example, warranties)
Children's Television Act (1990)	Promotion (for example, children's advertising)
Nutrition Labeling and Education Act (1990)	Packaging (for example, food and drug labeling)
National Do Not Call Registry (2003)	Promotion (for example, telemarketing)
Credit CARD Act (2009)	Pricing (for example, limiting interest rate hikes) Promotion (for example, limits on college campus marketing)

Marketers do have a bit of leeway in making statements and claims regarding their products and services. Claims of product superiority that cannot be proven as true or false are called **puffery** and are a generally accepted marketing practice. For example, saying "ABC cola tastes great!" is puffery, but saying "ABC water filters remove harmful chemicals from tap water" is not. Some company claims are presented as unique characteristics that create value to consumers yet, in reality, are not distinctive. Wegmans Bread boasted that it was "bromate free." But then so is all bread. Bromate, an additive, has never been found in bread at harmful levels, according to *Popular Science*.[25] On the other hand, **exaggerated claims** are restricted by the FTC. Every marketer that makes an explicit or implicit claim about its products or services should have substantiation or a reasonable basis for that statement. For example, ads for health products may boast that a product is a "medical breakthrough" or that it was "tested across the world." By law, anyone making these claims should have solid evidence in place before running these ads.

EXAMPLE REGULATIONS

Makers of the dietary supplement Airborne advertised and labeled their product as an effective treatment to prevent illnesses contracted when traveling on airplanes or in other public environments. The FTC investigated and found that Airborne "did not have adequate evidence to support its advertising claims in which its effervescent tablet was marketed as a cold prevention and treatment remedy." As a result, the makers of Airborne reached a $30 million settlement with the FTC, and consumers who purchased the product were able to file claims for refunds.[26]

PHOTO: Mark Stout Photography/Shutterstock.

>> END EXAMPLE

Another organization that issues regulations that affect marketing is the Consumer Product Safety Commission (CPSC). The CPSC is a watchdog organization whose charter is the protection and safety of consumers. It issues regulations on the ingredients and processes marketers can use when manufacturing their products. It also carries the authority to ban or seize potentially harmful products. Marketers who violate its regulations face severe penalties.

MARKETING and Social Responsibility (pp. 46–47)

DEFINED **Social responsibility** *is concern for how a person's (or company's) actions might affect the interests of others.*

EXPLAINED

Marketing and Social Responsibility

A business cannot be separated from the society in which it operates. A business's influence is felt through its products and services, its production methods, its pricing, its advertising, its distribution methods, and how it distributes its profits. Recognizing the interrelationships between companies and society, many firms have adopted a policy of **corporate social responsibility (CSR)** that encourages decision makers to take into account the social consequences of their business actions.

Profitability has been the traditional yardstick used to measure the success, or failure, of a business. As a result of using such a yardstick, the interests of society become secondary to monetary goals. Proponents of corporate social responsibility argue that companies should earn profits in an ethical manner that respects people and communities. They also suggest that companies ought to promote **sustainability** through careful stewardship of our natural resources and the environment.

Some people believe that marketing should not only avoid creating harm to society, but should also be used to benefit society. The **social marketing concept** asserts that marketing techniques may be employed for more than selling things and making a profit. Marketing tools can be applied to causes that improve the lives of individuals and society. One of the best examples of social marketing in action is the TRUTH antismoking advertising campaign. Using a variety of nontraditional and traditional media such as TV, promotional items (T-shirts), posters, and graffiti, TRUTH ads were credited with significant reductions in the number of middle- and high school students who began smoking.

APPLIED

Marketing and Social Responsibility

"To my mind, industry must aim for, exist for, and everlastingly operate for the good of the community. The community cannot ride one track and business another. The two are inseparable, interactive, and interdependent."
Cleo F. Craig, President, AT&T (1951–1956)

Corporate social responsibility is not a notion confined to textbooks and academia. Many major corporations now accept the tenets of CSR and weigh their marketing decisions accordingly. Coca-Cola, Ford Motor Company, Marathon Oil, Bayer, Colgate-Palmolive, Nestlé, Motorola, and Starbucks are just a few companies that have issued formal corporate social responsibility reports.

CSR is closely related to principles of ethical business behavior. **Ethics** are a system of moral principles and values, as well as moral duties or obligations. A simple way to think about ethics is that they determine which actions are "good," or correct, from a philosophical or social point of view. A similar set of principles, called **marketing ethics**, is rules for evaluating marketing decisions and actions based on marketers' duties or obligations to society (see Marketing Ethics below).

CSR assumes that marketers have a responsibility to behave in an ethical manner, and that decisions that negatively impact society are often unethical. There is even talk about a "triple bottom line," asserting that firms should be evaluated not only on their economic performance but also on their environmental and social impacts. Ethics codes, like the one published by the American Marketing Association, are an attempt to lay down general norms and guidelines for ethical marketing behavior.[27]

Marketing Ethics

1. Marketers must do no harm. This means doing work for which they are appropriately trained or in which they are experienced so that they can actively add value to their organizations and customers. It also means adhering to all applicable laws and regulations and embodying high ethical standards in the choices they make.
2. Marketers must foster trust in the marketing system. This means that products are appropriate for their intended and promoted uses. It requires that marketing communications about goods and services are not intentionally deceptive or misleading. It suggests building relationships that provide for the equitable alignment and/or redress of consumer grievances. It implies striving for good faith and fair dealing so as to contribute to the efficacy of the exchange process.
3. Marketers must embrace ethical values. These basic values are intended to be values to which marketers aspire and include *honesty, responsibility, fairness, respect, openness,* and *citizenship.*

Sometimes what is permitted legally is not necessarily ethical. For instance, a company might stop selling a product in developed nations where consumer safety regulations are strict and the product is found to be harmful. Although the firm could begin selling its product in less developed countries where legal restrictions are more lax, some people might find this action unethical. If a product is unsafe for human consumption in one country, it is equally unfit for another. An ethical lapse such as this sometimes happens because it is difficult to choose between what is legally permitted and what is ethical when profits or personal advancement are at stake.

EXAMPLE **SOCIAL RESPONSIBILITY**

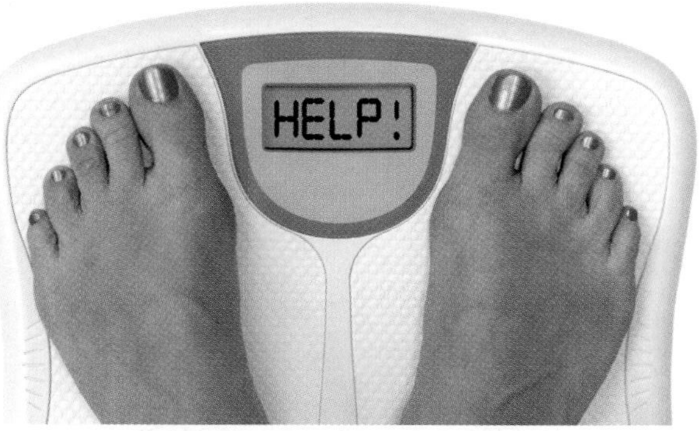

Food marketing is big business, and young people are a particularly attractive target. Soda, snacks, candy, fast food, and other high-energy but nutrient-poor foods have been marketed to youth in North America, Europe, and Australasia (New Zealand, Australia, Papua New Guinea, and neighboring islands in the Pacific Ocean) for years. In the United States, over $12 billion is spent annually marketing food to young consumers; a new emphasis has been placed on promotion in schools and on the Internet. In 2006, the Institute of Medicine concluded that food and beverage marketing is a "likely contributor to less healthful diets" and that it "may contribute to negative diet-related health outcomes and risks among children and youth." Childhood obesity has become a worldwide problem, with 10% of children worldwide estimated to be overweight or obese. Given the link between marketing, food choices, and health problems among youth, what should companies such as Coca-Cola, Frito-Lay, and Burger King do? Should they take a short-term view, focus on profits, and continue with "business as usual" while contributing to a growing health problem? Or should they focus on long-term social benefits by offering healthier food options, but possibly alienating customers who have been conditioned to prefer less healthy foods?[28]

PHOTO: Amy Walters/Shutterstock.

>> **END EXAMPLE**

Defenders of CSR suggest that a company's reputation depends on the totality of its actions, and that "doing the right thing" at all times will have long-term economic benefits. Surveys have indicated that consumers are willing to pay a higher price for products from firms that give priority to ethical behavior.[29] However, businesses in poorer countries or those in financial distress may be faced with the choice of either complying with CSR principles or going out of business. Like most conceptual frameworks, the application of ethics and social responsibility in the real world is sometimes a delicate balance.

EXAMPLE **CORPORATE SOCIAL RESPONSIBILITY**

When you think of corporate social responsibility, a bank may not be the first business that comes to mind. For years, Wells Fargo has provided financial services such as banking, insurance, investments, and mortgages while still guiding its marketing decisions by CSR principles. Here are some examples of socially responsible marketing actions taken by Wells Fargo in 2008:[30]

- **Serving customers responsibly**—The company adopted responsible lending principles and marketing practices for education financing.
- **Supporting homeownership**—The company launched Hope Now, an alliance of mortgage servicers, not-for-profit counselors, and investors in the capital markets to help homeowners at risk of foreclosure.
- **Building communities**—The company invested $6.4 billion in community-development loans to support projects for affordable housing, schools, economic development, community revitalization, and job creation. $226 million in direct assistance was provided to charitable organizations.
- **Volunteering**—1.4 million volunteer hours worth $27.3 million in person hours were contributed by team members.
- **Financial education**—In addition to its Hands on Banking financial education curriculum, Wells Fargo launched the Teen Checking project to improve young people's financial knowledge.
- **Protecting the environment**—The company committed to purchasing 550 million kilowatt-hours of renewable energy certificates each year for three years, making Wells Fargo the second largest purchaser of renewable energy.
- **Putting our people first**—Wells Fargo offers flexible work arrangements and work/life programs to support team members. *BusinessWeek* ranked Wells Fargo among the top 50 best places to launch a career in 2008.

PHOTO: Yuri Arcurs/Shutterstock.

>> **END EXAMPLE**

Visual Summary

Chapter 4 Summary

From a broader perspective, marketing involves society, the legal environment, and ethics. Consumers, companies, and culture interact in ways that can be either mutually beneficial or destructive. The force of law, both official and unofficial, is intended to curb marketing excesses and to encourage proper conduct. Consumer-driven agendas, such as consumerism, environmentalism, and corporate social responsibility, are topics companies must learn to integrate into their marketing strategies.

Marketing and Society p. 39

intertwined

Society is a collection of individuals who share common traditions, institutions, activities, and interests. Marketing is intertwined with society as a competitive marketplace with a wide range of consumer choices that must be balanced with safety and ethical business practices.

Marketing and Culture pp. 40–43

reflection

Culture is the shared values, beliefs, and preferences of a particular society. Marketing is both a reflection of culture and a powerful influence upon it.

Marketing and the Law pp. 44–45

rules

Laws are rules of conduct, binding customs and community practices. Areas of marketing that are of particular interest to legislators include false advertising, deceptive pricing, tobacco advertising, children's advertising, product safety, nutritional labeling, consumer privacy, and fairness in lending practices.

Marketing and Social Responsibility pp. 46–47

ethics

Social responsibility, based on the principles of ethical behavior, reflects the idea that business cannot be separated from the society in which it operates and the actions of one affect the interests of the other. Marketing ethics are rules for evaluating marketing decisions and actions based on marketers' responsibilities to society.

Capstone **Exercise** p. 50

Chapter Key Terms

Marketing and Society (p. 39)

Society *refers to a community, nation, or group that shares common traditions, institutions, activities, and interests. (p. 39)*
Opening Example (p. 39)

Key Terms (p. 39)

Gross Domestic Product (GDP) measures the total dollar value of goods and services a country produces within a given year. **(p. 39)**

Nongovernmental organizations (NGOs) are groups of private individuals who monitor the behavior of marketers or governments. **(p. 39)**

Marketing and Culture (pp. 40–43)

Culture *refers to the shared values, beliefs, and preferences of a particular society. (p. 40)* **Example: Culture (p. 40)**

Key Terms (pp. 41–43)

Boycotts happen when consumers refuse to do business with a company or nation in order to signal their disapproval of its actions and encourage change. **(p. 41) Example: Consumerism (p. 42)**

Consumerism is the organized efforts on the part of consumer groups or governments to improve the rights and power of buyers in relation to sellers. **(p. 41) Example: Consumerism (p. 42)**

Environmental sustainability is achieving financial objectives while promoting the long-term well-being of the earth. **(p. 42)**

Environmentalism is an organized movement of citizens, businesses, and government agencies to protect and improve our living environment. **(p. 42) Example: Consumerism (p. 42) Example: Environmentalism (p. 43)**

Green marketing refers to marketing efforts to produce more environmentally responsible products and services. **(p. 42) Example: Environmentalism (p. 43)**

Organic foods are foods grown naturally without the use of pesticides or synthetic fertilizers. **(p. 43)**

Marketing and the Law (pp. 44–45)

Laws *are rules of conduct or action prescribed by an authority, or the binding customs or practices of a community. (p. 44)*
Example: Regulations (p. 45)

Key Terms (pp. 44–45)

Exaggerated claims are extravagant statements made in advertising, either explicitly or implicitly, that have no substantiation or reasonable basis in truth. **(p. 45) Example: Regulations (p. 45)**

Puffery refers to claims of product superiority that cannot be proven as true or false. **(p. 45)**

Regulations are rules or orders issued by an official government agency with proper authority and which carry the force of law. **(p. 44) Example: Regulations (p. 45)**

Marketing and Social Responsibility (pp. 46–47)

Social responsibility *refers to a concern for how a person's (or company's) actions might affect the interests of others. (p. 46)*
Example: Social Responsibility (p. 47) Example: Corporate Social Responsibility (p. 47)

Key Terms (p. 46)

Corporate social responsibility (CSR) is a philosophy that encourages decision makers to take into account the social consequences of their business actions. **(p. 46) Example: Corporate Social Responsibility (p. 47)**

Ethics are a system of moral principles and values, as well as moral duties or obligations. **(p. 46) Example: Corporate Social Responsibility (p. 47)**

Marketing ethics are rules for evaluating marketing decisions and actions based on marketers' duties or obligations to society. **(p. 46) Example: Social Responsibility (p. 47)**

Social marketing concept asserts that marketing techniques may be employed for more than selling things and making a profit. **(p. 46) Example: Corporate Social Responsibility (p. 47)**

Sustainability is a term used to describe practices that combine economic growth with careful stewardship of our natural resources and the environment. **(p. 46)**

Capstone Exercise

This chapter deals with many of the cultural, social, legal, and ethical aspects of marketing. Today, *sustainability* has become a business buzzword. When we discuss "sustainability" we are looking at social (cultural), economic, and environmental sustainability—not just the eco-friendly or "green" movement. Marketers are responsible for promoting products while at the same time serving the "triple bottom line," a term coined by John Elkington in 1994, referring to people, planet, and profits.

A recent study by a consumer health organization, Families USA, reported that pharmaceutical drug companies spend over $57 billion per year on promotion. Direct-to-physician activities accounted for the bulk of spending, on a practice called "detailing"—visits to physicians by pharmaceutical sales representatives in order to promote their firm's drugs. Free drug samples distributed during these visits represent another significant expense. It is estimated that in total pharmaceutical companies spend over $61,000 in "promotion per physician." The other major piece of the marketing "pie" is spent on consumer-direct marketing—ads that suggest we "ask our doctor" about drugs we may not even need for ailments we may not even have. The report also states that each of the top 10 pharmaceutical companies spends more than twice as much on marketing as on research and development. This would confirm the public image that the pharmaceutical industry is a market-driven industry and supports public opinion that the industry should spend more on research and less on promotion.

Answer the following questions:

1. If prescription drugs can only be ordered by a physician, what is the purpose of marketing directly to consumers?
2. In your opinion, what are the positive and negative effects of the current pharmaceutical marketing strategy?
3. What might be some ethical issues connected with the practice of providing physicians with free samples?
4. Do you think legislation controlling pharmaceutical consumer-direct marketing would benefit the consumer? How?
5. Assume you are the marketing director for a major pharmaceutical company. Also assume that your company has "come under fire" for high costs of prescription drugs. How would you propose improving the public image of your company?

Application Exercise

Use the marketing concepts in this chapter to tackle and solve a marketing problem: culture, consumerism, environmentalism, and green marketing.

First, start by thinking about a category of products that is ecologically responsible, sometimes named "green." In general terms, green products are responsive to the sustainability and balance of the environment within the structure of the product and its packaging. There are many products available in stores within this category for us to consider purchasing.

The Marketing Problem

Choose a product in the green category after considering the following situation.

> You feel the environment and its sustainability may be affected by buying decisions that are being made by the ordinary consumer.

The Problem

Describe a product that helps or is neutral to the environment. What is the product's value? Did environmentalism prompt you to buy it? Would you pay more for a green product?

The Solution

Complete the following two Problem/Solution briefs using your product in the green product category, chapter concepts, and college resources.

1. From the Marketing Manager's Point of View
   a. Problem Definition
   b. Environmental Analysis
   c. Product's Value
   d. Solution

2. From the Consumer's Point of View
   a. Problem Definition
   b. Price Analysis
   c. Product's Value
   d. Solution

Resources:

Marketing Defined, Explained, Applied 2e, Michael Levens
The College Library
Retail or Online Field Trip
Assigned Reading—*Brand Week, Advertising Age, WSJ,* scholarly publications, category trade journals
Blog your problem from either point of view, gather responses/posts (www.blogger.com/start)

Global Marketing

Chapter Overview The practice of marketing becomes increasingly complex when it is extended globally. However, significant opportunities exist for businesses that carefully consider those factors that influence successful global marketing. This chapter considers concepts of contemporary global marketing as well as the global marketing environment consisting of global trade, economics, politics, law, and culture, and global marketing processes.

Chapter Outline

Global MARKETING (pp. 53–54)

DEFINED **Global marketing** *includes all marketing activities conducted at an international level by individuals or businesses.*

EXPLAINED

Global Marketing

Our world today is made up of about 6.8 billion people who are connected by global communications networks and relatively inexpensive transportation. This interconnectedness is closely tied to the concept of **globalization**, which is the outcome of cultures intermingling, sharing experiences, news, and commerce. Richard N. Haass, president of the Council on Foreign Relations, described globalization as "the increasing volume, speed, and importance of flows across borders: people, ideas, greenhouse gases, manufactured goods, dollars, euros, television and radio signals, drugs, germs, emails, weapons, and a good deal else."[1]

Global trade (and marketing) is one of the driving forces behind globalization. Brazil, Russia, India, and China, referred to as the BRIC countries, are quickly strengthening their ability to compete in the global marketplace mainly through their relatively inexpensive labor market and expanding manufacturing capacity, and their influence on mainstream American culture is already being felt. The growing popularity of Indian Bollywood films and Chinese *feng shui,* the ancient folk art of organizing buildings and objects to optimize the flow of life force, are just two examples. BRIC countries accounted for over a third of world economic growth from 2000–2009. Goldman Sachs forecasts that the economies of BRIC countries, in aggregate, will overtake the U.S. economy by 2018. Brazil's economy is forecasted to be larger than Italy's economy by 2020 and the individual economies of India and Russia will be larger than the economies of Spain, Canada, and Italy by 2020.[2]

Some of the benefits of global trade to businesses and nations include the following:

- Access to new and possibly growing consumer and business markets
- Obtaining scale economies (that is, reducing costs by increasing production volume)
- Access to lower cost labor or materials
- Ability to offset domestic economic cycles
- Enhanced brand image and perceptions
- Access to foreign investment incentives

APPLIED

Global Marketing

Even on a global scale, the basic functions of marketing do not change. A product must still be offered at a fair price whether it is sold in Paris, Texas, or in Paris, France. However, a "fair price" could be defined quite differently in those two locations. Different competitors exist in different countries, creating new consumer choice options, and product characteristics need to be adjusted for varying consumer desires. Supply chains and distribution options also differ between countries. Advertising and sales promotion must be adapted for foreign languages,

Li-Ning, the largest Chinese shoe and apparel company, opened its first U.S. showroom in 2010. Founded in 1990 by former Chinese Olympic gymnast Li Ning, the business has grown to sales of almost $1 billion. Even growing at 37% per year, however, it will take some time to catch industry leader Nike with sales of $19 billion. Located in Portland, Oregon, the same town that houses the world headquarters of Nike and the North American headquarters of Adidas, Li-Ning hopes to draw on local talent to further expand its business.

Li-Ning has been innovative since its inception. It was the first company of its kind to franchise throughout China in 1993, and it was the first to open a facility devoted to design and development of its apparel and footwear in 1998. In 2005, Li-Ning partnered with the National Basketball Association and other sporting organizations and began sponsorship of international athletes including Shaquille O'Neal, Baron Davis, Jose Calderon, Hasheem Thabeet, Yalena Isinbaeva, and Ivan Ljubicic. Li-Ning established a North American office in Portland, Oregon, in 2007, and it was a major sponsor of the Beijing Olympics in 2008. Li-Ning used the 2008 Olympics to debut its basketball, table tennis, and badminton lines to Western customers. China, once known mainly as a manufacturing location for U.S. shoe brands, now has a home-grown brand establishing a foothold in the U.S. market.[3]

PHOTO: Zimmytws\Shutterstock.

customs, legal requirements, and media options. National, regional, and local differences make global marketing more complex and difficult than single country marketing.

When consumer tastes differ at a local level, marketers are tempted to modify products, services, prices, distribution methods, and communications to cater to those tastes. However, extensive customization also defeats one of the primary benefits of global trade, which is lowering production costs through standardization. Successful global marketers do not think solely in terms of "local" versus "global." Instead, they are "**glocal**"—acting either globally, locally, or both, as needed. About 60% of McDonald's food items sold in India are also sold at McDonald's restaurants around the world, while 40% of its items, like the Paneer Salsa Wrap or McAloo Tikki, are specially designed to satisfy local tastes.[4]

EXAMPLE GLOBAL MARKETING

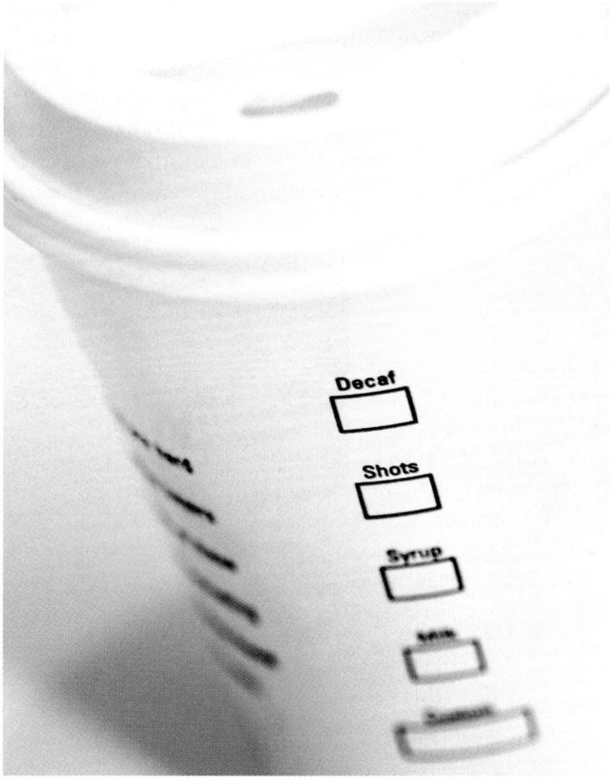

Starbucks operates in over 50 countries, and 70% of its consumers are located outside of the United States. Its largest audiences are in countries that vary greatly from one another—the United Kingdom, Indonesia, and Turkey. To serve the many and varied countries in which it does business, Starbucks uses Facebook and its portfolio to operate as a glocal company. Starbucks, owner of the largest fan base on Facebook with over 6 million fans, has created a central fan page, which primarily serves the U.S. market, and individual pages for local markets. Using the different pages, specific marketing communications including promotions and localized content can easily be distributed.

Responses to marketing communications, including advertising campaigns on Facebook, can be measured by individual countries rather than at the global level, and this knowledge allows Starbucks to manage resources and provide users with relevant content that increases the chance of achieving marketing objectives.[5] In addition to using Facebook, Starbucks also provides a combined global and local portfolio to its customers in different markets. Starbucks mixes some standardized products available throughout the world, such as bottled Frappuccino and the instant coffee Via, with local products, such as black sesame green tea Frappuccinos in the People's Republic of China and marmite (a yeast-based spread) and cheese Paninis in the United Kingdom.

PHOTO: Hadi Djunaedi\Shutterstock.

>> END EXAMPLE

Global MARKETING ENVIRONMENT (pp. 55–60)

DEFINED **Global marketing environment** *is the environment in different sovereign countries, with characteristics distinct to the home environment of an organization, influencing decisions on marketing activities.*

EXPLAINED

Global Marketing Environment

Businesses that are active in global markets are exposed to a wide range of environmental factors beyond those experienced in their home markets. The macroenvironment becomes increasingly complex when global dimensions of trade, economics, politics, law, and culture are introduced. As firms have, essentially, no control over the external environment, their success depends upon how well they adjust to that environment. The way a business operates globally has much to do with its potential for marketing and business success. There are three main categories of companies operating globally:

- **International companies** have no investment outside their home country other than the direct purchase of products or services and are, essentially, importers and exporters.
- **Multinational companies** maintain assets and operations in more than one country and concentrate on adapting products and services to the specific needs of each country.
- **Global companies** maintain assets and operations in more than one country and concentrate on penetrating multiple countries with a minimally customized marketing mix.

Whereas you may see different images and brands in each country served by a multinational company, a global company seeks to present a coordinated image and brand in each country. The global company model can be successful if enough common characteristics are found among different countries to allow for cost and volume efficiencies to be achieved. It is far less costly to design, manufacture, market, and sell one type of product rather than multiple versions of the same product. Regardless of the type of company, many businesses **outsource** parts of their operations, procuring certain services from third-party suppliers to decrease labor costs, access human capital not readily available within the business, or implement specific strategies. Outsourcing can occur within the home country or overseas. **Offshoring** is a type of outsourcing in which business activities are completed in another country. Offshoring occurs for many of the same reasons as outsourcing, but must comply with foreign legal requirements. Offshoring can also result in complex supply chains that span a variety of countries.

Global Trade

Economies are typically classified by their **gross domestic product (GDP)**, which measures the total dollar value of goods and services a country produces within a given year. GDP can also apply to entities that are not countries. Some multinational and global companies are among the largest economic entities in the world. Two-thirds of the world's largest economies as measured by GDP are not countries, but corporations. Much of the growth of these corporations has been fueled by global trade. The balance sheets of companies such as ExxonMobil, Walmart, and Royal Dutch Shell exceed the amounts of goods and services produced in countries such as Sweden, Switzerland, and Chile.[6] The influence on the global marketing environment of these corporate entities operating across national borders cannot be underestimated.[7] Corporations of this scale are capable of influencing trade practices and creating marketing opportunities.

Despite the power of some corporations, certain individual and groups of countries with special trade relationships remain the largest economic powers on the planet. The European Union boasts the largest economy on Earth while the United States is second, followed by the People's Republic of China and Japan. While the European Union and the United States currently produce over 40% of the world's economic power, the People's Republic of China is expected to overtake the United States prior to 2020.[8] Each of these markets prices goods and services differently and, to account for this, GDP is generally reported at **purchasing power parity (PPP)**, which is a model of exchange rate determination stating that the price of a good or service in one country should equal the price of the same good or service in another country, exchanged at the current rate. For example, suppose that one U.S. dollar (USD) is selling for $1.10 Canadian (CAD), and a highly desired composite ice hockey stick is selling for 180 CAD in Canada and 220 USD in the United States. The idea of purchasing power parity is that increased demand from individuals in the United States for the composite ice hockey stick in Canada will also increase demand for Canadian dollars, and prices and exchange rates will adjust to create purchasing power parity. Of course a single product would have limited impact, but a portfolio of many goods and services could have a major impact over time. The concept of exchanges rates and other concepts of global pricing are discussed in greater detail in Chapter 13.

Economic communities are groups of countries that agree to take certain actions to manage resources of goods and services by lowering tariff barriers and promoting trade among members. Countries create these communities by signing a trade agreement. **Trade agreements** are treaties between countries to create a free trade area where business can be conducted without tariffs or other barriers. Trade agreements may include commitments on topics such as:

- Customs facilitation
- Environmental standards
- Foreign investment
- Government procurement
- Intellectual property rights
- Labor rights

The European Union, North American Free Trade Agreement, and Dominican Republic-Central America-United States Free Trade Agreement are just some examples of economic communities and trade agreements. The **European Union (EU)** is an economic and political partnership among 27 European countries. Founded in 1993, the EU has established frontier-free travel and trade, a single currency (the euro), food and environmental standards, joint action on crime and terror, and opportunities to work and study in any of the EU countries. A European Parliament representing the people of Europe, the Council of the European Union representing individual member governments, and the European Commission representing common EU interests have all been formed to support the partnership.[9] While there can be many benefits to economic communities, there can also be challenges. Recent stress in the EU has come from disparities between individual countries within the EU in the areas of government debt, economic policies, industrial competitiveness, labor markets, and retirement programs.

The **North American Free Trade Agreement (NAFTA)** was established in 1994 as a trading partnership among the United States, Canada, and Mexico. All investment limitations and trading barriers were removed in 2008. U.S. trade of goods and services through NAFTA totaled $1.1 trillion in 2008, and Canada and Mexico are the top two trading partners with the United States.[10] The **Dominican Republic-Central America-United States Free Trade Agreement (CAFTA-DR)** was established in 2004 as a partnership among the United States, the Dominican Republic, Costa Rica, El Salvador, Guatemala, Honduras, and Nicaragua. CAFTA-DR is the first free trade agreement between the United States and a group of smaller developing economies. Central America and the Dominican Republic represent the third largest U.S. export market in Latin America, behind Mexico and Brazil.[11] To help regulate powerful trade agreements such as these and to mediate other trade-related issues, the **World Trade Organization (WTO)** was established in 1995 as the preeminent organization dealing with the rules of trade at a global or near-global level. Essentially, the WTO is a place where the 153 member governments go to try to address the trade problems they face with each other. The WTO spends much of its time discussing opportunities to continue trade liberalization efforts, although some trade barriers are supported in certain cases to protect consumers, prevent the spread of disease, and protect the environment.[12]

Many of the issues brought before the WTO involve barriers to trade. One country may want to protect a particular industry due to perceived strategic value while another country feels that its businesses should have the opportunity to compete freely and fairly. The marketing implications of trade barriers are significant for companies because barriers alter the competitive environment and provide distinct advantages to local companies over global competitors. Barriers can take many forms, including tariffs and quotas. **Tariffs** are schedules of duties (or fees) applied to goods or services from foreign countries. **Quotas** are limits on the amount of product that can be imported into a country. Tariffs and quotas are both examples of anti-dumping strategies. **Dumping** is the practice of selling a product in a foreign country for a price less than either the cost to make the product or the price in the home country. This type of situation may escalate to the WTO.[13]

The WTO might also become involved in situations involving **non-tariff barriers (NTBs)**, which are restrictions on imports that are not in the usual form of a tariff. As tariffs decline, NTBs generally increase. NTBs may take the form of manufacturing or production requirements on goods, such as how a certain type plant is grown, with an import ban imposed on products that don't meet the requirements. For example, the European Union restricts importation of genetically modified organisms. Yet another type of barrier is **exchange controls,** which are put in place by governments to ban or restrict the amount of a specific currency that is permitted to be traded or purchased. These controls enable countries to achieve a greater degree of economic stability by limiting the amount of exchange rate volatility due to currency inflows and outflows.

The various trade barriers and controls affect the health of the economies that rely on them. One of the measures of the health of an economy is a country's balance of trade. The **balance of trade** is the difference between the monetary value of exports and imports of output in an economy over a specific period. A **trade surplus** occurs when the value of exports exceeds the value of imports. A **trade deficit** occurs when the value of imports exceeds the value of exports. As of 2009, the United States had a $517 billion trade deficit.[14]

EXAMPLE GLOBAL TRADE

What is the world's largest free trade area? It is neither the North American Free Trade Agreement (NAFTA) area nor the European Union (EU). The Association of Southeast Asian Nations (ASEAN) –China Free Trade Area (ACFTA) came into effect on January 1, 2010, and covers a population of 1.9 billion and a combined gross domestic product close to 6 trillion U.S. dollars. It is the world's largest free trade area in terms of population covered and the third largest in terms of trading volume. Countries involved in ACFTA include Brunei Darussalam, Cambodia, Indonesia, Laos, Malaysia, Myanmar, People's Republic of China, Philippines, Singapore, Thailand, and Vietnam.

Under ACFTA, the average tariff on most goods shipped between ASEAN countries and the People's Republic of China is either sharply reduced or eliminated over a period of five years. Chinese benefits from ACFTA are both economic, through increased free trade, and strategic, through balanced influence of global powers active in the region—the United States and Japan. ASEAN countries benefit from lower tariff barriers in the People's Republic of China and from leveraging their relationship with the People's Republic of China when dealing with other trading partners such as the United States and Japan.[15]

PHOTO: William Ju\Shutterstock.

>> END EXAMPLE

Economic

Trade policies can greatly influence the marketing environment within individual countries and provide either opportunities or challenges to businesses interested in operating in those countries. In addition to trade policies and the level of adherence to those policies, economic factors within countries also shape the viability of each country. A country's level of industrialization and **income distribution**, the way in which income and wealth are divided among the members of an economy, combine to influence market attractiveness.

The level of industrialization can be classified into five categories:

- **Subsistence economies** are generally represented by agrarian societies where enough is grown, hunted, and crafted to provide for the essential needs of the people and any surplus is bartered for basic goods and services.
- **Raw materials exporting economies** consist of countries that are plentiful in a particular raw material, yet deficient in other resources, and rely on the export of that raw material for the majority of revenue.
- **Industrializing economies** include countries where the manufacturing sector accounts for a small but growing share of the total economy and an increasing number of imported raw materials are required to support manufacturing.
- **Industrial economies** consist of countries with robust manufacturing, service, and financial sectors that are actively engaged in international trade.
- **Post-industrial economies** include countries where the manufacturing sector diminishes while service and information sectors become the primary sources of economic growth.

Industrializing and raw materials exporting economies are generally referred to as developing countries. As they attempt to develop their economies, developing countries are regularly interacting with industrial and post-industrial economies. Most developing countries produce an export good, an import-competing good, and a nontraded good.[16] The cost to obtain financing and produce the various types of goods required for different markets can create economic pressure in developing countries such as variances in wage rates. That pressure can manifest itself in how income and wealth are distributed.

Both level of industrialization and government practices have considerable influence on how citizens of a particular country obtain income and create wealth. Subsistence economies may contain households with limited differentiation between income levels, yet the average level may be rather small. Raw materials exporting, industrializing, industrial, and post-industrial economies may experience varying degrees of income disparity between households due to a limited number of people controlling raw materials and manufacturing resources. Government practices, such as taxation policies, can either exacerbate or mitigate disparities in income.

The International Monetary Fund (IMF), a 186-member specialized agency of the United Nations, assists its member governments in taking advantage of the opportunities and managing the challenges posed by globalization and economic development. The IMF promotes international monetary cooperation and exchange rate stability, facilitates the balanced growth of international trade, and provides resources to help members with balance of payments difficulties or assist with poverty reduction. The IMF monitors the economic health of its members, alerts them to potential risks, and provides policy advice. In some cases, the IMF lends money to countries in difficulty. The IMF has its own charter, governing structure, and finances, and its members are represented through a quota system based on their relative size in the global economy.[17]

Political

While the economic environment relates to all the factors that contribute to a country's attractiveness for foreign businesses, the political environment in a country influences the rules and regulations under which a foreign firm operates. The political environment can increase or decrease market attractiveness based on the levels of **risk**, the potential for loss of investment, and **instability**, the condition of being erratic or unpredictable. While businesses tend to like the idea of **privatization**, the transfer of government functions to the private sector that creates new business opportunities, businesses tend to worry about the potential for **nationalization**, the transfer of control or ownership of private property to the government. An example of privatization would be if the Federal Bureau of Investigation (FBI) were sold to private investors and no longer run through the government. An example of nationalization would be if a foreign government enacted a law transferring ownership of a private phone or utility company operating in its jurisdiction to the government.

Both the structure of a specific government and the attitudes that government has toward business practices can influence market attractiveness. There are many types of governments, including the following:[18]

- **Democracy** is a form of government in which the supreme power is retained by the people, but which is usually exercised indirectly through a system of representation and delegated authority periodically renewed.
- **Monarchy** is a form of government in which the supreme power is held by a monarch who reigns over a state or territory, usually for life and by hereditary right; the monarch may be either a sole absolute ruler or a sovereign—such as a king, queen, or prince—with constitutionally limited authority.
- **Parliamentary democracy** is a political system in which the legislature (parliament) selects the government—a prime minister, premier, or chancellor along with the cabinet ministers—according to party strength as expressed in elections; by this system, the government acquires a dual responsibility: to the people as well as to the parliament.
- **Totalitarianism** is a form of government that seeks to subordinate the individual to the state by controlling not only all political and economic matters, but also the attitudes, values, and beliefs of its population.

EXAMPLE POLITICAL

The government of Pakistan blocked access to Facebook and YouTube in 2010 due to what it considered "offensive" content. A federal republic that has at times been ruled by the military, Pakistan claims Islam as the state religion. Much of the offensive content related to unfavorable portrayals of the prophet Muhammad. Muslims were deeply offended by the drawings that appeared on a Facebook page in an answer to the call for an "Everyone Draw Muhammad Day." A Pakistani court ordered a block on Facebook, implemented by the Pakistan Telecommunications Authority (PTA), which then banned YouTube and restricted access to other Web sites, including Wikipedia.[19]

PHOTO: Karam Miri\Shutterstock.

>> **END EXAMPLE**

Legal

Organizations operating in one country are subject to the laws of that country when engaging in marketing activities. This becomes increasingly complex when operating globally as there are varying sets of laws and legal structures. Each country in the world follows its own system of law. A foreign company operating in a particular country has to abide with its system of law as long as it is operating in that country. For example, Sweden prohibits domestic advertising that targets children; Belgium prohibits the advertising of medicinal products by telephone, e-mail, or on airplanes or ships; France bans English language advertising; and the use of English language acronyms and abbreviations have been banned on Chinese television. The EU restricts comparative advertising between one product and another for a variety of reasons, including creating confusion among consumers, discrediting or denigrating a competitor, and not objectively evaluating one or more significant features or the price of the products being compared.

Businesses should be clear when they are subject to the **jurisdiction**, the power or right of a legal or political entity to exercise its authority over a specific geographic area, of a foreign country. In some cases, principles of **international law**, a body of rules and customs by which countries are guided in their relations with other countries and recognized international organizations, exempt an individual or business from the jurisdiction of a foreign country. **Extraterritoriality** holds certain individuals such as diplomats accountable to the laws of their home country while exempting them from the jurisdiction of a foreign country in which they may be operating.

There is a wide range of legal issues that businesses must understand when dealing in foreign markets. For example, **bribery** is the practice of offering something of financial value to someone in a position of authority to alter behavior and gain an illicit advantage. In some countries bribery is not considered illegal while in others it is. The **Foreign Corrupt Practices Act** was enacted in 1977 "for the purpose of making it unlawful for certain classes of persons and entities to make payments to foreign government officials to assist in obtaining or retaining business."[20] **Counterfeiting,** or the unauthorized copying of products, packaging, or other intellectual property of a registered brand, is another example. It is estimated by the European Union that product counterfeiting costs $500 billion globally. According to the International AntiCounterfeiting Coalition (IACC), U.S. businesses are estimated to lose over $200 billion annually as a result of counterfeiting.

Legal requirements and trade practices often inform one another. Regulations on foreign exchange sometimes require a transaction to be conducted without direct financial payment. **Countertrade** is a legal agreement where goods are paid for in a form other than cash. While countertrade can take many forms, one of the most basic is that of barter, where one good is exchanged for another. For example, a U.S. manufacturer could exchange buses for an equivalent value of bananas. Approximately 130 countries require some form of countertrade in their procurements, and countertrade accounts for 20%–30% of world trade.[21]

EXAMPLE LEGAL

General Electric Transportation, a $4.5 billion division of General Electric, develops and manufactures railroad, marine, drilling, wind, and mining products. General Electric Transportation entered into an agreement, through its international trading activity General Electric Trading, with the Malaysian Railway, Malaysian Ministry of Transport, and Pasir Gudang Edible Oils Group. Under this countertrade deal, the Malaysian Railway and Malaysian Ministry of Transport purchased locomotives from General Electric Transportation valued at $64.5 million. At the same time, payment equal to the value of the locomotives was made by General Electric Trading to Pasir Gudang Edible Oils Group to purchase palm oil. These types of agreements help countries such as Malaysia target certain export markets for their products and generate additional export revenue.[22]

PHOTO: Binkski\Shutterstock.

>> END EXAMPLE

Cultural

Culture refers to the shared values, beliefs, and preferences of a particular society. It is also the influence that a society or group has on the behavior of individuals. Culture can be reflected through and influenced by morality, artistic expression, and even habits. While seemingly all-encompassing, culture can be both formally promulgated through laws and informally encouraged by societal actions and reactions. Cultures can also exist within a larger whole. It would be incorrect to assume, for example, that Chinese culture is the same in Urumqui by the Mongolian border as it is in Beijing. However, there are common themes that exist across cultures that can help businesses understand the environments in which they compete. *Culture's Consequences*, written by Dutch author Geert Hofstede, explores the relationship between national and organizational culture and discusses "mental programs" that develop early in life and are reinforced through national culture.[23] Five dimensions are identified to differentiate cultural values:

- **Power distance**—Involves whether individuals are comfortable participating in decision making regardless of position. Low power distance downplays the differences between individuals' power and wealth and results in a more egalitarian society. High power distance is just the opposite and results in the stratification of society or development of caste systems.
- **Uncertainty avoidance**—Involves the desire to minimize uncertainty. Low uncertainty avoidance societies more easily accept change and are open to more risk taking. High uncertainty avoidance societies look for structure and rules to control actions.
- **Individualism versus collectivism**—Involves the prevalence of people feeling comfortable making decisions with or without the input of group members. Low individualism societies emphasize group efforts, extended families, and teams. High individualism societies stress the prominence of individual rights over group rights. Relationships are less formal in high individualism societies.
- **Masculinity versus femininity**—Involves traits that are considered either masculine or feminine. Low masculinity societies have limited differentiation between genders. High masculinity societies experience a great degree of gender differentiation and tend to have much stricter definitions of gender roles.
- **Long-term versus short-term orientation**—Involves the importance of the past versus the future. Low long-term orientation means that change can occur more rapidly and with less resistance than in other societies. High long-term orientation means that consistent strong efforts are expected to be rewarded over a longer time horizon. This has significant impact in business transactions.

Behavior can be demonstrated either by a group or by an individual. Thus, by applying Hofstede's cultural perspective, the differences between societies can be explored. Consider the differences between collectivist societies such as the People's Republic of China and individualist societies such as the United States:

- Chinese consumers spend more time searching for products than U.S. consumers.
- Chinese consumers consider more brands per product than U.S. consumers.[24]
- Chinese consumers are more risk-adverse than U.S. consumers.[25]
- Chinese consumers rely on personal sources of information, as opposed to U.S. consumers who tend to rely on market-provided information.[26]
- Symbolism is generally more important for Chinese consumers than for U.S. consumers and symbolism can greatly influence purchase decisions.[27]

Understanding these differences is essential when developing marketing propositions for collectivist countries such as China.

APPLIED

Global Marketing Environment

"God is dead. The WTO and Starbucks have replaced him." This provocative slogan appears on signs at regular anti-WTO protests. The reality is that the WTO exists and will probably exist for the foreseeable future as an all-powerful entity in the world of global trade. It is also unquestionable that both globalization and its offspring, the WTO, have dramatically changed the world economy, national governments, businesses, and the lives of individuals forever. The nature of that change, however, is not agreed upon universally. Most arguments about global trade policy imply a **zero-sum game**, where one or more parties benefit to the same degree as one or more other parties lose. While that can certainly be the case, there are many instances in economic transactions where everyone gains or everyone loses. Understanding the connection between businesses engaged in global trade, governments and relevant international organizations, and the environments that they function in is critical to determining who wins, if anyone.

The objectives of businesses are not always consistent with national governments and have conflicted as long as both entities have existed together. Businesses may want to exploit valuable resources while a government may want to protect the environment or use the resources in another way. The same conflict occurs between countries and between and within free trade areas. Consider potential conflicts as free trade runs into strategic imperatives such as bidding on military contracts. While these conflicts have existed in the past, the difference today is the increased pace of change created by innovations in transportation and communication.[28]

Global MARKETING PROCESSES (pp. 61–63)

DEFINED **Global marketing processes** *are a series of strategic marketing decisions including deciding to go global, determining which markets to enter, deciding how to enter the markets, and selecting the global marketing program.*

EXPLAINED

Global Marketing Processes

When conducting global marketing, the first step is to decide whether a company actually needs a global marketing strategy. The primary motivations for embarking on a global strategy are to offset sluggish economic growth in a home market, capitalize on market opportunities abroad, or directly compete with other global competitors. Some firms are completely local in nature, and conducting business on an international scale would add unnecessary cost and complexity.

The next step involves looking at potential markets, assessing their differences, and selecting some (or all) for eventual market entry. This is a critical step, as an incorrect market assessment could lead a firm to invest heavily in a market with little potential. The third step is to decide the method of entry into each selected market. Some markets are attractive only if they are handled at arm's length through exporting, while others are ripe for full-scale investment. Once the entry method has been selected, the firm can then develop and implement marketing programs. At this point, global marketing for the company has begun.

Market Selection

A **market** is a place, either physical or virtual, where buyers and sellers come together to exchange goods and services. Nations, regions, localities, or portions of the Web are all markets. It is not uncommon for large companies to operate in dozens of markets. For example, the Coca-Cola Company sells products in more than 200 markets, including Fiji, Morocco, Nigeria, and Bulgaria. More than 70% of Coca-Cola's net operating revenues come from its operations outside the United States.[29]

Not every market is equally attractive. Understanding the environmental considerations discussed in the previous sections can be useful. Some important differences to consider when evaluating a market are as follows:[30]

- Market potential
- Customer characteristics
- Business cycles
- Competition
- Local culture
- Economic outlook
- Political outlook
- Government policies
- Financial requirements
- Labor market
- Taxation
- Legal environment
- Crime and corruption
- Infrastructure
- Foreign trade environment
- Current and future costs of building a business and brand

In developed markets like the United States or Europe, it has become harder to sustain high rates of GDP growth. For example, revenue growth among developed countries averages around 1%–4%. Marketers are subsequently exploring opportunities in emerging markets like the Middle East and Asia. In 2009, firms in Qatar and the People's Republic of China were averaging 9% growth.[31]

EXAMPLE **MARKET SELECTION**

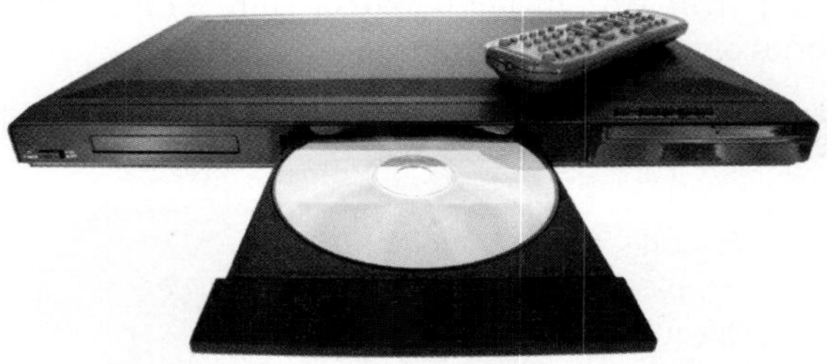

Samsung is a global manufacturer of consumer electronics, producing TVs, PDAs, mobile phones, DVD players, and other consumer electronics and appliances. By the late 1990s, Samsung decided to take aggressive action to close the gap between itself and market leader Sony in the international marketplace.

Formulating a global marketing strategy was daunting. Samsung marketed products in 14 different categories in more than 200 countries. To allocate resources and maximize return on investment, Samsung needed to prioritize each and every market and category. Data collected for each region included the following:

- Overall population and target buyer population
- Spending power per capita
- Category penetration rates
- Overall growth of categories

- Share of each of Samsung's brands
- Media costs
- Previous marketing expenditures
- Category profitability
- Competitor metrics

Samsung then created an information repository, called M-Net, that could be accessed by each region's marketing group, as well as by Samsung headquarters. Using analytic engines, marketing executives built predictive models to tell them both the current and the estimated future position of each market.

As a result, Samsung found that it was overinvesting in North America and Russia, and spending too little in Europe and China. Three product categories—mobile phones, vacuums, and air-conditioners—were also consuming too many marketing resources relative to their growth potential. Other categories, such as DVD players, TVs, and PC monitors, held greater growth and profit potential.

Based on its analysis of market differences, Samsung reallocated marketing resources and launched a new global branding campaign. Afterward, Samsung saw increases in its global brand equity and sales and net income rose sharply. Interbrand reported that Samsung had become the fastest-growing global brand name in 2002 and 2003. Samsung has maintained its strength, ranking 19th among top global brands in 2009.[32]

PHOTO: ZTS\Shutterstock.

>> **END EXAMPLE**

Market Entry Strategies

When selecting a market entry strategy, marketers balance how much risk, cost, and profitability they are willing to accept. Lower-risk strategies are usually cheaper, but profit opportunities are limited. Higher-risk strategies can be more expensive but have the potential for higher rewards. Figure 5.1 illustrates three categories of market entry strategies:[33]

FIGURE 5.1 Market Entry Strategies

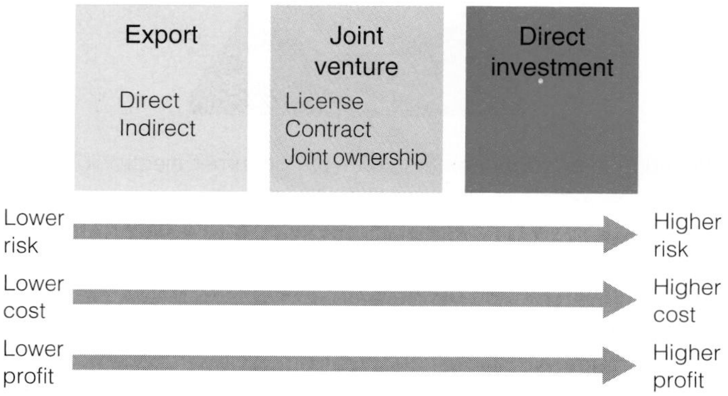

- **Exporting**—A common form of market entry, **exporting** occurs when a company produces in its home market and then transports its products to other nations for sale. Exporting may be either **indirect** (when a firm sells through intermediaries) or **direct** (when it establishes its own overseas sales branches). This entry strategy insulates marketers from risk because they remain distant from the market and it allows them to avoid costs associated with other forms of entry. However, it also limits profit potential, because exporting partners must be paid for their services.
- **Joint Ventures**—Marketers engaged in a **joint venture** must be willing to accept more risk, because this entry strategy means they are teaming with a host company in the particular market they are entering. Under a **licensing** approach, marketers are paid fees or royalties by partner firms in the host country for the right to use a brand, manufacturing process, or patent. Marketers may also directly hire **contract manufacturers** in the host nation to manufacture products on their behalf. The most expensive and risky form of joint venture is **joint ownership**, which occurs when a firm joins with a foreign investor to build its own local business. In some cases, joint ownership may even be required by a host country.
- **Direct Investment**—The riskiest and most expensive market entry strategy is **direct investment.** Firms pursuing a direct investment strategy establish foreign-based manufacturing facilities. Some benefits of direct investment include taking advantage of local cost differences and gaining better knowledge about the wants and needs of consumers in the local market. Because marketers do not need to share revenues with local partners, profit opportunities are greatest under a direct investment scenario.

Global companies use a variety of other market entry strategies as well. For example, McDonald's uses a form of licensing called **franchising,** in which local firms purchase the right to use its processes and brand in their restaurants. Automotive manufacturers like Nissan directly invest in markets, in part to gain a better understanding of local customers and to satisfy government requirements for local content in its products.

Global Marketing Strategy

Traditional marketing strategy is founded on the tenets of the marketing mix, including product, place, price, and promotion. Global marketing addresses the elements of the marketing mix as well as economic, political, legal, and cultural considerations. Global marketing strategy can be viewed as the extent to which a company standardizes its marketing mix strategy, coordinates its marketing initiatives, and integrates its competitive actions in country markets while predicating such strategies on the broadest possible market information. Global marketing strategies are intended to create marketing efficiencies by emphasizing four elements:[34]

- Cost efficiencies resulting from minimized duplication of efforts
- Opportunities to transfer products, brands, and ideas throughout various countries
- Emerging global customers
- Stronger links between country marketing infrastructures that support development of a global structure

APPLIED

Global Marketing Processes

The path toward global marketing is generally regarded as an incremental process that considers a wide range of environmental factors including global trade, economics, politics, law, and culture. In addition to the macroenvironment, many decisions to expand globally are influenced by other factors, including the desires and expectations of owners and leaders of businesses and the nature of the competitive environment in different business sectors. Businesses, if they choose to operate globally, typically gravitate toward countries that are similar in language and commercial practice to their home country. Sometimes affinity to one country supersedes the strategic value of a different, less similar, country.

In some cases, the process toward global marketing is anything but incremental. The idea of businesses being "**born global**" refers to businesses that, from their inception, intend to derive significant competitive advantage from the application of resources and commercial transactions in multiple countries.[35] The distinguishing characteristic of born global companies is the speed at which they became active in global markets. It has nothing to do with business size. Born global companies are created with a borderless view of the world and a desire to create value by generating a global advantage. Some companies are born global by necessity, such as those that are started in countries that have small domestic markets, or by choice. These companies generally are not innovators in the traditional sense of products and technologies, but they are innovative with their organizational structures and policies. The central office of a born global company acts as a coordinator of "cells" that leverage common technology, strategic goals, and attitudes. The structure of the company might make it difficult to attract investment capital, but such a structure has the potential to create significant market opportunities.[36]

EXAMPLE GLOBAL MARKETING PROCESSES

Some companies are thrust into a global environment by demand from international consumers. Vellus Products, Inc., an Ohio-based company that produces dog grooming products including shampoos, brushing sprays, conditioners, and detanglers, was founded to fill a gap of authentic salon grooming formulas for dogs. In 1993, shortly after launching the business in the United States, Vellus was contacted by a Taiwanese businessman interested in purchasing $25,000 in products for use at dog shows in Taiwan. Expansion into other countries quickly followed. Through increasing demand by foreign consumers and distributors, a business strategy of targeting the international dog show network, and the support of the U.S. Commercial Service, Vellus now sells its products in 34 countries.[37]

PHOTO: WilleeCole\Shutterstock.

>> END EXAMPLE

Visual Summary

Part 1 Explaining (Chapters 1, 2, 3, 4, 5)
Part 2 Creating (Chapters 6, 7, 8, 9)
Part 3 Strategizing (Chapters 10, 11)
Part 4 Managing (Chapters 12, 13, 14, 15, 16, 17)
Part 5 Integrating (Chapters 18, 19, 20)

Chapter 5 Summary

Global markets present complicated challenges for marketers, along with great opportunities and risks. Influenced by globalization, businesses are either expanding into new countries or facing new competitors in their home country. International entities such as the World Trade Organization exist to support trade liberalization and to arbitrate trade conflicts between countries. The North American Free Trade Agreement, European Union, and the China-Association of Southeast Asian Nations Free Trade Area are the largest of the growing number of trading blocs being formed across the world. Contemporary global marketing practices; the global marketing environment consisting of global trade, economics, politics, law, and culture; and global marketing processes are topics businesses must understand if they intend to expand outside their home country.

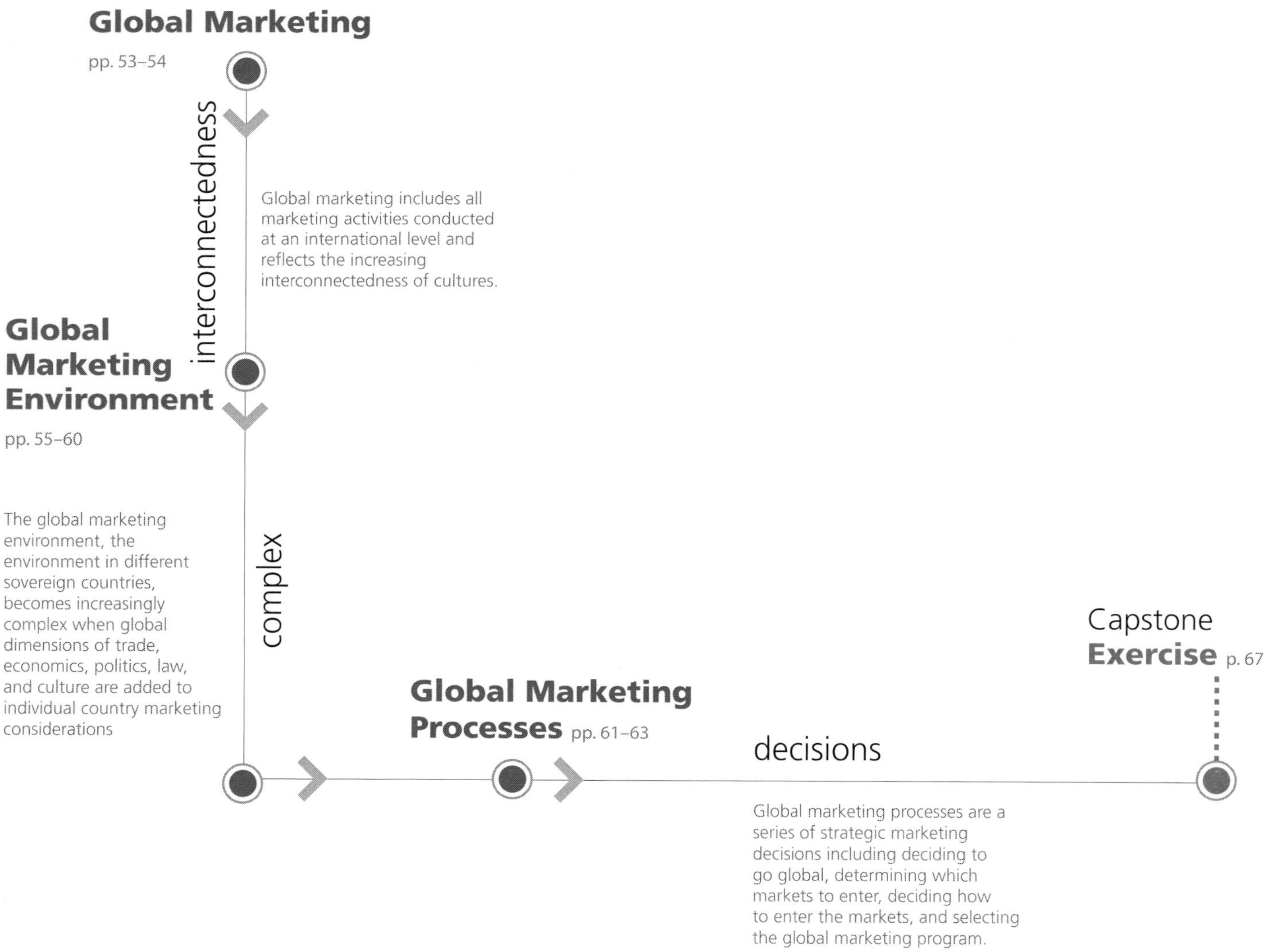

Global Marketing
pp. 53–54
interconnectedness
Global marketing includes all marketing activities conducted at an international level and reflects the increasing interconnectedness of cultures.
Global Marketing Environment
pp. 55–60
The global marketing environment, the environment in different sovereign countries, becomes increasingly complex when global dimensions of trade, economics, politics, law, and culture are added to individual country marketing considerations
complex
Global Marketing Processes pp. 61–63
decisions
Global marketing processes are a series of strategic marketing decisions including deciding to go global, determining which markets to enter, deciding how to enter the markets, and selecting the global marketing program.
Capstone Exercise p. 67

Chapter Key Terms

Global Marketing (pp. 53–54)

Global marketing *includes all marketing activities conducted at an international level by individuals or businesses. (p. 53)*
Opening Example (p. 53), Example: Global Marketing (p. 54)

Key Terms (pp. 53–54)

Globalization is the outcome of cultures intermingling, sharing experiences, news, and commerce. **(p. 53)**

Glocal describes a company that acts either globally, locally, or both, as needed. **(p. 54)**

Global Marketing Environment (pp. 55–60)

Global marketing environment *describes the environment in different sovereign countries, with characteristics distinct to the home environment of an organization, influencing decisions on marketing activities. (p. 55)*

Key Terms (pp. 55–60)

Balance of trade is the difference between the monetary value of exports and imports of output in an economy over a specific period. **(p. 56) Example: Global Trade (pp. 56–57)**

Bribery is the practice of offering something of financial value to someone in a position of authority to alter behavior and gain an illicit advantage. **(p. 58)**

Counterfeiting is the unauthorized copying of products, packaging, or other intellectual property of a registered brand. **(p. 58)**

Countertrade is a legal agreement where goods are paid for in a form other than cash. **(p. 58)**

Culture is the shared values, beliefs, and preferences of a particular society. **(p. 59) Example: Political (p. 58)**

Democracy is a form of government in which the supreme power is retained by the people, but which is usually exercised indirectly through a system of representation and delegated authority periodically renewed. **(p. 58)**

Dominican Republic-Central America-United States Free Trade Agreement (CAFTA-DR) is a trading partnership among the United States, the Dominican Republic, Costa Rica, El Salvador, Guatemala, Honduras, and Nicaragua that represents the first free trade agreement between the United States and a group of smaller developing economies. **(p. 56)**

Dumping is the practice of selling a product in a foreign country for a price less than either the cost to make the product or the price in the home country. **(p. 56)**

Economic communities are groups of countries that agree to take certain actions to manage resources of goods and services by lowering tariff barriers and promoting trade among members. **(p. 55)**

European Union (EU) is an economic and political partnership among 27 European countries. **(p. 56)**

Exchange controls are types of controls that governments put in place to ban or restrict the amount of a specific currency that is permitted to be traded or purchased. **(p. 56)**

Extraterritoriality holds certain individuals such as diplomats accountable to the laws of their home country while exempting them from the jurisdiction of a foreign country in which they may be operating. **(p. 58)**

Foreign Corrupt Practices Act is an act passed in 1977 that makes it "unlawful for certain classes of persons and entities to make payments to foreign government officials to assist in obtaining or retaining business." **(p. 58)**

Global companies are companies that maintain assets and operations in more than one country and concentrate on penetrating multiple countries with a minimally customized marketing mix. **(p. 55)**

Gross domestic product (GDP) is the measure of the total dollar value of goods and services an economy produces within a given year. **(p. 55)**

Income distribution is the way in which income and wealth are divided among the members of an economy. **(p. 57)**

Industrial economies are countries with robust manufacturing, service, and financial sectors that are actively engaged in international trade. **(p. 57)**

Industrializing economies are countries where the manufacturing sector accounts for a small but growing share of the total economy and an increasing number of imported raw materials are required to support manufacturing. **(p. 57)**

Instability is the condition of being erratic or unpredictable. **(p. 57)**

International companies are companies that have no investment outside their home country other than the direct purchase of products or services and are, essentially, importers and exporters. **(p. 55)**

International law is a body of rules and customs by which countries are guided in their relations with other countries and recognized international organizations. **(p. 58)**

Jurisdiction is the power or right of a legal or political entity to exercise its authority over a specific geographic area. **(p. 58)**

Monarchy is a form of government in which the supreme power is held by a monarch who reigns over a state or territory, usually for life and by hereditary right; the monarch may be either a sole absolute ruler or a sovereign—such as a king, queen, or prince—with constitutionally limited authority. **(p. 58)**

Multinational companies are companies that maintain assets and operations in more than one country and concentrate on adapting products and services to the specific needs of each country. **(p. 55)**

Nationalization is the transfer of control or ownership of private property to the government. **(p. 57)**

Non-tariff barriers (NTBs) are restrictions on imports that are not in the usual form of a tariff. **(p. 56)**

North American Free Trade Agreement (NAFTA) is a trading partnership among the United States, Canada, and Mexico. **(p. 56)**

Offshoring is a type of outsourcing in which business activities are completed in another country. **(p. 55)**

Outsourcing is procuring certain services from third-party suppliers to decrease labor costs, access human capital not readily available within the business, or implement specific strategies. **(p. 55)**

Parliamentary democracy is a political system in which the legislature (parliament) selects the government—a prime minister, premier, or chancellor along with the cabinet ministers—according to party strength as expressed in elections; by this system, the government acquires a dual responsibility to the people as well as to the parliament. **(p. 58)**

Post-industrial economies are countries where the manufacturing sector diminishes while service and information sectors become the primary sources of economic growth. **(p. 57)**

Privatization is the transfer of government functions to the private sector that creates new business opportunities. **(p. 57)**

Purchasing power parity (PPP) is the model of exchange rate determination stating that the price of a good or service in one country should equal the price of the same good or service in another country, exchanged at the current rate. **(p. 55)**

Quotas are limits on the amount of product that can be imported into a country. **(p. 56)**

Raw materials exporting economies are countries that are plentiful in a particular raw material, yet deficient in other resources, and rely on the export of that raw material for the majority of revenue. **(p. 57)**

Risk is the potential for loss of investment. **(p. 57)**

Subsistence economies are agrarian societies where enough is grown, hunted, and crafted to provide for the essential needs of the people and any surplus is bartered for basic goods and services. **(p. 57)**

Tariffs are schedules of duties (or fees) applied to goods or services from foreign countries. **(p. 56)**

Totalitarianism is a form of government that seeks to subordinate the individual to the state by controlling not only all political and economic matters, but also the attitudes, values, and beliefs of its population. **(p. 58)**

Trade agreements are treaties between countries to create a free trade area where business can be conducted without tariffs or other barriers. **(p. 56)** **Example: Global Trade (pp. 56–57)**

Trade deficits occur when the value of imports exceeds the value of exports. **(p. 56)**

Trade surpluses occur when the value of exports exceeds the value of imports. **(p. 56)**

World Trade Organization (WTO) was established in 1995 as the preeminent organization dealing with the rules of trade at a global or near-global level. **(p. 56)**

Zero-sum game is when one or more parties benefit to the same degree as one or more other parties lose. **(p. 60)**

Global **Marketing Processes** (pp. 61–63)

Global marketing processes *are a series of strategic marketing decisions including deciding to go global, determining which markets to enter, deciding how to enter the markets, and selecting the global marketing program. (p. 61)* **Example: Global Marketing Processes (p. 63)**

Key Terms (pp. 62–63)

Born global is a business that, from its inception, intends to derive significant competitive advantage from the application of resources and commercial transactions in multiple countries. **(p. 63)**

Contract manufacturer is an entry strategy in which a company directly hires a company in the host nation to manufacture products on its behalf. **(p. 62)**

Direct exporting is a form of exporting in which a firm establishes its own overseas sales branches. **(p. 62)**

Direct investment is an entry strategy in which a company establishes foreign-based manufacturing facilities. **(p. 62)**

Exporting is a common form of market entry that occurs when a company produces in its home market and then transports its products to other nations for sale. **(p. 62)**

Franchising is an entry strategy in which a local company purchases the right to use the processes and brand of another company. **(p. 62)**

Indirect exporting is a form of exporting in which a firm sells its products through intermediaries. **(p. 62)**

Joint ownership is an entry strategy in which a company joins with a foreign investor to build its own local business. **(p. 62)**

Joint venture is an entry strategy in which a company teams with a host company in the particular market they are entering. **(p. 62)**

Licensing is the practice of a company receiving fees or royalties from partner firms for the right to use a brand, manufacturing process, or patent. **(p. 62)**

Market is a place, either physical or virtual, where buyers and sellers come together to exchange goods and services. **(p. 61)** **Example: Market Selection (pp. 61–62)**

Capstone Exercise

Black Angus Steakhouse operates 46 restaurants in six western states of the United States. The company opened its first restaurant in Washington State in 1964. Currently, each restaurant serves an average of 3,000 guests each week. Black Angus operates under the mission:

> *To provide patrons with top quality, complete steak dinners at an affordable price, served in a warm, comfortable atmosphere with friendly service.* (www.blackangus.com)

Through market research, the marketing department has determined that a significant business segment comes from Asian visitors to the United States. The CEO has directed the marketing department to investigate and propose possible options for expansion into Asia.

1. What variables need to be considered in developing a list of potential countries?
2. From the list of top "candidates," what data should you collect on each market?
3. What market entry strategy would you suggest?
4. What are some of the internal and external challenges Black Angus may face in moving from a domestic business to a global business?
5. What country would you propose as having the #1 potential? Why?

Application Exercise

Use the following marketing concepts in this chapter to tackle and solve a marketing problem: global marketing, market selection, and market entry strategies.

First, start by thinking about product categories that are rich with product features, such as cell phones. In general terms, product features refer to basic, physical, or extended attributes of the product.

The Marketing Problem

Choose a product in the cell phone category after considering the following situation:

> College students tend to own cell phones and have significant interest in the category because they understand the product features very well. A domestic cell phone company in Brazil has asked you, as a marketing student, to determine their market selection and market entry strategy for a new smart phone that is eco-friendly, unbreakable, waterproof, and targeted to college students outside their home country.

The Problem

Describe your global marketing strategy and how, if at all, you would modify the product features or price by country in your market selection.

The Solution

Complete the following Problem/Solution brief using your product in the smart phone category, chapter concepts, and college resources.

1. From the Marketing Manager's Point of View
   a. Problem Definition
   b. Global Analysis
   c. Product's Value
   d. Target Market
   e. Solution
2. From the Consumer's Point of View
   a. Problem Definition
   b. Global Analysis
   c. Product's Value
   d. Solution

Resources:

Marketing Defined, Explained, Applied 2e, Michael Levens
The College Library
Retail or Online Field Trip
Assigned Reading—*Brand Week, Advertising Age, WSJ,* scholarly publications, category trade journals
Blog your problem from either point of view, gather responses/posts (www.blogger.com/start)

Value for Customers

Chapter Overview This chapter examines the principles that drive today's customer-focused companies, specifically those principles regarding creating value for customers. When customers receive value in excess of their expectations, their level of customer satisfaction with the brand is high, they are more likely to continue buying the brand, and they develop a loyalty to the brand. Successful companies seek to develop customer loyalty in an effort to build long-term relationships, which leads to higher revenue and greater profitability. To strengthen customer loyalty, companies focus their efforts on relationship marketing so as to fully understand customers and to stay abreast of their changing needs. The implementation of relationship marketing requires using customer relationship management techniques that allow companies to stay connected with their customers.

Chapter Outline

CUSTOMER Value (pp. 69–70)

DEFINED **Customer value** *is the difference between the benefits a customer expects to receive from a product and the total cost incurred from acquiring, using, and disposing of the product.*

EXPLAINED

Customer Value

The number of products that are available to potential buyers has increased significantly in recent decades. Products are offered with a variety of features, at different levels of quality, and at various prices. With so many different options, how do buyers determine which products to purchase? At the most basic level, buyers make a purchase decision based on the value they perceive a product will deliver. Buyers accomplish this by weighing the difference between the expected benefits gained from owning the product and the expected costs of the product. This can be shown with the following formula:

Customer Perceived Value = Expected Benefits – Expected Costs

Because buyers have different perceptions as to the benefits a product delivers, as well as different interpretations of its costs, the perceived value that a product delivers will vary. In most cases, buyers select the product they believe will offer them the greatest value. Some buyers will therefore select a high-quality, high-priced product loaded with features, while others will opt for a product that has a minimal number of features, but offers a low price.

APPLIED

Customer Value

Products deliver benefits to a customer in many different forms. The most basic and visible benefits of a product, which are referred to as functional benefits, relate to the specific attributes of the product. For example, the functional benefits of a digital camera are based on the number of megapixels, the size of the screen, and the magnification of the zoom offered by the camera. Additional benefits, referred to as psychological benefits, are created primarily through a company's branding efforts. These benefits include emotional benefits, self-expression benefits, and social benefits. The concept of branding will be discussed in greater depth in Chapter 9.

On the cost side, the cost of a product often includes much more than the purchase price. For example, there can be additional costs that should be taken into consideration, such as the costs of using, maintaining, and disposing of a product. For example, in addition to its higher purchase price, the total cost of owning an SUV is much higher than that of owning a smaller, more fuel-efficient automobile. These additional costs, such as operating costs (due to lower fuel efficiency) and higher disposal costs (due to lower resale values), have resulted in many buyers lowering the perceived value for SUVs. That reduced value has resulted in a dramatic drop in the sales of SUVs and an increase in the sales of smaller vehicles that are less expensive to operate. In the first quarter of 2008, as gasoline prices were rising toward $4 per gallon, the demand for trucks and SUVs decreased by 28%.[1] The trade-off between benefits and costs is shown in Figure 6.1.

To better understand the concept of customer value, the **value map** shown in Figure 6.2 examines the trade-offs customers make between costs and benefits (performance in this example) when making a purchase decision. Products that fall within the **fair value zone** are perceived to deliver benefits equal to the products' total cost. Products below, or to the right of, the zone are perceived to have greater benefits than their associated costs. Products above, or to the left of, the zone are perceived by buyers to deliver fewer benefits than what the products cost.

iTunes, first launched by Apple in 2001, is a free application for the PC or Mac that organizes and plays your digital video and music stored on a computer. It syncs media with a variety of Apple products, including the iPad, iPhone, iPod, iBook, and Apple TV. Additionally, iTunes can connect to the iTunes Store through the Internet to gain access to 13 million songs as well as movies, TV shows, audiobooks, podcasts, and applications. The iTunes Store was created in 2003 to provide value to customers through a virtual store where people can purchase and download digital music on demand. In 2009, Apple adjusted its uniform $0.99 download per song pricing to a three-tier pricing model to better reflect customer demand. The new pricing tiers were established as $0.69, $0.99, and $1.29. The most expensive songs are those deemed to create the greatest value to customers, such as top songs by the most popular artists. Business through the iTunes Store has grown significantly from 4 billion downloads in 2008 to surpassing 10 billion downloads in 2010.[2]

PHOTO: PSL Images/Alamy Images.

FIGURE 6.1 Customer Perceived Value

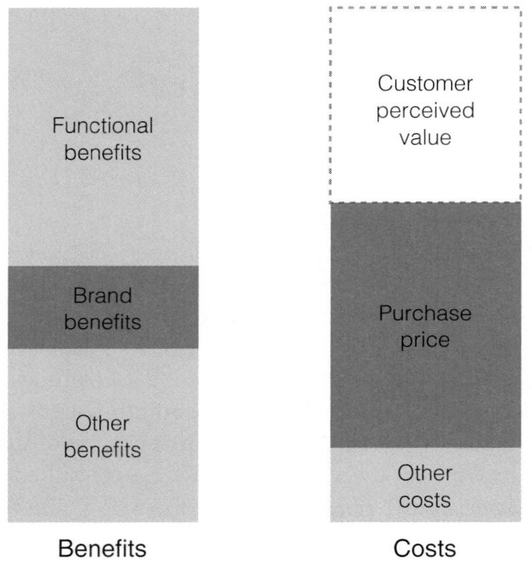

FIGURE 6.2 Price–Performance Value Map

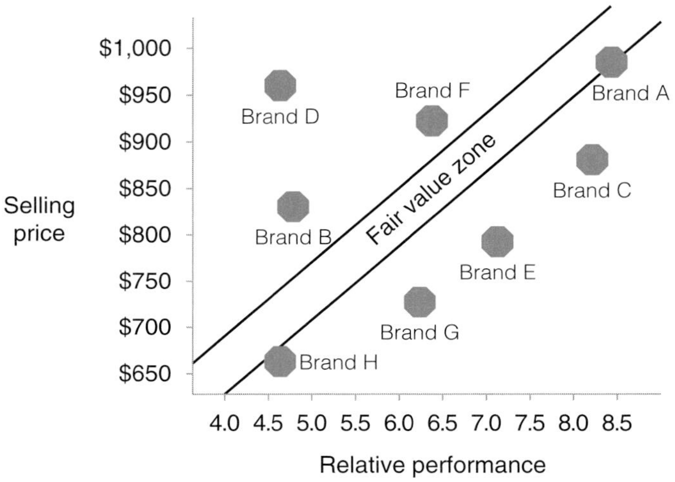

Managers use a value map to track and manage the perceived value customers assign to their brands, as well as to competitors' brands. The value map shown in Figure 6.2 highlights a market with eight competitors, each of which has various levels of performance and price. Brands B, D, and F all fall to the left of the fair value zone, which indicates low customer perceived value. The low perceptions by customers will translate into low market share for these brands. Brands C, E, and G are rated by customers as having high customer perceived value. Brands A and H are rated as having performance benefits equal to their selling price. In this example, brand C is priced around $200 higher than brand H. Is brand C worth the added cost? One could make the case that because brand C has a much higher performance rating, the additional $200 is acceptable.

Companies can alter the customer perceived value in one of three ways: increase the perceived benefits, decrease the perceived cost, or create a combination of the two. For example, perceived benefits can be increased by adding new features to a product while either maintaining the current price or increasing the price only slightly. Perceived costs can be altered through a price reduction or by improving a product's efficiency. An example of the latter would be an automobile manufacturer improving the gas mileage of one of its models. Improved fuel efficiency lowers the overall operating expenses, thereby reducing the perceived cost of the vehicle. Even if the perceived benefits remain the same, the reduction in overall costs results in an increase in the perceived value.

CUSTOMER Satisfaction (pp. 71–73)

DEFINED **Customer satisfaction** *is the degree to which a product meets or exceeds customer expectations.*

EXPLAINED

Customer Satisfaction

When customers have contact with a company, or an interaction with a product, they formulate an evaluation of their experience. This evaluation is based on the expectations they had before the experience. Customers' evaluation, or their level of satisfaction, will fall within one of three categories: The experience will either be positive, neutral, or negative. A negative feeling, or dissatisfaction, is the result when the product's performance does not live up to expectations. A neutral outcome occurs when a product's performance matches expectations. In this situation, a buyer has reached the baseline level of satisfaction. If expectations are exceeded, then a positive experience has occurred, leaving the buyer highly satisfied. This high level of satisfaction is referred to as delighted. The varying levels of satisfaction, and likely outcomes associated with each, are shown in Figure 6.3.

The initial level of satisfaction is normally determined at the time a product is purchased. However, for some products the level of satisfaction may change over time. For example, the purchase and consumption of a new flavor of soft drink will result in an initial level of satisfaction. In most cases, customers will make up their minds as to whether they would purchase that brand again in the first few sips. It is unlikely that a week after trying the new flavor that a person would alter his or her level of satisfaction without having a new experience with the product. This may not be the case for other types of products. Take the purchase of an ink-jet printer as an example. At first, the buyer may experience a high level of satisfaction due to a low purchase price and an acceptable quality of the pages being printed. However, over time the level of satisfaction may diminish as the customer seeks to replace the ink cartridge and finds the price to be much higher than expected. Where once there was initial delight, dissatisfaction takes over. For products where long-term ownership is expected, the company's product and customer service quality play an important role in customer satisfaction.

FIGURE 6.3 Outcomes of Varying Degrees of Satisfaction

Negative	Neutral	Positive
• Dissatisfied	• Satisfied	• Delighted
• Defect	• Switchable	• Loyal

APPLIED

Customer Satisfaction

Creating satisfied customers requires that a company manage the expectations customers have with the brand. While a company can generate higher initial sales volume by inflating claims of a product's superiority, if these claims are not delivered, customers will experience higher levels of dissatisfaction and are more likely to switch to a competing brand. As such, companies strive to manage expectations in an effort to not "overpromise and underdeliver." Even customers who have a neutral experience—that is, their experience matches expectations—are susceptible to switching to a competing offering. It is only customers who are delighted by their experience that can be counted on to remain loyal to the brand.

Companies with highly satisfied or delighted customers generate significant benefits for themselves in the following forms:[3]

- **Loyalty**—Customers who are satisfied are likely to continue to purchase the same brands, or do business with the same service provider.
- **Product champions**—Satisfied customers cannot wait to share their experiences with anyone who listens.
- **Reduced costs**—The costs benefits of having satisfied customers is found in multiple areas, from lower warranty expenses (satisfied customers have fewer problems, hence lower warranty expenses) to fewer phone calls to customer service representatives.
- **Larger share of wallet**—Satisfied customers are more likely to purchase other products from a company to which they are loyal.

These benefits in turn lead to greater profitability for the company, as well as an increase in revenue due to satisfied customers purchasing other products from the company. Satisfied customers may also become product advocates by referring the brand to their friends and colleagues. This word-of-mouth, or viral, advertising carries much greater weight with potential buyers than any advertising campaign a company could develop.

Measuring Customer Satisfaction

Because of its importance for long-term growth, companies make an effort to measure the satisfaction levels of their customers. The measurement of satisfaction can take the form of surveys where customers are asked to rate their level of satisfaction on a scale of 1 to 10. These types of surveys traditionally ask respondents questions such as the following: How satisfied are you with the product or service? Do you intend to purchase the product in the future? Would you recommend the product to a friend? Capturing ratings for customer satisfaction provides managers with insights into how well the company is performing in the marketplace. However, the data alone are of little use unless they are compared against the company's previous ratings or against the satisfaction ratings competitors have earned.

Independent rating organizations such as J.D. Power and Associates and the American Customer Satisfaction Index (ACSI) are also involved in the assessment of customer satisfaction. The ACSI conducts more than 65,000 customer interviews annually and links customer expectations, perceived quality, and perceived value to develop an overall ACSI score. Measures are taken across a wide variety of consumer and business-to-business product categories, allowing managers to see their customers' level of satisfaction in relation to industry averages and specific competitors.

EXAMPLE **CUSTOMER SATISFACTION**

According to the American Customer Satisfaction Index, Southwest Airlines customers are the most satisfied of the major air carrier customers in the United States. Southwest accomplishes this by consistently delivering superior customer service and customer value through its low prices, which in turn leads to high levels of customer satisfaction. In 2009, Southwest Airlines was awarded Best Customer Service in the Reader's Choice Awards by *Smarter Travel* and was named the top U.S. airline on the University of Michigan's American Customer satisfaction Index. Customers know exactly what to expect from Southwest: low fares, open seating, and limited amenities (you get a bag of peanuts and a soft drink). Southwest Airlines has shown a profit for 37 consecutive years, a record that has been unmatched in the airline industry.[4]

PHOTO: Yuri Arcurs/Shutterstock.

>> END EXAMPLE

Customer Loyalty

Customer loyalty is the degree to which a customer will select a particular brand when a purchase from that product category is being considered. Customer loyalty can also be described as a buyer's feeling of attachment to a particular product, brand, or company. Buyers exhibit varying degrees of loyalty toward the brands they purchase. Some buyers have high levels of loyalty to a particular brand and will purchase only that brand. Other buyers may split their loyalty among two or three brands in a category. Still others may hold loyalty to no brand and select perhaps the lowest priced product when a purchase decision must be made. It is the first group of customers, those who are loyal to a specific brand, that organizations strive to create and expand by delivering high levels of customer satisfaction. Companies also seek to ensure that highly loyal customers remain loyal. At the same time, companies try to move those customers who are only somewhat loyal into a state of high loyalty. To accomplish this, companies seek to ensure continued relationships with select groups of customers.

While it can be assumed that loyal customers will continue to purchase a specific brand, this does not mean they are the most profitable customers. Nor is it the case that the heavy users (customers who purchase in higher quantity) of a product are the most profitable. For example, heavy users may stock up on a product because of special deals or price promotions. In business-to-business markets, large volume buyers may also require additional company resources, such as higher levels of customer service or special product specifications. These additional resources result in higher costs and, thus, lower profitability. To determine which customers are profitable and which are not, an in-depth customer profitability analysis should be conducted. A profitability analysis of customers involves assigning actual marketing costs to customers, based on the actual costs that are required to perform various marketing activities, such as sales calls and product shipping. Looking at customers in this light allows the company to determine the overall value, in terms of profitability, that a customer generates for a company.

The Value of a Customer

It is important to note that not all customers are created equal. According to the Pareto Principle, or what is commonly referred to as the 80/20 rule, 80% of a company's profits are generated by 20% of its customers. Another 60% of customers generate the remaining profits for a company. This leaves an additional 20% of customers who generate a loss for the company. This observation has led many companies to offer tiered levels of service, with the most profitable customers receiving high levels of customer service and unprofitable customers receiving minimal levels of service. For example, credit card companies ensure that a "live" customer service representative answers a highly valued card holder's phone call in a matter of seconds; a phone call from a card holder that generates lower profits is generally routed through an automated phone system.

Customer Lifetime Value

Customer lifetime value (CLV) is the present value of all profits expected to be earned in the future from a customer. To determine the value of a customer, companies utilize metrics such as customer lifetime value. The benefit of using CLV can be seen in a simple example using a typical AT&T cell phone customer who pays $75 per month for service. The average customer generates $1,800 in revenue for AT&T over the life of a contract. If AT&T earns 20% profit on revenue from cell service, then the customer generates a total profit of $360 during the two-year contract period. At the most basic level, this $360 in profit can be viewed as the lifetime value of that customer. If the cost to recruit and retain the customer is less than $360, then this would be a profitable customer for AT&T.

Customer lifetime value goes much deeper than the preceding example demonstrates. Companies must also take into account the fact that revenue collected in the future is worth less than if that revenue were collected up front. To account for this, companies use what is known as a discount rate, which averages between 10% and 15%. The concept behind the discount rate is also referred to as the time value of money.

To calculate customer lifetime value, a company must know five pieces of information:

1. Customer average purchases per year
2. Profit margin earned on those purchases
3. Costs to service the customer
4. Customer retention rate (percentage of customers who remain customers)
5. The firm's discount rate

Customers represent different levels of value in terms of the amount of profits they generate for an organization. Because of the high expense and effort required, companies use metrics such as CLV to determine which customers should receive the focus of the company's relationship marketing efforts. Perhaps equally important, knowing a customer's lifetime value also allows a company to know with which customers to not seek to build relationships. For example, some companies have opted to "fire" unprofitable customers. Take the 2007 case of Sprint, which identified and terminated the contracts of over 1,000 customers who repeatedly contacted the company's customer service department an average of 40 times per month, some even after the original complaint was resolved. This move generated a great deal of negative publicity for Sprint, but other cell phone providers acknowledged that they had also cancelled customer contracts for similar reasons.[5]

Customers can add value to a company in addition to their lifetime value, because many highly satisfied customers may become champions for the products they buy. These loyal customers will go out of their way to refer a brand to anyone who will listen.[6] Research conducted by Purdue's Center for Customer Driven Quality shows that 87% of consumers follow the opinion of their friends and family.[7]

Customer Retention

Companies are continuously seeking to attract new customers to increase sales and profits. For many companies, attracting new customers is necessary to replace customers who defect to competing products, or who leave the market entirely. This is especially the case for those organizations that achieve low customer satisfaction scores, or even an entire industry, such as cellular phone service providers. Replacing lost customers is critical to growing a company's sales and profits, or to maintain current sales levels in those firms with high defection rates. However, companies that work to retain current customers are reaching higher levels of profitability. A majority of a company's marketing efforts are often geared toward recruiting new customers, but, in addition, today's savvy businesses are turning their attention to retaining current customers.

EXAMPLE **CUSTOMER RETENTION**

Searching for ways to connect with its "healthy, active, outdoor, aspirational" target customers, Nature Valley, a large health-oriented General Mill's cereal bar brand, called on consumers to post stories about their favorite nature activities, such as hiking and kayaking. The brand's Web site was redesigned in hopes of making the site a clearinghouse for information appealing to outdoor enthusiasts. Nature Valley also promoted a contest on YouTube where consumers posted videos highlighting their favorite place. The overall winner of the contest won two trips, one to Antarctica and the other to the North Pole. A total of 127 videos were submitted; they were viewed a total of 250,000 times. The Web site and contest gave Nature Valley the means to build a relationship with a core customer group and to retain this group of customers.[8]

PHOTO: Galyna Andrushko/Shutterstock.

>> END EXAMPLE

RELATIONSHIP MARKETING (p. 74)

DEFINED **Relationship marketing** *is the organizational commitment to developing and enhancing long-term, mutually beneficial relationships with profitable or potentially profitable customers.*

EXPLAINED

Relationship Marketing

In the past, companies would determine the value of customers based on their most recent purchase. Previous purchases or future purchases were of lesser concern. This transaction-based view gave way to the relationship-based view of an exchange with the emergence of the marketing concept. Today's successful companies have sought to focus their marketing efforts on building long-term, mutually beneficial relationships with profitable or potentially profitable customers. The primary goal for developing customer relationships is to increase customer loyalty and retention. In thinking about long-term customer relationships, companies understand that customer profitability may be limited or even at a loss at the beginning of a relationship, but over time, profits increase. Relationship marketing is especially important, given the following data:[9]

- A company can lose up to 50% of its customers over a five-year period.
- It costs 5–7 times more to recruit new customers than it does to retain existing customers.
- Even small increases in customer retention rates can have a profound impact on a company's profits.

According to Michael Porter, a world-renowned strategy guru, a business can differentiate itself from competitors based on the following: (1) the core product or service, (2) price, and (3) the total relationship and customer experience. Companies are finding that the first two are difficult in today's competitive environment and are focusing on the importance of developing strong customer relationships. Relationship marketing, or one-to-one marketing, requires that an organization be committed to the development of a customer relationship.

APPLIED

Relationship Marketing

Developing relationships with customers requires a complete, committed effort on the part of the organization. This is because a relationship requires the delivery of superior customer value that results from high product quality and exemplary customer service. Building relationships with customers is not a short-term undertaking; it requires a long-term plan and strong commitment from the organization, as well as the proper investment. It is important to understand that customers have different reasons for wanting to establish a relationship with a company. Customers may enter into a relationship because of the added value they receive, to reduce anxiety throughout the purchase/repurchase process, or to achieve a sense of belonging.

EXAMPLE RELATIONSHIP MARKETING

Seeking to establish a community with loyal customers, Patrón Spirits launched an online social networking Web site. The Patrón Social Club provides tequila aficionados with a central gathering place for Patrón (Spanish for "the good boss") enthusiasts. The site is interactive and open to members only. With the help of a worldwide, integrated marketing campaign, the brand is meeting the desires of its top customers. The information the company has gained from hosting the site has led to members receiving invitations for exclusive events and parties, including Super Bowl XLII. The addition of the Web site and the marketing campaign have raised awareness of the brand 61% from the previous year and increased case sales by 45%.[10]

PHOTO: Grant Terry/Shutterstock.

>> END EXAMPLE

CUSTOMER Relationship Management (pp. 75–77)

DEFINED **Customer relationship management (CRM)** *comprises the activities that are used to establish, develop, and maintain customer sales.*

EXPLAINED

Customer Relationship Management

Customer relationship management (CRM) seeks to ensure that every effort an organization undertakes has as its purpose the development and maintenance of a profitable customer relationship. The practice of CRM requires internal and external processes. External processes are those that connect the company with its customers, while internal processes involve the management of information acquired from customers. A breakdown in either process will result in the CRM experience not meeting the expectations of either the company or the customer.

APPLIED

Customer Relationship Management

Perhaps the most critical element of practicing CRM is in the information such a system can provide the organization. Companies should not only collect information regarding their customers, such as demographics and usage patterns, but also seek to gain information to help assess the customers' needs. The information that a company collects is stored in a customer database, which is an organized collection of information about a customer. The information in this database must be constantly updated and should be designed for ease of use.

There are four steps in the development of one-to-one relationships with customers:[11]

1. Identify and gather as much detail as possible about your customers.
2. Differentiate customers based on their needs and the levels of value they bring to the company.
3. Talk to your customers to find ways of improving cost efficiencies as well as the customer interaction experience.
4. Customize your products or services for each customer segment.

Customer Identification

For many companies, such as those in the business-to-business (B2B) market, taking the first step of identifying and collecting information about customers is relatively simple. However, the effort in the consumer market is much more challenging. In the B2B market, firms know who their customers are because of previous purchases. For example, ArcelorMittal, the world's largest steel manufacturer, can easily pull up a customer list from a previous order and begin building the necessary information needed for its CRM systems. However, in the consumer market, companies must make great effort to even identify their customers. Imagine the difficulty that Procter & Gamble (P&G) has determining which consumers purchase Tide detergent or Crest toothpaste. Although some of this information may be available from supermarkets that have implemented a loyalty program, issues abound when sharing information among firms.

In the process of identifying customers and collecting pertinent information, companies should seek to err on the side of having too much information, rather than too little. Information that should be collected includes the standard names and contact information, as well as other data that may be specific to your brand, company, or industry. For example, a consumer products company may benefit from knowing whether a customer is married, has children (along with their ages), or the type of job he or she holds. This information may allow the company to promote other products the company produces. Companies should also focus on ways to determine a customer's needs, for example, how the product is perceived, what features the customer finds valuable, and how the product is used. Perhaps the most critical piece of information that should be collected, either directly from the customer or from other sources, involves a customer's purchase history. This information will allow the company to perform a customer profitability analysis that, along with the other information mentioned, will be valuable in the next step of the process.

Customer Differentiation

The ability to differentiate customers based on the value they bring to the company in the form of profits and based on the customers' needs gives the company the means to find groups of customers who share similar characteristics. The information collected in Step 1 (customer identification) allows the company to identify its top customers in terms of sales and profitability. The differentiation step allows a company to detect customers whose purchases have been significantly fewer this quarter than they were last quarter. This might indicate that the customer has become less satisfied with the products. The company then might contact the customer to prevent the loss of this customer to a competitor. Companies that do not utilize a CRM system may not find out about a dissatisfied customer until it is too late.

Customer Interaction

Every contact a company has with a customer provides an opportunity to either strengthen or damage a relationship. Companies that make the effort to improve customer relationships look at their customer interactions as ongoing conversations. They seek to understand ways to improve customers' experiences with the company, for example, seeing a trend in the types of questions customers ask and including this information on a company Web site or automated information systems. Through customer interactions, companies can identify methods to deliver the resources that customers require in the most cost-effective ways, thus reducing overall costs and increasing customer profitability.

Customization

The first three steps, when implemented properly, can provide the company with increased revenue, decreased costs, and ultimately higher profitability. However, the fourth step may be the source of the greatest benefits to the organization. Taking the information learned and using this information to deliver what customers actually need generates enormous goodwill and loyalty. Customers see the value in continuing the relationship, and their degree of loyalty increases. Companies are better able to craft marketing messages through personalized direct-mail pieces, which leads to higher success rates for such advertising programs.

Loyalty Programs

Some brands lend themselves well to developing loyal customers based on the quality, customer service, or even price of the product. However, some product categories find that building repeat business requires the development of reward or loyalty programs. These types of efforts are found in many product categories and among retailers. They represent an attempt to entice customers to repurchase from the company in exchange for various rewards. Companies also benefit from loyalty programs by collecting information about customers, including contact information and a customer's spending habits. This type of information may even be the most beneficial part of a loyalty program. The various types of programs that are used include frequent flyer miles (airlines), cash back (credit cards), discounts on select products (supermarkets), and discounts on purchases (department stores), just to name a few. According to Jupiter Research, more than 75% of consumers are enrolled in at least one loyalty program. Consumer product manufacturers are also using various programs to build some degree of loyalty among their customers. Coca-Cola offers its customers free merchandise for the continued purchase of their beverages (see Mycokerewards.com). Retailers such as Nordstrom and Best Buy have implemented programs to encourage customer loyalty.

EXAMPLE **LOYALTY PROGRAMS**

In an effort to increase customer value, and thus build loyalty, online music retailer eMusic.com launched *A+R Access + Rewards* in early 2010. The program offers subscribers the chance to win concert tickets, discounts on accessories, and chances to meet musicians. Developing loyalty is critical for a firm like eMusic, which has access to significantly fewer songs than its largest competitor iTunes.[12]

PHOTO: HYEPSTOCK/Shutterstock.

>> END EXAMPLE

Technology

Implementing and utilizing a customer relationship management system requires a major investment in computer systems, including specialized software that allows for in-depth analysis of the information that is collected. Dedicated employees are also needed to manage the flow of information from customers to managers. Although a CRM system can provide managers with an instantaneous view of customers, these systems can be expensive. Over $14 billion was spent on CRM programs in 2007 and that amount is forecasted to expand to $22 billion in 2012.[13]

Formal CRM systems can be too expensive for small firms, but those companies can still realize the same benefits by using other, less expensive, methods such as basic databases created in Excel. Much greater effort is needed to generate the same level of information as systems costing millions, but companies may see greater returns because they might place a higher value on the information they receive. It is important to remember that no matter how much a company invests in its CRM program, if customer information is not maintained, the benefits will be minimal. A well-maintained database offers companies the potential to uncover market opportunities through the use of **data mining**. This statistical technique has been used successfully in direct marketing to uncover individuals or groups of individuals who are most likely to respond to an offer and the types of offers that will elicit a response. Data mining has helped reduce costs by eliminating duplicate customer entries. Retailers have also benefited from data mining techniques that identify local buying patterns, thus allowing them to tailor the types of merchandise carried by individual stores.

Special precautions must be taken with the sensitive information contained in databases because customers have great concern regarding privacy and security issues. There have been numerous incidents of customer information being compromised through security breaches or lost laptops. The expenses incurred because of lost or stolen customer information can reach into the millions, not counting the losses associated with the negative publicity. It is estimated that a company can incur a cost between $30 and $300 for every customer record that is compromised. A security breach at retailer T.J.Maxx in 2007, where over 45 million customer credit card and debit card numbers were stolen by computer hackers, cost the company more than $250 million.

Visual Summary

Part 1 Explaining (Chapters 1, 2, 3, 4, 5)
Part 2 **Creating (Chapters 6, 7, 8, 9)**
Part 3 Strategizing (Chapters 10, 11)
Part 4 Managing (12, 13, 14, 15, 16, 17)
Part 5 Integrating (18, 19, 20)

Chapter 6 Summary

A company's marketing efforts should be focused on developing profitable and loyal customers. Building customer loyalty is the result of delivering value to the customer in excess of their expectations. Exceeding expectations creates feelings of satisfaction with the brand or company. Higher levels of satisfaction, or delight, cause customers to continue to purchase the brand. Customer loyalty can be enhanced through the use of relationship marketing, where the focus is on the individual customer, not only at a single point in time, but over the lifetime of the relationship. However, not all customers are worthy of the effort and expense required to build a long-term relationship. It is only through in-depth analysis of customer lifetime value that a company can decide with which customers to build a relationship and which customers to fire.

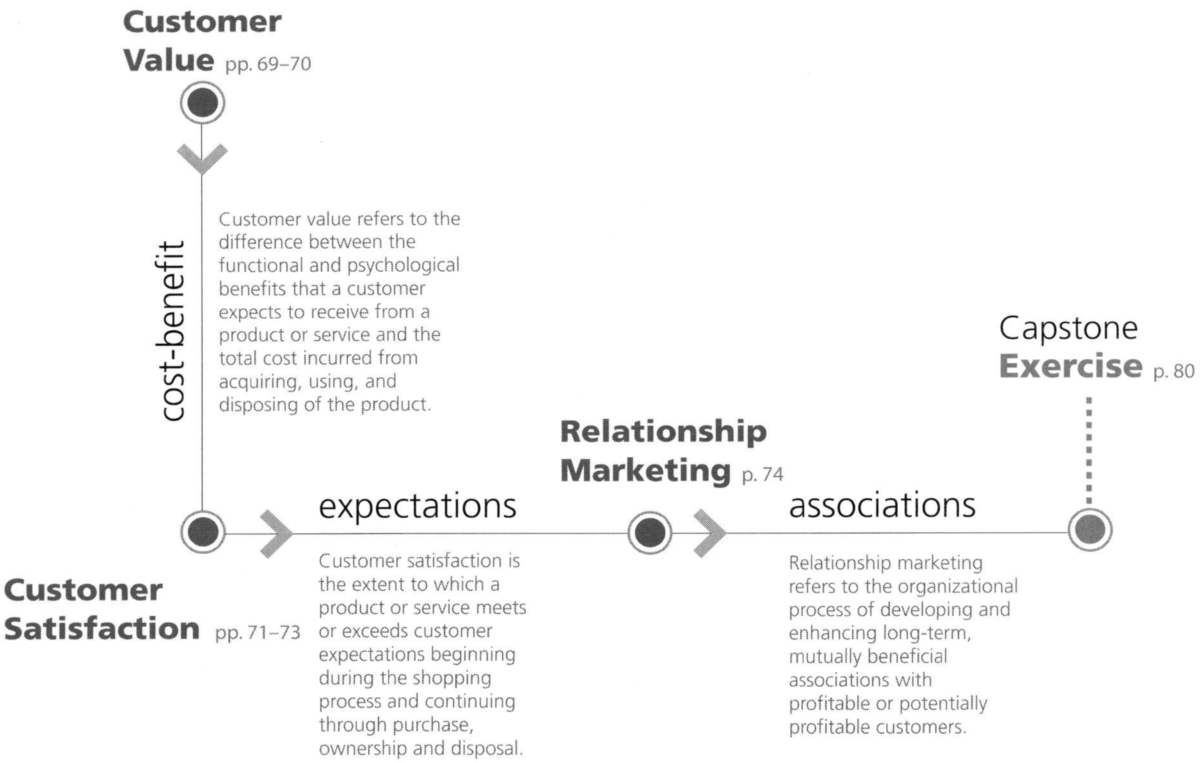
Customer Value pp. 69–70
cost-benefit
Customer value refers to the difference between the functional and psychological benefits that a customer expects to receive from a product or service and the total cost incurred from acquiring, using, and disposing of the product.
Customer Satisfaction pp. 71–73
expectations
Customer satisfaction is the extent to which a product or service meets or exceeds customer expectations beginning during the shopping process and continuing through purchase, ownership and disposal.
Relationship Marketing p. 74
associations
Relationship marketing refers to the organizational process of developing and enhancing long-term, mutually beneficial associations with profitable or potentially profitable customers.
Capstone Exercise p. 80

Chapter Key Terms

Customer Value (pp. 69–70)

Customer value *is the difference between the benefits a customer receives and the total cost incurred from acquiring, using, and disposing of a product. (p. 69)* **Opening Example (p. 69)**

Key Terms (p. 69)

Fair value zone is the area on a value map where customers' perceived benefits equal the customers' perceived cost. **(p. 69)**

Value map is a graphical representation of the ratio between customers' perceived benefits and the perceived total cost of a product. **(p. 69)**

Customer Satisfaction (pp. 71–73)

Customer satisfaction *is the degree to which a product meets or exceeds customer expectations. (p. 71)* **Example: Customer Satisfaction (p. 72) Example: Customer Retention (p. 73)**

Key Terms (pp. 72–73)

Customer lifetime value (CLV) is the present value of all profits expected to be earned from a customer over the lifetime of his or her relationship with a company. **(p. 73)**

Customer loyalty is the degree to which a customer will select a particular brand when a purchase from that product category is being considered. **(p. 72)**

Relationship Marketing (p. 74)

Relationship marketing *is the process of developing and enhancing long-term relationships with profitable customers. (p. 74)* **Example: Relationship Marketing (p. 74)**

Customer Relationship Management (pp. 75–77)

Customer relationship management (CRM) *is the activities that are used to establish, develop, and maintain customer relationships. (p. 75)* **Example: Loyalty Programs (p. 76)**

Key Term (p. 76)

Data mining is the statistical analysis of large databases seeking to discover hidden pieces of information. **(p. 76)**

Capstone Exercise

Video World is an independent video store—the only video store in a small town with a population of approximately 12,000. Video World rents movie DVDs and Blu-ray discs. Because it is located in a retirement community, Video World specializes in classic movies and movies of local interest. It also has previously viewed movies as well as new movies for sale. The average rental price is $4. The average price for a previously viewed movie is $10 and the average price for a new movie is $20. The average transaction is $10.

Video World has a customer base of nearly 2,000 members; however, only approximately 10% are "regular" customers—meaning they rent more than 10 movies each year. The store averages approximately 200 transactions each Friday, Saturday, and Tuesday. (Tuesday is the day the new releases are available.) There is an average of 100 transactions the other days of the week.

Currently, Video World offers two promotional specials: (1) after 90 days of inactivity, a "member" is called and offered a free movie for returning to the store, and (2) a "bundled" special of 2 movies, 2 candy items, 2 soft drinks (20 ounce), and popcorn for $15.

Recently, business has been seriously impacted by the competition from Netflix, Redbox, and On Demand pay-per-view. In addition, two of the local grocery stores have introduced movie rentals to their product line.

1. In what ways could a loyalty program help?
2. Do you think either of the current programs will support retention?
3. What type(s) of programs would you suggest? Be specific.
4. How would a loyalty program create value for Video World customers?
5. If a new program could increase "regular" customers to 20% of the total base and increase the average number of transactions on Sunday, Monday, Wednesday, and Thursday to 125 what would it be worth (in revenues) to Video World?

Application Exercise

Use the following marketing concepts in this chapter to tackle and solve a marketing problem: customer satisfaction, customer loyalty, customization, and customer relationship management.

First, start by thinking about a category of products in the entertainment market. In general terms, entertainment refers to a large number of sub-industries devoted to entertainment, some of which are music, gaming, film, theater, sports, and amusement parks.

The Marketing Problem

Choose a product in the entertainment category after considering the following situation.

> Young professionals are in touch with each other via social media. A regional theater company has asked you as a marketing student to give them a presence online that would resonate with this group.

The Problem

Describe how you would measure the success of your program in terms of customer satisfaction and customer loyalty. How would you go about maintaining a relationship with this target market?

The Solution

Complete the following Problem/Solution brief using your product in the entertainment category, chapter concepts, and college resources.

1. From the Marketing Manager's Point of View
   a. Problem Definition
   b. Analysis
   c. Product's Value
   d. Target Market
   e. Solution
2. From the Consumer's Point of View
   a. Problem Definition
   b. Analysis
   c. Product's Value
   d. Solution

Resources:

Marketing Defined, Explained, Applied 2e, Michael Levens
The College Library
Retail or Online Field Trip
Assigned Reading—*Brand Week*, *Advertising Age*, *WSJ*, scholarly publications, category trade journals
Blog your problem from either point of view, gather responses/posts (www.blogger.com/start)

A Perspective on **Consumer Behavior**

Chapter Overview In the previous chapter, you considered how companies create value for consumers and how businesses cultivate and maintain consumer relationships. To realize the potential of the value that can be created between consumers and companies, it is essential to understand how consumers behave—specifically, how they make decisions and how they solve problems. In this chapter, we explore the consumer decision-making and problem-solving processes to help us better understand consumer behavior.

Chapter Outline

CONSUMER BEHAVIOR (p. 83)

DEFINED **Consumer behavior** *is the dynamic interaction of affect and cognition, behavior, and the environment in which human beings conduct the exchange aspects (product and service purchases) of their lives.*[1]

EXPLAINED

Consumer Behavior

Consumer behavior represents the psychology of marketing. **Psychology** involves the study of the mind. The way a person's mind is wired plays an essential role in making purchase decisions. The process of how purchase decisions are made can be challenging to understand because the decisions consumers make are related to underlying human behavior. Consumer behavior has been explored through the lenses of marketing actions (for example, advertising and sales) and social psychology. **Social psychology** is a process used to understand social phenomena and their influences on social behavior. The process explores how individuals comprehend and relate to each other. Social psychology considers the influence of both the actual environment surrounding individuals as well as the beliefs and emotions of those individuals. The Theory of Planned Behavior, a social psychology theory, attempts to explain how attitudes, behaviors, and norms influence consumer behavior.[2] Attitudes toward behavior, social norms, and perceived control (as opposed to the amount of control one actually has) are determining factors of a consumer's intention. A consumer's intention is considered an indicator of how he or she will behave.[3]

APPLIED

Consumer Behavior

Consumer behavior is a familiar personal experience because consumers make product and service decisions on a regular basis. Consumers have considerable choices across a wide range of product and service categories. Consumers make purchase decisions based on several factors, for example, convenience, price, product or service characteristics, blogs about the product or service, and word-of-mouth recommendations. The decision-making process is often a combination of rational and emotional factors. Companies attempt to understand the consumer's process when that consumer makes a decision. Companies then develop marketing strategies to increase the likelihood that their products or services will be selected.

Consumer behavior involves not only a decision about purchasing a product or service, but it also involves the shopping process itself: how the relationships with the product and company evolve (including service and maintenance), how individual and societal perceptions of the product change, and how the relationship with the product develops over time.

Redbox, with its $1 dollar-a-night vending machines, has expanded from one kiosk in a McDonald's restaurant in 2004 to almost 30,000 in a wide range of locations including Walmart, Walgreens, 7-Eleven, and numerous grocery stores across the United States by the end of 2010. Owned by Coinstar, Inc., the coin-counting service found at many grocery stores, Redbox generated sales of $774 million in 2009. Redbox sales expanded to represent about one-fifth of a declining video rental market. Understanding how consumers shop and how they want to obtain access to videos allowed Redbox to create value for consumers through a simple consumer decision-making process. The price of $1 is significantly less than major competitor Blockbuster due mainly to much lower overhead. Consumers can reserve videos online—there is even an iPhone application—and then access the closest Redbox location. Alternatively, consumers can just go to a Redbox, select a movie, swipe a credit card, and go. This business model has proved so successful that existing competitors are struggling to react and new entrants such as NCR, the largest manufacturer of ATMs in the United States, have entered the market.

PHOTO: Johanna Goodyear/Shutterstock.

CONSUMER Decision-Making Process (pp. 84–90)

DEFINED *The* **consumer decision-making process** *is the steps that consumers take to identify and evaluate choice options.*

EXPLAINED

Consumer Decision-Making Process

The consumer decision-making process can range from a simple, low-involvement decision made without much investigation to a programmed response to a complex high-involvement cognitive task. Involvement is primarily classified into two segments: high and low. High involvement is typically considered a cognitive and verbal process that is referred to as left-brain processing.[4] Consumers under high-involvement conditions often reach deeper levels of information processing due to the significance of the decision being made.[5] However, some high-involvement situations may be considered nonverbal, emotional, and even metaphorical; these are referred to as right-brain processing.[6] Low-involvement situations are much like hypnotic suggestion and involve links to brain pathways that have been formed from prior experiences.[7] This is common with routine purchases that offer little risk.

It is important to understand that one person's low-involvement decision can be another's high-involvement decision. This can occur for a variety of reasons including level of interest in the product or service or level of income relative to the cost of the item. For someone interested in new computer technology, each new advancement may be studied carefully and new choices evaluated for their specific value. Others that are less interested in computer technology may simply rely on a friend's recommendation or just purchase whatever brand they purchased before.

In some cases decisions that were formerly low involvement for an individual can become high involvement. Throughout the most recent recession, many individuals changed their behavior by purchasing less expensive versions of products or service typically consumed, clipping coupons, setting budgets, or even forgoing certain items. For some this restrained spending behavior came from necessity while others chose to do so after personal reflection. In circumstances where income is reduced, individuals who previously may have shopped impulsively at gourmet grocery stores may now carefully compare prices at farmers' markets. When behavior change due to choice, as opposed to necessity, occurs, there is often a new emotional trigger for purchases that combines an understanding of societal economic circumstances, such as a recession, with trends in consumer attitudes, such as sustainability as discussed in Chapter 4. A consumer may choose to purchase a moderately priced shirt made of organic cotton from a lesser-known brand as opposed to a repeat purchase of a more expensive regular cotton shirt from a prestigious brand.

EXAMPLE **CONSUMER DECISION MAKING**

American Girl was founded in 1986 around the product concept of introducing historical character dolls to girls. Acquired by Mattel in 1998, the company is designed to appeal to "each stage of a young girl's development—from her preschool days of baby dolls and fantasy play through her tween years of self-expression and individuality." Given the relatively high cost of American Girl products and accessories such as the $95 Just Like You Doll, $85 Salon Station, and Dress Like Your Doll matching outfits selling for as much as $120, the purchase is generally considered high involvement. American Girl wraps its products into an experience that includes companion books, special events, and a collection of American Girl Place stores featuring cafes with special booster seats for dolls, a salon where girls and their dolls can get similar hair styles, an on-site theater featuring characters from the books, and even a doll hospital where damaged dolls can be fixed. Each of these services is intended to make the decision process easier for consumers. A positive ownership experience tends to build loyalty and satisfaction for American Girl.

PHOTO: JR Carvey/Streetfly Studio/Blend Images/Alamy.

>> END EXAMPLE

FIGURE 7.1 Decision-Making Process

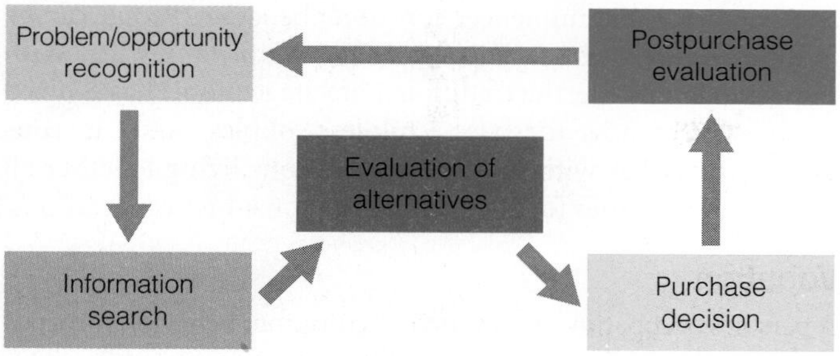

Decision making, influenced by involvement, is a problem-solving process that requires a selection of a particular type of behavior (see Figure 7.1).

The problem/opportunity recognition phase begins when a need or want is determined, such as the desire for a vacation. Information search involves exploring different sources of information to fulfill the need or want. In the case of a vacation, examples of information sources include travel agencies and travel Web sites. Different options are identified, based on certain criteria in the next step in the decision-making process. Travel choices could include places such as Florida, Mexico, or Puerto Rico. Those options could be evaluated based on criteria such as cost, ease of getting to and from the destination, and available activities at the destination. The purchase decision is made after evaluating alternatives. Postpurchase evaluation occurs when determining if the correct choice was made. Decisions on subsequent similar needs and wants, such as a vacation, are influenced by current experience.

APPLIED

Consumer Decision-Making Process

Developing marketing strategies that reflect an understanding of consumer decision making is important from a business perspective because strategies based on an understanding of consumer behavior enable marketing professionals to optimize the effectiveness of their investments. Effectiveness, even if strategically constructed and behaviorally aligned with consumer needs, can be either enhanced or limited by the type of product or service category, as well as by the interest level of certain consumers.

Products (and services) can be divided into three distinct categories based on how consumers interact with the respective categories. "Approach" products consist of products that consumers gain enjoyment from using and include categories such as automobiles, fashionable clothing, fine jewelry, and entertainment.[8] "Avoidance" products are those products that consumers would not regularly consider unless the use of such a product would reduce the likelihood of something unpleasant occurring.[9] Examples of avoidance products include insurance, automotive service, medical services, and deodorants. A third category includes "utilitarian" products that are products neither enjoyed nor used as a precaution.[10] Examples of utilitarian products include paper, pencils, and paper clips. It is much easier to create emotional connections with consumers when marketing approach products.

Consumer purchase decisions are influenced by personal, psychological, situational, and social factors. The extent to which businesses can understand these influences is significant when determining success. Each of these areas of influence is discussed in the following sections.

Personal Influence on Decision Making

Consumer behavior is influenced by a variety of personal characteristics. These personal characteristics include self-identity, personality, lifestyle, age and life stage (shared life events), vocation, and level of affluence (material comfort or wealth).

Self-Identity

Self-identity is an individual's understanding that he or she is unique. The implication is that through that uniqueness, different behavior can be expressed relative to other individuals. That behavior reflects personal values and is demonstrated through consumption choices. Self-identity has been shown to predict intentions, which we have previously shown extend to purchase behavior.[11] Individuals tend to select products and services that are consistent with their perception of self-identity.

Personality

Personality involves a "sense of consistency, internal causality, and personal distinctiveness."[12] Through interaction with one's environment, personality is expressed through particular patterns of behavior. Personalities can range from "rugged individualists" to "practical conformists." Products and services are often expressed, through characteristics of the product or service or through advertising, as having personalities that are relevant to the consumers identified as offering the most value to the company.

Lifestyle

Lifestyle is a way of life that individuals express by choosing how to spend their time and personal resources. Lifestyle is expressed through one's choices, for example, a home, car, travel, and music. Companies seeking to form deep emotional connections with consumers have worked to position their products and services in the environment in which those consumers live. Whether marketers are trying to reach scuba divers or dirt bike riders, they can connect with consumers through a variety of forms, including sponsoring events or advertising in lifestyle magazines.

Age and Life Stage

A person's age and age group influence consumer behavior. Different ages bring different societal requirements and product and service opportunities. Generation X consists of people born between 1965 and 1981, while Generation Y consists of people born between 1982 and 1994. Both groups have grown up experiencing successful and challenging economic times, but the groups have differences. Members of Generation X are moving into different life stages with more established careers, while many Generation Y members are still entering or becoming established with their careers. Experience with media is also different because Generation Y members are more immersed in social media than are Generation X members. This media experience changes the methods businesses use to communicate with these groups. Depending on your age and other factors, such as income, particular retirement investment choices are available. Age can also enable membership in certain organizations or the ability to live in certain communities where services are aimed at the typical member of that age group.

EXAMPLE AGE AND LIFE STAGE

AARP is a membership organization that operates in every state, the District of Columbia, Puerto Rico, and the U.S. Virgin Islands for people aged 50 and over. People aged 50 and older are the fastest-growing population in the United States and control the majority of America's financial assets. Therefore, it is critical that marketers are aware of how to reach this segment of the population. AARP provides a wide range of lifestyle-related information and services, ranging from travel to health. It operates a Web site, a magazine, and a monthly bulletin, as well as a Spanish-language newspaper. AARP also is involved in advocacy for its members on issues such as health care and Social Security.

PHOTO: Monkey Business Images/Shutterstock.

>> END EXAMPLE

In additional to chronological age, cognitive age contributes greatly to understanding an individual's perspectives, attitudes, and behaviors.[13] **Cognitive age**, also referred to as subjective age, is the age that one *feels*. Cognitive age influences one's self-image.[14] Cognitive age can link a 35-year-old with a 55-year-old and create marketing opportunities for particular products and services. For example, adventure sports such as triathlons, cycling, and skiing attract participants of varying ages. Interest in participating in such events has much to do with how one feels and how one is willing to work toward a particular goal.

Life stage, similar life events experienced by a group of individuals of varying chronological and cognitive ages, is yet another factor that influences consumer behavior. People can be in different life stages relative to their work or family life. With respect to family life, the traditional life-stage model has evolved to reflect alternative lifestyles. Childless couples, same-sex couples, and families with multiple generations living together all create opportunities for a wide range of consumer expectations.

Vocation

A person's occupation also influences consumer behavior. A corporate executive typically purchases different work-related products than a member of the clergy, an emergency room surgeon, or a factory worker, for example. Some occupations also provide more room for individual expression. An occupation might have great influence on work-related products, but it may have less influence on a person's personal choices outside the work environment.

Affluence

An individual's financial means determines the opportunity to purchase certain products or services, or the limitations on such purchases. Although some products, such as a Ferrari, are impossible for most individuals to afford, other products, such as a Burberry purse, are relatively expensive, yet possible for a broader range of people to purchase. The challenge for marketers of luxury products is to develop and manage an image of quality and prestige, while appealing to as broad a group of consumers as possible.

The process in which consumers purchase and consume luxury products is different from other products.[15] The consumer decision-making process for luxury items focuses on an item's meaning to the consumer and not necessarily on the physical presence of the item.[16] Meaning and corresponding motivation have changed over time. Instead of status and style as motivations for luxury purchases, other emotional factors now influence luxury purchases, ranging from jewelry to clothes and even homes, cars, and vacation clubs. The Boston Consulting Group has identified three emotional factors that influence the affluent purchase decision process:

- **Adventure or journey of reinvention**—This is the idea that individuals seek products and services, such as exotic vacations, that create excitement or enable introspection.
- **Desire to foster heath and wellness**—This idea is that individuals seek products and services such as spas and yoga retreats that are designed to assist in understanding and improving one's health.
- **Connecting and building personal relationships**—This is the idea that individuals seek products and services, such as team-building retreats and event planning, that engender shared experiences.

EXAMPLE **AFFLUENCE**

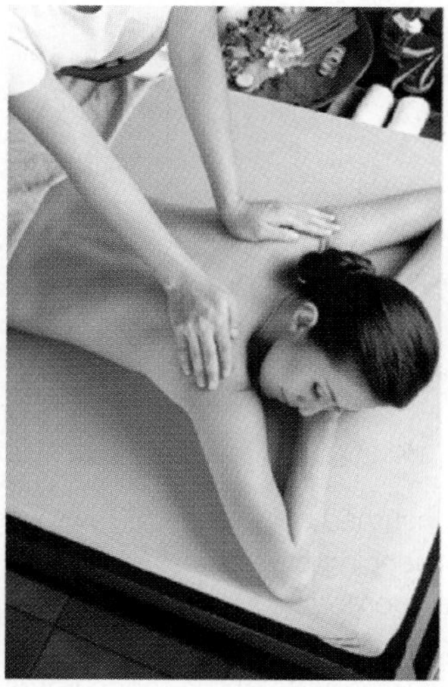

Golden Door, an upscale network of spas, has designed multiday health and wellness programs for affluent consumers. Capitalizing on the increased focus on improving health, Golden Door has expanded, with six locations across North America. The services range from personal fitness consulting to yoga, hiking, massage, and beauty services. Focusing on the desire for building relationships, Golden Door offers special events during its men's, women's, and co-ed weeks.

PHOTO: Hywit Dimyadi/Shutterstock.

>> **END EXAMPLE**

Psychological Influence on Decision Making

Consumer behavior is influenced by a variety of psychological characteristics. These personal characteristics include perception, motivation, attitudes and beliefs, and learning.

Perception

Perception is a cognitive impression of incoming stimuli that influences the individual's actions and behavior.[17] The stimuli are generated through the senses: hearing, smelling, tasting, seeing, and touching. How the information is processed through the senses is unique to each person. Stimuli, such as an advertisement with a picture of a new boat, or a magazine with the scent of a new perfume, must pass through a filtering process. With all the stimuli from the external environment as well as advertising, businesses try to understand those stimuli that generate desired responses from consumers.

Although stimuli are processed overtly, they can also be processed subconsciously. **Subliminal perception** is the processing of stimuli by a recipient who is not aware of the stimuli being received. The original intent of subliminal perception, which originated in the 1950s, was to influence behavior with embedded images in various forms of advertising. After significant research, this concept was proven to be ineffective other than to help remind people to do something they already were interested in doing. Subliminal advertising is considered unethical and is illegal in many countries.

Motivation

Although perception essentially involves working from the outside in to interpret external stimuli, motivation involves working from the inside out to match current conditions to a desired condition. Any gap between the current and desired state is a motive for action. **Motivation** is the set of conditions that creates a drive toward particular action to fulfill a need or want. Maslow's hierarchy of needs provides a context to understand motivation. The hierarchy is based on a theory that individuals need to secure their most basic needs, such as food and security, before trying to realize any higher-order needs, such as belongingness, self-esteem, or self-actualization.

Attitudes and Beliefs

Attitude is a state of readiness, based on experience, that influences a response to something. Attitudes involve a like, dislike, or ambivalence toward an idea, product, service, or just about anything. There are three components of attitudes, including what one feels, what one does, and what one knows. While attitudes are generally consistent over time, there are opportunities to influence attitudes through experience or education. A **belief** is a sense of truth about something. Beliefs are what an individual knows and they can influence attitudes.

Learning

Learning is knowledge that is acquired through experiences. The learning process includes drive, cue, response, and reinforcement.

- **Drive** is an internal stimulus that encourages action.
- **Cue** is an environmental stimulus that influences a particular action.
- **Response** is a consumer's reaction to drive and cues.
- **Reinforcement** is a reduction in drive resulting from a positive-response experience.

Businesses can use the learning process to create positive customer experiences and cultivate loyalty. For example, the need for a course textbook creates the drive to obtain one. Seeing the required textbook in the bookstore is a cue that can influence the purchase action. The actual purchase of the textbook is the response. Reinforcement occurs through using the textbook and eliminating the underlying drive to obtain the required course textbook.

Situational Influence on Decision Making

Consumer behavior is influenced by a variety of situation-specific characteristics. These characteristics include the purchase environment, time, digital environment, and context.

Purchase Environment

The shopping environment has considerable influence on consumer behavior. Energetic music can stimulate shoppers to make bold choices, whereas slow-paced music can encourage leisurely shopping that might translate into more purchases than might have otherwise been made. A shelf's organization can discourage shopping or encourage the education process for new products. Many businesses design aisles and overall store traffic flow to maximize the total purchase size.

EXAMPLE **PURCHASE ENVIRONMENT**

AutoZone, founded in 1979 with a single retail auto parts store, now has over 3,000 stores across the United States. Several years ago, AutoZone standardized how its stores used Plan-O-Grams (maps of how products should be displayed in a store environment). The idea was to place certain products that appeal to a particular customer next to each other instead of the more traditional way of displaying similar products next to each other. Instead of managing product lines independently, the entire portfolio is managed based on customer shopping behavior. For example, all chrome products used to be grouped together. Chrome tips were moved next to muffler clamps and hangers, allowing an easy purchase of the products necessary to update an automotive exhaust system, resulting in an overall increase in margin based on the new merchandising strategy.[18]

PHOTO: Andrjuss/Shutterstock.

>> END EXAMPLE

EXAMPLE **DIGITAL ENVIRONMENT**

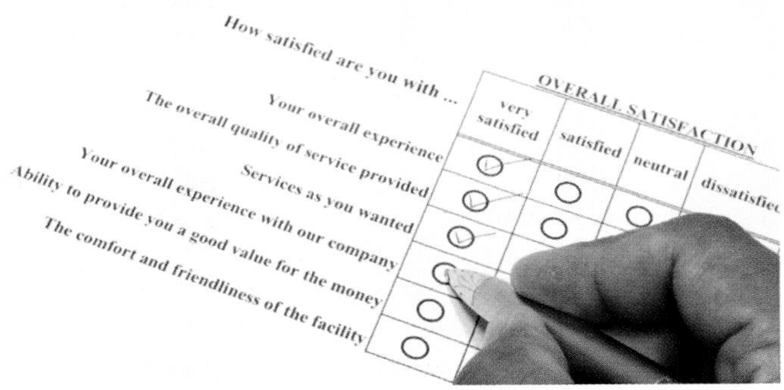

Epinions, a popular Web-based consumer reviews platform, is an example of how digital media is influencing consumer behavior. A service of Shopping.com, an eBay company, Epinions provides detailed product evaluations and personalized recommendations. Whether or not consumers purchase products online, consumers are increasingly conducting online product research prior to making purchases.

PHOTO: Ragsac/Shutterstock.

>> END EXAMPLE

Time

After the product decision is made, the length and amount of effort in the shopping process influence consumer behavior. If a consumer knows that a preferred product is in a store that typically has long lines and the secondary or tertiary product in a particular category is at a location that has short or efficient lines, the consumer may elect to purchase one of the less-desired products to avoid the long lines. Whether it is same-day dry-cleaning or fast food circumstances have the potential to override possible negative factors, such as lower quality, associated with the services.

Digital Environment

The digital environment influences consumer behavior through online social networking, blogs, product-ratings sites, and other activities that assist in online research, evaluation, and purchase. There is a tremendous wealth of information, of varying reliability, available instantly in the digital realm for consumers to consider when making decisions.

There is also a wide range of choices that are presented to consumers through digital technology, including emerging mobile applications.

Context

An individual may have very strong opinions about desired quality or ingredients. Depending on circumstances, the individual may create a different set of requirements for his or her purchases. If a consumer purchases only organic products, but is asked to purchase products for an office party, he or she may not elect to pay the price premium of the organic products because others may not expect or even appreciate the additional investment.

Social Influence on Decision Making

Consumer behavior is influenced by a variety of social characteristics. These characteristics include culture, subculture, groups, social class, gender roles, and family.

Culture

Culture refers to the shared values, beliefs, and preferences of a particular society. Culture can be reflected through and influenced by religious beliefs, morality, artistic expression, and even habits. Culture can be formally established through laws and informally encouraged by societal actions and reactions. Cultures can also exist within a larger whole. Consider the wide variety of cultures in the United States.

Culture is fundamental in the initial wiring of an individual's behavior. The influence of culture exists in all countries, but it varies in terms of the level of influence. Businesses must understand the extent to which culture influences consumer expectations and behavior.

Subculture

Subcultures are groups of people within a broader society who share similar behaviors and values. Subcultures influence, and are influenced by, the larger culture. Endurance athletes, such as triathletes and marathoners, make up a subculture within the larger sports culture. Innovations in training techniques or increasing interest in endurance sports could influence the larger sports culture through increasing gym memberships or through demand for new sports drinks or training products. Changes in attitudes toward sports, in general, could also influence the endurance athlete subculture. A large advertising campaign supporting the importance of physical activity could lead to more people eventually developing an interest in endurance sports. Many subcultures exist in the United States, including a wide range of ethnic and age groups, as well as religious, gender, professional status, and geographic subcultures.

By 2050, it is estimated that over 47% of the U.S. population will be composed of ethnic minorities.[19] Today, ethnic minorities account for more than 50% of the population in 48 of the 100 largest U.S. cities.[20] Hispanics and Asians will account for more than 45% of population growth in the United States through 2020.[21] The Asian population, the most affluent U.S. subculture, is growing at a rate of 9% annually, faster than Hispanics, but Hispanics are the largest minority in the total population.[22] African Americans have been supplanted as the largest minority group, and the African American population segment is growing at a much slower rate than Hispanics.

The subculture implications for marketers are that the various ethnic minorities do not necessarily follow general market-consumption patterns. AT&T has developed marketing programs to meet the needs of over 30 different cultures in 20 languages.[23] A unique marketing mix is necessary for each group, and there are opportunities to make a brand stand for different things to different groups, although at a significant cost.[24]

There is yet another factor when considering the ethnic minority subcultures. In 2000, seven million Americans considered themselves mixed-race, as recorded by the U.S census.[25] More mixed-race babies are born in Washington, California, and other western states than any other group except Caucasians.[26] Prominent individuals such as Tiger Woods, Keanu Reeves, Christina Aguilera, Alicia Keys, and Anne Curry all identify themselves as mixed-race.[27]

EXAMPLE SUBCULTURE

Matt Kelley, a 19-year-old freshman at Connecticut's Wesleyan University, launched MAVIN magazine in 1999. At the time of its inception, it was the only magazine dedicated to mixed-race people and families. Today, the MAVIN Foundation is involved in communities across the country through awareness-building and educational activities.[28]

PHOTO: Monkey Business Images/Shutterstock.

>> END EXAMPLE

The youth market can also be considered a subculture. Fifty million 13- to 23-year-old consumers spend over $150 billion annually.[29] However, the youth market influences a far greater number of expenditures by other people. Teenagers and young adults ages 13–21 exert varying degrees of influence on family decision making regarding different product or service categories.[30] In the clothing sector 89% decide or influence the purchase decision, 77% of 13- to 21-year-olds influence software decisions, and 61% influence vehicle purchase decisions.[31]

America's youth have generally been exposed to a greater variety of cultures than previous generations.[32] These diverse cultures are often integrated into the lives of the youth market and diverse messages are welcome and expected. Is it these youth who are defining diversity, as opposed to marketers?[33]

Groups

Throughout their lives, individuals will be influenced by a variety of groups. The extent of the influence will vary by group. Initially, group influence will come from one's parents, which will then expand to small groups of friends, and then to activities and organizations. In a particular group, there are standards of behaviors called **norms** that are imparted to members; norms in a group define membership in the group. One can also perform a particular role or roles within a group. In a group context, **roles** are specific actions expected from someone in a group as a member or from a particular position held. Through either belonging to or holding a position within a group, one can achieve status. **Status** is the position of one individual relative to others.

A **reference group** consists of people who directly or indirectly influence how an individual feels about a particular topic. Reference groups can provide a new perspective on how to live one's life. Businesses that understand the reference group dynamic can work through reference groups to link their products and services with changes in lifestyle. Within a given reference group are opinion leaders who can serve as the connection between consumers and businesses. **Opinion leaders** are individuals who have the greatest influence on the attitudes and behaviors of a particular group. The fact that consumers often look to opinion leaders for insight and direction provides marketers with opportunities to work through opinion leaders either directly, through paid activities, or simply by tracking consumer reactions to evolving trends. Opinion leaders can include celebrities, experts, or others who possess characteristics that individuals admire or respect. Social media, such as blogs, wikis, or networking sites, provide a forum for opinion leaders to establish their positions. For those opinions already established, social media provide a mechanism to quickly communicate perspectives on various topics.

EXAMPLE GROUPS

The American Federation of Labor and Congress of Industrial Organizations (AFL-CIO), founded in 1955, is a voluntary federation of 56 national and international labor unions. The AFL-CIO union movement represents 11.5 million members of the 15.4 million union members in the United States and includes a variety of professions including farm workers, engineers, pilots, doctors, and painters. The AFL-CIO encourages its membership to support its priorities, which include " . . . creating family-supporting jobs by investing tax dollars in schools, roads, bridges and airports; improving the lives of workers through education, job training and raising the minimum wage; keeping good jobs at home by reforming trade rules, reindustrializing the U.S. economy and redoubling efforts at worker protections in the global economy; strengthening Social Security and private pensions; making high-quality, affordable health care available to everyone; and holding corporations more accountable for their actions." The AFL-CIO also encourages its membership to support political candidates and legislative actions that support the organization's agenda. In the recent health care debate, AFL-CIO members made over 4 million phone calls in support of the legislation.[34]

PHOTO: James R. Martin/Shutterstock.

>> END EXAMPLE

Social Class

Social classes are characteristics that distinguish certain members of a society from others, based on a variety of factors, including wealth, vocation, education, power, place of residence, and ancestry. Social classes are based on shared life experiences. Many countries have a series of social class ranks that stratify individuals in one class above or below individuals in another class based on factors such as those previously mentioned. It is possible to change membership in a social class, such as an income class, but in some cases changing social class is not possible. For example, you cannot change family history. Membership in a particular social class generally influences how one presents oneself to society and influences consumer behavior in many lifestyle-related categories. Individuals in a particular social class may adopt purchasing behaviors that are reflective of general behavior of their peers in the same social class.

Gender Roles

Society defines expectations of appropriate attitudes and behaviors for men and women. Different societies have different gender roles that can affect the workplace and home. Gender roles can change or evolve over time. Only half of all women between the ages of 25–54 worked outside the home just 40 years ago; now that number is over 80%. Gender roles also differ depending on sexual orientation and gender identity.

Family

Family members are the first influencers of group behavior on an individual. The family group is considered one of the most important influencers of consumer behavior. Just as with other groups, there is normative behavior and distinct roles of family members. Norms and behavior can vary from one family to another and can evolve from one's birth family to one's family constructed through choice later in life. In a traditional family structure, one spouse can handle decision making for virtually all decisions, the decision making can be product and service specific, or both spouses may jointly make decisions. The construction of families has changed greatly from the traditional married household with children, and now includes same-sex households with or without children and an increasing number of single households.

CONSUMER Problem Solving (p. 91)

DEFINED **Consumer problem solving** *is how someone comes to a conclusion about a situation. This is determined by what kind of decision a consumer is facing.*

EXPLAINED

Consumer Problem Solving

Problem solving can be classified into three categories: limited problem solving, significant problem solving, and routine response problem solving. **Limited problem solving** occurs when a consumer is prepared to exert a certain amount of effort to make a purchase decision. This situation can occur when a consumer has considerable experience with a category and then encounters a new product option. **Significant problem solving** occurs when a consumer is prepared to commit considerable effort to make a purchase decision. This type of problem solving occurs when a new product is encountered that possesses characteristics that cause a consumer to reflect on his or her current perceptions of a category. Another scenario that warrants significant problem solving occurs when the product is expensive and there are great implications if a poor choice is made. **Routine response problem solving** occurs when a consumer has a well-developed process associated with fulfilling a need or want. An example of this problem-solving process is when a consumer purchases a new DVD from a series with which the consumer is familiar and enjoys. Each type of problem solving involves some level of risk. The more problem solving is involved in decision making, the more risk that must be managed.

APPLIED

Consumer Problem Solving

In practice, businesses constantly try to position products in such a way that the problem-solving process works to their advantage. If a business has a strong position in a particular market, that business is trying to make as many purchases as routine as possible. Alternatively, if a business is trying to grow significantly in a market, management may concentrate efforts on making consumers reconsider the characteristics that define the product category with respect to the attributes of its products or services.

EXAMPLE CONSUMER PROBLEM SOLVING

Eco-labels such as Energy Star, Fair Trade Certified, and the recycled logo are being used by a wide range of companies, including Marriott, Kohl's, and Hewlett-Packard (HP), to differentiate their products from competitors. Responding to consumer demand for more socially and environmentally friendly products, HP has created its Eco Highlights label for select HP products. Through disclosing energy-saving features and certifications, HP intends to help businesses and consumers "reduce the environmental impact of their imaging and printing." By focusing on the eco-friendly characteristics of its products, HP is hoping that consumers will prefer its "green" products to those of competitors.[35]

PHOTO: Arcady/Shutterstock.

>> **END EXAMPLE**

Visual Summary

Part 1 Explaining (Chapters 1, 2, 3, 4, 5)
Part 2 Creating (Chapters 6, 7, 8, 9)
Part 3 Strategizing (Chapters 10, 11)
Part 4 Managing (Chapters 12, 13, 14, 15, 16, 17)
Part 5 Integrating (Chapters 18, 19, 20)

Chapter 7 Summary

The concepts underlying consumer behavior are built on value creation and customer relationship management. Companies that understand the factors that influence consumer behavior as it is expressed through decision making can implement strategies based on consumer behavior. Decision making is influenced by personal, psychological, situational, and social factors. A consumer's decision-making process includes five main steps: problem/opportunity recognition, information search, evaluation of alternatives, purchase decision, and postpurchase evaluation. Depending on the type of decisions being made, certain levels of problem solving can occur, including limited problem solving, significant problem solving, and routine response problem solving. A commitment to understanding consumer behavior and implementing consumer behavior-based strategies can provide a business with the information necessary to create financially rewarding relationships with consumers.

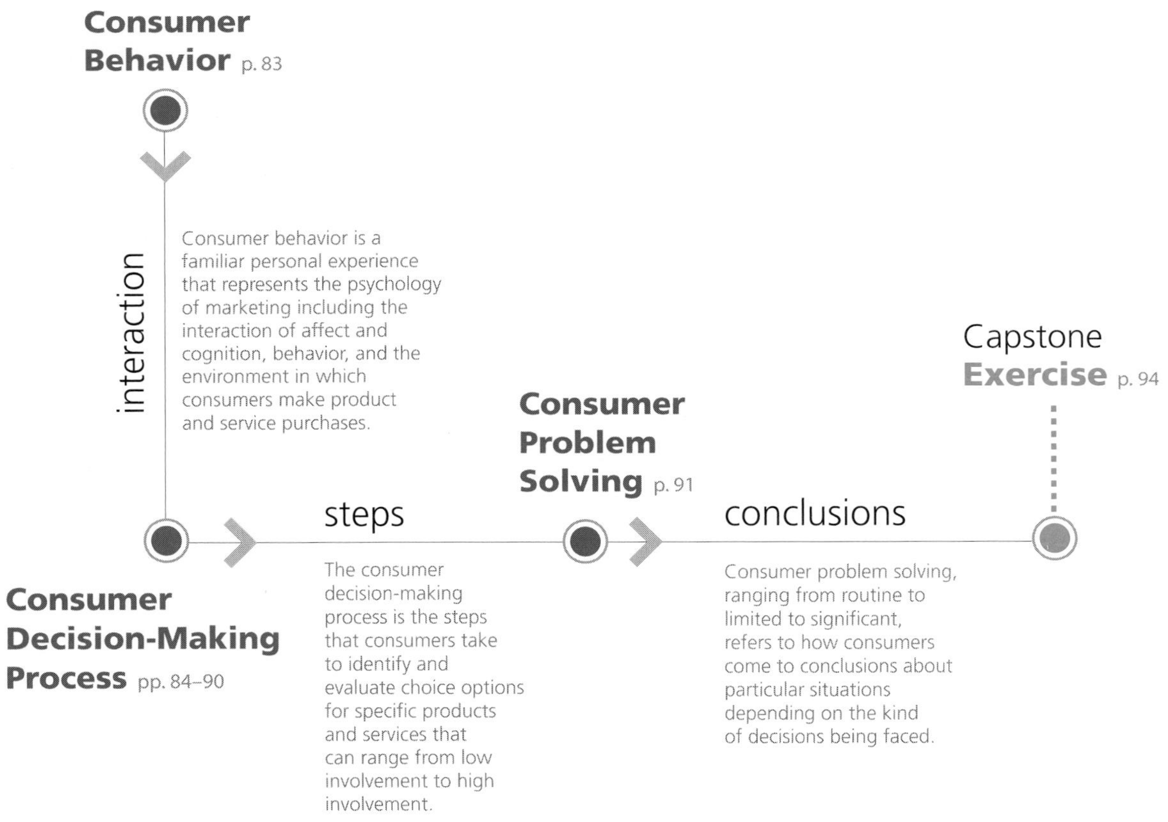
Consumer Behavior p. 83
interaction
Consumer behavior is a familiar personal experience that represents the psychology of marketing including the interaction of affect and cognition, behavior, and the environment in which consumers make product and service purchases.
Consumer Decision-Making Process pp. 84–90
steps
The consumer decision-making process is the steps that consumers take to identify and evaluate choice options for specific products and services that can range from low involvement to high involvement.
Consumer Problem Solving p. 91
conclusions
Consumer problem solving, ranging from routine to limited to significant, refers to how consumers come to conclusions about particular situations depending on the kind of decisions being faced.
Capstone Exercise p. 94

Chapter Key Terms

Consumer Behavior (p. 83)

Consumer behavior *is the dynamic interaction of affect and cognition, behavior, and the environment in which human beings conduct the exchange aspects of their lives. (p. 83)* **Opening Example (p. 83)**

Key Terms (p. 83)

Psychology involves the study of the mind. **(p. 83)**
Social psychology is the process to understand social phenomena and their influence on social behavior. **(p. 83)**

Consumer Decision-Making Process (pp. 84–90)

Consumer decision-making process *is the steps that consumers take to identify and evaluate choice options. (p. 84)* **Example: Consumer Decision Making (p. 84) Example: Purchase Environment (p. 88) Example: Digital Environment (p. 88)**

Key Terms (pp. 85–90)

Attitude is a state of readiness, based on experience that influences a response to something. **(p. 87)**
Belief is a sense of truth about something. **(p. 87)**
Cognitive age, also referred to as subjective age, is the age that a person feels. **(p. 86)**
Cue is an environmental stimulus that influences a particular action. **(p. 87)**
Culture refers to the shared values, beliefs, and preferences of a particular society. **(p. 88)**
Drive is an internal stimulus that encourages action. **(p. 87)**
Learning is knowledge that is acquired through experiences. **(p. 87)**
Life stages are similar life events experienced by groups of individuals of varying chronological and cognitive ages. **(p. 86) Example: Age and Life Stage (p. 86)**
Lifestyle is a way of life that individuals express through choosing how to spend their time and personal resources. **(p. 85)**
Motivation is the set of conditions that creates a drive toward a particular action to fulfill a need or want. **(p. 87)**
Norms are standards of behaviors imparted to members of a particular group that define membership. **(p. 89)**
Opinion leaders are those individuals who have the greatest influence on the attitudes and behaviors of a particular group. **(p. 89) Example: Groups (p. 90)**
Perception is a cognitive impression of incoming stimuli that influences the individual's actions and behavior. **(p. 87)**
Personality involves a sense of consistency, internal causality, and personal distinctiveness. **(p. 85)**
Reference group consists of people who directly or indirectly influence how an individual feels about a particular topic. **(p. 89) Example: Groups (p. 90)**
Reinforcement is a reduction in drive resulting from a positive response experience. **(p. 87)**
Response is a consumer's reaction to his or her drive and cues. **(p. 87)**
Roles are specific actions expected from someone in a group as a member or from a particular position held. **(p. 89)**
Self-identity is the understanding by an individual that he or she is unique. **(p. 85) Example: Age and Life Stage (p. 86)**
Social classes are characteristics that distinguish certain members of a society from others, based on a variety of factors, including wealth, vocation, education, power, place of residence, and ancestry. **(p. 90) Example: Affluence (p. 87)**
Status is the position of one individual relative to others. **(p. 89)**
Subcultures are groups of people, within a broader society, who share similar behaviors and values. **(p. 88) Example: Subculture (p. 89)**
Subliminal perception is the processing of stimuli by a recipient who is not aware of the stimuli being received. **(p. 87)**

Consumer Problem Solving (p. 91)

Consumer problem solving *is how someone comes to a conclusion about a situation. This is determined by what kind of a decision a consumer is facing. (p. 91)* **Example: Consumer Problem Solving (p. 91)**

Key Terms (p. 91)

Limited problem solving occurs when a consumer is prepared to exert a certain amount of effort to make a purchase decision. **(p. 91)**
Routine response problem solving occurs when a consumer has a well-developed process associated with fulfilling a need or want. **(p. 91)**
Significant problem solving occurs when a consumer is prepared to commit considerable effort to make a purchase decision. **(p. 91) Example: Consumer Problem Solving (p. 91)**

Capstone Exercise

This chapter deals with consumer behavior. The issue in this chapter is to understand the factors that influence a person's buying decisions. Why do people buy what they buy? For example, why would one woman spend $200 on a sweater when another comparable sweater could be bought for $50? To explore the buying process and how it works, it is helpful to talk to an individual who has bought a product or service and then dissect the buying decision.

This chapter's exercise is to interview two people who are not members of your marketing class. Preferably, the people should be from different demographic groups—age, income, education, and occupation. Don't just pick your fellow students, or that will skew your findings. Of the two people, one needs to have made a purchase decision of $25 or less, and the other a purchase decision of $100 or more. Evaluate and prioritize the information that influenced their purchase decisions.

Your task is to "get in the person's head." Try to understand why they bought what they did. Question the reasons they used to make their decisions.

Write a one- to two-page paper on each interview. Describe the person, what he or she bought, and what factors contributed to the person's purchase decision. Be creative in the questions that you ask. To get you started, here are some questions to ask:

- Was it an individual or family decision?
- Was it a want or a need?
- What motivated the purchase?
- What features or benefits seemed important to the buyer?
- Was it a first-time decision? Has the person bought this product before?
- How much thought went into the buying decision?
- Did the person search the Internet or speak to friends? Did he or she read reviews on a site such as Amazon or www.epinions.com?
- How did the person gather the information he or she used to make the decision?
- Was the choice a low- or high-involvement purchase?
- How many alternatives were evaluated?
- Was the person happy with his or her choice? Why or why not?
- Did service play a factor with the choice?
- Did the product/service meet the person's expectations? If so, why? If not, why not?
- What role did the brand name play?

Application Exercise

Use the marketing concepts in this chapter to tackle and solve a marketing problem: drive, lifestyle, life stage, and consumer decision-making process.

First, start by thinking about luxury goods and then choose a product within that category. Luxury goods are typically goods that are distinguished in design, quality, durability, or performance and are often priced higher than the general market can afford. There are many products available within this category for high-end consumers to consider purchasing.

The Marketing Problem

Think about your chosen product after considering the following situation.

> Luxury goods like yachts, private planes, vacation homes, and mansions are targeted to high-income consumers. When a country sustains an economic recession or an individual consumer loses income stature, high-income consumers may alter their lifestyle.

The Problem

How would you describe the life stage and lifestyle of a luxury good consumer? Describe the drive that compels their consumption.

The Solution

Complete the following two Problem/Solution briefs using your product in the luxury category, chapter concepts, and college resources.

1. From the Marketing Manager's Point of View
   a. Problem Definition
   b. Analysis
   c. Product's Value
   d. Consumer Decision-Making Process
   e. Solution

2. From the Consumer's Point of View
   a. Problem Definition
   b. Analysis
   c. Product's Value
   d. Consumer Drive
   e. Solution

Resources:

Marketing Defined, Explained, Applied 2e, Michael Levens
The College Library
Retail or Online Field Trip
Assigned Reading—*Brand Week*, *Advertising Age*, *WSJ*, scholarly publications, category trade journals
Blog your problem from either point of view, gather responses/posts (www.blogger.com/start)

Consumer Insight

Chapter Overview In the previous chapter, you considered how consumers made decisions and behaved in the marketplace. The reasons consumers behave the way they do, and the underlying motivations for that behavior, need to be understood for a company to make effective marketing decisions. This chapter considers the concepts, tools, and processes that companies can use to learn more about their customers (and potential customers). By exploring marketing research and marketing information systems, the concept of consumer insight will be developed.

Chapter Outline

CONSUMER INSIGHT (pp. 97–98)

DEFINED **Consumer insight** *is perceived meanings of data collected from the study of consumer behavior.*

EXPLAINED

Consumer Insight

With the increased competition for space on the shelves of retailers and the sheer number of new products entering the market each year, understanding what consumers want and why they want it is an essential marketing practice. Consumer insight is not insight that consumers have; it is insight about consumers. Consumer insight includes a broad range of information that is obtained and interpreted to create detailed perspectives on customers and other market members. **Insight** is defined as the act or result of apprehending the inner nature of things, or of seeing intuitively.[1] From this definition, we can see that insights are far more valuable than mere information. Insights place information in context; that context can extend to both consumers and businesses. The study of business behavior, for those involved in business-to-business activities, is just as important as the study of consumer behavior is to those involved in business-to-consumer activities.

The American Marketing Association (AMA) defines **consumer market insight** as "an in-depth understanding of customer behavior that is more qualitative than quantitative. Specifically, it describes the role played by the product/brand in question in the life of its consumers—and their general stance toward it, including the way they acquire information about the category or brand, the importance attached to generic and specific values, attitudes, expectations, as well as the choice-making process. It refers to a holistic appreciation, which used to be traditionally split by market researchers and brand managers as qualitative and quantitative research."[2] This definition illustrates the relationship of consumer insight to the study of consumer behavior. Exploring consumer behavior involves conducting marketing research and managing a marketing information system. Each of these topics will be addressed in subsequent sections.

APPLIED

Consumer Insight

Consumers interact with companies in many different ways, including responding to direct marketing, using call centers, shopping at retail outlets, using service locations, and responding to advertising. Each of these activities provides data (insights) that help companies determine who the most desirable consumers are, where they are, how best to talk to them, how to keep them happy, and how to sell them more things at higher margins.

Although consumer information is generated from many different areas within an organization, the responsibility for consumer insight is typically assigned to a person or group within the marketing or strategy departments. The specific department titles vary widely from Knowledge Management, Consumer Innovation, Marketing Intelligence, and Marketing Research to Consumer Insights. The specific functions of these groups may be similar, but this textbook treats the concepts of marketing intelligence, marketing research, and consumer insight differently.

The Nielsen Company, founded in 1923, is the largest global media measurement and information firm. Global research revenue reached almost $5 billion in 2009. Nielsen is best known for its daily metered system that monitors 25,000 U.S. households and produces the Nielsen ratings of TV show viewership. The Nielsen ratings are used to help calculate the amount that advertisers pay television networks to advertise during specific shows. Nielsen began measuring U.S. radio audiences in the 1930s but now provides measurement of TV, online, and mobile audiences. Nielsen's Three-Screen Media Measurement service uses a single-source TV and PC consumer panel to generate cross-screen insights, such as if a consumer uses Facebook while watching a TV program. A variety of research is generated including cause and effect analysis, such as if a TV advertisement encourages a consumer to visit a specific Web site.[3]

PHOTO: hfng/Shutterstock.

In practice, consumer insight can address a wide range of questions, including the following:

- What do people think about my brand?
- What do people think about the competing brands?
- What do people expect from my brand?
- What opportunities and threats exist for my brand?
- What factors influence purchase considerations for my brand?
- What types of advertising work best for communicating the essence of my brand?
- How consistently does price change with demand for my brand?
- With what other brands could my brand collaborate for mutual benefit?
- What is the personality of my brand, and how does that influence purchase consideration?
- Who are my brand's most loyal customers?
- What market conditions exist such that I have either greater or lesser opportunities than I did previously?

Understanding these consumer insights can lead to responsive product development processes, targeted marketing strategies, and efficiencies throughout the supply and distribution channels, as well as in marketing expenditures.

MARKETING RESEARCH (pp. 99–106)

DEFINED **Marketing research** *is the acquisition and analysis of information used to identify and define marketing opportunities that connect consumers to marketers.*[4]

EXPLAINED

Marketing Research

One of the first marketing research projects occurred in 1879 when advertising company N.W. Ayer & Son applied marketing research when creating ads for the Nichols-Shepard Company, makers of agricultural machinery. N.W. Ayer & Son wired state officials and publishers around the country asking for information on grain production.[5] The first continuous marketing research study is credited to Charles Parlin for his work with Curtis Publishing Company, beginning in 1911 and continuing for 27 years, to collect information about customers to help Curtis sell more magazine advertising for the *Saturday Evening Post.*[6]

Research is defined as "the studious inquiry or examination; *especially*: investigation or experimentation aimed at the discovery and interpretation of facts, revision of accepted theories or laws in the light of new facts, or practical application of such new or revised theories or laws."[7] Research can be classified as either applied or pure. **Applied research** attempts to answer questions related to practical problems. If a small business owner wants to know where to locate his or her new restaurant, the owner would conduct applied research on a variety of topics including competition, traffic patterns, and level of consumer affluence near the proposed locations. **Pure research** attempts to expand understanding of the unknown. Scientists searching for a cure for AIDS or cancer are conducting pure research. Applied research is much more common in business. Many different disciplines, from law to political history, utilize research, but marketing research is classified as either consumer marketing research or business-to-business marketing research. Consumer marketing research considers the behavior of individual consumers or groups of consumers. Business-to-business marketing research considers the behavior of businesses transacting with other businesses.

APPLIED

Marketing Research

The purpose of marketing research is to help decision makers make better decisions. Marketing research can produce valuable information, but that information is most valuable when it is effectively translated into consumer insight. Marketing research information is a tool that can be used to launch successful new products and assist in the creation of effective advertising. The uses of marketing research include the following:[8]

- Identify and define marketing opportunities and problems.
- Generate, refine, and evaluate marketing actions.
- Monitor marketing performance.
- Improve understanding of marketing as a process.

While potentially valuable, marketing research can also be misrepresented when not placed into proper context. The *Chicago Tribune* used a still-growing technology, the telephone, to project the winner of the 1948 presidential election. Collecting responses from a high-income, mainly Republican, group of telephone owners produced a skewed representation of the population. The result was the infamous front-page headline "Dewey Defeats Truman" running the day after the election, when, in fact, Harry Truman won the presidential election against New York Governor Thomas Dewey.[9]

EXAMPLE MARKETING RESEARCH

An example of misinterpretation of research is the 2000 Presidential election between George W. Bush and Al Gore. The results were announced, changed, changed again, and then thrust into confusion for many weeks. The election of George W. Bush was only made final after the Supreme Court case *Bush v. Gore* was decided in Bush's favor. Television network projections were incorrect for a variety of reasons, including bad information obtained from exit polling, sample results, and unofficial election returns from election sites throughout Florida. The rush to be the first network to announce election results and a lack of understanding of the methodology of how certain data were obtained caused much of the confusion.

PHOTO: Sergieiev/Shutterstock.

>> END EXAMPLE

The Internet has provided additional means to collect marketing research. The traditional methods of telephone, door-to-door, and mail have, although still used, essentially given way to

Internet-based marketing research. Given the speed to administer, ability to tailor questioning based on prior responses, opportunity to show pictures, cost-effectiveness for midsized to large surveys, and speed of responses, the Internet is transforming marketing research. One of the major concerns regarding Internet marketing research is the ability to translate results obtained from the Internet to the general population. Some argue that people on the Internet are different from the rest of the population because lower-income individuals have limited access to the Internet. A historical perspective on the current Internet research applications debate extends from the in-person versus telephone debate of the 1960s and 1970s. When phone penetration exceeded 90%, the argument became moot. Clearly, the Internet is moving in that direction. In 2009, Internet penetration in the United States was about 76%, compared to a global average of 27%, European average of 53%, African average of 9%, and Asian average of 20%. Companies that operate worldwide should understand that the Internet does not offer similar research opportunities in all countries.

When an organization has questions, marketing research may be appropriate. A formal process should be followed to determine if marketing research is warranted and, if warranted, then how best to structure and conduct the marketing research. There are five major steps in the marketing research process:

- Define the problem.
- Design the research.
- Conduct the research.
- Analyze the research.
- Address the problem in a research report.

These steps are each necessary and generally linear in nature, but there should be considerable feedback to ensure that no assumptions have changed during the research process.

Define the Problem

The first step in the marketing research process is the most important. It is the step when the specific problem is determined. At that time, the decision is made whether marketing research is necessary and viable as well as how to set limits on what will be studied. The **research question**, the question the research is designed to answer, is also defined in this step. Properly addressing this step provides necessary clarity for subsequent steps in the marketing research process.

Developing the problem statement involves considering the known facts as they relate to what is occurring and why. For example, a common trigger for a marketing research request is a significant decrease in sales of a product. Although the symptom of reduced sales is observed, there also may be other symptoms. The challenge lies in isolating symptoms from causes. The causes could vary, including a competitor's actions, a decrease in the size or number of distributors, a reduction in productivity of the sales force, or a production or operations issue. If I believe the perception of my product has changed, then the research question should evolve from "I need to know why my sales are down" to questions like the following: "How do customers evaluate my product relative to my competitors?" "What are the perceived strengths or weaknesses of my product?"

In some cases, research is not appropriate. Examples of marketing research being neither necessary nor viable include the following:

- The net benefit from conducting the research is significantly less than the cost of conducting the research, for example, when a business considers spending $50,000 to study the impact of purchasing $5,000 in computer software.
- The business is either unwilling or unable to take advantage of any potential results from the research, for example, when a business decides to test consumer interest in two advertising campaigns, even though the business has already committed to one of the campaigns.
- The business does not have time to wait for research before a business decision must be made or does not have the time to implement changes suggested by the research. An example is when a business has 24 hours to react to a competitor's dramatic price change and the business begins a viability study that will take several weeks to complete.

Once the appropriateness of conducting marketing research is determined, the next task involves designing the research.

Design the Research

With a clear research question determined, it is important to identify any available information that may assist in answering all or part of the question. Such information might be previous research or research conducted by others, for example, the government and trade associations. There also may be information available to help further clarify the research question. This information may come from inside or outside the company. In some cases new data must be obtained to answer specific questions. There are two classifications of information sources to consider:

- Primary data
- Secondary data

Primary data are information collected to address a current research question. The information is obtained directly from or about the object(s) being studied in the specific context of the research question. This type of research is generally more expensive than obtaining information from prior research. The main benefit is that primary research is targeted at the specific research questions being studied and is not being interpreted from a source that may or may not address the situation presented in the current research question. Primary data can be obtained through a variety of marketing research activities, including surveys and observational techniques. The techniques to obtain primary data will be discussed later in the chapter.

Secondary data are information previously collected for another purpose. Secondary data is not of lesser importance than primary data. The use of existing information can be cost effective and save time. Secondary data should be the first place to look for answers to research questions before making a decision to obtain primary data. While secondary data can be quite valuable, it is important to consider the quality of the source of the data by determining who collected the data, why the data were collected, where the data were collected, how the data were collected, and when the data were collected.

Secondary data come from a wide range of sources, including company reports, previous marketing research studies, sales performance reports, the Internet, government publications, and libraries. In many cases so much data are available that techniques must be employed to search for patterns that may lead to insights. **Data mining**, discussed in Chapter 6, is the statistical analysis of large databases seeking to discover hidden pieces of information. This technique can be used with both primary and secondary data.

Private research companies can provide primary, secondary, or both types of information. The data that private research companies provide are often called syndicated research. **Syndicated research** is information collected on a regular basis using standardized procedures and sold to multiple customers from a related industry. Examples of syndicated research include Nielsen Retail Indexes, managed and sold by the A.C. Nielsen Company, with inventory and purchase data from supermarkets, mass merchandisers, and drug stores throughout the United States, and Simmons Media/Market Service, managed and sold by Simmons Market Research Bureau, Inc., with U.S. household information on television viewing behavior as well as purchase and use behavior of products in 500 categories.

In many cases, secondary data can provide "close enough" answers to business questions. Quite often, businesses have considered the same research questions repeatedly. Determining the level of precision required to address a specific research question will indicate if secondary research might be acceptable, if the secondary research exists and is of sufficient quality.

EXAMPLE **MARKETING RESEARCH, SYNDICATED RESEARCH**

J.D. Power and Associates offers a variety of syndicated studies, including the Initial Quality Study for its automotive clients. The Initial Quality Study (IQS) provides in-depth diagnostic information on new-vehicle quality after 90 days of ownership. Owners and lessees are surveyed regarding problems with their new vehicles. Automotive brands use this secondary data to make business decisions instead of creating their own independent studies. Automotive brands consider the cost savings of secondary research over primary research and the ability to compare research results across automotive brands.[10]

PHOTO: JohnKwan/Shutterstock.

>> END EXAMPLE

Research Design Categories

Based on the research question, a research design can be developed. A **research design** is a framework or plan for a study that guides the collection and analysis of the data.[11] There are three general categories of research designs:

- Exploratory
- Descriptive
- Explanatory

Exploratory research is a marketing research design used to generate ideas in a new area of inquiry. This design is most useful in dividing a broad research problem into smaller problems for subsequent research. An example of exploratory research could involve a series of personal interviews with select consumers to determine why they purchase a particular product or service.

Descriptive research is a marketing research design that is used to describe marketing variables by answering who, what, when, where, and how questions. Descriptive research is more structured than exploratory research. An example of descriptive research could involve a survey among specific consumers that explores where they purchase groceries and how often they go shopping.

Explanatory research is a marketing research design used to understand the relationship between independent and dependent variables. This type of research, also known as causal research, is typically used to further study relationships identified from descriptive or exploratory research. An example of explanatory research could involve an experiment where a direct marketing campaign is tested against sales performance to determine effectiveness.

Research Types

Depending on the research design selected, a research classification will be selected. There are two types of research:

- Qualitative
- Quantitative

Qualitative research is a collection of techniques designed to identify and interpret information obtained through the observation of people. Qualitative research is generally considered subjective. It can be used in concert with **quantitative research**, a process to collect a large number of responses using a standardized questionnaire where the results can be summarized into numbers for statistical analysis. The analysis results can be used either to provide perspective prior to quantitative research or to further explore results from quantitative research. There is a variety of qualitative research techniques, including the following:

- Focus groups
- Structured interviews
- Ethnographic research

Focus groups are collections of a small number of individuals who were recruited using specific criteria with the purpose to discuss predetermined topics with qualified moderators.

Structured interviews are a series of discussions held between a trained interviewer and individuals, on a one-on-one basis. The individuals are recruited using specific criteria with the purpose to discuss predetermined topics.

Ethnographic research is a type of observational research where trained researchers immerse themselves in a specific consumer environment. Researchers using ethnographic research techniques may visit someone in their home and watch how breakfast decisions are made, or they may ride along in someone's vehicle to observe how shopping locations are selected when running errands.

EXAMPLE MARKETING RESEARCH, ETHNOGRAPHIC RESEARCH

On-Site Research Associates has been involved with digital ethnography for over 20 years. The company pioneered the use of nonobtrusive ethnographic techniques that do not require a videographer to record consumer reality in a person's home or in a retail environment. The company uses a small "hand cam" so it can record what consumers actually do with a given product. In 2004, On-Site conducted a cross-country ethnographic learning journey (The Pulse Of America) to collect information on American attitudes and cultural insights. Since 2008, On-Site has sponsored a syndicated ethnographic study of a facet of U.S. culture called the cyber census. In 2010 On-Site studied the impact technology has on lifestyles and how lifestyles are impacted by difficult economic conditions. On-Site offers a variety of products, including a YouTube channel called Ethnovision.[12]

PHOTO: Courtesy of www.istockphoto.com.

>> END EXAMPLE

The appropriate research technique depends on the scope of the project, the capabilities of the moderator/interviewer, the project timeline, and funding. The output from qualitative research can provide deep insight into the motivations of individuals. However, that output cannot be projectable to a larger group of similar people or to the general population.

Quantitative research is essentially survey research. The results are intended to be statistically valid and projectable to a larger group of the general population. While qualitative research tends to be more exploratory, quantitative research is more descriptive and explanatory.

Once a research classification is selected, a data-collection method must be identified. Several examples of qualitative techniques were identified earlier. Focus groups are typically conducted in person, but they are increasingly being conducted online. Much has changed since American Dialogue conducted the first documented online focus group in 1993. Many of those changes are due to the advent of broadband and other high-speed Internet options, as well as greater acceptance from businesses.[13] Still, individual interviews and ethnographic research are primarily conducted in person.

There is a variety of data-collection options when conducting quantitative research. These options include the following:

- Telephone
- In person
- Mail
- Online

Telephone interviewing can provide quick feedback, and the ability exists to react to specific responses. However, response rates are decreasing and there can be variability in how different interviewers ask questions and interpret responses. In-person interviewing can also provide quick feedback and flexibility to follow up on responses, but it can suffer from variability in interviewer questioning and it is very expensive. Mail questionnaires can be relatively cost effective and are not subjected to interviewer variability, but questionnaires have no flexibility for follow-up questions and can take a considerable amount of time to complete. Online questionnaires offer the lowest relative cost of all options and provide rapid responses. At the same time, online questionnaires control interviewer variation and allow some flexibility to follow up, based on some predetermined responses. Online questionnaires do not have the flexibility of in-person and telephone methods to deal with any respondent comprehension issues. Online questionnaires require valid e-mail addresses or access to a well-managed Internet panel. Response rates are considered lower for Internet research, unless an Internet panel is utilized, than other data collection options.[14]

Online research is one of the most popular forms of marketing research because an increasing number of consumers are online and an increasing amount of marketing and advertising investment is being made in the online environment. The four primary motivations for Web use by consumers are as follows:[15]

- Researching
- Shopping
- Socializing
- Surfing

Each of these motivations provides businesses with opportunities to connect with their customers. Marketing research can access consumers in any of these environments.

While a wide range of research can be conducted on the Internet, for example, online focus groups or tracking Web site visits, the decision on whether to conduct survey research on the Internet requires that several critical questions be answered. These questions include the following:[16]

- Can the survey be self-administered?
- Can the information about the product or service be effectively communicated on a computer monitor?
- Can the target respondent be reached through e-mail?
- Can members of the online population reflect the desired target market?

An Internet research panel can directly address the final two questions. An **Internet research panel** is a collection of individuals who agree, for some predetermined incentive, to participate in questionnaires on a variety of topics as determined by the owner and manager of the panel. These panels are typically owned and managed by marketing research companies and are used to provide services to their clients. A number of Internet research panels have been established for a single client of a marketing research company. These panels are known as online communities.

EXAMPLE MARKETING RESEARCH, INTERNET RESEARCH PANEL

e-Rewards, Inc., operates an invitation-only online marketing research panel with over 2,000 clients and 3.6 million panelists. e-Rewards offers panelists the opportunity to complete surveys, after matching individual profiles with specific business sponsor requirements, for e-Rewards currency that can be redeemed for gift cards. Joining e-Rewards is free, but consumers must join through one of e-Rewards' sponsors, such as the Delta SkyMiles frequent flyer program.[17]

PHOTO: Karen Roach/Shutterstock.

>> END EXAMPLE

It is important to understand that research collected from an Internet research panel is not typically representative of any given population because probability sampling is not used to recruit members. Internet research panels are often used to recruit specific types of people, such as adventurous individuals or owners of boats. Members often are invited from a variety of sources, including media placements or other Web sites. It is possible that special sampling, weighting, and other statistical techniques can be used to create representative data for certain populations. Panel maintenance is a critical issue to retain viability of the panel. Aspects of panel management include the following:

- Panelist relationship management (keeping panelists engaged in the panel)
- Incentive program development and administration
- Maintaining historical record of panelist activity
- Monitoring completion rates and response times of surveys
- Cleaning and refreshing the panel
- Periodic reprofiling
- Regular reporting on composition and response rates
- Compliance with laws and regulations

Many large businesses have transitioned much of their marketing research to the Internet. Brand-tracking studies, advertising copy tests, and customer satisfaction studies are all being conducted in an online environment. Some marketing research studies have transitioned easily, but others have had to be adjusted for the online environment. Some new marketing research techniques have evolved solely in an online environment. Virtual shopping environments can be created and used to simulate the actual choices that a consumer has in a store. The results can influence product development and positioning issues.

Much of the current work in moving marketing research from one data-collection method to another is from telephone to Internet. There are many differences between these two methods. It is often considered that online research limits the ability of a respondent to express emotion. However, the anonymity provided by an online environment does provide the opportunity for realistic opinions.[18] The Internet also uses a wider range of response types and can be considered less invasive and more satisfying for the respondent than other methods.[19]

Question structure can contribute significantly to accessing the benefits of Internet research. Core elements of a brand and advertising tracking study include questions relating to the consumer purchase funnel, brand imagery, and advertising recall and classification demographics and psychographics. Table 8.1 provides examples of the different wordings of questions for each topic.

Measurement

Measurement is the process of quantifying how much one variable's set of features or characteristics are possessed in another variable. A measurement plan involves two primary elements, including determining those features or characteristics, referred to as properties, that best represent the concept being studied from the research question. The second element of the plan is determining the appropriate scale to use to measure questions about the concept. The two aspects are closely linked by statistical requirements.

The first requirement is to determine what is to be measured. Will it be tangible (direct) or intangible (subjective)? The former allows for a direct rating, such as a demographic question of household income or age of respondent. The latter involves a respondent using a rating scale to choose which point on the scale best reflects the way they feel. This could involve a question such as the following: Which of the following statements best reflects the way that you feel about your vehicle's quality with respect to all vehicles? The possible responses would be as follows: Better than average. Average. Below Average.

The second requirement involves selecting the type of scale to use. There are four types of scales:

- Nominal
- Ordinal
- Interval
- Ratio

A **nominal scale** is a measurement in which numbers are assigned to characteristics of objects or groups of objects solely for identifying the objects.[20] The nominal scale is often used for classification and, therefore, is limited for analysis that can be conducted with the data. An **ordinal scale** is a measurement in which numbers are assigned to characteristics of objects or groups of objects to reflect the order of the objects,[21] such as the results of a 100-yard running race (John Smith came in first, Jack Johnson came in second, Jerry Jackson came in third). An ordinal scale allows rankings (first, second, third), but it does not allow us to know the specific differences between rankings; for example, John Smith finished in 10.5 seconds, Jack Johnson finished in 10.8 seconds, and Jerry Jackson finished in 11.1 seconds.

Table 8.1 Survey Question Format: Phone Versus Internet

Question Topic	Phone Question	Internet Question
Unaided brand awareness	Now, thinking of different makes and models of motorcycles, which make and model comes to mind first? Which comes to mind next? Which others?	Thinking of different makes and models of motorcycles, which makes and models come to mind? Please type in both the make AND the model for each motorcycle you can think of.
Familiarity	Now, I'd like to know how familiar you are with these various motorcycles. For each make and model I mention, can you tell me if you . . . ?	Which of these statements most applies to how familiar you are with the following?
Overall rating	Overall, how would you rate the . . . ?	Overall, how would you rate the . . . ?
Purchase consideration	Now, I'd like to know how likely you are to buy or lease these various motorcycles. For each make and model I mention, can you tell me if . . . ?	Thinking about the next time you purchase or lease a new motorcycle, how likely are you to purchase or lease the following?
Brand image	Based on anything that you've seen or heard or any impressions you may have . . . Which of these makes and models, if any . . . ?	We'd like you to indicate which motorcycle (companies/makes/models) is best described by the following statements. You can choose as many or as few as you wish, or none at all. Which is best described by these statements?
Advertising recall	Have you seen a commercial that (detailed description of commercial)?	We are now going to show you some pictures from a TV commercial. Have you seen this TV commercial before? Please wait for the images to completely load before answering the question.
Income	Is your total annual income before taxes over or under $50,000?	Please choose the category that roughly includes your total annual household income before taxes.
Age	For statistical purposes only, may I have your age please? That is, are you . . . ?	Which of the following groups include your age?
Ethnicity	Are you (read list of ethnicities)?	To ensure that we have a fair representation of diverse ethnic backgrounds, are you . . . ? Please select all that apply. If other, please specify your ethnic heritage.
Gender	What is your gender?	Are you? (male/female)
Psychographics	I am going to read you a list of statements that people have made about motorcycles and about what they are looking for when they are buying or leasing their vehicle. Please tell me if you agree strongly, agree somewhat, neither agree nor disagree, disagree somewhat, or disagree strongly that the statement describes you. The first statement is . . .	The following statements describe the way different people approach selecting the motorcycles they are going to buy. Please choose the one statement that best describes you.

An **interval scale** is a measurement in which the numbers assigned to the characteristics of the objects or groups of objects legitimately allow comparison of the size of the differences among and between objects.[22] An interval scale allows us to compare John Smith's time against Jack Johnson's time and Jerry Jackson's time. Interval scales are often used to rate satisfaction levels with some aspect of a product or service. A **ratio scale** is a measurement in which the numbers assigned to the characteristics of the objects have an identifiable absolute zero.[23] An example would be the number of days spent traveling in one calendar year. There is an absolute zero, so a person could travel one-third as much or twice as much as someone else could.

Questionnaire Development

A **questionnaire** is an organized set of questions that a researcher desires respondents to answer. Questionnaires perform a range of functions, including the following:

- Keeping respondents motivated to complete the survey
- Translating research objectives into research questions
- Providing a consistent question format for each respondent
- Facilitating ease of data analysis

The development of a questionnaire requires a decision on the answer choices presented to consumers. A **closed-ended**

question has specific survey answer choices available to respondents. The numbering of the answer choices for each question is known as **coding**. For example, "How many four-credit university courses do you anticipate registering for next term?" The choices are the following: A–0, B–1 to 2, C–3 to 4, and D–5 or more. An **open-ended question** allows for unrestricted survey responses. For example, "If you were the governor of your state, what would be your top policy priority?" Regardless of the choice of closed-ended, open-ended, or a combination of question types, the questions must be carefully worded, concise, and clear, so that respondents understand the precise meaning of each question being asked and responses are not biased by leading questions.

After determining the individual question structure, the overall design of the questionnaire must be considered. The primary elements of a questionnaire include the following:

- **Introduction**—An overview that introduces the general context of the survey.
- **Screening**—If any restrictions exist on the desired respondents for the survey, the restrictions are applied through screening questions.
- **Warm-up**—Opening questions that determine general knowledge of the topic of the questionnaire.
- **Body**—Main collection of survey questions.
- **Classification questions**—Questions that group respondents into various categories, such as age, income, gender, or level of education.

Sample Plan

The next design decision involves creating a sample plan. It is seldom either financially viable or physically possible (nor is it statistically necessary) to survey everyone within a specific consumer segment. A sample, if correctly identified, can represent the opinion of a broader population. A **sample** is a specific part of the population that is selected to represent the population. A **population** is the total group of individuals who meet the criteria being studied. A **census** is a survey that collects responses for each member of the population.

The **sample plan** identifies who will be sampled, how many people will be sampled, and the procedure that will be used for sampling. For example, if a company is interested in determining purchase consideration for its products relative to competitors, the company could ask a specific demographic target toward which its product is positioned, or the company could ask only those within that target who are aware of the brand and competitive brands in the category. The company then can select between a census and a sample. The actual number of the people in the target depends not only on the overall group being studied, but also on any subgroups within the overall group, such as gender or particular age cohorts. The calculation for the sample size is beyond the scope of this book. Ultimately, the sample plan should manage the risks of bias entering the marketing research project. **Sample error** refers to any differences between the sample results and the actual results that would emerge from a census of the population.

The **sampling procedure** involves selecting either a probability sample or a nonprobability sample as part of your sample plan. A **probability sample** is a procedure whereby each member of a population has a known and nonzero chance of possibly being selected to a sample. There are several probability sampling procedures, including simple random sampling, where each person has an equal chance of being selected; systematic sampling, where a skip interval is used from a list of the population to select the sample; and stratified sampling where the population is subdivided into specific groups and random samples are selected from those groups.

A **nonprobability sample** is a procedure whereby each member of a population does not have an equal chance, or, in some cases, any chance, of being selected to a sample. Results from nonprobability samples can describe only the characteristics of the sample and not the population. There are several nonprobability procedures, including a convenience sample, where samples are created out of convenience; a purposive sample, where judgment is used to create the sample based on a perception that the respondents meet the necessary requirements; a snowball sample, where respondents help identify subsequent respondents for the sample; and a quota sample, where predetermined categories are used to identify respondents based on that predetermined criteria.

Conduct the Research

Implementing the research design begins with data collection. Assuming that the survey instrument has been appropriately designed, the next concern is how to obtain viable data for analysis. If the collection is through the mail, then the area to watch is when data are transferred from the mail to a computer file. If collection is directly online, then the area to watch is the program that aggregates and analyzes the data, as well as the process to move the data from one program to another, if relevant.

When interviewers are involved, through either a telephone interview or an in-person interview, there are other concerns. The interviewer may not consistently execute the survey (either intentionally or unintentionally), the interviewer may record the responses incorrectly, the researcher may not understand the responses, or the researcher may improperly clarify or incorrectly clarify a question. **Nonsampling error** is any bias that emerges in the study for any reason other than sampling error. Nonsampling error includes not only interviewer error, but also respondent errors such as confusion, fatigue, or deceit.

The overarching concerns with the quality of the marketing research involve the levels of validity and reliability of the results. **Validity** is the strength of the conclusion. Were the results correct? **Reliability** is the level of consistency of the measurement. Is the marketing research repeatable with the same conditions? A variety of techniques are available to measure these factors, depending on how the scales were developed.

Analyze the Research

Analyzing the data involves creating a data file with the results and eliminating data-entry errors through cleaning and executing the warranted appropriate statistical analysis, given the scale of the data and the nature of the research question. With ratio data, there is the greatest flexibility to use a wide range of statistical techniques. The broad range of statistical techniques includes descriptive statistics used to describe findings and relationships, inferential statistics used to generalize sample results to a larger population, and other techniques that consider relationships between variables, differences between groups, and advanced modeling.

Address the Problem in a Research Report

Once the entire research process has been completed, it is essential to do more than simply document the results. Findings must be evaluated and conclusions developed. Most important, it is essential to attempt to answer the original research question. Think about who is receiving this information and understand that they may not have a marketing research background. Be sure to consider the findings of the research from various perspectives and ultimately try to synthesize the most viable recommendations from the findings and conclusions.

MARKETING INFORMATION SYSTEM (pp. 107–108)

DEFINED *A* **marketing information system (MIS)** *is a series of steps that include collection, analysis, and presentation of information for use in making marketing decisions.*[24]

EXPLAINED

Marketing Information System

A marketing information system functions much like a management information system except in support of the marketing activity. A management information system is a set of procedures and methods for the regular, planned collection, analysis, and presentation of information for use in making management decisions.[25] A marketing information system is intended to bring together various streams of marketing data within an organization. But a marketing information system is more than a repository of data. It is an ongoing collaboration of "people, equipment, and procedures."[26] The level of complexity can vary greatly from a manual system to a series of mainframe computers.

There are four primary elements of the marketing information system:

- Internal company data
- Marketing intelligence systems
- Marketing decision support systems
- Marketing research systems

Internal company data include everything from order status, stock levels, and production schedules to financial performance, human resource status, direct-mail redemption details, and Web site click-through details. These seemingly separate pieces of data can be combined to influence a wide range of marketing decisions, including product pricing, advertising copywriting, distribution partner selection, and packaging changes.

A **marketing intelligence system** is a system that gathers, processes, assesses, and makes available marketing information in a format that allows the marketing activity to function more effectively.[27] The information from a marketing intelligence system can also assist strategic planning and policy development. The procedures of a marketing intelligence system identify critical areas to be monitored, including market activity and trends, consumers, customers, and competitors. **Competitive intelligence** involves the systematic tracking of competitive actions and plans and is a significant activity within a business. Good competitive intelligence can help fend off a competitive attack or blunt a competitor's launch of a new product.

A **marketing decision support system (MDSS)** is the software and associated infrastructure that connect the marketing activity to company databases. This system is an important component of a marketing information system because it contains the analytical tools to provide critical data to marketing decision makers. An MDSS often contains modeling capability to create different marketing and financial models.

A **marketing research system** is a collection of the results of marketing research studies conducted by a company. The contents of this system are much more specific than those of the marketing intelligence system. The breadth of possible marketing research was discussed earlier in this chapter.

APPLIED

Marketing Information System

In practice, a marketing information system is often referred to as a customer relationship management (CRM) system. CRM comprises the activities that are used to establish, develop, and maintain customer relationships. There are many similarities because CRM is designed to create more valuable customer contact using databases. The two work together, but a marketing information system is more holistic; it includes more marketing inputs than CRM. Also, the sheer number of inputs into a marketing information system is growing. In addition to the many traditional sources of information feeding a marketing information system, the rapid proliferation of discussion forums, blogs, and other types of social media is forcing marketing information systems to evolve to keep up.

The sophistication of the marketing information system provides a marketing activity with everything needed to manage the portfolio, from scanner data from an individual store, to brand-switching data at a regional level, to cookies from online stores. Scanner data collected at the many retail checkout counters across the country can provide instant feedback on sales promotions and purchasing trends. Each person who uses a pharmacy or supermarket loyalty card provides inputs into a marketing information system when that card is swiped through a retail scanner. Scanner purchase data can be analyzed at the store level and at the state, regional, and national levels. **Cookies** are small files containing certain personal information and are sent from Web servers to a consumer's computer to be accessed the next time a consumer visits a particular Web site. Cookies are used to facilitate the completion of forms on Web sites, and they are also used to store online shopping cart information. Increases in online marketing and e-commerce practices have expanded the use of cookies and their importance as inputs to marketing information systems.

EXAMPLE MARKETING INFORMATION SYSTEM

Costco Wholesale, the largest wholesale club operator in the United States, uses a scanner-based point-of-sale tracking system developed by Information Resources, Inc. The Costco Collaborative Retail Exchange program provides information on sales performance, inventory control, and promotion performance.

PHOTO: Marcin Balcerzak/Shutterstock.

>> END EXAMPLE

Visual Summary

Chapter 8 Summary

The process of generating and utilizing consumer insight builds on the previous chapter's discussion of how consumers make decisions and behave in the global marketplace. Without a strong commitment to practicing a consumer-insight philosophy, businesses cannot effectively understand how they are perceived in the marketplace. Useful consumer insight builds on an active marketing research practice that identifies and defines marketing opportunities and problems; generates, refines, and evaluates marketing actions; monitors marketing performance; and improves understanding of the process of marketing. The marketing research is then included with marketing intelligence, internal reporting data, and the marketing decision support system to support a marketing information system. Ultimately, timely and detailed consumer insight is useful not only to the marketing function, but also to the business itself.

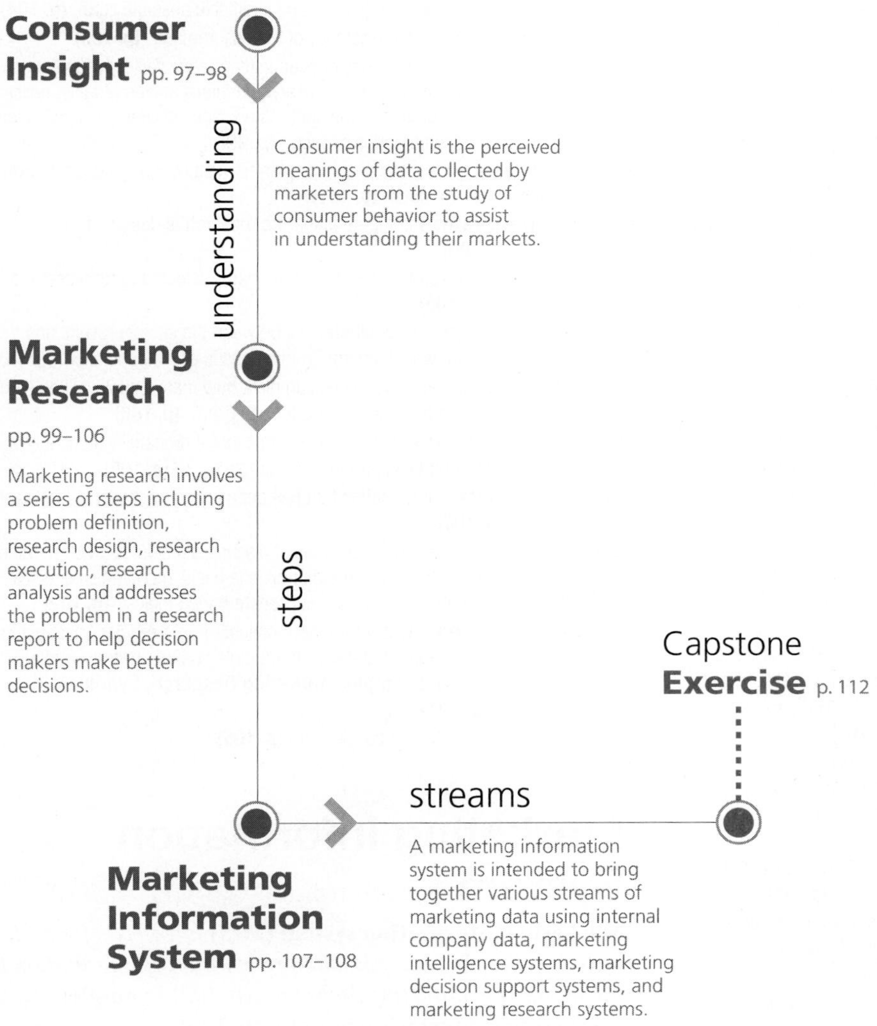

Consumer Insight pp. 97–98
understanding
Consumer insight is the perceived meanings of data collected by marketers from the study of consumer behavior to assist in understanding their markets.
Marketing Research
pp. 99–106
Marketing research involves a series of steps including problem definition, research design, research execution, research analysis and addresses the problem in a research report to help decision makers make better decisions.
steps
Capstone Exercise p. 112
streams
Marketing Information System pp. 107–108
A marketing information system is intended to bring together various streams of marketing data using internal company data, marketing intelligence systems, marketing decision support systems, and marketing research systems.

Chapter Key Terms

Consumer Insight (pp. 97–98)

Consumer insight *is perceived meanings of data collected from the study of consumer behavior. (p. 97)* **Opening Example (p. 97)**

Key Terms (p. 97)

Consumer market insight is an in-depth understanding of customer behavior that is more qualitative than quantitative. **(p. 97)**

Insight is the act or result of apprehending the inner nature of things, or of seeing intuitively. **(p. 97)**

Marketing Research (pp. 99–106)

Marketing research *is the acquisition and analysis of information used to identify and define marketing opportunities that connect consumers to marketers. (p. 99)* **Example: Marketing Research (p. 99)**

Key Terms (pp. 99–105)

Applied research attempts to answer questions related to practical problems. **(p. 99)**

Census is a survey that collects responses for each member of the population. **(p. 105)**

Closed-ended question is a question that has specific survey answer choices available to respondents. **(p. 104)**

Coding is the numbering of the answer choices for each survey question. **(p. 105)**

Data mining is the statistical analysis of large databases seeking to discover hidden pieces of information. This technique can be used with both primary and secondary data. **(p. 101)**

Descriptive research is a marketing research design that is used to describe marketing variables by answering who, what, when, where, and how questions. **(p. 101)**

Ethnographic research is a type of observational research where trained researchers immerse themselves in a specific consumer environment. **(p. 102) Example: Marketing Research, Ethnographic Research (p. 102)**

Explanatory research is a marketing research design used to understand the relationship between independent and dependent variables. **(p. 101)**

Exploratory research is a marketing research design used to generate ideas in a new area of inquiry. **(p. 101)**

Focus groups are collections of a small number of individuals recruited by specific criteria with the purpose to discuss predetermined topics with qualified moderators. **(p. 101)**

Internet research panel is a collection of individuals who agree, for some predetermined incentive, to participate in questionnaires on a variety of topics as determined by the owner and manager of the panel. **(p. 102) Example: Marketing Research, Internet Research Panel (p. 103)**

Interval scale is a measurement in which the numbers assigned to the characteristics of the objects or groups of objects legitimately allow a comparison of the size of the differences among and between objects. **(p. 104)**

Measurement is the process of quantifying how much of a variable's set of features or characteristics is possessed in another variable. **(p. 103)**

Nominal scale is a measurement in which numbers are assigned to characteristics of objects or groups of objects solely for identifying the objects. **(p. 103)**

Nonprobability sample is a procedure where each member of a population does not have an equal chance, or, in some cases, any chance, of being selected to a sample. **(p. 105)**

Nonsampling error is any bias that emerges in the study for any reason other than sampling error. **(p. 105)**

Open-ended question is a question that allows for unrestricted survey responses. **(p. 105)**

Ordinal scale is a measurement in which numbers are assigned to characteristics of objects or groups of objects to reflect the order of the objects. **(p. 103)**

Population is the total group of individuals who meet the criteria that is being studied. **(p. 105)**

Primary data is information that is collected to address a current research question. **(p. 100)**

Probability sample is a procedure where each member of a population has a known and nonzero chance of possibly being selected to a sample. **(p. 105)**

Pure research attempts to expand understanding of the unknown. **(p. 99)**

Qualitative research is a collection of techniques designed to identify and interpret information obtained through the observation of people. **(p. 101)**

Quantitative research is a process to collect a large number of responses using a standardized questionnaire where the results can be summarized into numbers for statistical analysis. **(p. 101)**

Questionnaire is an organized set of questions that a researcher desires that respondents answer. **(p. 104)**

Ratio scale is a measurement in which the numbers assigned to the characteristics of the objects have an identifiable absolute zero. **(p. 104)**

Reliability is the level of consistency of a measurement. **(p. 105)**

Research is the studious inquiry or examination; *especially* investigation or experimentation aimed at the discovery and interpretation of facts, revision of accepted theories or laws in the light of new facts, or practical application of such new or revised theories or laws. **(p. 99)**

Research design is a framework or plan for a study that guides the collection and analysis of the data. **(p. 101)**

Research question is the question the research is designed to answer. **(p. 100)**

Sample is a specific part of the population that is selected to represent the population. **(p. 105)**

Sample error refers to any differences between the sample results and the actual results that would emerge from a census of the population. **(p. 105)**

Sample plan identifies who will be sampled, how many people will be sampled, and the procedure that will be used for sampling. **(p. 105)**

Sampling procedure involves selecting either a probability sample or a nonprobability sample as part of your sample plan. **(p. 105)**

Secondary data is information that has been previously collected for another purpose. **(p. 100)**

Structured interviews are a series of discussions held between a trained interviewer and individuals, on a one-on-one basis, recruited by specific criteria, with the purpose to discuss predetermined topics. **(p. 102)**

Syndicated research is information collected on a regular basis using standardized procedures and sold to multiple customers from a related industry. **(p. 101) Example: Marketing Research, Syndicated Research (p. 101)**

Validity is the strength of a conclusion. **(p. 105)**

Marketing Information System (pp. 107–108)

Marketing information system (MIS) *is a series of steps that include collection, analysis, and presentation of information for use in making marketing decisions. (p. 107)* **Example: Marketing Information System (p. 108)**

Key Terms (p. 107)

Competitive intelligence involves the systematic tracking of competitive actions and plans and is a significant activity within a business. **(p. 107)**

Cookies are small files containing certain personal information that are sent from Web servers to a consumer's computer to be accessed the next time a consumer visits a particular Web site. **(p. 107)**

Marketing decision support system (MDSS) is the software and associated infrastructure that connects the marketing activity to company databases. **(p. 107)**

Marketing intelligence system is a system that gathers, processes, assesses, and makes available marketing information in a format that allows the marketing activity to function more effectively. **(p. 107)**

Marketing research system is a collection of the results of marketing research studies conducted by a company. **(p. 107)**

Capstone Exercise

One of the best ways to illustrate the value of good market research and the importance of applying the results of market research to your marketing strategy is to look at a corporate failure!

Pepsi and Coke have struggled for many years in what is called the Cola Wars. The Cola Wars are, for the most part, a reflection of how individuals chose to express themselves by the soft drink they like. Coca-Cola from its early beginnings and more recently Pepsi-Cola have used brands on a variety of lifestyle items (clothing, glassware, retro-signs, etc.) to help individuals promote their own preference through items used in their everyday life. Coca-Cola spent many years with this technique and millions of dollars building a brand image and a loyal customer base on a global basis.

In an effort to stop its eroding market share, Pepsi introduced the *Pepsi Challenge* in the mid-1980s. The resulting "research" from these simple taste tests showed that people really did prefer the taste of Pepsi to Coke. And, Coke knew it. Although there was no substantive research done by Coca-Cola and no significant change in its market share, in response to the Pepsi Challenge Coke changed the taste of Coke and re-branded it as New Coke. New Coke tasted a lot more like Pepsi than Coke and actually beat both Coke and Pepsi in blind taste tests.

Coca-Cola also conducted extensive qualitative and quantitative research on New Coke. The qualitative questions included determining how consumers felt about New Coke and why. Quantitative research was strictly by the numbers: How many people preferred the taste of New Coke? The numbers looked good. The quantitative analysis indicated that New Coke would be the "trendiest soft drink ever." The qualitative research was less definitive although it did indicate that some people were deeply unhappy with the change.

Coke executives ignored the qualitative research, focused on the quantitative research, and forged ahead with the plan to win the Cola Wars with New Coke. In 1990, Coca-Cola abandoned Coke for New Coke. There was a massive public backlash from loyal Coke folks and, within a few months of being dropped from the product line, Coke was back into the soft drink market as Coca-Cola Classic. New Coke or Coke II remained available in limited markets for several years but only managed to attract, at best, a 3% market share. It wasn't until 2009 that Coca-Cola finally conceded defeat and dropped the "classic" from Coke's name.

1. What information would have been important *before* introducing New Coke?
2. Does it appear that Coca-Cola was more interested in attracting new customers or keeping existing customers? Explain.
3. Do you think Coca-Cola adequately researched the potential risks of the change? Explain.
4. What variables did Coca-Cola neglect to take into consideration?
5. For marketers, what do you think is the most important function of market research?

Application Exercise

Use the marketing concepts in this chapter to tackle and solve a marketing problem: consumer insight, qualitative research, quantitative research, and secondary data.

First, start by thinking about the consumer electronic category. In general terms, consumer electronics include electronic equipment intended for everyday use. Consumer electronics are most often used in entertainment, communications, and office productivity. Some products classed as consumer electronics include personal computers, telephones, MP3 players, audio equipment, televisions, calculators, and GPS automotive navigation systems. There are many products available in stores within this category for us to consider purchasing.

The Marketing Problem

Choose a product in the consumer electronics category, and then choose a brand in that category after considering the following situation.

> You feel people your age are being underserved by manufacturers in the category and would like to obtain consumer insight to determine what has the greatest effect on your age group's propensity to purchase this product.

The most commonly used methods of primary research are surveys, interviews, and focus-group sessions.

The exercise is to design and run a small online survey. Your task is to design a 10-question online survey on consumer electronics. However, before you design the survey, remember to decide what information you are trying to gather. You need to get at least 10 responses and be able to write a short summary of your conclusions.

To make this task easier, here are a few Web sites that allow you to do online surveys. Each has a free option that allows you to do limited surveys.

- www.zoomerang.com
- www.surveymonkey.com
- www.questionpro.com

These are just suggestions; there are other sites that offer similar services.

To help you understand how to design your survey, refer to the following Web site:

- www.questionpro.com/survey-design.html

The Problem

In addition to the survey, describe how you would approach both qualitative and quantitative research. How could you utilize secondary data?

The Solution

Complete the following two Problem/Solution briefs using your product in the consumer electronics category, chapter concepts, and college resources.

1. From the Marketing Manager's Point of View
   a. Problem Definition
   b. Research Analysis
   c. Solution
2. From the Consumer's Point of View
   a. Problem Definition
   b. Category Insights Analysis
   c. Solution

Resources:

Marketing Defined, Explained, Applied 2e, Michael Levens
The College Library
Retail or Online Field Trip
Assigned Reading—*Brand Week*, *Advertising Age*, *WSJ*, scholarly publications, category trade journals
Blog your problem from either point of view, gather responses/posts (www.blogger.com/start)

The Brand

Chapter Overview In the previous chapters, you explored how companies create value, how consumers make decisions, and how consumer insights are generated. This chapter introduces the primary link between consumers and companies: the brand. The central concepts of branding will be discussed, including brand equity, building strong brands, and managing brands.

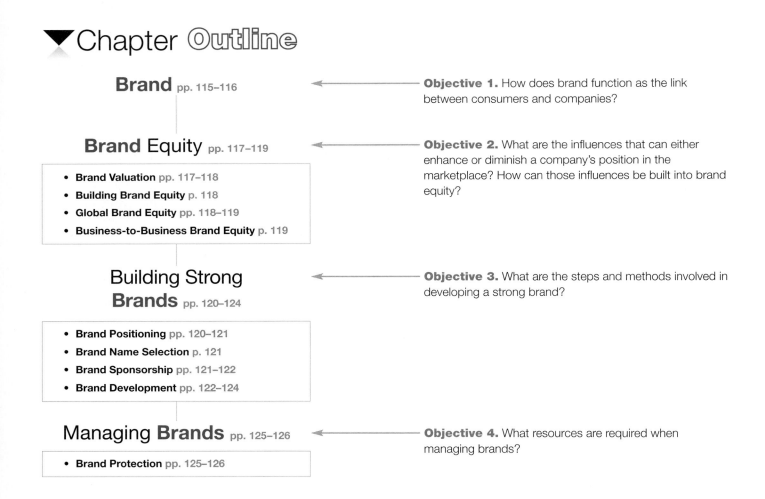

Chapter Outline

BRAND (pp. 115–116)

DEFINED *A* ***brand*** *is a promise to deliver specific benefits associated with products or services to consumers.*

EXPLAINED

Brand

Based on the Nordic word *brandr*, meaning to burn, brands began as a mark of possession that was applied to cattle.[1] Over time, brands have evolved not only to represent ownership, but also to stand for specific attributes that mean something to consumers. When the attributes that a brand possesses form a connection with consumers' desires, a perception of value is created.

A brand is more than simply a name; it is a promise. This promise manifests itself in everything that consumers can sense about a brand. If the promise is continually kept, the brand's image is solidified by its reputation. A brand can be represented by a name or symbol and can be perceived positively, negatively, or ambiguously by consumers. This perception is influenced by both marketing communications and experiences with the brand.

APPLIED

Brand

A brand differs considerably from a product or service as it exists in a consumer's mind. Consider the following:

- A product is something produced in a factory, while a brand is created through marketing communications and experience.
- A product can be duplicated by a competitor, while a brand is unique.
- A product can become outdated, while a successful brand is often timeless.
- A product is a generic term, while a brand has personality, characteristics, and associations.

The personality, characteristics, and associations of a brand can be thought of as layers. These layers provide richness to a brand that creates an emotional connection that is not typically generated from a product. The initial layer represents tangible features, while inner layers represent benefits, attitudes, and values. This richness can translate into many opportunities for brands, including the following:[2]

- Ability to command price premium
- Long-term financial strength
- Greater market share
- Higher perceived quality
- Greater supply and distribution chain advantage
- More brand extension opportunities to take an existing brand into a new category
- Greater purchase frequency

As consumers spend an increasing time online, the various mediums used to access online content are being targeted by brands. A **digital brand strategy** is a set of marketing activities that uses digital mediums to connect consumers to brands. A digital brand strategy is more than a Web site. Brand messages can be placed on many different digital devices including personal digital assistants (PDAs), mobile phones, and video games.

Brands are also being developed in a multicultural environment. Multicultural brands are brands that are created and managed to be relevant to more than one cultural group. For example, Yankelovich's 2007/2008 MONITOR Multicultural Marketing Study identified that Hispanic and African American consumers were likely to "enjoy looking at or listening to" advertising at a rate almost double of their peers of other races.[3] The study also revealed that marketing was generally perceived as neither culturally nor personally relevant.[4] The challenge for brands is to establish relevancy without over-commercializing culture.

Coca-Cola is sold in more than 200 countries. Produced by the Coca-Cola Company, its traditional soft drink product is often referred to simply as Coke. Originally intended as a patent medicine when Dr. John Pemberton created the product in the nineteenth century, Coca-Cola was eventually purchased by businessman Asa Candler, whose marketing efforts led Coke to its leadership in the world soft drink market throughout the twentieth and now twenty-first centuries. Coke is so well known that it can be recognized by a letter or two of typeface or simply the color of the container itself. The Coke name may also convey certain meaning to you that increases value of, and interest in, the Coke product.

PHOTO: RLN/Shutterstock.

EXAMPLE BRAND

Kodak invented the digital camera in 1975. After challenging times in the mid-2000s, Kodak has looked to digital media to help resurrect the company. The famous "Kodak moment" is now shared with others through social media. Kodak sees value both in the product as well as the digital services that can be activated. Kodak created a Web site, kodakmoments.com, where images can be submitted to a contest. Kodak also built functionality into its products to access social media, including share buttons and tagging capability for Flickr, YouTube, Facebook, and e-mail. Kodak has built its brand around its photographic heritage but has made the brand more relevant to consumers through the use of a digital brand strategy.

PHOTO: Photocreo Michal Bednarek/Shutterstock.

>> END EXAMPLE

BRAND Equity (pp. 117–119)

DEFINED **Brand equity** *is the power of a brand, through creation of a distinct image, to influence customer behavior.*[5]

EXPLAINED

Brand Equity

While brands are different from products and services, they definitely influence the perceived value of a company's products or services. This influence, or equity, can either enhance or diminish a company's position in the marketplace. Brand equity reflects the value consumers attach to the promise of the brand and evolves from the layers of the brand. Brand equity extends beyond products and services to include social movements, political parties, not-for-profit organizations, and individuals such as political candidates and other celebrities.

Branding expert Kevin Keller defines brand equity as "the differential effect of brand knowledge on consumer response to the brand's marketing activities. **Brand knowledge** is the set of associations that consumers hold in memory regarding the brand's features, benefits, users, perceived quality, and overall attitude as a result of prior brand marketing activities."[6] Effective marketing programs should apply Keller's brand equity definition to link desired images, perceptions, opinions, and feelings to their respective brands.[7]

APPLIED

Brand Equity

Brand equity can provide a sustainable competitive advantage that can be capitalized on in both good and bad times.[8] Given a competitive industry, a strong brand has the potential to sustain a **price war**, which is when businesses cut prices to take sales from competitors. Price wars often occur in the airline industry and better-known brands often use aggressive pricing against start-up airlines. Essentially, the brand premium that exists for a strong brand provides a differential position among consumers that lesser-established brands cannot match. The lesser brands generally become identified by the lower price. The stronger brand can trade off its premium tactically by reducing its price, but not to the level of competitors, or it can reinforce the quality of its product and attempt to stabilize the price war. Alternatively, growth opportunities can be capitalized on by a strong brand identity that attracts a large number of brand-loyal consumers. The situation facilitates less elastic demand that resists price changes and can translate into increased profits. Well-established supermarket brands are regularly faced with promotions by lesser-known brands and often use their equity to resist competitive discounting.

Although many companies acknowledge the financial potential of their brands, there is often a lack of understanding of many potential applications of brand equity. These applications include the following:[9]

- Brand alliances with other companies to expand marketing opportunities
- **Channel switching**, creating new product distribution or moving the distribution flow of products from one distribution channel to another, to project equity from one channel to another (A **channel** is a system with few or many steps in which products and services flow from businesses to consumers while payment flows from consumers to businesses.)
- Relationship building to connect faster and closer to customers and distribution partners
- **Brand stretching**, extending a brand to new products, services, or markets, to spread brand building costs across a larger base of activities provided there is a fundamental fit with consumers' perceptions of the brand
- **Outsourcing**, procuring certain services from a third-party supplier, to lower costs and focus resources on core competencies

Brand Valuation

Discussion of the practical importance of branding and brand equity leads us to consider the methods that consumers and businesses use to ascribe value to brands. **Brand valuation** is the process of quantifying the financial benefit that results from owning a brand. This process is important as companies try to understand what drives value in their business.

The history of modern brand valuation began in the mid-1980s when Interbrand began conducting a brand valuation for a United Kingdom business.[10] Interbrand continues to be involved with the brand valuation industry, including joining with *BusinessWeek* to publish a yearly ranking of the best global brands (see Table 9.1). Eight of the top-ranked global brands are U.S. owned.

Brand valuation has become increasingly important as certain countries require intangible items such as brand value to be included on a business balance sheet. There are two primary methods of brand valuation: additive and inclusive. The former,

Table 9.1 *BusinessWeek*/Interbrand's Annual Ranking of the Best Global Brands for 2009[11]

Rank	Company	2009 Brand Value $Millions	Percent Change (over 2008)	Country of Ownership
1	Coca-Cola	68,734	3%	U.S.
2	IBM	60,211	2%	U.S.
3	Microsoft	56,647	–4%	U.S.
4	GE	47,777	–10%	U.S.
5	Nokia	34,864	–3%	Finland
6	McDonald's	32,275	4%	U.S.
7	Google	31,980	25%	U.S.
8	Toyota	31,330	–8%	Japan
9	Intel	30,636	–2%	U.S.
10	Disney	28,447	–3%	U.S.

and more common application, refers to the idea that product and brand are separate, while the latter considers them to be one.[12] The problem with separation can be demonstrated by asking the questions "Can Coke be valued as a soda without the brand?" and "How many Jaguars would be sold without the brand versus with the brand?" An inclusive approach to brand valuation combines the brand with associated product attributes to determine true value. Product attributes can be translated into potential sales revenue in the inclusive approach.

Building Brand Equity

The process of creating or enhancing brand equity involves understanding the value of the brand as well those factors that can create a positive brand image. These factors include loyalty, commitment, and customer equity.

Loyalty

The equity ascribed to a brand is reflected behaviorally through loyalty. There are two components of **brand loyalty**: purchase loyalty and attitudinal loyalty. Attitudinal loyalty leads to a higher relative price while purchase loyalty leads to greater market share. These factors combine to influence brand profitability.[13]

Commitment

The psychological attachment that a consumer has to a brand will be a function of how relevant it is to that consumer, that is, does it touch on things that are truly important to him or her. Brand relationships can be placed in a continuum of very committed users to uninterested nonusers.

Customer Equity

Brand equity is also created from consumer knowledge that is translated into consumer behavior.[14] **Customer-based brand equity** is defined as the differential effect that brand knowledge has on the customer response to marketing efforts.[15] This concept is based on the idea that brand equity extends from what consumers have learned, heard, felt, and seen about a brand through their cumulative experiences. If this brand equity resides in the consumer's mind, managing and influencing experiences are critical.

EXAMPLE BRAND EQUITY

Victoria's Secret, a leading specialty retailer of intimate apparel with over 1,000 stores across the United States, launched the Pink brand in 2004 to target a younger audience of high school and college students. The Pink brand targeted a new audience for Victoria's Secret and has grown to become the leading loungewear brand in the world. The Pink brand is actively promoted across college campuses through its Pink Collegiate Collection, and through relationships with MTV; a co-branded merchandise arrangement with Major League Baseball; and on social media sites such as Facebook (with over 1.25 million fans for its VSPink page), MySpace, and other blogs that are frequented by its target consumers. Victoria's Secret is using the Pink brand to build loyalty that extends into the Victoria's Secret brand as girls grow older.[16]

PHOTO: Ken Inness/Shutterstock.

>> **END EXAMPLE**

Global Brand Equity

The concepts of loyalty, commitment, and customer equity and their contribution to building brand equity gain increased complexity when considered in a global context. Global brand equity is influenced by elements of the traditional marketing mix as well as additional issues such as geography, culture, legal and business environments, and political and economic realities. Four central ideas influence strategies to create global brand equity:[17]

- Identifying emerging global customers
- Building stronger links between country-specific marketing activities that support a global infrastructure
- Realizing opportunities to transfer products, brands, and ideas throughout various countries
- Gaining economies of scale by sharing human and financial resources in creating and managing brands

EXAMPLE GLOBAL BRAND EQUITY

IKEA, a Swedish furniture company, has cultivated unique global brand equity through its contemporary designs, creative promotions, and affordable pricing strategies. IKEA has grown steadily to over 220 stores in Europe, Asia, Australia, and North America by focusing on its consumers' lifestyles. The formula of quality, affordable contemporary furniture seems to reach across borders. IKEA endeavors to design and sell products that are aesthetically pleasing yet inexpensive and functional. Founded in 1943, the brand has not always fared well entering new markets. An entry into the United States in the early 1990s was met with challenges, including beds that were measured only in centimeters, sofas that were not deep enough, kitchens that did not accommodate U.S.-sized appliances, and curtains that were too short.[18]

PHOTO: Alexey Kashin/Shutterstock.

>> END EXAMPLE

Business-to-Business Brand Equity

Brands are as important in the business-to-business (B2B) environment as they are in the business-to-consumer (B2C) environment. As has been discussed in previous chapters, the purchase process is more formal in the B2B markets than in the B2C markets. However, the question remains as to how certain brands are selected for inclusion in the sourcing process. That decision is often based on the unique requirements of the contract, past experiences with brands in the appropriate category, and the established brand equity of potential brands. Successful brands like Cisco, Intel, and Akamai have all established clear B2B positions and have translated those positions into financial success. Businesses selling to other businesses tend to present their products and services while discussing more rational elements, such as product characteristics, than do B2C brands, but they also focus on both economic value and emotional benefits.

Building Strong BRANDS (pp. 120–124)

DEFINED *A* **strong brand** *occupies a distinct position in consumers' minds based on relevant benefits and creates an emotional connection between businesses and consumers.*

EXPLAINED

Building Strong Brands

Is there an innate purpose for brands? If there were such a reason, then companies could create demand for their brands by appropriately managing their image. It is possible that consumers are in need of brands as much as companies are in need of them. The clutter of products in the marketplace and the extensive choices available could drive consumers to look for reassurance in brands with which they have positive associations.[19]

Strong brands provide three things to consumers: They save time during the shopping process, they project the right message, and they provide an identity.[20] Consumers have established perspectives on known brands and, unless a unique new product or service has entered the market or there has been a large price adjustment or drastic change in the market, it is easy to repurchase a brand that has previously been selected and performed as expected. A brand can be used to project security, convenience, quality, or something else to consumers that can reinforce the ability of a product or service to meet consumer needs. The brand provides consumers with the ability to project style and preferences to others through the choices made.

The large numbers of brands that have stood the test of time demonstrate the value of brands. Over 60% of the best-known brands in the United States are 50 years old or older.[21] The power of a long-lasting brand can often resist but not necessarily prevent decline if not properly supported. Research that tracks consumer memorability of brands often identifies a latent memory of a brand's advertising even if it has not advertised for months or even years. Still, it is possible for a brand to be damaged beyond repair, such as the failed former energy giant Enron. Enron grew through the 1990s to a $70 billion company by operating gas lines and power plants as well as engaging in trading businesses for a variety of commodities. In 2001, it was revealed that Enron had misstated its income and that its value was billions less than its balance sheet claimed. Enron claimed bankruptcy and ultimately went out of business.[22]

Apparently, brands are just as important to CEOs as to consumers. A Marsh Inc. and Oxford University study conducted in 2000, based on input from senior business executives, revealed that 85% considered brands to be their company's most important asset. Brand management expert Leslie de Chernatony has identified three essential elements of a powerful brand:

- The values that will characterize the brand
- The purpose for the brand other than making money—the brand's reason for being
- The future environment that the brand aims to facilitate

A business with a powerful brand understands what its brand should stand for, what it does stand for, and what it can stand for in the future.

APPLIED

Building Strong Brands

How can a company capitalize on its brand and achieve a leading market position? This can be achieved, arguably, through a strong business model with desirable products and services of appropriate quality and a strong financial position, as well as strong brands. Strong brands can be built by considering the competitive category, level, and type of competitors; ability to differentiate; relevance to consumers; management acumen; corporate strategy; and corporate assets.[23] The nature of the category dictates the success criteria for competing businesses including consumer desires. The existing competitive environment, whether filled with many or few competitors, also influences the creation of strong brands. The basis for a brand to differentiate from competitors through elements such as patents, expensive or unique production equipment, or weaker elements can assist in creating strong brands. The relevancy of the brand to consumers, often presented using advertising and the characteristics of the product or service, also influences the strength of the brand. Business capabilities such as having capable management, having a clear vision, and possessing financial and human assets are additional factors that influence the creation of a strong brand.

Brand Positioning

The creation of a strong brand involves several different steps that collectively answer the question "What should my brand stand for?" The first step involves placing the brand in a distinct position in consumers' minds. **Brand positioning**, the location that a brand occupies in the marketplace relative to competitors, can be achieved on a hierarchy of three levels (see Figure 9.1).[24]

FIGURE 9.1 **Positioning Levels**

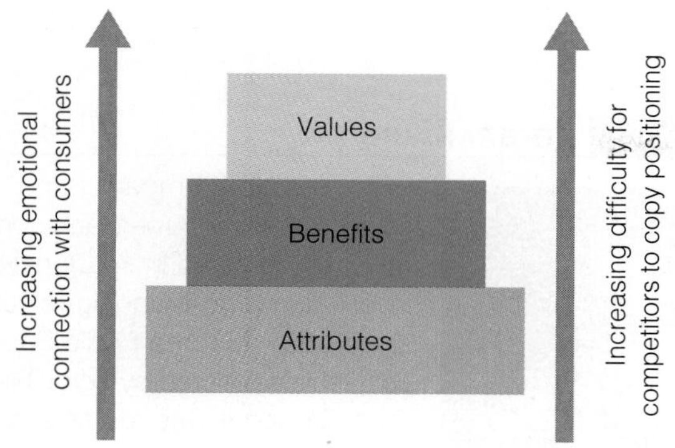

Attributes (either product or service) are the most basic levels of positioning and include smells, tastes, textures, and ingredients. Competitors can usually copy attribute positioning unless there is some type of intellectual property involved. The motivation for purchasing such products is typically what the attribute offers to the consumer instead of the brand itself.

The second level of positioning is benefit positioning, which involves focusing on the benefits that the attributes provide. Security, quality, performance, convenience, and value are all examples of benefits that products and services can provide. The benefits can also be communicated as a problem/solution position.

The third level is value positioning, which involves creating an emotional connection between the brand and consumer. Unlike beliefs and attitudes, values are the least likely to change. This type of positioning can appeal to aspirations as well. Each level creates value but the value positioning can create a relationship that engenders brand loyalty, commitment, and strong consumer equity.

Brand positioning is also strengthened if the positioning reflects the personality of the brand. **Brand personality** consists of characteristics that make a brand unique, much like human personality. Brand personalities vary widely, including rugged, sexy, and sophisticated.

Brand Name Selection

The right brand name can provide a tremendous advantage for the product or service. The brand name should fit with the attributes and benefits of the product or service and be relevant to the target consumers. Some important guidelines for brand name selection include the following:

- Use the name to distinguish as well as describe the product or service.
- Select a name that is memorable and distinctive yet appropriate for the category.
- Avoid limiting business opportunities to a particular market segment with a name that cannot be extended into new segments.
- Choose a name that is exportable to international markets.
- Ensure the name can be protected as intellectual property.

In many cases, a company is faced with a decision to create a new brand name for a new product or service or to add the product to an existing portfolio. This is a question regarding the company's brand architecture. **Brand architecture** involves the naming and organizing of brands within a broader portfolio. Sometimes these decisions are so critical that companies need to be hired to assist with naming research.

Brand Sponsorship

A product or service can be launched in two basic forms: manufacturer (national) brand and private label (retailer, reseller) brand. While the manufacturer, retailer, or reseller typically develops its own brand, some brands are licensed from other companies and others are co-branded with other brands. There are strategic advantages and disadvantages to each form and the most appropriate form must be carefully selected.

Comparing Manufacturer Brands to Private Label Brands

Manufacturer brands, which are owned by a manufacturer as opposed to a retailer or reseller, have traditionally dominated the brand choices available to consumers at retail stores. However, **private label brands** created by either a retailer or reseller have increasingly appeared in the retail environment. Private label brands have almost completely absorbed the "generic" or non-branded products of the 1980s and 1990s by realizing that branding can provide incremental profitability that non-branded products cannot. It is difficult to attach a brand promise to an unbranded product. This growth of private brands has expanded to small and midsize retailers primarily due to the profitability of these private label brands. Since retailers control more customer contact than manufacturers, they have the opportunity to realize the increased profit potential of private label products. Considerable effort goes into creating private brand products, from identifying and selecting a product to negotiating with the supplier and assessing and approving the product's level of safety and performance characteristics.

EXAMPLE **BRAND SPONSORSHIP**

Trader Joe's, established in 1958, has grown to 280 stores in 23 states. The company's strategy has included offering innovative, hard-to-find food with employees wearing Hawaiian shirts and selling in an environment that feels like a local market. The company also brands over 80% of its offerings as private label products, which allows development of the Trader Joe's brand as opposed to supplier brands and allows better control of advertising and promotion costs associated with the Trader Joe's brand. Trader Joe's private label strategy is part of the company's brand character. The net result is a loyal brand following translating into significant financial success. Interestingly enough, Trader Joe's has achieved its success without having to invest in traditional advertising. The company's only promotional effort is its newsprint circular.[25]

PHOTO: Shutterstock.

>> END EXAMPLE

Licensing

An alternative to the significant expense of creating and developing a brand is **licensing**. Licensing involves assigning rights, generally for a fee, for one company to use another company's brand for specific products and for a specific period. An existing brand can be used to provide brand equity and enhance the chances for the new product to be more rapidly accepted by consumers. The primary motivator for choosing which particular brand to license, beyond affordability, is the stature of the brand (including awareness, familiarity, and opinion) and the consistency and relevancy of the image to the company's target consumers and category. Typical types of properties that are licensed include characters, corporate trademarks and brands, fashion, sports, and art.

EXAMPLE LICENSING

Southern Comfort, a whiskey manufacturer, licensed its brand to Kemps Ice Cream, which created two products: Southern Comfort egg nog flavored ice cream and Southern Comfort vanilla spice flavored ice cream. Southern Comfort egg nog and Southern Comfort gourmet coffees are also in the marketplace. The benefit to the licensees is the unique brand flavor and brand equity. The Southern Comfort brand, founded in 1874, has also expanded to non-food product categories including apparel.[26]

PHOTO: Ljupco Smokovski/Shutterstock.

>> END EXAMPLE

Co-Branding

Co-branding involves the collaboration of multiple brands in the marketing of one specific product. The idea is that the attributes of each brand can be blended and loyalty from the separate brands may extend to the co-branded product. Any shortcomings of one brand may also be mitigated by positive equity from the other brand. These types of arrangements are seen in market sectors including automotive, fashion, hotels, financial service, and food products. A co-branding strategy can work for different reasons including generating marketplace exposure, positioning against private label brands, and sharing promotion costs with a partner. Many co-branding efforts are based on brand alliances. A **brand alliance** is a relationship, short of a merger, that is formed by two or more businesses to create market opportunities that would not have existed without the alliance. A brand alliance is one form of a brand extension.

EXAMPLE CO-BRANDING

Ford Motor Company and Eddie Bauer, a popular American sportswear company founded in 1920, have been involved in a co-branding relationship since 1983 with the Eddie Bauer edition vehicles offered by Ford. The 1984 Ford Bronco II was the first model to feature the Eddie Bauer premium trim package that was designed to reflect Eddie Bauer's brand character of unpretentious style and rugged capability. Other Ford models have subsequently offered the Eddie Bauer trim level, including the Aerostar minivan, F-Series truck, and Explorer, Expedition, and Excursion sport utility vehicles. Eddie Bauer edition vehicles offer unique paint schemes, special wheels, custom seats, and a variety of special interior and exterior features. Ford sells the vehicles through its dealer network while Eddie Bauer features the vehicles in its catalogs, promotional brochures, store displays, and on its Web site.[27]

PHOTO: Krivosheev Vitaly/Shutterstock.

>> END EXAMPLE

Brand Development

Brand equity can be developed and maximized not only for a single brand but also for a portfolio of brands. When a company has multiple brands, the decisions on the correct combination of brand names and attributes across the entire portfolio is part of a comprehensive brand strategy. **Brand strategy** is the process where "the offer is positioned in the consumer's mind to produce a perception of advantage."[28] The brand strategy defines the brand architecture that is used for brand development. The development of brands involves several different strategic options: line extensions, brand extensions, multibrand offerings, and entirely new brands.

Line Extensions

A **line extension** is an addition to an existing product line that retains the currently utilized brand name. Companies often use line extensions because they believe such use will keep customers from switching brands and allow firms to retain or increase their margins.

There are two primary methods to extend product lines: horizontal and vertical. The product attributes selected to distinguish the products will determine which method is being used. A vertical line extension involves varying the product line by price and quality. A horizontal line extension maintains products within a similar price and quality level but varies other attributes such as flavor or smell. Line extensions can provide new opportunities to reach different consumers but can also expose a brand to new levels of competition. Growth needs must be matched with any increased risks.

EXAMPLE **LINE EXTENSIONS**

Crayola, known for its crayons that made their initial debut in 1903, has a variety of products including clay, paints, markers, and coloring books for children. Silly Putty is also a Crayola brand offering. Crayola practices vertical line extension with its portfolio products marketed to adults and artists with an upscale version of its drawing pencils, oil pastels, colored pencils, acrylic paints, and watercolors. The use of a vertical line extension allows Crayola to present products to different market segments and to market different product characteristics and benefits while still building the overall Crayola brand.[29]

PHOTO: Judy Kennamer/Shutterstock.

>> END EXAMPLE

Bundling is a way to present the portfolio to customers without necessarily adding to the product lines. **Bundling** refers to the "practice of marketing two or more products and/or services in a single 'package.'"[30] The principle behind bundling is that a bundled offering is perceived by customers to offer more value than the individual components of the bundle sold separately.

Brand Extensions

A **brand extension** involves taking an existing brand into a new category. This practice can save marketing investment in a new brand and could build additional brand stature. The risks include losing focus of the core attributes and positioning of the brand and failing in the new category, which could damage perceptions of the brand. The greatest chance for success is if the brand is well positioned with consumers based on an emotional connection. Without an emotional connection, the brand can risk being overextended. Known for disposable razors, pens, and lighters, BIC attempted to extend its brand into women's underwear rather unsuccessfully.[31]

EXAMPLE **BRAND EXTENSIONS**

Entertainment and media giant Disney has extended its venerable brand with significant financial success. Disney has traditionally been involved in theme parks, television, and merchandising and recently has expanded into many different market segments. Disney uses its brand to enhance its relationships with its loyal customers by offering brand extensions such as Disney Vacation Club, Disney Cruise Line, and Radio Disney Network.[32]

PHOTO: Travelshots.com/Alamy Images.

>> END EXAMPLE

Multibrands

Some companies elect to launch several brands in the same category to appeal to the varying wants of the consumers and to take advantage of business conditions. In a fragmented market, a company may elect to compete with itself with the reasoning that owning 5 out of 14 brands will result in greater aggregate market share than owning 1 out of 10. Having individual brand names, while potentially expensive to develop, offers considerable flexibility in positioning different product attributes. Cannibalization is one particular problem associated with a multibrand approach. **Cannibalization** is the loss of sales of an existing product within a portfolio to a new product in the same portfolio. However, the risks of competing with oneself can be acceptable if there is a net overall gain. Many consumer product companies launch new products knowing that some sales will be cannibalized.

New Brands

A company can elect to create an entirely new brand because of an existing brand suffering from poor equity or because an existing brand does not extend well into a new category. New brands can offer a clean slate for positioning but require considerable financial investment to develop. Sometimes a new brand can be created based on the experience and positioning of another brand in the company's portfolio and positioned into a unique market niche.

EXAMPLE **NEW BRANDS**

In some market conditions, such as intense competition with clearly defined market segments, a new brand, often called a **flanker brand**, is created to expand an organization's portfolio into a new segment of an existing market category while retaining relevance with current customers. The idea is that the new brand will increase overall sales in a particular category by targeting consumers who are not currently purchasing products or services from a particular organization. In some cases, a brand currently owned by a parent organization is relaunched to compete as a

flanker brand. Sprint Nextel Corporation, one of the largest telecommunications companies in the United States, relaunched Boost Mobile, a wholly owned subsidiary brand that was mainly a regional business in the United States until 2006 when it became known nationally for its unlimited talk plan, as an unlimited talk time prepaid product. A flanker brand for Sprint Nextel in the expanding prepaid phone market, Boost Mobile offered unlimited calling, texting, and Web access for $50 at its 2009 relaunch. The new position for Boost directly competed with prepaid brands MetroPCS Communications Inc. and Leap Wireless International Inc. and put pressure on other large mobile phone companies such as AT&T and Verizon that did not have similar offers to the Boost Mobile product.[33]

PHOTO: Supri Suharjoto/Shutterstock.

>> END EXAMPLE

Managing **BRANDS** (pp. 125–126)

DEFINED **Brand management** *is the overall coordination of a brand's equities to create long-term brand growth through overseeing marketing mix strategies.*

EXPLAINED

Managing Brands

Just as the creation and development of brand equity involve significant resources, the ongoing management of brands requires significant resources as well. The intangible and tangible brand value that extends from strong brand equity requires ongoing management.

Brand management utilizes brand equity to create a shortcut to address market needs as business conditions change. **Category management** involves the management of multiple brands in a product line and **category managers** have responsibilities that tend to include what was traditionally handled by product managers and **brand managers,** including portfolio decisions and marketing activities across different products.

APPLIED

Managing Brands

The practice of brand management requires constant and consistent communication of a brand's desired positioning. That positioning is influenced not only by a brand's communication efforts but also by customer experience and more recently by social media. Blogs, discussion forums, and online evaluation services have considerable impact on the reputation of a brand. As a result, the media channels utilized by many companies have expanded and decentralized.

Even though social media has affected the relationship between consumers and brands, there are still opportunities for brands to use this media to their advantage. Just as small brands can look large to consumers by being active on the Internet, large brands can similarly look smaller to consumers when the Internet allows consumers to connect on an emotional level. Social relationships based on an emotional connection are some of the central principles of contemporary brand management.

Social media or not, it is still important to understand what a brand means to consumers. Just because a company brands its products does not guarantee that people will find the products either relevant or useful. With the average chief marketing officer's tenure at just over two years, the idea of either positioning or repositioning a brand seems daunting, but the core principles of brand management remain.[34]

Brand Protection

One of the critical elements of brand management is the protection of the brand. Beyond making strategic decisions about the creation and nurturing of the brand, there must also be decisions about **brand protection** and securing the brand's inherent value, including intellectual property. **Intellectual property** is a collection of non-physical assets owned by an individual or company that are the result of innovation and are legally protected from being copied or used by unauthorized parties. Examples include patents and trademarks. Failure to protect a brand's intellectual property can result in significant long-term problems:

- Devaluing corporate brands—recalls and bad publicity can hurt the perception of a brand
- Reducing legitimate profits—long- and short-term profits are reduced by the high cost of fighting counterfeits
- Damaging consumer confidence—consumers may feel unsafe or reticent to purchase products
- Creating liability-related exposure—lawsuits may result from the use of counterfeit products

The **United States Patent and Trademark Office (USPTO)** is a federal agency responsible for assigning rights for limited times to individuals or companies to use innovations. Protection is granted for inventions and new applications for existing products. The primary tasks of the USPTO are processing trademark and patent applications and providing trademark and patent information. Counterfeiting is one of the most common forms of brand protection violations. **Counterfeiting** is the unauthorized copying of products, packaging, or other intellectual property of a registered brand. There are three main effects:

- Indirect harm to the economy through lost tax revenues or foreign investment
- Direct harm caused to the manufacturer and distribution channel members
- Indirect social cost due to the redirection of public and private money to fight counterfeiting

Communication strategies can provide a front line of defense to fight counterfeiting. Examples of this include branded messages touting the risks of fake car parts and prescription drugs. By advertising the importance of purchasing the real product, quality, safety, durability, and other brand attributes can be leveraged on the demand side and subsequent pressure can be placed on the supply side of counterfeiting.

EXAMPLE **BRAND PROTECTION**

Louis Vuitton, a famous French fashion house established in 1854 with a wide range of luxury products ranging from handbags to sunglasses, is one of the most counterfeited brands in the world. In 2008, Louis Vuitton was part of a group of brands awarded a $63 million legal judgment in France against eBay for allowing individuals to auction counterfeit luxury goods on its Web site. In 2006, Louis Vuitton surveyed eBay and estimated that 90% of the perfumes, watches, and handbags sold under its brands were counterfeit. It is estimated that counterfeit fashion products constitute a $600 billion global industry.[35]

PHOTO: Bed Heys/Shutterstock.

>> END EXAMPLE

Visual Summary

Chapter 9 Summary

The process of creating, cultivating, and strategically managing brands builds on concepts of value creation, consumer decision making, and consumer insights discussed in preceding chapters. Strong brands provide a consumer with relevant and desired benefits and possess a distinct position in the consumer mind. Ultimately, brands form a connection between companies and consumers that, if properly nurtured, can provide the means to realize the financial potential of the company.

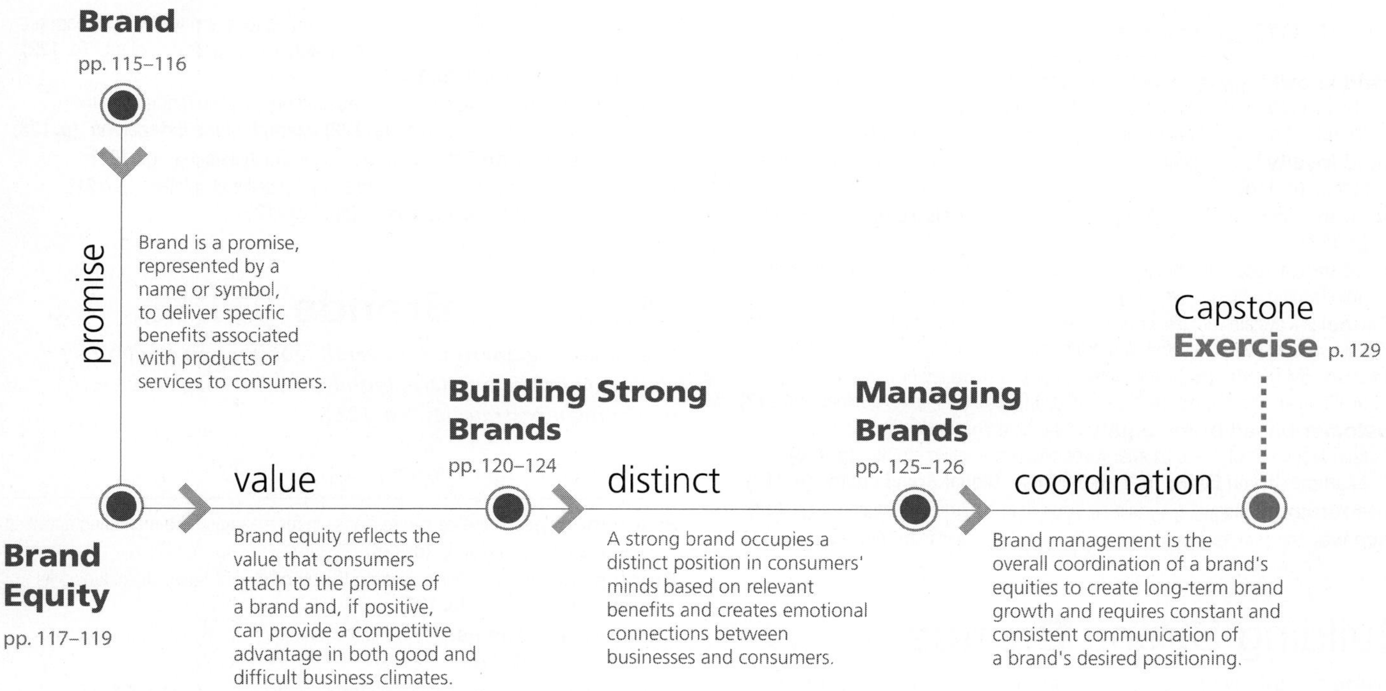

Brand
pp. 115–116
promise
Brand is a promise, represented by a name or symbol, to deliver specific benefits associated with products or services to consumers.
Brand Equity
pp. 117–119
value
Brand equity reflects the value that consumers attach to the promise of a brand and, if positive, can provide a competitive advantage in both good and difficult business climates.
Building Strong Brands
pp. 120–124
distinct
A strong brand occupies a distinct position in consumers' minds based on relevant benefits and creates emotional connections between businesses and consumers.
Managing Brands
pp. 125–126
coordination
Brand management is the overall coordination of a brand's equities to create long-term brand growth and requires constant and consistent communication of a brand's desired positioning.
Capstone Exercise p. 129

Chapter Key Terms

Brand (pp. 115–116)

Brand *is a promise to deliver specific benefits associated with products or services to consumers. (p. 115)* **Example: Brand (p. 116)**

Key Term (p. 115)

Digital brand strategy is a set of marketing activities that uses digital mediums to connect consumers to brands. **(p. 115)**

Brand Equity (pp. 117–119)

Brand equity *is the power of a brand, through creation of a distinct image, to influence customer behavior. (p. 117)* **Example: Brand Equity (p. 118) Example: Global Brand Equity (p. 119)**

Key Terms (pp. 117–119)

Brand knowledge is the set of associations that consumers hold in memory regarding the brand's features, benefits, users, perceived quality, and overall attitude as a result of prior brand marketing activities. **(p. 117)**
Brand loyalty is the extent to which a consumer repeatedly purchases a given brand. **(p. 118)**
Brand stretching is extending a brand to new products, services, or markets. **(p. 117)**
Brand valuation is the process of quantifying the financial benefit that results from owning a brand. **(p. 117)**
Channel is a system with few or many steps in which products flow from businesses to consumers while payments flow from consumers to businesses. **(p. 117)**
Channel switching is creating new product distribution or moving the distribution flow of products from one distribution channel to another. **(p. 117)**
Customer-based brand equity is the differential effect that brand knowledge has on the customer response to marketing efforts. **(p. 118)** **Example: Brand Equity (p. 118) Example: Global Brand Equity (p. 119)**
Outsourcing is procuring certain services from a third-party supplier. **(p. 117)**
Price war occurs when businesses cut prices to take sales from competitors. **(p. 117)**

Building Strong Brands (pp. 120–124)

Strong brand *occupies a distinct position in consumers' minds based on relevant benefits and creates an emotional connection between businesses and consumers. (p. 120)*

Key Terms (pp. 120–124)

Brand alliance is a relationship, short of a merger, that is formed by two or more businesses to create market opportunities that would not have existed without the alliance. **(p. 122) Example: Co-Branding (p. 122)**
Brand architecture is the naming and organizing of brands within a broader portfolio. **(p. 121)**
Brand extension takes an existing brand into a new category. **(p. 123)** **Example: Brand Extensions (p. 123)**
Brand personality consists of characteristics that make a brand unique, much like human personality. **(p. 121)**
Brand positioning is the location that a brand occupies in the marketplace relative to competitors. **(p. 120)**
Brand strategy is the process where the offer is positioned in the consumer's mind to produce a perception of advantage. **(p. 122)**
Bundling refers to the practice of marketing two or more products and/or services in a single package. **(p. 123)**
Cannibalization is the loss of sales of an existing product within a portfolio to a new product in the same portfolio. **(p. 123) Example: New Brands (pp. 123–124)**
Co-branding is the collaboration of multiple brands in the marketing of one specific product. **(p. 122)**
Flanker brand is created to expand an organization's portfolio into a new segment of an existing market category while retaining relevance with current customers. **(p. 123)**
Licensing is the practice of a company receiving fees or royalties from partner firms for the right to use a brand, manufacturing process, or patent. **(p. 122)** **Example: Licensing (p. 122)**
Line extension is an addition to an existing product line that retains the currently utilized brand name. **(p. 122) Example: Line Extensions (p. 123)**
Manufacturer brand is a brand owned by a manufacturer. **(p. 121)**
Private label brand is a brand owned by a reseller or retailer. **(p. 121)** **Example: Brand Sponsorship (pp. 121–122)**

Managing Brands (pp. 125–126)

Brand management *is the overall coordination of a brand's equities to create long-term brand growth through overseeing marketing mix strategies. (p. 125)*

Key Terms (pp. 125–126)

Brand manager is the person responsible for managing the marketing activities associated with a brand. **(p. 125)**
Brand protection involves securing the brand's inherent value, including its intellectual property. **(p. 125)**
Category management involves the management of multiple brands in a product line. **(p. 125)**
Category manager is the person responsible for managing a product line that may contain one or more brands. **(p. 125)**
Counterfeiting is the unauthorized copying of products, packaging, or other intellectual property of a registered brand. **(p. 125) Example: Brand Protection (p. 126)**
Intellectual property is a collection of non-physical assets owned by an individual or company that are the result of innovation and are legally protected from being copied or used by unauthorized parties. **(p. 125)**
United States Patent and Trademark Office (USPTO) is a federal agency responsible for assigning rights for limited times to individuals or companies to use innovations. **(p. 125)**

Capstone Exercise

In this chapter, you learned about the various issues relating to brands and how marketers develop brands. To better understand these concepts, let us examine the company that invented brand and category management. Founded in 1837 in Cincinnati, Ohio, as a soap- and candle-making venture, Procter & Gamble (P&G) is now a huge company. P&G has 23 brands with a combined revenue of over a billion dollars. In fact, P&G originated the term "soap opera" when it sponsored daytime radio programs and used them to sell soap.

Leading brands are based on consumer trust and loyalty and they are successful because they offer superior value. Sometimes, better value is measured by a more competitive price. Or, better value could be found in superior customer service or even because the product is unique.

Go to www.pg.com and look at the wide range of products and notice the brand names that are in the P&G product portfolio. Did you realize that all of these are P&G products?

The Chapter 9 learning objectives are:

Objective 1. How does brand function as the link between consumers and companies?

Objective 2. What are the influences that can either enhance or diminish a company's position in the marketplace? How can those influences be built into brand equity?

Objective 3. What are the steps and methods involved in developing a strong brand?

Objective 4. What resources are required when managing brands?

All of these are related to how P&G operates as a premier consumer products company.

1. Why do you think P&G emphasizes the brand name and not the company name?
2. Choose a P&G brand and explain what the image of the brand is and how P&G creates and conveys that image to the consumer.
3. As a P&G brand manager how do you improve your odds that when the customer makes the buying decision he or she will choose your brand and not your competitors' brands?

Application Exercise

Use the marketing concepts in this chapter to tackle and solve a marketing problem: brand equity, brand positioning, and brand name selection.

First, start by thinking about products with a distinct "high end" image. There are many products available in stores within this category for us to consider purchasing.

The Marketing Problem

Choose a category of products with a specific "high end" image; take, for example, designer apparel, and then choose a brand in that category after considering the following situation.

> Consumers seem to be confused as to the brand equity and brand positioning of your brand.

The Problem

Write a statement describing the brand's distinct image, its value and benefits, and its emotional connection. Does the brand name fit with the attributes and benefits?

The Solution

Complete the following two Problem/Solution briefs using your brand in the "high end" image category, chapter concepts, and college resources.

1. From the Marketing Manager's Point of View
   a. Problem Definition
   b. Brand Analysis
   c. Product's Value
   d. Solution
2. From the Consumer's Point of View
   a. Problem Definition
   b. Positioning Statement Analysis
   c. Product's Value
   d. Solution

Resources:

Marketing Defined, Explained, Applied 2e, Michael Levens
The College Library
Retail or Online Field Trip
Assigned Reading—*Brand Week*, *Advertising Age*, *WSJ*, scholarly publications, category trade journals
Blog your problem from either point of view, gather responses/posts (www.blogger.com/start)

Segmenting, Targeting, and Positioning

Chapter Overview In the previous chapter, you explored the brand-building process. The successful management of brands depends on an understanding of market potential. How efficiently a firm capitalizes on market potential can dictate success. This chapter introduces concepts related to the way brands can efficiently interact with consumers. The central elements of an efficient marketing strategy include the division of consumer markets into meaningful and distinct customer groups: segmenting, the selection of particular customer groups to serve; targeting; and positioning, the placement of the product or service offerings in the minds of consumer targets.

Chapter Outline

SEGMENTATION (pp. 131–132)

DEFINED **Segmentation** *(also referred to as* **market segmentation***) is the division of consumer markets into meaningful and distinct customer groups.*

EXPLAINED
Segmentation

There was a time when large companies such as McDonald's, Procter & Gamble, and Coca-Cola could market and sell their products by considering only the broad wants and needs of large groups of the U.S. population, if not the entire market. These companies could advertise their messages through a small number of radio and television stations that reached much of the population. This strategy is known as mass marketing.

Mass marketing is communicating a product or service message to as broad a group of people as possible with the purpose of positively influencing sales. The idea of mass marketing is that the broader the audience, the more potential for sales. In the past, this strategy proved successful for some businesses. Today, there are several problems with mass marketing. For one, there is no longer the ability to easily reach a large audience. Secondly, there are an increasingly vast number of product and brand choices for the consumer.

Communicating with the entire U.S. market or a large segment within the market was much easier decades ago. For example, in the 1960s, businesses could run advertising on three major television networks, ABC, CBS, and NBC, and reach 80% of U.S. women.[1] Reaching a similar level today would require advertising on over 100 television channels.[2] Even if a business purchased enough advertising and was able to reach such a large audience, it is not enough to tell consumers that the business exists and invite them to buy its products or services. Many product categories contain hundreds of different brand choices and consumers are often overwhelmed with options. Consider a typical supermarket shelf. Many brands in product categories offer specific attributes that appeal to certain consumers, but do not appeal to others.

Consumers differ in their wants, needs, perceptions, values, and expectations. It is these differences that form the foundation for segmentation. Segmentation identifies groups of consumers who have similar market responses, such as reacting to advertising or personal selling, within their group, but whose responses differ from other groups.[3] A response could be to product characteristics, or to a projected image, or the way a group learns about, purchases, and consumes a product or service.

To qualify as a true segment, a group should fulfill several criteria:[4]

- Be a homogeneous set
- Be different from other segments
- Be a critical mass
- Have core similarities of attitude, behavior, and economics
- Be robust and replicable over time

APPLIED
Segmentation

Market segmentation allows businesses to look at consumers as several different groups, instead of one mass market. Correctly segmenting consumers allows companies to target their marketing dollars effectively. The value of market segmentation can be measured through increased market share for a given segment, for example, an increase in sales for women ages 24–35.

The most basic form of market segmentation involves demographic or psychographic criteria, such as

Smartwater is the number one premium bottled water brand in the United States and is part of Glaceau's leading portfolio, along with Vitaminwater and Vitaminenergy, in the enhanced water category. Founded in 1996, Glaceau targets its products at people on the go who want to feel better, perform better, and live healthier lives through better hydration. Smartwater is targeted to healthy individuals who carefully watch what they put into their bodies. Smartwater is a zero-calorie, vapor-distilled, electrolyte-enhanced water product. As the segment of individuals who value health and wellness increases, Smartwater has differentiated its market position from spring water by having the lowest measurement of total dissolved solids, including minerals and metals, of any water on the market. Smartwater partnered with Jennifer Aniston, known for her healthy lifestyle including yoga and organic cooking, in 2007 to reinforce the product's market position.[5]

PHOTO: Deklofenak/Shutterstock.

age or gender. However, consumers seldom make purchase decisions based solely on demographics or psychographics. Instead, they rely on a wide range of other criteria, such as attitudes or values. There are similar levels of complexity in segmenting business markets (for B2B transactions) and segmenting international markets.

Businesses generally conduct market segmentation through marketing research studies among consumers or businesses. Large numbers of consumers or businesses are surveyed on a wide range of issues and the results are used to create segments based on a variety of factors. Additional information on various research techniques is included in Chapter 8.

SEGMENTATION Base (pp. 133–135)

DEFINED *The **segmentation base** is a group of characteristics that is used to assign segment members.*

EXPLAINED

Segmentation Base

The choice of a segmentation base can be one of the most critical decisions that influence the success of market segmentation. Consumers are divided into groups for marketing purposes. For example, if you market Smartwater, as we saw in the opening example, then you would market to health-conscious individuals who ascribe a high value to quality ingredients. You would focus your marketing in an effort to sell more units of Smartwater. Consumers are typically divided into groups by demographic, psychographic, values, behavioral, and needs variables.

Demographic segmentation divides the market into groups, based on criteria such as age, gender, family size, family life cycle, income, occupation, education, religion, ethnicity, generation, nationality, and sexual orientation. For example, some companies offer distinct products or marketing approaches for different age cohorts or life-stage groups, such as selling child insurance policies to new parents. Some may market to affluent consumers with premium goods or services. Others may market to men or women with gender-specific products or services.

FIGURE 10.1 Percentage of Age Groups That Watch 20 or More Hours of Television Each Week

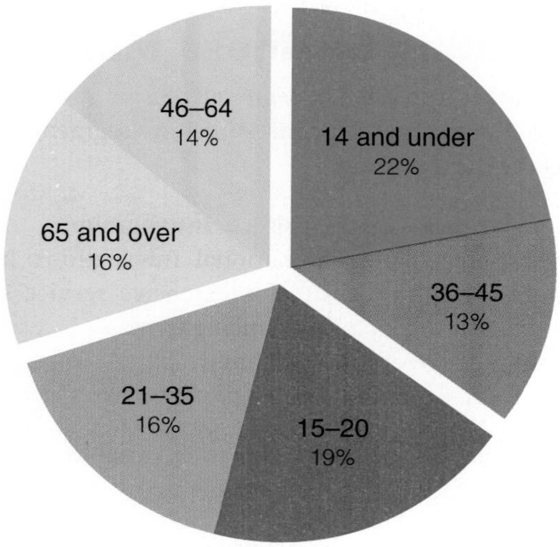

Demographic criteria provide the most common bases for segmenting customer groups and, while use of such criteria is typically the initial method of segmenting, other criteria can be used within demographic segments. Demographics can be the easiest information to obtain, but may not provide the greatest amount of insight into why consumers behave differently. A hypothetical example of demographic segmentation output that reflects the percentage of age groups that watch 20 hours or more of television each week is shown in Figure 10.1.

EXAMPLE DEMOGRAPHIC SEGMENTATION

Curves, the largest fitness franchise in the world, is designed to provide one-stop fitness facilities and exercise and nutritional information for women. With over 10,000 locations in 70 countries serving 4 million women, Curves offers a variety of products, including its 30-minute workout. By segmenting the market by gender, Curves has carefully defined itself to consumers and has made many women, both experienced athletes and novices alike, feel more comfortable about working out.[6]

PHOTO: Deklofenak/Shutterstock.

>> END EXAMPLE

Psychographic segmentation assigns buyers into different groups, based on lifestyle, class, or personality characteristics. People belonging to a particular demographic group can have dramatically different psychographic characteristics. For example, 18- to 24-year-old males represent a wide range of lifestyles that can dramatically influence the likelihood of whether they will select one type of product or service over another. Some may be adventurous and go camping when traveling, while others may enjoy staying in luxury hotels. In fact, these distinct groups of people may have more in common with people from a wide range of age groups rather than their fellow 18- to 24-year-olds.

EXAMPLE **PSYCHOGRAPHIC SEGMENTATION**

Moosejaw began as a small outfitter in Keego Harbor, Michigan. Over time, it became an iconic cult brand with sales across the country. Moosejaw flags are a common promotional tool and the company combines a savvy knowledge of consumer behavior with a broad range of products. Moosejaw uses lifestyle, a psychographic segmentation variable, to create an emotional connection with its customers; that connection is called Moosejaw madness. Moosejaw madness involves a variety of activities, such as reviewing proposed advertising copy and having people send in pictures of themselves with a Moosejaw flag in places around the world.[7]

PHOTO: Dana E. Fry/Shutterstock.

>> **END EXAMPLE**

Values segmentation considers what customers prefer and what motivates customer response to marketing activities. Individual values are among the most fundamental determinants of consumer behavior and are considered to be more closely related to motivations than attitudes. Once motivations are understood, behavior becomes easier to predict.[8] Values generally develop over many years and are very difficult to influence through marketing communication. However, values segmentation criteria can be used to segment consumers effectively by reflecting consumer perception. Examples of values variables include an interest in lifelong learning, enjoyment, integrity, respect, self-direction, and honesty.

Behavioral segmentation allocates consumers into groups based on their uses or responses to a product or service. For example, buyers can be grouped according to occasions or life events, such as graduations, when they get the idea to buy a product or service, actually make their purchase, or use the purchased item. Markets can be segmented into nonusers, ex-users, potential users, first-time users, and regular users of a product. Consumers could be grouped into high levels of usage or lower levels of usage. A market can be segmented by loyalty because consumers can be loyal to distribution outlets or product or service brands.

Needs segmentation assigns consumers into groups, based on their current and desired level of interaction with a particular market category. Consumers classified by needs segmentation are asked to rate their level of agreement with statements about how they feel about aspects of the category being studied. Automotive consumers can be classified based on their needs for storage space, horsepower, towing capacity, and many other characteristics of products in the automotive category.

APPLIED

Segmentation Base

The selection of a segmentation base is sometimes done by default if a business is unaware of the different ways to classify customers. Businesses may use readily available information, usually demographics, to conduct segmentation without considering if that available information best represents how consumers think about and interact with their business and the larger category. In many cases, more complex segmentation bases should be considered, such as psychographic, values, behavioral, and needs. Quite often, a combination of different bases provides the most useful segmentation.

Needs segmentation could be utilized to identify specific groups, but those groups could then be classified by demographic, psychographic, and behavioral characteristics. It is important to use a variety of criteria in creating segments because they may overlap in classification criteria. For example, two segments could both be females between the ages of 25 and 35, but the product needs could be completely different. One group may want to drive convertibles and the other group may consist of moms who want minivans. This would certainly require different marketing activities for each group.

Companies, however, can be wrong when trying to determine what different segments want. For example, a company could believe that it has a product that 18- to 25-year-olds will want, but in which 30- to 45-year-olds will not be interested. Believing this, the company targets its ads to the younger age group. However, sales information may indicate that both groups bought the product. For example, Toyota launched the Scion brand assuming young adults would be the primary purchasers. Ultimately, Toyota found that people of all ages were purchasing the product.

Marketers seldom restrict their segmentation analysis to variables from only one type of segmentation base, such as demographic. Instead, they are increasingly using multiple segmentation bases to locate better-defined target groups. For example, a jewelry designer could identify a group of individuals earning over $1 million each year who are interested in his or her products and, within that group, the designer could identify a large subgroup that enjoys tennis. By combining demographic and psychographic bases, the jewelry designer could produce products for high-income individuals that are either created in tennis themes or are marketed and sold at tennis events. Instead of simply targeting high-income individuals, there is another connection—tennis—that creates a stronger level of interest among certain consumers.

Segmenting Business Markets

Business markets can often be segmented using variables similar to consumer markets. The primary business segmentation variables include the following:

- **Demographics**—Business size, industry group
- **Geographics**—Regional, national, international locations
- **Benefits sought**—Desire for extensive service support, cutting-edge technology, financing terms
- **Loyalty**—Share of total purchases
- **Usage rates**—Amount, frequency of purchases

There are some unique business market variables that include the following:

- **Customer operating characteristics**—Customer capabilities and processes, and technology requirements

- **Purchasing approaches**—Where power resides in an organization and general purchasing policies
- **Situational factors**—Size of order, sense of urgency of order
- **Personal characteristics**—Loyalty, risk aversion of customer

Depending on the product, some businesses may place a high value on the service support offered by the supplier. That level of service may make the price less important. Like consumer markets, a combination of variables may provide the most effective segmentation.

EXAMPLE **SEGMENTING BUSINESS MARKETS**

JPMorgan Chase is a leading global financial services firm with assets of $2 trillion. Operating in over 60 countries, Chase offers consumer and business banking offerings. Business services include credit, payroll services, retirement services, and payment processing services. In addition, Chase offers special programs for certain business segments, including not-for-profits (through tax-exempt business retirement program management and access to potential grants through the JPMorgan Chase Foundation) and CPAs (through a dedicated CPA hotline and online access to client banking information). The programs are designed to meet the unique needs of these segments.[9]

PHOTO: David Gilder/Shutterstock.

>> END EXAMPLE

Segmenting International Markets

Consumers in one country's market can have more in common with certain segments in another country's market than with consumers in their own country. This could be due to immigration and shared heritage. Some Hispanic consumers in parts of the United States and some consumers in Mexico have the same brand preferences and consume similar media. Global marketing strategies can be successful by identifying consumer needs and wants that span national boundaries by increasing the overall market potential. Segments that span national boundaries can sometimes be more valuable to companies than segments that exist in a single country.

Countries, even those in close proximity, may differ significantly in their cultural, economic, and political composition. The basis for grouping consumers, whether across country borders or across county borders, involves identifying distinct buying needs and behaviors.

EXAMPLE **SEGMENTING INTERNATIONAL MARKETS**

Nokia, the world's leading mobile phone manufacturer, has sold over 1 billion phones in over 150 countries. Nokia has a global portfolio that is adapted to meet local customer needs as well as infrastructure and legal requirements. In the Middle East, Nokia launched a selection of mobile applications for the holy month of Ramadan. The Ramadan offering enables users to search, read, bookmark, and listen to Qur'an recitation. Locations of major mosques in Saudi Arabia, Egypt, Morocco, Pakistan, Jordan, and the United Arab Emirates are included through Nokia Maps. Additional mobile content includes wallpaper, ringtones, and Islamic songs. About 14% of Nokia global sales come from the Middle East and Africa.[10]

PHOTO: Josh Gow/Shutterstock.

>> END EXAMPLE

TARGETING (pp. 136–138)

DEFINED **Targeting** *(also referred to as* **market targeting***) is the process of evaluating and selecting the most viable market segment to enter.*

EXPLAINED

Targeting

Once the segmentation possibilities have been identified, the next step is to determine which customer groups to serve. Businesses often select more than one customer group based on criteria such as the following:

- Ability to meet requirements of the customers
- Overall cost to meet customer requirements
- Potential profitability of serving different customer groups

As many brands face an increasingly competitive and crowded market, the challenges are both strategic and tactical. Strategic questions generally involve "where" and "who" types of questions, such as "Who are those consumers who are most interested in what my brand stands for?" Tactical questions typically involve "what" and "how" types of questions, such as "What type of marketing offer would be most desired by those consumers who are most interested in my brand?"

Although market targeting often begins with an established product or service, target marketing occurs when a business identifies a market segment it wants to serve and then develops a product or service that is appropriate for that segment. For example, Baby Einstein, owned by Disney, has a wide product offering of DVDs and toys and markets its portfolio to moms, with a particular focus on first-time moms. The targeting process involves an understanding of the characteristics of the various segments and draws considerably from the choices made during segmentation. Ultimately, the concept of targeting involves the prioritization of segments and the allocation of resources.[11]

APPLIED

Targeting

Targeting allows businesses to build efficiencies through the use of appropriate advertising media and relevant messages for a given target. Targeting can be accomplished in a variety of methods, but ultimately should be based on the understanding of consumer preferences and needs. The result can be a competitive advantage that is essential to the overall marketing strategy.

With the growing number of ways to segment customers, targeting choices are also increasing. Generational marketing involves grouping consumers by age and socioeconomic factors. Cohort marketing looks at individuals with similar life experiences at different times in their history. Life-stage marketing considers those common events that individuals and families face regardless of age. Behaviors are another aspect, beyond age, that can provide valuable targeting options.

Behavioral targeting is a recent development that optimizes the online advertising potential for products and services. The ultimate idea is to increase interest in a particular product at a point when the consumer is actively shopping within the product category. Behavioral targeting works by placing a cookie, information that a Web site places on your computer to identify you at a later time, on a user's computer. The cookie then makes a note of the user's online behavior. An example would be a consumer searching a variety of automotive sites and then receiving an offer for vehicle insurance.

In some cases, products or services are developed before a market opportunity is sought. There is considerable risk with this scenario, particularly with technology companies.

EXAMPLE **TARGETING**

Iridium LLC, supported by Motorola, spent $5 billion to launch a system of satellites and to establish other infrastructure to support the development of a satellite telephone network in 1998. The global satellite telephone market proved unsustainable for Iridium and others in the late 1990s. Iridium filed for bankruptcy in 1999. While there was some demand for satellite telephones, the pricing structure, performance, and substitute products made companies such as Iridium not viable.[12]

PHOTO: Alistair Cotton/Shutterstock.

>> END EXAMPLE

There are several specific targeting choices available, but there are essentially three market coverage choices when targeting: undifferentiated, differentiated, and niche marketing.

Undifferentiated Marketing

Building on the concept of mass marketing introduced at the beginning of this chapter, **undifferentiated marketing** is when a company treats the market as a whole, focusing on what is similar among the needs of customers, rather than on what is different. By using this strategy, companies create products or services to appeal to the greatest number of potential buyers. The benefit of an undifferentiated strategy is that it can be cost-effective because a limited portfolio results in reduced production, advertising, research, inventory, and shipping costs. This strategy is typically most successful when used in a market with limited or no competition or when the product or service has wide appeal and the market is rapidly growing. A wide range of organizations could be classified as having practiced undifferentiated marketing at some point in their history; examples include local libraries, public utilities, Coca-Cola, and Disney.

EXAMPLE UNDIFFERENTIATED MARKETING

Henry Ford's early financial backers encouraged him to build cars for the rich to maximize his profits, just as the hundreds of other automotive start-ups were doing. Instead of taking this advice, Ford bought out his backers and embarked on a path that led to the launch of what Ford referred to as "the universal car." The Ford Model T was introduced in 1908 with the intention of being affordable for the general population. Over 15 million Model Ts were produced between 1908 and 1927. Ford practiced undifferentiated marketing that is best represented by his quote: "The customer can have any color he wants, so long as it's black." An excerpt from another quote acknowledges that he understood the market as well: "All Fords are exactly alike, but no two men are just alike. . . . " Ford was able to practice undifferentiated marketing because the automotive market was expanding rapidly and he had a unique selling proposition based on affordability, quality, and safety in the context of the time.[13]

PHOTO: Rob Wilson/Shutterstock.

>> END EXAMPLE

Differentiated Marketing

A firm practicing **differentiated marketing** separates and targets different market segments, with a unique product or service tailored to each segment. The result is a distinctive marketing plan for each segment. With a differentiated marketing strategy, companies can generally increase total sales because of broader appeal through greater relevance across market segments and a stronger position within each segment. Sometimes referred to as multisegment marketing, the strategy not only increases sales potential, but it also increases costs associated with targeting different market segments with relevant messages. Still, if done effectively, there is the potential for greater loyalty, resulting in repeat purchases.

EXAMPLE DIFFERENTIATED MARKETING

Just a decade ago, many people could have argued that McDonald's practiced undifferentiated marketing. McDonald's had a standard product portfolio that consisted of foods such as hamburgers, french fries, chicken nuggets, and fish sandwiches and essentially targeted the mass market with a standard marketing mix strategy. In recent years, McDonald's has taken steps to make its brand relevant to increasingly fragmented consumer segments by expanding its offerings. Those now include items such as salads and yogurt parfaits. Simply thinking beyond the core product of a hamburger led McDonald's to realize that convenience and enjoyment were reasons that its customers frequented its stores. These points became the foundation for McDonald's marketing. Today, McDonald's targets a wide range of consumer segments, from diversity groups to young people to healthy people of all ages. A recent entry into the coffee market has targeted yet another segment of the population.[14]

PHOTO: Jim Lopes/Shutterstock.

>> END EXAMPLE

Niche Marketing

The third market coverage strategy is known as the niche strategy. Also referred to as concentrated marketing, or focused marketing, **niche marketing** is serving a small but well-defined consumer segment. It is best suited for companies with limited resources, or companies with exclusive products. This approach allows companies to gain a strong position within their segments because they have a better understanding of consumer needs in those specific segments. The marketing plans for niche markets can be quite specialized.

EXAMPLE NICHE MARKETING

Movado Group, Inc., was founded in 1967 and designs, markets, and distributes jewelry and watches. The organization's portfolio includes popular watch brands such as Ebel, Concord, Movado, ESQ, Coach, HUGO BOSS, Juicy Couture, Tommy Hilfiger, and Lacoste. In 2007, Movado moved to retarget its premium offering, the almost 100-year-old Concord brand, to an even more upscale target. The Concord offering was reduced to a single line, the recently launched C1. The number of retail outlets was reduced significantly and average retail prices almost tripled to over $9,000. Concord's target was stated to be "hardcore watch aficionados and enthusiasts."[15]

PHOTO: Igor Grochev/Shutterstock.

>> END EXAMPLE

Global Targeting

There are many different ways that brands can adopt a global strategy. These methods include the following:

- Standardizing core products or services with limited localization for all markets
- Creating value-added elements for selective markets
- Practicing specific competitive-based strategies for each market
- Implementing a universal targeting strategy and marketing mix

Many luxury brands are practicing the strategy of targeting a group that exhibits similar characteristics across national boundaries. While this may be efficient, most brands are adopting some level of standardization with localization as necessary to reflect local conditions.

Selecting a Target

When choosing an appropriate market for a given product or service, three general factors should be considered:

- Attractiveness
- Size and growth potential
- Brand objectives and resources to form the basis for competition

The attractiveness of the segment is determined by the level of competition within the segment and the various strategies used by the brands competing in the segment. If many large competitors that practice differentiated marketing exist, it may be difficult for a smaller brand to stake out a particular market space. Alternatively, a small brand may have tremendous successes by entering an undifferentiated market with a specific point of differentiation.

The size and growth potential for the segment includes the variability and viability of the segment. A segment may be subjected to significant technology or legislative changes that might redefine opportunity in the near future. Brand objectives and resources represent the basis on which the company has to compete. There may be limited flexibility in the product portfolio, or there may be limited funding for advertising. Either reality might limit the potential for the brand to succeed, depending on the market being entered.

POSITIONING (pp. 139–141)

DEFINED **Positioning** *is the placement of a product or service offering in the minds of consumer targets.*

EXPLAINED

Positioning

Positioning involves the development of marketing programs to meet the requirements of target customers.[16] Ultimately, positioning is how your target customers define you in relation to your competitors. Therefore, customer perceptions have much to do with a brand's positioning. The process to establish positioning, provided you are not already positioned precisely where you want, involves competing with all your competitors' marketing communications. Communication of a **unique selling proposition (USP)** can provide a good basis for successful positioning. A USP is an expression of the uniqueness of a brand in a succinct manner. It can be a commitment that others cannot match, or it can be some distinct aspect of your product or service. There are three types of positioning:

- **Functional positioning** is based on the attributes of products or services and their corresponding benefits and is intended to communicate how customers can solve problems or fulfill needs. An example would be high quality.
- **Symbolic positioning** is based on characteristics of the brands that enhance the self-esteem of customers. An example would be the concept of physical appearance.
- **Experiential positioning** is based on characteristics of the brands that stimulate sensory or emotional connections with customers. An example would be the feeling of joy.

APPLIED

Positioning

The positioning of a brand results in a value proposition being presented to the target market. The value proposition is the entire set of benefits upon which the brand is differentiated. Similar to the USP, the value proposition is also unique. However, unlike the USP, it is intended to be specifically relevant to the target. Although a product can be unique, such as being organic or made in the United States, the brand target for that product may not value those characteristics. That same product may be of exceptionally high quality, which may be a desired benefit that could be conveyed in a value proposition. Value can be created from many different positioning strategies. Positioning strategies can be based on specific product attributes, different ways the product or service can be used, different types of users, differences between the product and a competitor's product, and a comparison to other product classes.

Sometimes a position needs to evolve, based on customer response. Federal Express invented the concept of delivering packages overnight. A significant point of differentiation was identified to be that the company owned its own fleet of planes. However, customers and potential customers did not care if Federal Express owned its own planes. Once the company determined that the primary benefit was the overnight delivery the positioning was cemented, and the success of Federal Express has been well documented.

EXAMPLE POSITIONING

The Apple iPod, with over 200 million units sold, controls the leading position in the global digital music player industry. Launched by Apple Computers in 2001, the iPod has enjoyed success from building on the Apple brand and using the Apple computer as a digital hub for consumers. The idea of a digital hub is that consumers will purchase additional Apple products to connect to their Apple computer. Beyond iPod, iTunes, iPhone, and iPad, there is iLife, iWork, iWeb, and iPhoto, not to mention Apple TV (renamed from iTV). While the iPod basically performs the same functions as the many different brands of MP3 players, it separates itself from other brands by being used by many different influential celebrities, from presidents to rock stars, and by generally being considered "cool." Being positioned as cool and being associated with celebrities have made the product iconic in countries across the world. Just as being popular has helped the iPod increase sales, it is that ubiquity that could, potentially, cause at least some of its consumers to look for less common brands of MP3s to express their individuality. That is where the digital hub strategy is designed to keep adding new and relevant products to the overall Apple offering.[17]

PHOTO: Michael Ledray/Shutterstock.

>> END EXAMPLE

Positioning is also important in an online environment. Since Internet search engines such as Google, Bing, and AltaVista have become ubiquitous, it makes sense to optimize one's position in this important medium. **Search engine optimization**, the process of enhancing Web site traffic through either organic or compensated means, can be an effective marketing tool and can assist in the positioning of your product or service during the consumer shopping process. The critical element of effective search engine optimization is the selection of the keywords, which should be based on the positioning of the product or service.

Using a Perceptual Map

A **perceptual map** defines the market, based on consumer perceptions of attributes, or characteristics, of competing products. Also referred to as a positioning chart, a perceptual map visually represents consumer perceptions of a group of brands by evaluating category attributes such as price, quality, speed, fuel economy, and appearance. Brands can be positioned in the context of competing brands on a perceptual map. The perceptual map can identify important competitors and indicate if the current positioning needs to be changed.

EXAMPLE **PERCEPTUAL MAP**

A perceptual map for the relationship between *Consumer Reports'* overall road-test scores and fuel economy ratings for a select list of compact sedans is illustrated in Figure 10.2.

This particular perceptual map combines subjective consumer road-test ratings with established fuel-economy numbers. The map could also have been constructed with two subjective criteria, such as consumer road-test ratings and consumer appearance ratings. In this example, although the Hyundai Elantra has the highest road-test score, the Toyota Prius has a similar road-test score, but with much higher fuel economy. The Toyota Corolla and Honda Civic are clear competitors for those consumers who consider road-test scores and fuel economy as the primary factors in their purchase decisions. This perceptual map assumes that road-test scores and fuel-economy ratings are the only relevant attributes in selecting a vehicle. This is seldom the case. Status, appearance, and ride could all factor into an evaluation. Still, Prius is the leading hybrid vehicle sold in the United States, and Civic and Corolla are two of the leading models in overall sales.[18]

>> END EXAMPLE

FIGURE 10.2 **A Perceptual Map**

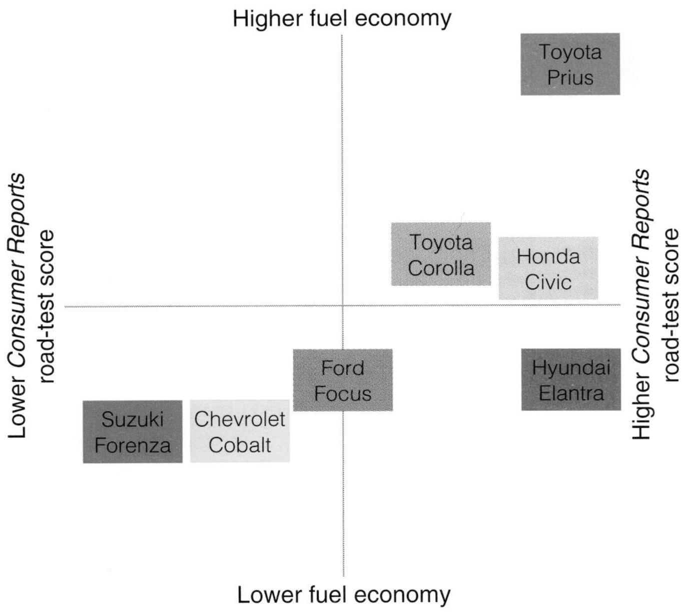

Selecting a Position

The selection of a position should reflect an understanding of the external marketing environment and the competitive advantage that can be created as a result of differentiation. It is necessary to understand how the brands, products, and services satisfy the needs of the target segment, as well as to switch costs for those target consumers who are using competitive products or services. Ultimately, the position selected should do the following:

- Deliver a valued benefit to the target
- Be distinctive with respect to competitors
- Offer a superior benefit that can easily be communicated
- Be difficult for others to copy
- Be affordable to the target
- Provide required revenues and profits to the brand

One way to communicate your position is through a brand position statement.

Developing a Brand Position Statement

The **brand position statement** is a summary of what your brand offers to the market. This statement is not seen by the public and is not the advertising tagline, although the tagline should support the brand position statement. The statement is a guide for marketing communication development and should be developed using the following form: To (consumer segment) our (brand) is (business concept) that (basis for differentiation).[19]

EXAMPLE **BRAND POSITION STATEMENT**

Focus: HOPE has been active as a Detroit-based community organization since 1967. Its brand position statement directed to potential donors is the following:

> To socially aware people and organizations who desire to financially support an organization dedicated to overcoming racism, poverty, and injustice, Focus: HOPE is the preeminent community-based organization that has a long history of addressing those issues through a holistic process by providing education and training for the disadvantaged, distributing packaged food to low-income seniors and young families, and revitalizing neighborhoods.[20]

PHOTO: Kuzma/Shutterstock.

>> **END EXAMPLE**

Visual Summary

Part 1 Explaining (Chapters 1, 2, 3, 4, 5)
Part 2 Creating (Chapters 6, 7, 8, 9)
Part 3 **Strategizing (Chapters 10, 11)**
Part 4 Managing (Chapters 12, 13, 14, 15, 16, 17)
Part 5 Integrating (Chapters 18, 19, 20)

Chapter 10 Summary

The process of segmenting, targeting, and positioning builds on concepts of building a brand and a marketing philosophy. Without a strong brand to which consumers ascribe equity and a company philosophy that places a brand at the forefront of its business, no segmentation effort can be successful. Well-crafted segmentation can provide a company with the means to efficiently identify and target consumers with a value proposition that is differentiated from its competitors. The process of identifying and selecting segments can be expensive and time-consuming, but the rewards can be significant. Ultimately, segmentation advances the marketing goals and creates an organization that grows with its customers.

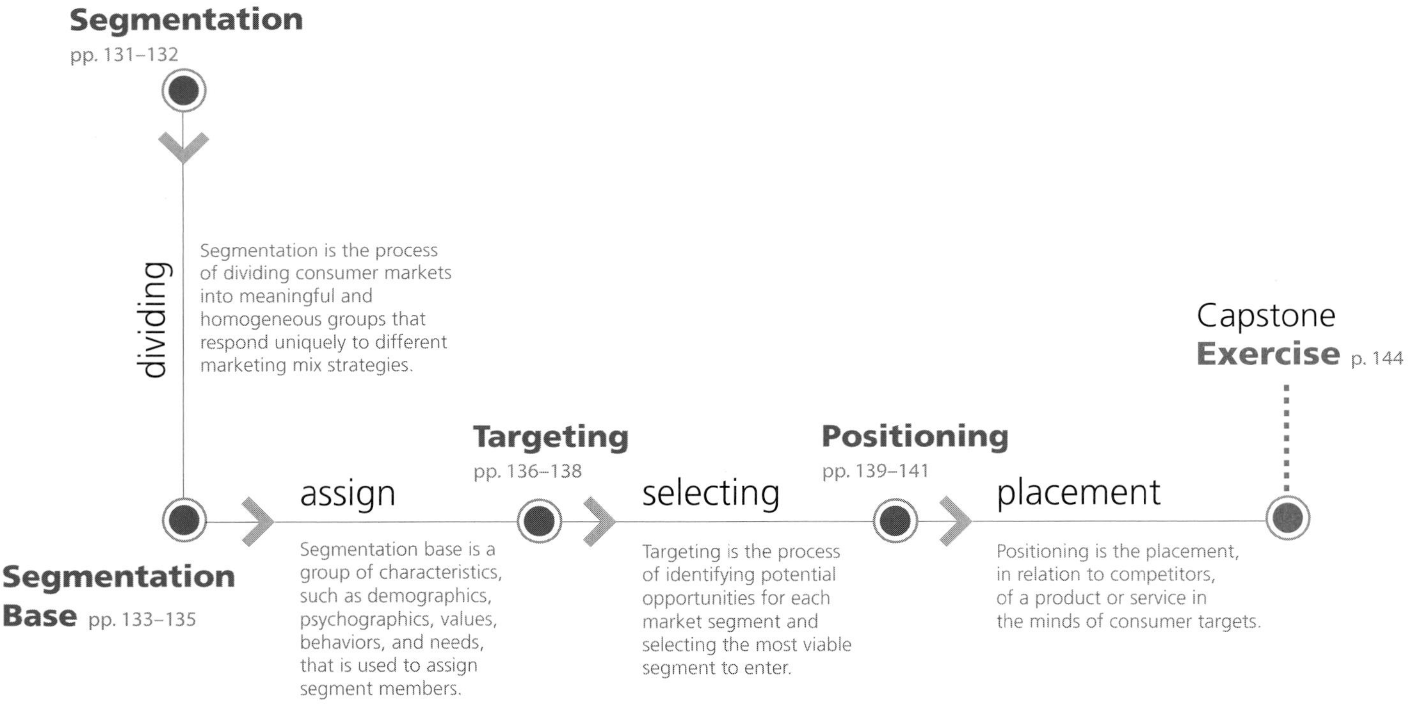
Segmentation
pp. 131–132
dividing
Segmentation is the process of dividing consumer markets into meaningful and homogeneous groups that respond uniquely to different marketing mix strategies.
Segmentation Base pp. 133–135
assign
Segmentation base is a group of characteristics, such as demographics, psychographics, values, behaviors, and needs, that is used to assign segment members.
Targeting
pp. 136–138
selecting
Targeting is the process of identifying potential opportunities for each market segment and selecting the most viable segment to enter.
Positioning
pp. 139–141
placement
Positioning is the placement, in relation to competitors, of a product or service in the minds of consumer targets.
Capstone Exercise p. 144

Chapter Key Terms

Segmentation (pp. 131–132)

Segmentation *(also referred to as* **market segmentation***) is the division of consumer markets into meaningful and distinct customer groups. (p. 131)* **Opening Example (p. 131)**

Key Term (p. 131)

Mass marketing is communicating a product or service message to as broad a group of people as possible with the purpose of positively influencing sales. **(p. 131)**

Segmentation Base (pp. 133–135)

Segmentation base *is a group of characteristics that is used to assign segment members. (p. 133)*

Key Terms (pp. 133–135)

Behavioral segmentation allocates consumers into groups based on their uses or responses to a product or service. **(p. 134)**

Demographic segmentation divides the market into groups, based on variables such as age, gender, family size, family life cycle, income, occupation, education, religion, ethnicity, generation, nationality, and sexual orientation. **(p. 133) Example: Demographic Segmentation (p. 133)**

Needs segmentation allocates consumers into groups, based on their product or service needs. **(p. 134) Example: Segmenting Business Markets (p. 135) Example: Segmenting International Markets (p. 135)**

Psychographic segmentation assigns buyers into different groups, based on lifestyle, class, or personality characteristics. **(p. 133) Example: Psychographic Segmentation (p. 134)**

Values segmentation considers what customers prefer and what motivates customer response to marketing activities. **(p. 134)**

Targeting (pp. 136–138)

Targeting *(also referred to as market targeting) is the process of evaluating and selecting the most viable market segment to enter. (p. 136)* **Example: Targeting (p. 136)**

Key Terms (pp. 136–138)

Behavioral targeting optimizes the online advertising potential for brands. **(p. 136)**

Differentiated marketing separates and targets several different market segments with a different product or service geared to each segment. **(p. 137) Example: Differentiated Marketing (p. 137)**

Niche marketing is serving a small but well-defined consumer segment. **(p. 137) Example: Niche Marketing (p. 138)**

Undifferentiated marketing is when a company treats the market as a whole, focusing on what is common to the needs of customers rather than on what is different. **(p. 137) Example: Undifferentiated Marketing (p. 137)**

Positioning (pp. 139–141)

Positioning *is the placement of a product or service offering in the minds of consumer targets. (p. 139)* **Example: Positioning (p. 139)**

Key Terms (pp. 139–141)

Brand position statement is a summary of what a brand offers to the market. **(p. 140) Example: Brand Position Statement (p. 141)**

Experiential positioning is based on characteristics of the brands that stimulate sensory or emotional connections with customers. **(p. 139)**

Functional positioning is based on the attributes of products or services and their corresponding benefits and is intended to communicate how customers can solve problems or fulfill needs. **(p. 139)**

Perceptual map defines the market, based on consumer perceptions of attributes of competing products. **(p. 140) Example: Perceptual Map (p. 140)**

Search engine optimization is the process of enhancing Web site traffic through either organic or compensated means. **(p. 140)**

Symbolic positioning is based on characteristics of the brand that enhance the self-esteem of customers. **(p. 139)**

Unique selling proposition (USP) is an expression of the uniqueness of a brand. **(p. 139)**

Capstone Exercise

In this chapter, you learned about segmenting markets and positioning your products to appeal to your best target customers. We will look in greater depth at how to apply these concepts by doing three exercises.

We will focus on another dominant consumer products company—Coca-Cola. Go to www.coca-cola.com to see the depth of products and the international areas served. Coca-Cola has 450 brands and does business in over 200 countries. Pick one of the international areas and see the brands offered there.

Go to www.virtualvender.coca-cola.com/vm/Vending.jsp to see the range of products to do the following exercises. From the virtual vendor page, pick soft drinks with all countries. Notice that the company sells 76 different brands of soft drinks worldwide. Look at each brand and notice the product description and how the company differentiates each brand in ways other than geography. This is clearly an example of differentiated marketing.

1. Think about the characteristics of the segment that Coke is trying to reach with each product. Pick four soft drinks and, based on the part of the chapter on **Segmentation Applied**, decide which of the major segmentation strategies apply and be prepared to identify which segment belongs to each product.

2. Make a perceptual map (see page 140) and plot 12 brands on this map. Remember that the trick is to think of what the axes represent.

3. Review the **Positioning Applied** section of the chapter. Decide how you want to position your four chosen brands in consumers' minds. Also decide what associations/images you want consumers to have when shown each bottle, for example, healthy, tasty, refreshing.

Application Exercise

Use the marketing concepts in this chapter to tackle and solve a marketing problem: targeting, needs segmentation, and unique selling proposition.

First, start by thinking about the pet food category and then choose a product within that category. There are many products available in stores within this category for us to consider purchasing.

The Marketing Problem

Think about your chosen product within that category after considering the following situation.

> Pet foods are becoming an important purchase for consumers and the category is becoming highly segmented. Consumers need to know what is best for their pet.

The Problem

How would you divide the category based on consumer needs? Write a list of close competitors to the product you chose in the pet food category. For each product, including the one you choose, write its unique selling proposition. Now choose a target for your product.

The Solution

Complete the following two Problem/Solution briefs using your product in the pet food category, chapter concepts, and college resources.

1. From the Marketing Manager's Point of View
   a. Problem Definition
   b. Analysis
   c. Target Market
   d. Product's USP
   e. Solution

2. From the Consumer's Point of View
   a. Problem Definition
   b. Analysis
   c. Product's USP
   d. Solution

Resources:

Marketing Defined, Explained, Applied 2e, Michael Levens
The College Library
Retail or Online Field Trip
Assigned Reading—*Brand Week*, *Advertising Age*, *WSJ*, scholarly publications, category trade journals
Blog your problem from either point of view, gather responses/posts (www.blogger.com/start)

The **Marketing Plan**

Chapter Overview At this point in the book, you have built a solid marketing foundation through explaining, creating, and strategizing fundamental aspects of marketing. This chapter provides a structure to document the marketing situation, marketing objectives, marketing strategy, and marketing initiatives through the creation of a marketing plan. Integrated throughout this chapter is a marketing plan for a fictitious company, Interior Views LLC. Interior Views, a home accessories shop specializing in fabrics and complementary services, is a relatively new company that has aggressive growth targets. Interior Views has a diverse group of competitors and distributes products both online and through a storefront location. Interior Views, which is unknown by many potential customers and deals with emerging and evolving trends, is promoting itself through a variety of media channels. This focus on Interior Views provides a vibrant example to support exploring the elements of a marketing plan.

In addition, components of the marketing plan and business plan are introduced and contrasted. In subsequent chapters, you will be introduced to management and integration issues based on specific marketing mix elements. As you are exposed to those concepts, it will be helpful to apply the framework of the marketing plan covered in this chapter to assist in building a holistic perspective on marketing.

Chapter Outline

BUSINESS PLAN (pp. 147–148)

DEFINED *A* ***business plan*** *is a written document that defines the operational and financial objectives of a business over a particular time, and defines how the business plans to accomplish those objectives.*

EXPLAINED

Business Plan

The business plan is a comprehensive document that identifies the nature of the business. Varieties of plans exist within the business plan, including the marketing plan. The business plan also contains objectives, decision-making processes, and policies. A well-crafted business plan guides optimal utilization of resources within a business. The elements of a business plan generally include the following:

- Title Page
- Executive Summary
- Business Overview
- Product or Service Overview
- Market Overview
- Competitive Overview
- Operations Overview
- Management Overview
- Financial Overview

Depending on the type of business, the business plan may include different sections. The identified sections are common for an established business. A start-up business would also need to include start-up expenses and information on capitalization. Not-for-profit businesses also benefit from developing a business plan. A not-for-profit business plan should identify the capacity of the business to benefit its customer target.

APPLIED

Business Plan

A business plan is a road map, based on current business and market understanding, to navigate the near future. It is used to guide decisions and to communicate the performance and direction of the business to potential investors and to stakeholders, people who are, or may be, affected by actions a business takes. A business plan is different from individual department plans, such as marketing or finance. A business plan identifies responsibilities of management and how those responsibilities pertain to each area. The plan also identifies the capital requirements to manage each area. Marketers contribute a variety of inputs into the business plan, including the following:

- A comprehensive review and assessment of a business's marketing environment
- An explanation of what the marketing function is attempting to achieve in support of the business plan
- A discussion on how a business intends to achieve its marketing objectives
- A process to allocate resources and monitor results

Most business plans include three types of financial statements: the income statement, cash-flow statement, and balance sheet. The income statement identifies business revenues, expenses, and profits. The cash-flow statement identifies how much cash is needed to

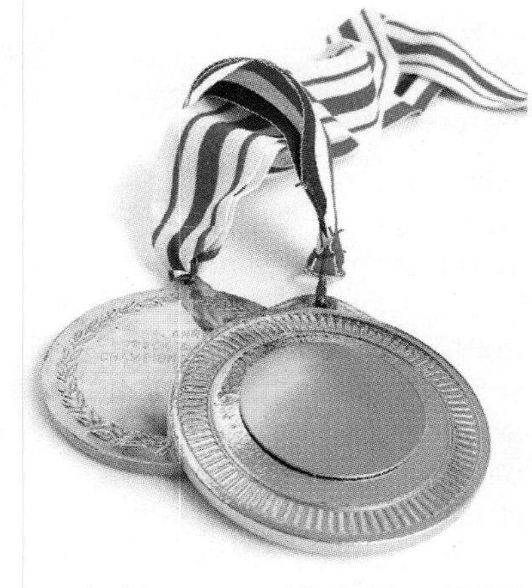

In July 2005, shortly after being awarded the 2012 Olympic Games, London began translating its bid proposal into specific plans. The London Olympics will sponsor 26 Olympic sports in 34 venues and 20 Paralympic sports in 21 venues, while hosting 10,500 Olympic athletes and 4,200 Paralympic athletes, along with 20,000 members of the press. It is anticipated that over 9 million tickets will be sold.

One specific area of planning relates to the marketing activities associated with the games. Both the London 2012 Organizing Committee and the International Olympic Committee will share in the revenues and costs, to varying extents, associated with the 2012 Olympic and Paralympic Games. The London 2012 Organizing Committee receives a share of the broadcasting revenue from the global sales of TV rights to the games and a share from The Olympic Partners program. The Olympic Partners is an International Olympic Committee program featuring companies that have purchased international marketing rights of association with the Olympic movement. Those companies include Coca-Cola, Acer, Atos Origin, GE, McDonald's, Omega, Panasonic, Samsung, and Visa. The London 2012 Organizing Committee will also receive income from domestic sponsorship, ticketing, and merchandising programs, including coins, stamps, official mascots, clothing, and pins.[1]

PHOTO: Johnny Lye.

meet financial obligations and the source of that cash. The balance sheet is used to determine the net worth, which is the assets less liabilities, of a business.

Anyone from one individual to an entire staff can create business plans. It is not the number of people involved in creating the business plan that matters, but how the various activities within a business are represented throughout the planning process. The support of the various levels of management is also essential for successful development and implementation of the business plan. Businesses should have a business plan in place at inception, and may have one well in advance of start-up if external financing is required. That plan must be reviewed on a regular basis if either external market or internal company conditions change.

EXAMPLE BUSINESS PLAN

Petfinder.com built its business plan on providing a searchable database of animals needing homes and a directory of more than 13,000 animal shelters and adoption organizations across the United States, Canada, and Mexico. Established in 1995, Petfinder claims more than 13 million adoptions. Pet lovers can search for a pet that best matches their needs from the convenience of their computer. They can then reference a shelter's Web page and learn about available services. Petfinder also includes classified ads, discussion forums, and a library of animal welfare articles. Petfinder.com was sold to Discovery Communications in 2006 as part of an acquisition strategy included in Discovery's business plan. The Web site is now part of Discovery's Animal Planet Media Enterprises and is featured on Discovery's and Animal Planet's Web sites.[2]

PHOTO: Suponev Vladimir Mihajlovich.

>> END EXAMPLE

MARKETING PLAN (pp. 149–158)

DEFINED *A* **marketing plan** *is a document that includes an assessment of the marketing situation, marketing objectives, marketing strategy, and marketing initiatives.*

EXPLAINED

Marketing Plan

A marketing plan can be an independent document, or it can be contained within a business plan. The marketing plan outlines those actions that are intended to communicate value, generate interest, and persuade target customers to purchase specific products or services. Many of the inputs to the plan come from consumer insight, marketing intelligence, marketing research, and strategic thinking. There can be one or more marketing plans, depending on the product or service portfolio. A **marketing program** is a consolidated plan of all individual marketing plans. A marketing program is intended to ration and optimize resources across brands, products, or services in a portfolio.

The marketing plan consists of six basic sections:

- Executive Summary
- Company Description, Purpose, and Goals
- Marketing Situation
- Forecasting
- Marketing Strategy
- Measurement and Controls

Creating and updating the marketing plan is the responsibility of the marketing department. Just as with business plans, the breadth of activities and levels of management represented in the marketing plan process are essential. Implementation of the marketing plan requires support of the entire business.

APPLIED

Marketing Plan

Marketing plans are used, just as are business plans, to guide decisions and provide valuable information to stakeholders. In practice, some businesses confuse the roles of the business and marketing plans, while others pay little attention to developing either plan. Still others commit resources and time to developing, implementing, and monitoring successful plans. The most successful marketing plans meet the following criteria:

- The plan is realistic and achievable.
- The plan can be measured.
- The plan has committed organizational resources for implementation.
- The plan requirements are clear.

We will now look at a marketing plan section by section. As each section of the marketing plan is introduced, the corresponding section from Interior Views LLC's marketing plan is presented.

Executive Summary

The executive summary provides a brief overview of the primary goals, recommendations, and planned actions included in the marketing plan. The executive summary is intended to communicate essential information to senior leadership and business stakeholders.

EXAMPLE INTERIOR VIEWS LLC EXECUTIVE SUMMARY

Interior Views is a home accessories shop specializing in fabrics and complementary services that is now in its third year. This destination store offers the advantage of providing fabrics specifically designed for home decorator use in fabric widths of 54 inches and greater. Over 900 fabrics are available on the floor at any time, with more than 3,000 sample fabrics available for custom "cut" orders. Customers can see, touch, feel, and take the fabric to their home as they work through their purchase decision. Market research indicates a specific and growing need in the area for the products and services Interior Views offers in the market it serves. The market strategy will be based on a cost-effective approach to reach this clearly defined target market. The three-phase approach will utilize resources to create awareness of the store and encourage customers to benefit from the convenience and services it offers. Interior Views will focus on its selection, accessibility of product, design services, and competitive pricing. The marketing objective is to actively support continued growth and profitability through effective implementation of the strategy.

PHOTO: Doroshin Oleg/Shutterstock.

>> **END EXAMPLE**

Company Description, Purpose, and Goals

The company description identifies the history of the business, its portfolio, and value proposition. The core competencies of the business, those characteristics that create a competitive advantage, are identified in this section, as is the purpose for the business to exist and its goals, both financial and nonfinancial.

EXAMPLE INTERIOR VIEWS LLC COMPANY DESCRIPTION, PURPOSE, AND GOALS

The Company—Interior Views is a home accessories shop specializing in fabrics and complementary services that is now in its third year. This destination store offers the advantages of providing fabrics specifically designed for home decorator use in fabric widths of 54 inches and greater. Over 900 fabrics are available on the floor at any time, with more than 3,000 sample fabrics available for custom "cut" orders. Customers can see, touch, feel, and take the fabric to their home as they work through their purchase decision.

Judy Wilson, the owner, is primarily responsible for marketing activities. This is in addition to her other responsibilities. She depends on outside resources for mailing (Donna at Postal Connection) and some graphic design work. Judy delegates responsibilities to Julie Hanson to assist with television advertising. Julie and the other staff members are also responsible for at least one special event throughout the year.

The Mission—Interior Views LLC is a store for discerning, quality-conscious buyers of decorator fabrics and complementary home accessories and furniture. The store celebrates the home through the color and texture of fabric. The experience informs, inspires, and shows people how to transform their home into a unique and personalized expression of themselves. Interior Views encourages people to imagine what can be and helps make their vision a reality.

The Offer—Our primary points of differentiation offer these qualities:

- The most extensive access to in-stock, first-quality decorator fabrics within 100 miles of our primary geographic market, offered at affordable prices
- The largest selection of special-order fabrics, with arrangements to have most of those products shipped to the store within 10 days of placing the order
- Personal assistance from a design-oriented staff that is qualified and capable of meeting the needs of discerning customers with high expectations
- Complementary product offerings, including hard-covering window treatments; hardware; home accessories; made-to-order upholstered furniture; and antiques that are designed, selected, and displayed in a way to emphasize the use of fabric in home design

Interior Views will qualify for the most attractive retail discount through select suppliers, offering greater profit margins and more competitive pricing for bolt purchases in quantities of 50 to 60 yards, or in half of that yardage with a "cutting fee" that increases cost per yard by an average of 50 cents. The primary product lines will include fabrics from the following textile sources:

- Robert Allen Fabrics
- Fabricut
- Waverly Fabrics
- Spectrum
- Art Mark
- Covington
- P/Kaufmann

Complementary accessories, including fabric trims, drapery hardware, and hard-covering window treatments, are supplied from the following sources:

- Hunter Douglas—Hard-window coverings
- Kirsch—Rods and selected window hardware and accessories
- Conso—Trims and fabric accessories
- Petersen-Arne—Trims and accessories
- Graber—Selected window hardware
- Grumman—Threads

Positioning—For the person creating a personalized and unique impression of his or her home, Interior Views is the best local source for selection and price points of the fabric, customer-oriented design services, and a variety of other home accessory and furniture products. Customers will be impressed with, and return for, the great in-stock selection, value-oriented pricing, and excellent customer service. Unlike JoAnn's, Warehouse Fabric, or catalogs, Interior Views is a pleasant and tasteful resource that encourages everyone in the process of decorating their home. Unlike employing an interior decorator, Interior Views allows the individual to participate in design choices to the extent he or she chooses and realize greater value for the dollars invested.

Value Proposition—Interior Views sells more than fabric; it sells a personalized and unique vision for your home. Interior Views helps you revive your home and your living experience.

Goals:

- Achieve growth rate in sales of 12% for the year 2008, to total in excess of $341,200 in total revenues
- Generate average sales per business day (305 days per year) in excess of $1,000
- Reduce the existing credit line by a minimum of $26,400
- Maintain a gross margin of 45% each month
- Generate an average of $1,000 of sales each business day each month

- Experience a $5,000 increase in quarterly sales with each newsletter
- Realize an annual growth rate of approximately 25% in the year 2008

>> END EXAMPLE

Marketing Situation

The marketing situation section includes an assessment of customers, competitors, product portfolio, distribution channel, business, and the marketing environment, including economic, political, legal, cultural, social, and technological factors. Tools such as the SWOT analysis and BCG growth-market matrix, discussed in earlier chapters, can also assist in completing the marketing situation section.

EXAMPLE INTERIOR VIEWS LLC COMPANY MARKETING SITUATION

Situation Analysis—Interior Views is a retail store heading into its third year of operation. The store has been well received, and marketing is now critical to its continued success and future profitability. The store offers the most extensive selection of in-stock decorator fabrics as well as a resource for special-ordered fabrics. The basic market need is to offer a good selection of decorator fabrics at reasonable prices, for the "do-it-yourself" and the "buy-it-yourself" customers, through a personalized retail store that offers excellent service, design assistance, and inspiration for people to redecorate their homes.

Market Needs—Interior Views is providing its customers the opportunity to create a home environment to express who they are. They can select their fabric and go in whatever direction they choose—to fabric it themselves or have it done for them. They have the opportunity to actively participate in the design, look, and feel of their home. They desire their home to be personal, unique, and tasteful as well as communicate a message about what is important to them. We seek to fulfill the following benefits that we know are important to our customers:

- **Selection**—The company carries a wide choice of current and tasteful decorator fabrics.
- **Accessibility**—The buyer can walk out of the store with the fabric needed to begin a project.
- **Customer Design Services**—Employees have a design background to make them a resource for the customer. This enables customers to benefit from suggestions regarding the selection of their fabric and related products in a manner to complement their design choice.
- **Competitive Pricing**—All products will be competitively priced in comparison to stores in the Boise, Idaho, market (best price comparison) and other channels of distribution, such as catalog sales.

The Market—We possess good information about our market, identified in Table 11.1, and know a great deal about the common attributes of our most prized and loyal customers. We will leverage this information to better understand who we serve, their specific needs, and how we can better communicate with them.

Market Demographics—The profile of the Interior Views customer consists of the following geographic, demographic, psychographic, and behavior factors:

- **Geographics**—Our immediate geographic market is the Boise area, with a population of 168,300. A 50-mile geographic area is in need of our products and services. The total targeted area population is estimated at 568,800.
- **Demographics**—The typical Interior Views customer is female, married, and has children but not necessarily at home; has attended college; has a combined income in excess of $50,000; has an age range of 35–55 years with a median age of 42; and owns a home, townhouse, and/or condominium valued at over $125,000. If the customer works from home, it's by choice in a professional/business setting. The individual belongs to one or more business, social, and/or athletic organizations, which may include:
  - Downtown Athletic Club
  - Boise Country Club
  - Junior League of Boise
  - American Business Women's Association
- We know the following regarding the profile of the typical residents of Boise:
  - 67% have lived in Boise for 7 years or more
  - 23% are between the ages of 35 and 44
  - 40% have completed some college
  - 24% are managers, professionals, and/or owners of a business
  - 53% are married
  - 65% have no children living at home
  - 56% own their residence
- **Psychographics**—The typical Interior Views customer believes the appearance of his or her home is a priority; enjoys entertaining and showing his or her home; and perceives him- or herself as creative, tasteful, and able, but seeks validation and support regarding decorating ideas

Table 11.1 Market Analysis

Potential Customers	Growth	2008	2009	2010	2011	2012
Country Club Women	25%	73,500	91,875	114,844	143,555	179,444
Boomers in Transition	20%	28,500	34,200	41,040	49,248	59,098
Professional Youngsters	18%	23,000	27,140	32,025	37,790	44,592
Home Builders	12%	18,000	20,160	22,579	25,288	28,323
Total	21%	143,000	173,375	210,488	255,881	311,457

and choices. The customer reads one or more of the following magazines:

- *Country Living*
- *Martha Stewart Living*
- *Home*
- *House Beautiful*
- *Country Home*
- *Metropolitan Home*
- *Traditional Homes*
- *Victoria*
- *Architectural Digest*
- *Elle Décor*

- **Behaviors**—The customer takes pride in having an active role in decorating his or her home. The customer's home is a form of communicating "who he or she is" to others. Comparisons within social groups are made on an ongoing basis, but rarely discussed.

Market Trends—The home textile market, considered to include sheets, towels, draperies, carpets, blankets, and upholstery, accounts for 37% of all textile output. The trade publication *Home Textiles Today* estimates the size of the U.S. home textiles market at the wholesale level, excluding carpets, to be between $6.5 billion and $7 billion annually. The industry is expected to realize a steady increase over the next few years.

The industry is driven by the number of "household formations," which is expected to continue for several years. This is primarily due to the solid growth in the number of single-parent and nonfamily households. This growth also comes from baby boomers needing bigger houses to accommodate growing and extended families and, as people get older, they are buying homes rather than renting to realize tax and equity-building benefits. Favorable mortgage rates will also enable others to invest in their existing home.

The "do-it-yourself" (DIY) market continues to grow and closely parallels the professional home-improvement market. DIY market growth is attributed to an increased presence of products, the personal satisfaction experienced, and the cost savings customers realize. A portion of the do-it-yourself market is the "buy-it-yourself" (BIY) market. Consumers are buying the product and arranging for someone else to do the fabrication and/or installation. This is more expensive than the do-it-yourself approach, but less costly than buying finished products from other sources.

Market Growth—The publication *American Demographics* projected the number of U.S. households will grow by 16% between 1995 and the year 2010, an increase from 98.5 million to 115 million. Of the households composed of people from 35 to 44 years old, almost half are married couples with children under the age of 18. Based on research by *American Demographics*, households in the 45 to 65 age range are anticipated to increase 32% from 2000 totals to 45 million in 2010 as baby boomers add to this peak-earning and spending age group. With approximately 46.2% of the nation's 93.3 million dwellings built before 1960, many of these homeowners are also expected to update. These factors contribute to an increased need for home decorator fabrics for window treatment, upholstering, pillows, bedding, and other fabric accessory needs.

One important factor is that married couples in the 35 to 65 age range represent a growth segment and enjoy larger incomes than other family structures. They enjoy the choice to spend their disposable income on life's amenities. They may demonstrate "cocooning" by making their home a more comfortable and attractive haven. They choose to spend resources here rather than on vacations and other discretionary options. This group represents a larger subsegment of the target market.

Macroenvironment—The following trends and issues influence the success of Interior Views:

- **National economic health**—The store does better when the country experiences "good times" regardless of its direct impact on the local economy. Sales decrease when the stock market falls. An upbeat State of the Union address correlates with an increase in sales.
- **New home construction activity**—More closely related to what is taking place in our local economy, new home construction has a significant impact on sales across all product lines.
- **Shifts in design trends**—Major changes in design trends increase sales. The Boise market lags behind metropolitan design trends by 6 to 12 months. This offers a buying advantage for the store, offering a preview of what is coming and how we should adjust our in-stock inventory.

SWOT Analysis—The following SWOT analysis captures the key strengths and weaknesses within the company and describes the opportunities and threats facing Interior Views.

- **Strengths**
  - Strong relationships with suppliers that offer credit arrangements, flexibility, and response to special product requirements
  - Excellent and stable staff, offering personalized customer service
  - Great retail space that offers flexibility with a positive and attractive atmosphere
  - Strong merchandising and product presentation
  - Good referral relationships with complementary vendors, local realtors, and some designers
  - In-store complementary products through "The Window Seat" and "Antique Bureau" add interest, stability, and revenue
  - High customer loyalty among repeat and high-dollar purchase customers
- **Weaknesses**
  - Access to capital
  - Cash flow continues to be unpredictable
  - Owners are still climbing the "retail experience curve"
  - Location is not in a heavily traveled, traditional retail area
  - Challenges of the seasonality of the business
- **Opportunities**
  - Growing market with a significant percentage of our target market still not knowing we exist
  - Continuing opportunity through strategic alliances for referrals and marketing activities
  - Benefiting from high levels of new home construction

- Changes in design trends can initiate updating and therefore sales
- Increasing sales opportunities beyond our "100-mile" target area
- Internet potential for selling products to other markets

- **Threats**
  - Competition from a national store, or a store with greater financing or product resources could enter the market
  - Catalog resources, including Calico Corners and Pottery Barn, are aggressively priced with comparable products
  - Continued price pressure, reducing contribution margins
  - Dramatic changes in design, including fabric colors and styles, creates obsolete or less profitable inventory

Competition—Competition in the area of decorator fabric comes from three general categories: traditional fabric retail stores, catalog sales, and discounters. The other local fabric retailers are direct competition, but we have seen strong indirect competition from catalog sales and discounters.

- **Retail Stores**
  - **House of Fabrics**—Nationwide recognition and buying power of numerous types of dated fabric with strong product availability. This store has experienced financial difficulty in recent years and has closed several locations throughout the country.
  - **Warehouse Fabrics**—Locally owned, offering low-cost products with a wide selection of discontinued fabrics and only a limited number of "current" fabrics. This warehouse concept offers marginal customer service with what many "upper-end" customers consider to be an "undesirable" shopping environment.
  - **JoAnn's**—Nationwide chain with strong buying power. The company has a broad fabric selection for clothing with a limited number of in-store decorator fabrics available. Its primary target market is the clothing seamstress, with an increasing emphasis on craft items.
  - **Interior Designers**—Interior Designers make profit off markup of fabric in addition to its hourly services charges. Its costs per yard are typically higher since they do not benefit from retail or volume discounts. Therefore, the costs to the customer are often two to four times higher than the price per yard from Interior Views.
  - **Web site providers**—Fabric sales over the Web are limited at this time, and this will be a source of competition for the future to watch. Currently, there is no measurable impact on our market through competitive Web sites.
- **Catalog Competitors**—An increasing level of competition is anticipated from catalog sales. Recent trends, such as those demonstrated in the well-established but evolving catalog *Pottery Barn*, indicate increased interest in offering decorator fabric, window designs, and other home decorating products through this increasingly popular channel of distribution. Catalog sources do not offer customers the option to see, touch, and have the fabric in their homes. Price is the most significant competitive factor this product source presents. The most aggressive catalog competitor is *Calico Corners* followed by *Pottery Barn* and other home-accessory-based providers.
- **Discounters**—Channels of distribution continue to shift in favor of discounters, who account for a significant portion of the growth in the industry. As consumers experience lower levels of disposable income, discounters leverage frequent store promotions to entice frugal, value-oriented consumers. One of the biggest criticisms of discounters is their failure to offer a quality service experience and their failure to present inviting displays to promote sales. These discounters, along with specialty store chains, present one of the most severe competitive threats for individually owned specialty stores. This is partially due to extensive promotional efforts, price advantages, and established relationships with their vendors. One example of these discounters is the "home improvement" chains, such as Home Base. This aggressive retailer has adopted a strategy to include complete decorator departments in their metropolitan stores. Currently existing in the Los Angeles market, this strategy is anticipated to be introduced into the Seattle area and other select metropolitan markets within the year. Although the Boise Home Base store sells basic curtain rod hardware and other hard-cover window treatment, there are no known plans at this time for the Boise Home Base store to implement this in the foreseeable future. This will be an important issue to monitor for competitive purposes.

>> END EXAMPLE

Forecasting

The forecasting section includes the anticipated outcomes based on achieving predefined marketing goals. Revenues and expenses are both forecasted in this section. A mix of judgment and data analysis is used to consider past performance and the characteristics influencing that performance, as well as current and future opportunities and threats. The outcome of the forecasting process is essential when exploring alternative marketing strategies.

EXAMPLE INTERIOR VIEWS LLC FORECASTING

Financials—Our marketing strategy is based on becoming the resource of choice for people looking for decorator fabrics, do-it-yourself, and buy-it-yourself resources to create a look in their home. Our marketing strategy is based on superior performance in the following areas:

- Product selection
- Product quality
- Customer service

Our marketing strategy will create awareness, interest, and appeal from our target market for what Interior Views offers our customers.

This section will offer a financial overview of Interior Views as it relates to our marketing activities. We will address break-even information, sales forecasts, expense forecasts, and how those link to our marketing strategy.

- **Break-even analysis**—The break-even analysis (detailed in Tables 11.2 and 11.3) illustrates the number of single sales, or units, that we must realize to break even. This is based on average sale and costs per transaction.

Table 11.2 Fixed Costs

Utilities	$ 400
Web Site Hosting	200
Recurring Marketing Expenses	1,200
Payroll	6,000
Rent	1,500
Total	$9,300

Table 11.3 Break-Even Analysis

Monthly Revenue Break-even	$20,427
Assumptions:	
Average Percent Variable Cost	54%
Estimated Monthly Fixed Costs	$ 9,300

- **Sales Forecast**—The sales forecast (Table 11.4) is broken down into the four main revenue streams: direct sales, Web sales, consignment sales, and sublease revenues. The sales forecast for the upcoming year is based on a 25% growth rate. This is a slower growth rate than what was experienced in previous years at 33%, and also less than what is expected for future sales, estimated to be approximately 28%. These projections appear attainable and take the increasing base into consideration. Future growth rates are based on percentage increases as follows:
  - Direct sales: 20% growth rate per year
  - Web sales: 50% growth rate per year
  - Consignment sales: 20% growth rate per year
  - Sublease revenues: 10% growth rate per year
- **Expense Forecast**—Marketing expenses (Table 11.5) are to be budgeted at approximately 5% of total sales. Expenses are tracked in the major marketing categories of television advertisements, newspaper advertisements, the newsletter and postcard mailings, Web marketing support, printed promotional materials, public relations, and other.

Table 11.4 Sales Forecast

Sales	**2008**	**2009**	**2010**	**2011**	**2012**
Direct Sales	$322,000	$386,400	$463,700	$556,400	$667,700
Web Sales	12,500	18,750	28,125	42,190	63,280
Consignment Sales	1,360	1,632	1,960	2,350	2,820
Sublease Revenue	5,340	5,600	6,165	6,780	7,460
Subtotal Sales	$341,200	$412,382	$499,950	$607,720	$741,260
Direct Cost of Sales	**2008**	**2009**	**2010**	**2011**	**2012**
Direct Sales	$178,850	$214,000	$255,500	$307,000	$370,000
Web Sales	6,875	10,400	12,000	18,000	20,000
Consignment Sales	71	85	102	123	150
Sublease Revenue	60	66	73	80	88
Subtotal Direct Cost of Sales	$185,856	$224,551	$267,675	$325,203	$390,238

Table 11.5 Marketing Expense Budget

Expenses	**2008**	**2009**	**2010**	**2011**	**2012**
Television Ads	$ 3,900	$ 4,600	$ 5,620	$ 6,740	$ 8,200
Newspaper Ads	1,800	2,160	2,592	3,110	3,800
Newsletter/Postcard	6,450	7,700	9,200	11,150	13,400
Printed Promotional Materials	960	1,150	1,380	1,660	2,000
Web Marketing/Support	1,500	1,950	2,535	3,295	4,300
Public Relations	240	345	415	500	600
Promotional Events	1,700	1,950	2,300	2,800	3,400
Web Site Expenses	2,400	2,600	2,800	3,000	3,000
Other	400	480	575	700	850
Total Sales and Marketing Exp.	$19,350	$22,935	$27,417	$32,955	$39,550
Percentage of Sales	5.67%	5.56%	5.48%	5.42%	5.32%

Marketing expenses are evenly allocated based on the type of inventory in the store. Marketing expenses are allocated 60% to invest in our current customer base, 30% in prospective customers that match our known profile, and 10% in creating greater awareness in the community. A key component of our marketing plan is to try to keep gross margins at or above 45%.

>> END EXAMPLE

Marketing Strategy

The marketing strategy section identifies the procedures that businesses intend to follow to meet their marketing objectives. The section also identifies the target market, positioning, marketing-mix strategies, and investment requirements. An example might be a company targeting 25- to 35-year-old females with a new personal care product that is positioned as a premium offer against the current market leader. If the brand is new, then the expenditure might be significant to support a wide range of marketing-mix strategies. Detailed marketing-mix strategies, including product, promotion, distribution, and pricing, will be discussed in subsequent chapters.

EXAMPLE INTERIOR VIEWS LLC MARKETING STRATEGY

Target Market Strategy—The target markets are separated into four segments: Country Club Women, Boomers in Transition, Professional Youngsters, and Home Builders. The primary marketing opportunity is selling to these well-defined and accessible target market segments that focus on investing discretionary income in these areas:

- **Country Club Women**—The most dominant segment of the four is composed of women in the age range of 35 to 50. They are married, have a combined income of greater than $80,000, own at least one home or condominium, and are socially active at and away from home. They are members of the Boise Country Club, the Downtown Athletic Club, the Junior League of Boise, AAUW, and/or the Doctor Wives Auxiliary. They have discretionary income, and their home and how it looks are priorities. The appearance of where they live communicates who they are and what is important to them. This group represents the largest collection of "Martha Stewart Wannabees," with their profile echoing readers of *Martha Stewart Living* magazine, based on the current demographics described in the *Martha Stewart Living Media Kit.*
- **Boomers in Transition**—This group, typically ranging in age from 50 to 65, is going through a positive and planned life transition. The members of the group are changing homes (either building or moving) or remodeling due to empty nest syndrome, retirement plans, general downsizing desires, or to just get closer to the golf course. Their surprisingly high level of discretionary income is first spent on travel, with decorating their home a close second. The woman of the couple is the decision maker, and often does not include the husband in the selection or purchase process.
- **Professional Youngsters**—Couples between the ages of 25 and 35 establishing their first "adult" household fall into this group. They both work, earn in excess of $50,000 annually, and now want to invest in their home. They seek to enjoy their home and communicate a "successful" image and message to their contemporaries. They buy big when they have received a promotion, a bonus, or an inheritance.
- **Home Builders**—People in the building process, typically ranging in age from 40 to 60, are prime candidates for Interior Views.

Messaging—Interior Views can help you create the personalized and unique vision you have for your home, with the best local source for fabric selection and price, customer-oriented design services, and a variety of other home accessory and furniture products. Revive your home today! Table 11.6 identifies messaging for each target market.

Branding—Our name is our brand. "Interior Views" represents our mission of celebrating the home through the color and texture of fabric. The brand invokes the fact that the home should be a unique and personalized expression of the person living there. The home is a "view" of the home's owner. The word "view" also evokes the vision of what a homeowner wants his or her home to be. In addition to our name, our logo reflects the architectural quality of the work that we do. Our products are more than just decoration; they enhance and reflect the home itself.

Objectives and Strategies—The single objective is to position Interior Views as the premier source for home decorator fabrics in the Greater Boise area, commanding a majority of the market share within six years of being founded. The marketing strategy will seek to first create customer awareness regarding the products and services offered, develop that customer base, establish connections with targeted markets, and work toward building customer loyalty and referrals. Interior Views's four main marketing strategies are as follows:

- Increased awareness and image
- Leveraging existing customer base
- Cross selling
- New home construction promotion

Marketing Mix—Our marketing mix is composed of these approaches to pricing, distribution, advertising and promotion, and customer service.

- **Pricing**—A keystone pricing formula plus $3 will be applied for most fabrics. The goal is to have price points within 5% of the list price of Calico Corners' retail prices. This insures competitive pricing and strong margins.

Table 11.6 Target Market Messaging

Country Club Women	Make your home new again
Boomers in Transition	It's time for a new look
Professional Youngsters	It's your first home—make it yours
Home Builders	Presentation is everything

- **Distribution**—All product is distributed through the retail store. The store does receive phone orders from established customers and we will be developing a Web site.
- **Advertising and Promotion**—The most successful advertising has been through the *Boise Herald* and through ads on *Martha Stewart* and *Interior Motives* television shows. The quarterly newsletter has also proven to be an excellent method to connect with the existing customer base, now with a mailing list of 4,300 people.
- **Customer Service**—Excellent, personalized, fun, one-of-a-kind customer service is essential. This is perhaps the only attribute that cannot be duplicated by any competitor.
- **Product Marketing**—Our products enable our customers to experience support, gather ideas and options, and accomplish their decorating goals. They will be able to create a look that is truly unique to their home. They will not be able to do this in the same way through any other resource.
- **Pricing**—Product pricing is based on offering high value to our customers compared to most price points in the market. Value is determined based on the best quality available, convenience, and timeliness in acquiring the product. We will consistently be below the price points offered through interior designers and consistently above prices offered through the warehouse/seconds retail stores, but we will offer better quality and selection.
- **Promotion**—Our most successful advertising and promotion in the past has been through the following:
  - **Newspaper Advertisements**—*Boise Herald*
  - **Television Advertisements**—*Martha Stewart* and *Interior Motives* television shows
  - **Quarterly Newsletter and Postcard**—A direct-mail, 4-page newsletter distributed to the customer mailing list generated from people completing the "register" sign-up list in the store. The mailing list now totals more than 4,300 people.
  - **In-Store Classes**—"How-to" classes, most of which are free, have been successful because of the traffic and sales they generate after the class. The most popular classes are typically 90 minutes in length and held on Saturday.
- **Advertising**—Expand newspaper advertisements to surrounding towns, and buy two half-page ads every month. Continue television ads.
- **Public Relations**—Our public relations plan is to pitch a twice-monthly column in the "Home" section of the local paper, covering our in-store classes, with profiles of our customers and their redecorated rooms. Readers will see how our classes directly relate to individual decorating projects.
- **Direct Marketing**—Improve the quality of the newsletter, increase the number of one-time customers who sign up for it, and offer an email-newsletter option to catch the more tech-savvy customers.
- **Web Plan**—Over 1,000 fabrics are available on the floor at any time with more than 8,000 sample fabrics for custom orders. The goal of this Web plan is to extend the reach of the store to others outside the area and add to the revenue base. Interior Views currently has a Web site but has not given it the attention or focus needed to assess its marketing potential. The site offers basic functions and we consider it to be a crude version of what we can imagine it will become through a site redesign that will produce revenue and enhance the image of the business. Market research indicates a specific and growing need in the area for the products and services Interior Views offers in the market it serves and there are indications that Web sales will play an increasing role in connecting customers with sellers. The most significant challenge is that the core target customer, women between the ages of 35 and 50, are some of the least likely of groups to shop on the Web. Shopping for decorator fabric presents an additional challenge. The online marketing objective is to actively support continued growth and profitability of Interior Views through effective implementation of the strategy. The online marketing and sales strategy will be based on a cost-effective approach to reach additional customers over the Web to generate attention and revenue for the business. The Web target groups will include the more Web-savvy younger customer base that the store currently serves (women between the ages of 25 and 35) and out-of-area potential customers who are already shopping on the Web for the products Interior Views offers. The Web site will focus on its selection, competitive pricing, and customer service to differentiate itself among other Internet options.
- **Web Site Goals**—Our Web site will generate revenue through initiating product sales to the targeted audience that we would not have realized through the retail store. It will be measured based on revenue generated each month compared to our stated objective. On a secondary basis, we will also measure and track traffic to the site and document what activities that traffic contributes to the other objectives of the site, including sales leads and information dissemination.
- **Objectives**—Increase revenues through Web-based sales by $2,400 per month with a 5% growth rate thereafter. Enhance "information channels" with the established customer base to provide additional options to receive information from the store. Meet the needs of customers outside the immediate serving area through Web accessibility.
- **Web Site Marketing Strategy**—Our Web site strategy will be to reach these key groups listed in order of importance based on their expected use and purchases from the site.
  1. **Professional Youngsters**—Expected to be the most likely of the targeted segments to use this resource because of their relatively high Internet use compared to the other segments. This group should offer the greatest online revenue opportunity.
  2. **Outsiders**—Composed of people outside the area with Internet access who have come in contact with the physical store or learned of it through a referral or promotion. This group, most commonly located in rural areas of the Western United States and Hawaii, is expected to be a small but faithful sector of buyers.

3. **Online Fabric Shoppers**—Most often find the site through search engines; these online decorator fabric shoppers are browsing multiple sites for a best buy or access to discontinued and hard-to-find fabric. They hold potential, but are typically the most work for the lowest return.
4. **Internet Learners**—Represents all of the targeted segments that are just beginning to become familiar with the site and will increase their use of the Internet over time. Revenue expectations from this group are low at this point and it is viewed as an investment in the future.

Three Web strategies have been developed:

Strategy #1—Increasing Awareness and Image
Informing those not yet aware of what Interior Views offers.

- Search engine presence
- Leveraging the newsletter and mailing programs

Strategy #2—Leveraging Existing Internet-Savvy Customers
Our best sales in the future will come from our current customer base.

- Newsletter information
- Web-only promotions

Strategy #3—Upselling and Cross-selling Activities
Increasing the average dollar amount per transaction.

- Additional and complementary fabric
- Other product sales:
  - Additional sales of trims, notions, and accessories
  - Promoting sales of furniture

Service—The first goal is to recognize everyone as they come into the store. If the person is a repeat customer, he or she is referred to by name. If he or she is a new customer, the person is asked, "How did you hear about us?" Help is always available and never invasive. The store is staffed to be able to dedicate time and energy to customers who want assistance when they need it. The store is designed so a customer can sit as long as he or she wants to look at books, fabric samples, and review the resources in the store. The customer's children are also welcome, with a television, VCR, and toys available in the children's area in clear view of the resource center. We provide service in a way that no other competitive retail store can touch. It is one of our greatest assets and points of differentiation. Insight, ideas, inspiration, and fun are the goals. Repeat, high-dollar purchases from loyal customers are the desired end product.

Implementation Schedule—Table 11.7 identifies the key activities that are critical to our marketing plan. It is important to accomplish each one on time and on budget.

>> **END EXAMPLE**

Measurement and Controls

The measuring and control section identifies the process to monitor achievement of the marketing objectives. The objectives are attained through successful implementation of the marketing strategies. Measuring and controlling consider both financial and nonfinancial factors. Underperforming products and services can be identified and necessary actions taken in context to overall marketing objectives. Information can be collected and processed through market intelligence systems to address a wide range of issues, from customer satisfaction to loyalty. Operational control, considering results with respect to the stated marketing plan or marketing program, and strategic control, considering the appropriateness of overall strategies based on internal and external conditions, should be addressed in this section.

EXAMPLE INTERIOR VIEWS LLC MEASUREMENT AND CONTROLS

Controls—The following will enable us to keep on track. If we fail in any of these areas, we will need to reevaluate our business model:

- Gross margins at or above 45%
- Month-to-month annual comparisons indicate an increase of 20% or greater
- Do not depend on the credit line to meet cash requirements

Table 11.7 Milestones

Marketing Activity	Start Date	End Date	Budget	Manager
Marketing Budget			$20,000	Tara
Television Ads	February 1	February 20	$ 3,000	Julie
Newspaper Ads	March 15	April 15	$ 1,000	Julie
Newsletter/Postcard	May 1	May 21	$ 3,000	Kandi
Special Event	June 10	June 10	$ 700	Julie
Printed Promotional Materials	July 13	July 26	$ 2,000	Kandi
Web Marketing/Support	August 1	August 30	$ 2,000	Pat
Public Relations	August 15	August 15	$ 300	Julie
Newsletter/Postcard	September 13	October 1	$ 3,000	Kandi
Promotional Events	Ongoing		$ 2,000	Kandi
Web Site Expenses	Ongoing		$ 3,000	Pat

- Continue to pay down the credit line at a minimum of $24,000 per year
- Retain customers to generate repeat purchases and referrals
- Generate average sales in excess of $1,000 per business day

Implementation—We will manage implementation by having a weekly milestones meeting with the entire staff to make sure that we are on track with our milestones and readjust our goals as we gather new data. Once a quarter, we will review this marketing plan to ensure that we stay focused on our marketing strategy and that we are not distracted by opportunities simply because they are different from what we are currently pursuing.

Market Research—The staff notes customer responses to the "How did you hear about us?" question. We attempt to correlate that with our advertising and promotional activities and referral-generation programs. The store suggestion box is another method to gain additional information from customers. Some of the most productive questions are as follows:

- What suggestions do you have to improve the store?
- Why did you visit the store today?
- What other products or services would you like to have available in the store?

We continually shop other stores. We visit each store in our market at least once each quarter for competitive information, we also visit stores in the nearby Seattle and Portland markets for merchandising and buying insight, and we subscribe to every catalog we know that has decorator fabrics as any part of their product line.

Contingency Planning

- **Difficulties and Risks**
  - Slow sales resulting in less-than-projected cash flow
  - Unexpected and excessive cost increases compared to the forecasted sales
  - Overly aggressive and debilitating actions by competitors
  - A parallel entry by a new competitor
- **Worst Case Risks Might Include**
  - Determining the business cannot support itself on an ongoing basis
  - Having to liquidate the inventory to pay back the bank loan
  - Locating a tenant to occupy the leased space for the duration of the five-year lease
  - Losing the assets of the investors used for collateral
  - Dealing with the financial, business, and personal devastation of the store's failure

CRM Plans—Our best sales in the future will come from our current customer base. In order to build this customer base, we need to provide exceptional customer service when customers visit the store, have regular follow-up correspondence to thank them for their business (as well as to notify them of special promotions, etc.), and provide personal shopper support so that each visit to the store meets their needs. In order to keep track of these activities, we will need to create a spreadsheet showing follow-up correspondence with customers and what, if any, feedback we have received from them. At least quarterly, we will plan to meet and discuss if we are, in fact, retaining our current customers and whether that base has grown, or what changes may need to be made.

SOURCE: Adapted from a sample plan provided by and copyrighted by Palo Alto Software, Inc. This plan was created using Marketing Plan Pro®.

>> **END EXAMPLE**

EXAMPLE MARKETING PLAN

Bombardier Flexjet, Bombardier Aerospace fractional jet ownership activity, and Bombardier Skyjet, an online booking service, created a strategic marketing agreement with Ultimate Resorts, a destination resort service. Each has named the other the "official" service for their businesses. The marketing plan application is for each business to increase access to the other's customers.[3]

PHOTO: Dragan Trifunovic.

>> **END EXAMPLE**

Visual Summary

Chapter 11 Summary

By building on explaining, creating, and strategizing fundamental aspects of marketing, this chapter provides a structure to develop a marketing plan. The relationship between the business plan and marketing plan is discussed. A business plan is different from individual department plans, such as those for marketing or finance. A business plan identifies the responsibilities of general management as they pertain to each functional area and identifies the capital requirements to manage each area. The marketing plan outlines actions that are intended to communicate value, generate interest, and persuade target customers to purchase specific products or services. The marketing plan consists of six basic sections:

- Executive Summary
- Company Description, Purpose, and Goals
- Marketing Situation
- Objectives and Forecasting
- Marketing Strategy
- Measurement and Controls

The most successful marketing plans meet several criteria:

- The plan is realistic and achievable.
- The plan can be measured.
- The plan has committed organizational resources for implementation.
- The plan requirements are clear.

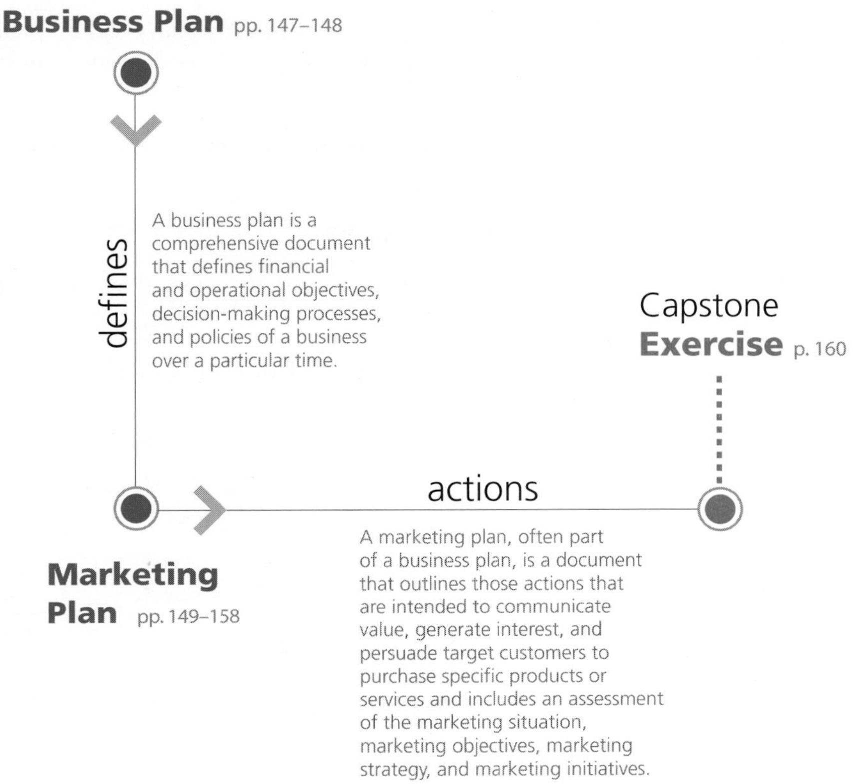
Business Plan pp. 147–148
defines
A business plan is a comprehensive document that defines financial and operational objectives, decision-making processes, and policies of a business over a particular time.
Capstone Exercise p. 160
actions
Marketing Plan pp. 149–158
A marketing plan, often part of a business plan, is a document that outlines those actions that are intended to communicate value, generate interest, and persuade target customers to purchase specific products or services and includes an assessment of the marketing situation, marketing objectives, marketing strategy, and marketing initiatives.

Chapter Key Terms

Business Plan (pp. 147–148)

Business plan *is a written document that defines the operational and financial objectives of a business over a particular time, and how the business plans to accomplish those objectives. (p. 147)* **Example: Business Plan (p. 148)**

Marketing Plan (pp. 149–158)

Marketing plan *is a document that includes an assessment of the marketing situation, marketing objectives, marketing strategy, and marketing initiatives. (p. 149)* **Example: Interior Views LLC Executive Summary (pp. 149–150) Example: Marketing Plan (p. 158)**

Key Term (p. 149)

Marketing program is a consolidated plan of all individual marketing plans. **(p. 149)**

Capstone Exercise

The Inn at Prescott Ranch is a small, boutique hotel located in Prescott, Arizona. It opened in 1998. The Inn has identified its main competition as the Prescott Resort, owned and operated by the Yavapai Nation, and the Hassayampa Inn, a historic hotel in downtown Prescott, adjacent to Whiskey Row.

The Inn has 65 rooms on two floors, each with a private balcony. The nightly room rates are the highest in Prescott. The Inn offers a full array of amenities both in the public areas and in the rooms. The Inn offers complimentary van service to the Gateway Mall, Bucky's Casino, and Whiskey Row, as well as complimentary valet parking services with covered parking. There is nightly entertainment in the lobby. In-room amenities include high-thread-count linens, terry robes, organic soaps and toiletries, flat-screen TVs with DVD players, and Bose stereo systems.

The Inn maintains a full bar and has an agreement with Wildflower Bakery to provide daily continental breakfast either as an additional charge to nightly rates or included in the Bed & Breakfast Special. Boxed lunches may also be pre-ordered from Wildflower Bakery.

The Inn is not "flagged" or branded. The management is highly involved in local organizations. There is an existing contract with Yavapai College for sponsorship of its performing arts series and with Paramount Studies for a project being filmed in the Prescott area. In addition, the Inn at Prescott Ranch has been featured on *Arizona Highways TV*, *Arizona Highways* magazine, and in the *Arizona Republic* travel section. The Inn also participates in the local chamber of commerce and tourism promotional efforts for the Prescott area.

Management is looking for a marketing plan for 2011.

1. If you were preparing a marketing plan for this hotel, how would you describe the company, its positioning strategy, and its value proposition?
2. What do you want to know about the market—demographics and psychographics?
3. Describe each of the 4Ps.
4. Without doing further research, who is the perceived target market?
5. Does the hotel have a brand image? If so, define.

Application Exercise

Use the marketing concepts in this chapter to tackle and solve a marketing problem: marketing plan, marketing situation, and marketing objectives.

First, start by thinking about the skin care category. The skin care category is large and contains products including soap, sunscreen, anti-aging cream, lip balm, lotion, and moisturizers. Choose a product within that category. There are many products available for us to consider purchasing.

The Marketing Problem

Think about your chosen product after considering the following situation.

> The skincare industry is highly competitive and has begun to target U.S. men as key users. Male consumers, most being fairly new to the category, need to know which manufacturer and which product represents the best choice for them.

The Problem

Your target market is U.S. men 18 to 24 years old. Think about the important elements of a sample marketing plan of the product you have chosen. Write a description of your marketing situation first, then provide three marketing objectives for your marketing plan.

The Solution

Complete the following two problem/solution briefs using your product in the skin care category, chapter concepts, and college resources.

1. From the Marketing Manager's Point of View
   a. Problem Definition
   b. Analysis
   c. Target Market
   d. Marketing Situation, Objectives
   e. Solution

2. From the Consumer's Point of View
   a. Problem Definition
   b. Analysis
   c. Product's Value
   d. Solution

Resources:

Marketing Defined, Explained, Applied, Michael Levens, 2e
The College Library
Retail or Online Field Trip
Assigned Reading—*Brand Week*, *Advertising Age*, *WSJ*, scholarly publications, category trade journals
Blog your problem from either point of view, gather responses/posts (www.blogger.com/start)

Product and **Service** Strategies

Chapter Overview The previous chapters explained how companies select target customers, position their brands, and construct a marketing plan. This chapter discusses how firms implement their marketing plan through product and service strategies. This effort involves effective management of new product development, a product portfolio, and the product life cycle.

Chapter Outline

PRODUCTS AND SERVICES (pp. 163–168)

DEFINED **Products** *are items consumed for personal or business use.* **Services** *are activities that deliver benefits to consumers or businesses.*

EXPLAINED

Products and Services

In the United States, tens of thousands of new products are introduced every year: shampoos, video games, soups, T-shirts, credit cards, and home security systems, to name just a few. Every product is defined by a set of **attributes** that include its features, functions, benefits, and uses. For example, the Dyson DC07 vacuum cleaner has a brush control (a feature) that deactivates its brushes at the touch of a button (a function). This feature helps protect delicate rugs (a benefit) when vacuuming carpets and other floor surfaces (a product use). The following are other examples of product attributes: product design (including visual appearance and ease of use), brand name, level of quality and dependability, logos or identifiers, packaging, and warranty.

The basic purpose of a product is to deliver benefits to consumers. **Benefits** define a product's utility, or what that product *does* for a customer. When choosing between two or more products, consumers evaluate the attributes and benefits of each. They select the product that offers them the maximum set of benefits.

The term "product" is often used as an umbrella term to refer to both goods and services. According to the Central Intelligence Agency World Factbook, services produced by private industry accounted for 76.9% of the U.S. gross domestic product in 2009.[1] Products can be thought of as falling on a continuum, from pure goods (for example, a hairbrush) to pure services (for example, a haircut). Most products are neither purely goods nor purely services, but a blend of both. Products that appear on the surface to be pure goods usually contain services, like the lifetime warranty on a Craftsman hammer. And services are often associated with goods, such as souvenir T-shirts at a Coldplay concert.

Four ways in which services differ from physical goods are as follows:

- **Intangibility**—A service cannot be perceived by the five senses before it is purchased and delivered.
- **Inseparability**—A service cannot be separated from whomever is providing the service. It must be bought, and then produced and used simultaneously.
- **Variability**—Service quality is sometimes inconsistent because it depends on factors that are difficult to control. For instance, the skill of the people providing the service can vary.
- **Perishability**—A service cannot be stored for later use. Once it is actually produced, it must be immediately consumed, or its value perishes forever.[2]

The ways that services differ from products create challenges and opportunities. While it can be difficult to easily demonstrate benefits in advance of a service, in some cases it is possible to customize a service to create even greater benefits to a particular customer. This is generally not possible with a product.

APPLIED

Products and Services

All parts of the marketing mix are important, but a sound product strategy is essential. It is through the sale and use of products or services that benefits are delivered to customers. Product strategy refers to all decisions that have an impact on a firm's product offerings, while service strategy refers to decisions about a company's services.

Successful companies spend a large amount of time and effort on product management because it presents a great opportunity to grow sales, improve margins, and increase customer satisfaction. How should products be developed? What attributes and benefits should they have? Will they need to fit into a larger portfolio (or collection) of other products? What marketing strategies should be employed based on product type? The answers to questions such as these compose a product strategy.

As an example of sustained innovation, Nintendo's Wii is the best-selling console in the world. Launched in 2006, Nintendo designers added a revolutionary level of physical interaction between players and games. The core features included wireless motion-sensitive remote controllers and built-in Wi-Fi capability. The simplicity of the Wii and its playability make it popular with all age groups. Residents at senior centers compete in nationwide Wii bowling tournaments. Nintendo launched the Wii Fit in 2008, Wii Fit Plus in 2009, and created a wide range of downloadable Wii games for 2010. These new offerings have helped the Nintendo Wii retain its dominant market position.[3]

PHOTO: Alamy Images.

Levels of Product

Marketers recognize that consumers buy products for a variety of reasons and distinguish between various **levels of a product** (also called layers). At the most basic level, all sodas quench thirst. Beverage brands such as Pepsi or Mountain Dew add a level of differentiation to their products through unique combinations of color, flavor, sweetness, carbonation, packaging, and brand image. Products can be viewed on three levels:[4]

- **Core benefits**—The fundamental product benefits that the customer is buying. For instance, people buy cars to have a means of transportation.
- **Actual product**—The combination of tangible and intangible attributes that delivers the core benefits. Each automobile has a particular combination of attributes, such as horsepower and fuel economy, that determine its acceleration and cost of ownership. For some owners, the vehicle brand may also be a status symbol, for example, BMW or Lexus, and provide emotional rewards in addition to functional ones.
- **Augmented product**—Additional services or benefits that enhance the ownership of the actual product. For example, new vehicle purchases can also secure financing or extended warranties.

Looking beyond the core level of a product may create an opportunity to compensate for a product deficiency or to add a product benefit. Consider the case of Kia automobiles. To address concerns about its quality among U.S. consumers, Kia augmented its product by offering a 10-year/100,000-mile power train warranty. When all products in a category have similar core benefits, the appeal of one can also be enhanced by differentiating it at the actual or augmented level.

EXAMPLE **LEVELS OF A PRODUCT**

Dell manufactures computers for the home and office. One of its most popular items is the laptop computer, used by many college students studying at home or away at school.

- At the core product level, a Dell laptop computer allows its user to manage information, enjoy personal entertainment, and connect to the Internet.
- Dimensions of the actual product include its color, screen size, weight, memory capacity, processor, software, and video card. The Dell brand image may also represent good value and quality to the laptop's owner.
- At the level of the augmented product, Dell offers financing, warranties, tech support, and customer service for every laptop that it sells.[5]

PHOTO: ArchMan/Shutterstock.

>> END EXAMPLE

Product Classifications

Marketers classify products based on customer behavior, as shown in Table 12.1. Depending on the classification, there are clear implications for shopping behavior, and thus marketing strategy. **Consumer products** are products that directly fulfill the desires of consumers and are not intended to assist in the manufacture of other products. **Convenience products,** such as potato chips or chewing gum, are bought frequently with little or no advanced planning. They usually have low prices and are widely distributed, so people can buy them easily when the mood strikes. For example, candy is usually prominently displayed near cash registers to motivate impulse purchases. Brand loyalty for convenience products is low, so manufacturers try to build awareness and preference through advertising and other forms of promotion, such as coupons.

Shopping products are more complex and are bought less frequently than convenience products. Consumers will spend more time cross-comparing product features and benefits—for example, product quality, brand name, and special features—before purchasing shopping products. Blue jeans or airline flights are examples of shopping products. Their prices are higher than convenience products and they are distributed through fewer locations, because customers are willing to make a greater effort to find them. Along with advertising, personal selling at point-of-sale plays a major role in promoting shopping products because salespeople are able to carefully explain product attributes and benefits.

Specialty products have unique characteristics, like highly prized brand names or one-of-a-kind features. Luxury cars, high-end designer clothes, and gourmet chocolates are some examples. Specialty products are purchased infrequently, and consumers are willing to expend more effort, search more locations, and spend more time to find exactly what they want. Because customers are willing to exert extra resources and effort, these items usually carry high prices and are distributed in far fewer locations. Promotional activities are highly targeted to particular audiences or lifestyles because mass communication would be far too inefficient.

Unsought products, such as life insurance or funeral planning, are items consumers often do not like to think about purchasing. People are generally unaware of brand names or specific product benefits. Purchases are made infrequently, often with a minimum amount of shopping effort. Price and distribution strategy will vary, based on the type of product sold. Life insurance is relatively low priced and easily available, but funeral services are fairly expensive and available at only a few locations. Heavy promotion and personal selling are common marketing strategies, because consumers will not actively seek out these products and marketing messages must be aggressively taken to them.[6]

Industrial products sold to businesses and governments, like factory equipment or legal services, may also be classified. Types of products consumed by the business-to-business market are the following:

- **Equipment**—Factory buildings or copy machines are classified as equipment, and their marketing strategy frequently involves personal selling and product customization.

Table 12.1 Consumer Product Classifications

Marketing Implications	Convenience Products	Shopping Products	Specialty Products	Unsought Products
Purchase frequency	Frequent	Less frequent	Infrequent	Infrequent
Amount of comparison and shopping effort	Minimal	Moderate	High	Minimal
Brand loyalty	Low	Higher	High	Low
Price	Low	Higher	High	Low to high
Distribution	Widespread	Fewer outlets	Few outlets	Low to high
Promotion	Mass promotion (for example, advertising, sampling) by manufacturer	Advertising and personal selling by manufacturer and retailer	Targeted promotion by manufacturer and retailer	Heavy advertising and personal selling by manufacturer and retailer
Examples	Chewing gum, potato chips, magazines	Blue jeans, TV sets, sofas	Luxury cars, deluxe vacations, fine crystal	Funerals, life insurance, retirement plans

- **MRO products**—Items used for the maintenance, repair, and operation of a business are called MRO products. Because they are purchased frequently, prices for MRO products are kept as affordable as possible. Screws, nails, and washers are all MRO products.
- **Raw materials**—Raw materials include products such as lumber, wheat, or cotton. Offering lower prices and superior customer service are two common strategies for marketing raw materials.
- **Processed materials and services**—Firms also purchase processed materials and services, like fabric for clothing or copy-machine repair services.
- **Components**—These are finished products that organizations use to fabricate their own products. For example, liquid crystal displays are components in the manufacture of cell phones and computer monitors.[7]

EXAMPLE PRODUCT CLASSIFICATIONS

Wrigley's chewing gum is perhaps the ultimate convenience product. The marketing strategy for Wrigley gum is an almost textbook example for how to market convenience products. Chewing gum is purchased frequently, so every Wrigley product package is small and lightweight, making it easy to purchase and carry. On average, consumers spend 16 seconds shopping for confections such as candy or gum. Because consumers often buy on impulse with little or no product search, intensive distribution for these items is critical. Wrigley is committed to building strong relationships with its retailer partners, which helps to keep its products on shelves in locations as diverse as grocery stores, convenience stores, gas stations, drug stores, mass merchandisers, and wholesale clubs. Prices for Wrigley gum products are always affordable and competitive, so they are easily attainable for customers. Regarding promotion strategy, Wrigley follows the precept laid down by its founder William Wrigley Jr.: "Tell 'em quick, and tell 'em often." The company consistently invests in advertising and other promotional activities to support its brands. Traditional print and TV ads are combined with new media to reach on-the-go, tech-savvy consumers. By strengthening the equity of its brands, Wrigley is able to create primary demand for its gum and avoid excessive discounting.[8]

PHOTO: Pablo Eder/Shutterstock.

>> END EXAMPLE

New Product Development

For companies to remain vital, they must develop a steady stream of new products. Unfortunately, the failure rate for new products in the packaged goods sector is as high as 80%.[9] To improve these odds, a **new product development** process incorporates insight into a firm's customers and its environment. The steps involved in new product development follow and are illustrated in Figure 12.1:[10]

- **Idea generation**—Formulate an idea for a new product or service.
- **Idea screening**—Review the idea to ensure that it meets customer wants and company goals.
- **Concept development**—Concretely define the features and benefits of the new product.
- **Marketing strategy**—Create a marketing strategy for the product's introduction.
- **Business analysis**—Validate that the new product will meet all sales and profit objectives.
- **Concept testing**—Develop prototypes of the product for test marketing.
- **Commercialization**—Launch the new product in the marketplace.

FIGURE 12.1 **Product Development Stages**

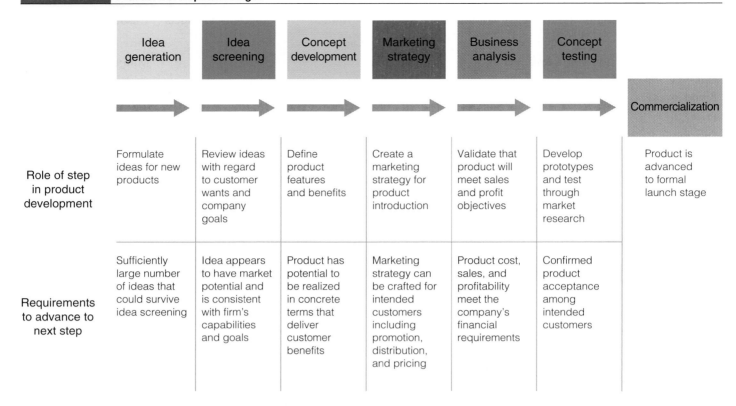

	Idea generation	Idea screening	Concept development	Marketing strategy	Business analysis	Concept testing	Commercialization
Role of step in product development	Formulate ideas for new products	Review ideas with regard to customer wants and company goals	Define product features and benefits	Create a marketing strategy for product introduction	Validate that product will meet sales and profit objectives	Develop prototypes and test through market research	Product is advanced to formal launch stage
Requirements to advance to next step	Sufficiently large number of ideas that could survive idea screening	Idea appears to have market potential and is consistent with firm's capabilities and goals	Product has potential to be realized in concrete terms that deliver customer benefits	Marketing strategy can be crafted for intended customers including promotion, distribution, and pricing	Product cost, sales, and profitability meet the company's financial requirements	Confirmed product acceptance among intended customers	

Product concepts must pass through each stage of the process to move on to the next. At each step, ideas that fail to make the grade are weeded out. As a result, companies strive to generate a large number of ideas up front, knowing that only a few of those ideas will survive to commercialization. During the concept-development step, focus groups or other qualitative research techniques are often used to refine product ideas based on customer feedback. Before commercialization, a company may also invest in test marketing, during which actual products are introduced into select geographic areas. Test markets involve full-scale launch activities, including advertising, pricing, sampling, and distribution. Although costly, test markets help firms avoid more costly mistakes and can suggest ideas for product improvements.

EXAMPLE **NEW PRODUCT DEVELOPMENT**

To broaden the appeal for their brand, marketers at Yoplait were looking to introduce a new product. At that time, yogurt was available in three styles: sundae-style (with fruit on the bottom), Swiss-style (with fruit mixed in), and plain. To uncover a new opportunity, Yoplait followed a classic product-development process:[11]

- **Idea generation**—According to market research, consumers liked Yoplait's flavor, but its smooth consistency led some to reject the brand. The Yoplait marketing team, along with its advertising agency, generated 26 new product ideas to address this problem.
- **Idea screening**—To pass through the screening stage, new product ideas had to meet specific sales volume objectives. Only 7 out of the original 26 ideas met those criteria.
- **Concept development**—The most promising idea was a new custard-style yogurt. The product needed to be firm and thick, yet smooth and creamy. Yoplait refined the product concept by experimenting with combinations of fat, fruit, color, and texture.
- **Marketing strategy**—Yoplait marketers were faced with several product strategy options:
  - Should the new product be positioned as a snack, meal substitute, or dessert?
  - Should it use the traditional conical Yoplait package?
  - Would a 4-oz or 6-oz serving be more appealing?
  - What should be the fat level (full or low)?
- **Business Analysis**—Yoplait marketers needed to ensure the new products would meet business requirements. The overall financial impact of the new portfolio was reviewed.
- **Concept Testing (Product development)**—Hundreds of prototypes were developed in search of the right combination of fruit, color, feel, and other attributes. Marketers sampled batches and used their judgment to narrow down the number of product concepts.

- **Concept Testing (Test marketing)**—Seven product concepts were tested in a minimarket test in Eau Claire/La Crosse, Wisconsin. Each concept used a different positioning and mix of package, size, and fat level. The "winning" alternative was positioned as a full-fat snack in a traditional 6-oz Yoplait package. Market test results suggested that the new product would add 36% incremental volume to the Yoplait line with a low risk of cannibalization.
- **Commercialization**—Based on favorable concept test results, Yoplait custard style yogurt was launched nationwide in six flavors.

Yoplait custard style yogurt is now available in a dozen flavors, such as Key Lime Pie and Peaches 'N Cream.

PHOTO: David Davis/Shutterstock.

>> **END EXAMPLE**

Product-Development Steps—Roles and Requirements

There is no single, best way to encourage innovation and new ideas. Some firms establish new product teams that are multidisciplinary groups (including representatives from marketing, finance, manufacturing, and other departments) that meet on a regular basis to discuss new product ideas. Other companies maintain formal R&D (research and development) groups responsible for presenting new product concepts to brand managers.

Some new product ideas are **discontinuous innovations** that change our everyday lives in dramatic ways. Personal computers and portable phones are some examples. But innovations are not only revolutionary, breakthrough ideas. According to Peter Fisk, there are typically three kinds of new product ideas:[12]

- **Cosmetic change**—The most basic type of innovation, involving some evolutionary change to an existing product or service. New versions of existing automotive nameplates (such as Toyota Camry or Ford Escape) are introduced every few years, although they are rarely total product redesigns.
- **Context change**—When an existing product or service is taken into a new context or market. The context for the Bacardi Breezer was repositioned from a big bottle in the supermarket to a cool club drink.
- **Concept change**—This is an advanced innovation that changes everything. IKEA rethought home decoration and do-it-yourself shopping, and brought affordable Scandinavian design to the masses.

Ideas for new products come from almost anywhere. Mistakes can even be a source of innovation. In the 1970s, a researcher at 3M was trying to find a strong adhesive. His experiments led to an adhesive that was the opposite of strong; in fact, it was so weak that after sticking to a surface it could be easily removed. Years later, 3M came to understand the hidden potential in this discovery, and the product known as 3M Post-it Notes was born.

Another source of product innovation is packaging. One aspect is packaging design, which delights consumers by making products more attractive and easy to use. In 2006, CARGO Cosmetics won a DuPont Award for packaging for its ColorCards single-use portable eye shadows. Each ColorCard is the size of a credit card and employs a patented printing process that deposits a thin layer of eye shadow onto a 12-point decorated board. Marketers are also searching for ways to incorporate recyclable and environmentally safe ingredients into packages. The wedge-shaped Tetra Pak is designed to heat sauces in microwave ovens and is made with over 70% renewable materials.[13]

Product and Service Quality

Consumers will pay for a product (or service) only if it has an adequate level of quality at a fair price. But quality is in the eye of the beholder, and no two people define quality in exactly the same way. Quality is most frequently defined as the customer's overall reaction to the attributes of a product or service. For example, consider a trip to the dentist. For one patient, a quick visit with minimal discomfort is a "quality" experience, while another person will be satisfied only if their dentist also has an engaging, personable manner.

A product quality strategy, therefore, specifies a level of performance for each product attribute relative to the target market's perception of quality and value. Not every product needs to have superior performance on every attribute. In fact, few customers will pay for products that offer "the best of everything." Higher quality usually means higher costs, due to better engineering, superior materials, or a more highly trained workforce. A quality product for many people is one that excels on those few dimensions that are important to them, and is merely adequate on others. In this instance, they will give up some benefits for a lower price.

To implement a product and service quality strategy, marketers set performance level targets for attributes in alignment with customer wants and needs. Then, every activity of the firm, from research and development to customer service, is aligned to deliver those objectives. QFD (quality function deployment) is a method some companies use to translate customer needs into product and quality requirements. Process tools like Six Sigma use statistical analysis to continually reduce manufacturing defects. Firms compliant with ISO 9000 and ISO 9001 standards follow a strict set of rules governing internal processes from record keeping to annual reviews. A well-thought-out and well-executed product quality strategy will reduce costs, improve customer satisfaction, reduce customer defection, increase sales, and improve profitability.

Product Design

Although often overlooked, product design is a critical element of product strategy and has the potential to add differentiation and value. The term **product style** refers to the visual appearance of a product, but **product design** is a broader term that includes a product's style, its tactile appeal, and its usability. Consider two products with identical core benefits. The well-designed product is more pleasurable to look at, feels better in your hands, and is easier to use. The page you are currently reading was designed by graphic artists to make it legible and easy to understand.

Good design evokes positive feelings in the customer and is a source of strategic advantage. The OXO brand specializes in ergonomically designed tools for household tasks such as cooking, repairing, and gardening. Each OXO tool is designed to be visually appealing and comfortable to hold. Services as well as goods may be well designed. Online marketers often apply experience design principles to improve their services. Amazon.com has redesigned the online buying experience by offering a "1-Click" feature that stores personal credit card information so returning customers can make quicker, easier purchases with a single mouse click.

EXAMPLE **PRODUCT DESIGN**

How can design be used to make an everyday product, such as a prescription bottle, more useful and attractive? After her grandmother accidentally took her grandfather's medication, designer Deborah Adler looked for a better way to design medicine bottles. Her ideas became the inspiration for the ClearRx prescription bottles offered exclusively through Target stores.

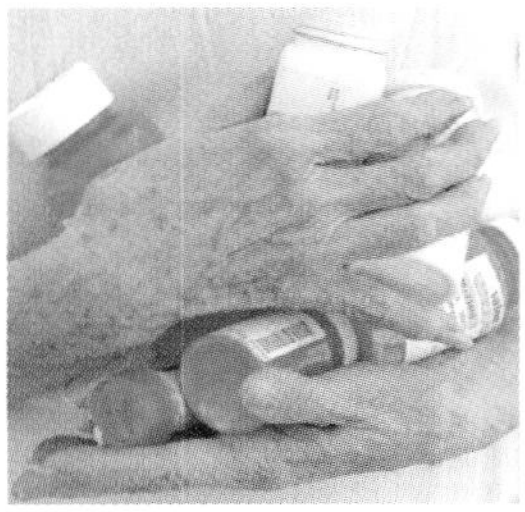

Every ClearRx bottle has numerous features to improve the way medicine is used and stored:[14]

- An easy-to-read label with large type
- A color-coded ID ring with a color for each family member
- A top label with the name of the drug clearly printed for easy identification in case the bottle is stored in a drawer
- A slide-in information card with important patient and drug information
- An oral syringe to make measuring liquid doses easier
- Free flavoring for liquid medicine, with flavors such as watermelon or bubble gum
- A free magnifier to make label reading easier

PHOTO: Elena Ray/Shutterstock.

>> END EXAMPLE

PRODUCT Portfolio (pp. 169–170)

DEFINED *A **product portfolio** (also called a **product mix**) is the collection of all products and services offered by a company.*

EXPLAINED

Product Portfolio

Most companies sell more than one kind of product or service. If a product is successful, a firm usually introduces additional variations on the basic product, or additional new products, into its product portfolio. When a firm targets multiple customer segments, it may also need to offer a range of products tailored for each target group.

A company's product portfolio includes all of the brands, subbrands, and varieties of products or services that it offers. The number of products in a portfolio can add up quickly, so managing them might become overwhelming. A product that is popular today could go out of fashion tomorrow. The strategic challenge is to keep the firm's product portfolio fresh and relevant in the marketplace.

APPLIED

Product Portfolio

Portfolio management comprises all of the decisions, or strategic wagers, a company makes regarding its portfolio of current and future products. Managing the product portfolio is an important component of the marketing strategy because company resources are finite. Even the most successful firms have limits on the amount of time and money they can devote to any one product. Resource-investment decisions are made based on which products the company believes have greater, or lesser, potential in the marketplace. The company must choose which products to keep within, remove from, or add to the portfolio. Because the success or failure of any particular product is uncertain, the resulting set of investment decisions adds up to a firm's collective wagers, or "bets," on the future performance of the portfolio.

When discussing product portfolios, several terms are used. A **product line** is a group of closely related products. Table 12.2 is an example of Sony's U.S. product lines in the spring of 2010.

Some organizations employ a **full-line product strategy** by offering a wide range of product lines within a product portfolio. Procter & Gamble sells a variety of household products in categories such as oral care, cleaning products, and child care. Other companies pursue a **limited-line product strategy** and focus on one or a few product lines. The product portfolio is managed along three dimensions:[15]

- **Product mix width** refers to the number of product lines a company offers.
- **Product mix length** is the total number of products offered.
- **Product mix depth** is the number of versions of products within a line.

These terms are helpful when thinking about ways to expand or contract a portfolio. A firm may decide to change the width of its product mix by adding or eliminating a product line. **Line extensions** are additions to an existing product line and are one way to increase the depth of a product line. Developed as a stand-alone product, the popular Swiffer cleaning brush has inspired a series of line extensions, including Swiffer SweeperVac, Swiffer WetJet, Swiffer Dusters, and Swiffer CarpetFlick. Another way to increase the depth of a line is to stretch it upward (or downward) by introducing products of superior (or lesser) quality or price. **Line expansions** occur when entirely new lines are added to a product mix. For example, Pepsi added the Naked Juice health-drink line to its beverage portfolio by acquiring the brand's parent company in 2007.

EXAMPLE **PRODUCT PORTFOLIO**

The Hershey Company is the largest maker of chocolate and sugar confectionery products in North America. Although it is most famous for its Hershey bars and Kisses, the Hershey Company maintains a product mix of great width, length, and depth. Reese's, Almond Joy, Mounds, Twizzlers, Heath, and Jolly Rancher are just a sampling of its chocolate and confectionery brands. The Hershey premium product lines include Cacao Reserve chocolate bars, Joseph Schmidt handcrafted chocolate gifts, and Dagoba organic chocolate products. Ice Breakers mints and Bubble Yum gum are some of Hershey's refreshment product lines.[16]

PHOTO: Joseph/Shutterstock.

>> **END EXAMPLE**

Table 12.2 Sony U.S. Product Portfolio, Spring 2010

	PRODUCT CATEGORY					
	Computers	**Cameras and Camcorders**	**TV and Home Entertainment**	**MP3 and Portable Electronics**	**Movies and Music**	**Games**
PRODUCT LINES	VAIO notebooks	Cyber-shot digital cameras	Televisions	Walkman Video MP3 players	DVD movies	PlayStation systems
	VAIO desktops	Digital SLR cameras	Home theater systems	Reader Digital Book	Blu-ray Disc movies	PlayStation 3
	Digital Home	Handycam camcorders	Blu-ray Disc	Sony Ericsson	UMD videos for PSP	PlayStation Portable (PSP)
	Disc burners	Digital picture frames	DVD players	Mobile phones	Music	
	Personal Internet Viewer	Photo printers	Home Entertainment Servers (HES)	GPS navigation		
	Accessories	Photo services	Home audio components	Portable DVD and CD players		
	Software and media		Mini stereo systems	Bluetooth devices		
				Radios and boom boxes		
				Headphones		
				Voice recorders		
				iPod accessories		

When adding products to a portfolio, marketers should pay attention to the possibility of cannibalization, which occurs when a new product takes market share from an established product. Cannibalization is not necessarily to be avoided, but it has the potential to ruin a business if a new, less profitable product is an attractive substitute for an older, more profitable entry. It could even become necessary when an aging product needs to be replaced by a newer, fresher alternative due to changes in consumer tastes or technological innovation. In the late 1990s, Charles Schwab recognized a potential opportunity in the emerging online stock-trading business. It deliberately cannibalized its own traditional brokerage business by instituting a common price for both online and offline stock trades. By cannibalizing itself, within six months $51 billion in assets poured into Charles Schwab and the firm captured 42% of the online stock-trading market.[17]

PRODUCT Life Cycle (pp. 171–173)

DEFINED *The* ***product life cycle (PLC)*** *is a model that describes the evolution of a product's sales and profits throughout its lifetime. The stages of the product life cycle are as follows: Introduction, Growth, Maturity, and Decline.*

EXPLAINED

Product Life Cycle

The popularity of a product evolves over time, growing and fading as consumer tastes change or as a newer, more desirable product is introduced in that product's place. The PLC, illustrated in Figure 12.2, assumes that products follow a common pattern of evolution through a series of life stages. The PLC is based on an analogy taken from the realm of biology, where organisms evolve in a predicable pattern. Although only a model, or picture, of how the real world operates, the PLC can still be valuable because it contains implications for marketing strategy at each stage of evolution. The four stages of the PLC are as follows:

- **Introduction stage**—During this stage, a new product is introduced to the marketplace. Sales volume increases as potential customers gain awareness of the product.
  - Highly innovative tablet PCs (like Apple's iPad) will continue to be in the introduction stage for the near future as new products come to market with even more exciting features.
- **Growth stage**—Many products fail during the introductory phase of the PLC. Those gaining acceptance in the marketplace progress to the growth stage, where sales increase rapidly. For marketers, this is an exciting time, because the new product also becomes very profitable.
  - Plasma or LCD widescreen TV sets are currently in the growth stage of the PLC, with a greater range of brands and models on sale as demand for these items continues to grow.
- **Maturity stage**—At some point, markets become saturated. Customers are sated with products and all of their variations. At this point, the product has graduated to the maturity stage, where sales growth peaks and eventually flattens. Although a few first-time buyers are coming to market, most product sales are replacements for previous purchases.
  - For many years, the DVD player has been in the maturity stage of the PLC. Prices are now so affordable that DVD players are within the budget of the majority of U.S. consumers. Many purchases are sales made to replace older or broken products.
- **Decline stage**—Every product eventually reaches a decline stage where sales and profits fall. A product may go into decline for many reasons, including technological obsolescence, an erosion of brand equity, increased competition, and changes in customer preferences. One product may fade away slowly and gracefully, while another vanishes abruptly.
  - In the mass consumer market, VHS players are in decline due to technological advances like DVD players, laptops with video capability, and TiVo. Previously easy to purchase and rent, VHS tapes and players are now difficult to find as manufacturers scale back models and production.

The PLC is not fixed, unchangeable, and true for each and every marketing situation. The PLC is a model for how products generally behave, based on past experience. Each product is unique; it has its own set of customers, benefits, competitors, brand names, and other attributes. Any of these could shorten, lengthen, or change the shape of an individual product's life cycle.

FIGURE 12.2 Product Life Cycle

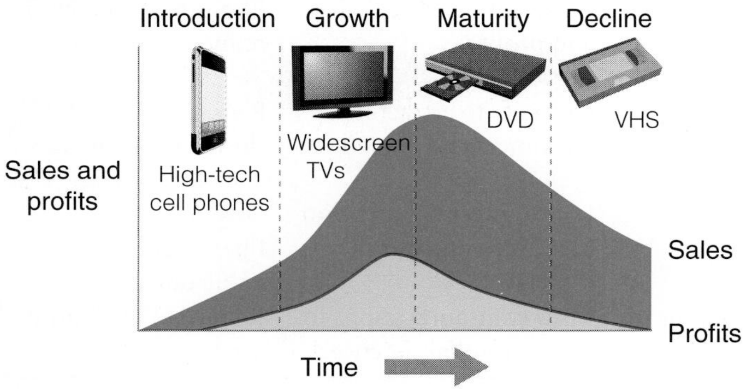

APPLIED

Product Life Cycle

The PLC is a useful tool for marketers because it provides a clear, predictable framework for sales and profit levels over time. Marketers may take advantage of general rules or strategies that have been devised for each stage of the PLC. Although accurately estimating sales volume or profit at each stage can be difficult, and products may follow different life-cycle patterns, the PLC remains a useful source of ideas for marketing strategies throughout a product's lifetime.

Product Life Cycle and Marketing Strategies

The PLC model assumes that sales build through successive stages of the life cycle until a product reaches maturity, and that each stage has different implications for marketing mix strategy (product, pricing, placement, and promotion), as shown in Table 12.3. In contrast, profits are low (or negative) in the introduction stage, rise to a peak during growth, and then begin to decline over time, until they are essentially eliminated.

During introduction, the goal is to gain acceptance for the new product in the marketplace so companies will invest heavily in promotion and distribution. Prices may be high or low, depending on whether the firm has chosen to pursue a **penetration strategy** (holding price low to gain share) or a **skimming strategy** (keeping price high to maximize return).

Upon reaching the growth stage, the emphasis shifts to capitalizing on an expanding market opportunity. Competitors are attracted to the new profit opportunity and introduce their own variations of the successful product. Pioneer firms respond by attempting to build preference for their brands or by adding features to the basic product. Defending a high-market-share position during the growth stage can be expensive. Although investments in new product development or brand advertising may forfeit short-term profits, they can also leave a firm well-positioned to compete in the maturity stage.

As sales growth slows during the maturity stage, competitors struggle over a more finite pool of available customers. Downward pressure is exerted on profits as most firms are forced to invest in marketing incentives and/or to reduce prices. This is usually the longest stage because some products may remain in maturity for decades. Recognizing the challenges of the maturity stage, companies take steps to extend its duration as long as possible.

During the decline stage, some firms choose to simply pull out of the market, thus **divesting** themselves of a product. The declining product could be discontinued or sold outright to another firm. Others prefer licensing the brand name or product design to another company, allowing the original owners to maintain a degree of profitability without significant expense. LEGO licenses its brand name to the Clic Time Company, which manufactures clocks and watches using LEGO's distinctive colors and product design. **Harvesting** is a third option in which a firm continues to sell a product while gradually reducing, and eventually eliminating, all of its marketing investment.

Duration of the Product Life Cycle

Innovations take time to spread through the marketplace. Not every business or consumer is equally willing to try new things. **Diffusion of innovations** refers to the speed with which consumers and businesses adopt a particular product. Marketers segment populations into five groups with various degrees of openness toward innovations (see Figure 12.3):

- **Innovators** (2.5% of population):
  The innovators are the most willing to adopt innovations. They are open-minded, adventurous, and tend to be

FIGURE 12.3 Innovation Segments

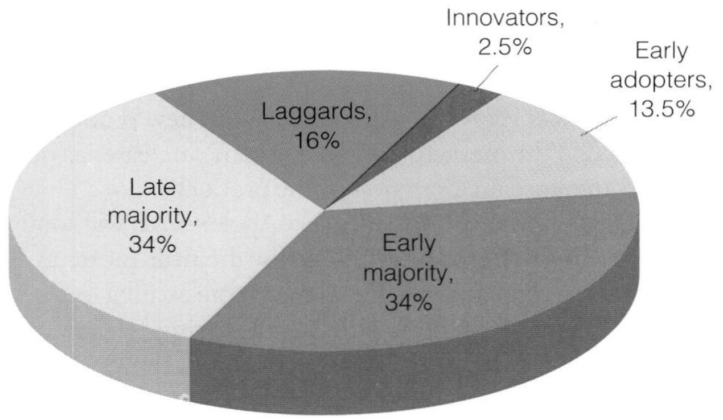

Table 12.3 Stages of the Product Life Cycle

Marketing Implications	Introduction	Growth	Maturity	Decline
Sales	Low	Growing	Peak—Sales curve flattens out	Declining
Profit	Low or even negative	Rising	Falling	Low and eventually negative
Marketing goals	Build awareness for product category; encourage trial	Take advantage of growing demand; build brand preference	Maximize market share and profit	Eliminate product or reduce investment
Product	Basic	Add features and product line extensions	Diversify to attract new customers and extend life cycle	Reduce costs and slow-selling versions
Price	May be high or low	Lower	Low to meet competition	Low
Distribution	Selective, with few outlets	More outlets	Maximize number of outlets	Phase out unprofitable outlets
Promotion	Heavy expenditure to build targeted awareness	Mass communications to build general awareness	Mass communications to build brand preference	Reduce to minimum level

younger, better educated, and more financially secure. They try new things just because they like having something new and unusual.

- **Early adopters** (13.5% of population):
  Early adopters are more socially aware than innovators and consider the prestige or social implications of being seen using a new product. They are media savvy, and more mainstream groups look to early adopters for cues as to what is the "next big thing."
- **Early majority** (34% of population):
  Members of the early majority do not want to be the first or the last to try a new product. Instead, they wait to see what excites the early adopters, and only then do they begin to buy a product. Once the early majority adopts a product, it is no longer a cutting-edge item, but has become part of the mainstream.
- **Late majority** (34% of population):
  Older and more conservative than other groups, the late majority will not adopt a product they consider to be too risky. They will purchase something only if they consider it to be a necessity or when they are under some form of social pressure.
- **Laggards** (16% of population):
  Laggards are heavily bound by tradition and are the last to adopt an innovation. By the time laggards take up a product, it may already have been rendered obsolete by another innovation.

When launching a new product, marketers will focus their efforts on innovators and early adopters to get the diffusion process rolling. Depending on how readily these groups adopt the new product, the PLC may be quite short or very long.[18]

Although the average human lifetime is approximately 78 years, the estimated life cycle for a product or service is only 13 years.[19] Not every PLC is this short, however, because some products may be long lived. Colt pistols, Stetson hats, Vaseline emollient, and Pepsi-Cola have endured for more than 100 years. Marketers can extend a product's life span by doing the following:

- Promoting the product to new customers or markets
- Finding new uses or applications for the product
- Repositioning the product or brand
- Adding product features or benefits
- Offering new packages or sizes
- Introducing low-cost product variations and/or reducing price

Graphical representations of the PLC usually depict all four of its stages as roughly equal in duration. In reality, some stages might be longer or shorter than others. For example, when a product is a fad, it rapidly gains and then loses popularity in the marketplace, resulting in a PLC with a tall, narrow shape. The PLC graph for a style of product has a more wave-like appearance, as its popularity rises or falls over time. For instance, consider women's hemlines. Ankle-length skirts (or miniskirts) may be fashionable for a while, lose their appeal, and then become stylish again years later.

Limitations of the Product Life Cycle

One should keep in mind that the PLC is a model, or theory, about how products behave in the marketplace. Like most models or approximations of the real world, the PLC has limitations. In reality, the PLC is most applicable to classes of products (like the Blu-ray player category) and less predictive of behavior for individual products or brands (like Sony Blu-ray players). The PLC works best in modeling categories of product innovations, and not individual products. Determining the life stage for a class or category of products is fairly straightforward, because the sales and profits for all brands can be rolled up into a single metric. However, identifying the life stage for a particular brand can be more difficult. Although the overall product category may continue to hold appeal for consumers, not all brands may be equally preferred. Therefore, each one may perform differently.

It may also be difficult for marketers to identify the exact stage of their products in the life cycle because PLC curves come in many different shapes, for example, fads and styles. Your product's profit curve is rising, but does this mean it is progressing within the growth stage, or has it reached its peak of maturity? A "normal" life-cycle curve shows profits rising over a reasonable period of time, but in the case of a fad, sales and profits peak very quickly.

Perhaps the biggest controversy surrounding the PLC is that some say it stifles original marketing thought. If you believe a product is in decline, and you follow the suggestions of the PLC model completely, you will cut back R&D investment and promotion. Although the product may have had the potential to be resurrected, this disinvestment may simply force it into decline, as needed resources are pulled away. The PLC can serve as inspiration for marketing strategy, but it should never be the final word about what actions to take in each and every marketing situation.

Visual Summary

Chapter 12 Summary

It is through the creation and management of products and services that a company delivers value to its customers. Portfolio management and new product development are two methods companies employ to keep their assortment of products and services relevant and vital. The product life cycle model suggests ways to improve performance at each stage in a product's life. Carefully formulated product and service strategies, when aligned with the marketing plan, will pave the way for the remaining elements of the marketing mix.

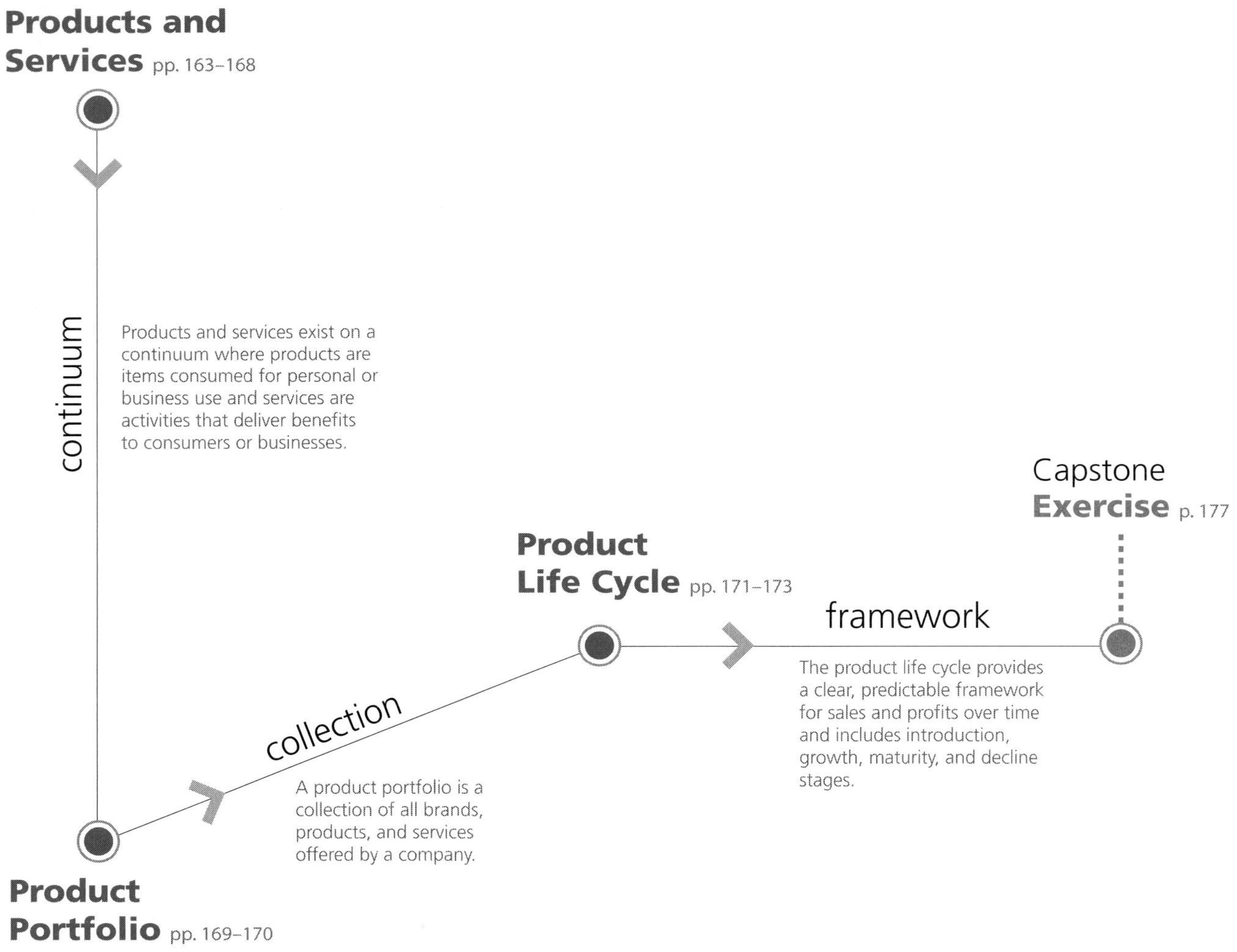

Products and Services pp. 163–168
continuum
Products and services exist on a continuum where products are items consumed for personal or business use and services are activities that deliver benefits to consumers or businesses.
Product Portfolio pp. 169–170
collection
A product portfolio is a collection of all brands, products, and services offered by a company.
Product Life Cycle pp. 171–173
framework
The product life cycle provides a clear, predictable framework for sales and profits over time and includes introduction, growth, maturity, and decline stages.
Capstone Exercise p. 177

Chapter Key Terms

Products and Services (pp. 163–168)

Products *are items used or consumed for personal or business use. (p. 163)* **Opening Example (p. 163)**

Services *are activities that deliver benefits to consumers or businesses. (p. 163)*

Key Terms (pp. 163–168)

Actual product is the combination of tangible and intangible attributes that delivers the core benefits of the product. **(p. 164)**

Attributes are the unique characteristics of each product, including product features and options, product design, brand name, quality, logos, identifiers, packaging, and warranty. **(p. 163)**

Augmented product is the additional services or benefits that enhance the ownership of the actual product. **(p. 164)**

Benefits, realized through product attributes, define the utility (or usefulness) of a product for the customer. **(p. 163)**

Business analysis is the process of validating that the new product will meet all sales and profit objectives. **(p. 165)**

Commercialization is the process of launching a new product in the marketplace. **(p. 165)**

Components are finished products companies employ to manufacture their own products, for example, microchips or engines. **(p. 165)**

Concept change is an advanced, breakthrough innovation that changes everything. **(p. 167)**

Concept development is the process of concretely defining the features and benefits of the new product. **(p. 165)**

Concept testing is developing prototypes of the product for product testing. **(p. 165)**

Consumer products are products that directly fulfill the desires of consumers and are not intended to assist in the manufacture of other products. **(p. 164)**

Context change is when an existing product or service is taken into a new context or market. **(p. 167)**

Convenience products are products that are purchased frequently with little or no shopping effort, for example, grocery staples, paper products, and candy. **(p. 164) Example: Product Classifications (p. 165)**

Core benefits are the fundamental product benefits the customer receives from a product. **(p. 164)**

Cosmetic change is an evolutionary change to an existing product or service. **(p. 167)**

Discontinuous innovations are new product ideas that change our everyday lives in dramatic ways. **(p. 167)**

Equipment is a group of products used in the everyday operation of a business, for example, factories and copy machines. **(p. 164)**

Idea generation is the process of formulating an idea for a new product or service. **(p. 165)**

Idea screening is the process of reviewing a product idea to ensure that it meets customer wants and company goals. **(p. 165)**

Industrial products are products sold to business customers for their direct use or as inputs to the manufacture of other products. Classifications of industrial products include equipment, MRO products, raw materials, processed materials and services, and components. **(p. 164)**

Inseparability recognizes that a service cannot be separated from its means or manner of production. **(p. 163)**

Intangibility recognizes that a service cannot be perceived by the five senses (sight, hearing, touch, smell, or taste) before it is produced and consumed. **(p. 163)**

Levels of a product consists of three classifications: core benefits, actual product, and augmented product—and each additional level has the potential to add greater value for the customer. **(p. 164) Example: Levels of a Product (p. 164)**

Marketing strategy is a statement of how a business intends to achieve its marketing objectives. **(p. 165)**

MRO products are products used in the maintenance, repair, and operation of a business, for example, nails, oil, or paint. **(p. 165)**

New product development is the process of creating, planning, testing, and commercializing products. **(p. 165) Example: New Product Development (pp. 166–167)**

Perishability that services cannot be stored for later use and must be consumed upon delivery. **(p. 163)**

Processed materials and services are products or services used in the production of finished products or services, for example, lumber, steel, or market research. **(p. 165)**

Product design is a product's style, tactile appeal, and usability. **(p. 167) Example: Product Design (p. 168)**

Product style is the visual and aesthetic appearance of a product. **(p. 167)**

Raw materials are unfinished products that are processed for use in the manufacture of a finished product, for example, wood, wheat, or iron ore. **(p. 165)**

Shopping products are products that are purchased with a moderate amount of shopping effort, for example, clothing, linens, housewares. **(p. 164)**

Specialty products are products with unique characteristics that are purchased with a high degree of shopping effort, for example, luxury items, vacations, and homes. **(p. 164)**

Unsought products are products that consumers do not usually search for without an immediate problem or prompting, for example, life insurance, funerals, or legal services. **(p. 164)**

Variability recognizes that service quality may vary from experience to experience. **(p. 163)**

Product Portfolio (pp. 169–170)

Product portfolio *(also called a* ***product mix****) is the collection of all products and services offered by a company. (p. 169)* **Example: Product Portfolio (p. 169)**

Key Terms (p. 169)

Full-line product strategy is offering a wide range of product lines within a product portfolio. **(p. 169)**

Limited-line product strategy is focusing on one or a few product lines within a product portfolio. **(p. 169)**

Line expansions are the addition of entirely new product lines to a product mix. **(p. 169)**

Line extensions is an addition to an existing product line that retains the currently utilized brand name. **(p. 169)**

Portfolio management comprises all of the decisions a company makes regarding its portfolio of current and future products. It involves deciding which products to add, keep, and remove from the overall product portfolio. **(p. 169)**

Product line is a group of closely related products. **(p. 169) Example: Product Portfolio (p. 169)**

Product mix depth is the number of versions of products within a product line. **(p. 169)**

Product mix length is the total number of products a company offers. **(p. 169)**

Product mix width is the number of product lines a company offers. **(p. 169)**

Product Life Cycle (pp. 171–173)

Product life cycle (PLC) *is the model that describes the evolution of a product's sales and profits throughout its lifetime. The stages of the product life cycle are as follows: Introduction, Growth, Maturity, and Decline. (p. 171)*

Key Terms (pp. 171–173)

Decline stage is the stage at which the demand for a product falls due to changes in customer preferences. Sales and profits eventually fall to zero. **(p. 171)**

Diffusion of innovations is a theory concerning how populations adopt innovations over time. **(p. 172)**

Divesting is the process of discontinuing the production and sale of a product. **(p. 172)**

Early adopters are consumers who are more socially aware than innovators and consider the prestige or social implications of being seen using a new product. **(p. 173)**

Early majority are middle-class consumers who do not want to be the first, or the last, to try a new product. They look to the early adopters for direction about product innovations. **(p. 173)**

Growth stage is the stage at which a product is rapidly adopted in the marketplace. Sales grow rapidly and profits peak. **(p. 171)**

Harvesting is the process of continuing to sell a product in spite of declining sales. **(p. 172)**

Innovators are consumers who are the most willing to adopt innovations. They tend to be younger, better educated, and more financially secure. **(p. 172)**

Introduction stage is the stage at which a new product is introduced to the marketplace. Sales begin to build, but profits remain low (or even negative). **(p. 171)**

Laggards are consumers who are heavily bound by tradition and are the last to adopt an innovation. **(p. 173)**

Late majority are older and conservative consumers who avoid products they consider to be too risky. They will purchase something only if they consider it to be a necessity or when they are under some form of social pressure. **(p. 173)**

Maturity stage is the stage at which the product has been purchased by most potential buyers and future sales are largely replacement purchases. Sales plateau and profits begin to fall. **(p. 171)**

Penetration strategy is the process of offering a product at a low price to maximize sales volume and market share. **(p. 172)**

Skimming strategy is the process of offering a product at a high price to maximize return. **(p. 172)**

Capstone Exercise

In 1885, Binney & Smith had a product line of ONE—An-Du-Septic dustless chalk. While promoting this product to teachers across the United States, the company founders discovered that teachers were importing expensive wax crayons from Europe. In the early 1900s, nearly 20 years after starting the company, Binney & Smith introduced a new product, eight colored crayons packaged in a green and yellow box. Crayola Crayons remain a staple in American classrooms today. The size of the boxes and the selection of colors have changed over the decades, but the basic product remains essentially the same. (The "Big Box" with a mind-boggling 96 crayons was introduced in 1993.)

In 1964, Binney & Smith acquired Permanent Pigments, an acrylic paint manufacturer, and in 1977, it acquired the rights to Silly Putty. In 1984, the Binney & Smith company became a wholly owned subsidiary of Hallmark Cards, Inc.

In 2007, the Binney & Smith corporate name was changed to Crayola because of the brand familiarity. The name Crayola has a 99% recognition among U.S. consumers. Eighty percent of all the crayons sold in the United States today have the Crayola brand name. Crayola products are sold in 80 different countries and packaged in 12 languages.

The name change also reflected the company's new direction. For nearly 100 years, Crayola targeted children and their parents with a product line of back-to-school products. The products had expanded from crayons to water paints, markers, chalk, colored pencils, and poster paints. However, in an effort to expand the market and generate revenues throughout the year, Crayola entered the toy industry. Bath tub art, glow stations, Color Explosion products, Mess-Free Art, flavored drinking water, and even a colorful computer keyboard and mouse are just some of the products added to the Crayola line. Today in any big box store, Crayola will have shelf space in both the art and school supply aisle AND the toy section.

1. How would you define the attributes and benefits of Crayola products?
2. Define the core, actual, and augmented product benefits.
3. Where was Crayola in the product life cycle *before* it entered the toy market? Where do you think they are now? Explain.
4. Do you see the move from school supply products to toys as product development? Explain.
5. Describe the Crayola product portfolio strategy.

Application Exercise

Use the marketing concepts in this chapter to tackle and solve a marketing problem: new product development, discontinuous innovations, concept development, and benefits. First, start by thinking about new products you have seen in the last two or three years, then choose a new product in any category. There are many new products available in stores for us to consider purchasing.

The Marketing Problem

Think about your chosen new product after considering the following situation.

> Consumers have myriad products to choose from. There is risk to the manufacturer and retailer in introducing a new product and it may take some time for a new product to obtain a loyal base.

The Problem

Describe the steps most likely taken in the development of your new product to mitigate risk before it was available. Is the new product you have in mind a discontinuous innovation? How would you describe its benefits?

The Solution

Complete the following two Problem/Solution briefs using your product in the new product category, chapter concepts, and college resources.

1. From the Marketing Manager's Point of View
   a. Problem Definition
   b. New Product Concept Analysis
   c. Product's Benefits
   d. Solution
2. From the Consumer's Point of View
   a. Problem Definition
   b. Analysis
   c. Product's Benefits
   d. Solution

Resources:

Marketing Defined, Explained, Applied, Michael Levens, 2e
The College Library
Retail or Online Field Trip
Assigned Reading—*Brand Week*, *Advertising Age*, *WSJ*, scholarly publications, category trade journals
Blog your problem from either point of view, gather responses/posts (www.blogger.com/start)

Pricing Strategies

Chapter Overview The previous chapter addressed the product and service elements of the marketing mix. This chapter examines pricing and pricing strategies, which are critical to generating revenue and earning profits. It explains how to establish a price by understanding a product's value, its supply-and-demand curves, and its costs. General pricing practices are discussed, including the need to comply with legal requirements, price quotes, competitive bidding, and global pricing. The chapter concludes by exploring pricing strategies for specific marketing situations, such as the introduction of new products, online versus storefront pricing, auctions, portfolio pricing, and making price adjustments.

Chapter Outline

Objective 1. What are the roles of price and value in the marketing mix? How do market structures, costs, and demand affect prices?

Objective 2. What are the most important market factors influencing pricing decisions?

Objective 3. How do marketers use pricing strategy and pricing objectives to achieve their goals?
Objective 4. What procedures and strategies do marketers use when making pricing decisions?

Establishing PRICES (pp. 179–183)

DEFINED *A* **price** *is the exchange value of a product or service in the marketplace.*

EXPLAINED

Establishing Prices

Science fiction author Robert Heinlein is credited with popularizing the acronym TANSTAAFL, which stands for "There Ain't No Such Thing As A Free Lunch."[1] Whether you prefer to eat at Subway or Panera Bread, this saying holds true. Whenever you make a purchase, an exchange is taking place—you are giving up one thing in order to have another. A price is the formal expression of the value of this exchange.

Although consumers weigh a price carefully when making a purchase decision, the literal price is only part of a product's value. It is a product's perceived value that determines whether it will be purchased, not just its price. Value is a consumer's subjective evaluation of the ratio of the benefits of a product or service to its price. This concept is captured in a simple formula:

$$\text{Value} = \frac{\text{Benefits}}{\text{Price}}$$

A "good value" or a "good deal" is an instance where the ratio of product benefits to price is large. These benefits could be functional benefits, emotional benefits, or a combination of both. Your jacket may not only keep you dry in the rain (a functional benefit), but if it carries a prestigious brand name, it may also make you feel special when wearing it (an emotional benefit).

Price is the marketing mix variable that translates a product's or service's value into monetary terms. If a product is seen to have greater value, it should also have a higher price. The converse is also true, because marketers are forced to cut prices when items decline in perceived value.

Value is a relative concept, because customers will compare alternative products to find the one that offers the most benefits at the least cost. Because price is part of the value equation, whenever any competitor in a market raises (or lowers) its price, the value of every other product is affected. Beyond price, marketers add value for customers by improving the following:

- Product reliability
- Product performance
- Longevity
- Cost (both initial cost and lifetime cost)
- User and environmental safety
- Service (delivery reliability, speed, and flexibility)
- Superior aesthetics or design
- Prestige

Fair prices are those consumers perceive as offering good value and meeting personal and social norms. Unfair prices can evoke strong negative emotion. Companies must be careful to establish fair prices, which convey both value and fair dealing, or they risk alienating customers.

APPLIED

Establishing Prices

Among the elements of the marketing mix, price is most closely linked with revenue. The activities of product development, promotion, and distribution are considered to be costs with, at best, only an

The Apple iPod has been an incredible success, with sales ranging from 50 to 60 million units per year. In addition to breakthrough design and innovative advertising, pricing has been a cornerstone of the iPod marketing strategy. Apple follows a price-lining strategy that positions newer versions of its players or those with the most advanced features at higher price points. For example, consider the following:

- The iPod Shuffle is the smallest and most portable version of the iPod, but has the least amount of storage. Its price begins at $49.
- The iPod Nano is larger than the Shuffle, but can hold more songs and play video. Its price starts at $149.
- The iPod Touch responds to touch and movement like the iPhone and has a starting price of $199.
- The iPod Classic boasts 160GB of storage that can hold 40,000 songs, 200 hours of video, or 25,000 photos and begins at $249.

By offering players at a range of prices, Apple has expanded the number of customers who can afford an iPod. An additional benefit is the opportunity to up-sell a consumer to a $149 Nano when that customer was originally interested in a $49 iPod Shuffle. Apple's profit stream does not end with the sale of its MP3 players. By selling individual songs on its iTunes Web site for around a dollar, the company further extends its revenue stream over time and enhances the value of each iPod.[2]

PHOTO: Joseph Moore/Shutterstock.

indirect ability to encourage sales. For example, although a clever advertising campaign may encourage brand preference over the long term (and possibly an increase in sales), it is easier to understand how a price adjustment leads to a short-term change in revenue.

Prices are dynamic and constantly changing, but they are a clear reflection of marketplace value in a free market system. They are affected by changes in economic conditions, such as recessions, in which the disposable incomes of consumers fall, or to the introduction of a new product by a competitor, which may offer customers a better value. Pricing must also be aligned with the firm's overall marketing strategy and the product's brand positioning. If the products of an upscale brand (like Gucci) are priced too low, are always on sale, or are a "deal," the company risks an erosion of its brand equity. Price can even be an indicator of quality or superiority. The **price–quality ratio** describes this relationship: Higher-priced products are assumed to have better quality. Lower-priced products are assumed to have lesser quality, regardless of actual product performance. Prices must be carefully calibrated with regard to pricing objectives, market structure, cost, and customer demand.

Market Structure

Market structure refers to the state of a market with respect to competition. Market structure defines the boundaries of a firm's pricing flexibility. In theory, an individual firm is either a price "maker" with the ability to set prices above those of its competitors, or a price "taker" who must accept the marketplace price for its products or services. Economists recognize four types of market structures:

- **Monopoly**—A single firm is able to act as a price "maker," often due to product exclusivity (such as a patent) or high barriers to competitive entry. This gives a monopoly substantial **pricing power**, which is the ability to set a high price without a significant deterioration in market share. For example, patents on new drugs grant pharmaceutical companies monopoly power by restricting competition. Only the owner of a patent can sell the formulation of a drug, and any firms caught copying or simulating the patented product face legal sanctions. Although they are defended as essential for funding advanced drug research and development, monopolies resulting from patent protection can lead to prices almost 10 times above the competitive market price.
- **Oligopoly**—A small group of firms that shares pricing power through its collective ability to control prices, usually by restricting product supply. Cartels such as OPEC are the modern-day equivalent of oligopolies. For oligopolies to function, they depend on cooperation between member companies, who must agree to meet price and production targets. This can lead to a market price for the products of all member firms that is higher than any single company could achieve on its own.
- **Monopolistic competition**—A limited number of firms compete by offering products with varying degrees of differentiation. In this market structure, individual firms have a moderate ability to set higher prices, depending on customer demand for their specific brand. Nike, Reebok, and Adidas all make tennis shoes. But their products differ in terms of design, materials, and brand image. Each company may charge a price premium to the degree that its shoes are more appealing than those of its competitors. At the same time, monopolistic competition cannot function like a monopoly because if prices are raised too high, customers will defect to competitors.
- **Pure competition**—A large number of producers sell mostly undifferentiated products, like wheat or soybeans. No particular brand of wheat or soybeans is preferred by consumers, so no producer has any appreciable pricing power. In purely competitive situations, companies usually deemphasize price as part of the marketing mix.

Due to globalization and the proliferation of product choices, today's marketplace is highly competitive. Evidence of this is the increasing failure of both start-up and long-standing businesses. Once-healthy and vibrant sectors like banks, automobiles, and airlines are under increasing pressure to reduce prices, cut costs, and consolidate operations. In response, some American firms have outsourced portions of their business, such as customer service or finance, to countries with lower labor costs. Economic cycles, globalization, the proliferation of product choices, and business failures lead to increased competition on the basis of price and downward pressure on profits. It is essential for marketing managers to aggressively manage costs in these situations.

Cost-Based Pricing

In addition to market structure, the cost to manufacture a product or deliver a service should be taken into account. Three common ways to group costs are as follows:

- **Fixed costs** (or **overhead**) are those costs associated with a product incurred regardless of any production or sales taking place.
- **Variable costs** are costs directly attributable to the production of a product or the delivery of a service.
- **Total cost** is the sum of fixed and variable costs.

For example, the Air Transport Association reports the Quarterly Cost Index on U.S. Passenger Airlines, which divides airline operating expenses into various categories. Variable costs such as fuel, food, labor, and marketing add up to about 85% of total operating cost. Insurance, landing fees, aircraft rents, and other miscellaneous items make up the remainder of the costs.[3]

To earn a profit, a firm must generate revenue that exceeds its total costs. The relationship between a company's profit, revenue, and costs is as follows:

$$\text{Profit} = \underset{\text{(Price)} \times \text{Sales}}{\underset{\uparrow}{\text{Revenue}}} - \underset{\text{Fixed Cost} + \text{Variable Cost}}{\underset{\uparrow}{\text{Total Costs}}}$$

A product's **profit margin** is the difference between its price and total cost per unit. Because revenue is a function of sales volume times price per unit, improving the margin will also increase profitability. **Cost-based pricing** (or cost-oriented) approaches to pricing recognize the need to establish a price that offsets costs and results in a reasonable profit margin or rate of return.

A traditional cost-based method for setting margins is the **cost-plus pricing** approach, which adds a fixed amount to the cost of each item sufficient to earn a desired profit. The additional amount, or margin, added to each product is called a **markup** and is calculated as a percentage of unit variable cost. Although some people use the terms interchangeably, a markup is technically not the same thing as a margin. A markup determines a price based on product cost, while a margin is determined by the difference between the final price and unit cost. Table 13.1 compares margin and markup for a hypothetical product.[4] Let's take the first and last examples from the table and demonstrate how margin and markup are calculated:

> You buy a $9.00 widget from ACME company and sell it to your customer Sue for $10.00. Your margin is $1.00, or 10% of the sales price of $10.00. Your markup is $1.00, or 11% of your purchase price of $9.00.
>
> Let's say that you buy a $2.50 widget from ACME company and sell it to your customer Sue for $10.00. Your margin is $7.50, or 75% of the sales price of $10.00. Your markup is $7.50, or 300% of your purchase price of $2.50.

Margin and markup, therefore, are two methods that calculate profit from different perspectives. From this example, you can see that a 10% margin generated more profit than a 10% markup.

Another cost-based technique for setting price is to calculate a product's **break-even point,** which is a projected price and sales volume where a company "breaks even," or earns revenue exactly equal to its total cost.

At the break-even point, profits are zero. If a firm can sell one additional unit beyond the break-even point, it will earn a profit equal to the margin on that product. Because each additional sale contributes to the bottom line, the gap between price and variable cost is also called a **contribution margin**. The formula used to calculate a break-even point (in units) is as follows:

$$\text{Break-Even Volume} = \frac{\text{Fixed Cost}}{\text{Price} - \text{Variable Cost}}$$

Table 13.1 Relationship Between Margin and Markup

Price	Cost	Margin	Markup
$10.00	$9.00	10%	11%
$10.00	$7.50	25%	33%
$10.00	$6.67	33%	50%
$10.00	$5.00	50%	100%
$10.00	$4.00	60%	150%
$10.00	$3.33	67%	200%
$10.00	$2.50	75%	300%

For instance, suppose a product sells for $50. If the product costs $10 per unit to manufacture, and the company's fixed costs are $60,000, then break-even volume is 1,500 units, or

$$1{,}500 \text{ units} = \frac{\$60{,}000}{\$50 - 10}$$

Break-even analysis is helpful to marketers because it clarifies, for a given price, the minimum number of products a company must sell to stay in business. When performing a break-even analysis, marketers find it helpful to calculate the break-even formula at various price points. In Figure 13.1, the firm's variable cost per unit is $5, fixed costs are $40,000, and price per unit is $10.

In this example, the break-even point is 8,000 units. It should be immediately apparent that any quantity to the left of the break-even point (below 8,000 units) will result in a net loss for the firm, because total cost will be greater than total revenue (represented by the red shaded area). Any sales volume above 8,000 units will be profitable (the green shaded area). Based on this information, the product price is adjusted upward or downward until a volume is reached that the marketing group believes is both achievable and profitable. A firm might use a rate of return on investment (such as 10% or 15% on total cost) or a target amount of profit as its criteria.

The main advantage to using cost-based pricing methods is that they are relatively easy to calculate. Once costs have been estimated, you simply determine the markup needed to earn a target amount of revenue (or offset fixed costs plus a satisfactory amount of profit). One drawback, however, is that this approach ignores customer demand for the product. It is based solely on cost and desired profit. If fixed or variable costs are too high relative to competition, then using a cost-based approach can lead to an uncompetitive price. If the products offered by competitors are comparable in terms of brand image and performance, a cost-based pricing method will dictate a price that is too high for the marketplace. Customers will not pay a higher price without added benefits. The marketing challenge then becomes how to find a way to make the product more attractive without adding cost, or to reduce fixed, variable, or total costs.

FIGURE 13.1 The Break-Even Formula at Various Price Points

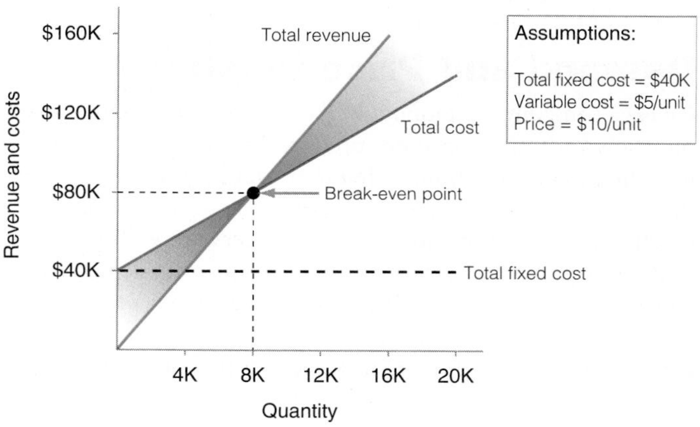

EXAMPLE COST-BASED PRICING

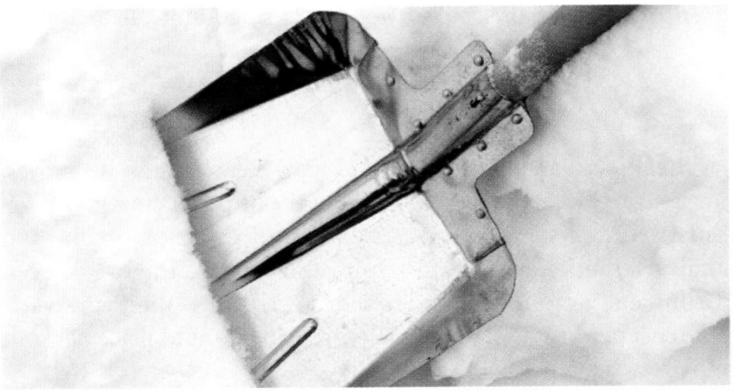

Dr. Sarah Maxwell is an expert in the theory and practice of fair pricing. Two components of fairness are personal fairness and social fairness. Personal fairness is how people perceive that a price affects them personally. Social fairness is how people judge that a price is fair to society in general.

All price increases may be personally unfair to a degree, but the situation can be made worse, depending on how socially unfair they seem. Dr. Maxwell conducted an interesting study that asked two separate groups of people to consider two different imaginary pricing scenarios:

- The first group was told that a hardware store had been selling snow shovels for $15, but raised the price to $20 after a snowstorm. They were then asked to rate this action as completely fair, acceptable, unfair, and very unfair.
- For the second group, the scenario and questions were identical to the first, with the omission of any reference to a snowstorm.

When a storm was not mentioned, 69% of people in the second group found the price increase to be unfair, compared with 86% in the first group. Both groups perceived the price increase to be unfair, most likely due to the negative personal impact of paying a higher price (that is, personal fairness). But the second group also saw the price change as socially unfair, as evidenced by the higher percentage who rated the store's action unfavorably. Raising prices to "take advantage" of a snowstorm was perceived as unfair both to individuals and to society.[5]

PHOTO: Fedor A. Sidorov/Shutterstock.

>> END EXAMPLE

Demand and Price Elasticity

Unless a company is a monopoly, it cannot set prices based solely on its own whims. Consumer preferences also must be factored into the pricing equation. A **demand curve** (or **demand schedule**), as illustrated in Figure 13.2, charts the projected sales for a product or service for any price customers are willing to pay. Each point along the curve represents the quantity demanded by consumers for a product at a given price. When plotted on a graph of quantity demanded versus price, a typical demand curve begins in the upper-left corner, and then slopes downward and to the right. This is because customers usually buy more of a product at lower prices than at higher ones.

FIGURE 13.2 The Demand Curve

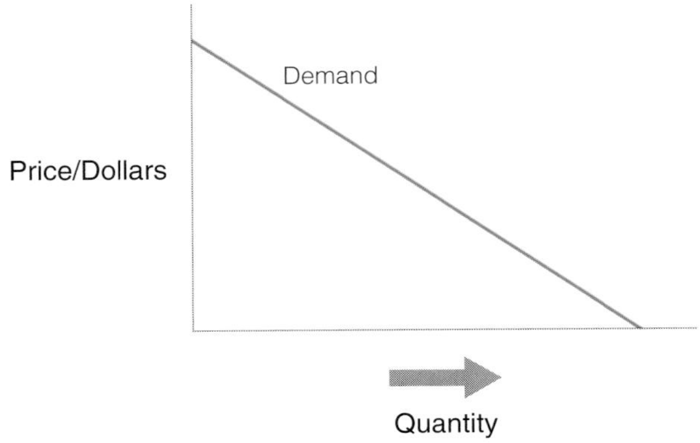

Using a break-even analysis, a marketer can estimate a target volume and price. The demand curve can then be employed as a quick validation of the feasibility of these assumptions. Are customers willing to purchase the target quantity at the desired price? If the price is too low, can it be changed without a substantial impact on sales? At first glance, the break-even price is sometimes below what a firm would like to charge to cover its fixed costs. Appropriate responses include reductions in fixed costs, variable costs, or tactics such as innovative advertising campaigns to enhance perceived product value.

Marketers may also attempt to stimulate customer demand for product categories or individual brands through nonprice methods. Developing improved versions of products or launching clever new advertising campaigns are just a couple of ways companies attempt to shift their demand curves upward, thereby maintaining higher prices.

EXAMPLE DEMAND AND PRICE ELASTICITY

In 1993, the California Milk Processor Board (CMPB) decided that something needed to be done to turn around 15 consecutive years of falling milk sales. Although prices could be lowered to increase demand, this would be a short-term strategy at best and could threaten the survival of California's milk producers. Instead, the CMPB chose to use advertising to stabilize and reverse milk sales.

"Got Milk?" became the tagline for a memorable advertising campaign designed to stimulate demand for an entire category of products. Every ad was based on a single consumer insight: Milk is usually consumed along with food, and people care passionately about the product if it runs out while they are eating. Marquee TV ads included a game show contestant who eats a peanut butter sandwich but cannot give the winning answer because he has run out of milk.

The ad campaign achieved 90% awareness in California by 1995, aided by national news coverage. Tracking studies and sales figures from the California Department of Food and Agriculture showed that milk was being used more often. It may be quick and simple to lower prices to improve sales,

Tennis whites.
On or off the court, the calcium in milk
keeps bones strong and helps prevent osteoporosis.
got milk?

but sometimes marketing techniques can shift the demand curve itself.[6]

PHOTO: Courtesy of Lowe Worldwide as agent for the National Fluid Milk Processor Promotion Board.

>> END EXAMPLE

A product's **price elasticity** measures the percentage change in quantity demanded relative to a percentage change in price. Also called price elasticity of demand, this metric is helpful to marketers because it provides a guideline as to how much, or how little, a price should be increased or decreased. Elasticity can be measured at any point along the demand curve. The formula for estimating price elasticity is as follows:

$$\text{Price Elasticity} = \frac{\%\Delta \text{ Quantity}}{\%\Delta \text{ Price}}$$

Suppose demand falls by 6% when a price is increased by 2%. The price elasticity at this point along the demand curve is –3. This situation is said to be price **elastic** because the quantity is highly responsive to a change in price. Marketers consider lowering their prices when demand is elastic, because the relatively greater change in volume may lead to higher total profits. When elasticity is less than one, the situation is said to be price **inelastic**. Quantity demanded is largely unresponsive to a change in price. At inelastic points along the demand curve, marketers often increase prices and thus maximize profits. A monopoly has an inelastic demand curve, because it can raise prices with little fear that large numbers of customers will defect to other products.

By encouraging brand preference among their customers, some firms attempt to change the slope of their demand curves. Powerful brands are more price inelastic, allowing marketers to charge higher prices for moderately differentiated goods or services. For instance, a comparison of prices on the Blue Cross and Blue Shield Web site from 2009 showed that a brand name 750 mg tablet of a popular prescription pain medication was $1.26, while a generic version of the drug was only $0.06.

PRICING Practices (pp. 184–186)

DEFINED **Pricing practices** *are considerations (such as legal requirements or bidding practices) that must be taken into account when establishing a price for a product or service.*

EXPLAINED

Pricing Practices

Establishing prices relies on an understanding of market structure, costs, and marketplace demand. Measuring price elasticity, in particular, requires data on customer demand at numerous price points. But it also requires marketers to consider other factors that may present constraints or opportunities for pricing strategy.

Marketers do not have total freedom when setting prices. But neither do they have to simply accept the market price for a product or service. Marketing can influence customer perceptions, and thereby affect prices. Products that are perceived as different and unique due to higher quality or a more exciting brand image often command higher prices.

A number of considerations to take into account when crafting a pricing strategy include legal requirements, the character of the competitive bidding process, and setting prices in a global marketing environment.

APPLIED

Pricing Practices

Pricing practices are basically rules that marketers should follow when setting prices. Some of these, like legal requirements, restrict marketers' freedom of action. Others, like global pricing, allow marketers to maximize the effectiveness of their pricing strategies across national borders.

Implementing smart pricing practices and strategies represents a huge opportunity for marketers to improve the bottom line. In their book *Six Sigma Pricing* authors Manmohan Sodhi and Navdeep Sodhi estimate that well-managed pricing strategies add between 8% and 11% to operating profit, more than cost or sales volume (see Table 13.2).[7]

One of the more interesting aspects of pricing is its relationship to psychology. Beyond cost estimation, demand curves, and elasticity calculations, pricing strategy depends on how people make decisions. And this process is not always rational. For example, **odd-even pricing** is a practice that sets prices at fractional numbers instead of whole ones. An example is an item that is priced at $9.99 instead of $10.00. Logically, a price that is lower by one penny should make little difference, but research shows consumers will buy more of an item priced at $9.99 than $10.00.

Table 13.2 Average Impact of 1% Improvement on Operating Profit

Driver	Compustat Companies	S&P 500 Companies
Price management	11.1%	8.2%
Variable cost	7.8%	5.1%
Sales volume	3.3%	3.0%
Fixed costs	2.3%	2.0%

Marketers also engage in **price bundling** to make two or more items appear more attractive at a single price than individually. A McDonald's value meal is a classic example of price bundling, where a sandwich, beverage, and fries are sold in a bundle. Computer manufacturers such as Dell and Gateway also sell computers with preinstalled devices, such as DVD drives along with preloaded software. In some instances, the price bundle offers a discount on the collected items. Another benefit for customers is the psychological effort they are saved in terms of product search and price evaluation.

Legal Requirements

The federal government, state governments, and private groups (like the Better Business Bureau) have taken an active interest in encouraging fair pricing practices. The goal of federal laws, state laws, and other guidelines is to promote fairness in pricing both for customers and for members of the distribution network. Marketers must keep one eye on their own strategic imperatives, for example, cost and marketplace demand, and the other eye on the legal requirements for fair pricing.

In terms of federal law, pricing is the most heavily regulated aspect of the marketing mix. **Antitrust law** is the catchall phrase for federal legislation meant to prohibit anticompetitive actions on the part of manufacturers, wholesalers, or resellers. The name for these laws dates back to the turn of the twentieth century, when industries like tobacco, oil, and steel were dominated by monopolies or oligopolies (also called "trusts"). A key assumption underlying this legislation is that actions on the part of private firms that lessen competition could force consumers, wholesalers, or resellers to pay unnecessarily inflated prices. The major U.S. antitrust laws are presented in Table 13.3.[8]

Table 13.3 Summary of U.S. Antitrust Laws

Federal Legislation	Purpose of Legislation	Concerns
Sherman Antitrust Act of 1890	Make acts in restraint of trade illegal	• Price fixing • Bid fixing (rigging) • Monopolization (interstate)
Federal Trade Commission Act (FTC Act) of 1914	Establishes FTC in order to investigate unfair trade practices	• Price discrimination • Price fixing
Clayton Act of 1914	Outlaws unfair trade practices	• Price discrimination • Predatory pricing
Robinson-Patman Act of 1936	Outlaws price discrimination	• Price discrimination

A violation of federal antitrust legislation can incur severe penalties. For example, individuals can be fined up to $350,000 and receive up to three years in prison for each offense under the Sherman Antitrust Act. Corporations can be fined up to $10 million for each offense, and fines can go even higher. Although the Clayton Act carries no criminal penalties, if found guilty of an infringement, a firm may be forced to pay triple damages as well as court and lawyer fees.

Types of unfair pricing activities prohibited by antitrust law are as follows:

- **Price fixing**—This occurs when two or more companies discuss prices in an effort to raise the market price for their products. Working together in this manner is also called collusion. Under the Sherman Antitrust Act, it is illegal to discuss prices with a competitor or even to mention prices in the competitor's presence, because this would reduce competition.
- **Price discrimination**—This occurs whenever a firm injures competition by charging different prices to different members of its distribution channel. Price discrimination that lessens competition in interstate commerce is illegal under both the Robinson-Patman Act and the Clayton Act. A marketer cannot offer a discount, rebate, coupon, or other benefit to one customer and not another, with a few exceptions. If a company has lower costs, a physically different product, or must adjust its price to meet competition, it is not considered to be guilty of price discrimination.
- **Predatory pricing**—When a firm sells its products at low prices to drive competitors out of the market, it is acting in a predatory manner. If the intention of an extremely low price is to bankrupt competitors and leave the low-priced firm as the sole survivor, this is considered to be a predatory strategy and is illegal under the Sherman Antitrust Act. An acceptable defense to these charges is that the firm has a more efficient cost structure that allows it to still earn a profit at much lower prices.

Antitrust cases may be brought against companies in one of three ways: by the Antitrust Division of the Department of Justice, by the Federal Trade Commission, or by private parties against each other. Today, private firms initiate the majority of antitrust cases in an attempt to curtail what they perceive to be unfair pricing practices.

EXAMPLE LEGAL REQUIREMENTS

Price fixing is prohibited not only in the United States, but also in other countries. In 2002, the Hasbro toy company was found guilty of fixing prices on games such as Monopoly and on *Star Wars* merchandise. Hasbro was accused of forcing 10 of its distributors to enter price-fixing agreements. "These [price-fixing] agreements prevented the distributors from selling Hasbro toys and games below Hasbro's list price without permission," said a representative for Britain's Office of Fair Trading (OFT). As punishment, the OFT imposed its largest fine in history on the company—£4.95 million ($7.7 million).[9]

PHOTO: Gualbereto Becerra/Shutterstock.

>> **END EXAMPLE**

Other federal and state laws attempt to curtail **deceptive pricing**, which occurs when a price is meant to intentionally mislead or deceive customers. Deceptive pricing can take many forms. Perhaps the most well-known is **bait-and-switch pricing**. In this scenario, an unscrupulous marketer advertises a low price on a desirable product. When customers attempt to buy the advertised product, they discover it has "sold out," but that many higher-priced items just happen to be readily available. The law is that an advertised price must be a bona fide offer, or one made legitimately in good faith.

Some states have prohibited **loss-leader pricing** as an unfair sales act that harms consumers. Traditionally used as a form of **promotional pricing** by retailers such as grocery stores, loss-leading pricing involves selling items below cost to drive floor traffic. Laws restricting this kind of pricing are intended to protect smaller competitors whose cost structures do not allow them to conduct similar promotional activities.

Quotations, Competitive Bidding, and Negotiated Pricing

Every product and service has a price, whether it is sold to consumers or to businesses. A price offered by a business to a consumer is often called a **sticker price,** or an **MSRP (manufacturer's suggested retail price)**. Prices for most consumer products are preestablished by the manufacturer or retailer. In some instances, the seller may allow a customer to discuss a price, but in the vast majority of cases, this is not allowed. When purchasing paper towels, paint, or dog food, the average customer will accept the sticker price and not attempt to haggle.

In the business-to-business realm, the process for reaching a price acceptable to both buyer and seller is often complex. This is because businesses may need to acquire sophisticated and expensive products like buildings, machinery, or specialized components. Purchases are made by a group of employees instead of an individual and can take weeks, or even months. The purchasing process is usually initiated by a **request for quote (RFQ)**, which specifies the characteristics of the product or service a company wants to purchase. A price **quotation** (or quote) is a supplier's response to an RFQ from a potential customer.

A customer may submit requests to multiple firms to compare quotes. In a **competitive bidding** process, each supplier receives an identical RFQ and is asked to submit a price quote. All bids are "blind," so communication between buyer and sellers remains strictly confidential. After all quotes have been received, they are reviewed. Each supplier is evaluated based on its ability to fulfill the terms of the RFQ at an acceptable price. All things being equal, the supplier that can meet the RFQ criteria at the lowest cost will be chosen. A good purchasing representative will consider not only cost, but also the reputation or track record of a supplier when making a final sourcing decision.

As part of the competitive bidding process, a company's purchasing department often engages in some degree of negotiation with suppliers. A **negotiated price** is the result of a back-and-forth discussion between a buyer and seller regarding the final price of a product or service. Purchasers attempt to trim costs from a bid to obtain a lower price, while sellers try to protect their profit margins. Price negotiation may occur face-to-face or online, through a variety of commercial Web portals. And negotiation is not limited to the business-to-business marketplace, because consumers may also negotiate prices. Negotiation is a common practice when buying a new car or home.

Global Pricing

It used to be that transportation expense and limited access to global communications kept pricing information fairly contained within national borders. The globalization of commerce and travel has led to consumers who are more aware of prices in multiple nations. And the Internet has made it simple to acquire a product or service from almost anywhere in the world. Almost every firm is affected, because although one firm may not engage in multinational operations, other firms can export their products into the firm's home market. Increased competition and downward pressure on prices are the result.

At the same time, there is also opportunity in the global market. Consumers differ from country to country. Brands are different. Products are different. The price of an item in one country could be more than twice as much as in another country. Marketers who recognize and act on market differences customize prices based on individual regional, national, or local characteristics. Prices should be set recognizing the product costs, customer demand, brand equity, and the power of distributors in each market.

As in the United States, legal requirements also impact global pricing strategies. Marketers must set prices, taking into account limitations imposed by possible quotas or tariffs. **Quotas** are limits on the amount of a product that can be imported into a country. Limiting product supply may create the opportunity to raise prices if the product is in high demand, but it also constrains revenue. A **tariff** is a schedule of duties (or fees) applied to goods and services from foreign countries. When a tariff is imposed on a product, the net effect is to increase the product's price, and marketers must take this into account. **Antidumping laws** in some countries are activated when the government perceives that a price has been set too low in an attempt to harm local manufacturers or producers. Quotas, tariffs, fines, and other penalties may result if a firm is found guilty of dumping.

Currency exchange rates specify the price of one currency in terms of the price of another. Currencies flow freely on the global capital market, and their values are constantly changing. Even though a marketer may have taken great care in setting the price for a product, a fluctuation in currency exchange may have the net effect of raising (or lowering) the product's price overnight. There is nothing a marketer can do to influence exchange rates, but when pricing opportunity (or risk) is presented due to a currency fluctuation, the marketer must act quickly.

PRICING Strategies (pp. 187–191)

DEFINED *A* **pricing strategy** *identifies what a business will charge for its products or services.*

EXPLAINED

Pricing Strategies

A pricing strategy includes all activities that convey and enhance the value of a purchase. As already discussed, a price must convey a product's value to customers. It also needs to be fair, or consumers will defect to competitors. There are dimensions to pricing strategy that go beyond the traditional notion of a "price," however. Each of the following is also an example of a pricing strategy:

- Offering a discount when a customer pays within 30 days
- Giving a new-car buyer a trade-in value for his or her old vehicle
- Earning points for purchases when using a retailer's credit card

None of these examples change the literal "price" of the product. The quoted or sticker price remains unchanged. But they all have an impact on the perceived value the customer is receiving and, as a result, are part of pricing strategy.

Pricing objectives are goals that keep marketing actions in alignment with overall business objectives. Any marketing strategy or tactic that influences price or perceived customer value should meet the firm's pricing objectives. Different pricing objectives include the following:

- **Profitability**—to maximize profit or to achieve a target profit level
- **Volume**—to maximize volume or market share
- **Meeting competition**—to remove price as a differentiator by matching competitor prices
- **Prestige**—to create an image of exclusiveness and quality by setting a high price

APPLIED

Pricing Strategies

Should the price for a product be set above, equal to, or below its competition? When setting prices, marketers follow a stepwise process:

1. Develop pricing objectives.
2. Estimate demand.
3. Determine costs.
4. Evaluate the pricing environment.
5. Choose a pricing strategy.
6. Develop pricing tactics.

Steps 1 through 4 have already been discussed in this chapter. Step 5 involves choosing the pricing strategy that is most appropriate, given the product or service. Strategies vary depending on the newness of the product, as well as where it will be sold. In Step 6, a company implements its strategy and monitors the results.

EXAMPLE PRICING STRATEGIES

Many of us enjoy a really tasty hamburger. But not all hamburgers are created (or priced) equal. Restaurants charge different prices for their burgers, according to the unique characteristics of their products and their pricing objectives. Here are some examples:

- **Profitability**—Applebee's sells a cheeseburger for about $7. It is not the cheapest burger, nor the most expensive, but it is sold at a price adequate to cover costs and earn a little profit.
- **Volume**—White Castle sells cheeseburgers for about 70 cents. This low price is designed to maximize sales volume—and encourage you to buy a sack full of cheeseburgers!
- **Meeting competition**—Both McDonald's and Burger King sell cheeseburgers for around $1. Because their cheeseburgers are basic, prices are essentially equal, and marketing emphasis shifts to promotions, for example, movie tie-ins or kids' meal prizes.
- **Prestige**—A Burger Royale at the DB Bistro Moderne in New York City sells for $32. It is a sirloin burger stuffed with short ribs and foie gras (maybe the restaurant will add a slice of cheese gratis). The ingredients are high quality, but customers are also paying for the prestige of a burger prepared by some of New York's top chefs.[10]

PHOTO: Joao Virissimo/Shutterstock.

>> END EXAMPLE

New Product and Service Pricing Strategies

Suppose that you are planning to introduce a totally new product into the marketplace. Perhaps it is an amazing innovation that offers customers surprising benefits they simply will not be able to find anywhere else. The fixed and variable costs for this product are known to you, but what price should you charge? There is probably a segment of customers who are eager to obtain the product at almost any price, or who will certainly pay a premium for it. At the same time, there is another group who like the product, but are unwilling to pay a higher price. This segment will try the product only if it is sold at a low price, which reduces their risk of purchase.

A **skimming price** is set above the marketplace price for similar products or services, usually with the objective of maximizing revenue or profit. Much like a farmer might skim cream from a pail of milk, this strategy attempts to skim out of the market those customers who are willing to pay a higher price. Early adopters who want the latest and greatest technology will pay more for a new product when it is first introduced, even though prices may fall dramatically 12 to 18 months later. Using a skimming price is only feasible when the new product or service has clear, meaningful advantages over alternatives in the market. The main advantage of a skimming price is that it "does not leave money on the table" and it earns the maximum possible margin for the company on each product sold.

When a **penetration price** is used, the product or service is offered at a low price compared to its competition. Although a product may be sufficiently appealing to command a higher price, and therefore is a candidate for a skimming strategy, a marketer might prefer to set a low price so as to quickly generate sales volume, market segment penetration, and production scale. According to the **experience curve** theory, costs to manufacture a product will decline as volume increases. This is because when manufacturing is done at higher volumes, companies are able to buy their inputs in larger, cheaper quantities. They also become more skilled and efficient in their manufacturing processes. As a result, even though margins and profits may be slight at first, they should increase over time as costs fall. The firm also gains from brand recognition as a top-selling product in its category. Table 13.4 outlines when a skimming or a penetration price is most appropriate.[11]

Most products and services are not breakthrough, market-changing innovations. Instead, they are incremental improvements to existing products or line extensions under already well-known brand names. Skimming or penetration pricing strategies can be appropriate, but marketers must fully understand consumer perceptions of the product and its pricing power. Marketers should also keep in mind that competitors will react to whatever pricing strategy is employed and attempt to capitalize on vulnerabilities.

EXAMPLE NEW PRODUCT AND SERVICE PRICING STRATEGIES

Every day, ballpoint pens are used by millions of people. The basic design of each pen is similar and includes a barrel, ink cartridge, and pocket clip. Simple versions employ a cap to keep ink fresh, while others are spring activated by a push button. For some customers, ballpoint pens are merely a means to an end: a way to write a school paper or a quick note. For other customers, they might be a high-involvement specialty product and convey an image of prestige or exclusiveness based on the brand of pen or its heritage. As a result, marketers of ballpoint pens follow different pricing strategies:

- The BIC brand uses a penetration pricing strategy to generate high sales volume. BIC targets a large segment of consumers who view ballpoint pens as purely functional, disposable devices. A package of 12 BIC pens might sell for $3 to $4 (or as little as 25 cents per pen).
- Mont Blanc targets a smaller group of customers who are highly involved with their pens and view them as fashion items or exclusive collectibles. The brand uses a skimming pricing strategy because its buyers will pay a premium for top quality and craftsmanship. Mont Blanc rollerballs can run $300, or more than 2,000 times the price of a disposable pen.[12]

PHOTO: Dusan Zidar/Shutterstock.

>> END EXAMPLE

Table 13.4 Proper Uses of Skimming and Penetration Pricing

Use a skimming price when . . .	Use a penetration price when . . .
• The product performs better than alternatives.	• Demand is very elastic.
• Early adopters will value the product highly.	• Producing higher quantities can reduce costs.
• Demand is initially inelastic.	• The threat of competitor imitation is strong.
• A company cannot meet expected demand.	• No segment is willing to pay a higher price.
• The goal is to position the product as high quality.	• A low price may prevent competitors from entering the market.
• A company wants to avoid a price war.	

Online and Storefront Pricing Strategies

Before the Internet emerged as another place for customers to buy (or sell) products, people bought the majority of their goods and services through traditional retail channels like grocery stores, mass merchandisers, or other "brick and mortar" businesses. **Storefront pricing** (also called offline pricing) refers to prices established for products or services sold through these kinds of traditional sales channels.

Today, the Internet is an important part of global commerce, with players like Amazon.com becoming a major force in online retailing. **Online pricing** is the process of setting prices for products or services sold over the Internet or through an electronic medium. When developing a pricing strategy, depending on its distribution methods, a firm may use online pricing, offline pricing, or a combination of both.

The Internet's primary effect on pricing strategy has been in the area of **cost transparency,** which is the ability of consumers to understand a firm's true costs. Information about prices is readily abundant, easy to find, and free to anyone with a computer and Internet connectivity. A seller's costs and profit margins become more transparent to its customers. In the past, if you wanted to understand the true cost of a product or whether a price was fair, you had to visit many different storefront locations to collect pricing data. Few customers had the time or willingness to do this. Internet pricing sites like Priceline.com will provide this information quickly and for free. Table 13.5 displays price differences for contact lenses sold both online and offline.[13]

From the marketer's perspective, although cost transparency may be good for consumers' pocketbooks, it also makes online pricing more difficult. Cost transparency has four effects on pricing strategy:[14]

- It erodes high margins because consumers have a better understanding of product costs.
- It can turn products and services into commodities that can be sold only at a common market price.
- It may weaken customer loyalty to brands (if margins are perceived as unfair).
- It can create a perception of price unfairness (if customers feel they are paying too much).

Although marketers can never put the Internet genie back into the bottle, there are strategies marketers can deploy to offset the impact of online cost transparency. A company may use **price lining** (also called **tiered pricing** or **versioning**) to create different prices for different products and services. This technique is commonly used by telecommunications companies that offer various plans at different price points based on customer needs. **Dynamic pricing** (or **"smart" pricing**) is the practice of varying prices based on market conditions, differences in the cost to serve customers, or in the value customers place on a product. When airlines charge a higher fare to business travelers who attempt to book a flight at the last minute, they are leveraging the power of dynamic pricing. Marketers should be cautious in setting dynamic prices, because customers may feel they have been treated unfairly or could even bring accusations of price discrimination.

Auction Pricing Strategies

"Going once . . . going twice . . . sold!" is the phrase we commonly associate with **auctions,** in which buyers and sellers engage in an adjudicated process of offer and counteroffer until a price acceptable to both parties is reached. A **forward auction** happens when a buyer puts forth what he or she is seeking to purchase and sellers respond in kind with bids (or prices). Forward auctions end when a bid that is high enough for the seller and low enough for the buyer is reached. In contrast, a **reverse auction** takes place when a buyer communicates not only his or her specifications for the product or service, but also an exact price he or she is willing to pay. If one or more companies are willing to accept the buyer's price, then the reverse auction is complete.

Until recently, the auction process has been used most often in business-to-business contexts. Online auction sites, such as eBay.com, have popularized the notion of negotiating prices in the business-to-consumer and consumer-to-consumer realms. Many customers no longer accept the sticker price and expect that they will be able to negotiate. Respected brands, unique products, and store location (screen placement) can help protect margins. However, new competitors and more powerful price comparison sites are popping up on a daily basis, so marketers must be prepared to negotiate without giving up too much profit.

It is critical for marketers conducting online auctions or price negotiations with customers to understand the **incremental cost** leading to an online sale. These costs include not only the wholesale costs of the product or service, but also the expected clickthrough fees paid to platforms. **Clickthrough fees** are the amount one online entity charges another online entity for passing along a Web user who clicks an ad or link. On price-comparison sites, these fees range from 40 cents to as much as $1.50 or more. Knowing the incremental cost helps marketers more accurately gauge their potential profitability during an auction and establish a price "floor," which tells them when to stop or decline a sale.

Table 13.5 Online and Storefront Pricing Comparisons for Contact Lenses

	Average All Lenses	Average Spherical	Average Specialty
All online	$ 87.92	$65.51	$119.85
All offline	$107.95	$81.89	$146.36
Offline premium	$ 20.03	$16.38	$ 26.51

EXAMPLE AUCTION PRICING STRATEGIES

Many consumers view eBay and similar auction services available at Yahoo!, Amazon.com, or Google as the modern-day alternative to classified ads, flea markets, or plain old word of mouth. You do not need to be a corporation with a multimillion dollar marketing budget to be a retailer. Just make your sales pitch on eBay and see who turns up!

eBay has become the world's most popular online auction site, selling over $60 billion worth of gross merchandise volume annually through its marketplace channels. One of the main selling points for eBay, or for any online auction, is that it keeps prices low by "cutting out the middleman" and encouraging negotiation. Buyers and sellers are able to interact one-on-one without the need for additional markups (except for commissions or listing fees charged by the site). Dedicated shoppers use strategies like sniping, where they hold off making a bid until the last seconds before an auction expires. Professional snipers even install software such as Auction Sentry or HammerSnipe on their PCs to let them monitor multiple auctions simultaneously and bid more quickly.[15]

PHOTO: Dmitriy Shironosov/Shutterstock.

>> END EXAMPLE

Portfolio Pricing Strategies

As defined in Chapter 12, a product portfolio is the collection of all products and services offered by a company. When a company owns a large portfolio of products, pricing decisions focus on whether to charge a similar price across brands or to vary a price according to brand and product type. For example, Samsung sells LCD, plasma, and DLP (digital light projection) televisions under a variety of subbrand names (such as Series 6). Should all of these products be priced in a similar fashion? Should some have higher percentage margins than others? Should all products within a related product line follow a line pricing strategy?

Each product line usually has a **price ceiling,** which is the price below which all products in that line will be priced. A product line also might have a **price floor,** which is the price above which all products within a line will be priced. The price ceiling and floor create a price range for the product line, and individual products are priced anywhere between the two bounds. Over time, price ranges come to be associated with brand names. If a marketer sets a price outside the brand's normal price range, either higher or lower, the product's value may be suspect. The brand's image must be broad enough to accommodate this kind of stretch in its price range. Figure 13.3 illustrates how different products may be priced within a brand's price floor and ceiling.

FIGURE 13.3 Price Ceiling, Price Floor, and Their Effects on Product Pricing

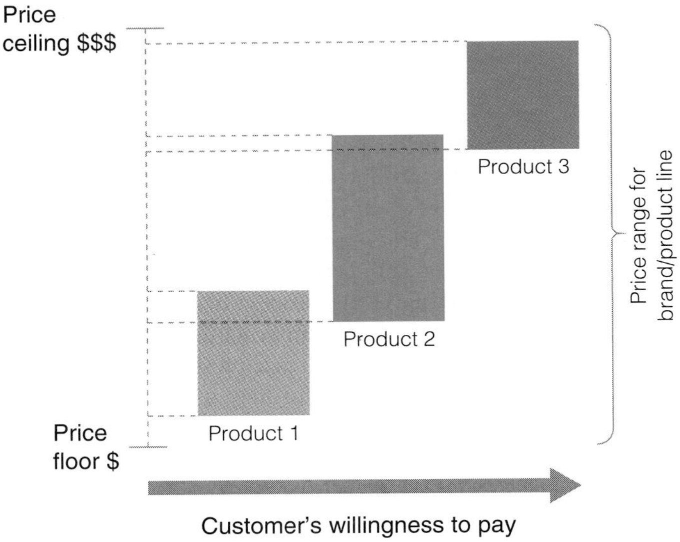

Although there is a degree of overlap in pricing between some products, all prices remain within the price range for the entire product line. They do not exceed the boundaries established by the price ceiling and floor. The same principles apply to portfolios that include multiple product lines and brands. In the illustration, simply replace "Product 1" with "Product Line A" or "Brand X."

As with the majority of pricing questions, a sound portfolio pricing strategy begins with an understanding of customer wants, needs, and willingness to pay. Marketers should then overlay individual product performance compared to competition. If portfolio pricing is not properly managed, then the firm will risk product cannibalization (due to excessive overlaps in price) or erosion in brand equity.

Price Adjustment Strategies

A quoted or sticker price is not necessarily the final price that a customer pays. In some cases, marketers may choose to reduce prices due to competitive pressures, cost advantages, or product improvements. The most straightforward method is to cut the selling price, but once a price is lowered, it may be tough to raise it again. As an alternative, marketers employ several price adjustment strategies to lower the actual price paid by customers, while leaving the MSRP intact:

- **Cash discount**—Customers paying in cash are given a percentage or fixed amount off the quoted price.
- **Quantity discount**—Buying a larger quantity of an item results in a discount per item purchased.
- **Trade-in**—A customer is given cash value for an item in trade toward the new purchase.

- **Rebate**—A manufacturer makes a cash payment back to a customer who has purchased their product at full price.

Reducing prices too often can lead to damaging **price wars** with other firms. Suppose one firm reduces the price of its products. A competitor may react by lowering its prices in turn. Then, the first company may be tempted to reduce price even further. A price war happens when two firms become locked in a downward spiral of constantly reducing prices in reaction to each other. No one wins a price war because if it continues long enough, it will eventually wipe out everyone's profits.

EXAMPLE PRICE ADJUSTMENT STRATEGIES

Pizza restaurants have had difficult times in recent years. Foreign demand for dairy products has sent cheese prices skyrocketing, and droughts in the United States propelled flour prices to all-time highs. All this combined with economic challenges in the U.S. economy have diminished demand.

In the past, product quality and customer service drove market share. With more customers looking for discounts in today's tighter economy, pizza retailers are using low prices as the primary tool to win more business. Combined with higher ingredient costs, price wars among pizza makers are squeezing profit margins.

To avoid the negative consequences of price competition, pizza makers are looking for new ways to maximize revenue and reduce cost. Technology is an answer for some, and more stores are giving customers the option of ordering online or by cell-phone texting. Operators say that check averages for online orders are 10% higher because the Web allows customers to discover items they did not know about. A Papa John's in Louisville, Kentucky, even uses a computer-controlled oven that does not burn at full power until a sufficient number of orders are received.[16]

PHOTO: Hywit Dimyadi/Shutterstock.

>> END EXAMPLE

Visual Summary

Chapter 13 Summary

Pricing is perhaps the most dynamic element of the marketing mix because it is constantly changing in reaction to competitive pressures and marketplace shifts. At the most fundamental level, prices depend on marketplace structure, costs, demand, and price elasticity. Once these factors are understood, marketers overlay pricing practices such as legal or bidding requirements. Final pricing strategies are then developed based on the nature of the product (new or existing), where it will be sold (online, offline, or in an auction), its role in a portfolio, and the need to make pricing adjustments.

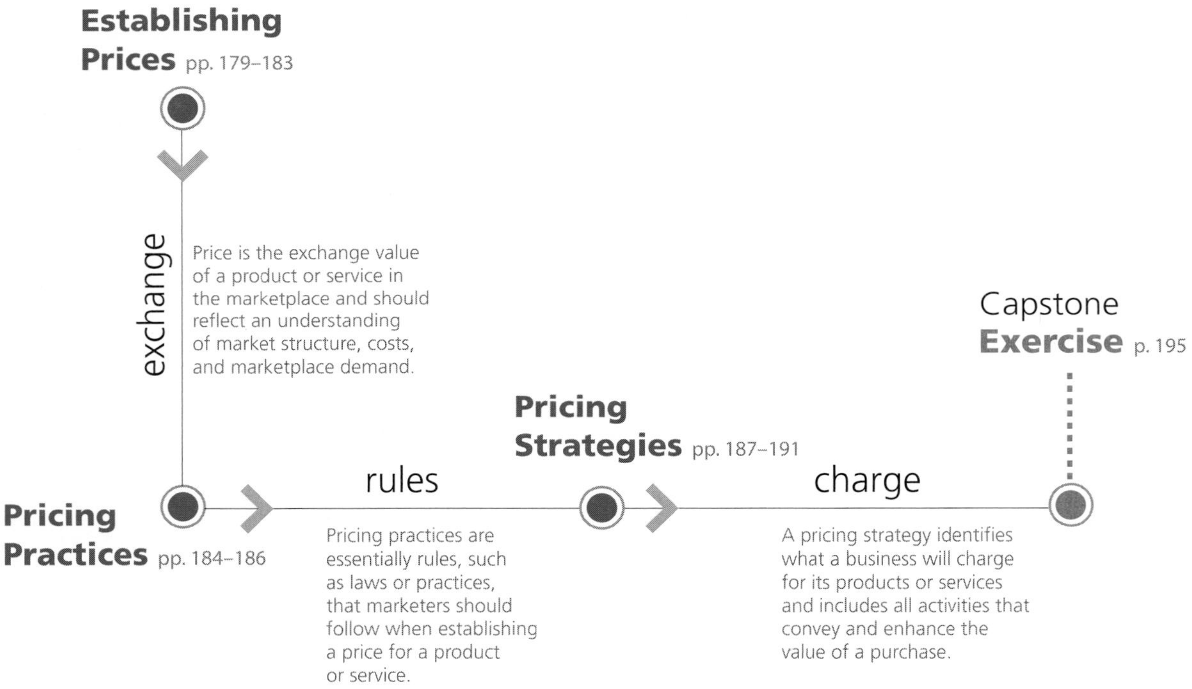
Establishing Prices pp. 179–183
exchange
Price is the exchange value of a product or service in the marketplace and should reflect an understanding of market structure, costs, and marketplace demand.
Pricing Practices pp. 184–186
rules
Pricing practices are essentially rules, such as laws or practices, that marketers should follow when establishing a price for a product or service.
Pricing Strategies pp. 187–191
charge
A pricing strategy identifies what a business will charge for its products or services and includes all activities that convey and enhance the value of a purchase.
Capstone Exercise p. 195

Chapter Key Terms

Establishing **Prices** (pp. 179–183)

Price *is the exchange value of a product or service in the marketplace. (p. 179)* **Opening Example (p. 179)**

Key Terms (pp. 179–183)

Break-even point is the volume or price at which a company's revenue for a product exactly equals its fixed cost. **(p. 181)**

Contribution margin is the difference between a product's price and its variable cost. **(p. 181)**

Cost-based pricing establishes a price based on the cost to manufacture a product or deliver a service. **(p. 181) Example: Cost-Based Pricing (p. 182)**

Cost-plus pricing adds a fixed amount to the cost of each product or service sufficient to earn a desired profit. **(p. 181)**

Demand curve (or **demand schedule**) charts the projected sales for a product or service for any price customers are willing to pay. **(p. 182) Example: Demand and Price Elasticity (pp. 182–183)**

Elastic refers to the situation in which price elasticity is greater than one or when demand is highly responsive to a change in price. **(p. 183) Example: Demand and Price Elasticity (pp. 182–183)**

Fair prices are those consumers perceive as offering good value and meeting personal and social norms. **(p. 179)**

Fixed costs (or **overhead**) are costs that are incurred regardless of any production or sales. **(p. 180)**

Inelastic refers to the situation in which price elasticity is less than one or when demand is relatively nonresponsive to a change in price. **(p. 183)**

Market structure refers to the type of marketplace situation the company faces: monopoly, oligopoly, monopolistic competition, or pure competition. **(p. 180)**

Markup is a percentage or fixed amount added to the cost of a product or service. **(p. 181) Example: Cost-Based Pricing (p. 182)**

Monopolistic competition refers to a market composed of firms with somewhat differentiated products and limited pricing power sufficient to influence the price of their own products to a degree. **(p. 180)**

Monopoly refers to a market composed of a single firm with pricing power sufficient to set the marketplace price for all products or services. **(p. 180)**

Oligopoly refers to a market composed of a small group of firms that share pricing power sufficient to set the marketplace price for their products or services. **(p. 180)**

Price elasticity is the measure of a percentage change in quantity demanded for a product, relative to a percentage change in its price. **(p. 183) Example: Demand and Price Elasticity (pp. 182–183)**

Price–quality ratio is the ratio between the price of a product and its perceived quality. **(p. 180)**

Pricing power is the ability of a firm to establish a higher price than its competitors without losing significant market share. **(p. 180) Example: Cost-Based Pricing (p. 182)**

Profit margin is the difference between the price of a product and its total cost per unit. **(p. 181)**

Pure competition refers to a market composed of a large number of firms that together lack sufficient pricing power to influence the market price for their products. **(p. 180)**

Total cost is the sum of fixed and variable costs. **(p. 180)**

Variable costs are costs directly attributable to the production of a product or the delivery of a service. **(p. 180)**

Pricing Practices (pp. 184–186)

Pricing practices *are considerations (such as legal requirements or bidding practices) that must be taken into account when establishing a price for a product or service. (p. 184)*

Key Terms (pp. 184–186)

Antidumping laws are laws designed to prevent predatory pricing. **(p. 186)**

Antitrust law is a catchall phrase for federal legislation meant to prohibit anticompetitive actions on the part of manufacturers, wholesalers, or resellers. **(p. 184) Example: Legal Requirements (p. 185)**

Bait-and-switch pricing occurs when a firm advertises a low price on a desirable product but, in an attempt to trade customers up to more expensive items, it does not make a good faith effort to carry sufficient quantities of that product. **(p. 185)**

Competitive bidding involves suppliers in a bid process that receive identical RFQs and then return quotes in secret to the buyer. **(p. 186)**

Currency exchange rates are variable rates that specify the price of one currency in terms of the price of another. **(p. 186)**

Deceptive pricing occurs when a price is meant to intentionally mislead or deceive customers. **(p. 185)**

Loss-leader pricing involves the sale of items below cost to drive floor traffic. **(p. 185)**

Negotiated price is the result of a back-and-forth discussion between a buyer and seller regarding the final price of a product or service. **(p. 186)**

Odd-even pricing is a practice that sets prices at fractional numbers, instead of whole ones. **(p. 184)**

Predatory pricing occurs when a firm sells its products at a low price to drive competitors out of the market. **(p. 185)**

Price bundling occurs when two or more items are priced at a single, combined price instead of individually. **(p. 184)**

Price discrimination occurs when a firm injures competition by charging different prices to different members of its distribution channel. **(p. 185)**

Price fixing occurs when two or more companies discuss prices in an effort to raise the market price for their products. **(p. 185) Example: Legal Requirements (p. 185)**

Promotional pricing is the strategy of using price as a promotional tool to drive customer awareness and sales. **(p. 185)**

Request for quote (RFQ) is a document a buyer sends to a potential supplier that outlines the criteria for the goods or services to be purchased. **(p. 186)**

Quotas are limits on the amount of a product that can be imported into a country. **(p. 186)**

Quotation is a supplier's response to an RFQ from a potential customer. **(p. 186)**

Sticker price (MSRP [manufacturer's suggested retail price]) is the quoted or official price for a product. **(p. 186)**

Tariff is a schedule of duties (or fees) applied to goods and services from foreign countries. **(p. 186)**

Pricing Strategies (pp. 187–191)

Pricing strategy *identifies what a business will charge for its products and services. (p. 187)* **Example: Pricing Strategies (p. 187)**

Key Terms (pp. 187–191)

Auctions are markets in which buyers and sellers engage in a process of offer and counteroffer until a price acceptable to both parties is reached. **(p. 189)** **Example: Auction Pricing Strategies (p. 190)**

Cash discount is a percentage or fixed amount off the quoted price of an item and is given when a customer pays in cash. **(p. 190)**

Clickthrough fees are the amount one online entity charges another online entity for passing along a Web user who clicks an ad or link. **(p. 189)** **Example: Auction Pricing Strategies (p. 190)**

Cost transparency is the ability of consumers to understand a product's actual cost. **(p. 189)**

Dynamic pricing (or **"smart" pricing**) is the practice of varying prices based on marketplace conditions. **(p. 189)**

Experience curve is an economic model that presumes costs will decline as production volume increases. **(p. 188)**

Forward auction is a market in which a buyer states what he or she is seeking to purchase and sellers respond in kind with bids (or prices). **(p. 189)** **Example: Auction Pricing Strategies (p. 190)**

Incremental cost is the additional cost to produce or sell one more product or service. **(p. 189)**

Online pricing is the process of setting prices for products or services sold over the Internet or through an electronic medium. **(p. 189)** **Example: Auction Pricing Strategies (p. 190)**

Penetration price is a price that is set low to maximize volume and market share. **(p. 188)** **Example: New Product and Service Pricing Strategies (p. 188)**

Price ceiling is the price all products in a product line must be priced below. **(p. 190)**

Price floor is the price above which all products in a product line must be priced. **(p. 190)**

Price lining (or **tiered pricing, versioning**) is a strategy used to create different prices for different, but related, products or services. **(p. 189)**

Price wars occur when businesses cut prices to take sales from competitors. **(p. 191)** **Example: Price Adjustment Strategies (p. 191)**

Pricing objectives are goals that keep marketing actions in alignment with overall business objectives. **(p. 187)**

Quantity discount is a discount per item purchased that is given to customers buying a larger quantity of a product. **(p. 190)**

Rebate is a cash payment made back to a customer who has purchased his or her products at full price. **(p. 191)**

Reverse auction is a market in which a buyer states what he or she is seeking to purchase, as well as the price he or she is willing to pay. **(p. 189)** **Example: Auction Pricing Strategies (p. 190)**

Skimming price is a price that is set high in order to maximize revenue and profit. **(p. 188)** **Example: New Product and Service Pricing Strategies (p. 188)**

Storefront pricing (also called offline pricing) refers to prices established for products or services sold through traditional sales channels like grocery stores, mass merchandisers, or other "brick and mortar" businesses. **(p. 189)**

Trade-in is the cash value given to a customer when he or she offers his or her own product in trade toward a new purchase. **(p. 190)**

Capstone Exercise

Garland's Lodge is an independent boutique resort located in Oak Creek Canyon just north of Sedona, Arizona. The resort features 16 individual cabins, situated along the banks of Oak Creek, and a full-service gourmet restaurant. The property is open April 2nd through November 20th each year and closes each Sunday at 1 PM until Monday at 11 AM.

Garland's appeals to the discriminating traveler. Its clientele demands excellent service, luxury accommodations, and privacy. Many dates on the reservations calendar are booked a full year in advance. However, overall, occupancy averages 80% for the 198 nights it is open. Garland's manager has recently hired a full-time marketing coordinator to develop a promotional strategy and a revenue management strategy.

The new marketing coordinator learned that the current rate is $295 per night for two persons, which includes afternoon tea, a four-course dinner, and breakfast. This rate applies to all arrival dates throughout the season. The resort requires a two-night minimum stay. In researching occupancy, the coordinator learned that occupancy Fridays and Saturdays throughout the season average nearly 100%. However, Tuesdays and Wednesdays occupancy averages drop to only 60%. With such a small number of rooms, the coordinator is concerned about the financial impact of the perishability of unoccupied rooms.

The coordinator presented a proposal to the manager to adopt a tiered pricing strategy with full rates for Fridays and Saturdays; a 15% discount on Mondays and Thursdays; and, a 20% discount on Tuesdays and Wednesdays. Further, the coordinator is looking at offering a joint package with a local Jeep tour company. The coordinator forecasts that the new rate program will increase overall occupancy average to 90% and, although rooms will be discounted four nights each week, overall revenues will increase as a result. In addition, because of increased occupancy bar and restaurant revenues will also increase.

1. What type of pricing strategy is currently being used? Explain.
2. If total cost associated with an occupied room is $75, what is the lost revenue for each room that remains unoccupied?
3. Based on the new rate structure, if the coordinator can increase overall occupancy to 90% for the following year (assuming Fridays and Saturdays remain at 100%) will the resort increase overall revenues? Explain. Do you need more information?
4. Should the resort consider introducing an Internet rate to reservations booked online through its Web site? Why or why not?
5. What types of pricing strategies would you suggest?

Application Exercise

Use the marketing concepts in this chapter to tackle and solve a marketing problem: price bundling and pricing practices.

First, start by thinking about the products you may buy in a bundle (for example, cable, phone, and Internet service; software suites; combination fast food meals), then choose a set of products that are available both as bundles and as individual items. There are many products available for us to consider purchasing.

The Marketing Problem

Think about your chosen products after considering the following situation.

> Marketers use price bundling as a strategy to increase awareness, interest, and sales. Consumers are under the impression that bundled products are cheaper when purchased together than when they are purchased separately.

The Problem

How often would you say you are motivated to buy more product bundled than when it is priced individually? Are you always getting a "better deal"?

The Solution

Complete the following two Problem/Solution briefs using your products, chapter concepts, and college resources.

1. From the Marketing Manager's Point of View
   a. Problem Definition
   b. Pricing Strategy Analysis
   c. Product's Value
   d. Solution

2. From the Consumer's Point of View
   a. Problem Definition
   b. Individual Item/Bundle Cost Analysis
   c. Product's Value
   d. Solution

Resources:

Marketing Defined, Explained, Applied, Michael Levens, 2e
The College Library
Retail or Online Field Trip
Assigned Reading—*Brand Week*, *Advertising Age*, *WSJ*, scholarly publications, category trade journals
Blog your problem from either point of view, gather responses/posts (www.blogger.com/start)

Supply Chain and Distribution Strategies

Chapter Overview After a product has been created and priced, the next step is to determine how to get the product to the customer for purchase. This chapter deals with the physical distribution (the "Place" element of the marketing mix) of products to consumers or businesses. The various members of a marketing channel, the functions they perform, and the strategies that can be employed are discussed. Other important aspects of the distribution process, including logistics, transportation, and warehousing, are also covered.

Chapter Outline

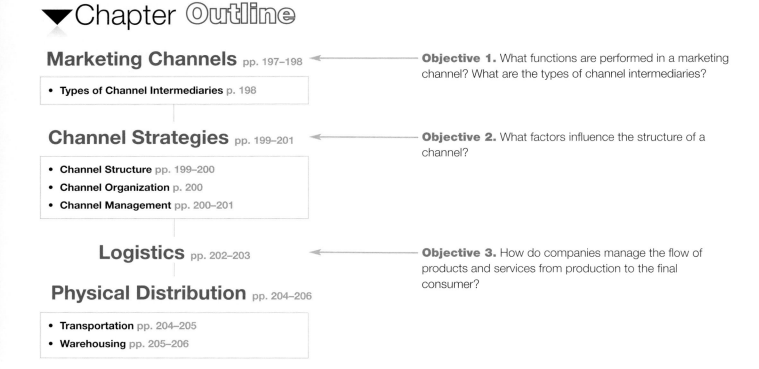

Objective 1. What functions are performed in a marketing channel? What are the types of channel intermediaries?

Objective 2. What factors influence the structure of a channel?

Objective 3. How do companies manage the flow of products and services from production to the final consumer?

MARKETING CHANNELS (pp. 197–198)

DEFINED *A* **marketing channel** *is the network of parties involved in moving products from the producer to consumers or business customers.*

EXPLAINED

Marketing Channels

Think back to the last time you bought groceries. With your shopping list in hand you probably weaved your way through the aisles of a grocery store filling your cart with the items on your list (and probably some that weren't). Could you imagine how different life would be if there were no retailers? The opportunity for you to choose from a wide selection of products, in a single location (such as a grocery store), is made possible through the power of **distribution**. Distribution (or the Place element of the 4 Ps) is the process of making products available to customers. It is essential because without it, products will not be available for customers to purchase.

Several different businesses, or middlemen, participate in the movement of products from production to the point of sale. A marketing channel (or a channel of distribution) includes all the parties that are involved in the distribution process. Channels are composed of one or more intermediaries, such as a wholesaler and a retailer, with each performing a role in producing, collecting, sorting, transporting, promoting, pricing, and selling products to customers. These activities directly relate to the three marketing functions (exchange function, physical function, and facilitating function) that were outlined in Chapter 1. Examples of the specific marketing functions performed by channel members include:

Exchange Function: Negotiate price; make sales; place orders; develop communications
Physical Function: Transport and store products; break bulk; create assortments
Facilitating Function: Gather information; provide credit and other purchase options

Moving products through a marketing channel is expensive; 30% to 50% of the ultimate selling price of a product is attributed to distribution costs.[1] These costs entail more than freight or storage expenses; they also include the profits earned by intermediaries such as wholesalers and retailers. Manufacturers are willing to share the profits with intermediaries in exchange for the functions that they perform. A manufacturer could decide to keep more of the profits by eliminating wholesalers from the channel, but they cannot eliminate the functions that the intermediary performed.

APPLIED

Marketing Channels

In addition to the functions they perform, channel intermediaries provide significant benefits to manufacturers. One key benefit gained through marketing channels is **contact efficiency**, which is explained with a hypothetical example. Assume there are six manufacturers of digital cameras and six consumers who want to buy a digital camera. As shown in Figure 14.1, each manufacturer has to directly contact six consumers, resulting in a total of 36 contact points. If a retailer was added to the mix, as shown in Figure 14.2, the number of contact points is reduced to 12. The addition of a retailer decreased the number of contacts by 67%, making the process more efficient for the consumer and the manufacturer. A retailer provides additional benefits to both consumers and other manufacturers by offering accessories for the digital camera, such as tripods, camera bags, batteries, and memory cards.

At midnight on July 21, 2007, the final installment of the Harry Potter series of books, *Harry Potter and the Deathly Hallows*, went on sale in bookstores around the world. Anticipation among fans was palpable; some stood in line for hours so they could be among the first to own a copy. A year earlier, in 2006, the book's publisher, Scholastic, began distribution plans for 12 million copies—a record number of books for a first printing. To keep the book from slipping out in advance of the official release date, every copy had to arrive in customers' hands as close to 12:01 A.M., July 21, 2007, as possible. Given the enormity of the task, and the book's importance to its readers, Scholastic worked with printers, trucking companies, warehouses, and retailers to make Harry's final bow a complete success. If all the trucks delivering the books were lined up end to end, they would have stretched for 15 miles. The publisher used GPS (Global Positioning System) trackers on every truck to prevent shipments from getting lost. Upon receiving the books, Barnes & Noble.com separated copies according to zip code. A complicated formula was used to calculate exactly when to release a copy to the post office or UPS to guarantee simultaneous arrival across the United States.[2]

PHOTO: Scott Rothstein/Shutterstock.

FIGURE 14.1 Manufacturer-to-Customer Channel

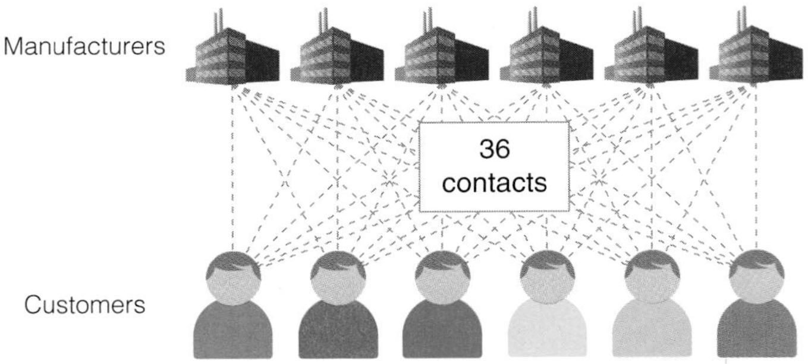

FIGURE 14.2 Manufacturer-to-Retailer-to-Customer Channel

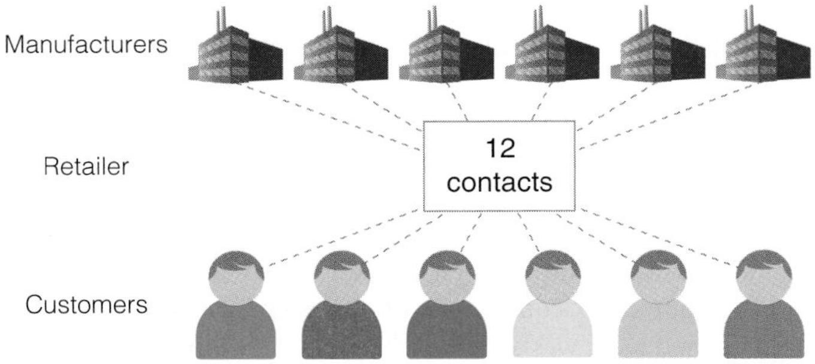

The use of marketing channels can also help to alleviate the differences between the desires of the manufacturer and those of the customer. For example, in a manufacturer's ideal world, the manufacturer would prefer to sell every product it produces, at the time it is produced, and in the location where it is produced. The customer, on the other hand, wants to buy a single unit of the product, at the time he or she needs it, and as close to home as possible. Marketing channels help overcome these differences.

Types of Channel Intermediaries

The role of intermediaries is to improve the overall efficiency and effectiveness of the marketing channel. Channel intermediaries are classified based on whether they take ownership, or title, to the product. Resellers, which include wholesalers and retailers, take ownership of the product, while brokers and facilitators do not.

Resellers

- Wholesalers—firms that acquire large quantities of products from manufacturers and then sort, store, and resell them to retailers or businesses.
- Retailers—all channel members who are involved in selling products or services to consumers.

Brokers

- Agents—people who facilitate the exchange of products but do not take title (i.e., purchase) anything that they sell.

Facilitators

- Transportation Companies—organizations that assist in the distribution of products but do not take title or negotiate sales.

EXAMPLE MARKETING CHANNELS

Have you ever wondered how a bottle of Listerine mouthwash ends up in your local drugstore or grocery store? Every bottle travels through a series of manufacturing and distribution partners that work together to form a marketing channel:

- Warner-Lambert, the maker of Listerine, purchases eucalyptol, synthetic alcohol, sorbitol, menthol, citric acid, and other ingredients. These are transported to Warner-Lambert's manufacturing and distribution facility, where they are mixed together to create Listerine mouthwash.
- The product is bottled, capped, labeled, and then put in large boxes. The boxes are organized into pallets, which are then transported to the distribution center where they will remain for about two to four weeks.
- When Warner-Lambert receives an order from a retailer (such as a drugstore), the order is screened to ensure that it can be filled. Software calculates the price for the order and how much product is already in stock. If there is a shortage, additional production is scheduled.
- When the order can be filled, pallets are transported by forklift to the appropriate shipping door. Trucks are loaded with the product, and those trucks depart for the customer's warehouse.
- The trucks are unloaded at the retailer's warehouse where the Listerine is stored for as long as three weeks until it is needed.
- When one of the retailer's stores begins running low on Listerine, that store requests a shipment of additional product from the warehouse. Another software program optimizes delivery schedules for all the retailer's stores that are requesting product, and boxes of Listerine are shipped.
- Trucks unload their cargo of Listerine at each of the destination stores, where staffers place bottles on shelves.[3]

PHOTO: EuToch/Shutterstock.

>> END EXAMPLE

CHANNEL STRATEGIES (pp. 199–201)

DEFINED *A* **channel strategy** *involves the decisions a manufacturer makes to effectively and efficiently move its products to the customer.*

EXPLAINED

Channel Strategies

The goal of a channel strategy is to determine the best way of making a product available to the target market. However, the strategy must also ensure that the overall marketing objectives of the product are being supported. While a properly crafted channel strategy cannot guarantee the success of a product, an incorrect strategy will generally ensure its failure.

APPLIED

Channel Strategies

Because a principal goal of marketing is to deliver high levels of customer satisfaction, formulating a channel strategy must begin with the target customer. Based on this, marketers must decide on the structure of the channel and how it should be organized.

Channel Structure

One of the initial decisions that marketers face in developing a channel strategy is determining how many levels of intermediaries should be used to connect the manufacturer to the end customer. Figure 14.3 illustrates the various types of business-to-consumer (B2C) and business-to-business (B2B) channels.[4] The shortest possible channel is a **direct marketing channel**, where the manufacturer sells directly to the end customer. One benefit of a direct channel is that it gives the manufacturer greater control over every step of the distribution process. In this case the manufacturer must perform all the functions normally conducted by intermediaries, including sales, payment processing, delivery, and product returns.

Indirect marketing channels contain at least one intermediary, and allow manufacturers to leverage the growing importance of intermediaries. In a B2C channel, for example, many consumers have a strong affinity for specialized retailers. Stores such as The Home Depot, Best Buy, and Bed Bath & Beyond are

FIGURE 14.3 Business-to-Consumer and Business-to-Business Channels

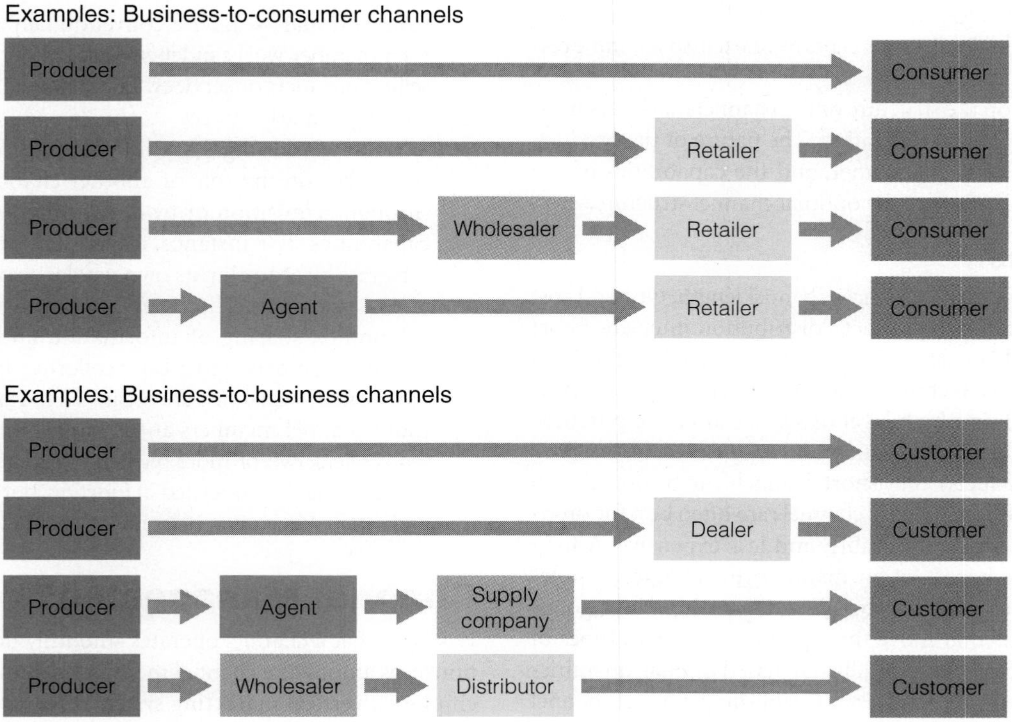

increasingly "where customers go first" for hardware, home electronics, or housewares. Indirect channels allow manufacturers to capitalize on the specialized skills of intermediaries in the performance of transportation, storage, return, and transaction functions.

Due to changes in customer preferences and the emergence of new channel options, manufacturers are adopting **multichannel distribution systems**. The use of multiple distribution channels allows a manufacturer to better satisfy the needs of different customer segments more efficiently than any single channel could offer. For example, a manufacturer can sell directly to consumers through an online store, and sell its products through traditional retailers. The company's own sales force assumes the responsibilities for large retailers, while wholesalers service smaller, local or regional retailers. Under this system the consumer will have multiple locations in which to purchase the product.

In addition to the channel's length, marketers must decide on the **distribution intensity**, or the width of a channel level. Intensity describes the number of outlets or locations where a product will be sold. Distribution intensity is determined by a combination of a product's classification (recall from Chapter 12 as convenience, shopping, or specialty products) and the branding strategy. Convenience products generally follow an **intensive distribution** strategy and are sold through a large number of retail outlets so they are readily available. For example, Coca-Cola places its products in a wide variety of locations so consumers can easily locate and purchase its soft drinks. The locations are not limited to retail outlets as Coke has invested heavily in developing and placing vending machines in areas with high foot traffic. In contrast, shopping products employ a more **selective distribution** strategy. Consumers are willing to exert a bit more time and effort to buy an HD TV or a computer, so these kinds of shopping products are distributed more selectively, through retailers like Best Buy or department stores. Many luxury or high-ticket items use **exclusive distribution**, where retailers or wholesalers are given exclusive rights to sell a product. This level of intensity is frequently used to maintain a perception of exclusivity and prestige for these products.

Before deciding on the structure of the channel marketers must take several factors into consideration. The nature of the product, the characteristics of the customer, and the capabilities of the organization will all influence the optimal channel structure.

Product Factors

The nature of the product influences channel length, type and cost of transportation, and the product's distribution intensity. Short channels (i.e., few channel members) are better suited for products that require extensive technical knowledge before the purchase (such as airplanes) or a high level of service after the purchase (such as automobiles). For products such as perishables (such as flowers or dairy products), only short channels can be used due to the potential for spoilage. Longer channels are often best for products that are standardized, durable, and less expensive. A long channel structure is beneficial for manufacturers because wholesalers and retailers assume risks by taking ownership of the goods they carry. Products that move through long channels, tubes of toothpaste, for example, are typically purchased in small quantities by consumers, at retailers of all sizes. Establishing a direct channel with consumers, or a sending a sales team to every retailer who sells toothpaste, is impractical for manufacturers.

Customer Factors

Marketers must determine how customers prefer to buy the product. For some customers, such as those in the business market, professional buyers prefer to purchase directly from the manufacturer. A face-to-face meeting provides the opportunity to negotiate in areas such as price and payment terms. In the B2C market, consumers are becoming more comfortable purchasing a wide range of products on the Internet. However, these consumers may require that a local retailer carry the product so they can examine the product firsthand. In business markets, if customers are concentrated in a relatively small area a short channel can be used. For example, Silicon Valley, which is located outside of San Francisco, California, is home to a high concentration of companies involved in the high-tech or computer industry. If customers require a high level of service after the sale, a shorter channel is needed. If customers require or prefer a wide assortment of products, longer channels, such as the use of retailers, will be required.

Organizational Factors

An organization may select a specific channel structure due to its own limitations. Small firms, or firms with a narrow product line, may have no other option but to utilize middlemen to reach customers. The organization may also decide to focus its efforts on product development and turn over the responsibility for sales and marketing to intermediaries such as agents or wholesalers.

Channel Organization

Channel organization defines how channel members will work together and the role each one should play. Three methods for channel organization are as follows:

- **Conventional**—Under a conventionally organized channel, each member works independently of the others, buying and selling products or services. The channel is self-regulating according to market forces.
- **Vertical Marketing System (VMS)**—A VMS exists when a firm takes on the role of another channel member, either through acquisition or by developing its own distribution capabilities. For instance, a manufacturer could vertically integrate by acquiring its own wholesale or retail business. As a result, the channel becomes more efficient due to reductions in conflict, sharing of information and resources among channel members, and greater collective-bargaining power.
- **Horizontal**—Channels are organized horizontally when two or more channel members at the same level (e.g., two or more wholesalers, two or more retailers) form an alliance. The firms may be related or unrelated in function, but they share resources and services as a means to improve channel performance.

Channel Management

Ensuring that a channel operates smoothly depends on the relationships among the channel members. Unless the manufacturer employs a vertical marketing system, each channel member will have its own objectives and profit targets. At times, the interests of one channel member will conflict with that of another, which can negatively impact the entire channel functions. Even if the conflict is between the wholesaler and a retailer, the manufacturer must be aware of and be willing to work to resolve the issue. Four general types of conflict can occur in a channel:

- **Channel conflict** refers to situations in which there is a disagreement among two or more parties in a distribution channel. For instance, a retailer may think that a wholesaler's terms and conditions are unreasonable.
- **Vertical conflict** occurs between two channel members at different levels. A wholesaler's argument with a manufacturer over access to a popular item is an example.
- **Horizontal conflict** involves channel members at the same level, such as two retailers, arguing over sales territories.
- **Multichannel conflict** refers to conflicts among multiple channel types. A manufacturer selling products through its own Web site might experience conflict with its independent brick-and-mortar retailers over pricing strategy.

A **channel leader** (also called a channel captain) is a firm with sufficient power over other channel members to take a leadership role, enforcing norms and processes. A strong leader who can establish and enforce "rules of engagement" for the channel is also a leader who can reduce conflict. Manufacturers have traditionally been channel leaders due to their ownership of powerful brands, desirable products, and access to customer information. However, retailers are increasingly taking on leadership roles because of the number of customers they influence and the increasing sophistication of their marketing approach.[5]

Marketers who successfully manage their distribution channels carefully select their channel partners on the basis of expertise and ability to cooperate. These successful marketers also work to motivate members to achieve shared objectives for the entire channel, often through training and financial incentives. The performance of channel participants is also carefully measured according to stated objectives, such as volume, profitability, and market share. Underperforming members are removed from the channel and replaced.

EXAMPLE CHANNEL STRATEGIES

When Hyundai decided to offer its customers a 10-year warranty on its products, it also had to begin planning for a decade-long period when repair parts might be needed to fulfill this promise.

PHOTO: Jamzol/Shutterstock.

>> END EXAMPLE

LOGISTICS (pp. 202–203)

DEFINED **Logistics** *is the coordination of all activities related to the movement of raw materials and finished goods that occur within the boundaries of a single business or organization.*

EXPLAINED

Logistics

Logistics is about getting several things right. Products and services must reach the right customers, in the right place, at the right time, in the right quantities, at the right price, and with the right level of service. Logistics involves the coordination of every activity within a company that influences the flow of products from production to final customer. Production forecasting, information systems, purchasing, inventory management, warehousing, and transportation are all aspects of logistics.

Supply chain management broadens the concept of logistics to include all firms or organizations, both inside and outside a company, that impact the distribution process. Finance, new product development, and customer service operations also fall under the definition of supply chain management. Some supply chains are simple, involving only a few players; others are more complex, spanning every distribution activity from raw materials to retailing.

APPLIED

Logistics

Logistics involves managing the flows of products and information. There are three main types of logistics (see Figure 14.4):[6]

- **Outbound logistics** controls the movement of products from points of production (factories or service delivery points) to customers.
- **Inbound logistics** deals with the flow of products or services from suppliers to manufacturers or service providers.
- **Reverse logistics** addresses the methods consumers use to send products backward through a channel for return or repair. For instance, Estée Lauder created a $250-million product line from returned cosmetics, which were then sold in discount stores and in developing countries.[7]

Marketing specialists called **logistics managers**, or supply chain managers, are responsible for coordinating the activities of all members of a company's distribution channel. Well-managed logistics and supply chains have several benefits. By coordinating activities among channel members, distribution costs can be reduced, leading to higher profits and potentially lower prices for customers. Well-managed chains can result in improved customer service due to improved information flows, faster delivery, and easier product returns.

Different segments of customers are looking for different things from a distribution channel. One segment may value low prices, so a logistics manager will focus on minimizing delivery costs. Another segment may want exceptional service, which means added cost to hire and train qualified customer service personnel. A central part of the logistics manager's role is to satisfy customer demands, yet at the same time maximize channel profit. This is done by making trade-offs between cost and service.

Instead of handling its logistics systems internally, a firm may hire a **third-party logistics company (3PL)** to manage all or part of its distribution network. At least 70% of companies worldwide use a 3PL for one or more key supply chain tasks. For example, UPS Supply Chain Solutions operates a two-million-square-foot campus that services more than 70 companies.[8] Third-party logistics firms help marketers save money by performing functions more efficiently, giving them access to more sophisticated distribution networks, and allowing them to focus

FIGURE 14.4 Logistics

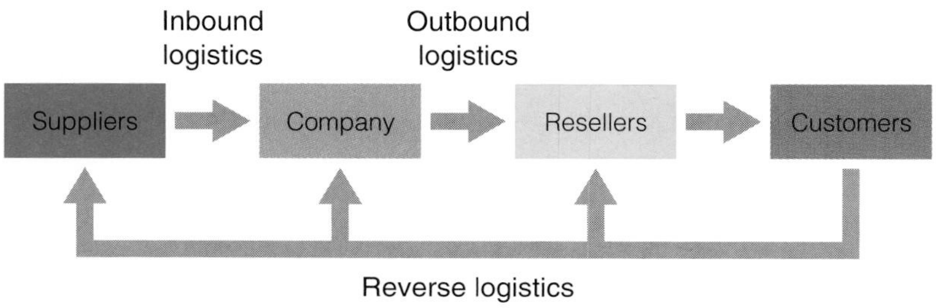

on their core business. Some 3PLs even handle product returns or manage repair centers for their clients.

Holding inventory for long periods of time is expensive due to storage and maintenance costs. As a result, manufacturers and retailers look for ways to minimize the time they have possession of physical inventory. Minimizing possession time keeps carrying costs as low as possible and maximizes production capability or the use of manufacturers' and retailers' sales floors. Initially developed and implemented by Toyota, **just-in-time (JIT)** inventory management is a technique in which goods are delivered within a predefined time "window." This time slot corresponds to exactly when the goods are needed, so they arrive "just in time" to be used or sold, thus ensuring that the firm's storage costs are minimal.

EXAMPLE LOGISTICS SYSTEMS

Walmart became the world's largest retailer by promising "Every Day Low Prices." Its logistics systems are aligned in the following five areas to reduce costs and pass those savings along to customers:[9]

- **Production**—Although Walmart is a mass-market retailer, it manufactures some of its own products by partnering with low-cost global suppliers.
- **Inventory**—Walmart stores follow a "big box" format, allowing the company to combine a store and warehouse in one location, and to gain operating efficiencies by doing so.
- **Location and Transportation**—Sites for large distribution centers (DCs) are identified, and then Walmart stores are located near DCs. Supply chain costs, such as transportation, are minimized as a result.
- **Information**—Walmart's electronic data interchange (EDI) systems automate ordering and payment processes with its suppliers, thereby reducing costs and improving order accuracy.

PHOTO: Infomages/Shutterstock.

>> END EXAMPLE

PHYSICAL DISTRIBUTION (pp. 204–206)

DEFINED **Physical distribution** *is the process of moving finished goods to customers through various transportation modes.*

EXPLAINED

Physical Distribution

A basic function of marketing channels is to facilitate the movement of products from point A to point B. Physical distribution (or freight transportation) deals with the transport and storage of the finished goods, which are products that have been manufactured but not yet sold or delivered to the customer. Transportation services, such as air carriers, railroads, and trucking companies, physically move products, while warehouses handle product storage and manage product inventory. The term **inventory** refers to the storage of goods awaiting transport or shipping. Because holding inventory can be expensive, marketers try to keep inventory quantities low, but still large enough to satisfy customer demand. Distribution planners coordinate these activities, balancing costs with the need for quick delivery and customer service.

APPLIED

Physical Distribution

Best-in-class distribution is not a solo activity. It is a group performance, with participants acting in a manner that benefits themselves as well as the whole distribution network. Three parties are involved in the distribution process:

- **Shippers** who own the goods being distributed. Bobs Candies acts as a shipper when it sends candy canes from its factories in Albany, Georgia, to retailers on the West Coast.
- **Consignees** who receive the distributed goods. In the case of Bobs Candies, its consignees are food and candy resellers who take delivery of the candy canes in time for the holiday season.
- **Carriers** who physically transport the goods from shippers to consignees. Like most consumer products, the majority of Bobs Candies are shipped by truck from its factory.[10]

For carriers to take physical possession of the goods, shippers must have the correct quantities of products ready to ship at the appointed time. Consignees rely on carriers to deliver their shipments efficiently and on schedule. In turn, shippers depend on both carriers and consignees to transport products and to make the actual sales. A breakdown anywhere along this network may result in products not being available for customers to purchase.

Transportation

U.S. companies spend hundreds of billions of dollars each year transporting products between manufacturers and customers. In determining the best way to transport a product, shippers must consider factors such as cost, dependability, speed, and the accessibility of the mode in connecting shippers and customers. Shippers have five options in deciding which method, or mode, of transportation to employ: trucks, airplanes, railroads, waterways, and pipelines. Each mode has its advantages (such as speed for airplanes) and disadvantages (such as costs for airplanes). Shippers must weigh the differences before selecting the optimal transportation mode.

- **Trucks**—Trucks are the most widely used form of transport in part due to the widespread accessibility of roads. Trucks have the ability to deliver products directly from the manufacturer to the customer, which other transportation modes cannot provide on a broad scale. As such, trucks are used to facilitate the transportation of goods through other modes by moving product from the manufacturer to the airport, terminal, or port. Truck transport is relatively fast, highly dependable, and offers a high frequency of shipments (as evidenced by the number of trucks on America's highways). However, the cost of using trucks is second only to air.
- **Air**—Airplanes are the fastest mode of transport, but the high cost limits their use. Airplanes are limited in the type of products they can deliver, but because they take off and land based on set schedules, they are highly dependable. As such, a firm like Jim's Lobster Co. in South Harpswell, Maine, can catch a lobster in the morning and have it arrive in Los Angeles later that night due to speed of air transport. Of course, using this option will result in a very expensive dinner. Many companies, such as FedEx and UPS, have built their business around the speed of delivery and could not operate without the use of airplanes.
- **Rail**—Although slower than truck or air, rail transport is attractive due to its low cost and the high flexibility in the types of goods that can be shipped. Railroads are ideal for bulk goods, such as coal, or heavy items, such as paper, that do not need to be delivered quickly. However, nearly every type of product, including consumer goods and automobiles, are shipped by train. The importance of railroads in transportation is evidenced by warehouses and manufacturing facilities being located along rail lines.

- **Water**—Waterway transport can be performed by oceangoing cargo ships or on barges that move goods on rivers and canals. Water is the least expensive form of transportation, but it is also the slowest. Like rail travel, water shipping has limits. Goods can be transported by water only to locations with navigable waterways and docks. In 2008, over 2 billion metric tons of goods were shipped over water.[11]
- **Pipelines**—The most limited form of transportation is pipelines, as this transportation mode is suitable for only limited goods such as petroleum or natural gas. Compared with moving these goods via truck, train, or waterway, pipelines are very inexpensive. However, the initial construction of the pipeline is costly. For example, the Trans-Alaskan Pipeline, which runs 800 miles from Prudhoe Bay to Valdez, Alaska, was completed in 1977 at a cost of $8 billion.[12]

For many shippers, a single mode, such as waterways, is not sufficient as not all customers are accessible by a river or canal. As such, companies employ **intermodal distribution systems**, which combine the use of multiple modes of transportation. To accommodate intermodal transportation, companies use standardized shipping containers that can be used on cargo ships, rail cars, or trucks. To manage the complexity of transportation decisions, some companies install **transportation management systems (TMS)**, which are software packages that automate shipping processes. A TMS can make recommendations on everything from carrier selection to scheduling. In spite of initial prices ranging from $50,000 to as much as $1 million, cost savings from these systems often allow firms to recoup their up-front investment within one year.[13]

Warehousing

A **warehouse** is a physical facility used primarily for the storage of goods held in anticipation of sale or transfer within the marketing channel.[14] Most businesses or retailers don't require large quantities of products all at one time, so it's more cost-effective to store items at warehouses and then ship items to their ultimate destination in smaller, more frequent orders. Warehouses help other distribution channel members by **breaking bulk**, or reducing large product shipments into smaller ones more suitable for individual retailers or companies. Another function warehouses serve is to **create assortments** of products from the wide variety they carry. When one truck carries an assortment of five orders to a single destination, five different trucks no longer have to make the same trip.[15]

Inventory management is the focus of efficient warehousing operations. Carrying too much inventory is wasteful, because the storage space could be used for more profitable items. However, having too little inventory is a missed opportunity as products may not be available when customers wish to buy. Inventory levels vary based on time of year, the type of industry being serviced, and customer demand. Items are tracked within a warehouse and throughout the distribution process by using **stock-keeping unit (SKU)** numbers, which serve as identification codes that are unique for each product.

A large warehouse may also be called a **distribution center**. As mentioned earlier in this chapter, Walmart locates its stores near its own centralized distribution centers to minimize transportation costs. The planning for a distribution network determines the number and locations of warehouses or distribution centers a company needs. For example, Walmart plans for each distribution center to serve approximately 120 stores. Some key questions to answer when developing a warehouse or distribution center strategy are as follows:[16]

- How many warehouses or distribution centers do you need?
- Where should they be located?
- How much inventory should be stocked at each one?
- Which customers should each warehouse or distribution center service?
- How often should shipments be made to each customer?
- What additional services should be provided?

Some warehouses or distribution centers use **RFID (radio frequency identification)** tags to track the movement of goods electronically. An RFID tag carries an electronic chip and an antenna, which sends the precise location of each item to a computer. Using RFID, marketers can follow a product all the way from production to shipment. A study by Kurt Salmon Associates estimates that RFID can reduce the amount of time needed to track inventory by as much as 90%.[17]

Bar codes (or **barcodes**) are another form of identification used to monitor inventory. Every product carries a bar code with unique numerical identifiers that can be scanned within a warehouse to confirm the product's storage location, to ensure its correct destination when being shipped, or to record its final sale at checkout. Retail bar codes specify a product's **Universal Product Code** (or **UPC**), which is a series of numbers uniquely identifying that product.

More sophisticated supply chains use **cross-docking** to minimize inventory holding costs and improve delivery time. Goods that are cross-docked are not warehoused, but are simply unloaded at a distribution center, immediately sorted by destination, and then reloaded onto trucks for dispatch.

EXAMPLE **PHYSICAL DISTRIBUTION**

As one of America's largest retailers, Sears, Roebuck and Co. manages physical distribution for three major categories of products:

- **Seasonal products**, such as snowblowers or lawn mowers, which must be fully stocked during times of peak demand
- **Fast-moving products**, like home improvement or DIY items, which must arrive at and depart from the distribution centers quickly

- **Slow-moving products**, such as washing machines and dryers, which can be transported more slowly and economically

Cross-docking helps Sears keep its inventory moving efficiently. For example, when a shipment of high-definition TVs arrives at one of Sears' regional distribution centers, the load is broken down and single TVs are then loaded onto trucks headed for different stores or homes across the United States.[18]

PHOTO: Baloncici/Shutterstock.

>> END EXAMPLE

Visual Summary

Chapter 14 Summary

A marketing channel can be short and direct such as when a manufacturer sells directly to a customer. Or it can include intermediaries, such a wholesalers and retailers that facilitate the movement of product from the manufacturer to the end customer. No matter which channel a manufacturer chooses to use, the functions of a channel must be performed by someone. Channel strategy involves decisions regarding the number of levels a channel will contain, how it should be organized, and how it should be managed. Logistics and supply chain management are employed to oversee the physical transportation and warehousing of products.

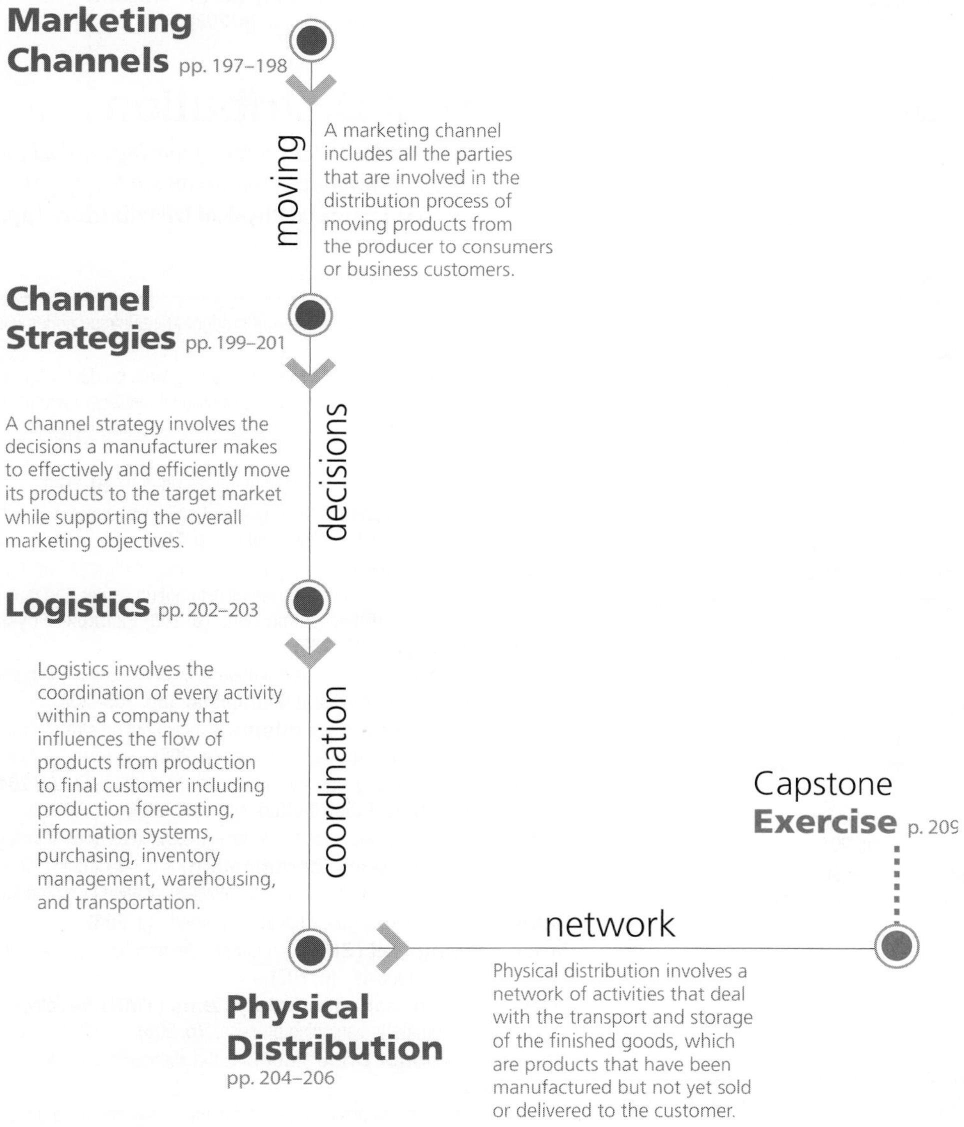
Marketing Channels pp. 197–198
moving
A marketing channel includes all the parties that are involved in the distribution process of moving products from the producer to consumers or business customers.
Channel Strategies pp. 199–201
decisions
A channel strategy involves the decisions a manufacturer makes to effectively and efficiently move its products to the target market while supporting the overall marketing objectives.
Logistics pp. 202–203
coordination
Logistics involves the coordination of every activity within a company that influences the flow of products from production to final customer including production forecasting, information systems, purchasing, inventory management, warehousing, and transportation.
Physical Distribution pp. 204–206
network
Physical distribution involves a network of activities that deal with the transport and storage of the finished goods, which are products that have been manufactured but not yet sold or delivered to the customer.
Capstone Exercise p. 20

Chapter Key Terms

Marketing Channels (pp. 197–198)

Marketing channel *is the network of parties involved in moving products from the producer to consumers or business customers. (p. 197)* **Example: Marketing Channels (p. 198)**

Key Terms (pp. 197–198)

Contact efficiency is the efficiency gained in terms of a reduction in the number of contacts required through the use of channel intermediaries. **(p. 197)**

Distribution is the process of delivering products and services to customers. **(p. 197) Example: Marketing Channels (p. 198)**

Channel Strategies (pp. 199–201)

Channel strategy *describes the levels, organization, and distribution intensity of a marketing channel. (p. 199)* **Example: Channel Strategies (p. 201)**

Key Terms (pp. 199–201)

Channel conflict occurs when two or more channel members disagree. **(p. 201)**

Channel leader is a firm with sufficient power over other channel members to take a leadership role in the channel. **(p. 201)**

Direct marketing channel is a single channel member that produces and distributes a product or service. **(p. 199)**

Distribution intensity determines the number of outlets or locations where a product will be sold. **(p. 200)**

Exclusive distribution refers to the distribution of products in only a few locations. **(p. 200)**

Horizontal conflict occurs between channel members at the same level in a channel (e.g., two retailers). **(p. 201)**

Indirect marketing channel is a channel involving one or more intermediaries between producer and customer. **(p. 199)**

Intensive distribution refers to the distribution of products in a relatively large number of locations. **(p. 200)**

Multichannel conflict refers to conflict between different types of channels. **(p. 201)**

Multichannel distribution system is a system where the consumer has multiple locations to purchase the product. **(p. 200)**

Selective distribution refers to the distribution of products in relatively few locations. **(p. 200)**

Vertical conflict refers to conflict between channel members at different levels in a channel (e.g., a wholesaler and a retailer). **(p. 201)**

Vertical Marketing System (VMS) is a channel that is vertically integrated based on acquisition or formal agreement, or by a firm developing its own distribution capabilities. **(p. 200)**

Logistics (pp. 202–203)

Logistics *is the coordination of all activities related to the transportation or delivery of products and services that occur within the boundaries of a single business or organization. (p. 202)*

Key Terms (pp. 202–203)

Inbound logistics controls the flow of products or services from suppliers to manufacturers or service providers. **(p. 202)**

Just-in-time (JIT) is an inventory management technique in which goods are delivered within a predefined time "window" that corresponds to exactly when the goods are needed. **(p. 203)**

Logistics manager is a person responsible for coordinating the activities of all members of a company's distribution channel. **(p. 202)**

Outbound logistics controls the movement of products from points of production (factories or service delivery points) to consumers. **(p. 202)**

Reverse logistics addresses the methods consumers use to send products backward through a channel for return or repair. **(p. 202)**

Supply chain management is the management of all firms or organizations, both inside and outside a company, that impact the distribution process. **(p. 202) Example: Logistics Systems (p. 203)**

Third-party logistics company (3PL) manages all or part of another company's supply chain logistics. **(p. 202)**

Physical Distribution (pp. 204–206)

Physical distribution *is the process of moving finished goods to customers through various transportation modes. (p. 204)* **Opening Example (p. 205) Example: Physical Distribution (pp. 205–206)**

Key Terms (pp. 204–206)

Bar codes (or **barcodes**) are unique product identification codes used to monitor inventory. **(p. 205)**

Breaking bulk refers to the process of reducing large product shipments into smaller ones that are more suitable for individual retailers or companies. **(p. 205)**

Carrier is the entity that physically transports goods from shipper to consignee. **(p. 204)**

Consignee is the receiver of goods being distributed. **(p. 204)**

Creating assortments is the process of collecting an assortment of products into a single shipment to a destination. **(p. 205)**

Cross-docking is a warehousing technique that minimizes holding costs by unloading products at a warehouse or distribution center and then reloading them almost immediately for transport. **(p. 205) Example: Physical Distribution (pp. 205–206)**

Distribution center is a large warehouse used to store a company's products. **(p. 205) Example: Physical Distribution (pp. 205–206)**

Intermodal distribution systems is a distribution strategy that uses more than one kind of transportation mode. **(p. 205)**

Inventory is a store of goods awaiting transport or shipping. **(p. 204) Example: Physical Distribution (pp. 205–206)**

Pipeline is a transportation mode used for liquids such as oil or natural gas. **(p. 205)**

RFID (radio frequency identification) is an electronic chip and an antenna that can identify the precise physical location of a product. **(p. 205)**

Shipper is the owner of goods being distributed. **(p. 204)**

Stock-keeping unit (SKU) is a unique identification number used to track and organize products. **(p. 205)**

Transportation management systems (TMS) are software programs used to automate the shipping process. **(p. 205)**

Universal Product Code (or **UPC**) is the standard format for retail bar codes. **(p. 205)**

Warehouse is a physical facility used primarily for the storage of goods held in anticipation of sale or transfer within the marketing channel. **(p. 205) Example: Marketing Channels (p. 198) Example: Physical Distribution (pp. 205–206)**

Capstone Exercise

Starbucks is one of the world's leading retailers of specialty coffee beverages, beans, and related merchandise. Starbucks owns nearly 7,000 retail stores and has licensed nearly 4,000 airport and shopping center locations in 41 countries. Starbucks' revenues exceeded $6.0 billion in 2009. In addition to direct retailing, Starbucks has joined forces with Dreyer's Ice Cream (premium coffee-flavored), Kraft Foods (distribution of coffee beans to more than 18,000 supermarkets), Barnes & Noble Booksellers, Jim Beam distillers, United Airlines, Sheraton Hotels, Holland America Cruises, and PepsiCo (ready-to-drink Frappuccino) to expand both its product portfolio and distribution channels.

Starbucks has a very well-defined and developed value chain (supply chain and distribution channels). It obtains its supply of coffee beans from many different growers in South America, Asia, and Africa. Starbucks buys over 2% of the total world's supply of coffee beans. It uses exporter agents and domestic brokers for inspection and transportation of the coffee beans from the growers to warehouses and roasting facilities. Starbucks operates roasting facilities in several locations across the United States and in Europe and Asia, strategically placed for proximity to major markets. The roasted beans are moved to a contracted packaging manufacturer and on to one of several major distribution centers.

Starbucks' strategy for distribution is three-pronged: retail outlets (owned and licensed), specialty sales (business accounts and joint ventures), and direct sales (Internet and mail orders).

1. Draw a simple flow chart identifying the channel members from production to consumption.
2. Do you see any potential for channel conflict in the existing value chain? Explain.
3. Within the channel structure, identify the conventional, vertical, and horizontal channel segments.
4. Would Starbucks benefit from ownership of coffee plantations? Why or why not?
5. Of the three major distribution channels, which one do you think offers the greatest growth potential. Why?

Application Exercise

Use the marketing concepts in this chapter to tackle and solve a marketing problem: channel strategy and physical distribution.

First, start by thinking about the confectionery category (candy, gum, and mints) and then choose a product within that category. There are many products available in stores within this category for us to consider purchasing.

The Marketing Problem

Think about your chosen product after considering the following situation.

> Confectionery products are typically sold in most distribution points (food stores, drug stores, convenience stores, big box stores, department stores, etc.). The category is highly competitive and consumers buy this category on impulse, so the manufacturers and retailers rely on up to the moment information at the store level to have the right candy in the right place for the target market.

The Problem

Select a target market, for example, teenage boys, and describe the channel strategy that would be most appropriate for the first 90 days of introduction. Discuss how the finished goods would be transported from the plant to stores across the globe.

The Solution

Complete the following two Problem/Solution briefs using your product in the confectionery category, chapter concepts, and college resources.

1. From the Marketing Manager's Point of View
   a. Problem Definition
   b. Channel Strategy Analysis
   c. Solution

2. From the Consumer's Point of View
   a. Problem Definition
   b. Analysis
   c. Solution

Resources:

Marketing Defined, Explained, Applied, Michael Levens, 2e
The College Library
Retail or Online Field Trip
Assigned Reading—*Brand Week*, *Advertising Age*, *WSJ*, scholarly publications, category trade journals
Blog your problem from either point of view, gather responses/posts (www.blogger.com/start)

Retailing and Wholesaling Strategies

Chapter Overview As discussed in the previous chapter, intermediaries serve a critical role in moving a product through its marketing channel. This chapter focuses on the final stages of the marketing channel by examining retailers and wholesalers. Because they serve to connect manufacturers and consumers, retailers are perhaps the most important member of a marketing channel. The retail landscape is evolving as shoppers are becoming more comfortable with purchasing products over the Internet, through kiosks and vending machines, or using smart phones.

Chapter Outline

Objective 1. What role do retailers and wholesalers play in a marketing channel?
Objective 2. What impact does retailing have on the U.S. economy?
Objective 3. How are retailers classified? What are the major types of retailers?
Objective 4. How will the growth of nonstore retailing affect traditional retailers?

Objective 5. What are the strategic decisions faced by a retailer?

Objective 6. What is the principal criterion used to classify wholesalers? What are the major types of wholesalers?

RETAILING (pp. 211–213)

DEFINED **Retailing** *is the activities involved in the sale of products to consumers for their personal, nonbusiness use.*

EXPLAINED

Retailing

The sale of products to consumers, or retailing, is performed by a broad range of organizations. For example, some manufacturers sell directly to consumers over the Internet or through their own factory outlets, and many wholesalers operate limited retail operations. However, the majority of retail sales are made through **retailers**, which are businesses whose primary source of revenue is generated through retailing.

APPLIED

Retailing

To understand how important retailing is to the U.S. economy, consider these facts. Retailers generated $4.4 trillion in retail sales in 2008,[1] which represents 6.2% of the U.S. gross national product.[2] They represent almost 10% of the total businesses in the United States and employ 10.5% of the country's workforce. U.S.-based retailers are also major players in the global economy, and five of the world's largest retailers are U.S.-based companies. The top 10 U.S. retailers for 2009 are listed in Table 15.1.

Retailers are typically classified based on the products they offer, the level of service they deliver, or on the prices they charge compared to direct competitors. Products sold at retail are broadly divided into durable and nondurable goods. **Durable goods**, or hard goods, are products that are expected to last for three or more years. Examples of durable goods include automobiles, appliances, electronics, and furniture. Nondurable, or soft goods, are products that have a short lifespan (less than three years) and include food, apparel, health and beauty aids, and office supplies. The major types of retailers are found in Table 15.2.

Types of Retailers

Specialty stores concentrate on satisfying the specific needs of a select group of customers. These retailers typically carry a broad range of choices for a narrow product line. Employees will generally have much greater expertise in the product category and offer a higher degree of service. Examples include David's Bridal, Radio Shack, and the 150-year-old toy retailer FAO Schwarz.

Another form of specialty store that has emerged is the **category killer**. These retailers, which include the likes of Staples, Toys "R" Us, Best Buy, and The Home Depot, offer a wide selection of merchandise in a narrow product category. These stores provide a moderate level of service and expertise to customers, and generally offer lower prices than smaller competitors. The size of these stores varies based on the product category. For example, stores for office product retailer Staples average about 20,000 square feet, while home improvement retailer The Home Depot averages 100,000 square feet.

Department stores, such as Nordstrom, Macy's, and Sears, carry a wide selection of products organized by departments, such as housewares, men's and women's apparel, appliances, and luggage. Each department is generally operated as a stand-alone entity inside the store, with each having its own dedicated group of buyers. Department salespeople are usually well trained and typically work under some type of commission structure. Shoppers expect top-of-the-line brands; however, many department stores have begun establishing their own branded product lines in order to capture higher margins. Department stores average about 150,000 square feet of selling space and generate $124 to $160 in sales per square foot. Typically, apparel accounts for 50% or more of total sales.

Discount stores, such as Walmart or Target, share many similarities with department stores in that they offer a wide variety of products and are organized by departments. However, these retailers operate under an entirely different philosophy. Discount stores focus on turning products over more quickly than traditional department stores by offering lower prices.

One of the busiest shopping days of the year, the Friday following Thanksgiving, is more commonly referred to as "Black Friday"—a reference to the day retailers begin showing a profit for the year. In 2009, over 80 million shoppers, many of whom camped in line for up to 12 hours, spent more than $10 billion on Black Friday. Retailers spend up to six months planning for this event and, after numerous incidents where employees or shoppers were injured, the focus has been on ensuring that customers have a positive experience. As a result, many retailers have turned to experts experienced at handling events that draw large crowds, such as the Super Bowl or the Olympics, to help them manage the retail spectacle of Black Friday.

PHOTO: Dmitrijs Dmitrijevs/Shutterstock.

Table 15.1 Top 10 U.S. Retailers for 2009

Rank	Name	Headquarters	Revenue (in billions)	Store Count
1	Walmart	Bentonville, AK	$405.0	7,873
2	Kroger	Cincinnati, OH	76.0	3,654
3	Costco	Issaquah, WA	72.5	544
4	Home Depot	Atlanta, GA	71.2	2,274
5	Target	Minneapolis, MN	64.9	1,682
6	Walgreens	Deerfield, IL	59.0	6,934
7	CVS Caremark	Woonsocket, RI	48.9	6,981
8	Lowe's	Mooresville, NC	48.2	1,649
9	Sears	Hoffman Estates, IL	46.7	3,918
10	Best Buy	Richfield, MN	45.0	3,942

Source: www.stores.org/stores-magazine-july-2009/top-100-retailers. Copyrighted 2011 NRF Enterprises Inc. 70389-nlcd.

While lower prices generally mean lower retail margins, discount stores typically have lower expenses as they offer limited service to customers. Discounters also seek cost efficiencies wherever possible. Many of these retailers, most notably Walmart, have focused on supply chain management to keep prices low. The average discount store occupies 100,000 square feet of space and generates $300 to $450 of sales per square foot.

Off-price retailers typically sell name-brand apparel and accessories at prices 20% to 50% less than specialty or department stores. These retailers continuously change the merchandise they carry based on the availability of closeout merchandise, production overruns, or factory seconds, which are products that have slight irregularities. Off-price retailers, including T.J. Maxx, Ross, and Big Lots, can acquire inventory only through manufacturer imperfections, including production mistakes and misjudgments in consumer demand. Apparel designers rely on off-price retailers to sell products that would otherwise be destroyed.

Warehouse clubs carry a limited selection of merchandise, typically about 10% to 20% of the number of items sold in grocery stores. In addition, the products offered by warehouse clubs come in large quantities or multi-packs that deliver higher value for customers and generate greater unit volume for manufacturers. Groceries typically account for the largest portion of sales revenue for warehouse clubs, followed by health and beauty products and apparel. Warehouse clubs have two streams of revenue: margins earned on the sale of products and membership fees received from consumers and businesses. With members paying between $35 to $100 per year just for the opportunity to shop, larger warehouse clubs, such as Sam's Club and Costco, can generate revenue in excess of $3 billion from membership fees alone.

Grocery stores/supermarkets are self-service retailers that carry food and nonfood items. A typical supermarket, or grocery store, can exceed 47,000 square feet and can stock up to 45,000 different SKUs, all of which are arranged in departments. Stores

Table 15.2 Major Categories of Retailers

Retailer Type	Examples	Product Line/Product Assortment	Level of Service	Average Size (Sq. Ft.)	Sales per Sq. Ft.
Specialty Stores	David's Bridal, FAO Schwartz	Narrow/Deep	High	1,000–2,500	$250–$400
Category Killer	Office Max, Home Depot, Toys "R" Us	Narrow/Broad	High	20,000–150,000	$250–$350
Department Stores	Nordstrom, Sears, Kohl's	Broad/Broad	High	150,000	$124–$160
Discount Stores	Walmart, Target, Kmart	Broad/Narrow	Limited	100,000	$300–$450
Off-Price Retailers	T.J. Maxx, Big Lots	Varies	Limited	30,000	$125–$250
Superstores	Walmart Supercenter, SuperTarget	Broad/Broad	Limited	200,000	$300
Warehouse Clubs	Sam's Club, Costco	Broad/Very Narrow	Limited	150,000	$600
Supermarkets	Kroger, Publix, Safeway	Broad/Broad	Limited	47,000	$95–$115
Convenience Stores	Circle K, 7-Eleven	Narrow/Narrow	Limited	2,500	$160

are normally located close to residential centers and are built to serve a relatively small area, typically a radius of between one and five miles. The U.S. retail grocery industry, to which supermarkets belong, generates over $460 billion in revenue per year and is dominated by major chains such as Kroger, Publix, and Safeway. However, the size of the industry has attracted new competitors, including Walmart, which opened a chain of 42,000-square-foot grocery stores known as Neighborhood Markets. Supermarkets face stiff competition from superstores like SuperTarget and Walmart Supercenters, and have begun offering shoppers greater convenience by leasing space to other retailers such as banks, dry cleaners, and hair salons. Grocers are also facing pressure from changes in consumer lifestyles, as Americans are spending more of their food budget eating outside the home.[3] Supermarkets are introducing prepared and ready-to-eat food sections that expand traditional deli offerings and include other ready-to-eat items such as sushi, roasted chicken, and even Thai food.

Superstores are the combination of a discount store and a grocery store. These retailers, including Walmart Supercenters, Meijer, and SuperTarget, require high customer traffic to justify their existence. A typical superstore averages around 200,000 square feet of space and offers a wider variety of products, including food, electronics, housewares, and home and garden supplies, all under a single roof. The inclusion of a broad range of products allows superstores to provide customers greater convenience and lower prices.

Convenience stores are small, self-service retailers that offer few product choices outside their primary offerings of beer, soft drinks, and snacks. These retailers, such as 7-Eleven and Circle K, average 2,500 square feet and have annual sales per square foot of $325 to $650. There are over 140,000 convenience stores in the United States, and the majority are located in high traffic areas and remain open 24 hours a day. However, shoppers pay for this convenience because these stores have higher prices than other retailers offering the same products. Eight out of 10 convenience stores also sell gasoline, and these stores sell an average of 100,000 gallons of gas each month.

Nonstore Retailing

A physical retail location is not always required to sell products to consumers. **Nonstore retailing** involves the sale of products through the use of vending machines, self-serve kiosks, the Internet, and smart phone applications. Nonstore retailing currently accounts for 4% to 6% of all retail sales, and it is expected to grow to 10% of sales within a decade. This growth is due to the key benefit that consumers gain from using nonstore retailers—convenience. Given that consumers face great constraints on their time, the ability to buy products without waiting in line or from the comfort of home is very appealing. Additionally, the shopping behaviors of Gen Xers and millennials are vastly different from those of baby boomers. Window shopping is out; browsing online is in.

Vending machines generate over $6 billion in revenue each year and sell a wide range of products including soft drinks, snacks, hot and cold meals, gumballs, and toys. An average vending machine costs between $4,000 and $8,000 and generates sales of about $300 per week. Many retailers are installing automated retail stores (upscale vending machines) to vend products that previously could not be stocked due to security concerns. For example, Macy's is now selling personal electronics, such as iPods, GPS units, and digital cameras, through vending machines.[4]

Internet retailers recorded sales in excess of $150 billion in 2009 and this number is expected to reach almost $230 billion by 2014.[5] Retailing via the Internet is becoming more widely accepted by consumers, and 71% of adults in the United States have made a purchase online.[6] While a wide range of products can be purchased online, certain product categories tend to do especially well. For example, in 2008 more than half of all computer hardware and software sales were made online, followed by books (28%), toys and games (16%), and jewelry/luxury goods (14%).[7] Retailing on the Internet has allowed a new breed of retailers to compete without the presence of a physical store. Although Walmart is the world's largest retailer, the $3.5 billion in online sales it recorded pales in comparison to Amazon's $24.5 billion in sales.[8]

The newest form of nonstore retailing, known as **M-Commerce**, is conducted through the use of mobile devices such as smart phones. By the end of 2010, more than 126 million U.S. consumers are expected to own a smart phone. This is nearly double the 51 million smart phones that were being used in 2008. That year, consumers purchased products totaling $346 million using smart phones.[9] To date, the most popular uses of M-Commerce are in financial services such as mobile banking or stock transactions. However, as smart phone ownership grows and cellular network capabilities improve, mobile commerce will allow consumers to purchase movie tickets and snacks from vending machines, and to participate in online auctions. To capitalize on the emergence of M-Commerce, retailers have begun offering customers specially designed "apps" (short for applications) that can be used to conduct transactions with the retailer. For example, eBay offers an app that allows customers to bid on items up for auction.

EXAMPLE NONSTORE RETAILING

Visa Inc., a global payments technology company, released an iPhone application in 2009 that allows consumers to complete mobile financial purchase transactions by waving their handset in front of a contactless payment terminal. According to the Smart Card Alliance, 150,000-plus merchant locations in the United States accept contactless payments, including Office Depot, AMC movie theaters, Walgreens, CVS, 7-Eleven, Arby's, McDonald's, PetCo, and Subway.

PHOTO: Khomulo Anna/Shutterstock.

>> END EXAMPLE

RETAIL STRATEGIES (pp. 214–216)

DEFINED **Retail strategies** *are the decisions to be made regarding the establishment and ongoing operations of a retailer.*

EXPLAINED

Retail Strategies

A retail strategy is established in order to satisfy the business objectives of the organization. As the primary business objective is profitability, a retailer must balance its desires with potential margins. A **retail margin** is the difference between a product's retail selling price and its wholesale cost. As such, a retailer's overall profitability is determined by: (1) the amount of merchandise sold, (2) the retail margin on the merchandise, and (3) the store's overall operating expenses. The strategy crafted by the retailer will impact all three of these elements, and each of these elements influences the others. For example, a retailer can't offer top-quality designer clothing, provide a high level of service to customers, and offer discounted prices. While volume may be high, the retail margin will be too small to cover the high operating costs.

FIGURE 15.1 The Retail Marketing Mix

APPLIED

Retail Strategies

Developing a retail strategy begins with an understanding of the wants and needs of the target customer. As such, retailers face the same type of decisions that manufacturers address in developing new products. They use segmentation to select a target market and then establish a position in the retail market space that is appealing to target customers. Next, they decide on the elements of the **retail marketing mix**, which are the product, price, place, and promotion. The product in this case involves decisions about **merchandise assortment**, the **level of service** to offer, and the store's atmospherics, which are the design and décor of the store. The elements of the retail marketing mix are shown in Figure 15.1.

Merchandise Assortment

Decisions regarding merchandise assortment determine the breadth and depth of product lines to carry, as well as the amount of each product to stock. For example, Toys "R" Us carries a broad selection of products in a single category, while Walmart carries a narrow selection of products across many categories. In making merchandise decisions, retailers must account for target customers, as well as current and future competitors. Merchandise decisions should be made with the goal of attracting a large enough target market while differentiating the retailer from competitors. Retailers must also take into account the demographics of the local population to ensure that the right styles, sizes, and colors are available when customers are ready to purchase. Retailers must determine if the focus will be on well-known name brands or if **private label products** should be offered. Private label goods have grown in importance for retailers over the past few decades as the products offer retailers higher margins. For example, Kirkland Signature, Costco's private label brand, currently accounts for 20% of the retailer's total sales. As margins are significantly higher than national brands, the company is aggressively working to increase private label sales to 37%.

Level of Service

The service level of a retailer typically ranges between full-service and self-service. **Full-service retailers** are typically high-end specialty and department stores where sales personnel provide assistance during, and even after, a customer's visit. Salespeople have a high degree of knowledge of the product category and their expertise is valued by customers. **Self-service retailers**, on the other hand, provide only a minimal level of service; contact between customers and employees is typically limited to when the sale is made. **Limited-service retailers** provide assistance to customers upon request. These retailers, such as Best Buy or Sears, allow customers to serve themselves, but also have knowledgeable sales associates available to offer guidance. The products a retailer stocks typically determine the level of service offered—specialty goods require more services than do convenience goods—however, the retail strategy determines the degree of service provided. For many retailers carrying similar merchandise, especially those competing for the same target customers, offering more services is often the only means of differentiation. Providing more services increases labor costs, resulting in lower margins.

Atmospherics

A store's **atmospherics**, which include layout, furnishings, color scheme, and music, establish the image customers have of a retailer. The physical environment will determine if shoppers enter a retailer and how long they remain. The layout of a store determines how easy it is for shoppers to navigate the aisles. Grocers, such as Kroger, design stores so that shoppers need to navigate through the majority of the store to find the most often purchased products, such as bread, produce, and milk. Fixtures and furnishings also signal the image of the retailer. Warehouse clubs, such as Costco, use steel racks to stack pallets of merchandise. This no-frills, low-expense approach matches the low price expectations of shoppers. High-end specialty stores are appointed with fine wood displays and decorative lighting to convey luxury and elegance.

The music a retailer plays is carefully selected to reinforce the store's image. As such, apparel retailers like American Eagle Outfitters use decidedly different music than upscale women's clothing stores like Ann Taylor. Music is also used to influence shopper behavior. For example, shoppers spend less time, on average, in a store that plays up-tempo music and spend more time in stores that feature slower, softer music. Older shoppers are typically more sensitive to a store's selection of music than are younger shoppers, and 40% of consumers surveyed indicated that they have left a store because of the music being played.[10]

Location

Assuming that the decision has been made to have physical locations, a retailer has a wide range of options regarding where stores are placed. The decision about where to locate a store is determined by multiple factors, including the product and the target customer. For example, many shoppers will drive several hundred miles to visit an Ikea store; however, they will not drive more than a few minutes to visit a grocery store or pharmacy. When making their selection, retailers must balance a location's cost with the area's traffic, which is the number of people or cars that pass by a location. A destination retailer, such as Bass Pro Shops, can choose a low-cost location away from population centers. The retailer's popularity ensures that consumers will shop at their location. However, most retailers require locations with high traffic counts and, thus, locate within malls or shopping centers. Even in the face of competition, many retailers have elected to open locations close to each other to ensure an adequate level of traffic.

Promotion

A retailer's promotional efforts often focus on creating awareness of a store's grand opening or an upcoming sale. Retailers use a wide variety of promotional tools, including advertising, public relations, and sales promotion, to generate customer traffic in the store. No matter the promotional tool, retailers must ensure that the message being sent is consistent with the store image. Because of its local content and customer expectations, newspapers are used by many retailers, especially specialty stores and supermarkets. Retailers are also using the Internet to reach out to customers by providing information on upcoming sales or offering special deals and discounts.

Retail Price Policy

A retail price policy establishes the level at which prices will be set compared to competitors. Retailers must ensure that the policy is consistent with the positioning or image of the store. Retailers can take an upscale approach, trading lower volume for higher margins, or they can offer discount prices that result in higher volume. Retailers can also use parity pricing by setting prices at the same level as competitors. This strategy is effective if the retailer can differentiate itself in some other way such as service level, merchandise assortment, or location. In many instances, a retailer's pricing strategy is narrowed considerably by the decisions made about the other elements of the retail marketing mix. Retailers with higher expenses, whether due to enhanced services, upscale furnishings, and/or an expensive location, typically require higher retail margins to achieve profitability.

EXAMPLE **RETAIL STRATEGIES**

Known for its innovative approach to cosmetics retailing, Sephora operates more than 750 stores on three continents. Most cosmetics have traditionally been sold in department stores, alongside furniture, electronics, and hardware. Sephora has built a niche for itself as a specialty retailer, similar to chains like Ikea, Best Buy, or The Home Depot. Sephora offers customers a unique shopping experience by focusing its retailing strategy on innovation, exclusivity, and customer service. The following are key points in that strategy:

- **Merchandise**—Sephora carries exclusive product brands, such as Benefit Cosmetics, Stila, Philosophy, and Perricone

MD, that aren't widely available. As Bare Escentuals CEO Leslie Blodgett said, "Sephora is a trailblazer . . . it takes brands that seemingly no one else will and turns them into stars."

- **Promotion**—Unlike department stores, Sephora doesn't invest heavily in advertising but relies on positive customer experiences to generate favorable word-of-mouth promotion.
- **Location**—Sephora attempts to secure high-traffic locations in cities or malls. Such locations draw people into the stores. There is a Sephora store on the Champs-Elysées in Paris and on Fifth Avenue in New York City.
- **Atmosphere**—The concept for Sephora stores is perhaps its greatest innovation. Products are displayed in an open-sell environment without glass cases, so shoppers can touch, compare, and sample the items. Each store's distinctive black-and-white decorating scheme draws attention to the colorful product packages that are on display.
- **Pricing**—Prices are generally on par with department stores, but Sephora attempts to deliver better value through product selection, store atmosphere, and customer service. Coaches are even trained to create made-to-order products for customers by mixing cosmetics to match individual color and skin tones.
- **Customer service**—Sephora invests heavily in employee training, so that its salespeople become "beauty coaches" who provide detailed information and assistance to customers.

As of 2009, Sephora continues to increase its sales through expansion into worldwide markets.[11]

PHOTO: Brian Chase/Shutterstock.

>> END EXAMPLE

WHOLESALING (pp. 217–219)

DEFINED **Wholesaling** *is the sorting, storing, and reselling of products to retailers or businesses.*

EXPLAINED

Wholesaling

Wholesaling involves the redistribution of products to retailers, institutions, and government agencies. A **wholesaler** is a firm that purchases products from manufacturers and resells them to retailers and industrial buyers. There are more than 430,000 wholesalers in the United States, and these channel members handle over 50% of all products sold.[12] In addition to the physical movement of products, wholesalers perform other essential functions in distribution channels. They store goods until consumers need them. They simplify product, payment, and information flows between producers and customers. They inject capital into businesses by providing cash in advance of product sales to customers. They may even assume responsibility for technical support and order processing, thereby making life easier for manufacturers.[13]

APPLIED

Wholesaling

Although wholesalers have been in existence for centuries, their widespread use began in the nineteenth century as manufacturers began to mass-produce products. Wholesalers expanded the market coverage area of a manufacturer and enabled regional brands to become national brands. Even today, many retailers would not have access to the products on their shelves without wholesalers. The same is also true for manufacturers because they would not have access to the markets being served by smaller retailers.

Wholesalers sell a variety of products, from components essential for the manufacture of finished goods (e.g., bicycle seats) to supplies used to conduct everyday business activities (e.g., paper clips). Some wholesalers specialize in a particular category of products, while others sell a broad range.

EXAMPLE WHOLESALING

With more than 15 million square feet of storage space spread out across 11 states, C&S Wholesale Grocers is the largest food wholesaler in the United States. The 90-year-old company carries more than 95,000 different products, including produce, meat and dairy products, health and beauty aids, and candy. C&S Wholesale services over 4,000 independent supermarkets and regional chain stores such as Target, Safeway, Pathmark, and Giant Food Stores.

In 2008, *Forbes* magazine ranked C&S Wholesaler the 12th largest private company in the United States. The wholesaler strives to deliver value to its retail customers, and part of the company's vision is to have "Braggingly happy customers."

PHOTO: Kenneth V. Pilon/Shutterstock.

>> END EXAMPLE

Types of Wholesalers

Wholesalers can be classified in a number of ways. They can be identified based on the products they carry, how products are distributed, or by the services they perform. The most often used method of classifying a wholesaler is based on if they **take title**, or ownership, of the product. The U.S. *Census of Wholesale Trade* uses this method and classifies wholesalers as either (1) merchant wholesalers, (2) agents and brokers, or (3) manufacturers' branches. Table 15.3 identifies the types of wholesalers, along with the products they typically carry and their likely customers.

Merchant Wholesalers

Merchant wholesalers encompass the broad group of wholesalers that take title to the products that are purchased from manufacturers. While most of these wholesalers take possession of the products, not all do. Wholesalers purchase merchandise in bulk from manufacturers and then sell in smaller quantities to their customers, which are retailers, businesses, or other wholesalers. Wholesalers are typically granted the exclusive rights to sell a manufacturer's products in a protected geographic area.

Table 15.3 Categories of Wholesalers

Wholesaler Type	Products Carried	Customer	Description
Merchant Wholesalers			
Full-service			
General merchandise	Pharmaceuticals, groceries, machine parts	Supermarkets, hardware stores	Offers high level of service to customers; can offer narrow or broad range of products
Specialty line	Health food, oriental foods	Specialty retailers	Typically offers a single product line, provides high level of service and support
Limited-service			
Cash-and-carry	Groceries, building materials, office supplies	Small businesses	Buyers purchase products at wholesaler's location, pays cash, and self-transports
Mail-order	Computer hardware, jewelry, sporting goods	Small retailers, industrial firms	Catalogs are used in place of a sales force; customers may have no other means of acquiring products
Drop shippers	Bulk products such as coal, timber	Retailers, wholesalers	Take title to products, but generally do not take possession; orders are shipped by manufacturers
Truck jobbers	Produce, bread, milk	Supermarkets, restaurants	Sales of perishable goods to regular group of customers who pay in cash
Rack jobbers	Nonfood items such as toys, magazines and books, health/beauty aids	Supermarkets, small retailers	Merchandise placed in stores on consignment; jobber keeps merchandise in stock and fresh
Agents and Brokers			
Manufacturers' agents	Apparel, furniture, raw materials	Retailers, manufacturers	Are used in place of a manufacturer's sales force; agents work assigned territories; little control over pricing
Selling agents	Coal, textiles, timber	Manufacturers	Assume full marketing duties for the producer; have authority over pricing and promotional decisions
Commission merchants	Agricultural goods such as wheat, livestock	Industrial buyers, manufacturers	Take possession, but not title. Earn a commission on the sale; seek to sell at highest possible price
Merchandise brokers	Food, insurance, real estate	Retailers, manufacturers, developers	Hired by either the buyer or the seller; paid when transaction is completed

Manufacturers will contract with enough merchant wholesalers to ensure that products are available throughout the entire market. There are two broad types of merchant wholesalers, full-service wholesalers and limited-service wholesalers.

Full-service wholesalers assume many responsibilities that otherwise would be performed by manufacturers. In addition to the sales function, these wholesalers service customers by extending credit and providing delivery of products. Full-service wholesalers usually have a broader understanding of the market and share this expertise with their customers and manufacturers. **General merchandise wholesalers** carry a wide assortment of merchandise in a broad product category, such as pharmaceuticals or groceries. Customers for these wholesalers vary between nationwide retail chains and small regional wholesalers. General merchandise wholesalers work with their customers to help sell more products and may include advertising and promotional allowances or shelf design services. **Specialty line wholesalers** focus on a single product line, such as health food, and may cover a wide geographic area. They are highly knowledgeable about the product category and the consumer. Specialty line wholesalers are willing to share their knowledge with customers to increase product sales.

Limited-service wholesalers perform fewer services for manufacturers but may be the best or only way to reach the markets they serve. **Cash-and-carry wholesalers** provide few services but offer low prices on the limited number of goods they carry. Customers must travel to these wholesalers' locations, pay for their purchases in cash, and transport their purchases back to their retail store or business. For retailers who are unable to establish accounts with larger, full-service wholesalers, cash-and-carry wholesalers offer the only means necessary to acquire products. **Mail-order wholesalers** employ catalogs or the Internet as their sales force. Many small businesses must use mail-order wholesalers because they lack access to other types of wholesalers due to their location or size. Computer hardware, office supplies, and costume jewelry are all commonly sold through mail-order wholesalers. **Drop shippers** take title to products but never take possession. By taking title, drop shippers assume all risks until the product is delivered to the buyer. These wholesalers carry no inventory, instead placing an order with the manufacturer after a sale is made. Drop shippers are used primarily for products that require a lot of space, such as coal and timber. **Jobbers** are wholesalers that operate on a relatively small scale and sell and provide services primarily to retailers. Jobbers are active in many industries ranging from automotive parts to textiles.

Agents and Brokers

Agents and brokers are independent businesses that may take possession of products but never take title. Compensation is typically commission-based, payable upon the completion of a transaction. Where some agents and brokers perform only sales, others may assume greater responsibilities over all of a manufacturer's marketing activities. **Manufacturers' agents**, for example, are used as a replacement for a manufacturer's sales team. These independent agents are responsible for all sales in an assigned territory, and they represent several manufacturers of noncompeting, related products. Manufacturers' agents have little control over the selling price of the products they carry. **Selling agents**, on the other hand, are often responsible for a wider range of marketing activities in addition to the sales function. These agents have more flexibility with regards to pricing and promotional activities than do manufacturers' agents. **Commission merchants** take physical possession of products but do not take title. Once the products are sold, these merchants collect payment from the buyer, subtract the agreed-upon commission, and then make payment to the seller. They are widely used for commodity products such as copper, livestock, and wheat. In a retail setting, eBay and Sotheby's Art Auction House are examples of commission merchants. **Merchandise brokers** focus on linking buyers and sellers together. They are generally well known in the area they specialize in and can be hired by either the buyer or the seller. Merchandise brokers are often used to assist in the negotiation process and are paid a fee or commission upon the completion of the transaction.

Manufacturers' Branches

In lieu of a wholesaler, many organizations elect to perform all channel duties themselves. A **manufacturer-owned intermediary** offers benefits in a number of ways. For example, manufacturers will earn greater profit margins and have more control over inventory and the sales process by eliminating an intermediary such as a wholesaler. As a form of a vertically integrated channel, manufacturer-owned intermediaries create efficiencies for large firms. A **sales branch** maintains inventory for a company in different geographic areas. On the other hand, **sales offices** carry no inventory but provide selling services for specific geographic areas. A **manufacturer's showroom** is a facility where a firm's products are permanently on display for customers to view. Any purchases are then fulfilled from distribution centers or warehouses.[14]

Visual Summary

Chapter 15 Summary

Retailers and wholesalers provide valuable services to manufacturers, for which they earn a percentage of the retail selling price. From buying merchandise in bulk from manufacturers to providing a location for consumers to buy, the wide assortment of brands that is available to consumers would not be possible without these two channel members. Retailing accounts for a significant portion of America's economy and retailers continuously look for ways to attract customers to their stores. Nontraditional forms of retailing, such as Internet merchants and the emergence of M-Commerce, impact the retail landscape by altering how, when, and where consumers shop for products.

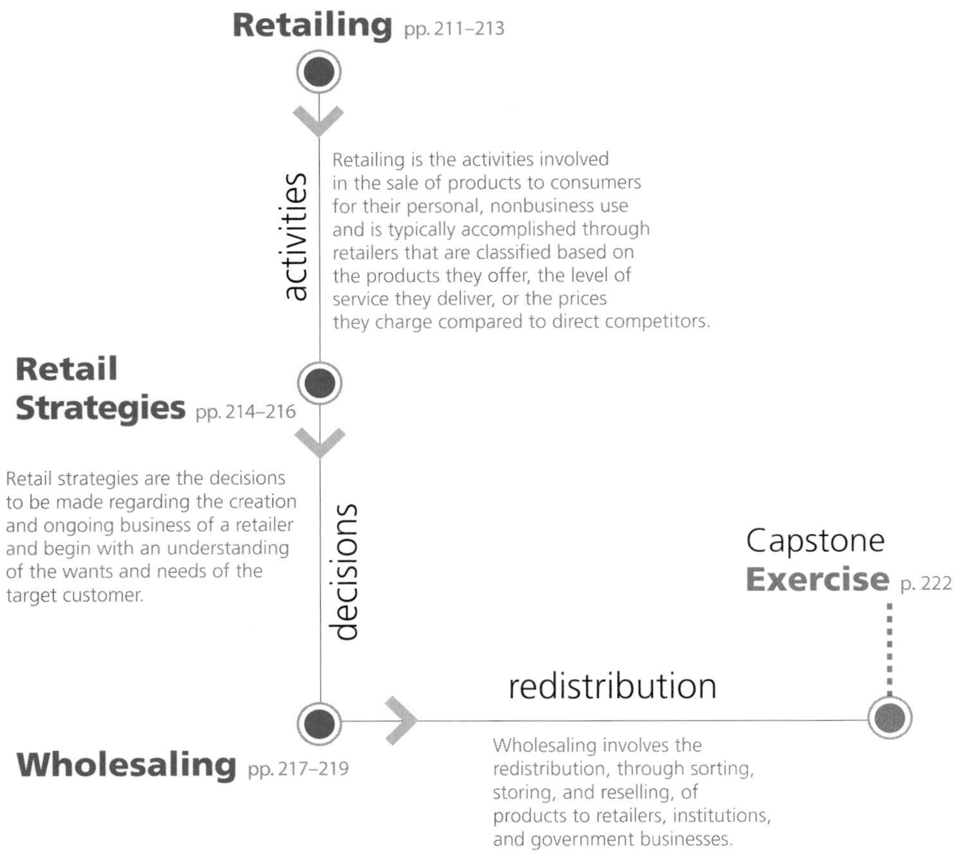
Retailing pp. 211–213
activities
Retailing is the activities involved in the sale of products to consumers for their personal, nonbusiness use and is typically accomplished through retailers that are classified based on the products they offer, the level of service they deliver, or the prices they charge compared to direct competitors.
Retail Strategies pp. 214–216
Retail strategies are the decisions to be made regarding the creation and ongoing business of a retailer and begin with an understanding of the wants and needs of the target customer.
decisions
Capstone Exercise p. 222
redistribution
Wholesaling pp. 217–219
Wholesaling involves the redistribution, through sorting, storing, and reselling, of products to retailers, institutions, and government businesses.

Chapter Key Terms

Retailing (pp. 211–213)

Retailing *is the activities involved in the sale of products to consumers for their personal, nonbusiness use. (p. 211)*

Key Terms (pp. 211–213)

Category killers are retailers that offer a wide selection of merchandise in a narrow product category. **(p. 211)**
Convenience stores are small, self-service retailers that offer few product choices outside their primary offerings of beer, soft drinks, and snacks. **(p. 213)**
Department stores carry a wide selection of products organized by departments, such as housewares, men's and women's apparel, appliances, and luggage. **(p. 211)**
Discount stores are a type of department store focused on turning over products more quickly than traditional department stores by offering lower prices. **(p. 211)**
Durable goods are products that are expected to last for three or more years. **(p. 211)**
Grocery stores/supermarkets are self-service retailers that carry food and nonfood items. **(p. 212)**
Internet retailers offer a wide range of products that are sold online. **(p. 213)**
M-Commerce is a form of nonstore retailing conducted through the use of mobile devices such as smart phones. **(p. 213)**
Nonstore retailing involves the sale of products through the use of vending machines, self-serve kiosks, the Internet, and smart phone applications. **(p. 213) Example: Nonstore Retailing (p. 213)**
Off-price retailers sell name-brand products at prices 20% to 50% less than specialty or department stores by acquiring closeout merchandise, production overruns, or factory seconds. **(p. 212)**
Retailers are businesses whose primary source of revenue is generated through retailing. **(p. 211)**
Specialty stores concentrate on satisfying the specific needs of a select group of customers. **(p. 211)**
Superstores are the combination of a discount store and a grocery store. **(p. 213)**
Vending machines sell a wide range of products including soft drinks, snacks, hot and cold meals, gumballs, and toys. **(p. 213)**
Warehouse clubs carry a limited selection of merchandise in large quantities that deliver higher value for customers and greater unit volume for manufacturers. **(p. 212)**

Retail Strategies (pp. 214–216)

Retail strategies *are the decisions to be made regarding the establishment and ongoing operations of a retailer. (p. 214)* **Example: Retail Strategies (pp. 215–216)**

Key Terms (pp. 214–215)

Atmospherics are the layout, furnishings, color scheme, and music that establish the image customers have of a retailer. **(p. 215)**
Full-service retailers are typically high-end specialty or department stores where sales personnel provide assistance to customers during and after their visit to the store. **(p. 214)**
Level of service is the service offered to customers on the continuum between full- and self-service. **(p. 214)**
Limited-service retailers provide assistance to customers upon request. **(p. 214)**
Merchandise assortment is the breadth and depth of product lines a store carries, as well as the amount of each product the store stocks. **(p. 214)**
Private label products are store brand items that offer higher profit margins for retailers than name brand products. **(p. 214)**
Retail margin is the difference between a product's retail selling price and its wholesale cost. **(p. 214)**
Retail marketing mix consists of the product, price, place, and promotion of merchandise by a retailer. **(p. 214)**
Self-service retailers provide a minimal level of service and contact between customers and employees. **(p. 214)**

Wholesaling (pp. 217–219)

Wholesaling *is the sorting, storing, and reselling of products to retailers or businesses. (p. 217)* **Example: Wholesaling (p. 217)**

Key Terms (pp. 217–219)

Agents and brokers are independent businesses that may take possession of products but never take title. **(p. 219)**
Cash-and-carry wholesalers provide few services but offer low prices on the limited number of goods they carry. **(p. 218)**
Commission merchants are brokers who take physical possession of products but do not take title and subtract an agreed-upon commission from the buyer's payment to the seller. **(p. 219)**
Drop shippers are wholesalers who take title to products but never take possession of them. **(p. 219)**
Full-service wholesalers typically assume supply chain responsibilities that would otherwise be performed by manufacturers. **(p. 218)**
General merchandise wholesalers carry a wide assortment of merchandise in a broad product category, such as pharmaceuticals or groceries. **(p. 218)**
Jobbers are wholesalers that operate on a relatively small scale and sell and provide services primarily to retailers. **(p. 219)**
Limited-service wholesalers perform fewer services for manufacturers but may be the best or only way to reach the markets they serve. **(p. 218)**
Mail-order wholesalers employ catalogs or the Internet as their sales force. **(p. 218)**
Manufacturer-owned intermediaries are wholesaling or similar entities owned by the manufacturer as a way of controlling the inventory and sale processes and increasing profit margins. **(p. 219)**
Manufacturers' agents are independent agents used in place of a manufacturer's sales team. **(p. 219)**
Manufacturer's showroom is a facility where a firm's products are permanently on display for customers to view. **(p. 219)**
Merchandise brokers are brokers that specialize in linking buyers and sellers together and are generally well known in their area of specialization. **(p. 219)**
Merchant wholesalers are a broad group of wholesalers that take title to the products that are purchased from manufacturers. **(p. 217)**
Sales branches maintain inventory for companies in different geographic areas. **(p. 219)**
Sales offices carry no inventory but provide selling services for specific geographic areas. **(p. 219)**
Selling agents are independent agents who take responsibility for a wide range of marketing activities in addition to sales functions. **(p. 219)**
Specialty line wholesalers focus on a single product line, such as health food, and may cover a wide geographic area. **(p. 218)**
Taking title refers to the practice of a wholesaler taking ownership of the products it purchases. **(p. 217)**
Wholesalers are firms that purchase products from manufacturers and resell them to retailers and industry buyers. **(p. 217)**

Capstone Exercise

Barnes & Noble Inc. owns and operates the largest chain of bookstores in the United States. In 1917, the company was formed by combining the C.M. Barnes Company, a seller of new and used books, and Noble & Noble, an educational bookstore. The company's primary business was wholesaling to schools, libraries, and dealers. Barnes & Noble entered the retail sector rather reluctantly. It agreed to "tolerate" (not encourage) sales to individual college students who contacted the company directly. Customer demand for individual book sales grew. In 1932, Barnes & Noble opened its first retail store in New York at Fifth Avenue and 18th Street. This flagship store became a model for college bookstore operations as the target market remained college students. For the next 20 years, Barnes & Noble successfully operated its retail division alongside its original business of wholesaling to schools and libraries. In 1969, a "crippled" Barnes & Noble was purchased for $750,000 by a young entrepreneur, Leonard Riggio. He developed Barnes & Noble into an educational bookseller with a broader focus that included all kinds of how-to and nonfiction books. By 1976, the company operated 21 campus bookstores and Riggio had grown the wholesale and retail divisions to $32 million in sales. This financial success made possible the creation of the first book supermarket. The original Barnes & Noble superstore opened across the street from the original flagship store. It provided a warehouse environment for educational books, children's books, fiction, nonfiction, and gift books. This original model was designed to attract the average shopper, not the academician or bibliophile. It was a unique marketing technique.

Between 1980 and 1990, Barnes & Noble acquired BookMasters, Marlboro Books, Doubleday Book Shops, and B. Dalton Bookseller. In 1990, Barnes & Noble operated a total of 23 superstores. Each store was large, carrying as many as 150,000 titles, and offered a pleasant customer-friendly atmosphere encouraging shoppers to browse, read, and linger. In 2009, the total number of stores had grown to nearly 800 in all 50 states. In addition, it operates 636 college bookstores. In spite of concerns that rapid expansion would saturate the book market, Barnes & Noble seemed to understand the importance of an environment equally suited to bargain hunters, book lovers, and socializers. Today, in addition to a vast offering of books, Barnes & Noble offers magazines, newspapers, DVDs, audio books, gifts, games, and music.

By 2000, Barnes & Noble, the number one bookseller in the United States, met a major threat. The fact that Barnes & Noble held a 15% share of all book sales in the United States was less important than the fact that Amazon.com held a 75% share of online book sales. The result was a sudden halt to store expansions and new emphasis on developing barnsandnoble.com. Today, Barnes & Noble is the second largest online retailer, carrying over 1 million titles.

In 2003, Barnes & Noble expanded its product further with the acquisition of Sterling Publishers. Management saw publishing as a way to create revenues from both the publishing and the selling of the same title. In 2009, Barnes & Noble introduced its digital book reader, the Nook.

Revenues for fiscal year 2009 totaled $5.8 billion—10% of which came from Internet sales. Amazon remains the online market leader with 70% of total online book sales compared to Barnes & Noble's 20%. Global revenues for Amazon.com for fiscal year 2009 totaled $24.5 billion.

1. Define the major types of retail operations utilized by Barnes & Noble.
2. Did the development of the "superstore" change the primary type of retail operation? Explain.
3. Explain how the "atmospherics" of Barnes & Noble serves the perceived needs/wants of the consumer. Do the atmospherics serve Barnes & Noble Inc.?
4. How did the growth strategies of the 1980s differ from the 1990s?
5. Was the reassignment of resources from bricks and mortar store operations to barnesandnoble.com a good decision? Explain your opinion.

Application Exercise

Use the marketing concepts in this chapter to tackle and solve a marketing problem: retail strategy, retail marketing mix, merchandise assortment, customer service, and atmospherics.

First, start by thinking about the sports equipment category. The sports equipment category is large and contains sports gear, footwear, and apparel. Then choose a product within that category. There are many products available for us to consider purchasing.

The Marketing Problem

Think about your chosen product after considering the following situation.

> The sports equipment industry is highly fragmented; consumers' interests are typically within specific segments. Consumers need to know which retailer and which product represents the best choice for them.

The Problem

How would you choose the right retail strategy and marketing mix for the product you have chosen? Think about the merchandise assortment you would need to be efficient as a retailer and satisfied as a customer. What type of store atmospherics and level of customer service would best suit your product?

The Solution

Complete the following two Problem/Solution briefs using your product in the sports equipment category, chapter concepts, and college resources.

1. From the Marketing Manager's Point of View
   a. Problem Definition
   b. Analysis
   c. Retail Category (refer to Table 15.2)
   d. Retail Marketing Mix
   e. Solution

2. From the Consumer's Point of View
   a. Problem Definition
   b. Analysis
   c. Customer Service Level
   d. Solution

Resources:

Marketing Defined, Explained, Applied, Michael Levens, 2e
The College Library
Retail or Online Field Trip
Assigned Reading—*Brand Week, Advertising Age, WSJ*, scholarly publications, category trade journals
Blog your problem from either point of view, gather responses/posts (www.blogger.com/start)

Advertising and Sales Promotion Strategies

Chapter Overview Over the next three chapters the final piece of the marketing mix, promotion, is discussed. The term *promotion* is broadly used to describe the communication efforts that marketers use to build awareness and demand for products and services. These chapters will outline the vast array of promotional tools marketers have available to build relationships with customers. These tools include advertising, sales promotion, public relations, sponsorships, personal selling, and direct marketing. This chapter discusses how marketers use indirect forms of communication, namely, advertising, public relations, sales promotion, and sponsorships, to shape customer perceptions. Chapter 17 will discuss personal selling and direct marketing and Chapter 18 will focus on how marketers integrate their promotional efforts.

Chapter Outline

Objective 1. How can marketers influence the way consumers think, feel, and act toward a brand?
Objective 2. What are the elements of the marketing communication process?

Objective 3. What steps do marketers follow when developing an advertising plan?

Objective 4. Who are the two groups targeted by sales promotions?
Objective 5. How do sales promotions create incentives to buy?

Objective 6. How does public relations influence consumer perceptions?

MARKETING COMMUNICATIONS (pp. 225–227)

DEFINED **Marketing communications** *are the messages sent from organizations to members of a target market in order to influence how they think, feel, and act toward a brand or market offering.*

EXPLAINED

Marketing Communications

Developing, pricing, and distributing a product or service will get it into the market, but how do consumers learn about and become motivated to buy? This is the role promotion, or marketing communication, plays in the marketing mix. Whether the communication is through a multi-million dollar Super Bowl commercial or a coupon in a local newspaper, the goal is the same—to influence the thoughts, feelings, and/or actions of consumers.

APPLIED

Marketing Communications

Communication can be viewed as an exchange of information between two parties. To communicate with the target market, marketers can use direct communications, such as personal selling, or mass communications, such as advertising, sales promotions, sponsorships, or public relations. No matter which method is used, marketers must understand how to effectively communicate with the intended audience.

Marketing communication requires two parties. The sender initiates the process by *encoding* a marketing idea, which is translating the meaning into a *message* (for example, by using language, graphics, and music) to be conveyed through a *medium* that serves as a channel to convey the idea. By *decoding*, the receiver interprets the sender's message to understand its meaning. Then, the receiver completes the process by providing the sender with *feedback*—a reaction to the message (see Figure 16.1).

Feedback may take the form of a purchase, a comment on a product blog, a request for additional information, or a consumer-created commercial for the marketer's brand. In traditional models of the communication process, the marketer is the sender and the consumer is the receiver. However, consumers today frequently act as the sender by initiating communication with a marketer. A consumer might encode a message (such as a question about a product's warranty) and choose a medium (such as an e-mail) to reach the marketer. After decoding the message, the marketer would use feedback to respond in an appropriate way, such as e-mailing a copy of the product warranty.

Noise is anything that might distort, block, or otherwise prevent the message from being properly encoded, sent, decoded, received, and/or comprehended. Competing messages represent noise, for instance, which is why the Chinese government limited billboard and airport advertising by marketers who were not official sponsors during the Beijing Olympics. This cleared the way for messages from official sponsors, such as McDonald's and Panasonic, to be noticed and received by visitors to the Olympic Games.

Communication Objectives

The overall goal of marketing communication is to elicit some form of buyer action. The action could be a search for more information, or it could result in the sale of a product. Marketers realize, however, that all buyers are not ready to purchase at the same time or make decisions at the same pace. Some buyers may be unaware of the product, while others may be aware, but have no need or interest.

Bringing new meaning to the phrase "captive audience," the media firm Captivate specializes in place-based advertising like video terminals in elevators. Are you bored with watching floor numbers change? Just watch a minute of programming on Captivate, which mixes snippets of news and entertainment content with paid ads. The company has installed more than 8,200 digital, wireless screens in buildings in 23 major North American markets. Captivate screens deliver almost 55 million impressions (or ad views) per month, and reach the often hard-to-find, college-educated business professional. Every time they ride the elevator, 88% of riders watch the Captivate programming, and over half report increased interest in a product or service they saw advertised.[1]

PHOTO: Creatas/Thinkstock Royalty Free.

FIGURE 16.1 The Marketing Communication Process

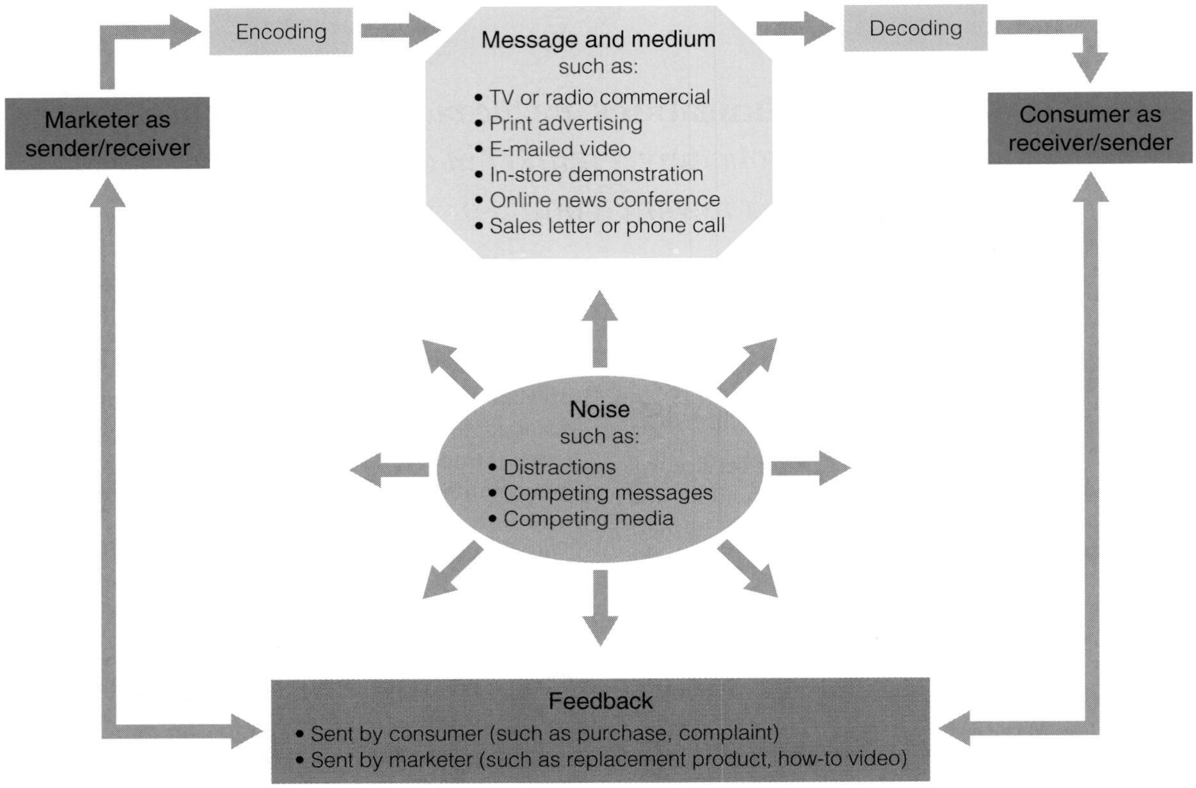

As such, marketing communications can be used to address the following objectives:

- Help the consumer recognize a need (influence how the consumer thinks about a problem or need).
- Build awareness and interest (influence how the consumer thinks and feels about a category, brand, or company, and encourage the consumer to find out more).
- Inform about benefits (influence how the consumer thinks about the brand's ability to satisfy the recognized need).
- Persuade about value (influence how the consumer thinks and feels about the brand's competitive superiority in satisfying needs).
- Stimulate action (influence the consumer to take the next step toward buying, such as forming an intention to buy or placing an order for that brand).
- Reinforce the buying decision (influence the consumer's thoughts and feelings about having purchased that brand).
- Remind about brand (influence the consumer's thoughts about the brand's value and encourage trial or repeat purchasing).

Nonprofit organizations also set marketing communication objectives, such as building awareness of a social problem or soliciting donations. A recent United Way campaign used television, print, billboard, and online advertising to encourage consumers to volunteer their time for local causes and to donate money to the United Way.

Consider the following two ads and compare them. What marketing objectives do these ads seek to achieve?

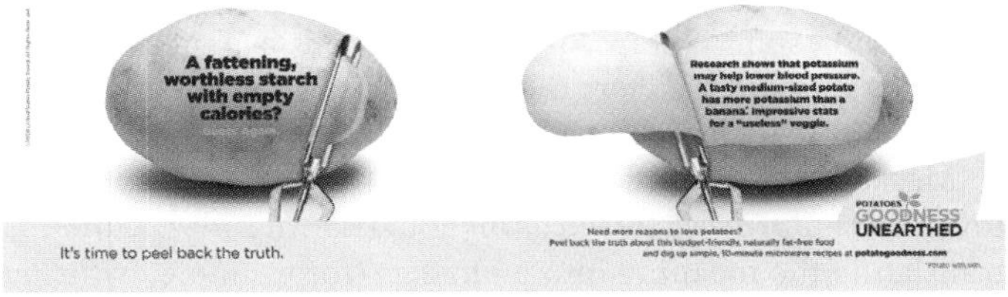

EXAMPLE COMMUNICATION OBJECTIVES

Mini Cooper uses print, television, and online advertising to influence how consumers think and feel about its car. Showing a Mini poised to plunge into a half-pipe helps consumers

imagine that the experience of driving a Mini is as exciting as extreme sports.

PHOTO: Courtesy of BMW Worldwide.

>> **END EXAMPLE**

Control and Credibility

When it comes to controlling the message, and the credibility of the message, all forms of marketing communications are not created equal. For example, marketers have the highest amount of control over the message in direct marketing. The control exists because the marketer determines the message to be delivered and who receives the message. Unfortunately, direct marketing is saddled with negative perceptions, which results in low credibility among consumers and business buyers. On the other hand, **word of mouth**, in which consumers communicate with each other about a brand, marketing offer, or marketing message, enjoys a high degree of credibility yet a very low level of control of the message. People are more likely to believe that their friends, relatives, neighbors, and colleagues are more credible sources of information than company-controlled sources. Many marketers seek to stimulate word of mouth through **viral marketing**, activities that encourage consumers to share a company's marketing message with friends. However, marketers have little to no control over the message because people can change, distort, or exaggerate the intended message. Plus, the person may not like the product, which is a message no marketer wants shared. Figure 16.2 shows the level of control and the degree of credibility for the various forms of marketing communication.

FIGURE 16.2 **Credibility and Control of Marketing Communications**

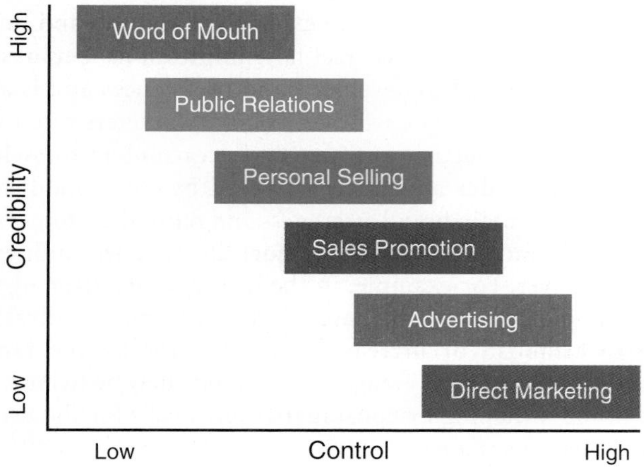

EXAMPLE **WORD OF MOUTH**

Adidas has been running hard to catch Nike, the market leader in athletic shoes. Its "Basketball Is a Brotherhood" campaign, which focused on Adidas basketball shoes, included viral marketing as well as print, television, and online advertising. Adidas invited consumers to sign up via text message to receive recorded voice messages from an NBA star, for example, Tim Duncan of the San Antonio Spurs. The messages sent consumers to a Web site where they could personalize and download ringtones featuring the voices of NBA players. The novelty prompted many consumers to talk about Adidas and forward the Web site address so their friends could mix their own ringtones.[2]

PHOTO: Dan Thomas Brostrom/Shutterstock.

>> **END EXAMPLE**

Relationship Building

For maximum impact, marketers should use communications tools that allow two-way interaction with customers. Starting a dialogue with consumers helps the marketer better understand and respond to the target audience's needs and behaviors. Keeping the dialogue going strengthens the marketer's relationship with the target, which leads to higher brand loyalty and sales. Many companies build relationships by sending birthday cards to customers and calling to check on product satisfaction.

In the earlier viral marketing example, Adidas wanted only to get consumers talking about its brand and its unique basketball-star ringtones, not make an immediate sale. Feedback, such as the number of consumers who signed up to receive messages and the number who mixed personalized ringtones, told Adidas whether it was reaching its target audience and whether its message was of interest. Other messages in other media were designed to motivate consumers to actually buy Adidas products.

ADVERTISING (pp. 228–230)

DEFINED **Advertising** *is the paid, nonpersonal communication of a marketing message by an identified sponsor through mass media.*

EXPLAINED

Advertising

Advertising is a cost-effective, creative way to communicate with groups of people, educate the audience about a product or category, and help initiate or maintain a dialogue with a target market. It can alert consumers to products that satisfy their needs, let them know when and where offerings are available, or suggest how to compare competing brands. As the preceding definition states, advertising is a paid, nonpersonal message that is sent from an identified sponsor through a mass medium such as television, radio, newspapers, magazines, or the Internet.

APPLIED

Advertising

Worldwide, over $550 billion is spent on advertising each year,[3] with $117 billion spent in the United States.[4] Automobile manufacturers were the top spending category in the United States in 2008, spending over $8.1 billion, which is almost double the second ranked category, pharmaceuticals, which spent over $4.5 billion. Procter & Gamble, the makers of Tide, Charmin, and hundreds of other household products, spent over $3.3 billion in 2008 on television, magazine, newspaper, and online advertising.[5] Table 16.1 highlights the top 10 U.S. advertisers for 2008.

Table 16.1 Top 10 Advertisers in 2008

Company	Ad Spending (in billions)	% Change from 2007
Procter & Gamble	$3.3	–6.0%
Verizon Communications	2.4	4.1%
General Motors	2.2	11.3%
AT&T	1.9	–10.4%
Johnson & Johnson	1.4	1.0%
Time Warner	1.3	–20.8%
Walt Disney Co.	1.2	–5.4%
General Electric Co.	1.2	18.4%
GlaxoSmithKline	1.0	–11.3%
Toyota Motor Corp.	1.0	–3.8%

FIGURE 16.3 Main Components of the Advertising Plan

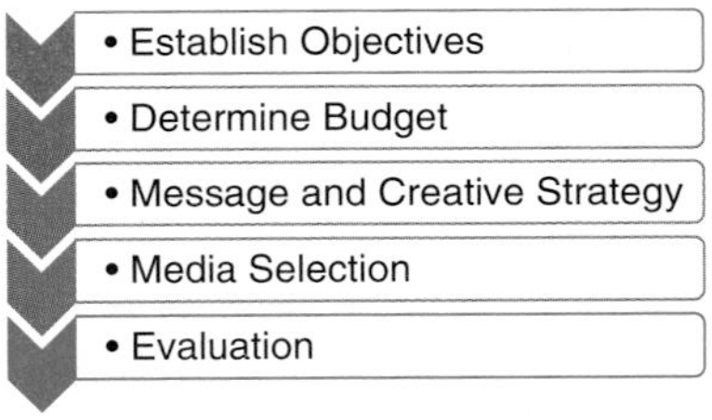

For advertising to be effective as a communication tool, marketers develop an advertising plan. The plan, shown in Figure 16.3, outlines the key decisions that must be made. First, marketers establish the objectives to be met through advertising. Next, a budget is determined based on achieving the objectives. Strategic and creative elements of the advertising plan are then developed before the decision on the type or types of media that will be used.

Finally, marketers establish how they will evaluate the effectiveness of the advertising. Most companies, such as Procter & Gamble, hire advertising agencies to plan and implement ad campaigns for every brand, including researching the audiences, creating the messages, choosing the media, placing the ads, and researching the results.

Advertising Objectives

Advertising has three primary objectives—to inform, to persuade, and to remind. **Informative advertising** is used to provide consumers with information on the product or service, as well as to build awareness and initial demand of a new product. It can also be used to explain the features and functions of a product or to correct false impressions. **Persuasive advertising** is used to develop brand preferences and is also effective at increasing customer loyalty. Marketers often use comparative advertising to persuade consumers to switch brands. **Reminder advertising** is used by well-established brands to maintain brand awareness and remind customers to buy. The brand's stage in the product life cycle will influence the objectives. For example, in the introductory stage of the product life cycle the objective will use informative advertising to establish or increase awareness among the target market. In the maturity stage, the objective may be to encourage brand switching by consumers, which calls for the use of persuasive advertising.

Advertising Budget

The size of the ad budget will depend on several factors including the objectives, anticipated competitor reactions, and economic circumstances. Several methods are available that can assist marketers in determining the size of the budget. Perhaps the easiest method to use is the **percentage of sales method**, where the size of the budget is based on a percentage of sales. The percentage to be used can be based on the average for the industry, or it may be set in relation to a competitor. The key here is to remember that while the percentage may be the same, larger companies will still have a bigger advertising budget. Under the **competitive budget method** though, the ad budget is set to match, dollar for dollar, that of an important competitor.

Message and Creative Strategy

The advertising message is the information that is to be delivered to the target audience. The creative strategy is how the message will be encoded. In developing the message, marketers must understand the thoughts, feelings, and behaviors of the target audience. In general, messages focus on the functions or benefits of the brand and are meant to influence the perceptions that the target audience has of the brand. Messages should also convey the unique selling proposition (USP), which was introduced in Chapter 10. From an advertising perspective, the USP is the point of differentiation that "sells" the brand in a positive way that the target audience values and believes. For example, the USP for GEICO is that it saves consumers money on insurance.

The creative aspect of advertising carries many responsibilities, such as making sure that the message is received and properly decoded by the target audience. Given that consumers are exposed to a great many advertising messages each day, creating an advertisement that cuts through the clutter is critical. There are a number of different **message execution** styles that can be used to attract attention, including slice of life, lifestyle, mood or image, fantasy, personality symbol, music, scientific evidence, or technical expertise. These styles are highlighted in Table 16.2.

The **advertising appeal**, or the reason to purchase a product, must also be determined. Advertising appeals work well if they are able to connect with the target market on an emotional or rational level. Examples of advertising appeals include economic savings, love or romance, fear, health, admiration (celebrity endorsers), and vanity/ego. In an effective ad the execution style and the advertising appeal will complement each other. For example, GEICO's use of humor as an execution style and an economic advertising appeal ("15 minutes will save you 15% on your car insurance") is partly responsible for the company's success.

Media Selection

Messages can be transmitted to the target audience through a variety of media types. Media types include newspapers, television, radio, magazines, outdoor advertising, and the Internet. The selection of the media depends on the target audience and which types of media they consume. It also depends on which media provides the necessary **reach** (percentage of the target market exposed to the ad) and **frequency** (the number of times they are exposed to the ad) required to meet the objectives. Even after a specific type of media is selected (television, for example), decisions must be made on which specific media vehicles (in this case, which channels to broadcast the commercial) to use. Marketers must balance the reach and frequency with the cost of the media. More specifics regarding the various media types are discussed in Chapter 18.

Evaluation

Because advertising accounts for a significant portion of the marketing budget, the effectiveness of the ad should be measured before and after it reaches the target market. Testing an ad before launch (pretesting) involves showing the ad to a small sample of the target market to find out if the message was received as intended. Changes to the ad can be made, and then the ad can be retested, before launching the ad. After an ad has been launched additional testing should be conducted to check if the intended message is being delivered as well as the

Table 16.2 Advertising Message Execution Styles

Message Execution	Description
Slice of Life	Shows "real-life" people using a product in a normal setting, such as a family sitting at the dinner table.
Lifestyle	Shows how a product relates to the lifestyle of the target market.
Mood or Image	Ads using this style build an image (or mood) around a product such as peace or love.
Fantasy	The use of the product creates a fantasy for the viewer. Car commercials use this so viewers can imagine themselves behind the wheel.
Personality Symbol	Uses a character, such as the GEICO gecko, to represent the product.
Music	Uses music to convey the intended message. Also includes the use of jingles.
Humor	Uses comedy to deliver the message to capture and maintain attention.
Scientific Evidence	Presents scientific evidence to highlight a product's superiority.
Technical Expertise	Highlights some form of expertise that is perceived to be valuable by the target market, such as an expertise in product design or quality.

ability of viewers to recall the ad. Recall testing can be aided or unaided. Unaided recall involves asking viewers to recall the ads they have seen in a particular product category. If the ad was effective at attracting viewers, they should be able to list the name of the brand. Aided recall narrows the focus by showing the viewer a copy of the ad and asking if they have seen the ad before. Taken together, these forms of testing can be used to determine awareness, preferences, and intentions to purchase. In time, testing should focus on the financial influence of the ad by determining the ad's effect on product sales. Additional discussion of advertising evaluation occurs in Chapter 20.

EXAMPLE ADVERTISING

H.J. Heinz invited consumers to create and submit 30-second commercials that expressed their passion for the company's market-leading ketchup. The company announced the contest online and on its product labels. "The most powerful vehicle for us to communicate with consumers is our own bottle," explained the ketchup brand manager. Feedback came in the form of thousands of video entries that were collectively viewed more than 10 million times on YouTube and TopThisTV.com. From all the entries submitted, 10 finalists were selected and viewers were asked to vote for their favorite. Heinz gave the winner $57,000 and aired the commercial on national television.[6]

PHOTO: Dirk Herzog/Shutterstock.

>> END EXAMPLE

SALES PROMOTION (pp. 231–232)

DEFINED **Sales promotion** *is marketer-controlled communication to stimulate immediate audience response by enhancing the value of an offering for a limited time.*

EXPLAINED

Sales Promotion

Sales promotions are used to achieve short-term marketing objectives by offering buyers incentives to take immediate action. They can be targeted toward consumers or business customers, or members of the trade (retailers and wholesalers). **Consumer promotions** take many forms, including coupons, product samples, contests and sweepstakes, bonus offers, and rebates. They are designed to motivate consumers to try a product or buy it again by offering an economic incentive. Consumer promotions offer marketers a higher degree of control and their effect can be easily measured through product sales, coupon redemption, and other consumer responses.

Trade promotions are incentives offered to retailers and wholesalers that take the form of discounts or allowances. Members of the trade are offered discounts, typically a percentage off the list price, for a limited time. Allowances are also offered to encourage retailers to feature a manufacturer's product in the store's weekly sales ad or for the use of special displays.

APPLIED

Sales Promotion

Companies can use a variety of consumer sales promotion techniques, including the following:

- **Coupons** encourage consumers to try a new product or keep buying an existing product at a limited-time discount.
- **Samples and trial offers** allow consumers to try and evaluate a good or service for free or at a low price.
- **Refunds and rebates** return some or the entire purchase price to the buyer to encourage product trial or repurchase.
- **Loyalty programs** reward consumers for repeat purchases of a product or brand.
- **Contests and sweepstakes** offer prizes to build excitement and involve customers in a brand-related activity.
- **Premiums** give buyers free (or low-cost) items in the product package, in the store, or by mail to encourage buying.
- **Point-of-purchase displays** draw shoppers' attention to particular products with eye-catching in-store displays.

EXAMPLE **SALES PROMOTION**

The Arby's fast-food chain frequently uses coupons to bring consumers into its restaurants and boost sales of specific menu items. Now Arby's is reaching out to a wider audience by delivering coupons by cell phone. Instead of handing a printed coupon to the cashier, the consumer shows the coupon on his or her cell phone screen. According to the vice president of marketing, "Arby's does a lot of couponing in newspaper and direct mail, so it was a natural transition to do a mobile couponing offer. We look for alternative media opportunities to reach different audiences and we felt that mobile was the perfect way to reach a younger audience."[7]

PHOTO: Jainie Duplass/Shutterstock.

>> **END EXAMPLE**

Trade sales promotion techniques include the following:

- **Trade show exhibits** showcase products to many buyers during industry events.
- **Trade allowances** reward retailers or wholesalers with discounts or payments for promoting a product to consumers.
- **Co-operative advertising allowances** pay part of the cost for wholesalers and retailers that include a product in their local advertising.
- **Sales contests** reward salespeople for meeting or exceeding sales goals.
- **Training** improves the trade's product knowledge and sales skills.

Sales promotion can be fun and engaging, but it can also be controversial. Pharmaceutical companies have invested billions of dollars in consumer coupons, free samples, and payments to doctors for attending product-training courses. Critics worry that these promotions will prompt consumers to ask doctors for unneeded or inappropriate drugs. They also worry that doctors will be swayed to prescribe drugs unnecessarily or prefer the promoted drugs over other alternatives. In response, some states have restricted pharmaceutical sales promotions targeting doctors. And the Pharmaceutical Research and Manufacturers of America, an industry group, has adopted voluntary guidelines limiting payments and gifts to doctors.[8]

PUBLIC RELATIONS (pp. 233–234)

DEFINED **Public relations** *is two-way communication designed to improve mutual understanding and positively influence relationships between the marketer and its internal and external publics.*

EXPLAINED

Public Relations

The target audiences of public relations—the **publics**—are people inside or outside the company who have a "stake" in what it does. These publics include all stakeholders; customers, employees, suppliers, distributors, government officials, industry groups, community members, reporters, and others who may influence or be influenced by the marketer in some way.

The objectives of public relations are as follows:

- To gauge what various publics think and feel about the marketer's brands and about business issues
- To establish a dialogue about various publics' interests and concerns
- To enhance the marketer's image
- To build or rebuild trust and goodwill
- To build a solid foundation for ongoing marketing efforts

Table 16.3 Commonly Used Publicity Techniques

Technique	Use
News release	Printed, electronic, or video information about a product or the company delivered to the media for news purposes
Media kit	General information about the company, personnel, products, history, and activities delivered to the media as background for news
News conference	A meeting with media representatives to publicly communicate company or product news and answer questions
Public appearance	Live appearances by company or celebrity spokespeople to call attention to a brand, product, issue, or cause
Sponsorships	Financially linking a company or brand with a cause, issue, or event

APPLIED

Public Relations

A marketer can use **corporate public relations** to evaluate and shape or reshape long-term public opinion of the company. The focus is on polishing the company's image over time, rather than on achieving an immediate marketing objective. Sometimes companies spotlight their involvement with causes or organizations that are important to its publics, the way McDonald's communicates its support of the Ronald McDonald House Charities. Similarly, The Home Depot builds goodwill through its connection with Habitat for Humanity in many communities.

In contrast, **marketing public relations** seeks to achieve specific marketing objectives by targeting consumers with product-focused messages. For example, Kraft Foods has six Oscar Mayer Wienermobiles touring the country to introduce new products and reinforce brand awareness. One of the most visible forms of marketing public relations is **product placement**, in which the company arranges for its brand or product to appear in a movie or other entertainment vehicle. For example, Cisco Systems' videoconferencing products have appeared on *CSI* episodes, and branded Coca-Cola cups have been prominently featured on *American Idol*. Integrating a product into a movie, TV show, video game, concert tour, or stage show sends a more subtle message about the brand than does marketer-controlled advertising.

Note that **publicity**, generating unpaid media coverage about a company or its products, is only one part of public relations and can be used for either corporate or marketing purposes. Table 16.3 shows some of the most common techniques used for publicity purposes.

One major function of public relations is to allow a company to engage in two-way communication during times of crisis caused by natural disasters, illegal activity, product recalls, or other problems. What a company says and does during such difficult situations will affect its image, reputation, and relationships. Despite the very real potential for damage, a crisis can also be an opportunity to demonstrate genuine concern for the safety and welfare of employees, customers, and other publics.

EXAMPLE **PUBLIC RELATIONS**

Mattel faced a serious crisis when the paints on some of its toys imported from China were found to contain dangerous levels of lead. Even before the company and the U.S. government

completed their investigations, Mattel's CEO decided to recall millions of toys, increase supplier scrutiny, and expand safety testing. The CEO also publicly apologized to consumers, retailers, legislators, and business leaders, seeking to regain their trust by highlighting Mattel's actions to head off future problems. "When my children tell me to trust them," the CEO told a Chamber of Commerce meeting, "I tell them, 'deeds, not words.' That's never been more true for us at Mattel than in recent months."[9]

PHOTO: Iwona Grodzka/Shutterstock.

>> END EXAMPLE

Another form of public relations is sponsorships. **Sponsorship** financially links a company, or brand, with a cause, issue, or event. Whereas advertising conveys a specific message and sales promotion sparks immediate action, sponsorship influences brand awareness, attitudes, and feelings. According to a senior marketer at the British cell phone company Vodafone, "The emotional connection with people is what is valuable."[10] The positive thoughts and feelings provoked by sponsorship lay the groundwork for making the sale using other tools in the promotional mix. Sponsorship can also target internal audiences, building pride in the company and using event attendance to reward employees.

Brand activation can be defined as the marketing process of bringing a brand to life through creating brand experience.

The key to successful sponsorship is to choose an event or activity that reaches the right audience, is important to that audience, and has a natural connection with the brand. This process of bringing a brand to life by creating an experience that reflects the values of a brand is known as **brand activation**. Depending on the brand and the audience, the company can sponsor anything from a sports event, museum exhibit, or rock concert to an entertainment convention, charity fundraiser, or special online event. McDonald's reaches out to young men by sponsoring the Midnight Gamers Championships because this tournament is a natural fit with the target audience and the chain's promotion of its late-night hours.[11]

EXAMPLE SPONSORSHIP

Anheuser-Busch InBev links its Budweiser brand with the excitement of NASCAR racing by sponsoring Kasey Kahne's car, as well as the Budweiser Shootout at Daytona. It sponsors Bud Light Bleachers at Chicago's Wrigley Field to link the brand with major league baseball. And it reaches nearly 100 million viewers every winter as one of the longtime sponsors of the Super Bowl (and a major advertiser during the game). The goal is to have fans who attend the events and fans who watch on television associate the brand with their enjoyment of sports.[12]

PHOTO: Rob Byron/Shutterstock.

>> END EXAMPLE

Visual Summary

Part 1 Explaining (Chapters 1, 2, 3, 4, 5)
Part 2 Creating (Chapters 6, 7, 8, 9)
Part 3 Strategizing (Chapters 10, 11)
Part 4 **Managing (Chapters 12, 13, 14, 15, 16, 17)**
Part 5 Integrating (Chapters 18, 19, 20)

Chapter 16 Summary

Companies use marketing communications to shape how the target audience thinks, feels, and acts toward a brand. For effective communications to occur, a message must be encoded so that the receiver decodes the message the same way, or the way the marketer intended. Even then, a message may not be received because of noise, which is anything that can distort or block a message from being received. Developing an advertising plan requires marketers to set the objectives and budget, decide the message and creative strategy, determine which media to use, and finally to evaluate the message before and after it is released to the target market. Sales promotions are incentives that encourage consumers and members of the trade to take immediate action. Public relations involve two-way communication designed to improve understanding and positively influence relationships between the marketer and its internal and external publics.

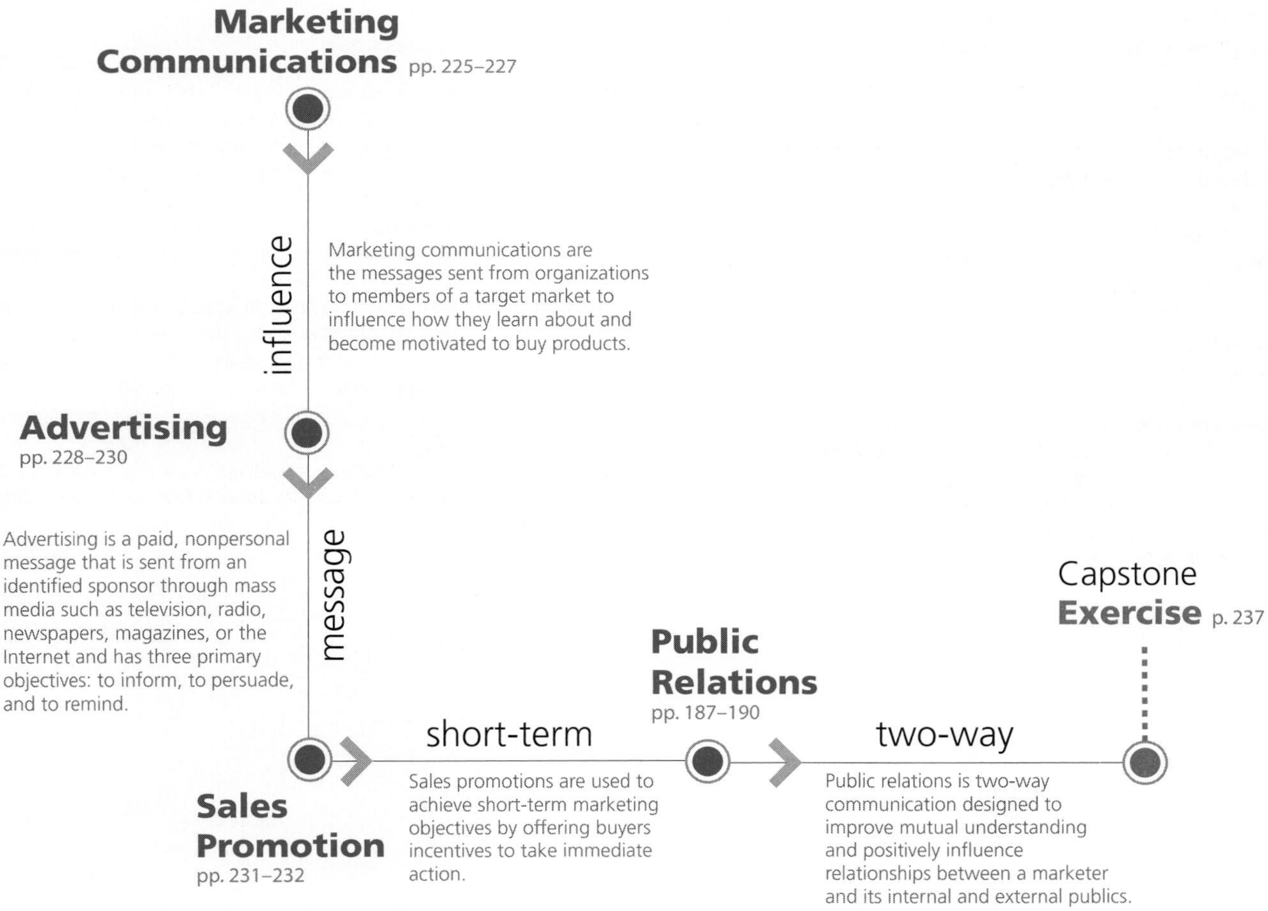
Marketing Communications pp. 225–227
influence
Marketing communications are the messages sent from organizations to members of a target market to influence how they learn about and become motivated to buy products.
Advertising pp. 228–230
message
Advertising is a paid, nonpersonal message that is sent from an identified sponsor through mass media such as television, radio, newspapers, magazines, or the Internet and has three primary objectives: to inform, to persuade, and to remind.
Sales Promotion pp. 231–232
short-term
Sales promotions are used to achieve short-term marketing objectives by offering buyers incentives to take immediate action.
Public Relations pp. 187–190
two-way
Public relations is two-way communication designed to improve mutual understanding and positively influence relationships between a marketer and its internal and external publics.
Capstone Exercise p. 237

Chapter Key Terms

Marketing Communications (pp. 225–227)

Marketing communications *are the messages sent from organizations to members of a target market in order to influence how they think, feel, and act toward a brand or market offering. (p. 225)*

Key Terms (pp. 225–226)

Noise is anything that might distort, block, or otherwise prevent the message from being properly encoded, sent, decoded, received, and/or comprehended. **(p. 225)**

Viral marketing is activities that encourage consumers to share a company's marketing message with friends. **(p. 227)**

Word of mouth is communication between consumers about a brand, marketing offer, or marketing message. **(p. 226) Example: Word of Mouth (p. 228)**

Advertising (pp. 228–230)

Advertising *is the paid, nonpersonal communication of a marketing message by an identified sponsor through mass media. (p. 228)* **Example: Advertising (p. 230)**

Key Terms (pp. 228–229)

Advertising appeal is the reason to purchase a product or service. **(p. 229)**

Competitive budget method is a method of setting the advertising budget where the budget is set to match, dollar for dollar, that of an important competitor. **(p. 229)**

Frequency is the number of times people are exposed to the ad. **(p. 229)**

Informative advertising provides consumers with information on the product or service. **(p. 228)**

Message execution is how the message is delivered. **(p. 229)**

Percentage of sales method is a method of setting the advertising budget where the size of the budget is based on a percentage of sales. **(p. 229)**

Persuasive advertising entices consumers to increase brand preference by communicating unique product or service benefits. **(p. 228)**

Reach is a measure of the number of people who could potentially receive an ad through a particular media vehicle. **(p. 229)**

Reminder advertising keeps a known product or service in the mind of consumers. **(p. 228)**

Sales Promotion (pp. 231–232)

Sales promotion *is marketer-controlled communication to stimulate immediate audience response by enhancing the value of an offering for a limited time. (p. 231)* **Example: Sales Promotion (p. 231)**

Key Terms (p. 231)

Consumer promotions are designed to motivate consumers to try a product or buy it again by offering an economic incentive such as coupons. **(p. 231)**

Trade promotions are incentives offered to retailers and wholesalers that take the form of discounts or allowances. **(p. 231)**

Public Relations (pp. 233–234)

Public relations *is two-way communication to improve mutual understanding and positively influence relationships between the marketer and its internal and external publics. (p. 233)* **Example: Public Relations (pp. 233–234)**

Key Terms (pp. 233–234)

Brand activation is the process of bringing a brand to life by creating an experience that reflects the values of a brand. **(p. 234)**

Corporate public relations is how management evaluates and shapes or reshapes long-term public opinion of the company. **(p. 233) Example: Public Relations (pp. 233–234)**

Marketing public relations is how marketers seek to achieve specific marketing objectives by targeting consumers with product-focused messages. **(p. 233)**

Product placement is an arrangement in which the company has its brand or product appear in a movie or other entertainment vehicle. **(p. 233)**

Publics are the target audiences of public relations; the people inside or outside the company who have a "stake" in what it does. **(p. 233)**

Publicity is generating unpaid, positive media coverage about a company or its products. **(p. 233)**

Sponsorship is a way of publicly associating a brand with an event or activity that the company supports financially. **(p. 234) Example: Sponsorship (p. 234)**

Capstone Exercise

"I melt for no one." This from America's favorite *spokescandy*, Ms. Green. She speaks to the core competency of M&Ms candy—the candy that "melts in your mouth, not in your hand." Today, central to the M&M candy marketing strategy are the colorful spokescandies (Red, Green, Yellow, Blue, and Orange) who are responsible for delivering the marketing message. Since its inception in 1941, M&Ms has continued to implement an effective marketing program. A subsidiary of Mars Snackfood US, M&Ms has become a global competitor. The M&M brand is a global icon and represents colorful, chocolate fun to consumers around the world.

M&Ms places over 50% of its media budget in TV advertising—primarily with cable and syndication. M&Ms spent another 40% of its media budget in magazines supporting various promotions in high-reaching popular titles like *People, InStyle,* and *ESPN The Magazine*. The remaining 10% supports digital promotion and sponsorships.

The M&Ms interactive Web site features games, recipes, and current promotions. Visitors are invited to create their own customized character. The M&M Facebook page has nearly 500,000 fans and provides promotional and informational material every few days. M&Ms maintains three Twitter accounts: @mmsgreen, where consumers can find updates on promotions and interact with M&Ms through Ms. Green, and @RidinWithRowdy, which deals with the NASCAR racing sponsorship of Kyle "Rowdy" Busch.

M&Ms merchandise stores, like the flagship store on the Las Vegas Strip, offer thousands of branded items and collectibles. M&Ms has conducted favorite-color voting around the world. M&Ms created a variety of character spokescandies dressed as characters from Star Wars, Transformers, Pirates of the Caribbean, and Zorro, all for special promotions. M&Ms also offers cross-promotional Disney-themed candy in M&Ms Memorable Moments and a joint venture with Dreyer's Ice Cream. M&Ms Colorworks allows customers to choose candy by color, and the custom-printing option first offered in 2004 allows individuals and businesses to put their own message alongside the M&M brand.

M&Ms supports the Susan G. Komen Breast Cancer Foundation through the sale of specially packaged pink and white M&Ms. M&Ms has a strong brand relationship with the Special Olympics through the "Keep Wrappers to Keep Dreams Alive" program.

Each day, more than 400 million M&Ms are consumed.

1. Identify each of the communication tools being used by M&Ms.
2. What do you see as the objective(s) of the M&Ms communication strategy?
3. In what ways do you think the M&M strategy encourages consumers to take ownership of the brand?
4. How would you describe customer perception of the brand?

Application Exercise

Use the marketing concepts in this chapter to tackle and solve a marketing problem: marketing communications and viral marketing. First, think about the many charities that are active in your area such as the American Red Cross or a local soup kitchen.

The Marketing Problem

Choose a charity after considering the following situation.

> Consumers, in general, believe in charitable giving, especially when the cause makes sense to them and they believe that the charity is well run. Consumers typically do not expect charities to spend their money on perceived expensive advertising activities. Still, charities need to communicate with current and potential donors.

The Problem

How would you develop the marketing communication process for your chosen charity? Think about how to integrate the marketing communication across all media within the advertising campaign while remaining frugal with expenditures. How could you utilize viral marketing to help your charity?

The Solution

Complete the following two Problem/Solution briefs using your charity, chapter concepts, and college resources.

1. From the Marketing Manager's Point of View
   a. Problem Definition
   b. Analysis
   c. Marketing Communications
   d. Viral Marketing
   e. Solution
2. From the Consumer's Point of View
   a. Problem Definition
   b. Analysis
   c. Message Consistency
   d. Viral Marketing
   e. Solution

Resources:

Marketing Defined, Explained, Applied 2e, Michael Levens
The College Library
Retail or Online Field Trip
Assigned Reading—*Brand Week, Advertising Age, WSJ*, scholarly publications, category trade journals
Blog your problem from either point of view, gather responses/posts (www.blogger.com/start)

Personal Selling and Direct Marketing Strategies

Chapter Overview The previous chapter discussed the ways organizations communicate with customers on a mass scale. This chapter examines how organizations communicate with specific customers through personal selling and direct marketing. The examination of personal selling will outline its advantages and disadvantages, the ways salespeople can be classified, the selling process salespeople follow, and how organizations manage their sales forces. The chapter concludes with a look at direct marketing, including the methods that can be used, as well as the conditions when it should be used.

Chapter Outline

PERSONAL SELLING (pp. 239–240)

DEFINED **Personal selling** *is when a representative of a company interacts directly with a customer to inform and persuade him or her to make a purchase decision about a product or service.*

EXPLAINED

Personal Selling

Whether it was homemade lemonade, Girl Scout cookies, or wrapping paper for a school fundraiser, almost everyone has sold something. And no matter which career path you choose, you will be engaged in personal selling at different times throughout your life. For example, when searching for your first job, you will assume the role of a salesperson in selling yourself to an employer.

Personal selling is one of the oldest and most effective forms of marketing communication. What makes it effective is that it allows a representative of the company, a salesperson, to have a one-on-one interaction with a customer or prospect (a potential customer). This interaction allows the salesperson to present the features and benefits of the product based on the specific needs of the customer. A salesperson can also alter the message, or provide additional information, based on the immediate feedback gained during a sales call.

More and more companies are relying on personal selling to generate product sales. These salespeople are employed in a number of industries and meet with customers in a variety of locations such as:

- A retail environment, for example, store, bank, or a dealership
- A business environment, for example, client office, sales office, real estate site, or job site
- A nonbusiness environment, for example, trade show, event, fair, golf course, restaurant, or new home site
- A customer's or prospect's home, for example, door-to-door selling or personal consultation
- On the phone
- Over the Internet

APPLIED

Personal Selling

Although personal selling can be the most expensive promotional activity, it offers numerous advantages over other forms, such as advertising. Personal selling allows the company to:

- Develop long-term, personal relationships with customers
- Precisely target the most desirable customers
- Directly address customers' questions or concerns
- Demonstrate the product firsthand
- Deliver complex information to the customer

Salespeople not only deliver information, they also gain information. By being out in the field, members of the sales team are often the first to learn of new opportunities and potential threats that often arise in the market. For example, a salesperson can learn about the customer's plans for expansion or is informed about a competitor's new product. Just by being out of the office, a salesperson can discover potential new customers.

The biggest disadvantage of personal selling is the high average cost of a sales call. Some estimates place this figure as high as $300 in the B2B market. Given that a salesperson may need to make multiple trips before a prospect becomes a customer, the costs of gaining a new customer can approach $1,500 or more. The cost of a sales call involves more than the salesperson's compensation. Other costs, including travel expenses, sales support, sales training, employee retention, and the recruitment of salespeople, must also be taken into account.

For many companies, and in many industries, recruiting salespeople is an expensive and ongoing process. A high **turnover rate**, which is the percentage of the sales force that leaves a company per year, can significantly increase the costs of personal selling. Attracting and training new salespeople takes time, which often leaves a sales territory without a salesperson. This usually results in little to no sales being generated. It can also have a long-term impact if a customer decides to switch to a competitor.

Richard Santulli, CEO of NetJets, a company that specializes in fractional jet ownership, once telephoned a prospective customer who was worried that he would never be important to NetJets. The prospect told him, "You guys are big and successful, and I'm just a little guy." Richard said that it was 12:10 P.M., and that he was getting married at 1:00 P.M. that day. As he spoke, his wife-to-be was yelling at him to get off the phone. Richard said, "I insisted that I give you a call to show you we do care." The prospect has been a customer since 1998—and a happy one.[1]

PHOTO: USTIN/Shutterstock.

Further, the customer may have established a personal, working relationship with the salesperson, and in some cases salespeople may "take the customer with them" if they are hired by a competitor.

Personal selling can be used for a wide variety of products and services in both the consumer and business market. However, personal selling is best used when the product or service:

- Is complex
- Is purchased infrequently
- Is expensive
- Is customized
- Requires a "push" strategy
- Has a long consideration period
- Has a small target market
- Has a purchase price that is negotiable

EXAMPLE PERSONAL SELLING

According to *Selling Power* magazine, the top 500 companies in America, based on the size of their salesforce, employ a total of 21 million salespeople. These firms are found across a variety of industries, including services, manufacturing, and direct selling. The greatest number of salespeople are employed by direct-sales firms such as Amway, Mary Kay, and Tupperware. The top 30 firms in this sector employ just over 19 million salespeople. The service sector, composed of companies such as AFLAC, AT&T, and Citigroup, have a total of 662,250 salespeople. Firms such as Microsoft, Coca-Cola, and Pfizer make up the manufacturing sector, which employs just over 500,000 salespeople. As far as productivity goes, each salesperson in the manufacturing sector generates an average of $7.6 million in sales, while the average sales per salesperson in the service sector is $3.9 million.

PHOTO: Yuri Arcurs/Shutterstock.

>> END EXAMPLE

PERSONAL SELLING PROCESS (pp. 241–242)

DEFINED *The* ***personal selling process*** *is a set of activities that salespeople follow in acquiring new customers.*

EXPLAINED

Personal Selling Process

A company's growth, and often its survival, depends on the ability of the sales team to obtain new customers. And although they may be offering different products, to distinct groups of customers, virtually every salesperson follows the personal selling process to recruit new business for their company.

APPLIED

Personal Selling Process

In the seven-step process, shown in Figure 17.1, the salesperson identifies (prospecting), researches (preapproach), and contacts (approach) potential customers. During her meeting with the prospective customer (the sales presentation) the salesperson outlines the benefits of the product and responds to any issues raised by the prospect (overcomes objectives). After the salesperson has addressed the concerns of the prospect, she asks for the order (closes the sale). Even at this point, the personal selling process is not over. The salesperson needs to contact the customer (follow-up) to ensure that the order was delivered as promised. Whereas each particular company may use unique terms, descriptions, or requirements, the general process is widely accepted.

FIGURE 17.1 Steps in the Personal Selling Process

1. Prospecting
2. Preapproach
3. Approach
4. Sales Presentation
5. Overcome Objections
6. Close the Sale
7. Follow-up

Step 1: Prospecting

Because they have limits on their time, salespeople must be able to identify those individuals or companies that are most likley to be interested in the products or services being offered. This process, called **prospecting**, results in a list of potential customers, or prospects, for the salesperson to pursue.

A prospect list can be developed through external or internal sources. External sources include lists from trade associations (e.g., American Hospital Association), business research firms (e.g., Hoovers, Inc.), or commercial databases (e.g., InfoUSA.com). Many companies generate their own prospect list by using other elements of the promotion mix such as advertising or trade shows. A prospect list that was generated internally is often considered more valuable because the prospect must take action to be included.

Professional online social networks, such as LinkedIn.com, Ryze.com, Biznik.com, or WomanOwned.com, are becoming valuable tools for sales professionals. These sites allow salespeople to network online with people they already know, and to also request "introductions" to people they want to know. Professional social networking is a fast, efficient way to establish a connection with people to whom salespeople might not otherwise have access. Today, many salespeople are using social networking as a replacement for cold calling.

Step 2: Preapproach

The objective of the preapproach step is for the salesperson to learn as much as possible about the prospect. For business prospects, this includes identifying the prospect's business needs and challenges and determining how to help solve the problem and add value to the prospect's business. This step also includes identifying the correct person in the organization with whom to make initial contact, as well as identifying other key decision makers and key influencers who will have an impact on the final purchasing decision.

Sources such as financial analysis firms (e.g., Standard & Poor's), local and national business publications (e.g., *Wall Street Journal*), and the company's own Web site are ideal places to build knowledge of the prospect. A salesperson may also find information on a prospect from an internal company database. Here, the salesperson can learn if there was any previous contact with the prospect and, if so, the timing of the contact, the response, and the reasons the prospect chose not to purchase at that time. This is why it is critical that salespeople maintain excellent records of their activities.

Step 3: Approach

After a prospect has been qualified and researched, the salesperson is ready to approach the prospect. The approach is the first formal contact with the prospect and allows salespeople to make a professional introduction of themselves and their company. The approach provides a great opportunity for salespeople to enhance their understanding of the prospect's needs. The approach phase is a critical step in the personal selling process because the prospect will decide whether to go to the next step, which is agreeing to a formal meeting with the salesperson. The old saying, "you never get a second chance to make a first impression," is never more true than during the approach phase.

Step 4: Sales Presentation

The **sales presentation**, or sales call, is the formal meeting between the salesperson and the prospect. A sales call is not just about presenting information; it also serves as a means of gaining information. A question that broadly addresses the prospect's need and offers an all-encompassing solution can be effective at the beginning of a sales presentation. This ensures that the salesperson accurately understands the needs of the prospect. This type of questioning can also signal to the prospect that the salesperson engages in **consultative selling**, in which the salesperson is focused more on solving the problems of the prospect rather than just trying to sell a product. A problem-solving approach will generally result in long-term relationships that are mutually beneficial.

Because it can take multiple sales calls before a prospect places an order, the initial sales call is the first step in building a professional relationship. As such, the salesperson should seek to build rapport with the prospect in order to build understanding and to develop trust. This can be accomplished by observing the décor of the prospect's office. Most people will have some items of personal interest in their office that can offer cues as to what topics will be of interest to the prospect that can be used to break the ice.

Step 5: Overcome Objections

Prospects will almost always raise objections when the salesperson asks for the order. The most frequent objections given relate to price, quality, timing, or existing contracts. A good salesperson has already anticipated these objections prior to the sales presentation and developed a means to overcome them. In handling objections, the salesperson should ask questions of the prospect to clarify the concerns. In many cases, the objections can be overcome if the salesperson fully understands the prospect's concerns by providing new information. Supporting information such as testimonials, references, and case studies can help salespeople successfully overcome objections.

Step 6: Close the Sale

If all objections have been satisfied, the salesperson should **close the sale** by asking for the order. Although this task may seem daunting to inexperienced salespeople, the close is a natural outcome of the well-prepared sales effort. Deciding when to close is perhaps the most difficult part of this step, but often prospects provide signals to indicate they are ready to buy. These buying cues can be verbal, such as questions about price or credit terms, or nonverbal, such as relaxed facial muscles or a natural smile.

A variety of techniques can be used to close the sale. Many times a salesperson will use a **trial close** to gauge the prospect's interest. Under a trial close the salesperson might ask, "Now that your concerns have been addressed, is there anything else that can impact your decision to buy?" The **alternative close** seeks to have the prospect make a choice not between buy or not buy, but rather between product features or options. For example, the salesperson could ask the prospect "Would you prefer it in red or blue?"or "Should I have it delivered tomorrow or next Tuesday?" The **assumptive close** takes a more direct approach by asking the prospect specific questions such as "Will 200 cases be enough for the first order?"

Step 7: Follow-up

After the sale has been made, the salesperson needs to finalize the process by following up with the customer to ensure that the order was received on time and the product was delivered to the customer as promised. This simple effort can serve multiple purposes, including solving any problems that may have occurred with the order and also to show the customer that the salesperson cares as much after the sale as before receiving the order. This is especially true if the salesperson wishes to have future business with the new customer.

EXAMPLE PERSONAL SELLING PROCESS

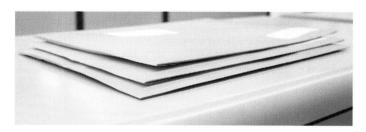

At Pitney Bowes, a global provider of physical and digital mailing products and services, sales representatives rely on vital customer and inventory information available on their mobile devices. They can, for example, get information about their next sales call, ensure they have the proper parts and inventory within their vans, and access client sales and service histories. Sales reps are able to make more calls in a day because they spend less time on each call.[2]

PHOTO: Galina Barskkaya/Shutterstock.

>> **END EXAMPLE**

SALES MANAGEMENT (p. 243)

DEFINED **Sales management** *is the process of planning, implementing, and controlling the personal selling function.*[3]

EXPLAINED

Sales Management

Because sales are the lifeblood of every company, proper sales management is a requirement for success. Sales management clearly communicates company objectives, strategies, and product information so the salespeople can communicate with customers. For most companies, a senior sales executive, with titles such as vice president of sales or general sales manager, is responsible for overseeing the selling function. These executives organize, motivate, and lead the sales team, with the purpose of ensuring that sales targets or objectives are met. Many companies split their sales team into regions, which are led by regional sales managers. These midlevel executives will manage a small group of district managers, who in turn supervise groups of 8 to 10 salespeople.

APPLIED

Sales Management

Effective sales managers provide leadership, which, in turn, outlines priorities and direction to salespeople. Sales managers are constantly looking for ways to reduce nonselling functions, such as paperwork and internal meetings, so salespeople have more time to focus on selling activities, such as meeting with customers and prospects.

Sales managers use an organizational structure to help provide accountability and increase salesperson productivity. Although all sales forces are not structured exactly the same, some general functions are used by most selling organizations. Sales managers may oversee different types of salespeople. Salespeople who are physically located inside the office and rarely, if ever, have face-to-face contact with customers or prospects are called **inside sales**. Salespeople who spend the majority of their time outside the office meeting with customers and prospects are called **outside sales**. Sales managers may exclusively use one type of sales force or combine the two types, based on the company's sales strategy and financial structure. An inside sales force is usually less expensive because it does not generate travel expenses. However, outside salespeople enable the development of personal relationships with customers, which generates long-term benefits for the company.

Some key sales roles include order taker, customer service representative, technical or product specialist, sales representative, sales support, and new business development. All these roles can be performed either as inside or outside sales functions.

EXAMPLE **SALES MANAGEMENT**

Rebecca Herwick, CEO of Harley-Davidson licensee Global Products, knew her sales strategy wasn't working when seven of her nine independent sales representatives quit carrying her products during August 2006. Herwick had been using independent sales reps to sell her products—everything from Harley-Davidson–branded bandanas to coffee mugs—to over 800 Harley dealerships nationwide. Although the use of independent sales reps was a cost-effective strategy, there were problems, including a lack of clear expectations, a limited performance tracking system, and few penalties for violating established rules. The independent sales reps were selling other product lines that didn't compete with her products, but she still felt that her company wasn't getting the attention it deserved. Rather than hiring a dedicated but expensive internal sales staff, she learned to better manage her independent sales reps. She laid down ground rules, including new commission rates, new requirements for customer visits, and customer feedback surveys to help assess sales representative performance. The changes are paying off. Sales are up, and more important, customers have noticed a difference in attention and service.[4]

PHOTO: Kaspars Grinvalds/Shutterstock.

>> **END EXAMPLE**

SALES MANAGEMENT PROCESS (pp. 244–246)

DEFINED *The **sales management process** is a comprehensive approach used by sales managers to determine how the sales force is organized and managed and how they will hire, recruit, manage, motivate, and evaluate the performance of the individual salespeople.*

EXPLAINED

Sales Management Process

Establishing a sales force requires long-term vision on the part of senior sales executives. The decisions they make at the start will determine the structure and size of the sales force. However, the sales management process should be examined from the operational perspective, which determines how salespeople are recruited, compensated, trained, managed, motivated, and evaluated. The goal of the sales management process is to ensure that the sales force is organized to effectively and efficiently meet the sales objectives of the company.

APPLIED

Sales Management Process

The sales management process entails four key areas, and the decisions made provide the blueprint to manage salespeople and deliver results.

Setting Sales Force Objectives

The overall sales objectives for a company are established on an annual basis by the firm's top management team. However, the objectives that are set for the sales force will vary depending on the goals of the company. While one company will set its objectives based on sales volume, another company may focus the sales force on generating new customers. Once established, the objectives will filter down to individual salespeople who will be responsible for meeting their specific objectives.

Take, for example, a company with a national sales team that is structured around five regional offices. If the overall objective of the company is to increase sales by $10 million, then, on average, each regional office is responsible for $2 million in additional sales. If each regional office has five districts, then each district must increase sales by $400,000. Taking this further, if each district has eight salespeople, then each salesperson is responsible for $50,000 in additional sales. Of course, this is a very simple example. A more likely scenario would be to allocate a percentage of the $10 million objective based on each region's previous year's sales, with larger regions and districts being expected to account for a larger share. These objectives express exactly what the sales force needs to accomplish and by when.

Objectives also help sales managers develop even more specific goals for each salesperson in terms of how many sales should be generated from each existing customer, how many sales should come from new customers, and how many new business calls must be made to meet the overall sales objective. The specific sales objectives then become the basis of sales staff compensation.

Developing the Sales Force Strategy

The sales force strategy is the approach that sales management uses to meet a company's sales objectives. To develop this strategy, sales managers determine the number and type of sales positions needed to meet sales objectives. These people and positions must then be organized in the most efficient manner possible. Sales managers can organize their sales forces by:

- **Geography.** This approach ensures there is coverage in all key geographic areas. This so-called geographic or territory strategy is common because it is among the most cost-efficient approaches in that it minimizes the amount of time salespeople spend traveling between calls.
- **Product line.** This means that each salesperson specializes in selling a particular product or product line. This strategy is effective in putting the focus on individual products or product lines, but it can be difficult and expensive to implement because it means that each salesperson might have to travel to various geographic areas to meet with customers or prospects. This approach may also require that some customers or prospects have multiple salespeople calling on them from the same company.
- **Industry.** In organizing by industry, each salesperson calls on companies in a single industry, such as retail, financial services, or pharmaceuticals. This strategy is successful when products or services are complex and have different applications in different industries. Here, salespeople have the opportunity to learn from each customer and apply this knowledge to help others in the industry.
- **Key accounts.** This strategy recognizes that the major customers of a product or service are the most important, so those customers should receive dedicated personal-selling resources. The key account strategy can be used alone, or it can be

supplemented with any of the strategies mentioned earlier. For instance, a company may have some salespeople dedicated to calling on key accounts, while the balance of its sales force may be organized by territory, product line, or industry.

Recruiting, Compensating, Training, and Motivating the Sales Force

Building a successful sales force is key to meeting the company's objectives.

Recruiting

Recruiting and hiring the right salespeople is one of the most important activities a sales manager can perform. The salesperson is an ambassador for the company and, in many cases, the customer's exclusive point of contact with the company. A salesperson can make the difference between success and failure in meeting both the customer's and his or her company's objectives. Most companies therefore make a significant investment in training, managing, motivating, and recognizing salespeople.

Salespeople must possess specific characteristics, such as good personal and listening skills, the ability to work both independently and as part of a team, the ability to manage a budget, and the ability to resolve problems in a timely manner. They must also be able to identify and research a qualified prospect, close a sale, and follow up. They must have the drive and passion to move forward, even when everything is not going smoothly.

There is no ironclad method for hiring the right salespeople. Some companies administer tests to see whether sales candidates have the characteristics and skills needed to succeed. Other companies use an extensive interviewing process in which the candidates meet with several people inside the company and accompany existing staff on sales calls.

Compensating

In most companies, the sales function is based on a **pay-for-performance compensation strategy**. This strategy means that a large part or all of a salesperson's income is based on the amount of sales or profit he or she delivers to his or her company in a given time frame. When this is the case, salespeople are paid on **commission**. Commission is a percentage of the sales or profit the salesperson generates. In some companies, a salesperson may earn commission, plus an incentive or bonus for sales or profit delivered over a stated goal. A bonus may be an additional commission rate, a set dollar amount, a trip, or some other incentive. In many companies, there is no limit to how much money a salesperson can make, because the company wants to sell as much of its products and services as possible.

Training

To ensure that their salespeople are successful, most companies invest in training for all members of the sales force. There are several types of training. Usually, sales management provides a combination of types of training for salespeople on an ongoing basis. The types of training include the following:

- Product training is information about the features and benefits of specific products or product lines.
- Sales training can focus on information about the company, its product offerings, or specific skills that help salespeople improve their relationship building or closing skills.
- Personal-development training includes exposure to areas that help prepare salespeople to advance to the next level. This can include topics such as management training and leadership skills.

Sales meetings are the traditional method used to train salespeople. A sales meeting allows salespeople to meet their peers; all salespeople hear the company message at the same time and feel the energy of the meeting. In addition, technology plays a significant role in all types of sales training, with the use of webinars, podcasts, video conferences, audio conferences, on-demand training videos, Web-based knowledge centers, and video games. Sales managers know that in-person meetings with technology-based training can be a powerful combination.

Motivating

Maintaining a highly motivated sales force is key for any company. Although money and incentives can be effective, the effect is generally short-lived. Great sales managers realize that it takes more than money or prizes to motivate and engage salespeople. Rather, motivating a sales force requires constant communication and recognition. Communication keeps an organization on track by maintaining the focus on goals and providing updates about successes. One of the best ways to motivate and retain salespeople is to recognize them for their efforts. Many companies have recognition programs that highlight high achievers in a variety of areas. For instance, in addition to recognizing sales achievements, many companies also recognize salespeople who have provided extraordinary customer service, supported other employees, or otherwise gone above and beyond the call of duty. Recognition programs may include rewards such as being invited to a recognition dinner, receiving a plaque, or being inducted as a member of a performance "club."

Evaluating the Sales Force

The last area that sales managers focus on—evaluating the sales force—links back to the first step in the process. Each salesperson will have one or a series of objectives for the sales territory set by the sales manager. Typical objectives used include sales volume, average number of sales calls per day, sales per customer, or new customer orders. Once the objectives are established, regular reports must be made available to all salespeople so that they can track their performance.

Evaluation is an ongoing process. Formal evaluations usually take place on a regular basis, such as monthly, quarterly, or annually. New objectives for the upcoming time period are established, based on each salesperson's performance. Some companies are beginning to include customer feedback as a means to evaluate salespeople. In these cases, the company issues a survey (by mail, phone, or online) and gathers feedback about the performance of the company and the salesperson.

EXAMPLE **EMPLOYEE TRAINING**

Michael Dell began selling computers from his dorm room at the University of Texas in 1984. The company he founded, Dell Inc., grew into one of the largest technology companies selling computers directly to consumers through ads placed in national computer magazines. While the direct-to-consumer market remains an integral part of its business, the decision to use a sales force to target corporate, institution, and government accounts enabled the company to generate sales exceeding $50 billion in 2008.

Facing increased competition in the computer market, the company is adding over 4,000 new salespeople as it seeks to expand its product offerings to include integrated business solutions, which involves a complex combination of computer hardware, software, and services. This shift will require the company's existing sales force to undergo intensive technical training to be able to effectively communicate the benefits to potential customers. The additional salespeople, along with training for the company's 11,000 existing salespeople, will cost Dell more than $500 million over the next three years.

PHOTO: joyfull/Shutterstock.

>> **END EXAMPLE**

DIRECT MARKETING (pp. 247–250)

DEFINED **Direct marketing** *is any communication addressed to a consumer that is designed to generate a response.*

EXPLAINED

Direct Marketing

Direct marketing is an interactive process that uses communication that is addressed to an individual consumer to generate an action or response from that consumer. The desired response could be an order, a request for further information, or a visit to a store or other place of business to purchase a product.[5] Direct marketing is considered interactive because the consumer actually interacts with the marketer as a direct result of the marketing communication.

Direct marketing is sometimes referred to as "one-to-one" marketing because marketers can target the communication and even personalize the message to each individual. Direct marketing can employ this high degree of targeting because it involves the use of consumer databases. A database may include demographic information, such as name, address, income, age, gender, number of children in the household, home ownership status, and prior purchases of specific products or services. Some consumer databases also include psychographic information, such as hobbies, travel preferences, personal aspirations, or perceptions of certain products, services, brands, or stores. Direct marketers use the information in such databases to target specific messages to specific consumers at specific times to increase the likelihood of getting the desired response. Marketers can create their own proprietary databases of customer information based on previous inquiries, transactions (such as frequent purchasers), and surveys; this type of database is called a **house file**. Alternatively, marketers can rent consumer information from companies that collect and maintain databases. These rented lists are called **outside lists**, and they can be used alone or in conjunction with a house file.

APPLIED

Direct Marketing

The types of direct marketing can be seen in Table 17.1.

The key benefits of direct marketing are as follows:

- **Targeting**—As previously discussed, direct marketing allows marketers to deliver their message only to those consumers who meet their target audience characteristics.
- **Measurability**—Direct marketing is trackable and measurable. Marketers can calculate a true ROI (return on investment) based on the consumer responses.
- **Testing**—With direct marketing, marketers can test offers, creative approaches, and responsiveness of specific customer segments. Testing makes it possible to fine-tune a company's marketing efforts before launching a full campaign.
- **High ROI**—The Direct Marketing Association reports that, on average, direct marketing generates a return on investment of $11.69, compared to $5.24 for nondirect marketing expenditures.[6]

On the other hand, the key weaknesses of direct marketing include the following:

- **Expensive**—The cost per contact (that is, the cost to reach each consumer) is usually higher for direct marketing than for other media. Paper, printing, and postage have a significant impact on the costs of direct marketing. Although the upfront cost of direct marketing is high, the return on the investment is high and helps offset the expense.
- **Low response rates**—Direct marketing usually yields a response rate of 1%–5%. That means that 95%–99% of the consumers who receive a particular direct marketing communication do not respond to it.
- **Lack of general brand awareness**—When companies use direct marketing alone, consumers who do not receive the direct marketing may not be aware of the brand or product.

Direct marketing should be considered as part of the communication mix when one or more of the following conditions holds true:

- The product or service is used only by a clearly defined segment or portion of consumers.
- The product or service purchase is time sensitive.
- The product or service is available in a particular geographic location.
- The marketer wants to reach previous purchasers of the product or service to encourage a repeat purchase or trial of a related product.
- The marketer wants to make an offer to a select group of consumers.

Direct marketing includes catalogs, direct mail, direct-response TV and radio, infomercials, and the Internet. Direct marketing has evolved significantly over the years. What started with a flyer sent to customers about products in the nineteenth

Table 17.1 Types of Direct Marketing

Type	Response Rate[7]	Cost per Order	Advantages	Disadvantages	Examples
Mail Order					
Catalogs	2.5%	Mid	Can present a wide selection of products, can target specific groups of buyers	High cost to produce and mail, saturation of mail pieces	Pottery Barn, L.L. Bean, TigerDirect
Direct Mail	1%–3%	Mid	Personalized message, high control, wide coverage, flexible	Delivery delays, saturation	Financial/insurance offers
Phone-based					
Telemarketing	6%–10%	Highest	Interactive, personal, high impact, wide reach	Negative image, high costs for equipment/training, use of caller ID, Do Not Call list	For-profit and nonprofit organizations
Direct Response Advertising					
DRTV Infomercials	4%	High	Ability to demonstrate product, holds attention	High production costs, long lead time	ShamWow, OxiClean, George Foreman Grill
Internet					
E-mail	1.7%	Mid	Lower costs, quick to implement, can be targeted, broad reach, easy response	Negative image, low response rate, spam filters can block messages	Variety
Paid Search	3.8% (clickthru)	Low	Can target specific search terms, measurable results	High competition, click fraud	Variety
Internet Display	4.4% (clickthru)	Low	Ability to reach target market, flexible, quick to implement, measurable results	Difficult to gain and maintain attention of viewer	Variety

century has developed into sophisticated and customized communications to consumers on the Internet, via mobile phones, and even on video game consoles. Technology has become a major force behind the evolution of direct marketing, with over 1.8 billion people around the world using the Internet. The diversity of direct marketing is discussed in the following sections.[8]

Mail Order

In 1872, Aaron Montgomery Ward and two partners created a one-page flyer that listed their merchandise with prices, hoping to generate some interest in their retail store.[9] But it was Richard Sears, who in 1888 published a flyer to advertise his watches and jewelry, who truly revolutionized the direct marketing business. Sears promised his customers that "we warrant every American watch sold by us, with fair usage, an accurate time keeper for six years—during which time, under our written guarantee we are compelled to keep it in perfect order free of charge."[10] It was the promise of satisfaction guaranteed that changed the face of mail-order marketing.

Today, mail order includes two types of marketing—catalogs and direct mail. The term **mail order** describes "the business of selling merchandise through the mail."[11]

Catalogs are a common marketing strategy for many marketers, such as Pottery Barn, J. Crew, and PC Mall. Over 19 billion catalogs are distributed annually.[12] They provide marketers an opportunity to showcase a large selection of product and service offerings to their target audience.

Catalogs are an effective element in the communication mix because they are targeted, can generate high returns per catalog mailed, and can be accurately measured for the sales and profit they generate. However, catalogs are extremely expensive to print and mail; costs range from $0.50 to over $3.00 or more per catalog mailed, depending on the number of pages, quantity printed, and paper quality.

Direct mail differs from catalogs because it does not showcase an entire assortment of products. Instead, direct mail usually involves only a pamphlet or flyer that focuses on a specific product or service. Direct mail may also include a postcard, letter, brochure, or product sample. Charities, political groups, retail stores, and packaged goods companies are major users of direct mail. Some Internet companies such as Netflix also use direct mail to drive traffic to their Web sites.

Although there are many variations of direct mail, all successful direct mail campaigns include three major elements:

- **Offer**—A compelling offer should be apparent to the recipient. An offer is usually promotional in nature to provide incentive for the recipient to respond. Examples of common offers are "Save 20%," "Free shipping," or "Buy One, Get One Free."

- **Mailing list**—When conducting a direct-mail campaign, identifying the proper target is as important as crafting the message. The mailing list should include only those consumers who have the highest likelihood of responding. For example, if a local grocer wants to mail coupons for baby products, the mailing list should include only those households with children under the age of one that are located within a five-mile radius of each store.
- **Call to action**—A **call to action** describes the response the company wants to elicit from the consumer. Examples of a call to action are the following: "Call 800-555-5555 to make an appointment," "Visit www.si.com and order today," or "Visit your nearest Lexus dealership." The call to action should be clear and easy to act on.

Direct mail can be an effective medium because it is targeted. However, like catalogs, direct mail can be an expensive option due to the cost of paper, printing, and postage.

Telemarketing

Telemarketing, direct marketing conducted over the phone, can be an effective part of a marketer's media mix because it provides a real-time, personal conversation with a potential customer. The types of marketers that often rely on telemarketing include charities, political parties, financial services, and retailers. Because of the negative perceptions of telemarketing that stem from calls being received at inconvenient times and the use of unscrupulous selling techniques, some marketers avoid telemarketing. Telemarketing is an expensive means of communicating with potential customers. Many firms, in order to reduce the cost, have turned to specialized firms that benefit from economies of scale. One key reason that many firms have abandoned telemarketing was the passage of the national **Do Not Call Registry** in 2003. This legislation, which was updated in 2008, prohibits telemarketers from calling any phone number registered with the Federal Trade Commission.

Direct-Response Advertising

Direct-response advertising is designed to have customers respond to specific offers or calls to action by marketers. The delivery of the enticement is through broadcast media, including newspapers and magazines, TV, radio, and the new medium of choice, the Internet. The benefit of direct-response advertising is that the effectiveness of different campaigns and media is quantifiable.

DRTV (direct-response TV) includes any form of television commercial or home shopping television show that advertises a product or service and allows the viewer to purchase the product or service directly. Although the investment in production and media can be significant, when produced and targeted properly DRTV can be an effective marketing tool. Companies such as QVC and Home Shopping Network made DRTV mainstream. Newer forms of DRTV are emerging that can deliver targeted television commercials based on selected criteria and provide a personalized call to action.

Infomercials, television shows that are a combination of an information session and a commercial, are considered direct-response marketing when they include a method for viewers to purchase the product or service directly. Infomercials vary in their length and can range from a few minutes to an hour or more. The growth of cable television has provided a significant amount of programming time, which has appealed to producers of infomercials. Once the flagship of entrepreneurs and some unscrupulous marketers, infomercials have come of age; they now generate over $1 billion in sales annually. Major marketers such as Volkswagen, American Airlines, and Procter & Gamble successfully use this format to drive consumer response, such as a dealer visit or request for additional information.

Infomercials are effective because they are targeted based on the television or radio stations on which they air. In addition, they give marketers an opportunity to describe and demonstrate the features and benefits of a product or service. Infomercials are well suited for new product introductions as well as complex products because the format provides more selling time than a traditional 30-second commercial. However, producing, testing, and airing infomercials can be expensive.

EXAMPLE **DIRECT-RESPONSE ADVERTISING**

Billy Mays was one of the most successful direct-response marketing salespersons, often called pitchmen, in history. Prior to his death in 2009, Mays was a regular presence on television advertisements with his emotional sales pitch, distinctive voice, and trademark beard selling products including Orange Glo, OxiClean, and a wide range of home-based cleaning and maintenance products. Mays and Anthony Sullivan, another well-known direct-response personality, starred in a 2009 Discovery Channel series *Pitchmen*. In each episode, the pitchmen became potential backers for inventors' products such as a broken-screw extractor and shark repellent device.

PHOTO: s70/ZUMA Press/Newscom.

>> END EXAMPLE

Internet

The Internet is an ideal direct-marketing medium. It is quickly evolving to offer unique, personalized experiences for users and targeted audiences for marketers. The different kinds of online direct-marketing opportunities continue to expand, based on technological advancements and consumer behavior. Internet-based direct marketing, offering increased targeting, quick connection to consumers and good measurement capability, is the fastest growing segment of direct marketing with expected annual growth in business investment of 18.5% per year through 2014.[13]

E-mail has evolved from an approach of "blasting" a message to all customers in a company's e-mail database to sophisticated **life cycle marketing**, with e-mail messages targeted specifically to individual consumers as each progresses through a specific life stage or life cycle (such as pregnancy to birth for marketers of baby products). Some companies use **dynamic imaging** to systematically populate individual e-mails with products targeted specifically to each consumer, based on behavior patterns and inventory.

Personalized experiences, including Web pages and offers, are also being developed and tested by several companies. The use of personalized URLs (PURLs) and landing pages (the page on which you land when you enter a URL or Web site address) allows a marketer to create a completely customized Internet experience in the form of a "mini Web site" that is personalized with the consumer's name, relevant information, and product or content that is appropriate to his or her interests. For instance, if a consumer named Sarah Morrison receives a direct mail piece or e-mail that includes a call to action to visit www.sarahmorrison.abccompany.com, and the landing page includes customized information and an offer, the response rate can increase significantly.[14] PURLs are not yet widely tested, so cutting-edge marketers can use this marketing approach to target their message in a new way.

Consumer Privacy

The nature of direct marketing is that it involves personal and targeted communications from marketers to consumers. Some marketers have abused this relationship by sending too much "junk" mail, calling consumers at dinner time, and sending unsolicited e-mails. Because of this, the Direct Marketing Association (DMA), which has more than 3,600 members (including the majority of companies on the *Fortune* 100 list), has established a **Do Not Mail List** for consumers who do not want to receive direct marketing. In addition, in 2007 the DMA created the Commitment to Consumer Choice, which requires that member companies notify consumers of the opportunity to modify or eliminate future mail solicitations.[15]

Various laws also require that companies must clearly inform consumers of their **privacy policy**, which includes the company's policy on renting its list of customer names, physical addresses, and e-mail addresses. To this end, most companies post their privacy policy on their Web site.

When illegitimate marketers began sending millions of unsolicited, misleading, and inappropriate e-mails, Congress passed the **CAN-SPAM Act of 2003** (Controlling the Assault of Non-Solicited Pornography and Marketing Act). This law has the following requirements regarding Internet marketers:

- It bans false or misleading e-mail header information, such as in the "To" and "From" fields.
- It prohibits deceptive e-mail subject lines.
- It requires that e-mails provide recipients with opt-out methods.
- It requires that commercial e-mail be identified as an advertisement and include the sender's valid physical postal address.

The CAN-SPAM Act specifies significant fines, including banning advertising, for any violators.[16]

Visual Summary

Part 1 Explaining (Chapters 1, 2, 3, 4, 5)
Part 2 Creating (Chapters 6, 7, 8, 9)
Part 3 Strategizing (Chapters 10, 11)
Part 4 Managing (Chapters 12, 13, 14, 15, 16, 17)
Part 5 Integrating (Chapters 18, 19, 20)

Chapter 17 Summary

The power of targeted marketing is demonstrated in personal selling and direct marketing. These methods allow marketers to target and communicate directly with potential customers who are most likely to respond. Either on their own, or as part of the overall communication plan, personal selling and direct marketing can be effective at generating sales.

Personal Selling pp. 239–240

one-on-one

Personal selling occurs when a salesperson has a one-on-one interaction with a current or potential customer to inform and persuade the customer to make a purchase decision by presenting the features and benefits of the product or service based on the specific needs of the customer.

Personal Selling Process pp. 241–242

acquiring

The personal selling process is a set of seven activities that salespeople follow in acquiring new customers including prospecting, preapproach, approach, sales presentation, overcome objectives, close the sale, and follow-up.

Sales Management p. 243

structure

Sales management provides structure to the process of planning, implementing, and controlling the personal selling function.

Sales Management Process pp. 244–246

approach

The sales management process is a comprehensive approach used by sales managers to determine how the sales force is organized and managed and how they will hire, recruit, manage, motivate, and evaluate the performance of the individual salespeople.

Direct Marketing pp. 247–250

interactive

Direct marketing is an interactive process that uses communication addressed to an individual consumer to generate an action or response such as an order, request for further information, or a visit to a store or other place of business to purchase a product or service.

Capstone Exercise p. 253

Chapter Key Terms

Personal Selling (pp. 239–240)

Personal selling *is when a representative of a company interacts directly with a customer to inform and persuade him or her to make a purchase decision about a product or service. (p. 239)* **Opening Example (p. 239) Example: Personal Selling (p. 240)**

Key Term (p. 239)

Turnover rate is the percentage of the sales force that leaves a company per year **(p. 239)**

Personal Selling Process (pp. 241–242)

Personal selling process *is a set of activities that salespeople follow in acquiring new customers. (p. 241)* **Example: Personal Selling Process (p. 242)**

Key Terms (pp. 241–242)

Alternative close is a sales closing technique that seeks to have the prospect make a choice between product features or options. **(p. 242)**
Assumptive close is a sales closing technique that involves direct and specific questions. **(p. 242)**
Close the sale refers to the part of the selling process in which the salesperson asks for an order. **(p. 242)**
Consultative selling is when the salesperson is focused more on solving the problems of the prospect rather than trying to sell a product. **(p. 242)**
Prospecting is the process of researching multiple sources to find potential customers or prospects. **(p. 241)**
Sales presentation is the formal meeting between a salesperson and a sales prospect. **(p. 242)**
Trial close is a sales closing technique to gauge a prospect's interest in buying. **(p. 242)**

Sales Management (p. 243)

Sales management *is the process of planning, implementing, and controlling the personal selling function. (p. 243)* **Example: Sales Management (p. 243)**

Key Terms (p. 243)

Inside sales are members of the sales team who reside inside the office or company location and rarely, if ever, have face-to-face contact with customers or prospects. **(p. 243)**
Outside sales are salespeople who meet face-to-face with customers and prospects. **(p. 243) Example: Sales Management (p. 243)**

Sales Management Process (pp. 244–246)

Sales management process *is a comprehensive approach used by sales managers to determine how the sales force is organized and managed and how they will hire, recruit, manage, motivate, and evaluate the performance of the individual salespeople. (p. 244)* **Example: Employee Training (p. 246)**

Key Terms (p. 245)

Commission is the part or all of a salesperson's income that is based on the amount of sales or profit delivered in a given time frame. **(p. 245)**
Pay-for-performance compensation strategy is the compensation system in which salespeople are paid based on the amount of sales or profits they deliver to the company. **(p. 245)**

Direct Marketing (pp. 247–250)

Direct marketing *is any communication addressed to a consumer that is designed to generate a response. (p. 247)* **Example: Direct-Response Advertising (p. 249)**

Key Terms (pp. 247–250)

Call to action is the response that a marketer wants a consumer to take as a result of receiving a direct-mail communication. **(p. 249)**
CAN-SPAM Act of 2003 (Controlling the Assault of Non-Solicited Pornography and Marketing Act) is the law that requires e-mail marketers to abide by certain requirements when e-mailing consumers. **(p. 250)**
Catalog is a printed direct-mail piece that showcases an assortment of products or services offered by a company. **(p. 248)**
Direct mail is a printed advertisement in the form of a postcard, letter, brochure, or product sample that is sent to consumers who are on a targeted mailing list. **(p. 248)**
Direct-response advertising is a direct marketing approach that includes a specific offer and call to action for the consumer to immediately contact the marketer to purchase or inquire about the product. **(p. 249) Example: Direct-Response Advertising (p. 249)**
Do Not Call Registry is a list of consumers who do not want to receive phone calls from telemarketers. Consumers can contact the Federal Trade Commission to be added to the Do Not Call Registry. **(p. 249)**
Do Not Mail List is the list of consumers who do not want to receive direct mail. Consumers can contact the Direct Marketing Association to be added to the Do Not Mail List. **(p. 250)**
DRTV (direct-response TV) is any kind of television commercial or home shopping television show that advertises a product or service and allows the viewer to purchase it directly. **(p. 249)**
Dynamic imaging is the process of systematically populating individual e-mails with products targeted specifically to each consumer, based on behavior patterns and inventory. **(p. 250)**
House file is a proprietary database of customer information collected from transactions, inquiries, or surveys from the company. **(p. 247)**
Infomercial is a television show that is a combination of an information session and a commercial. **(p. 249)**
Life cycle marketing is a series of targeted messages to customers and prospects based on their experience during a sequence of events that takes place during a specific stage in life. **(p. 250)**
Mail order is the term that describes the business of selling merchandise through the mail. **(p. 248)**
Outside lists consist of consumer information compiled by an outside company and rented to a marketer. **(p. 247)**
Privacy policy is a company's practice as it relates to renting customer information to other companies. **(p. 250)**
Telemarketing is a phone call placed to a specific consumer to offer products or services for sale. **(p. 249)**

Capstone Exercise

Tupperware Brands Corporation (TBC) makes and sells household products and beauty items. Tupperware parties became an integral part of suburban life in the United States beginning in the 1950s. Though the original Tupperware party is a nostalgic memory of another era, Tupperware has become a global competitor. Today, Tupperware is one of the largest direct marketers in the world and has a sales force of more than 2 million independent contractors in more than 100 countries.

The original Tupperware products were made from a durable plastic named Poly-T that is lightweight, flexible, and unbreakable. Over the years, the Poly-T material was improved and refined to also be clear, odorless, and non-toxic. These unique containers were further refined with a unique lid seal. Between 1950 and 1970 Tupperware parties created a strong brand awareness and sales multiplied 10-fold every year. For many women, Tupperware was their entry into the workforce.

By 1970, international sales represented a significant source of income for Tupperware. By the mid-1980s, sales were slipping and the original concept of the Tupperware party was outdated. Management introduced new ideas of parties—in the office, cocktail parties, and shorter sales presentations. Management improved delivery speed with several new warehouses and distribution centers. New, more contemporary items like microwave cookware were added to the product portfolio. The company introduced a direct-mail catalog and increased national print and television advertising.

By 2000, international sales represented 85% of total revenues and 95% of profits. Between 1995 and 2000, Tupperware introduced more than 100 new product items catering to the specific needs of the international consumer. Tupperware diversified its distribution strategy by selling over the Internet; through television infomercials, and at shopping mall kiosks. The product portfolio continued to expand with kitchen tools, small appliances, and children's products.

With an understanding that cosmetics were more in vogue than domestic products, Tupperware acquired BeautiControl, Inc., in 2001 and Sara Lee's direct-sale, beauty-supply line (operating primarily outside the United States) in 2005. Reflecting its identity as a "multi-brand, multi-category direct sales company," the corporate name was changed to Tupperware Brands Corporation. In 2009, beauty products accounted for nearly 50% of Tupperware's total sales revenues.

1. Compare and contrast the original Tupperware party with today's social networking. Can you see a way in which social networking might be used as part of Tupperware's strategy? Explain.
2. How would you describe Tupperware's sales force strategy?
3. How do you think Tupperware's management supports the individual sales efforts? Be specific.
4. What are the major components or Tupperware's direct marketing strategy?

Application Exercise

Use the marketing concepts in this chapter to tackle and solve a marketing problem: personal selling, sales management, and direct marketing.

First, start by thinking about the automobile category and then choose a make, such as Honda or Ford, and model, such as a Civic or Escape. There are many makes and models available for us to consider purchasing.

The Marketing Problem

Think about your chosen make and model after considering the following situation.

> The automobile industry is highly competitive and finds itself under increased scrutiny in terms of both consumer safety and environmental sustainability. Consumers need to know which manufacturer and which product represent the best choice for them.

The Problem

How would you apply the seven-step personal selling process to the product you have chosen? Compile a list of three close competitors to the make and model you chose in the automobile category. For each competitor, including the one you chose, define its target and describe how you would use direct marketing.

The Solution

Complete the following two Problem/Solution briefs using your make and model in the automobile category, chapter concepts, and college resources.

1. From the Marketing Manager's Point of View
   a. Problem Definition
   b. Analysis
   c. Sales Management Objectives, Strategy
   d. Direct Marketing Approach
   e. Solution
2. From the Consumer's Point of View
   a. Problem Definition
   b. Analysis
   c. Product's Value
   d. Solution

Resources:

Marketing Defined, Explained, Applied 2e, Michael Levens
The College Library
Retail or Online Field Trip
Assigned Reading—*Brand Week*, *Advertising Age*, *WSJ*, scholarly publications, category trade journals
Blog your problem from either point of view, gather responses/posts (www.blogger.com/start)

The Communications Mix

Chapter Overview The previous two chapters examined various marketing communications tools, which include advertising, sales promotions, personal selling, and direct marketing. This chapter explains how these tools are integrated to achieve marketing objectives. The chapter begins by describing the current media environment, and then explains the advantages and disadvantages of various types of media. The process for media selection (planning and buying) and the techniques used to optimize media are also discussed.

Chapter Outline

INTEGRATED MARKETING COMMUNICATIONS (p. 255)

DEFINED **Integrated marketing communications** *is the coordination of advertising, sales promotion, public relations, and personal selling to ensure that all marketing communications are consistent and relevant to the target market.*

EXPLAINED

Integrated Marketing Communications

Marketing messages are delivered through a variety of communication tools including advertising, sales promotions, personal selling, and public relations. In most cases, two or more of these communication tools are used to reach a target market. To ensure that all messages being sent to the target market are consistent, companies adhere to the principles of integrated marketing communications (IMC). Not only does this ensure that a single cohesive message is delivered, but it also promotes the use of multiple delivery methods as a more effective way than any single delivery method to deliver that message.

APPLIED

Integrated Marketing Communications

Most major companies use ad agencies that assume the responsibility of developing all forms of advertising. Some companies use one agency for ads geared toward traditional media (such as newspapers or television), another agency that handles public relations, and a third agency that deals with all things digital. In addition, companies also produce in-house marketing communications, such as sales promotions or personal selling. Subscribing to the concept of integrated marketing communications ensures all messages are consistent and work toward building long-term relationships with customers.

EXAMPLE **INTEGRATED MARKETING COMMUNICATIONS**

One GEICO campaign features a wisecracking gecko, while another features modern-day cavemen. Both campaigns highlight the insurance company's key benefit of saving customers money. Using a variety of media and creative interpretations enables GEICO to target audiences that respond to different versions of the core money-saving message. All marketing communications—whether they air on television or radio, appear in print or on billboards, arrive in the mailbox or flash across the computer screen—use the humorous, irreverent tone that sets GEICO apart from its competitors. Even the company's wildlife conservancy efforts reinforce the association of the gecko with the GEICO brand. With an annual communications budget that tops $500 million, GEICO aims to increase market share and soon become the third largest U.S. insurance company.[1]

PHOTO: Fedor Selivanov/Shutterstock.

>> END EXAMPLE

Dove's "Campaign for Real Beauty" has put a fresh face on skincare advertising and reenergized a decades-old brand. Rather than focusing on supermodels, Dove's magazine, television, billboard, and online ads for soaps, creams, and body washes showcase the beauty of real women of all ages, sizes, and shapes. Unilever, Dove's parent company, has also invited consumers to share their thoughts about beauty on the campaign's Web site and create their own television commercials using the "real beauty" theme. The campaign not only won awards for creativity and effectiveness, it also helped Dove increase its worldwide market share and launch profitable new products.[2]

PHOTO: The *New York Times*.

COMMUNICATIONS MIX (pp. 256–257)

DEFINED *The* **communications mix** *is the various elements companies can use to communicate with the target market, including advertising, public relations, sales promotion, and personal selling.*

EXPLAINED

Communications Mix

The various elements companies can use to communicate with the target market are referred to as the communications mix. These elements include advertising, public relations, sales promotion, and personal selling. Marketers must decide how to integrate these elements in an effective way to deliver the right marketing message at the right time. While one company will focus all its communication efforts on a single element, such as advertising, others will use two, three, or even all four elements in concert with each other.

EXAMPLE COMMUNICATIONS MIX

Hoping to reinvigorate a long neglected brand, Old Spice launched its "The Man Your Man Could Smell Like" ad campaign during the 2010 Super Bowl. Although the ad, featuring Isaiah Mustafa, scored with viewers during the game, no one could imagine that the ad would become an online sensation almost overnight. Within months, the commercial was viewed over 10 million times on YouTube, with subsequent commercials also being released online. Looking to maintain the buzz, Old Spice turned to Facebook and Twitter by inviting people to post questions to Mustafa. Over a two-day period the former NFL wide receiver responded, in near real-time, with over 180 video responses to select messages he received. Those responses have been viewed over 40 million times and the Old Spice brand has received over 110 million brand Web views.[3]

PHOTO: Christina Leohr/Shutterstock.

>> END EXAMPLE

APPLIED

Communications Mix

Deciding which communication element to use depends on several factors, including the marketing objectives, target market, type and age of product, and promotional resources. For example, limited financial resources will generally exclude a national television campaign as a consideration. High-priced products, such as automobiles, typically employ personal selling because buyers prefer more interaction to gain information and access to product demonstration (test drive). Brands in the early stages of the product life cycle benefit from increased awareness, which can be accomplished through advertising.

Companies typically establish the communications mix based on a set of objectives. These objectives guide the marketer in determining what message should be sent and how to send it. Determining objectives requires that marketers understand that before consumers buy they first must be aware of the product. The AIDA model, which is an acronym for Awareness, Interest, Desire, and Action, assists the marketer in developing the communications mix. Each element of the communications mix is beneficial at one stage of the AIDA model, but is ineffective at another. Figure 18.1 shows that advertising and public relations are effective at generating awareness, but they lack the capability to move consumers to take action or buy. Personal selling and sales promotions are effective at stimulating desire and encouraging action, but do little in the way of building awareness. As such, multiple elements of the communications mix are often needed to reach the desired objectives.

In many cases, companies must decide whether to use a pull or push strategy. Companies use a **pull strategy** by promoting directly to consumers, who then request the product from retailers. Retailers in turn request the product from the wholesaler, who orders it from the manufacturer. A **push strategy**, on the

FIGURE 18.1 AIDA Model and the Effectiveness of Communication Tools

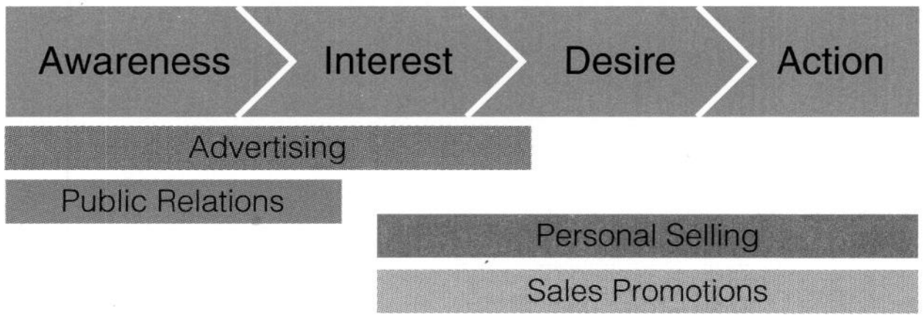

	Awareness	Interest	Desire	Action
Advertising	High	High	Limited	None
Public Relations	High	Limited	None	None
Personal Selling	None	Limited	High	High
Sales Promotions	None	Limited	High	High

FIGURE 18.2 **Push-Pull Strategies**

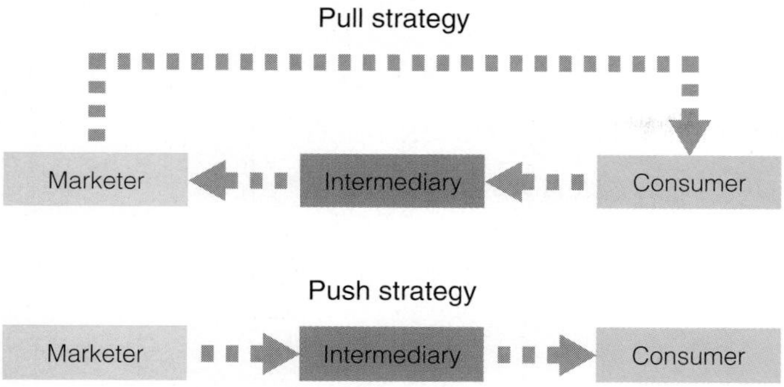

other hand, targets wholesalers and retailers and encourages them to order the product, thus *pushing* it through the channel to consumers (see Figure 18.2). A pull strategy often employs advertising and consumer sales promotion while personal selling and trade promotions are used with a push strategy.

Companies should also consider the time that some objectives require. For example, communication tools such as advertising and public relations require longer periods of time for maximum benefits to be realized. The same is true for building brand loyalty and strong customer relationships. Sales promotions, on the other hand, are designed for short-term sales increases. However, sales promotions should be used wisely and on a limited basis. Because promotions typically result in lower prices, their continued use will run the risk of shifting the expected price of a product downward.

The media environment is constantly evolving, and marketers must understand how members of the target market use media. For example, 30 years ago, media options were relatively limited. Network television dominated the American media landscape, along with print (including newspapers and magazines), radio, and outdoor advertising such as billboards. In the twenty-first century, television still plays a role in consumers' media choices, but new forms of communication are rapidly emerging, creating a variety of choices for consumers. As evidence, consider the complexity of an average American's media habits:[4]

- Americans spend more than 3,200 hours a year consuming some form of media.
- Over 1,900 hours are spent watching television (including broadcast, cable, and satellite).
- Over 550 hours are spent listening to the radio.
- Almost 350 hours are spent on the Internet.
- About 158 hours are spent reading newspapers.
- Over 90 hours are spent reading magazines or books.
- Over 220 hours are spent playing video games.

To make things even more complicated, some consumers use multiple types of media at the same time. It is not uncommon for consumers to simultaneously watch TV, talk or text on their cell phones, and surf the Internet on a laptop. As consumers gain more control over media and have a broader range of media choices, companies will need to alter where media dollars are spent. Many companies have already begun to shift from traditional media, such as TV and radio, toward digital media such as the Internet and mobile (see Figure 18.3).[5]

Although our media choices are increasing, our ability to pay attention remains limited because no one has found a way to add hours to a day. To communicate effectively, marketers need to create innovative media strategies that deliver relevant messages to consumers wherever and whenever they are prepared to receive them.

FIGURE 18.3 **Past and Future Media Mix**

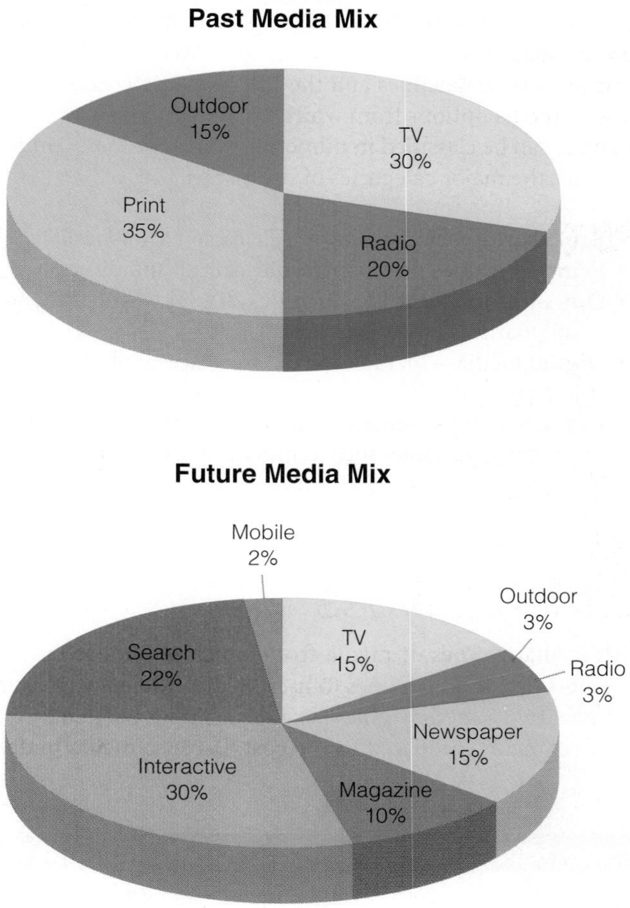

MEDIA Types (pp. 258–262)

DEFINED *A* **media type** *(or* **media vehicle***) is a form of media used for marketing communications, including types such as broadcast, print, digital, and branded entertainment.*

EXPLAINED

Media Types

The various forms of media enable people to have options for how they receive news, sports, or entertainment. While many people spend a lot of time watching shows or movies on TV, many others use their TVs for video games. While some people read newspapers, others turn to the Web. Technological advances such as satellites and the Internet have created a wide range of media options from which to choose.

Media can be classified in numerous ways. For mass communications, the major categories of media are:

- **Broadcast**—Includes network TV, cable TV, and radio
- **Print**—Includes newspapers, magazines, and direct mail
- **Out-of-home (OOH)**—Includes display advertising such as billboards, signs, and posters
- **Digital media**—Includes media such as e-mail, Web advertising, and Web sites
- **Branded entertainment**—Incorporates brand messages into entertainment venues such as movies or TV shows

APPLIED

Media Types

With so many types of media from which to choose, how do marketers decide which ones to use? **Media efficiency** measures how effective a media vehicle is at reaching a particular customer segment, compared to the cost. Because media budgets are not infinite, marketers weigh efficiency carefully. More efficient forms of media are less expensive, but less able to finely target niche demographics or behavioral segments.

Media impact is a qualitative assessment of the value of a message exposed in a particular medium. For example, consumers might view an ad in the *New York Times* as having more credibility than if it appeared in the *National Enquirer*. Marketing research companies collect measures of **media engagement**, which evaluates how attentively audiences read, watch, or listen to media. Two television shows might deliver audiences of equal size, but viewers of one show might be significantly more engaged and involved in their experience than viewers of another show. For example, viewers of drama shows, such as *NCIS* or *Grey's Anatomy*, are more actively involved in the show from week to week than are viewers of other genres such as news or comedy. Product or service characteristics are also taken into account. Does the product need to be demonstrated for consumers to understand what it does? If so, visual media such as television or online advertising are required. Are customers located in a fairly tight geographic area? If so, local newspapers or local radio would be a great solution. Each type of medium has relative advantages and disadvantages that are weighed when developing a media mix.[6] Table 18.1 highlights the capabilities and limitations of the major media types.

Broadcast

For decades, broadcast was the media type of choice among U.S. advertisers. Broadcast sends messages to large numbers of people extremely quickly, at a fraction of the cost of other media. The two traditional forms of broadcast are television and radio.

Table 18.1 Capabilities and Limitations of Major Media Types

	Television	Radio	Newspapers	Magazines	Internet	Out-of-Home
Reach mass audience	Yes	No	No	No	Yes	No
Target market	Limited	Yes	Limited	Yes	Yes	No
Target geographically	Limited	Yes	Yes	Limited	Limited	No
Lead time	Long	Short	Short	Long	Short	Limited
Shelf life	Short	Short	Short	Long	Short	Long
Expense	High	Low	Low	High	Low	High
Measureable results	Limited	Limited	Limited	Limited	High	None

Network television (for example, CBS, NBC, ABC, and FOX) refers to the over-the-air broadcast of programming and paid advertising through a nationwide series of affiliate television stations. Although network television commands the majority of broadcast spending, **cable television** (for example, CNN, MTV, and USA Network) is gaining advertising dollars. Unlike network television, which started by broadcasting over free public airwaves, cable TV networks require cable or satellite dishes to deliver their signals. Some cable networks are funded by paid ads, whereas others charge viewers a fee to watch.

Among all types of media, television has the greatest capability to deliver audiences en masse. **Reach** measures the number of people who could potentially receive an ad through a particular media vehicle. It can be expressed as a raw number of individuals or as a percentage of a target audience. An **impression** is a single delivery of an advertising message. Another way to think about television is that it offers high reach, because it can generate a huge number of impressions. Nielsen Media reports television and radio **ratings** that are the percentage of the total available audience watching a television show or tuned in to a radio program.[7]

Television is also attractive to marketers because it serves up big audiences at a low cost per viewer. **CPM** (or **cost per thousand**) is a metric that calculates the cost for any media vehicle to deliver one thousand impressions among a group of target customers. The "M" in CPM comes from the Latin word *mille*, which stands for thousand. To calculate CPM, all a marketer needs to know is total media cost and the number of impressions. Cost is then divided by impressions converted into thousands.

EXAMPLE **CPM**

An advertising campaign costs $4,000 and generates 120,000 impressions. The CPM can be calculated using the following formula:[8]

$$\text{Cost per Thousand (CPM)} \quad \frac{\text{Advertising}}{(\text{Impressions Generated}/1{,}000)}$$

$$= \frac{\$4{,}000}{(120{,}000/1{,}000)}$$

$$= \frac{\$4{,}000}{120} = \$33.33$$

>> **END EXAMPLE**

Despite its strengths, television has a few disadvantages. In addition to concerns over declining viewership, marketers balk at the high up-front costs of television advertising. Production expenses on a polished TV commercial will often run into millions of dollars. In addition, television is a better choice for marketers targeting broad population groups, such as adults aged 18–54. As targets become smaller and more narrowly defined, the efficiency of television is lost.

Growth in the use of DVRs (digital video recorders) also poses a threat to television advertising. **Time-shifting** is the practice of recording a television program at one time to replay it at another. Research shows that during playback, 53% of viewers with DVRs skip over the commercials, which is troubling to networks with business models based on television advertising.[9] If fewer people are watching commercials, advertisers will demand lower rates or will shift advertising dollars to other forms of media.

In contrast with television, radio is a low-cost medium. Media rates to advertise on radio stations are much lower than for network or cable television. Network and cable signals may cover an entire country, but radio broadcasts are mostly confined to the geographic reach of a station's signal transmitter. Radio ads are also purchased to target specific local or regional areas. It should therefore come as no surprise that local businesses like automotive dealers or restaurants use significant amounts of radio advertising.

Radio also does an excellent job of targeting audiences with specific interests. Programming ranges across diverse genres such as music, talk, sports, and news. Even within the music format, listeners can find almost any kind of channel they want, from hip-hop to classical music. This ability to target audiences is why marketers who segment customers based on their lifestyles or interests find radio appealing.

A major disadvantage of radio is that advertising messages cannot include visuals. The entire ad must succeed, or fail, based on a virtual "theater of the mind" where consumers imagine products or services based solely on what they hear. This poses a creative challenge for many ad agencies, but radio ads have a significant impact on listeners when done well. Because they involve only the sense of hearing, radio ads may also leave a more fleeting impression on listeners. This problem is compounded because our attention is usually divided while listening to radio. Most of us are doing something else, such as driving a car or cooking, while tuned in.

Because of the increasing popularity of digital media, spending on broadcast-station-based terrestrial radio will continue to decline. However, this does not mean that radio will disappear. Both television and radio are looking for new ways to distribute their programming content. Some television networks and radio stations are broadcasting or streaming shows online to laptops or mobile devices. Satellite radio is a fairly recent addition to the media landscape and uses space-based satellites to broadcast instead of local antennas. As the listener base increases, satellite radio companies might begin to offer limited on-air advertising opportunities to marketers.

Print

Magazines and newspapers are the two most frequently used forms of print advertising. Posters, flyers, signs, and other printed communications are included under the heading of "print" but are used by marketers much less frequently.

There are thousands of magazines published in the United States every year. You can find a magazine devoted to almost any interest or hobby imaginable. If you're a news junkie, you can read *Time Magazine* or *The Week*. If you love pets, then perhaps you should check out *Pet Fancy*. Are you a high school science teacher? *Science Teacher* magazine might be right for you. Companies selling products or services related to occupations, lifestyles, or interests use magazines because they can pinpoint their target audiences. For instance, it would be efficient and effective for a business manufacturing yoga mats to run ads in *Yoga* magazine.

Magazines also have a degree of credibility and prestige, due in part to their capability to reproduce high-quality images. As any reader of *GQ* or *Vogue* will testify, there is no medium with ads as beautiful as those found in glossy magazines. The credibility of such magazines is further enhanced by the professionally written stories and editorials they contain. Magazines also have fairly long lives; monthlies may be kept around and read for 30 days or longer.

The number of published and distributed copies of a magazine is called its **circulation**. A magazine's circulation can be thought of as a measure of its readership, or reach. The long life span of magazines creates a pass-along effect, where a single issue might have multiple readers. Copies of magazines that you might read in a doctor's office are an example of a single issue "passing along" from one patient to another.

One disadvantage of magazines is their high CPM relative to other types of media. Marketers justify the added expense of magazines based on their capability to deliver specific target audiences, their credibility, and their longer life spans. **Lead time** is the amount of preparation time a media type requires before an advertisement can be run. Four-color magazines require longer lead times than television or newspapers, and the position—for example, front cover or back cover—of an ad in a particular issue is usually not guaranteed.

EXAMPLE MEDIA TYPES

Grape juice sales have been falling due to rising competition and parents' concerns over beverages with high sugar content. Marketers for Welch's brand noticed that traditional media plans emphasizing television ads with pictures of smiling, happy kids weren't as effective as in the past. Welch's revamped its entire message and media strategy.

Instead of emotional appeals, new ads emphasize the fact that Welch's has twice the antioxidant power of orange juice. With a total budget of $10 million and the need to provide consumers with an information-intensive message, a breakthrough approach to media was also needed. Special print ads with "Peel 'n Taste" strips attached appeared in magazines such as *People* and *Cookie*, inviting readers to experience Welch's bold flavor. After peeling back the strip and then licking it, consumers were able to read about the juice's health benefits. News coverage for the innovative ad included stories in the *Wall Street Journal* and on *Good Morning America*, and dramatically expanded the campaign's reach. Best of all, during the campaign period, sales of Welch's grape juice increased 10%.[10]

PHOTO: David P. Smith/Shutterstock.

>> END EXAMPLE

Local newspapers focus the bulk of their coverage on a city or regional area, like the *Chicago Tribune* or *Miami Herald*. Messages that are relevant to specific geographic areas, like ads for 24-hour sales at a neighborhood furniture store, are well suited to local papers. Similar to magazines, ads in newspapers are surrounded by independently written stories that may lend credibility to their marketing messages. Newspapers also have more advertising flexibility than magazines because they usually publish on a daily basis. Compared with television, local papers are a somewhat less expensive media option, but this advantage can be offset by their limited geographic coverage. National newspapers like *USA Today* or the *Wall Street Journal* can achieve nationwide coverage; however, readers tend to be more upscale, such as businesspeople and travelers. They offer the same advantages of timeliness and credibility as local newspapers, but their overall audience numbers are small when compared with television or other types of media.

A major drawback of using newspapers as part of a media mix is their declining readership. Fewer people are reading newspapers, as evidenced in a study by the Pew Research Center for the People & the Press. In 2008, only 34% of people reported reading a newspaper the previous day, down 6% from just two years prior.[11]

Web readership is increasing, but there are not yet sufficient numbers of online readers to offset declines in printed newspapers. To offset weaker ad sales, publishers are creating online versions of their papers as new outlets for content. Over the next decade, advertising spending on online newspaper sites is expected to grow to $10 billion.[12]

Compared with a magazine, the average newspaper has a very short life. Readers may be exposed to an ad for only a single day before a paper is consigned to the recycle bin. As a result, opportunities for pass-along readership are limited. Image reproduction quality is also relatively poor. To keep newspaper prices low, publishers use less expensive paper and most ads are printed in black and white.

Out-of-Home

Media channels aren't limited to delivering messages into our homes or into our hands. Because people are often in transit at some point during the day, marketers place brief advertising messages along people's travel routes. Out-of-home (OOH) media is a term that covers the following three main types of media:[13]

- **Outdoor boards** are large ad display panels, usually near highways or other heavily trafficked locations.
- **Posters** are smaller than outdoor boards and are frequently used at bus or train stops.
- **Transit advertising** appears on and inside buses, in air terminals, in taxis, and wherever people are being transported from one place to another.

OOH is a popular type of media among advertisers, with spending exceeding $8 billion annually. This is due in part to the implementation of new OOH technology like digital billboards, which can rotate ad messages, generating 10 times the advertising revenue of a static board.[14] As an example of applying new technology to outdoor advertising, Nike installed an electronic billboard in New York's Times Square that displayed a tennis shoe that passersby could modify by using their cell phones. One advantage of out-of-home media is that it can result in high message frequency among people who often travel the same route past an outdoor board or transit ad. **Frequency** is the number of times an individual is exposed to an advertising message by a media vehicle.

Marketers use OOH media when they have a short message that needs to be exposed to a broad audience. OOH media does an excellent job of delivering sheer numbers of impressions at a low CPM. It is also a good choice for messages that have a geographic component, such as an ad sited along a highway that says "For a great meal, exit here!" The OOH media environment is fairly uncluttered compared with magazines or television. Marketers also have total control over the location of their messages; they choose the size, site, and duration of their advertising. Some boards are even movable, allowing expanded market coverage.

Although its CPM is low, OOH advertising can have significant out-of-pocket costs. In a top national market, the monthly cost for outdoor boards can add up to millions of dollars. The time for passersby to process messages is also fleeting, so advertising copy must be kept to a minimum. If you need a lot of words to explain your product or service, then outdoor advertising is not the most appropriate medium.

Digital Media

Digital media are certainly the new media "kid on the block," with broadband penetration in the United States estimated at 48.3% (or 139.4 million people).[15] Definitions and categories of digital media change almost daily, but some of the most frequently recognized types are as follows:

- **Banner advertising**—The placement of advertisements (called banners) onto various Web sites that link to the sponsor's Web page.
- **Classified advertising**—The online version of traditional classified ads.
- **Search marketing**—The optimization of Web site keywords and marketing agreements with search engines to drive traffic to Web sites.
- **Mobile advertising**—Refers to advertisements delivered over portable communication devices such as mobile phones and PDAs.
- **User-generated content**—Social networks (such as Facebook or MySpace), user blogs, and filesharing (such as Flickr or Snapfish) are sources of both word-of-mouth communications and advertising.

Digital media spending topped $22.7 billion in 2009,[16] propelled mainly by display ads, search, and online classifieds.[17] One of the most attractive aspects of digital media for marketers is the capability to target Web users based on their previous behavior, interests, or other factors. To give a simple example, a search of Google for "refrigerators" might serve up a banner ad for a GE refrigerator along with the results. CPM per contact can also be fairly low, and the message result can be immediate. Unlike ads in any other form of media, customers can interact directly with ads, clicking or texting in response to a sponsor's messages. This characteristic adds another level of accountability for digital media, which is vital for marketers who must prove a return on investment from their advertising campaigns.

Social networks, such as Facebook and MySpace, connect people with common interests and those who are looking to make friends online. These sites are growing in popularity, and marketers are experimenting with their advertising potential. Electronic publishing, such as blogs, e-magazines, and e-books, are also emerging marketing opportunities. Marketers are even exploring virtual worlds, such as SecondLife or CyWorld, where users have avatars that act as cyberspace "selves" who work, play, and interact online. Advertisements may be placed or virtual market tests conducted in these new media environments.

Digital media also has some limitations. Penetration of digital media is growing, but large portions of the U.S. population are not yet online. Research has shown that on the question of television or Internet advertising, the answer is not "either/or," but "both." There are parts of the population who can be reached only through the Web. And there are others who can be reached only by using traditional media communications. Campaigns have been proven to be more effective when using combinations of media instead of using one type exclusively.

Marketers need to adopt a completely different perspective when thinking about digital media. For the most part, consumers are in control of the communication process. At any given time, consumers' personal interests dictate when and where they will end up on the Web. Most advertisements are not so much "transmitted" in an Internet world as they are "found." In addition, surfers are only a click away from any ad they find offensive or boring.

EXAMPLE DIGITAL MEDIA

The United States Air Force stages recruiting events at state fairs and other locations around the country. At many of these events, real fighter jets are often available for attendees to touch, and thus increase excitement about the Air Force. But once a potential recruit leaves an event, how does the USAF maintain that excitement and interest? One way is through the use of mobile media. Event attendees can download 17 different types of USAF-related content to their cell phones, including videos, wallpaper, and ringtones. Signs at events display SMS short codes, which can be sent as phone text messages to unlock videos detailing specific careers in the Air Force. Quick response (QR/2D) code messaging is also possible, whereby attendees with phones containing special software may scan a bar code granting them access to USAF promotional material. Event staffers are also on hand to provide visitors with training in the use of these advanced features, if needed. For prospects who will not or cannot attend formal events, the USAF also places a variety of ads on mobile sites from channels such as MTV and Comedy Central, which direct viewers to resources offering additional content.[18]

PHOTO: Tebnad/Shutterstock.

>> END EXAMPLE

Branded Entertainment

The integration of brands or brand messages into entertainment vehicles, such as movies, television shows, video games, or sporting events, is referred to as branded entertainment. Companies spent over $24 billion in 2009 on product placement, product integration, and event sponsorships, which are some of the elements of branded entertainment. This use of branded entertainment can be used to develop a connection with an audience in a much deeper way than traditional advertising. Well-known examples include a can of Coke being prominently displayed on *American Idol* (product placement), James Bond driving an Aston Martin in *Casino Royale* (product integration), and Dodge Ram sponsoring the 2010 Kentucky Derby (event sponsorships).[19]

Branded entertainment can deliver a large number of impressions and is well suited for brands that already have mass awareness, so marketers don't need to worry if audiences understand a product's basic purpose. But exposure in entertainment lends an aura of prestige or credibility, especially if a well-known movie, music, or TV star is using the product. In addition, many audience members might prefer to avoid advertising, but will sit for two hours watching a movie embedded with brands. Product placements are immune to DVR or TiVO as well, because viewers may zip past ads, but they would never skip their recorded programs.

Like television advertising, branded entertainment ventures have low CPM but often carry high initial costs. Studios and publishers are quite aware of the value of branded entertainment, and the price for its use is rising. These prices are inflated as marketers bid against each other for the right to appear in the hottest properties. In the majority of instances, onscreen brand impressions are fleeting, so the impact of audience exposures may be questionable. Even the most savvy media maven can't accurately predict the success or failure of a film, song, book, or TV show. Branded entertainment is partially a "roll of the dice" because marketers have to guess a year or more in advance which are the special properties that audiences, listeners, and readers will embrace.

EXAMPLE BRANDED ENTERTAINMENT

Even branded entertainment can become a cluttered media environment. In the 2001 film *Driven*, Brandchannel identified 102 different brand or product placements. These included both paid and unpaid brand exposures, which can be frustrating for those companies who invested significant dollars to be part of the movie. Brands represented in this movie included Kool-Aid, Marlboro, Snapple, and Nextel.

In part, this was due to the film's storyline about racing, which naturally contains a large number of brand identifications. Unfortunately for everyone involved, the film only grossed $54.7 million on a production budget of $94 million.[20]

PHOTO: Konstantin Sutyagin/Shutterstock.

>> END EXAMPLE

The effectiveness of any mass media advertising campaign can be greatly increased through the use of personal selling, sales promotions, and direct marketing. Personal selling involves marketing messages delivered face-to-face, from salespeople to customers. The impact of a mass-media campaign is multiplied when salespeople are able to clarify and build on its basic message at the point of sale. With personal selling, communication with prospects is customizable on the spot. Questions can be answered, products demonstrated, or additional information provided.

On a CPM basis, however, personal selling is expensive because its reach is extremely limited. Training is required to ensure that salespeople have the knowledge needed to deliver the right messages, which increases the total cost for the campaign. The quality of personal selling also varies; it depends on an individual salesperson's personality, knowledge, and selling ability.

Direct marketing is another useful complement to broader-reach media. Similar to personal selling, direct marketing is highly targeted, because each recipient is preselected based on his or her product usage, demographics, interests, or geography. Marketers leverage the wider audience of mass media like broadcast or even print, and then reinforce the impact of this advertising with specific target audiences via direct marketing.

MEDIA Selection (pp. 263–265)

DEFINED **Media selection** *refers to the process of choosing which media types to use and when, where, and for what duration in order to achieve marketing objectives.*

EXPLAINED

Media Selection

Marketing communication campaigns involve the definition of a target customer, specification of communication objectives, development of a creative strategy, and media selection. Because the first part of this list has previously been discussed, the remainder of this chapter focuses on media selection, implementation, and measurement. Marketers follow a step-by-step process to select, implement, and measure advertising media (see Figure 18.4).

The process starts by establishing a media budget and media objectives. A media budget is a subset of the marketing communications budget, which also includes funds for nonmedia activities such as sales force support and public relations. In turn, the marketing communications budget is a portion of the company's overall marketing budget. The **media budget** specifies the total amount a firm will spend on all types of advertising media.

As a first step, along with the media budget, an understanding of **media objectives** is required. A media objective is a clear, unambiguous statement as to what media selection and implementation will achieve. This statement should convey, in as much detail as possible, what the media will accomplish and when. Some examples of media objectives are as follows:[21]

- Within the $10 million budget, create national awareness for our product before the end of the year.
- During the launch period, reach 80% of target customers an average of five times, and reach 50% of target customers an average of three or more times.
- Sustain product awareness by reaching 30% of target customers at least once a month.

Media budgets and media objectives are interrelated, because it would be impossible to fully achieve an objective without sufficient funding. The optimal way to set budgets is by using a **task-and-objective** approach and by allocating dollars sufficient to attain media objectives. In reality, many firms have limited budgets, and simply decide to use an easily calculated method, for example, a percentage of sales revenue, or to spend whatever they can afford.

APPLIED

Media Selection

Marketing decisions should be based on an in-depth understanding of the customer, and media are no exception. The next step in the media-selection process is to build a detailed profile of the target customers and their media habits. This profile will include data on the following characteristics of target customers:

- **Demographics**—Who are they?
- **Geographic location**—Where do they live?
- **Media consumption habits**—What types of media do they consume? At what times of day?
- **Lifestyles and interests**—How do they live? What are their likes and dislikes?

Marketers use these profiles to guide their media-selection decisions. A hypothetical profile may suggest that a target customer is a heavy user of print media, an occasional user of the Internet, and never listens to radio. The target may also live on the West Coast of the United States and make product purchases twice a month. All these findings will have implications for media strategy.

Once the media objectives have been established, the media budget has been set, and the target customer media

FIGURE 18.4 Media Selection

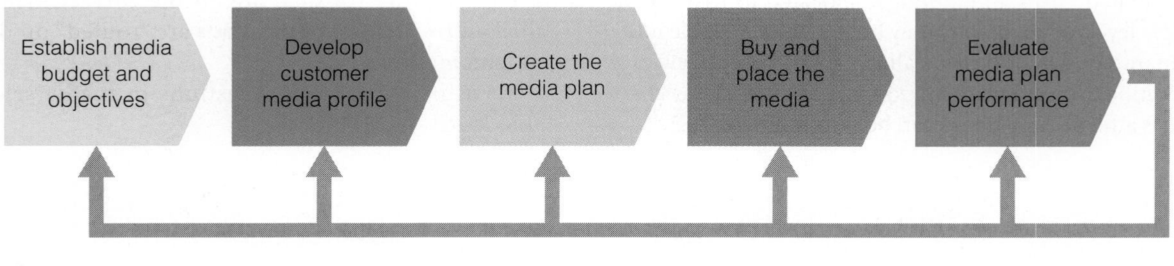

profile has been developed, then media planning can begin. **Media planning** involves the creation of a **media plan**, which is a document that describes how an advertiser plans to spend its media budget to reach its objectives. A media plan specifies the types and amounts of media to be used, the timing of media, and the geographic concentration—national, regional, or local.

The media plan is implemented through media buying and placement. **Media buying** is the negotiation and purchase of media. These purchases should correspond to the direction as given in the media plan. **Placement** is the implementation of the media plan via the purchased media vehicles. Ads must be sent (or trafficked) to media companies in time for them to run as scheduled. Because the plan and buying are implemented in real time, their performance is monitored and evaluated. Real-time conclusions and insights from the plan are fed back into the process for continuous improvement.

Media Planning

Media planning is a complicated activity; it requires advertisers to balance many different inputs. For a large advertiser, the planning department of the company's advertising agency writes the media plans. A **media planner** has extensive knowledge about media vehicles and expertise in formulating media plans.

Planners consider several issues when building a media plan. When formulating a plan, media planners take into account not only the suitability of each medium, but how different types could work together to deliver the advertising message. The impact of a message viewed on television is multiplied when heard on the radio or seen on a billboard. Working with creative teams, planners also look for ways to combine or link media vehicles. For instance, TV ads sometimes contain Web addresses directing customers to the Internet or to 800 numbers to call to obtain additional product information or make purchases. Some advertisers include special codes in magazine ads that readers can scan with Webcams or enter into cell phones to unlock additional online content.

Gross Rating Points (GRPs) are a way for planners to approximate the impact of media decisions. A GRP is the product of reach multiplied by frequency. For example, if an ad is scheduled to air two times in a single TV show (frequency), where the show has a 5.0 rating (reach), the plan will result in 10 GRPs. Demographics are always specified for GRPs (like ratings among adults aged 25–54).

A **media flowchart** (or **media footprint**) is a visual representation of the media plan. Expressed in worksheet or project software, the flowchart is essentially a calendar with time periods as columns and media types as rows. Whenever the plan dictates a media vehicle should be used, the column and row intersection contains estimated GRPs and a budget allocated to that media type. Multiple levels of geography may be shown on a single footprint or separately. The footprint allows planners to view at a glance the complete media plan. An example of a media flowchart for a women's athletic shoe brand can be seen in Figure 18.5.[22]

FIGURE 18.5 Media Flowchart

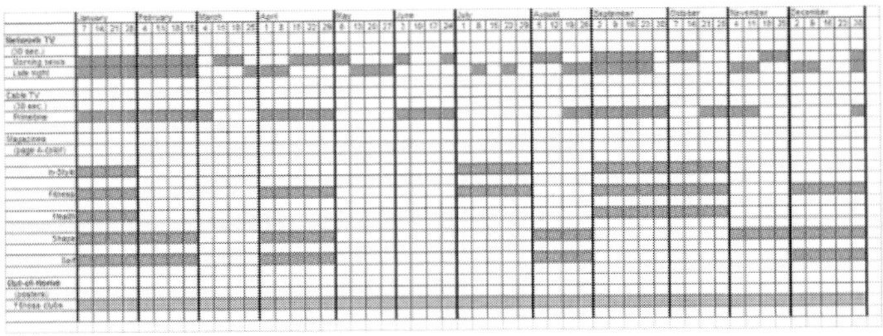

Media Buying

Based on the media plan, a group of agency experts called **media buyers** negotiate and purchase media properties. All media are sold on an open market, with media companies trying to sell their properties for top dollars and advertisers looking to scoop up the best deals. Media prices vary according to marketplace demand and the skill of negotiators on both sides of the table.

The bulk of network television is sold in an **upfront market**, which is a long-lead marketplace where TV networks and advertisers negotiate media prices for the fourth quarter of the current year, plus the first three quarters of the following year. In an upfront market, advertisers commit to purchase media and, in return, the networks set aside ad time for their upcoming programs. Advertisers can usually lock in the best pricing and programming by participating in an upfront market, but their ability to cancel or sell off any commitments is limited. Ads that are not purchased in advance via an upfront market, but are secured on a quarterly basis, are called **scatter buys**. Although scatter buys can be less efficient, media buyers can use them to react to changes in the marketplace and they allow greater spending flexibility.

Magazines, newspapers, radio, and OOH are purchased on the basis of **rate cards**, which are officially published prices for different types of media. Rate cards are often negotiable, and with the merger of large media companies, packages featuring a single price for combined offline and online media buys are increasingly common.

Internet advertising is usually priced on a CPM basis, and prices vary according to the size and type of ad. Advertisements could take many forms, such as banners or interstitial ads (also called "pop-ups"). Search advertising operates differently, with advertisers paying search engines or directories only after Web surfers have clicked their ad or link.

After media have been purchased, the advertising agency or marketing firm must deliver ads to the various media companies for broadcast, publication, or posting. The procedure for getting finished ads to the correct media firms is called **ad trafficking** because ads are "routed" on their way to implementation.

For a list of strategic questions in media selection, see Table 18.2.

Table 18.2 Strategic Questions in Media Selection

Issue	Strategic Questions (Examples)	Impact
Reach versus frequency	Should the plan maximize the number of customer impressions (reach), the number of times each customer is communicated with (frequency), or both?	Maximizing reach will require heavy investments in mass media, such as broadcast; maximizing frequency may more heavily employ vehicles with less reach.
Scheduling	Should the plan be continuous, where advertising is running constantly? Should the plan involve a flight, where advertising is running for only brief periods? Should the plan be some combination of the two?	Continuous plans can be expensive, but are well suited to products or services in demand year-round, for example, food, beverages, and telecommunications. Flights are less expensive and are good for products that are more seasonal, for example, Halloween costumes and snow blowers, or for brand-reminder advertising.
Geography	Should the plan cover the entire world? A single country? Regions within a country? Cities or localities?	A plan could have national, regional, or local coverage, or combinations of any of the three. The media plan's geographic coverage is determined by the location of target customers.
Product type	How frequently is the product purchased? How much information do customers need?	Products that are used frequently require more continuous media. Ones that are information intensive suggest plans that employ print, digital, or direct media.
Media cost	What does this media type cost? What is its CPM to deliver the target audience?	All issues are weighed in relation to media cost. A media type may be effective in terms of achieving objectives, but highly inefficient. It may also be efficient, but do a poor job of reaching the target audience.

MEDIA Optimization (pp. 266–267)

DEFINED **Media optimization** *is the adjustment of media plans to maximize their performance.*

EXPLAINED

Media Optimization

When a media plan is developed, it is based on the estimated performance of each broadcast program, magazine, newspaper, outdoor board, Web site, or any other media vehicle that it contains. A **media audit** measures how well each selected media vehicle performs in terms of its estimated audience delivery and cost. In the real world, some media will achieve target levels, whereas others will under- or overdeliver on their projections. For instance, a television ad could be preempted by a special news report. Or an issue of a magazine might have blockbuster sales because of a movie star's photo or a scandalous lead story on its cover. Audit reports include metrics such as GRPs delivered, CPM, response rates, Web traffic, and click-through rates.

Media companies can correct for preemption or significant audience underperformance in several ways. Additional media may be credited to the advertiser's account with the media supplier. Advertisers could use this extra media inventory for future advertising, or they might claim some portion of the original amount as a refund. **Make-good ads** may be offered, which are essentially replacements for any media that did not run as scheduled. Some media vehicles come with **guarantees** that estimated audience numbers will be achieved, or part of the vehicle's cost will be returned to the advertiser. Guaranteed media are usually more expensive, because the media supplier is accepting financial risk.

Although actions by media companies are one way to bolster media plan implementation, marketers also make changes on their own. Media optimization is the process of adjusting media plans to improve their performance. Advertisers review the media audit reports and, whenever possible, reallocate media weight away from weak properties and toward strong ones. Optimization can take place on many levels, such as an overall spend-by-media category (for example, radio versus OOH) or by individual media vehicles (for example, a particular radio station versus a particular outdoor board). Marketers also optimize media by changing plans in reaction to marketplace conditions. Competitive actions and economic conditions may lead to a plan adjustment. For instance, if a competitor increases advertising spending in a geographic region, a firm may reallocate its own media dollars to this area to blunt the attack.

APPLIED

Media Optimization

Media planning and buying are complex, with many interrelated components. As a result, the task of optimizing a full-blown media plan can be incredibly daunting. **Modeling** is a tool that many large advertisers use to guide their media planning and plan optimization. In an advertising context, economic modeling decomposes the impact of individual media vehicles on a target variable such as sales. For example, an econometric model would calculate how the amount of money spent in each category of media influences product sales.

Live test markets are sometimes used to conduct a "test run" of a proposed national media plan. Geographic markets are selected where the plan will be implemented on a limited basis. Products are manufactured, priced, and distributed into the test market, so that as the media run, advertisers are able to track actual sales in response to the campaign. Any market chosen should have a range of media channels, demographics, purchase behavior, and other characteristics that reflect the media profile of the broader geography to be used in the overall plan as much as possible.

In addition, advertisers consider the potential for spill-in or spill-out. **Spill-in** occurs when ads from outside the test market "spill into" the area, which may confuse reach and frequency calculations. **Spill-out** happens whenever ads meant for the test market "spill out" and touch people in adjacent markets. Because advertised products are available only in the test market, potential customers affected by spill-out may become frustrated if they attempt to make a purchase. As a result, they may ignore any future roll-out of a national campaign.

A control market has a profile similar to those of the test markets, but it does not receive any special treatment. Everything remains "normal," or constant, in the control market, so in terms of marketing, it resembles the remainder of the nontest markets to be included in the overall media plan. If metrics such as product awareness or sales increase in test markets more than in the control market, then it is a reasonable assumption that the media campaign is having a positive impact on customers. Conversely, if sales fall in test markets or are unchanged, then the creative strategy, media plan, or both should be revised before implementation.

EXAMPLE MEDIA OPTIMIZATION

When Ford launched the newest version of its best-selling F-150 pickup truck, during a six-month launch period the media plan targeted males, aged 25–54. The media plan included heavy television advertising, magazines such *Car & Driver* or *Western Horseman*, as well as online advertising. A relatively new form of advertising at the time, digital roadblocks, was also employed. Digital roadblocks are ads automatically served to visitors at Web portals like AOL.com, Yahoo.com, or MSN.com. To understand the effectiveness and efficiency of its media choices, Ford conducted a study to model the impact and net cost of each media type. The study found the following:

- Although TV was expensive, it bolstered the overall performance of the other media channels.
- At half the cost of television, magazines could deliver a similar impact on purchase intent.
- Digital roadblocks were very efficient in terms of cost-per-person influenced.

Extending the impact of suggested media changes from sales to revenues, the study estimated that optimization of the F-150 media plan would lead to a significant incremental profit for Ford.[23]

PHOTO: Marek Slusarczyk/Shutterstock.

>> END EXAMPLE

Visual Summary

Chapter 18 Summary

To ensure that all marketing communications deliver a consistent message, companies embrace the concept of integrated marketing communications. The communications mix consists of all the elements or tools that can be used to deliver a marketing message and include advertising, public relations, personal selling, and sales promotion. The target market, product characteristics and age, objectives, and budget all influence the make-up of the communications mix. Media selection involves allocation of spending across the various types of media, which include broadcast (television and radio), print, (magazines and newspapers), OOH, and digital media. Comprehensive media strategies also take into account the impact of personal selling and direct marketing. Media plans specify the media vehicles to be used as well as scheduling, geographics, and cost considerations. Plans are implemented through the purchase and placement of media. Measurement and optimization of media plans complete the process, thus improving current performance and providing insight for future campaigns.

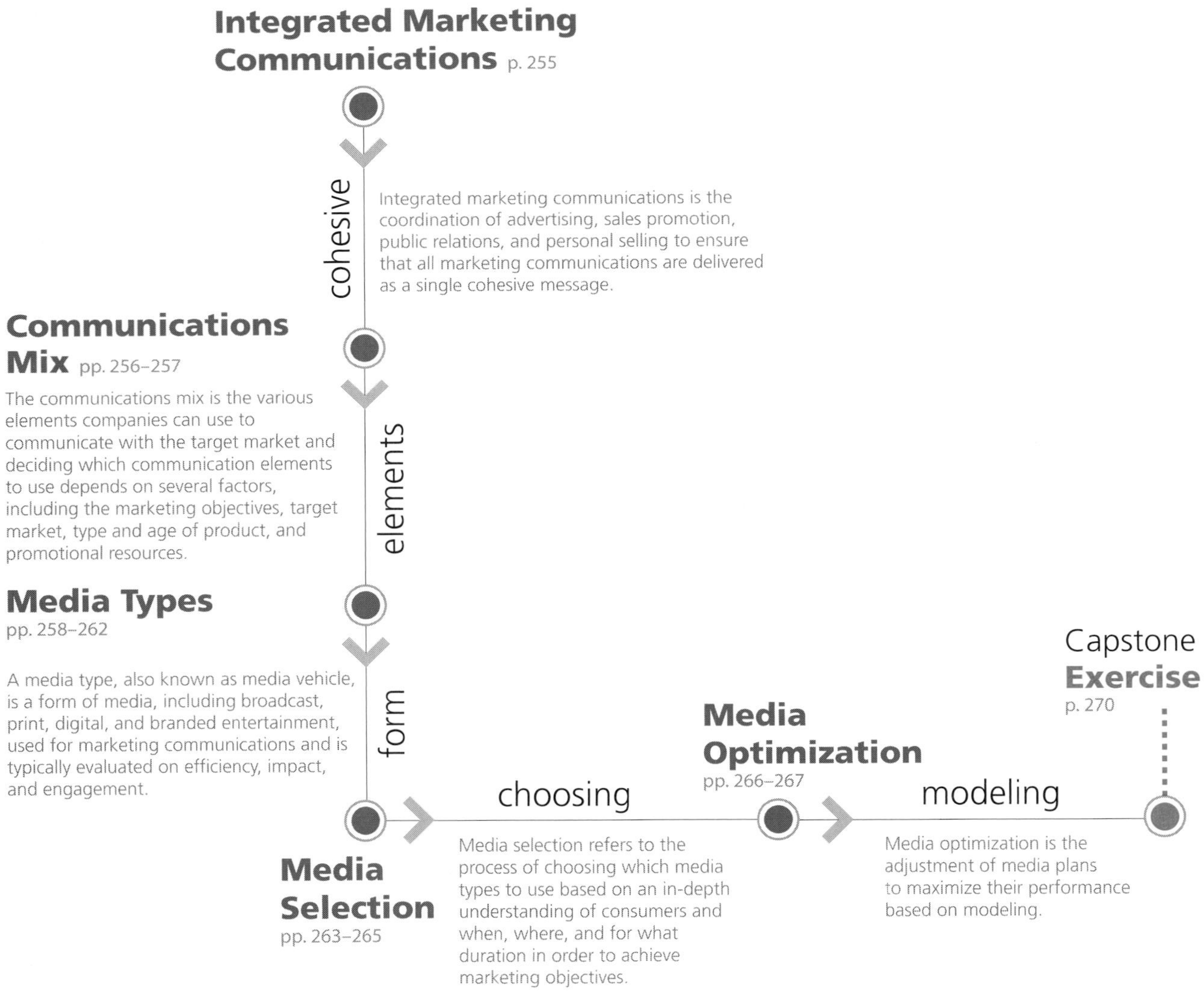

Integrated Marketing Communications p. 255
cohesive
Integrated marketing communications is the coordination of advertising, sales promotion, public relations, and personal selling to ensure that all marketing communications are delivered as a single cohesive message.
Communications Mix pp. 256–257
The communications mix is the various elements companies can use to communicate with the target market and deciding which communication elements to use depends on several factors, including the marketing objectives, target market, type and age of product, and promotional resources.
elements
Media Types pp. 258–262
A media type, also known as media vehicle, is a form of media, including broadcast, print, digital, and branded entertainment, used for marketing communications and is typically evaluated on efficiency, impact, and engagement.
form
Media Selection pp. 263–265
choosing
Media selection refers to the process of choosing which media types to use based on an in-depth understanding of consumers and when, where, and for what duration in order to achieve marketing objectives.
Media Optimization pp. 266–267
modeling
Media optimization is the adjustment of media plans to maximize their performance based on modeling.
Capstone Exercise p. 270

Chapter Key Terms

Integrated Marketing Communications (p. 255)

Integrated marketing communications *is the coordination of advertising, sales promotion, public relations, and personal selling to ensure that all marketing communications are consistent and relevant to the target market. (p. 255)* **Opening Example (p. 255) Example: Integrated Marketing Communications (p. 255)**

Communications Mix (pp. 256–257)

Communications mix *is the various elements companies can use to communicate with the target market, including advertising, public relations, sales promotion, and personal selling. (p. 256)* **Example: Communications Mix (p. 256)**

Key Terms (p. 256)

Pull strategy promotes products directly to consumers, who then request the product from retailers. Retailers in turn request the product from the wholesaler, who orders it from the manufacturer. **(p. 256)**

Push strategy targets wholesalers and retailers and encourages them to order the product, thus *pushing* it through the channel to consumers. **(p. 256)**

Media Types (pp. 258–262)

Media type *(or* **media vehicle***) refers to a form of media used for marketing communications, including types such as broadcast, print, digital, branded entertainment, and social networks. (p. 258)* **Example: Media Types (p. 260)**

Key Terms (pp. 258–261)

Banner advertising is the placement of advertisements (called banners) onto various Web sites that link to the sponsor's Web page. **(p. 261)**

Branded entertainment is the integration of brands or brand messages into entertainment media, for example, films, television, novels, and songs. **(p. 258) Example: Branded Entertainment (p. 262)**

Broadcast media include network television, cable television, and radio. **(p. 258)**

Cable television refers to television broadcasts using cables or satellite dishes. **(p. 259) Example: Media Types (p. 260)**

Circulation is the number of published and distributed copies of a magazine. **(p. 260)**

Classified advertising is the online version of traditional classified ads. **(p. 261)**

CPM (or **cost per thousand**) is a metric that calculates the cost for any media vehicle to deliver one thousand impressions among a group of target customers. **(p. 259)**

Digital media includes electronic media such as e-mail, Web advertising, and Web sites. **(p. 258) Example: Digital Media (pp. 261–262)**

Frequency is the number of times an individual is exposed to an advertising message by a media vehicle. **(p. 261)**

Impression refers to the single delivery of an advertising message by a media vehicle. **(p. 259)**

Lead time is the amount of preparation time a media type requires before an advertisement can be run. **(p. 260)**

Media efficiency measures how inexpensively a media vehicle is able to communicate with a particular customer segment. **(p. 258)**

Media engagement evaluates how attentively audiences read, watch, or listen to a particular media vehicle. **(p. 258)**

Media impact is a qualitative assessment as to the value of a message exposed in a particular medium. **(p. 258)**

Mobile advertising refers to advertisements delivered over portable communication devices. **(p. 261)**

Network television refers to the broadcast of programming and paid advertising through a nationwide series of affiliate TV stations. **(p. 259)**

Out-of-home (OOH), or display, advertising includes media types that are encountered outside the home, such as billboards, signs, and posters. **(p. 258)**

Outdoor boards are large ad display panels, usually near highways or other heavily trafficked locations. **(p. 260)**

Posters are smaller than outdoor boards and are frequently used at bus or train stops. **(p. 260)**

Print media include newspapers, magazines, and direct mail. **(p. 258) Example: Media Types (p. 260)**

Ratings are the percentage of the total available audience watching a TV show or tuned in to a radio program. **(p. 259)**

Reach is a measure of the number of people who could potentially receive an ad through a particular media vehicle. **(p. 259)**

Search marketing is the optimization of Web site keywords and marketing agreements with search engines to drive traffic to Web sites. **(p. 261)**

Social networks, such as Facebook and MySpace, connect people with common interests and those who are looking to make friends online. **(p. 261)**

Time-shifting is the practice of recording a television program at one time to replay it at another. **(p. 259)**

Transit advertising appears on and inside buses, in air terminals, in taxis, and wherever people are being transported from one place to another. **(p. 260)**

User-generated content such as social networks (for example, Facebook or MySpace), user blogs, and filesharing (for example, Flickr and Snapfish) are sources of word-of-mouth communications and advertising. **(p. 261)**

Media Selection (pp. 263–265)

Media selection *refers to the process of choosing which media types to use and when, where, and for what duration in order to execute a media plan. (p. 263)*

Key Terms (pp. 263–264)

Ad trafficking is the procedure for delivering finished ads to the correct media firms for placement. **(p. 264)**

Gross Rating Points (GRPs) are a way for planners to approximate the impact of media decisions and are the product of reach multiplied by frequency. **(p. 264)**

Media budgets specify the total amount a firm will spend on all types of advertising media. **(p. 263)**

Media buyers negotiate and purchase media properties according to the media plan. **(p. 264)**

Media buying is the negotiation and purchase of media. **(p. 264)**

Media flowcharts (or **media footprints**) are visual representations of the media plan. **(p. 264)**

Media objectives are clear, unambiguous statements as to what media selection and implementation will achieve. **(p. 263)**

Media planners create media plans based on their extensive knowledge about media vehicles and expertise. **(p. 264)**

Media planning involves the creation of a media plan, which is a document that describes how an advertiser plans to spend its media budget to reach its objectives. **(p. 264)**

Media plans specify the types and amounts of media to be used, the timing of media, and the geographic concentration (national, regional, or local). **(p. 264)**

Placement is the implementation of the media plan via the purchased media vehicles. **(p. 264)**

Rate cards are officially published prices for different types of media. **(p. 264)**

Scatter buys are ads that are not purchased in advance via an upfront market, but are secured on a quarterly basis. **(p. 264)**

Task-and-objective is an approach to media budgeting that allocates dollars sufficient to attain media objectives. **(p. 263)**

Upfront markets are long-lead marketplaces where TV networks and advertisers negotiate media prices for the fourth quarter of the current year plus the first three quarters of the following year. **(p. 264)**

Key Terms (p. 266)

Guarantees are promises made by media companies that estimated audience numbers will be achieved, or part of the cost of advertising will be retuned to the advertiser. **(p. 266)**

Make-good ads are given by media companies as replacements for any media that did not run as scheduled. **(p. 266)**

Media audits measure how well each selected media vehicle performs in terms of its estimated audience delivery and cost. **(p. 266)**

Modeling is a tool that many large advertisers use to guide their media planning and plan optimization. **(p. 266)**

Spill-in occurs when ads from outside a test market "spill into" the test market area. **(p. 266)**

Spill-out happens whenever ads meant for a test market "spill out" and touch people in adjacent markets. **(p. 266)**

Media Optimization (pp. 266–267)

Media optimization *is the adjustment of media plans to maximize their performance. (p. 266)* **Example: Media Optimization** (p. 267)

Capstone Exercise

Staples, the inventor of the office supply superstore category, opened its first store in 1986 in Framington, Massachusetts. The company targeted small to medium-size businesses selling everything for the office under one large roof. Between 1986 and 1996 Staples expanded rapidly by the addition of new stores, acquisition of existing office supply companies by region, and international expansion through joint ventures. In 1996, its tenth anniversary, sales exceeded $3 billion—only the sixth company in U.S. history to achieve this level of sales within the first 10 years of operation.

In the second half of the 1990s, Staples embarked upon a very aggressive marketing strategy. With the company slogan, "Yeah, we've got that" at the focus, it launched staples.com and staplesLink.com for contract customers. It produced catalog editions for both the United States and Europe. Staples integrated its e-commerce site into the retail store locations. It signed a contract for naming rights to the Staples Center in Los Angeles, which was home to several athletic teams, including the NBA's L.A. Lakers, and special entertainment events like the Grammy Awards. Staples sponsored recycling projects for both paper and ink cartridges. In 2000, Staples launched the Staples Foundation for Learning to support organizations that "teach, train, and inspire."

However, all was not well with this corporate giant. The slogan, "Yeah, we've got that" was no longer resonating with customers. Office Depot, a key competitor, was poised to overtake Staples as the #1 office supply retailer and additional competition from retailers like Walmart and Best Buy was cutting further into market share. After extensive market research including focus groups and interviews, Staples' management found that price was not a major consideration for customers—they wanted a simple, straightforward shopping experience. They wanted knowledgeable and helpful associates and hassle-free shopping. Staples simplified store organization and created a tagline and icon to match those changes. "That was easy!" and the Easy Button reflected a simplified shopping experience and was complementary to the corporate brand promise, "Staples. We make buying office products easy."

For the 2009 back-to-school program, Staples focused on television. It revived "The Most Wonderful Time of the Year" spot and the mom-and-teen targeted Easy Button. In addition, it used public relation campaigns ("Do Something 101" to encourage donating school supplies for needy children), promotional partnerships (with Bed Bath & Beyond in a "Shop Smart for College" promotion), online display, social media, and event sponsorship—all to drive its back-to-school message. Product placement embedded in TV's *The Office*, direct mail pieces, and its tiered loyalty program, Staples Rewards, continue to target the core customer, the small to medium-size business.

1. Identify the major elements of the communication mix for Staples.
2. Describe how each element is being used for pull strategy and/or push strategy.
3. How would you define Staples' targeted market(s)?
4. Do you think Staples has created a strategy that communicates one consistent message? Explain.
5. Is the message relevant to the target market? Explain.

Application Exercise

Use the marketing concepts in this chapter to tackle and solve a marketing problem: media type, digital media, and media optimization.

First, start by thinking about the baby toy category and then choose a product within that category. There are many products available in stores within this category for us to consider purchasing.

The Marketing Problem

Think about your chosen product after considering the following situation.

> Baby toys are an important purchase for consumers and the category is becoming highly competitive. New parents, who are first-time serious consumers of this category, need to know what is best for their child.

The Problem

Which media type would you use to reach new parents? Assuming that your client would like to fully explore digital media, which type would you select specifically? Now assume that market testing led you to believe that digital media was underperforming your goals, how would you approach media optimization?

The Solution

Complete the following two Problem/Solution briefs using your product in the baby toy category, chapter concepts, and college resources.

1. From the Marketing Manager's Point of View
   a. Problem Definition
   b. Analysis
   c. Target Market
   d. Optimized Media Mix
   e. Solution

2. From the Consumer's Point of View
   a. Problem Definition
   b. Analysis
   c. Lifestage Media Habits
   d. Solution

Resources:

Marketing Defined, Explained, Applied 2e, Michael Levens
The College Library
Retail or Online Field Trip
Assigned Reading—*Brand Week*, *Advertising Age*, *WSJ*, scholarly publications, category trade journals
Blog your problem from either point of view, gather responses/posts (www.blogger.com/start)

The **Marketing Mix**

Chapter Overview The previous chapter explored how various marketing communication tools are integrated to achieve marketing objectives. This chapter expands on those concepts to explore how all the marketing mix elements are integrated to support a marketing strategy. Building on the concept of the marketing mix introduced in Chapters 1 and 3 and consideration of individual marketing mix components in Chapters 12–17, this chapter is designed to explore how the marketing mix is constructed, managed, and modeled. Contemporary marketing-mix classifications are introduced and the concept of optimizing elements of the marketing mix is discussed.

Chapter Outline

Objective 1. What choices do marketers make to achieve their marketing goals?

Objective 2. How do marketers select a particular marketing mix to achieve their marketing goals?

Objective 3. How do marketers measure the effects of each component in a marketing program?

MARKETING MIX (pp. 273–274)

DEFINED *A* **marketing mix** *is a group of marketing variables that a business controls with the intent of implementing a marketing strategy directed at a specific target market.*

EXPLAINED

Marketing Mix

The marketing mix can be considered a marketing manager's tool box. The tools are the individual marketing-mix elements. Different tools are needed depending on the particular task; while there are many possible combinations of tools to accomplish a specific task, some combinations work better than others. Even if the most appropriate set of tools is used at the onset of the job, conditions may change and require a different set of tools.

The concept of a marketing mix was originally discussed in the 1950s and included 12 categories of marketing variables that were deemed important to a marketing plan:[1]

- **Product planning**—Which products to offer and where to sell them
- **Pricing**—Product price and margin structure
- **Branding**—How the product will be branded and whether any intellectual property will be involved
- **Channels of distribution**—How to move the product from manufacturer to consumer
- **Personal selling**—Extent to which personal selling will be utilized
- **Advertising**—Product image, type of advertising, and how much will be spent
- **Promotions**—Role and type of promotion to be used
- **Packaging**—Labeling and package design
- **Display**—Location and type of point-of-sale display
- **Servicing**—Type of after-sales service
- **Physical handling**—Warehousing, inventory control, and transportation
- **Fact finding and analysis**—Securing and analyzing marketing information

The 12 categories were later organized into what is now referred to as the **4 Ps:** product, price, place, and promotion.[2]

The 4 Ps remain the most common classification of a marketing mix. It is important to think of the 4 Ps from a managerial perspective because they help organize business activities. Businesses must be sure that they are marketing the right *product* to the right *person* through the right *promotion* at the right *price* in the right *place* at the right *time.*

Each of the 4 Ps influences the other elements of the marketing mix. A failure in one marketing-mix variable could undermine good choices made with the other marketing-mix variables. Consider a manufacturer of backpacks that are targeted at typical college students and their options (see Table 19.1).

It is essential to understand the marketing objectives and the needs and wants of target segments. It is important to select a target that can deliver the necessary sales volume, revenue, and profitability.

APPLIED

Marketing Mix

In practice, businesses make decisions about marketing-mix variables either by reacting to changes in the market, strategically changing position to achieve desired business results, or by default when not responding to market changes.

H&R Block, formed in 1955 as a tax-preparation and bookkeeping business, is the world's largest tax preparation business with almost 14,000 offices in the United States, Canada, the United Kingdom, and Australia. H&R Block became famous in the late 1980s with its "Rapid Refund" service, which allowed its customers who filed their taxes electronically to receive refunds much more quickly than through the mail. H&R Block was well established with mature taxpayers and wanted to appeal to younger individuals by creating a marketing mix that includes various types of social media and tailored products. H&R Block is active on Second Life, MySpace, Facebook, YouTube, and Twitter and uses these sites to communicate with customers and manage the company image. Some examples of social media activities by H&R Block have included using Twitter to respond to consumer questions, comments, and concerns and the Me & My Super Sweet Refund competition that included video submissions on YouTube on how consumers might spend refunds. Another social media activity is Ask a Professional nights in digital shops in Second Life. H&R Block also formed strategic marketing alliances with AOL Time Warner, Amazon.com, Microsoft, Disney, Sprint, and Blockbuster and modified its products to be available where its target customers prefer to be reached—in a retail office, online, or a combination of the two.[3]

PHOTO: Comstock Images/Corbis RF.

Table 19.1 Options for a Backpack Manufacturer Targeting College Students

Marketing-Mix Element	It would be more desirable to market:	As opposed to marketing:
Product	A stylish and functional backpack	A high-fashion designer backpack that emphasizes appearance over function
Price	An affordable price	A high price
Place	Through mass merchandisers, bookstores, and moderately priced retailers	Through exclusive designer boutiques
Promotion	Through direct-mail, word-of-mouth, and point-of-sale material	Through invitation-only events and high-gloss magazine advertisements in magazines that target affluent readers

Consumer responses to marketing-mix decisions differ for many reasons including macroenvironmental factors of greater technological sophistication and an increasing number of competitors. While many businesses organize themselves to manage elements of the 4 Ps, the businesses that practice a marketing orientation actually must consider more than the 4 Ps. Broadening the definition of the marketing mix to include elements beyond the 4 Ps is discussed later in this chapter, and factors such as employees, customers, and processes are often considered when developing marketing-mix strategies.

MARKETING-MIX Strategies (pp. 275–278)

DEFINED **Marketing-mix strategy** *is the logic that guides the selection of a particular marketing mix to achieve marketing objectives.*

EXPLAINED

Marketing-Mix Strategies

Although there are many marketing-mix possibilities for any marketing situation, certain marketing mixes are more desirable than others for some of the following reasons:

- Ability to achieve business and marketing objectives
- Time available to fulfill objectives
- Resources, human and financial, available to fulfill objectives
- Influence of market factors, such as competition and consumer interest
- Consistency with business mission and vision
- Level of risk and exposure to business

The most effective marketing-mix strategies consider those factors mentioned previously as well as how each marketing-mix element interacts with the other elements.

Once a marketing-mix decision has been made, it is important to monitor market performance and the target market to determine if changes need to be made. A variety of changes could occur that would require a reevaluation of marketing-mix strategies:

- Competitors could enter or leave the market or reposition themselves.
- New products or services could be offered in the market.
- The market could grow or shrink.
- Target consumers could change their attitudes.
- New trends could emerge.
- Technology could evolve or change the cost structure for products or services.
- New distribution channels could emerge or evolve.

Consider the U.S. market for sport utility vehicles. The segment grew rapidly throughout the 1990s and into 2007 before gas prices increased and the economy declined rapidly. Many automakers dedicated a large share of their manufacturing capacity to sport utility vehicles, as opposed to sedans. In addition, many of the product decisions also involved a slow adoption of alternative propulsion systems such as hybrid technology. Pricing decisions reflected the perception of strong product demand and margins were used to subsidize product development of other vehicles. Fewer incentives were offered for sport utilities, as opposed to other vehicles such as small cars. Considerable promotional investment was dedicated to communicating a new sport utility vehicle launch, as opposed to other vehicles. A large volume of sport utility vehicles was built and distributed through the dealer networks.

When the market changed, significant marketing-mix decisions needed to be made relative to sport utility vehicles. Fewer sport utility vehicles were produced, but that reduced overall margins for all vehicles. Therefore, less money was available for product development, unless money was diverted from other parts of the business. Promotional dollars were severely reduced from sport utility vehicles to support other vehicle types, such as small cars, which saw a significant increase in demand. Many sport utility vehicles were in the distribution pipeline and automotive dealers and manufacturers had to discount prices and offer special financing to help reduce inventory. The result is structural change among companies and suppliers in the automotive sector that will take several years to adjust. In the meantime, careful decisions must be made regarding the marketing mix for sport utility vehicles.

APPLIED

Marketing-Mix Strategies

Businesses are constantly reevaluating and re-creating marketing-mix strategies. A change of business objectives or marketing objectives is a common reason to reconsider a marketing-mix strategy. Business acquisitions of brands, such as is common with packaged-goods companies, change brand portfolios and may require repositioning or retargeting existing brands through new marketing-mix strategies. Sometimes market conditions change and new marketing-mix strategies need to be developed. In other cases, the existing marketing-mix strategies are not effective. Examples of marketing-mix strategies with the underlying marketing situation are considered next.

Situation 1:

Managing products with different targets within the same product portfolio requires an understanding of how each product contributes to portfolio performance.

EXAMPLE **MARKETING-MIX STRATEGIES: SITUATION 1**

Cadillac, founded in 1902 and historically one of General Motors' most prestigious brands, has experienced a sales renaissance over the past decade with edgy high-performance products. The Cadillac product portfolio consists of sedans (CTS, DTS, and STS), a crossover (SRX), and a sport utility (Escalade). There are some variations within the portfolio, such as the CTS also being available as a coupe and sport wagon; different engine sizes; and a V-series premium performance version of most of the vehicles including the CTS coupe, CTS sedan, and CTS sport wagon. Although the CTS and CTS-V are both manufactured at the same facility, there are many differences, including the marketing-mix strategies for each vehicle.[4]

Targets—The CTS-V is targeted at individuals with household incomes over $200,000. The CTS-V targets tend to also consider vehicles like the BMW M3. The CTS is targeted in the entry luxury segment that is more expensive than most vehicles, but includes a much wider target range of individuals, particularly those who are trendy and younger and who might typically purchase non-American brands. CTS targets often consider a variety of other entry luxury brands, including Mercedes C-Class, Audi A4, and BMW 3-Series.

Pricing—The CTS and CTS-V represent both ends of the price range of the product portfolio. The CTS starts at around $35,000, and the CTS-V starts above $62,000.

Product—The CTS-V is the fastest production sedan in the world with a 556-horsepower supercharged engine, whereas the CTS is a midsize sport sedan that shares a platform with the Chevrolet Malibu.

Place—Both the CTS and the CTS-V are sold through the Cadillac dealer network. The CTS-V is sold in limited volumes and not all dealers have them in stock. The CTS-V is often used as a "halo" vehicle, one that is used to create interest in other vehicles and increase showroom traffic.

Promotion—Both vehicles are shown in national television advertising as part of the entire Cadillac portfolio and in individual campaigns. The CTS advertising emphasizes being named a *Car and Driver* 10 Best whereas CTS-V advertising emphasizes being the world's fastest production sedan. Both the CTS and the CTS-V have their own microsites within the Cadillac Web site. The CTS-V, as a niche vehicle, has also utilized some specialized advertising, including the promotion of its CTS-V coupe by sponsoring *Automobile* magazine's iPhone application. Both models reflect Cadillac's performance luxury positioning, but in the context of their respective market segments.

PHOTO: Transtock Inc./Alamy Images.

>> END EXAMPLE

Situation 2:

Using alternative media to build emotional connections with people across the globe requires an understanding of how different media types work together and how different people throughout the world use media.

EXAMPLE **MARKETING-MIX STRATEGIES: SITUATION 2**

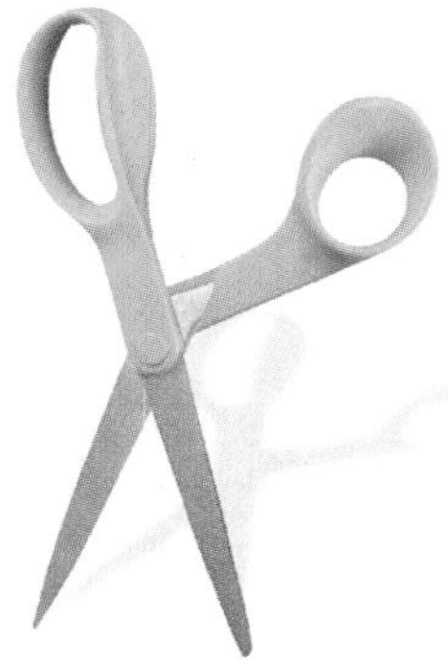

Fiskars is one of the oldest companies in the world. It was founded in 1649 in Finland. Fiskars began as an ironworks and expanded through the centuries to manufacture a wide range of consumer and industrial products, ranging from cutlery to steam engines. Fiskars employs 4,300 people across the globe and operates four manufacturing divisions: garden, housewares, outdoor recreation, and craft. Fiskars Orange, products with an iconic orange color, has become ubiquitous, with almost 1 billion orange-handled scissors sold. Fiskars manages a marketing mix that incorporates a significant amount of word-of-mouth marketing and social networking, including viral marketing, online videos, and blogs. The Fiskars marketing mix focuses on creating an emotional connection with its customers. Project Orange Thumb provides community garden groups with plants, tools, materials, and grants needed for beautification and education. Fiskars has also created "Fiskateers," a social network ambassador program, for its most loyal customers that has increased loyalty, online interaction, and sales.[5]

PHOTO: Vrjoyner/Shutterstock.

>> END EXAMPLE

Situation 3:

Introducing a new product to an established market segment through a unique positioning requires a thorough understanding of market competitors and their products, as well as the wants and needs of the market.

EXAMPLE **MARKETING-MIX STRATEGIES: SITUATION 3**

Axe, owned by the consumer products company Unilever, is a brand of male grooming products that includes Axe Body Spray, Axe Dry, Axe Shower Gel, and Axe Deodorant Stick. Axe was launched in the United States in 2003 with an award-winning advertising campaign that was targeted at males aged 18–24 with the message that the more men spray, the more likely they are to get the girl. The advertising campaign has drawn some criticism as being sexist, degrading, and encouraging sexual promiscuity. Initially, Axe's marketing mix utilized a Web presence prior to launching traditional television communication. The decision to utilize digital initiatives was based on the idea that the target segment would like to learn about products such as Axe in an environment to which they are more accustomed, such as the Web.[6]

PHOTO: Tomasz Trojanowski/Shutterstock.

>> **END EXAMPLE**

Situation 4:

Repositioning an established brand for a different target audience requires understanding the wants and needs of the new targets, which products they currently are purchasing, and what other substitute products are important to the target.

EXAMPLE MARKETING-MIX STRATEGIES: SITUATION 4

Godiva Chocolatier, an 80-year-old company founded in Brussels, Belgium, produces and sells a wide range of premium chocolates as well as coffee and liqueur through its 450 global stores. Owned by Campbell Soup Company for 30 years, Godiva was sold in 2007 to the Turkish company Yildiz Holding. The iconic gold boxes are brand cues Godiva uses to support its relationship with consumers. Those customers are increasingly younger than its customers from the previous decade. The typical target is now 25- to 35-year-olds. Godiva made a strategic decision several years ago to broaden its appeal to younger consumers with a marketing campaign resembling fashion advertisements. One advertisement for Godiva's Limited Edition Truffles featured Victoria's Secret model Frankie Rayder and appealed to women's "inner divas." Other promotion includes advertising in magazines such as *Vogue*, *Harper's*, and *Vanity Fair*. Although Godiva chocolates are typically more expensive than average chocolate, Godiva's target tends to consider a group of premium chocolates in addition to Godiva. Chocoladefabriken Lindt & Sprüngli A.G, known mainly for its Ghirardelli brand; See's Candies, Inc.; Ferrero USA Inc., known mainly for its Ferrero Rocher brand; Lake Champlain Chocolates; and Scharffen Berger are all considered premium brands and influence Godiva's marketing planning. Godiva does not limit its competition to other premium chocolate brands. Other Godiva competitors include champagne and flowers. Godiva chocolates are available in Godiva retail stores and online, and now can be purchased through a new mobile application for BlackBerry that uses an individual's stored contact list.[7]

PHOTO: Ronald Sumners/Shutterstock.

>> **END EXAMPLE**

Situation 5:

Reacting to a change in consumer preference that transforms an important mass-market product into a niche product requires a focus on the portfolio development and the innovation process.

EXAMPLE MARKETING-MIX STRATEGIES: SITUATION 5

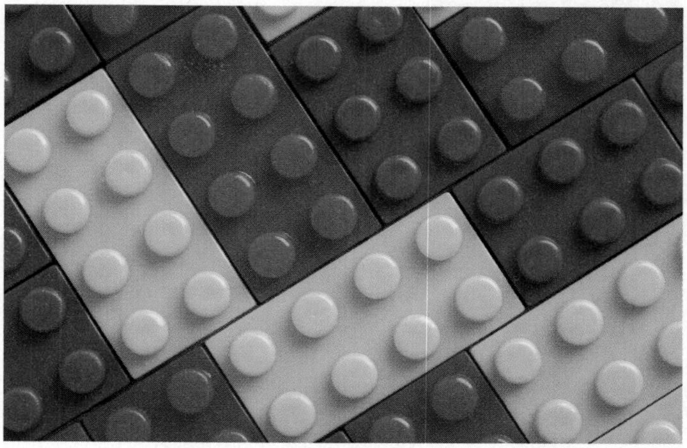

LEGO, founded in Denmark in 1932, is the world's fifth largest manufacturer of play materials. Known primarily for its colorful interconnecting plastic bricks, LEGO produces a wide range of toys, teaching materials, and experiences for children in 130 countries. In the early 2000s the ubiquity of the LEGO brick, with over 300 billion pieces sold, and other traditional toys could not continue to grow with the increasing choices that children had for toys. Computers, video games, cell phones, and other electronics attracted an increasing share of children's time. As traditional toys, including most of LEGO's portfolio, decreased in demand the former mass-market products became niche products. LEGO as a company had also suffered from some poor product launches such as the Galidor line and expiration of important patents. LEGO decided that innovation and design would be the path to success. While not new concepts to LEGO, the novelty was the process of injecting marketing and manufacturing personnel early into the product development process to ensure customer requirements and financial discipline are considered along with creative ideas. LEGO introduced board games, co-marketed classic products with well-known Disney/Pixar brands, and broadened the portfolio with items such as the Duplo Play line with fewer and less complicated pieces to appeal to younger children. After almost a decade of challenging financial performance, LEGO posted a yearly net profit increase of 63% in 2009.[8]

PHOTO: Volodymyrr Krasyuk/Shutterstock.

>> **END EXAMPLE**

Situation 6:

Serving the needs of two different target segments demanding unique products and services requires different communications channels to realize the full potential of each target segment.

EXAMPLE MARKETING-MIX STRATEGIES: SITUATION 6

Figure skating has the largest fan base among any sport in the United States, more than the NFL, MLB, NBA, and all college sports, among females 12 and older. U.S. Figure Skating is the national governing body for the sport of figure skating in the United States and is a member of the International Skating Union, the

international federation for figure skating, and the U.S. Olympic Committee. U.S. Figure Skating is composed of over 700 member clubs, collegiate clubs, and school-affiliated clubs, over 900 Basic Skills programs, and over 170,000 individual members. The organization desires to expand interest and participation in the sport of figure skating. While the fan base spans a wide range of ages, over 70% of members are under the age of 25. In order to address the different needs of the various figure skating constituents, U.S. Figure Skating decided to create two separate online environments. U.S. Figure Skating partnered with Major League Baseball Advanced Media to create icenetwork.com to which all interactive media rights were assigned. Launched in 2007, icenetwork.com is a subscription service that hosts live events, news, athlete information, videos, schedules, results, shopping, and other fan-oriented material. U.S. Figure Skating also manages usfigureskating.org, which contains information for members, athletes, coaches, judges, and officials. Membership in U.S. Figure Skating has increased 38% from 1994 while the first full year of icenetwork.com included 221,000 hours of video streamed and recorded 49 million page views.[9]

PHOTO: Denise Levens

>> END EXAMPLE

Beyond the 4 Ps

The 4 Ps were developed in the manufacturing economy of the 1960s when large consumer goods firms were serving mass markets.[10] The 4 Ps were intended to refer to the combination of elements that a business controls to satisfy customers, and each element was considered both distinct and interdependent.[11] In the contemporary environment, market segmentation, targeting, and positioning are practiced and entities other than manufacturing businesses practice marketing. In view of this environment, concepts such as relationship marketing and the marketing strategies of not-for-profit businesses, places, and events create the need for a broader perspective on the elements of the marketing mix. There are many contemporary perspectives that challenge the sufficiency of the 4 Ps as the only marketing-mix framework. These include Booms and Bitner's 7 Ps and Kotler's 4 Cs.

Primarily responding to the growth of service businesses, Booms and Bitner proposed 3 additional Ps to add to the traditional 4 Ps to create a **7 Ps** classification. The additional 3 Ps include the following:[12]

- **People**—The role that people play in satisfying the customer
- **Physical evidence**—The environment of the service
- **Process**—The way the service is delivered

An example of an important marketing mix that includes people involves employee attitudes toward their business's brand. Employees can either enhance brand image or undermine brand image through their actions or inaction. Research by Market & Opinion Research, Ltd., claims that 30% of employees in the United Kingdom are brand neutral and a further 22% are brand saboteurs. The remaining 48% are considered brand champions and will spread the brand message. One-third of all employees would talk positively about the brand if asked, and 15% claim they would talk positively about the brand spontaneously.[13] This provides an opportunity to differentiate not only on the traditional marketing mix, but also on another P—people. With an entire organization focused on the brand, such differentiation can be possible. Without such a focus, a brand's marketing investment is undermined.

Kotler challenged the relevancy of the 4 Ps from a buyer perspective. Considering the traditional 4 Ps, which Kotler views to be a seller's model, Kotler proposes the **4 Cs.** The variables include the following:[14]

- Customer value
- Cost
- Convenience
- Communication

Customer value takes the place of product from the traditional classification. Cost to the customer replaces price decisions. Convenience replaces place. Communication takes the place of the promotion mix. Kotler bases these recommendations on the idea that customer relations is more important than customer acquisition.[15]

The appropriateness of the various marketing-mix perspectives should be considered in the context of how businesses relate to their customers, which is typically through transactional methods, relational methods, or some combination of the two. Current marketing practice remains mainly transactional, which fits with the traditional perspective of the marketing mix.[16]

However, as companies increasingly focus on customer retention and strong supply-chain management, marketers are increasing their use of technology. In addition, increased competition and consumerism are influencing more demanding consumer expectations.[17] The result is the need to increasingly consider relational marketing perspectives such as those offered by the 7 Ps and 4 Cs marketing-mix classifications.

MARKETING-MIX Models (pp. 279–280)

DEFINED **Marketing-mix models** *evaluate the contribution that each component of a marketing program makes to changes in market performance.*

EXPLAINED

Marketing-Mix Models

Marketing-mix models began as a result of increasingly available scanner data—data obtained from checkout scanners at supermarkets and other retail stores—and has grown in its use among many different industries. Marketing activities can be tracked on databases with statistical modeling as a measurement tool. Scanner data or other sales data can be compared with sales price and volume. Overlaying performance data with marketing events, such as the launch of a new television advertising campaign or direct mail, can assist with developing marketing-mix models (see Figure 19.1).[18]

Baseline data are developed from historical information to predict what sales performance might occur without any changes in marketing activity. The accumulated effect of advertising, public relations, brand usage, and experiences such as testimonials and word-of-mouth is considered to be the brand's baseline.[19] Sales-lift models, based on those things that contribute to incremental sales, can be developed from considering the various marketing-mix elements as defined for a particular business. The costs for specific marketing-mix elements are also factored into an analysis. The variables are processed through a software package that maximizes marketing-mix elements with respect to particular financial outcomes. The result is an optimized marketing plan. **Marketing-mix optimization** involves assigning portions of the marketing budget to each marketing-mix element so as to maximize revenues or profits. An example of an optimized marketing mix that relates media and promotions to sales performance follows.

FIGURE 19.1 Contribution to Sales

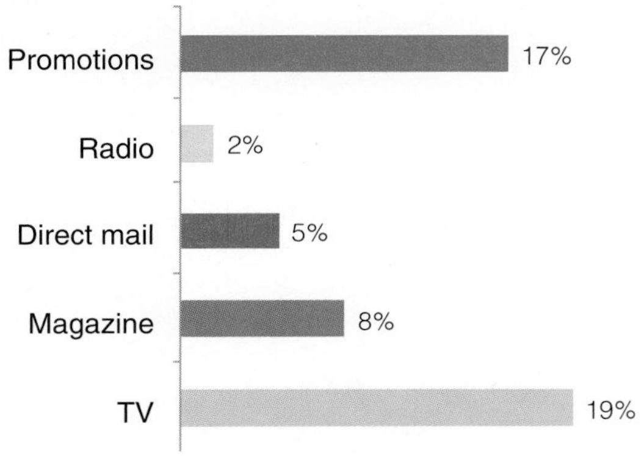

Using the example in Figure 19.1, TV has the greatest contribution to total sales, and, assuming similar media costs across channels, money that might have been allocated to other media such as radio and magazines could be redirected to television. Alternatively, if an optimum level of spending for television can be determined, then excess funding can be redirected to the next-most-efficient medium of promotions or possibly magazines, provided brand image is not degraded by lowering prices.

There are a variety of applications of marketing-mix models. They can be used to measure the impact of temporary price adjustments, coupons, and displays, as well as to forecast future brand sales.

APPLIED

Marketing-Mix Models

Marketing departments are under constant pressure to demonstrate the benefits derived from the marketing budget. Modeling, as is used in media optimization discussed in Chapter 18, is increasingly being used as a data-driven mechanism to quantify benefits from marketing expenditures. Companies in the consumer packaged-goods sector were the first to adopt marketing-mix models. Implementing a marketing-mix model often requires moving from "gut" decisions to a more structured approach to decision making.

There can be challenges to developing marketing-mix models, such as the following:

- Establishing buy-in throughout organizations for using marketing modeling
- Determining a way to optimize nontraditional marketing activities such as events, product placement, and social media
- Creating a balance between creativity and a strict interpretation of marketing-mix model output

Effective implementation of marketing-mix models can provide strategic advantages relative to competitors, including efficient use of marketing funds across different media.

EXAMPLE MARKETING-MIX MODELS

Miller Brewing announced a major shift in its marketing strategy based on a marketing-mix assessment. Miller determined the relative contribution that public relations (PR), advertising, sales promotion, and other marketing variables had on its product sales. The conclusion was that PR was much more effective, when cost is considered, than other marketing activities. Miller identified that PR accounted for 4% of incremental sales. This can be contrasted to a 17% contribution for TV advertising at a significantly higher cost. The ratio was the basis for reallocating marketing dollars away from TV advertising and toward PR.[20]

PHOTO: Svry/Shutterstock.

>> **END EXAMPLE**

Visual Summary

Part 1 Explaining (Chapters 1, 2, 3, 4, 5)
Part 2 Creating (Chapters 6, 7, 8, 9)
Part 3 Strategizing (Chapters 10, 11)
Part 4 Managing (Chapters 12, 13, 14, 15, 16, 17)
Part 5 Integrating (Chapters 18, 19, 20)

Chapter 19 Summary

A marketing mix is a group of marketing variables that a business controls with the intent of implementing a marketing strategy directed at a specific target market. The most common classification of the marketing mix is referred to as the 4 Ps, consisting of product, price, place, and promotion. There are many contemporary perspectives that challenge the sufficiency of the 4 Ps as the only marketing-mix framework, including the 7 Ps and 4 Cs. The 7 Ps adds people, physical evidence, and process. The 4 Cs, a marketing-mix perspective that considers the buyer's perspective over the seller's perspective, consists of customer value, cost, convenience, and communication.

Marketing-mix models evaluate the contribution that each component of a marketing program makes to changes in market performance. There is a variety of applications of marketing-mix models. They can be used to measure the impact of temporary price adjustments, coupons, and displays, as well as to forecast future brand sales.

There can be challenges to developing marketing-mix models, such as the following:

- Establishing buy-in throughout the organization for using marketing modeling
- Determining a way to optimize nontraditional marketing activities such as events, product placement, and social media
- Creating a balance between creativity and a strict interpretation of marketing-model output

Effective implementation of marketing-mix models can provide strategic advantages relative to competitors, including efficient use of marketing funds across different media.

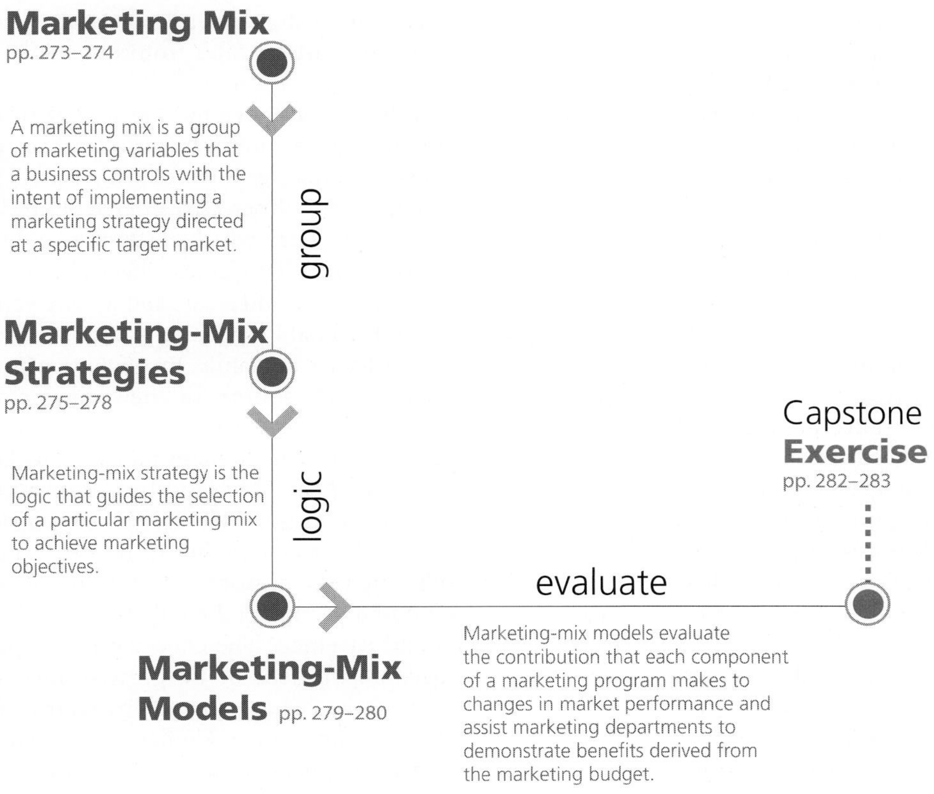
Marketing Mix
pp. 273–274
A marketing mix is a group of marketing variables that a business controls with the intent of implementing a marketing strategy directed at a specific target market.
group
Marketing-Mix Strategies
pp. 275–278
Marketing-mix strategy is the logic that guides the selection of a particular marketing mix to achieve marketing objectives.
logic
Marketing-Mix Models pp. 279–280
evaluate
Marketing-mix models evaluate the contribution that each component of a marketing program makes to changes in market performance and assist marketing departments to demonstrate benefits derived from the marketing budget.
Capstone Exercise
pp. 282–283

Chapter Key Terms

Marketing Mix (pp. 273–274)

Marketing mix *is a group of marketing variables that a business controls with the intent of implementing a marketing strategy directed at a specific target market. (p. 273)* **Opening Example (p. 273)**

Key Term (p. 273)

4 Ps are the most common classification of a marketing mix and consist of product, price, place, and promotion. **(p. 273) Example: Marketing-Mix Strategies: Situation 1 (p. 276)**

Marketing-Mix Strategies

(pp. 275–278)

Marketing-mix strategy *is the logic that guides the selection of a particular marketing mix to achieve marketing objectives. (p. 275)* **Example: Marketing-Mix Strategies: Situations 1, 2, 3 (pp. 275–277) Situations 4, 5, 6 (pp. 277–278)**

Key Terms (p. 278)

4 Cs are a classification of a marketing mix that includes customer value, cost, convenience, and communication. **(p. 278)**

7 Ps are a classification of a marketing mix that includes product, price, place, promotion, people, physical evidence, and process. **(p. 278)**

Marketing-Mix Models (pp. 279–280)

Marketing-mix models *evaluate the contribution that each component of a marketing program makes to changes in market performance. (p. 279)* **Example: Marketing-Mix Models (p. 280)**

Key Term (p. 279)

Marketing-mix optimization involves assigning portions of the marketing budget to each marketing-mix element so as to maximize revenues or profits. **(p. 279)**

Capstone Exercise

In November 2007, a small plane flew over the headquarters of Progressive Corp. pulling a huge banner featuring a big caveman and the word "GEICO." It wasn't enough that GEICO had recently surpassed Nationwide and Farmers Insurance in market share and was now threatening to overtake Progressive as the nation's third-largest auto insurer. Now GEICO was "buzzing" Progressive's 6,000-employee headquarters.

GEICO was spending over $600 million a year on marketing (twice that of Progressive) and the GEICO gecko and cavemen had become advertising sensations. Progressive management decided to "get back to the basics." They decided the company would reexamine its core competency, rethink the marketing mix, and reestablish its competitive advantage.

Progressive offers a portfolio of insurance policies with lower profit margins designed to attract more customers, more revenues, and more market share. The company chose to give up margin to gain customers, concentrating on long-term benefits. Progressive's core competency is assessing risk. The company has always been good at pricing strategy and predicting exactly who is likely to have an accident and cost the company money.

A key part of Progressive's market strategy is to tell consumers the company will shop around for them. Progressive believes that the easier a company makes it to buy insurance, the more likely the customer is to purchase the insurance. Therefore, the strategic objective is three-pronged: competitively priced insurance rates, excellent customer service, and the practice of giving customers comparison rates from other insurance companies.

Until the late 1990s Progressive had been sold through independent insurance agents. However, lack of brand recognition and limited policy offerings were reducing agency sales. As a result, beginning in 1997, Progressive offered online interactive customer services through which customers could look up their policy information, get quotes, check the status of claims, make online payments, and create and update personal account information. Personal Progressive was innovative and timed perfectly to customer demands. By 2005, the Internet was the most significant source of new business for Progressive.

In 2008, Progressive bought the naming rights to Jacobs Field (The Jake), home of the Cleveland Indians. And then, along came Flo in a heavy dose of clever television ads. Her overly perky and sarcastic persona, her retro style, and her bright red lipstick catch the customers' attention. It seems Progressive has found a pretty good competitor to GEICO's legendary gecko and cavemen. The cheery but deceptively sharp Flo has become the face of Progressive insurance. From the heavenly setting where customer dreams of low prices and high service come true to Flo herself, a connection is made. Flo is a genuine listener. She asks a question. She waits for the answer. And then she serves up a customized, cost-saving insurance solution from Progressive. Flo takes us back in time with her style and carries the message of painless online transactions with her "easy peasy" humor. Flo is old enough to be trusted and young enough to be "cool." Flo is an emotionally comforting persona offering rational insurance benefits.

In the Brand Keys Customer Loyalty Index for insurance brands, Progressive moved from #5 in 2009 to #2 in 2010.

1. Identify and describe the major variables in Progressive's marketing mix.
2. Do you think Progressive is successful in building an emotional connection with the consumer? Explain.
3. Do you think Progressive's marketing strategy serves the broader corporate strategic objective? Explain.
4. In what ways do you think Progressive demonstrates competitive advantage?

Application Exercise

Use the marketing concepts in this chapter to tackle and solve a marketing problem: marketing mix and 7 Ps.

First, start by thinking about the service industry and then choose a service, such as haircuts or tree trimming. There are many services available for us to consider purchasing.

The Marketing Problem

Think about your chosen service after considering the following situation.

> The service industry has become a large part of our global economy. Consumers generally find themselves confronted with many choices for any given service. Consumers need to know which service provider is best for them.

The Problem

How would you divide the consumer market for your service based on consumers' needs? Now choose a target market for your service. Describe each of the 7 Ps and determine the marketing mix you would use to reach your target audience.

The Solution

Complete the following two Problem/Solution briefs using your service, chapter concepts, and college resources.

1. From the Marketing Manager's Point of View
   a. Problem Definition
   b. Analysis
   c. The 7 Ps
   d. Solution

2. From the Consumer's Point of View
   a. Problem Definition
   b. Analysis
   c. The 7 Ps
   d. Solution

Resources:

Marketing Defined, Explained, Applied 2e, Michael Levens
The College Library
Retail or Online Field Trip
Assigned Reading—*Brand Week, Advertising Age, WSJ*, scholarly publications, category trade journals
Blog your problem from either point of view, gather responses/posts (www.blogger.com/start)

Marketing Performance Measurement

Chapter Overview In recent chapters, you considered how the communications mix and marketing mix are developed, managed, and optimized. This chapter expands those concepts by considering the overall performance of marketing activities as influenced by legislation, technology, and business practices. Ultimately, this chapter addresses the question many CEOs ask their marketing departments: "What am I getting from my marketing dollars?" The concept of marketing performance is explored through the topics of marketing accountability, marketing measurement, measuring advertising, brand health, and return on marketing investment.

Chapter Outline

MARKETING ACCOUNTABILITY (pp. 285–286)

DEFINED **Marketing accountability** *is the management of resources and processes to achieve measurable increases in both return on marketing investment and efficiency while increasing the value of the organization in compliance with all legal requirements.*[1]

EXPLAINED

Marketing Accountability

Business functions such as operations and finance are accountable for return on investment while marketing, until recently, is typically managed as more of an "art" rather than a "science." Aligning marketing goals with organizational goals and financial performance is critical to business success. Accomplishing this alignment requires the increasing quantification of the value of marketing activities. The traditional challenge of relating "cause" to "effect" resulted in gut-level, or opinion-based, marketing, which is being replaced with practices that are more quantitative.

Legislation has influenced the need for marketing accountability. The **Sarbanes-Oxley Act**, enacted in 2002, mandated that organizational leaders from publicly traded companies take responsibility for their business practices. The law is primarily focused on accounting reform, but the impact of the requirements extends into many other business activities including marketing. Marketing activities directly influence financial statements such as cash, accounts receivable, and accounts payable amounts on a balance sheet and revenue and general and sales administrative expenses on the income statement. As a result, marketing accountability processes play a critical role in determining compliance with Sarbanes-Oxley.

Managing the marketing accountability process involves activities such as the following:

- Conducting qualitative and quantitative marketing research
- Developing **data analytics**, an inference-based process to transform data into useful information
- Linking departmental goals and objectives throughout an organization
- Implementing and tracking **marketing metrics**, units of measure such as brand awareness and market share that allow for assessment of the effectiveness of marketing activities

Planning, forecasting, CRM software, and optimization models are tools to help manage marketing accountability.

EXAMPLE **MARKETING ACCOUNTABILITY**

Ad-ID is a Web-based digital tagging system for a wide range of media properties developed by the American Association of Advertising Agencies and the Association of National Advertisers.

This tracking system codes each marketing asset that an organization deploys, which enables marketing accountability by identifying the contribution of each marketing asset toward attainment of marketing objectives. Currently used by dozens of large companies, the system increases the ability to track assets across a wider range of media than previous systems. For example, BMW uses Ad-ID codes to track its television, radio, outdoor, online, and print advertisements from development to market launch.[2]

PHOTO: photoslb.com/Shutterstock.

>> **END EXAMPLE**

Home Depot, the world's largest home improvement retailer and the second largest retailer in the United States, uses a proprietary computer model to relate specific promotions and advertisements to sales performance. Because of this information, Home Depot can engage in certain marketing activity in one market, such as increasing direct mail offers in New York, while using a different marketing activity in another, such as increased in-store promotions in Illinois, to generate the largest and most profitable sales increases based on marketing investments. Home Depot believes that this information creates a competitive advantage.[3]

PHOTO: Pavel Kosek/Shutterstock.

APPLIED

Marketing Accountability

As organizations increase their focus on corporate responsibility and the associated compliance requirements, marketing accountability is gaining added importance. In addition, many organizations are using marketing accountability processes to make better business decisions by identifying and optimizing the contribution of different marketing activities. There is considerable disparity in how marketing accountability is practiced, ranging from a lack of knowledge of the subject or simply injecting the term into an organization's vocabulary to deploying marketing-mix models. While legislation requires a focus on accountability, some organizations simply do not know where to begin the process.

However, many organizations are beginning the marketing accountability process and are identifying required human and financial assets, processes, and tools. The more successful companies have deployed cross-disciplinary teams representing departments such as finance, marketing, and operations with senior leadership support to determine the appropriate accountability measures. The organizations use marketing accountability processes based on data analytics that track specific marketing metrics, which lead to better decision making.

Choosing to practice marketing accountability is only the first step. Implementation is another critical step. Challenges to implementing marketing accountability practices include:

- Lack of leadership support
- Lack of financial support
- Lack of trained resources
- Lack of technology
- Time constraints
- Legal and regulatory demands

Companies already engaged in marketing accountability face other challenges, including balancing creativity with accountability. An example of this would be trying to optimize a nontraditional marketing mix combining airline tray table advertising with mobile advertising and event sponsorship with each using different means of measuring performance. Another challenge to marketing accountability programs occurs when selected performance metrics, such as brand awareness, are not related to traditional financial data. Finance departments are typically more comfortable with revenues or profits. The relationship between finance and marketing activities is critical to successful marketing accountability implementation. The common language between the two activities must evolve beyond the popular argument that marketing is an "art" whose effects cannot be quantified to the idea that marketing is a "process" that can be managed and optimized. Thinking of marketing as a process allows for connecting business investment, such as the marketing budget, to business results, such as operating profit.

MEASURING MARKETING (pp. 287–288)

DEFINED **Marketing measurement** *is collecting and evaluating marketing metrics to determine the effectiveness of marketing activities in fulfilling customer, organizational, and marketing objectives.*

EXPLAINED

Measuring Marketing

A popular quotation, attributed to department store merchant John Wanamaker, is "Half the money I spend on advertising is wasted; the trouble is I don't know which half." Although the quote refers to advertising, the idea behind it is often extended to all marketing activities. The challenges to measuring marketing effectiveness are significant:[4]

- Difficulty in isolating marketing activities in complex distribution channels, such as when a manufacturer and retailer concurrently engage in advertising that could either complement or contradict the efforts of the other
- Significant investment required to implement information technology to support gathering marketing information
- A variety of marketing activities acting simultaneously with possibly different brand messages

Early marketing measurement efforts considered consumer attitudes such as brand awareness and intention to purchase, which could be calculated through surveys.[5] Current efforts to measure the effectiveness of marketing expenditures involve linking sales performance with marketing actions such as advertising.

By choosing to measure marketing activities, organizations are committing to relating their marketing activities to specific marketing objectives. An appreciation of how brand relationships are influenced by marketing communications and how the elements of marketing communication work together is also necessary. Understanding marketing measurement also requires a commitment to explore the financial implications of marketing decisions on individual advertising executions, complete advertising campaigns, and brands.

Effective measurement of marketing activities requires a more contemporary perspective on the role of marketing within an organization. A measurement-focused marketing activity is concerned with actions such as developing marketing campaigns that generate revenues and profits with a level of risk that is consistent with other business investments. This is in contrast to simply generating brand awareness or creating innovative artistic renderings of the brand.

Marketing measurement has both process and structural implications for a business. Process issues include how marketing information is generated and analyzed and how employees are rewarded for using measurement data. Structurally, staff needs to be assigned to perform the necessary measurement tasks and dedicated and qualified individuals are needed who ensure insights generated from marketing measurement are comprehended.

Organizations generally decide on activities to measure and the types of measurements to collect for each activity based on marketing objectives. **Key performance indicators** (KPIs) are measurements that assist an organization in quantifying progress toward achievement of marketing objectives. Examples of KPIs include average revenue per customer, cost to acquire a new customer, and cost to retain a customer. KPIs can be connected to the strategic planning process through models such as the balanced scorecard discussed in Chapter 3.

APPLIED

Measuring Marketing

The Adworks 2 study identified that, among the top 10% of consumer packaged-goods companies, TV advertising returned only 32 cents on the dollar for their brands.[6] The fundamental choice resulting from that study was either TV is not returning an adequate amount on its investment or the value of marketing is not being properly measured by current industry standards.

Managers need to know that their investment will increase sales or profitability before they engage in an expensive marketing campaign. Businesses create and administer customer relationship management (CRM) programs to build and maintain profitable relationships with customers, invest in consumer influence campaigns that can involve one or more media types, and implement marketing-mix strategies. Many customer KPIs are identified and managed through CRM programs. Firms attempt to measure the impact of marketing activities on loyalty, customer value, and, importantly, sales. Companies such as Coca-Cola, Kraft, and Procter & Gamble all have ways to measure marketing investment. Marketing measurement tools include advertising copy tests, brand health tracking studies, and return on marketing investment models. These terms are defined and discussed on the following pages.

EXAMPLE MEASURING MARKETING

Cadillac, which was founded in 1902 and is one of General Motors' most prestigious brands, regularly evaluates how consumers view its advertising prior to launching a new advertising campaign. The company does this by presenting a sample of target consumers with a collection of finished advertisements or artistic renderings of key elements of advertisements to determine consumer reactions such as interest in the advertisement, impact on interest in the brand, and impact on interest in competitors' brands. Low-rated advertisements are then changed or cancelled prior to launch. Cadillac also monitors consumers' attitudes toward its brand and products through regular consumer surveys.

PHOTO: Dongliu/Shutterstock.

>> **END EXAMPLE**

MEASURING ADVERTISING (pp. 289–290)

DEFINED **Advertising measurement** *is collecting and evaluating advertising metrics to determine the effectiveness of an advertisement or advertising campaign in fulfilling customer, organizational, and marketing objectives.*

EXPLAINED

Measuring Advertising

For most organizations, advertising is one of the largest marketing expenditures. The most important measure of advertising is its level of effectiveness in meeting marketing objectives such as increasing market share, building brand awareness, and changing brand perceptions. Advertising effectiveness can be considered on two levels, strategically and behaviorally. From a strategic perspective, attaining the communications objectives is paramount. Communications objectives range from introducing a new idea to asking consumers to act. The construction of an advertising campaign depends entirely on the communication objectives. The length of time to determine success of an advertising campaign varies with the communication objectives. Informing consumers and building the brand relationship is typically a longer-term effort, whereas call to action advertising is asking for an immediate response that often involves a sale of a product or service.

From a behavioral perspective, the effectiveness of advertising can be measured more specifically through outcomes up to and including sales. Advertising influences measurable items such as brand awareness and advertising awareness. Brand attributes, such as quality and convenience, can also assist in predicting consumer behavior since attributes define the positioning of one brand versus another. It is important to consider both the strategic and behavioral elements of advertising effectiveness.

Advertising effectiveness is ultimately measured as the ability to persuade. The influencing factors in moving from establishing an advertising objective to persuading consumer action include:

- Brand perception
- Category interest
- Consumer engagement
- Integrated marketing

The cumulative effect of advertising evolves from both short-term advertising actions, such as a direct mail offers, and longer-term advertising actions, such as magazine advertising.

APPLIED

Measuring Advertising

Advertising managers and advertising agency representatives alike would seldom question the necessity and benefits of advertising. Although advertising often has a significant impact on marketing results, it is important to evaluate critically the contribution that advertising makes to a product or service such as building brand equity. Advertising effectiveness can be measured qualitatively, such as by conducting focus groups, and quantitatively, such as through surveys.

A product category provides either an initial opportunity or a significant challenge when choosing advertising to assist in shaping consumer behavior. Customer loyalty ranges from pet food at 54% loyalty to soft drinks at 41% to canned goods at 14%.[7] The greater the loyalty, the stronger are the existing brand relationships, whereas the lower the levels of loyalty, the greater the opportunities to gain sales.

Many advertising campaigns take advantage of a variety of media channels. A successful integrated marketing campaign that uses different media channels must include consistent messaging. Even then, as we learned in Chapter 19, certain media is more effective than others for a given brand's marketing strategies. It may be the case that a brand is most efficient on radio but feels that it must be on TV simply because it is a big brand. The risk is sub-optimizing marketing expenditures by overlooking efficient, less costly media and spending marketing dollars on more expensive but relatively inefficient media choices.

Individual advertising also can be examined for effectiveness. Within a TV or radio spot, it is possible that a small percentage of the advertisement will account for a large percentage of recall. It is essential that the elements of the advertisement that are recalled contain both the brand and the critical messages. Music can serve as the component that induces recall. "Like a Rock" is attached to Chevrolet and the song, even without additional advertising content, can induce recall. Businesses often use a process known as copy testing to explore advertising effectiveness.

Copy testing is a survey-based process that can assist in measuring advertising and campaign effectiveness. The assessment of effectiveness can be performed prior to the airing of advertising, during the advertising campaign, and after the campaign. Testing

Table 20.1 Advertising Report Card

	Advertising Report Card				
Advertising Execution	**Recognition %**	**Brand Linkage %**	**Entertainment (1–10)**	**Creativity (1–10)**	**Grade**
Execution 1	30	65	4	2	C+
Execution 2	38	63	6	2	B-
Execution 3	30	50	6	8	B-

before media is launched to the public is particularly important so as not to expend advertising dollars for an advertisement that does not work toward the campaign objectives.

Often called a report card, such as the example in Table 20.1, by advertising agency creative directors, copy testing can be simply a report card or it can be a diagnostic tool to help evolve creative development into successful advertising campaigns. The more direct explanation of copy testing is the process of evaluating how well an advertising execution communicates the brand's strategic positioning and accomplishes the brand's objectives. In the report card example, Execution 2 is better recognized and better linked to the appropriate brand than Execution 3, but Execution 3 is considered to be considerably more creative. A decision still needs to be made based on desired quality level of the execution and the better fit to brand position and objectives.

Copy testing can explore alternative advertising campaign ideas, as well as the communication effectiveness of different campaigns. Copy testing can reveal connections between executional elements and performance dimensions while identifying what works and what does not. Ultimately, copy testing can suggest what elements might warrant changing to achieve optimal performance against stated objectives.

Ultimately, the copy test process must be versatile enough to address the needs of different advertising objectives. New product introduction advertising should be evaluated on criteria like basic enjoyment and brand awareness. Public service announcements can be evaluated differently based on whether they are related to established brands with a consistent message or if brand and message are relatively new or require an immediate response.

The measurement of new media, such as interactive advertising, is becoming increasingly important as a greater percentage of marketing budgets are being allocated to new media platforms. Everything from viral video to blogs to video game sponsorship are targets for research. Currently there is no standard tool to copy test the wide range of diverse media platforms.

EXAMPLE **MEASURING ADVERTISING**

Millward Brown, a leading global research agency specializing in advertising, marketing communications, media, and brand equity research and part of communications services giant WPP, has conducted over 65,000 advertising copy tests over 20 years using its proprietary model known as Link. Link exposes respondents to advertising in various forms of development and then asks a series of questions including what message was recalled, what brand was doing the advertising, and ability to recount the elements of the advertisement. Link also includes an interest trace, a process where respondents use a computer mouse to indicate what they like and what they dislike as the commercial plays, to address nonverbal measures that lead to persuasion, including involvement, integration, and interest.[8]

PHOTO: Helder Almeida/Shutterstock.

>> END EXAMPLE

MEASURING BRAND HEALTH (pp. 291–292)

DEFINED **Brand health** *is the collective consumer perceptions, attitudes, and expectations for a brand resulting from historical and current brand experiences.*

EXPLAINED

Measuring Brand Health

Advertising and other marketing activities as well as customer experience have a cumulative effect, over time, on consumer attitudes toward an organization and its products and services. This effect is often measured as the health of an organization's brand. We have already studied the idea, in Chapter 9, that a brand is essentially a promise to consumers. That promise provides context to everything that consumers can sense about a brand. If the promise is regularly fulfilled, then the brand's image is solidified and its reputation established and reinforced. This reputation can be enhanced or diminished depending on the ability of an organization to deliver on its brand promise.

Quantitative brand tracking among consumers is one means to monitor brand health. A brand tracking process typically begins with assessing the recognition and influence of advertising and other forms of marketing communications such as sponsorship and public relations on consumer attitudes toward the advertising brand and its competitors. By translating marketing communications into a linear communications model, a content outline can be developed for a brand tracking study. In Figure 20.1, media recognition—referring to which media channels on which

FIGURE 20.1 **Brand Tracking Model**

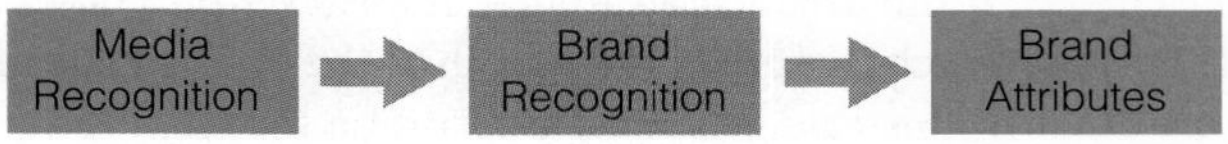

consumers claim to see a brand advertised, brand recognition, and brand attributes associated with the brand—form the basic architecture for a brand tracking process.

APPLIED

Measuring Brand Health

Brand tracking studies are common among large companies. These studies typically measure aspects of brand health and marketing communications and the interplay between the two. Some brands are tracked on a continuous basis with monthly or quarterly reports while others are measured once or twice each year. Reports are provided to a marketing or brand manager and the marketing team on issues such as the **purchase funnel**, a sequential consumer decision-making model encompassing awareness to loyalty (see Figure 20.2). Consider the stages in the

FIGURE 20.2 **The Purchase Funnel**

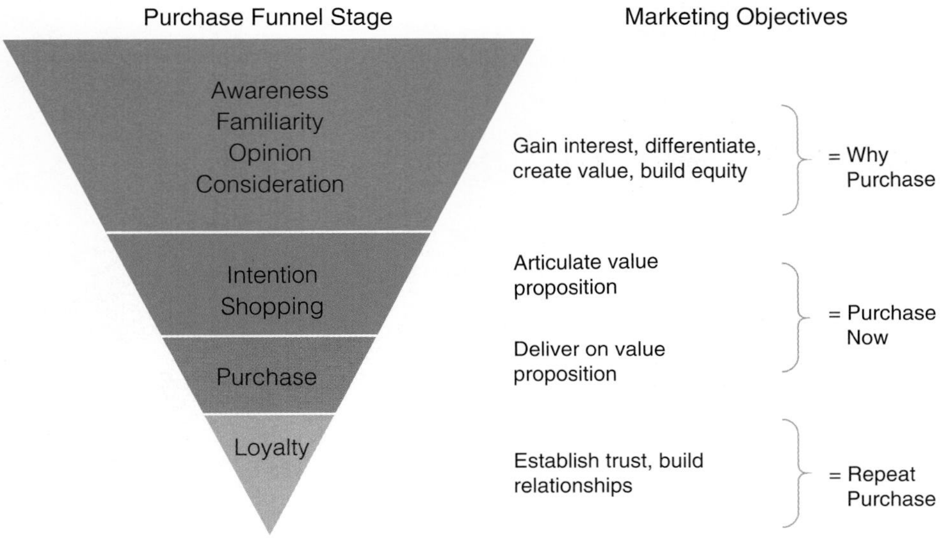

purchase funnel and the associated marketing objectives. Different marketing activities would be appropriate for different stages and objectives. Sponsorship may help build awareness for a brand while a direct mail offer may assist in the shopping stage and a reward program may assist in the loyalty stage.

Consider a situation where there is 15% unaided awareness for a brand of speedboat, meaning that only 15% could name the specific brand in question when asked "Thinking about brands of speed boats, which brands come to mind?" What if 90% of those aware of the boat subsequently purchased the boat? The purchase funnel would be very narrow and vertical. One possible interpretation is that the product is so desirable that the more people that become aware, the more sales that will be generated. If this interpretation is correct one might wish to increase advertising focused on increasing awareness. Alternatively, if the unaided awareness is 80% yet purchases are only 5%, the purchase funnel is wider than the one portrayed in Figure 20.2. In this case, one may interpret a problem lower in the purchase funnel because people are aware yet not satisfied about some aspect of the speedboat. Possibly the price is too high based on the value of the product or perhaps there is an inadequate distribution network. The purchase funnel can be a very useful tool in assessing brand health.

Other measures often tracked include brand image statements exploring topics such as value, convenience, and quality. Data from various measures are often trended—collected at specific time intervals such as every business quarter or every year—to determine if any change in market perception relative to a brand's competitors has occurred. The trending aspect is critical to the viability of the brand health data. If the topics studied change each month, then no trending is possible and there is limited strategic marketing value.

EXAMPLE **MEASURING BRAND HEALTH**

Tropicana, owned by PepsiCo, changed its packaging in January 2009 to reflect fresh taste with a simpler, cleaner design. There was extensive public outcry through letters and social media claiming that the brand looked generic and even "ugly." After sales plummeted and brand perceptions diminished, Tropicana quickly dropped the redesign and returned to the original packaging. By continually assessing brand health, Tropicana was able to identify a problem in its purchase funnel where a change in packaging altered opinions, which subsequently reduced purchase levels.[9]

PHOTO: Martin Poole/Thinkstock Royalty Free.

>> END EXAMPLE

RETURN ON MARKETING INVESTMENT (p. 293)

DEFINED **Return on marketing investment** *(ROMI) is the impact on business performance resulting from executing specific marketing activities.*

EXPLAINED

Return on Marketing Investment

ROMI is used to inform decisions on future marketing investments by measuring the overall effectiveness of marketing activities. Models are typically created to measure performance against near- and long-term objectives. A near-term objective could be to have a sale to lower inventory levels and a long-term objective could include a market share growth target of 10% higher than the current level. The primary difference between a traditional marketing evaluation perspective and a ROMI perspective is that financial performance metrics are established with ROMI as opposed to typically intangible objective criteria such as brand awareness.

ROMI provides insights into which types of marketing activities most effectively deliver on marketing objectives. ROMI should lead to improved marketing effectiveness, increased financial performance, and increased market share for the equivalent marketing expenditure without ROMI. ROMI models are developed over extended periods (often 18 months or greater) due to the considerable time it takes to measure the short- and long-term effects of different media channels on sales and can provide insights for brand marketing and media planning. Examples of specific benefits of ROMI include:

- Advertising investment can be allocated to the most efficient media executions.
- Advertising investment can be optimized to avoid overspending.
- Concurrent advertising activities can be measured to ensure they work together to achieve campaign objectives.
- Media placement and media weight can be scheduled to optimally influence sales.
- Campaign wear-out can be identified relative to other marketing activities.

APPLIED

Return on Marketing Investment

In practice, a ROMI model is generally used to explain the relative contribution of various marketing efforts to sales. Proper funding can then be allocated to the most effective marketing activity depending on the marketing objective such as sales revenue or market share. Based on the output from a ROMI model and efficiency projections of various media campaign elements, allocation of marketing funds can be made based on budgetary limitations and not guesswork. Although there are no specific industry standards, it is logical that ROMI should return something better than a 1-to-1 relationship between minimum expected incremental revenue from a specific marketing program in relation to the amount to be invested in that marketing program.

Consider a company that spends $300,000 for a direct marketing campaign that delivers $1,200,000 in incremental revenue. The ROMI factor is 4. If the incremental contribution margin based on the incremental revenue for the direct marketing campaign is 50%, then the program returns $2 (50% × 4) for each additional marketing dollar invested. Typically, there are ROMI factors for a set of alternative campaigns representing different media. Depending on the marketing objective and program **hurdle rate**, the minimum amount of financial return that an organization requires before making a financial investment, the direct marketing campaign will be evaluated relative to the financial return of any alternatives. Generally, the campaign with the highest financial return that meets marketing objectives is implemented.

Visual Summary

Part 1 Explaining (Chapters 1, 2, 3, 4, 5)
Part 2 Creating (Chapters 6, 7, 8, 9)
Part 3 Strategizing (Chapters 10, 11)
Part 4 Managing (Chapters 12, 13, 14, 15, 16, 17)
Part 5 Integrating (Chapters 18, 19, 20)

Chapter 20 Summary

Building on the concepts of marketing mix and media mix, this chapter expanded the idea of evaluating marketing performance. Marketing accountability is the management of marketing resources and processes to achieve measurable increases in both return on marketing investment and marketing efficiency while increasing the value of the organization. Marketing measurement allows companies to relate marketing expenditures on specific activities to marketing objectives, while advertising measurement, a subset of marketing measurement, enables an evaluation of the effectiveness of an advertisement or advertising campaign against marketing objectives.

Measuring brand health begins with assessing the consumer influence of advertising and other forms of marketing communications such as sponsorship and public relations. Brand tracking essentially provides on ongoing perspective on what a brand means to consumers relative to competitors. Brand health and the other concepts discussed within this chapter are typically included in ROMI calculations. The primary difference between a traditional marketing evaluation perspective and a ROMI perspective is that financial performance metrics are established with ROMI as opposed to typically intangible objective criteria such as brand awareness.

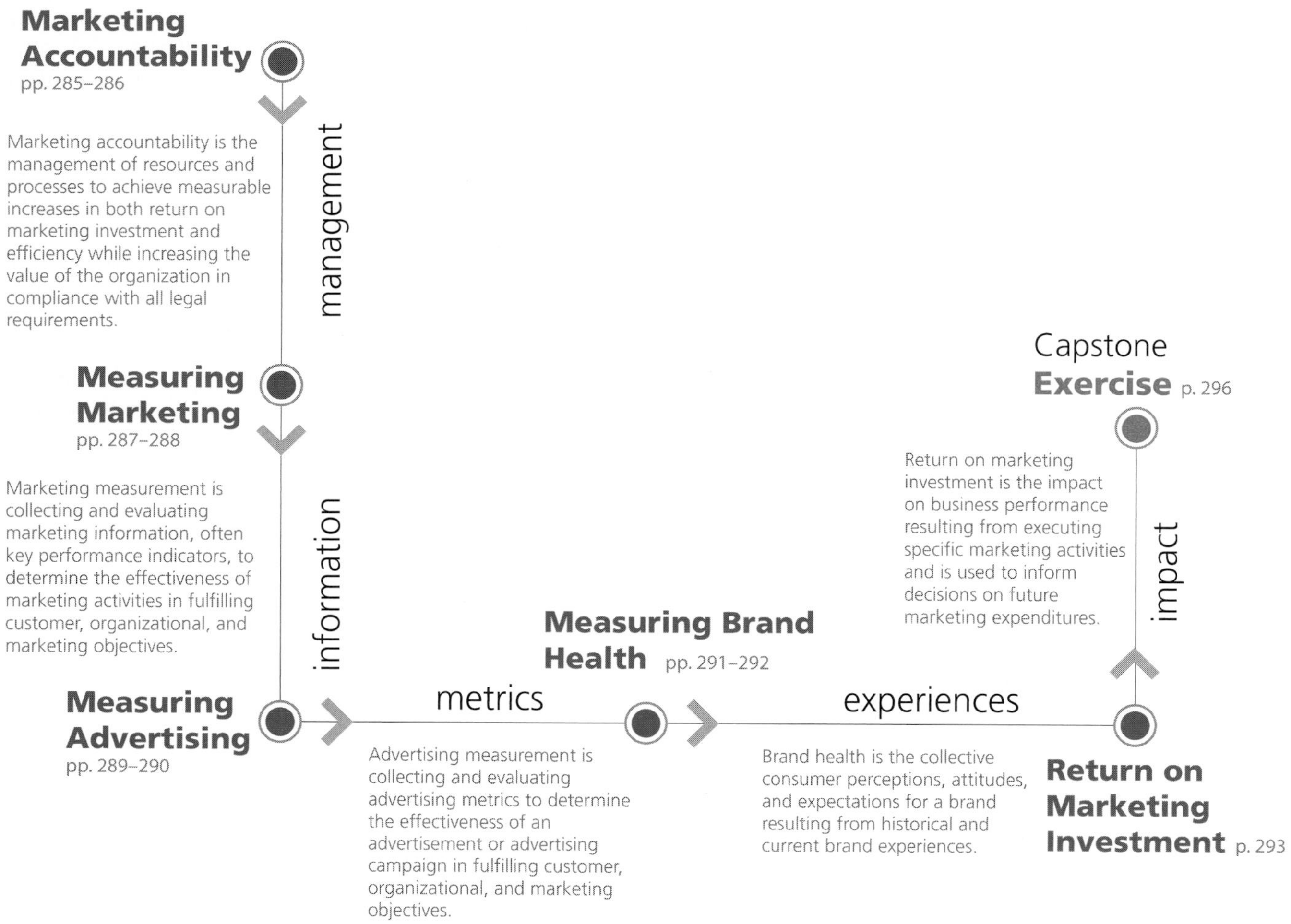
Marketing Accountability pp. 285–286
Marketing accountability is the management of resources and processes to achieve measurable increases in both return on marketing investment and efficiency while increasing the value of the organization in compliance with all legal requirements.
management
Measuring Marketing pp. 287–288
Marketing measurement is collecting and evaluating marketing information, often key performance indicators, to determine the effectiveness of marketing activities in fulfilling customer, organizational, and marketing objectives.
information
Measuring Advertising pp. 289–290
metrics
Advertising measurement is collecting and evaluating advertising metrics to determine the effectiveness of an advertisement or advertising campaign in fulfilling customer, organizational, and marketing objectives.
Measuring Brand Health pp. 291–292
experiences
Brand health is the collective consumer perceptions, attitudes, and expectations for a brand resulting from historical and current brand experiences.
Return on Marketing Investment p. 293
impact
Return on marketing investment is the impact on business performance resulting from executing specific marketing activities and is used to inform decisions on future marketing expenditures.
Capstone Exercise p. 296

Chapter Key Terms

Marketing Accountability

(pp. 285–286)

Marketing accountability *is the management of resources and processes to achieve measurable increases in both return on marketing investment and efficiency while increasing the value of the organization in compliance with all legal requirements. (p. 285)* **Example: Marketing Accountability (p. 285)**

Key Terms (p. 285)

Data analytics is an inference-based process to transform data into useful information. **(p. 285)**

Marketing metrics are units of measure that allow for assessment of the effectiveness of marketing activities. **(p. 285)**

Sarbanes-Oxley Act is a law passed in 2002 mandating organizational leaders from publicly traded companies take responsibility for their business practices. **(p. 285)**

Measuring Marketing (pp. 287–288)

Marketing measurement *is collecting and evaluating marketing metrics to determine the effectiveness of marketing activities in fulfilling customer, organizational, and marketing objectives. (p. 287)* **Example: Measuring Marketing (p. 288)**

Key Term (p. 287)

Key performance indicators (KPIs) are measurements that assist an organization in quantifying progress toward achievement of marketing objectives. **(p. 287)**

Measuring Advertising (pp. 289–290)

Advertising measurement *is collecting and evaluating advertising metrics to determine the effectiveness of an advertisement or advertising campaign in fulfilling customer, organizational, and marketing objectives. (p. 289)* **Example: Measuring Advertising (p. 290)**

Key Term (pp. 289)

Copy testing is a survey-based process that can assist in measuring advertising and campaign effectiveness. **(p. 289)**

Measuring Brand Health

(pp. 291–292)

Brand health *is the collective consumer perceptions, attitudes, and expectations for a brand resulting from historical and current brand experiences. (p. 291)* **Example: Measuring Brand Health (p. 292)**

Key Term (p. 291)

Purchase funnel is a sequential consumer decision-making model encompassing awareness to loyalty. **(p. 291)**

Return on Marketing Investment (p. 293)

Return on marketing investment (ROMI) *is the impact on business performance resulting from executing specific marketing activities. (p. 293)*

Key Term (p. 293)

Hurdle rate is the minimum amount of financial return that an organization requires before making a financial investment. **(p. 293)**

Capstone Exercise

The Quapaw Nation is located in the extreme northeast corner of Oklahoma on 275 acres adjacent to I-44. Beginning in 2005, Tribal leaders had a vision for a project that would pump dollars into the struggling local economy by providing jobs and requiring goods and services from local suppliers. In 2007, the $300 million Downstream Casino Resort project (named for the Quapaw's original name, O-Gah-Pah, meaning *downstream people*) was under way with personal loans from tribal members and development funds arranged through Bank of America and Merrill Lynch.

The resort opened in November 2008. It features 220 hotel rooms, five restaurants, a state-of-the-art Vegas-style casino, and two lounges. The director of marketing identified the tri-state area (Oklahoma, Missouri, and Arkansas) as the target market, and market studies project the resort will attract more than 2 million visitors each year. The amenities of the resort complex and the public space were designed with the recognition that the environment of the resort affects guest attitudes toward gaming, length of stay, and return visits to the property.

Unlike retail businesses where each transaction is recorded and therefore can become part of historical data for analysis, many casino-resort transactions go unrecorded or are not directly attributed to a particular person or marketing activity. The casino loyalty program is a way for casino management to identify its customers. Downstream offers the Q-Club, a rewards program for loyal gamers. The Q-Club is a three-tiered reward system with levels of bronze, silver, and gold. It's based on the individual level of play in the casino. Points can be redeemed throughout the resort complex.

Another challenge for casino-resort marketers is related to the identification of the source of revenues. For example, how much incremental gaming revenue was generated by a specific promotion? Other factors of the resort environment may simultaneously impact gaming volume: day of the week, hotel occupancy, special events, holiday periods, and special food offers. At the Downstream Casino Resort many of the marketing objectives are related to acquiring, retaining, and recovering players. Player databases are "mined" and players are graded and segregated into database tiers for the purpose of determining offer eligibility.

The advertising objective is to attract customers to the resort, and the objective of the Floor Host program is to identify valuable players, attempt to get them to become members of the Q-Club, and develop a lasting relationship with them. Downstream Resort Casino has also found that existing premium players are a valuable source for referral and acquisition of new players.

The accounting department at the Downstream Casino Resort produces a monthly analysis of all marketing expenses and together with the marketing department a report is prepared linking various marketing activities and expenses with revenue streams. These two departments also conduct a cost-benefit analysis each quarter for the Q-Club.

1. Do you think the Downstream Casino Resort is managing marketing accountability? Explain.
2. List ways that the resort casino is measuring marketing activities. What other ways do you think would be helpful?
3. If the majority of Downstream's advertising budget is spent on newspaper advertising in the tri-state area and in direct-mail campaigns, what measurement tool(s) do you recommend the marketers use to measure the advertising effectiveness?
4. If management's objectives are three-pronged—the customer experience, repeat or loyal gamers, and an average of $100 coin-in per gamer-visit—what types of measurement tools would you suggest? Be specific.

Application Exercise

Use the marketing concepts in this chapter to tackle and solve a marketing problem: marketing measurement.

First, start by thinking about the denim jeans category and then choose a product within that category. There are many products available in stores within this category for us to consider purchasing.

The Marketing Problem

Think about your chosen product after considering the following situation.

> Denim jeans are an important purchase for consumers and the category is becoming highly segmented. Consumers need to know what is best for them and marketers need to know that their marketing dollars are achieving organizational objectives.

The Problem

Denim jeans are being marketed to "baby boomers" (born between 1946 and 1964) since they represent a large and affluent part of the global population and may well represent a profitable investment in marketing dollars. How would you determine the extent to which the marketing dollars are achieving their goals?

The Solution

Complete the following two Problem/Solution briefs using your product in the denim jean category, chapter concepts, and college resources.

1. From the Marketing Manager's Point of View
   a. Problem Definition
   b. Analysis
   c. Target Market
   d. Solution

2. From the Consumer's Point of View
   a. Problem Definition
   b. Analysis
   c. Solution

Resources:

Marketing Defined, Explained, Applied, 2e Michael Levens
The College Library
Retail or Online Field Trip
Assigned Reading—*Brand Week*, *Advertising Age*, *WSJ*, scholarly publications, category trade journals
Blog your problem from either point of view, gather responses/posts (www.blogger.com/start)

interiorViews

Interior Views LLC

Marketing Plan

This sample marketing plan has been made available to users of *Marketing Plan Pro*, marketing planning software published by Palo Alto Software. Our sample plans were developed by existing companies or new business start-ups as research instruments to determine target market viability, explore marketing strategies, or prepare funding proposals. Names, locations, and numbers may have been changed, and substantial portions of text may have been omitted to preserve confidentiality and protect proprietary information.

You are welcome to use this plan as a starting point to create your own, but you do not have permission to reproduce, publish, distribute, or even copy this plan as it exists here.

Requests for reprints, academic use, and other dissemination of this sample plan should be addressed to the marketing department of Palo Alto Software.

Copyright Palo Alto Software, Inc., Confidentiality Agreement

The undersigned reader acknowledges that the information provided by ________________ in this marketing plan is confidential; therefore, reader agrees not to disclose it without the express written permission of ________________.

It is acknowledged by reader that information to be furnished in this marketing plan is in all respects confidential in nature, other than information which is in the public domain through other means and that any disclosure or use of same by reader may cause serious harm or damage to ________________.

Upon request, this document is to be immediately returned to ________________.

Signature

Name (typed or printed)

Date

This is a marketing plan. It does not imply an offering of securities.

Table of Contents

1.0 Executive Summary

Interior Views is a retail home decorator fabrics and complementary home accessories and services concept that is now in its third year. This destination store offers the advantages of providing fabrics specifically designed for home decorator use in fabric widths of 54 inches and greater. Over 900 fabrics are available on the floor at any time with more than 3,000 sample fabrics for custom "cut" orders. Customers see, touch, feel, and take the fabric to their home as they work through their purchase decision.

Market research indicates a specific and growing need in the area for the products and services Interior Views offers in the market it serves. The market strategy will be based on a cost-effective approach to reach this clearly defined target market. The three-phase approach will utilize resources to create awareness of the store and encourage customers to benefit from the convenience and services it offers. Interior Views will focus on its selection, accessibility of product, design services, and competitive pricing.

The marketing objective is to actively support continued growth and profitability through effective implementation of the strategy.

2.0 Situation Analysis

Interior Views is a retail store heading into its third year of operation. The store has been well received, and marketing is now critical to its continued success and future profitability. The store offers the most extensive selection of in-stock decorator fabrics as well as a resource for special ordered fabrics. The basic market need is to offer a good selection of decorator fabrics at reasonable prices, for the "do-it-yourself" and the "buy-it-yourself" customers, through a personalized retail store that offers excellent service, design assistance, and inspiration for people to redecorate their homes.

2.1 Market Needs

Interior Views is providing its customers the opportunity to create a home environment to express who they are. They have the choice to select their fabric and go whatever direction they choose—to fabric it themselves or have it done for them. They have the opportunity to actively participate in the design, look, and feel of their home. They desire their home to be personal, unique, and tasteful as well as communicate a message about what is important to them. We seek to fulfill the following benefits that we know are important to our customers.

- **Selection**—A wide choice of current and tasteful decorator fabrics.
- **Accessibility**—Buyers can walk out of the store with the fabric they need to begin their project.
- **Customer Design Services**—Employees have a design background to make them a resource for the customer. This enables customers to benefit from suggestions regarding the selection of their fabric and related products in a manner to complement their design choice.
- **Competitive Pricing**—All products will be competitively priced in comparison to stores in the Boise, Idaho, market (best price comparison) and other channels of distribution, such as catalog sales.

2.2 The Market

We possess good information about our market and know a great deal about the common attributes of our most prized and loyal customers. We will leverage this information to better understand who we serve, their specific needs, and how we can better communicate with them.

Table: Market Analysis

Market Analysis

Potential Customers	Growth	2008	2009	2010	2011	2012
Country Club Women	25%	73,500	91,875	114,844	143,555	179,444
Boomers in Transition	20%	28,500	34,200	41,040	49,248	59,098
Professional Youngsters	18%	23,000	27,140	32,025	37,790	44,592
Home Builders	12%	18,000	20,160	22,579	25,288	28,323
Total	21.48%	143,000	173,375	210,488	255,881	311,457

Market Analysis (Pie)

2.2.1 Market Demographics

The profile of the Interior Views customer consists of the following geographic, demographic, psychographic, and behavior factors:

Geographics

- Our immediate geographic market is the Boise area, with a population of 168,300.
- A 50-mile geographic area is in need of our products and services.
- The total targeted area population is estimated at 568,800.

Demographics

- Female.
- Married.
- Have children, but not necessarily at home.
- Have attended college.
- A combined annual income in excess of $50,000.
- Age range of 35 to 55 years, with a median age of 42.
- Owns their home, townhouse, and/or condominium valued at over $125,000.
- If they work out of the home, it's by choice in a professional/business setting.
- Belong to one or more business, social, and/or athletic organizations, which may include:
  - Downtown Athletic Club.
  - Boise Country Club.
  - Junior League of Boise.
  - American Business Women's Association.

We know the following regarding the profile of the typical resident of Boise:

- 67% have lived in Boise for 7 years or more.
- 23% are between the ages of 35 and 44.
- 40% have completed some college.
- 24% are managers, professionals, and/or owners of a business.
- 53% are married.
- 65% have no children living at home.
- 56% own their residence.

Psychographics:

- The appearance of her home is a priority.
- Entertaining and showing her home are important.
- She perceives herself as creative, tasteful, and able, but seeks validation and support regarding her decorating ideas and choices.
- She reads one or more of the following magazines:
  - Martha Stewart Living.
  - Country Living.
  - Home.
  - House Beautiful.
  - Country Home.
  - Metropolitan Home.
  - Traditional Homes.
  - Victoria.
  - Architectural Digest.
  - Ellé Decor.

Behaviors

- She takes pride in having an active role in decorating their home.
- Her home is a form of communicating "who she is" to others.
- Comparisons within social groups are made on an ongoing basis, but rarely discussed.

Table: Market Demographics

Market Demographics

Market Segments	Age	Annual Income	Average Sale	Focus	Characteristic
Country Club Women	35–60	$80,000	High	Social and High Profile	-
Boomers in Transition	50–60	Varies	High	Time and Security	-
Professional Youngsters	25–35	$50,000	Moderate	Image and Climbing	-
Home Builders	30–45	$60,000	High	Image and Security	-

2.2.2 Market Trends

The home textile market, considered to include sheets, towels, draperies, carpets, blankets, and upholstery, accounts for 37% of all textile output. The trade publication *Home Textiles Today* estimates the size of the U.S. home textiles market at the wholesale level, excluding carpets, to be between $6.5 billion to $7 billion annually. The industry is expected to realize a steady increase over the next few years.

The industry is driven by the number of "household formations," which is expected to continue through the first years of the new millennium. This is primarily due to the solid growth in the number of single-parent and non-family households. This growth also comes from baby boomers needing bigger houses to accommodate growing and extended families and, as people get older, they are buying homes rather than renting to realize tax and equity building benefits. Favorable mortgage rates will also enable others to invest in their existing home.

The "do-it-yourself" (DIY) market continues to grow and closely parallels the professional home-improvement market. DIY market growth is attributed to an increased presence of products, the personal satisfaction experienced, and the cost savings customers realize. A portion of the do-it-yourself market is the "buy-it-yourself" (BIY) market. Consumers are buying the product and arranging for someone else to do the fabrication and/or installation. This is more expensive than the do-it-yourself approach, but less costly than buying finished products from other sources. It also provides similar feelings of creativity, pride, and individuality associated with direct creative involvement. This sense of "participation" in home decorating is an important factor for many of these committed customers.

Market Analysis (Trends)

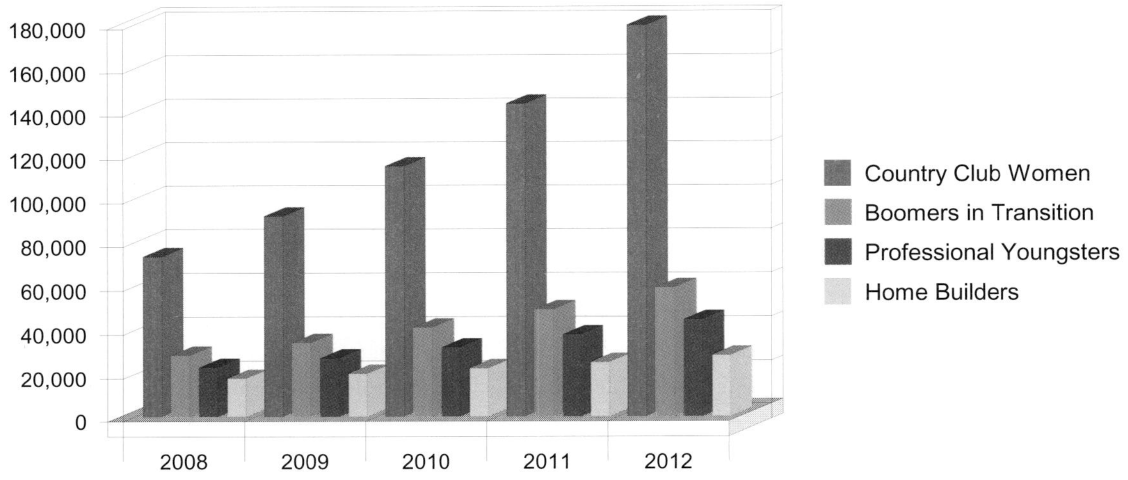

2.2.3 Market Growth

The publication *American Demographics* projected the number of U.S. households will grow by 16% between 1995 and the year 2010, an increase from 98.5 million to 115 million. Of the households composed of people from 35 to 44 years old, almost half are married couples with children under the age of 18. Based on research by *American Demographics*, households in the 45 to 65 age range were estimated to grow to 34 million by the year 2000. These households will increase another 32% from 2000 totals to 45 million in 2010 as baby boomers add to this peak-earning and spending age group. With approximately 46.2% of the nation's 93.3 million dwellings built before 1960, many of these homeowners are also expected to update. These factors contribute to an increased need for home decorator fabrics for window treatment, upholstering, pillows, bedding, and other fabric accessory needs. This demand is expected to be complemented by the growth in the Boise market. The majority of homeowners spend a large percentage of their disposable income on home goods within two years after buying a new house. Therefore, positive trends in new housing activity represents growth and opportunity for home textiles.

One important factor is that married couples in the 35 to 65 age range represent a growth segment and enjoy larger incomes than other family structures. They enjoy the choice to spend their disposable income on life's amenities. They may demonstrate "cocooning" by making their home a more comfortable and attractive haven. They choose to spend resources here rather than on vacations and other discretionary options. This group represents a larger sub-segment of the target market.

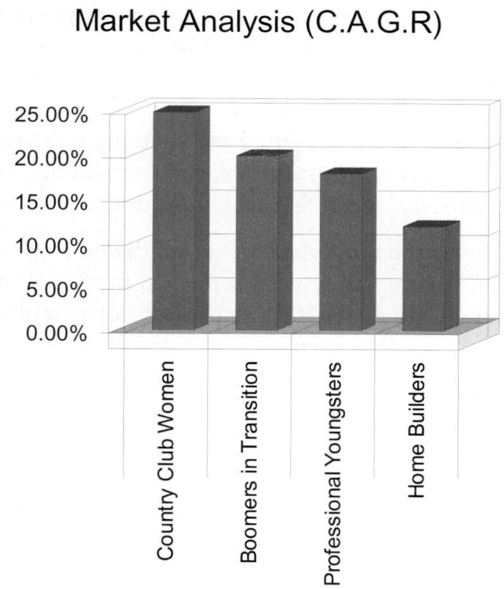

2.2.4 Macroenvironment

The following trends and issues impact the success of Interior Views.

- **National economic health** — The store does better when the country experiences "good times" regardless of its direct impact on the local economy. Sales decrease when the stock market falls. An upbeat State of the Union address correlates with an increase in sales.
- **New home construction activity** — More closely related to what is taking place in our local economy, new home construction has a significant impact on sales across all product lines.
- **Shifts in design trends** — Major changes in design trends increase sales. The Boise market lags behind metropolitan design trends by 6 to 12 months. This offers a buying advantage for the store, offering a preview of what is coming and how we should adjust our in-stock inventory.

2.3 The Company

Interior Views is a retail home decorator fabrics and complementary home accessories and services concept. This destination store offers the advantages of providing fabrics specifically designed for home decorator use in fabric widths of 54 inches and greater. Over 900 fabrics are available on the floor at any time with more than 3,000 sample fabrics for custom "cut" orders. Customers see, touch, feel, and take the fabric to their home as they work through their purchase decision.

Judy Wilson, the owner, is the one primarily responsible for marketing activities. This is in addition to her other responsibilities, and she does depend on some outside resources for mailing (Donna at Postal Connection) and some graphic design work. Judy does delegate responsibilities to Julie Hanson to assist with television advertising. Julie and the other staff members are also responsible for at least one special event throughout the year.

2.3.1 Mission

Interior Views LLC is a store for discerning, quality-conscious buyers of decorator fabrics and complementary home accessories and furniture. The store celebrates the home through the color and texture of fabric. The experience informs, inspires, and shows people how to transform their home into a unique and personalized expression of themselves. Interior Views seeks to encourage people to imagine what can be and help make their vision a reality.

2.3.2 Product Offering

Our primary points of differentiation offer these qualities:

- The most extensive access to in-stock, first quality decorator fabrics within 100 miles of our primary geographic market and offered at affordable prices.

- The largest selection of special-order fabrics, with arrangements to have most of those products shipped to the store within 10 days of placing the order.
- Personal assistance from a design-oriented staff that is qualified and capable of meeting the needs of discerning customers with high expectations.
- Complementary product offering, including hard-covering window treatment, hardware, home accessories, made-to-order upholstered furniture, and antiques that are designed, selected, and displayed in a way to emphasize the use of fabric in home design.

Interior Views will qualify for the most attractive retail discount through these suppliers, offering greater profit margins and more competitive pricing for bolt purchases in quantities of 50 to 60 yards, or in half of that yardage with a "cutting fee" that increases cost per yard by an average of 50 cents. The primary product lines will include fabrics from the following textile sources:

- Robert Allen Fabrics
- Fabricut
- Waverly Fabrics
- Spectrum
- Art Mark
- Covington
- P/Kaufmann

Complementary accessories, including fabric trims, drapery hardware, and hard-covering window treatments, are supplied from the following sources:

- Hunter Douglas — Hard-window coverings.
- Kirsh — Rods and selected window hardware and accessories.
- Conso — Trims and fabric accessories.
- Petersen-Arne — Trims and accessories.
- Graber — Selected window hardware.
- Grumman — Threads.

2.3.3 Positioning

For the person creating a personalized and unique impression of her home, Interior Views is the best local source for selection and price points of the fabric, customer-oriented design services, and a variety of other home accessory and furniture products. Customers will be impressed with, and return for, the great in-stock selection, value-oriented pricing, and excellent customer service. Unlike JoAnn's, Warehouse Fabric, or catalogs, Interior Views is a pleasant and tasteful resource that encourages everyone in the process of decorating their home. Unlike employing an interior decorator, Interior Views allows the individual to participate in their design choices to the extent they choose, and realize greater value for the dollars they invest.

2.3.4 SWOT Summary

The following SWOT analysis captures the key strengths and weaknesses within the company and describes the opportunities and threats facing Interior Views.

2.3.4.1 Strengths

- Strong relationships with suppliers that offer credit arrangements, flexibility, and response to special product requirements.
- Excellent and stable staff, offering personalized customer service.
- Great retail space that offers flexibility with a positive and attractive atmosphere.
- Strong merchandising and product presentation.
- Good referral relationships with complementary vendors, local realtors, and some designers.
- In-store complementary products through "The Window Seat" and "Antique Bureau" add interest, stability, and revenue.
- High customer loyalty among repeat and high-dollar purchase customers.

2.3.4.2 Weaknesses

- Access to capital.
- Cash flow continues to be unpredictable.
- Owners are still climbing the "retail experience curve."
- Location is not in a heavily traveled, traditional retail area.
- Challenges of the seasonality of the business.

2.3.4.3 Opportunities

- Growing market with a significant percentage of our target market still not knowing we exist.
- Continuing opportunity through strategic alliances for referrals and marketing activities.
- Benefiting from high levels of new home construction.
- Changes in design trends can initiate updating and therefore sales.
- Increasing sales opportunities beyond our "100-mile" target area.
- Internet potential for selling products to other markets.

2.3.4.4 Threats

- Competition from a national store; or a store with greater financing or product resources could enter the market.
- Catalog resources, including Calico Corners and Pottery Barn, are aggressively priced with comparable products.
- Continued price pressure, reducing contribution margins.
- Dramatic changes in design, including fabric colors and styles, create obsolete or less profitable inventory.

2.3.5 Historical Results

The following table shows estimated industry revenue as well as estimated market share, expenses, and net margin for Interior Views.

Table: Historical Data

Historical Data			
Variable	**2005**	**2006**	**2007**
Industry Revenue	$1,305,000	$1,650,000	$2,062,500
Company Market Share	11%	12%	13%
Company Revenue	$143,550	$198,000	$257,813
Industry Variable Costs	$717,750	$750,000	$1,179,750
Company Variable Costs	$78,953	$90,000	$147,505
Industry Gross Contribution Margin	$587,250	$900,000	$882,750
Company Gross Contribution Margin	$64,597	$108,000	$110,308
Marketing Expenses	$1,150	$12,560	$15,920
Company Net Contribution Margin	$63,447	$95,440	$94,388

2.4 Competition

Competition in the area of decorator fabric comes from three general categories: traditional fabric retail stores, catalog sales, and discounters. The other local fabric retailers are direct competition, but we have seen strong indirect competition from catalog sales and discounters.

2.4.1 Direct Competition

Retail Stores

Current local competition includes the following:

- **House of Fabrics** — Nationwide recognition and buying power of numerous types of dated fabric with strong product availability. This store has experienced financial difficulty in recent years and has closed several locations throughout the country.
- **Warehouse Fabrics** — Locally owned, offering low-cost products with a wide selection of discontinued fabrics and only a limited number of "current" fabrics. This warehouse concept offers marginal customer service with what many "upper end" customers consider to be an "undesirable" shopping environment.
- **JoAnn's** — Nationwide chain with strong buying power. They have a broad fabric selection for clothing with a limited number of in-store decorator fabrics available. Their primary target markets are the clothing seamstress, with an increasing emphasis on craft items.
- **Interior Designers** — Interior designers make profit off mark up of fabric in addition to their hourly services charges. Their costs per yard are typically higher since they do not benefit from retail or volume discounts. Therefore, their costs to their customer are often two to four times higher than the price per yard from Interior Views.
- **Website Providers** — Fabric sales over the Web are limited at this time, and this will be a source of competition for the future to watch. Currently, there is no measurable impact on our market through competitive websites.

Table: Growth and Share Analysis

Growth and Share

Competitor	Price	Growth Rate	Market Share
House of Fabrics	$80	5%	18%
Warehouse Fabrics	$75	8%	23%
JoAnn's Fabrics	$80	6%	16%
Interior Designers—Combined	$205	12%	25%
Interior Views	$135	25%	29%
Average	$115	11.20%	22.20%
Total	$575	56%	111%

Competitor by Growth and Share

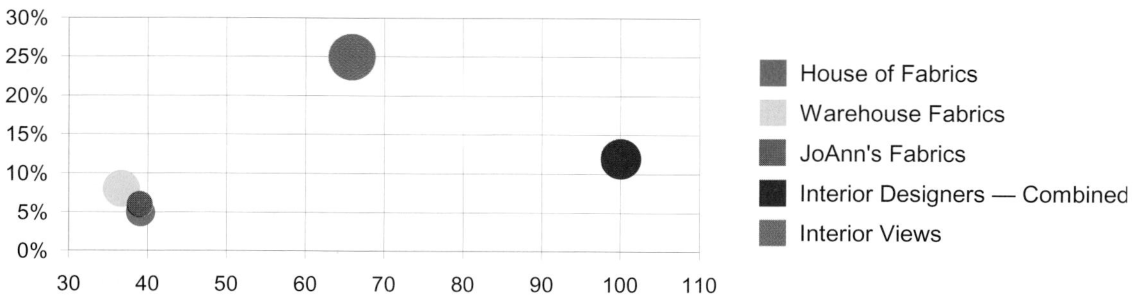

Table: Competitive Analysis

Competitive Analysis	#1	#2	#3	#4	#5
Competitor	House of Fabrics	Warehouse Fabrics	JoAnn's	Interior Designers	Interior Views
Product and/or Service	House of Fabrics	Warehouse Fabrics	JoAnn's	Interior Designers	Interior Views
Quality	7	8	6	2	6
Selection	6	7	3	1	8
Price	5	8	2	2	8
Other	0	0	0	0	0
Location and Physical Appearance	House of Fabrics	Warehouse Fabrics	JoAnn's	Interior Designers	Interior Views
Visibility	8	7	8	3	6
Convenience Factors	6	6	6	3	8
Other	0	0	0	0	0
Added Value Factors	House of Fabrics	Warehouse Fabrics	JoAnn's	Interior Designers	Interior Views
Pre and Post Sales Service	5	4	5	8	9
Experience	4	4	4	7	7
Expertise	6	5	6	9	8
Reputation	2	8	6	8	8
Image	3	3	3	6	8
Stability	0	0	0	0	0
Strategic Alliances	0	0	0	0	0
Other	0	0	0	0	0
Other Marketing Activities	House of Fabrics	Warehouse Fabrics	JoAnn's	Interior Designers	Interior Views
Established Sales Channels	6	6	4	3	6
Advertising	6	7	4	5	7
Post-Purchase Support	4	4	8	9	7
Incentives	4	5	2	1	8
Loyalty Components	6	5	2	1	8
Other	0	0	0	0	0
Total	78	87	69	68	112

2.4.2 Indirect Competition

Catalog Competitors

An increasing level of competition is anticipated from catalog sales. Recent trends, such as those demonstrated in the well-established but evolving catalog *Pottery Barn*, indicate increased interest in offering decorator fabric, window designs, and other home decorating products through this increasingly popular channel of distribution. Catalog sources do not offer customers the option to see, touch, and have the fabric in their homes. Price is the most significant competitive factor this product source presents. The most aggressive catalog competitor is *Calico Corners* followed by *Pottery Barn* and other home-accessory-based providers.

Discounters

Channels of distribution continue to shift in favor of discounters, who account for a significant portion of the growth in the industry. As consumers experience lower levels of disposable income, discounters leverage frequent store promotions to entice frugal, value-oriented consumers. One of the biggest criticism of discounters is their failure to offer a quality service experience and their failure to present inviting displays to promote sales. These discounters, along with specialty store chains, present one of the most severe competitive threats for individually owned specialty stores. This is partially due to extensive promotional efforts, price advantages, and established relationships with their vendors. One example of these discounters is the "home improvement" chains, such as Home Base. This aggressive retailer has adopted a strategy to include complete decorator departments in their metropolitan stores. Currently existing in the Los Angeles market, this strategy is anticipated to be introduced into the Seattle area and other select metropolitan markets within the year. Although the Boise Home Base store sells basic curtain rod hardware and other hard-cover window treatment, there are no known plans at this time for the Boise Home Base store to implement this in the foreseeable future. This will be an important issue to monitor for competitive purposes.

3.0 Marketing Strategy

This plan will further Interior Views' financial and marketing objectives:

Financial objectives: create sales growth of 12%, reduce existing credit line, and increase the average dollar amount per transaction

Marketing objectives: increase visibility of store for potential customers, and better retain existing customers

3.1 Value Proposition

Interior Views sells more than fabric: We sell a personalized and unique vision for your home. Interior Views helps you revive your home and your living experience.

3.2 Critical Issues

Interior Views is still in the "speculative" stage as a retail store. Its critical issues are:

- Relatively slow annual sales growth. With admirable results through the first 30 months of operation, the market continues to hold promise, but, as learned through the first two years of operation, it is still smaller than what it should be to support a store of this kind.
- Continue to take a fiscally conservative approach; downscale when necessary and modify our business model based on market response.

3.3 Financial Objectives

1. A growth rate in sales of 12% for the year 2008, to total in excess of $341,200 in total revenues.
2. An average sales per business day (305 days per year) in excess of $1,000.
3. Reduce the existing credit line by a minimum of $26,400.

3.4 Marketing Objectives

1. Maintain a gross margin of 45% each month.
2. Generate an average of $1,000 of sales each business day each month.
3. Experience a $5,000 increase in quarterly sales with each newsletter.
4. Realize an annual growth rate of approximately 25% in the year 2008.

3.5 Target Market Strategy

The target markets are separated into four segments; "Country Club Women," "Boomers in Transition," "Professional Youngsters," and "Home Builders." The primary marketing opportunity is selling to these well-defined and accessible target market segments that focus on investing discretionary income in these areas:

Country Club Women—The most dominant segment of the four is composed of women in the age range of 35 to 50. They are married, have a combined income of greater than $80,000, own at least one home or condominium, and are socially active at and away from home. They are members of the Boise Country Club, the Downtown Athletic Club, the Junior League of Boise, AAUW, and/or the Doctor Wives Auxiliary. They have discretionary income, and their home and how it looks are priorities. The appearance of where they live communicates who they are and what is important to them. This group represents the largest collection of "Martha Stewart Wanna Be's," with their profile echoing readers of *Martha Stewart Living* magazine, based on the current demographics described in the *Martha Stewart Living Media Kit.*

Boomers in Transition—This group, typically ranging in age from 50 to 65, is going through a positive and planned life transition. They are changing homes (either building or moving) or remodeling due to empty nest syndrome, retirement plans, general downsizing desires, or to just get closer to the golf course. Their surprisingly high level of discretionary income is first spent on travel, with decorating their home a close second. The woman of the couple is the decision maker and often does not always include the husband in the selection or purchase process.

Professional Youngsters—Couples between the ages of 25 and 35 establishing their first "adult" household fall into this group. They both work, earn in excess of $50,000 annually, and now want to invest in their home. They seek to enjoy their home and communicate a "successful" image and message to their contemporaries. They buy big when they have received a promotion, a bonus, or an inheritance.

Home Builders—People in the building process, typically ranging in age from 40 to 60, are prime candidates for Interior Views.

3.6 Messaging

Interior Views can help you create the personalized and unique vision you have for your home, with the best local source for fabric selection and price, customer-oriented design services, and a variety of other home accessory and furniture products. Revive your home today!

3.6.1 Branding

Our name is our brand. "Interior Views" represents our mission of celebrating the home through the color and texture of fabric. The brand invokes the fact that the home should be a unique and personalized expression of the person living there. The home is a "view" of the home's owner. The word "view" also evokes the vision of what a home owner wants their home to be.

In addition to our name, our logo reflects the architectural quality of the work that we do. Our products are more than just decoration; they enhance and reflect the home itself.

Table: Target Market Messaging

Target Market Messaging

Market Segments	Messaging
Country Club Women	Make your home new again
Boomers in Transition	It's time for a new look
Professional Youngsters	It's your first home—make it yours
Home Builders	Presentation is everything

3.7 Strategy Pyramids

The single objective is to position Interior Views as the premier source for home decorator fabrics in the Greater Boise area, commanding a majority of the market share within six years of being founded. The marketing strategy will seek to first create customer awareness regarding the products and services offered, develop that customer base, establish connections with targeted markets, and work toward building customer loyalty and referrals.

Interior Views' four main marketing strategies are:

1. Increased awareness and image.
2. Leveraging existing customer base.
3. Cross selling.
4. New home construction promotion.

The following Strategy Pyramid charts show the specific tactics and programs planned to achieve each planned strategy.

Strategy Pyramid: Increase Awareness/Image

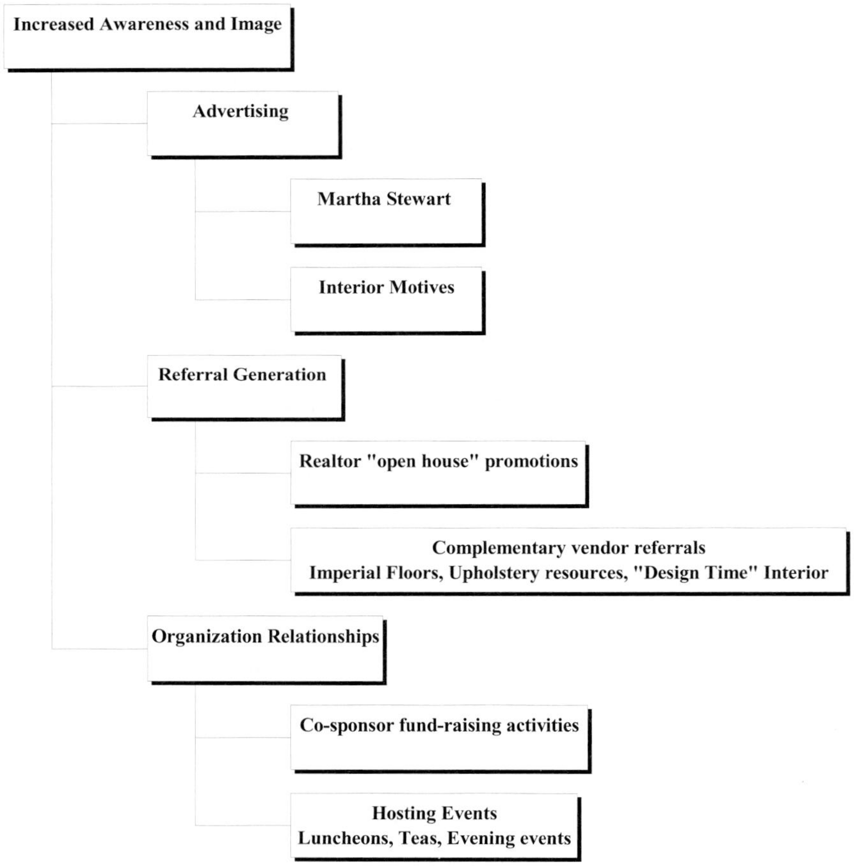

Strategy Pyramid: Leveraging Existing Customer Base

- **Leveraging Existing Customer Base**
  - **Newsletter**
    - **Sales promotions**
    - **Classes**
    - **Events**
  - **Customer Service Relationships (CRM)**
    - **Exceptional customer service in store**
    - **Follow-up contact**
    - **Personal shopper support**
  - **Additional Experiences**
    - **Classes**
    - **Demonstrations**

Strategy Pyramid: Cross Selling

- **Cross Selling**
  - **Internal**
    - **Additional sales of trims, notions, and accessories**
    - **Promoting sales of furniture; Chameleon and Scottie Mac lines**
  - **Sub-Lease Sales**
    - **Antiques through "Antique Bureau"**
    - **Accessories through "The Window Seat"**

Strategy Pyramid: New Home Construction Promotion

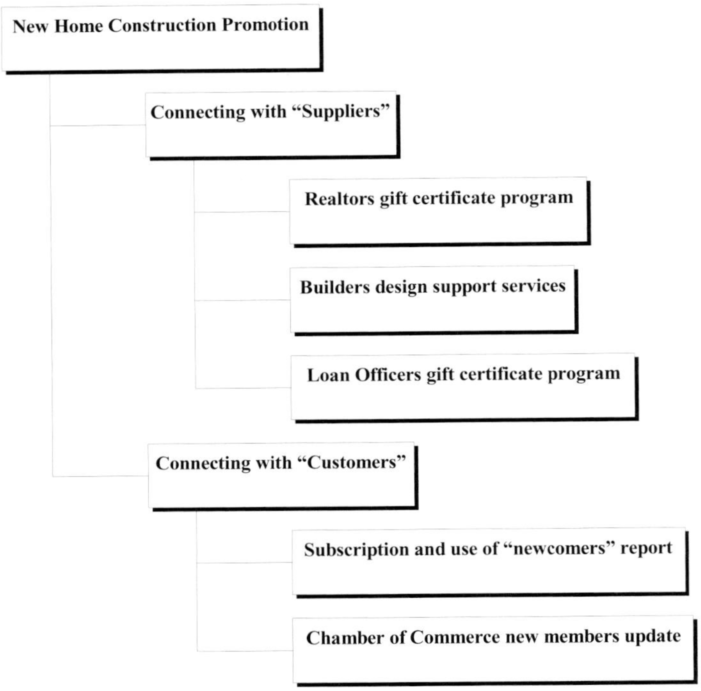

4.0 Marketing Mix

In brief, our marketing mix comprises of these approaches to pricing, distribution, advertising and promotion, and customer service.

Pricing — A keystone pricing formula plus $3.00 will be applied for most fabrics. The goal is to have price points within 5% of the list price of Calico Corners' retail prices. This insures competitive pricing and strong margins.

Distribution — All product is distributed through the retail store. The store does receive phone orders from established customers and we will be developing a website.

Advertising and Promotion — The most successful advertising has been through the *Boise Herald* and through ads on *Martha Stewart* and *Interior Motives* television shows. The quarterly newsletter has also proven to be an excellent method to connect with the existing customer base, now with a mailing list of 4,300 people.

Customer Service —Excellent, personalized, fun, one-of-a-kind customer service is essential. This is perhaps the only attribute that cannot be duplicated by any competitor.

4.1 Product Marketing

Our products enable our customers to experience support, gather ideas and options, and accomplish their decorating goals. They will be able to create a look that is truly unique to their home. They will not be able to do this in the same way through any other resource.

4.2 Pricing

Product pricing is based on offering high value to our customers compared to most price points in the market. Value is determined based on the best quality available, convenience, and timeliness in acquiring the product. We will consistently be below the price points offered through interior designers and consistently above prices offered through the warehouse/seconds retail stores, but we will offer better quality and selection.

4.3 Promotion

Our most successful advertising and promotion in the past has been through the following:

- **Newspaper Advertisements** — *Boise Herald.*
- **Television Advertisements** — *Martha Stewart* and *Interior Motives* television shows.
- **Quarterly Newsletter and Postcard** — A direct mail, 4-page newsletter distributed to the customer mailing list generated from people completing the "register" sign-up in the store. The mailing list now totals more than 4,300 people.
- **In Store Classes** — "How to" classes, most of which are free, have been successful because of the traffic and sales they generate after the class. Typically 90 minutes in length and most held on Saturday, these are the most popular classes:
  - "Pillow Talk" — Pillow fabrication.
  - "Speaking of Slip Covers" — Slip cover presentation and discussion.
  - "Shades of the Season" — Window treatment options with fabric.

4.3.1 Advertising

Expand newspaper advertisements to surrounding towns, and buy two half-page ads every month. Continue television ads.

Table: Advertising Milestones

Milestones					
Advertising	**Start Date**	**End Date**	**Budget**	**Manager**	**Department**
Television Campaign 1	1/1/2008	1/30/2008	$780	Julie	New
Television Campaign 2	9/1/2008	12/31/2009	$3,120	Julie	New
Total Advertising Budget			$3,900		

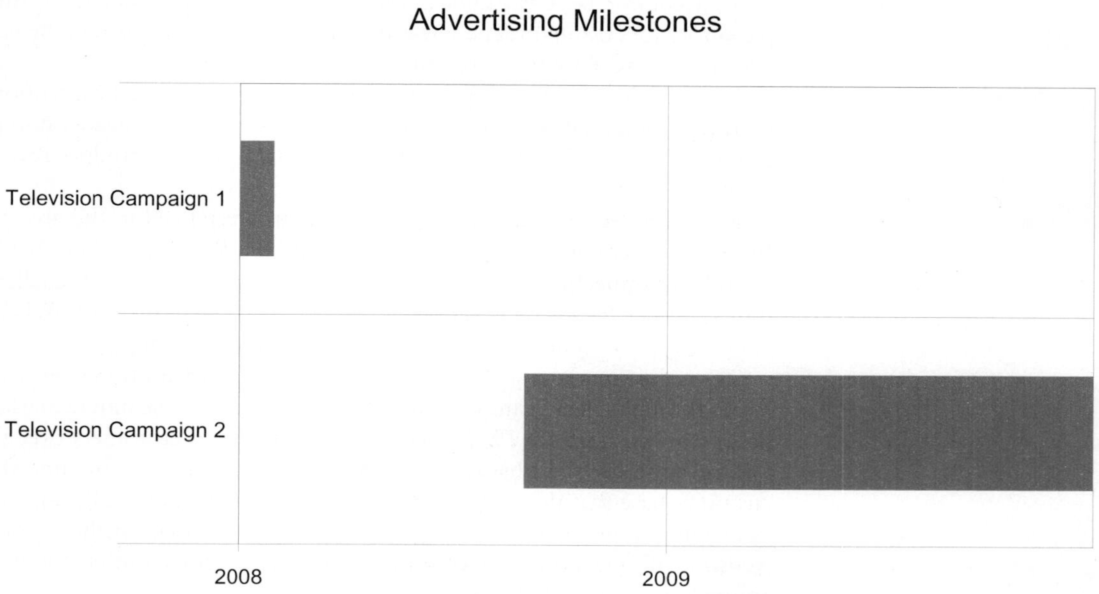

4.3.2 Public Relations

Our public relations plan is to pitch a twice-monthly column in the "Home" section of the local paper, covering our in-store classes, with profiles of our customers and their redecorated rooms. Readers will see how our classes directly relate to individual decorating projects.

Table: PR Milestones

Milestones					
PR	**Start Date**	**End Date**	**Budget**	**Manager**	**Department**
Event: Realtor Promotion	2/1/2008	2/28/2008	$400	Julie	New
Event: Junior League	5/1/2008	5/31/2008	$400	Kandi	New
Event: For the Arts	9/1/2008	9/30/2008	$400	Pat	New
Event: Relief Nursery	11/1/2008	11/25/2008	$400	Jo	New
Total PR Budget			$1,600		

4.3.3 Direct Marketing

Improve the quality of the newsletter, increase the number of one-time customers who sign up for it, and offer an email-newsletter option to catch the more tech-savvy customers.

Table: Direct Marketing Milestones

Milestones					
Direct Marketing	**Start Date**	**End Date**	**Budget**	**Manager**	**Department**
Newsletter Q1	12/1/2007	1/2/2008	$1,350	Judy	Existing
Newsletter Q2	2/15/2008	3/15/2008	$1,400	Judy	Existing
Newsletter Q3	6/1/2008	6/30/2008	$1,450	Judy	Existing
Newsletter Q4	9/1/2008	9/30/2008	$1,500	Judy	Existing
Postcard	11/15/2008	12/5/2008	$750	Judy	Existing
Total Direct Marketing Budget			$6,450		

4.4 Web Plan

Interior Views is a retailer of home decorator fabrics and complementary home accessories now in its fourth year. This destination store offers the advantages of providing fabrics specifically designed for home decorator use. Over 1,000 fabrics are available on the floor at any time with more than 8,000 sample fabrics for custom orders. The goal of this Web plan is to extend the reach of the store to others outside the area and add to the revenue base.

Interior Views currently has a website but has not given it the attention or focus needed to assess its marketing potential. The site offers basic functions and we consider it to be a crude version of what we can imagine it will become through a site redesign that will produce revenue and enhance the image of the business.

Market research indicates a specific and growing need in the area for the products and services Interior Views offers in the market it serves and there are indications that Web sales will play an increasing role in connecting customers with sellers. The most significant challenge is that the core target customer, women between the ages of 35 and 50, are some of the least likely of groups to shop on the Web. Shopping for decorator fabric presents an additional challenge.

The online marketing objective is to actively support continued growth and profitability of Interior Views through effective implementation of the strategy. The online marketing and sales strategy will be based on a cost-effective approach to reach additional customers over the Web to generate attention and revenue for the business. The Web target groups will include the more Web-savvy younger customer base that the store currently serves (women between the ages of 25 and 35) and out-of-area potential customers that are already shopping on the Web for the products Interior Views offers. The website will focus on its selection, competitive pricing, and customer service to differentiate itself among other Internet options.

Interior Views' website is for the person who wants her home to be an individual expression of who she is. Unlike other online fabric sites, Interior Views will provide these customers with first quality decorator fabric selections and complementary products to decorate their homes, as well as intelligent and helpful customer service and support for each sale. Interior Views is a pleasant and tasteful resource that encourages everyone in the process of decorating their home, allows the individual to participate in their design choices to the extent they choose, and offers greater value for the dollars they invest.

4.4.1 Website Goals

Our website will generate revenue through initiating product sales to the targeted audience that we would not have realized through the retail store. It will be measured on the basis of revenue generated each month compared to our stated objective. On a secondary basis, we will also measure and track traffic to the site and document what activities that traffic contributes to the other objectives of the site, including sales leads and information dissemination.

Objectives

- Increase revenues through Web-based sales by $2,400 per month with a 5% growth rate thereafter.
- Enhancing "information channels" with the established customer base to provide additional options to receive information from the store.
- Meet the needs of customers outside the immediate serving area through Web accessibility.

Future Development

The objectives of the site redesign will include:

- Increased speed.
- Enhanced navigation.
- Additional products added to the decorator fabric selections including "Oval Office Iron" hardware and select home accessories.

4.4.2 Website Marketing Strategy

Our website strategy will be to reach these key groups listed in order of importance based on their expected use and purchases from the site.

- **Professional Youngsters**—Expected to be the most likely of the targeted segments to use this resource because of their relatively high Internet use compared to the other segments. This group should offer the greatest online revenue opportunity.
- **Outsiders**—Comprising people outside the area with Internet access who have come in contact with the physical store or learned of it though a referral or promotion. This group, most commonly located in rural areas of the Western U.S. and Hawaii, is expected to be a small but faithful sector of buyers.
- **Online Fabric Shoppers**—Most often find the site through search engines and these online decorator fabric shoppers are browsing multiple sites for a best buy or access to discontinued and hard-to-find fabric. They hold potential, but are typically the most work for the lowest return.
- **Internet Learners**—Represents all of the targeted segments that are just beginning to become familiar with the site and will increase their use of the Internet over time. Revenue expectations from this group are low at this point and it is viewed as an investment in the future.

The online strategy supports the objective to position Interior Views as a preferred source for home decorator fabrics on the Web as we maintain the position of being considered the premier source in the geographic area of the store. The online sales strategy seeks to, first, inform visitors about the site and create a positive awareness regarding the products offered; second, provide successful purchasing experiences and establish connections with targeted markets; and third, work toward building customer loyalty and referrals.

The online sales approach will accomplish these four objectives:

1. Increased overall awareness and image.
2. Meet the online interests and needs of the existing customer base.
3. Expand the total out-of-area customer population.
4. Exploit upsell and cross-sell opportunities.

Strategy #1—Increasing Awareness and Image

Informing those not yet aware of what Interior Views offers.

- Search engine presence.
- Leveraging the newsletter and mailing programs.

Strategy #2—Leveraging Existing Internet-Savvy Customers

Our best sales in the future will come from our current customer base.

- Newsletter information.
- Web-only promotions.

Strategy #3—Upselling and Cross-Selling Activities

Increasing the average dollar amount per transaction.

- Additional and complementary fabric.
- Other product sales:
  - Additional sales of trims, notions, and accessories.
  - Promoting sales of furniture.

4.4.3 Development Requirements

Once we have determined the general look and navigation of the new site, we will accomplish the following tasks:

- Define initial site layout and general design characteristics;
- Fabric selection for site; and
- Product selection including decisions about "Oval Office Iron" and lighting products.

Front End

We currently have the basic elements of the site in place at www.fabric-online.com. It possesses some of the functional components that we want to keep including:

- A URL that is not ideal, but tolerable.
- Identifiable home page.
- The ability to select and view the most popular fabrics.
- Newsletter access.
- Contact information.

A sign redesign is desperately needed to attract additional traffic, support easier and quicker navigation, and hopefully result in increased sales. We are not satisfied with these components of the site:

- Graphic design characteristics—the look and feel of the site is dated and "amateurish."
- Speed—the site is slow in areas where we can speed the process.
- Basic navigation through the site—a consistent method to move throughout the site.
- The addition of other products including "Oval Office Iron" hardware and select home accessories.

Back End

Our back-end features should include the following:

1. Web hosting with 98% uptime through the local provider.
2. Statistics to determine page views, unique users, banner impressions, sponsorship impressions, and clickthroughs.
3. The ability to enable visitors to gain easy access to product information, visuals, newsletter information, and a robust email system.

Resource Requirements

The site has been, and will continue to be, supported through a local Internet provider and the consultant whom we have been working with. We have found that experience to be relatively economical and he has been highly responsive to our need. Employees do not have the expertise to do much more than respond to emails and check the status of the site, so this has been a good complement to what time and resource limitations impose.

The monthly budget, including Internet access, is $65.00 in addition to hourly consulting rates for redesign work and fabric scanning.

Table: Pay-Per-Click ROAS

Pay-Per-Click ROAS

Network	Monthly Cost	Clicks	Leads Generated	Orders	Monthly Revenue	ROAS	Cost-per-click	Cost-per-lead
Google	$2,000	4000	100	30	$3,000	150%	$0.50	$20.00
Yahoo!	$1,250	2000	45	14	$1,400	112%	$0.63	$27.78
Total	$3,250	6000	145	44	$4,400	131%	$0.56	$23.89

Table: Website Milestones

Milestones

Web Development	Start Date	End Date	Budget	Manager	Department
Site Redesign Plan	1/1/2008	1/15/2008	$1,200	Julie	New
Source Designers	1/1/2008	1/15/2008	$1,200	Julie	New
Other	1/1/2008	1/15/2008	$0	Julie	New
Total Web Development Budget			$2,400		

4.5 Service

The first goal is to recognize everyone as they come into the store. If they are a repeat customer, they are referred to by name. If they are a new customer, they are asked, "How did you hear about us?" Help is always available and never invasive. The store is staffed to be able to dedicate time and energy to customers who want assistance when they need it. The store is designed so a customer can sit as long as they want to look at books, fabric samples, and review the resources in the store. Their children are also welcome, with a television, VCR, and toys available in the childrens' area in clear view of the resource center. We provide service in a way that no other competitive retail store can touch. It is one of our greatest assets and points of differentiation. Insight, ideas, inspiration, and fun is the goal. Repeat, high dollar purchases from loyal customers are the desired end product.

4.6 Implementation Schedule

The following identifies the key activities that are critical to our marketing plan. It is important to accomplish each one on time and on budget.

Table: Marketing Milestones

Marketing Milestones					
Advertising	Start Date	End Date	Budget	Manager	Department
Media Campaign 1	1/1/2008	1/30/2008	$780	Julie	New
Media Campaign 2	9/1/2008	12/31/2009	$3,120	Julie	New
Total Advertising Budget			$3,900		
PR	Start Date	End Date	Budget	Manager	Department
PR: Realtor Promotion	2/1/2008	5/28/2008	$400	Julie	New
PR: Junior League	5/1/2008	5/31/2008	$400	Kandi	New
PR: For the Arts	9/1/2008	9/30/2008	$400	Pat	New
PR: Relief Nursery	11/1/2008	11/25/2008	$400	Jo	New
Total PR Budget			$1,600		
Direct Marketing	Start Date	End Date	Budget	Manager	Department
Newsletter Q1	12/1/2007	1/2/2008	$1,350	Judy	Existing
Newsletter Q2	2/15/2008	3/15/2008	$1,400	Judy	Existing
Newsletter Q3	6/1/2008	6/30/2008	$1,450	Judy	Existing
Newsletter Q4	9/1/2008	9/30/2008	$1,500	Judy	Existing
Postcard	11/15/2008	12/5/2008	$750	Judy	Existing
Total Direct Marketing Budget			$6,450		
Web Development	Start Date	End Date	Budget	Manager	Department
Site Redesign Plan	1/1/2008	1/15/2008	$1,200	Julie	New
Source Designers	1/1/2008	1/15/2008	$1,200	Julie	New
Other	1/1/2008	1/15/2008	$0	Julie	New
Total Web Development Budget			$2,400		
Total Other Budget			$0		
Totals			$14,350		

5.0 Financials

Our marketing strategy is based on becoming the resource of choice for people looking for decorator fabrics, do-it-yourself, and buy-it-yourself resources to create a look in their home. Our marketing strategy is based on superior performance in the following areas:

- Product selection.
- Product quality.
- Customer service.

Our marketing strategy will create awareness, interest, and appeal from our target market for what Interior Views offers our customers.

This section will offer a financial overview of Interior Views as it relates to our marketing activities. We will address break-even information, sales forecasts, expense forecasts, and how those link to our marketing strategy.

5.1 Break-Even Analysis

The break-even analysis below illustrates the number of single sales, or units, that we must realize to break even. This is based on average sale and costs per transaction.

Table: Fixed Costs

Fixed Costs	
Cost	
Utilities	$400
Web Site Hosting	$200
Recuring Marketing Expenses	$1,200
Payroll	$6,000
Rent	$1,500
Total Fixed Costs	$9,300

Table: Break-Even Analysis

Break-Even Analysis	
Monthly Revenue Break-even	$20,427
Assumptions:	
Average Percent Variable Cost	54%
Estimated Monthly Fixed Cost	$9,300

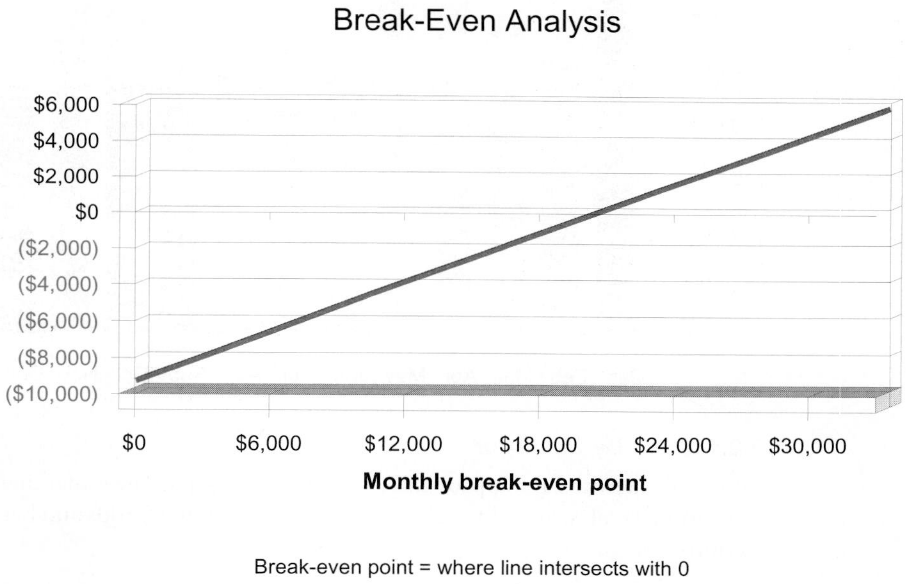

5.2 Sales Forecast

The sales forecast is broken down into the four main revenue streams: direct sales, Web sales, consignment sales, and sub-lease revenues. The sales forecast for the upcoming year is based on a 25% growth rate. This is a slower growth rate than what was experienced in previous years at 33%, and also less than what is expected for future sales, estimated to be approximately 28%. These projections appear attainable and take the increasing base into consideration. Future growth rates are based on percentage increases as follows:

- Direct Sales 20% growth rate per year.
- Web Sales 50% growth rate per year.
- Consignment Sales 20% growth rate per year.
- Sub-lease Revenues 10% growth rate per year.

Table: Sales Forecast

Sales Forecast					
Sales	**2008**	**2009**	**2010**	**2011**	**2012**
Direct Sales	$322,000	$386,400	$463,700	$556,400	$667,700
Web Sales	$12,500	$18,750	$28,125	$42,190	$63,280
Consignment Sales	$1,360	$1,632	$1,960	$2,350	$2,820
Sub-Lease Revenue	$5,340	$5,600	$6,165	$6,780	$7,460
Total Sales	$341,200	$412,382	$499,950	$607,720	$741,260
Direct Cost of Sales					
Direct Sales	$178,850	$214,000	$255,500	$307,000	$370,000
Web Sales	$6,875	$10,400	$12,000	$18,000	$20,000
Consignment Sales	$71	$85	$102	$123	$150
Sub-Lease Revenue	$60	$66	$73	$80	$88
Subtotal Direct Cost of Sales	$185,856	$224,551	$267,675	$325,203	$390,238

Sales Monthly

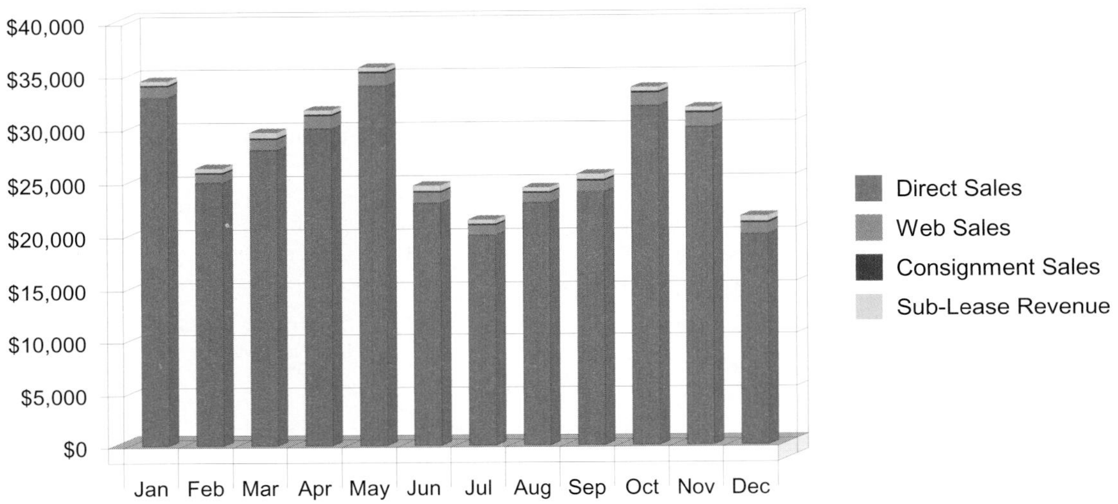

5.2.1 Sales by Manager

Fabric sales account for approximately 74% of total sales. The remaining sales result from complementary products sales, including trims, tassels, pillows, drapery rods and hardware, books, and upholstered furniture.

Table: Sales Breakdown by Manager

Sales by: Manager					
Sales	**2008**	**2009**	**2010**	**2011**	**2012**
Drapery Weight	$53,633	$65,351	$79,298	$96,470	$117,762
Upholstery Weight	$26,815	$32,675	$39,649	$48,235	$58,881
Mixed	$100,566	$122,533	$148,683	$180,882	$220,803
Special Order	$67,040	$81,688	$99,122	$120,588	$147,202
Other	$93,146	$110,135	$133,198	$161,545	$196,612
Total	$341,200	$412,382	$499,950	$607,720	$741,260
Average	$68,240	$82,476	$99,990	$121,544	$148,252

Sales Breakdown by Manager Monthly

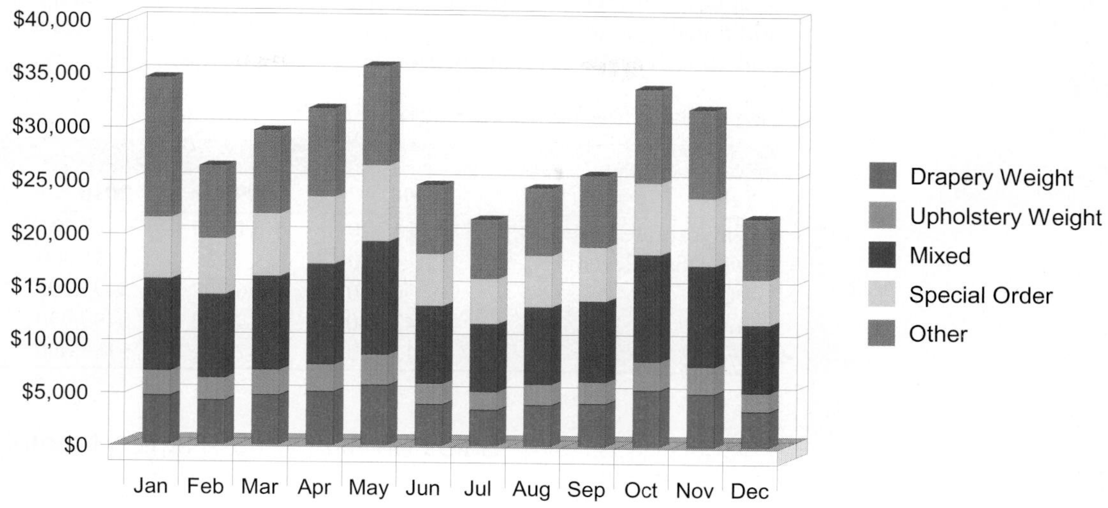

5.2.2 Sales by Segment

Consignment sales account for a relatively small portion of total sales and are primarily supported to create a better feel and look for the store. This is an area that does provide useful information feedback regarding other possible product sales the store may want to sell in the future.

Table: Sales Breakdown by Segment

Sales by: Segment					
Sales	**2008**	**2009**	**2010**	**2011**	**2012**
"The Window Seat"	$11,732	$14,295	$17,346	$21,103	$25,760
Antiques	$26,815	$32,675	$39,675	$48,235	$58,881
Other	$302,653	$365,412	$442,929	$538,382	$656,619
Total	$341,200	$412,382	$499,950	$607,720	$741,260
Average	$113,733	$137,461	$166,650	$202,573	$247,087

Sales Breakdown by Segment Monthly

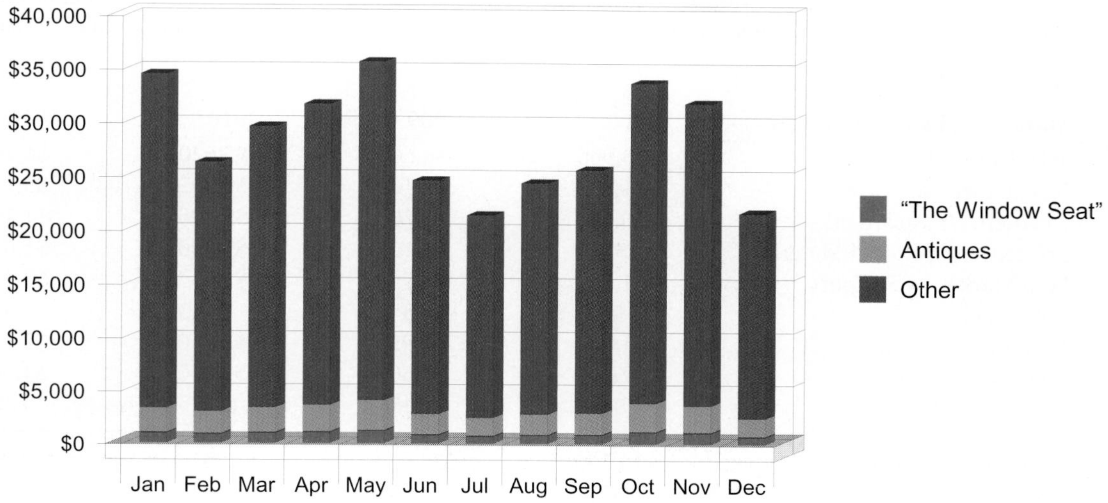

5.2.3 Sales by Region

The Antique Bureau sub-leases approximately 450 square feet. This store offers a selection of authentic antiques. It attracts additional customers and provides revenue for space that is currently unused. Two additional areas are available. The "conference room" space is available for special events, and the second office is available for an interior designer to sub-lease.

Table: Sales Breakdown by Region

Sales by: Region					
Sales	**2008**	**2009**	**2010**	**2011**	**2012**
The Antique Bureau	$4,320	$4,750	$5,225	$5,750	$6,325
Event/Sale Revenue	$840	$925	$1,020	$1,120	$1,230
Other	$336,040	$406,707	$493,705	$600,850	$733,705
Total	$341,200	$412,382	$499,950	$607,720	$741,260
Average	$113,733	$137,461	$166,650	$202,573	$247,087

Sales Breakdown by Region Monthly

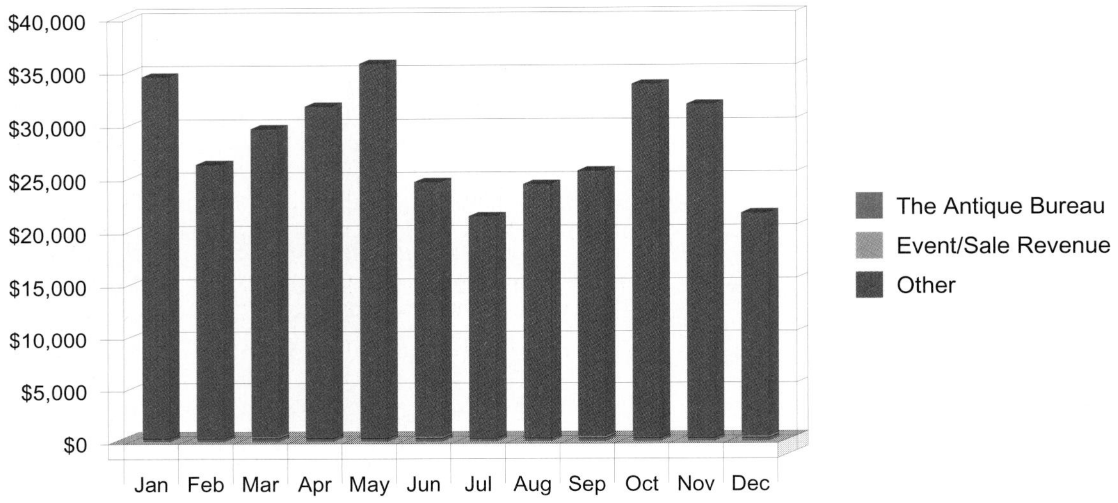

5.3 Expense Forecast

Marketing expenses are to be budgeted at approximately 5% of total sales. Expenses are tracked in the major marketing categories of television advertisements, newspaper advertisements, the newsletter and postcard mailings, Web marketing support, printed promotional materials, public relations, and other.

Table: Marketing Expense Budget

Marketing Expense Budget	**2008**	**2009**	**2010**	**2011**	**2012**
Television Ads	$3,900	$4,600	$5,620	$6,740	$8,200
Newspaper Ads	$1,800	$2,160	$2,592	$3,110	$3,800
Newsletter/Postcard	$6,450	$7,700	$9,200	$11,150	$13,400
Printed Promotional Materials	$960	$1,150	$1,380	$1,660	$2,000
Web Marketing/Support	$1,500	$1,950	$2,535	$3,295	$4,300
Public Relations	$240	$345	$415	$500	$600
Promotional Events	$1,700	$1,950	$2,300	$2,800	$3,400
Website Expenses	$2,400	$2,600	$2,800	$3,000	$3,000
Other	$400	$480	$575	$700	$850
Total Sales and Marketing Expenses	$19,350	$22,935	$27,417	$32,955	$39,550
Percentage of Sales	5.67%	5.56%	5.48%	5.42%	5.34%

Monthly Expense Budget

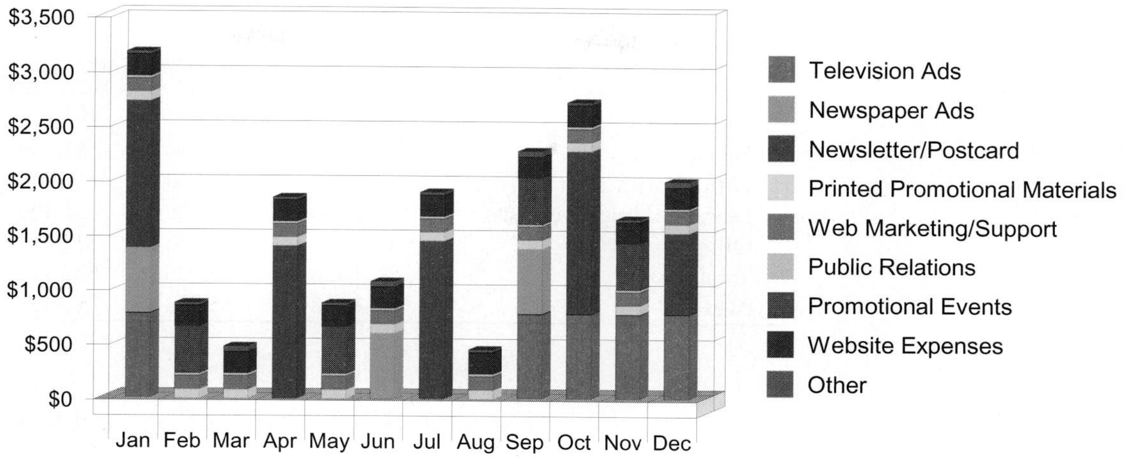

5.3.1 Expense by Manager

Marketing expenses are evenly allocated based on the type of inventory in the store.

Table: Expense Breakdown by Manager

Expenses by: Manager					
Expenses	**2008**	**2009**	**2010**	**2011**	**2012**
Drapery Weight	$2,546	$3,268	$3,965	$4,824	$5,888
Upholstery Weight	$1,265	$1,634	$1,982	$2,412	$2,944
Mixed	$2,230	$5,100	$6,400	$8,000	$9,000
Other	$13,309	$12,933	$15,070	$17,719	$21,718
Total	$19,350	$22,935	$27,417	$32,955	$39,550
Average	$4,838	$5,734	$6,854	$8,239	$9,888

Expense Breakdown by Manager Monthly

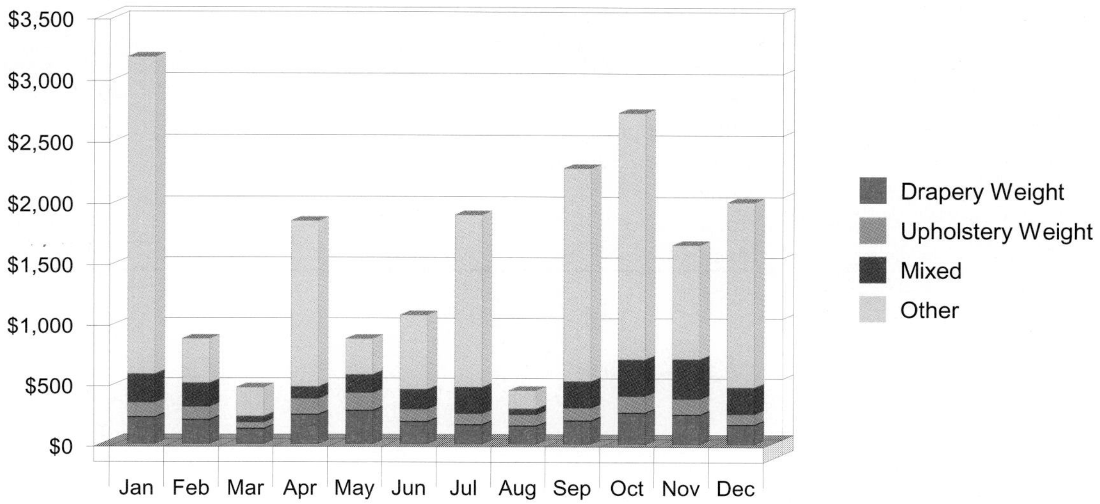

5.3.2 Expense by Segment

Fixtures and in-store improvements are important for us to track and allow us to better understand how we are using the space allocated.

Table: Expense Breakdown by Segment

Expenses by: Segment					
Expenses	**2008**	**2009**	**2010**	**2011**	**2012**
Fabric Racks	$1,200	$1,400	$1,500	$1,600	$1,700
Office Furniture	$600	$800	$900	$1,000	$1,100
Leasehold Improvements	$1,000	$1,200	$1,400	$1,600	$1,800
Other	$16,550	$19,535	$23,617	$28,755	$34,950
Total	$19,350	$22,935	$27,417	$32,955	$39,550
Average	$4,838	$5,734	$6,854	$8,239	$9,888

Expense Breakdown by Segment Monthly

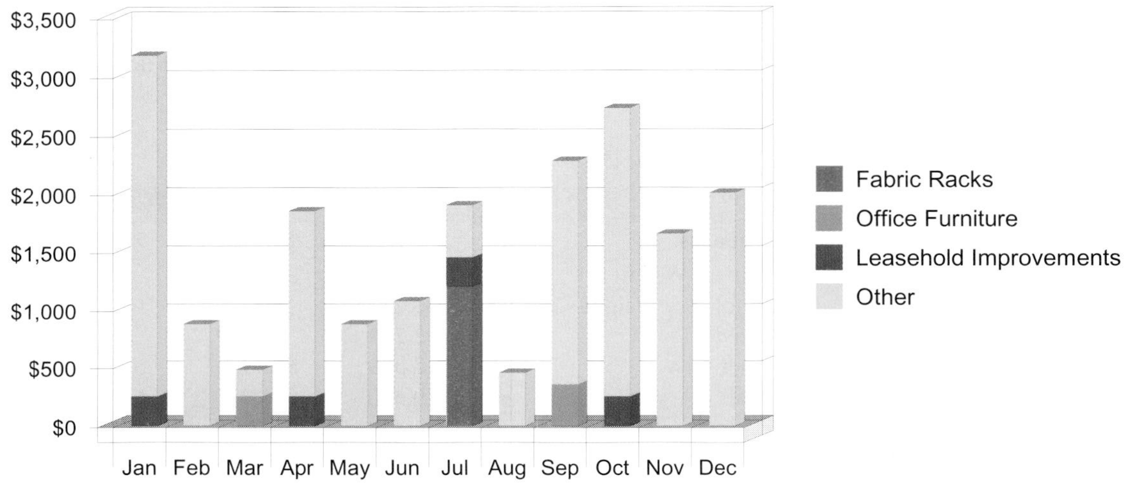

5.3.3 Expense by Region

Supplies are one of the more controllable expenses and will be important to monitor as we grow.

Table: Expense Breakdown by Region

Expenses by: Region					
Expenses	**2008**	**2009**	**2010**	**2011**	**2012**
Office Supplies	$420	$480	$540	$600	$660
Fabrication Supplies	$300	$340	$380	$420	$460
Other	$18,630	$22,115	$26,497	$31,935	$38,430
Total	$19,350	$22,935	$27,417	$32,955	$39,550
Average	$6,450	$7,645	$9,139	$10,985	$13,183

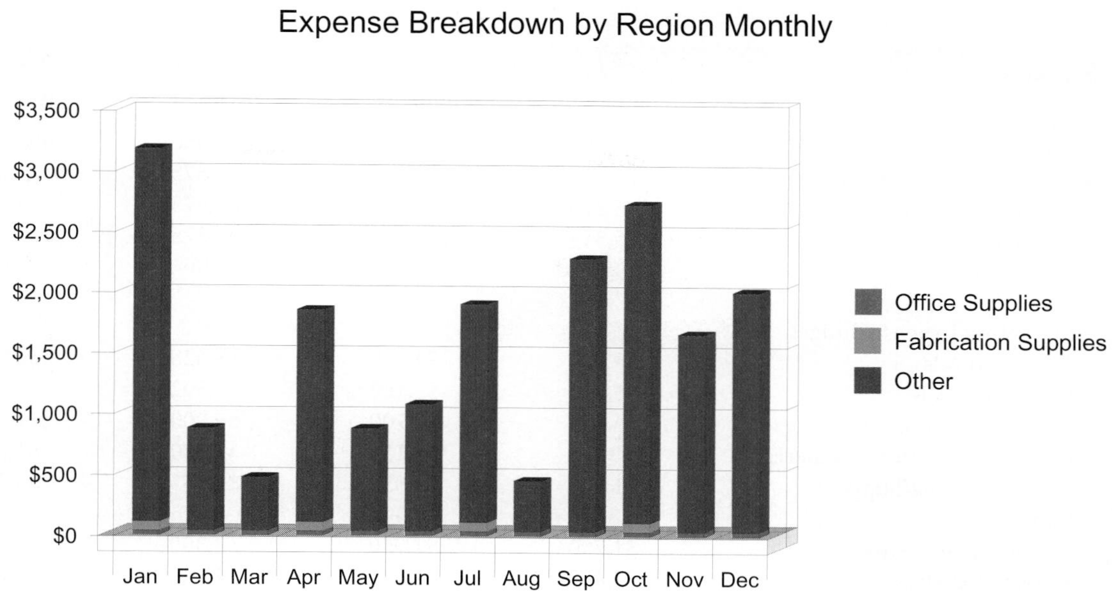

5.4 Linking Expenses to Strategy and Tactics

Our marketing expenses are allocated based on this prioritized approach:

1. Invest in our current customer base—60%.
2. Invest in prospective customers who match our known profile—30%.
3. Invest in creating greater awareness in the community—10%.

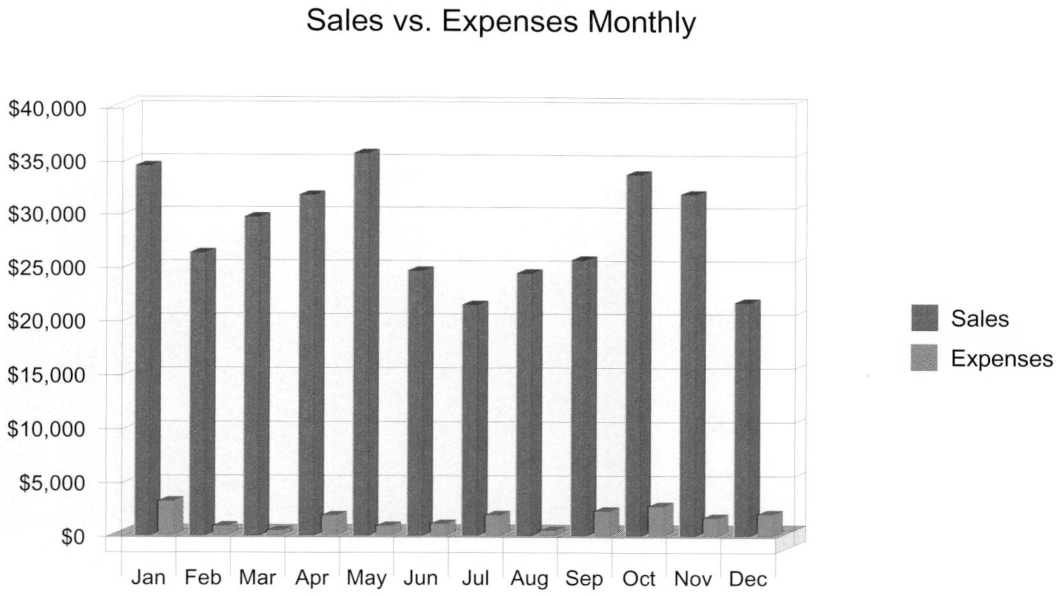

5.5 Contribution Margin

A key component of our marketing plan is to try and keep gross margins at or above 45%.

Table: Contribution Margin

Contribution Margin	2008	2009	2010	2011	2012
Sales	$341,200	$412,382	$499,950	$607,720	$741,260
Direct Costs of Goods	$185,856	$224,551	$267,675	$325,203	$390,238
Cost of Goods Sold	$185,856	$224,551	$267,675	$325,203	$390,238
Gross Margin	$155,344	$187,831	$232,275	$282,517	$351,022
Gross Margin %	45.53%	45.55%	46.46%	46.49%	47.35%
Marketing Expense Budget					
Television Ads	$3,900	$4,600	$5,620	$6,740	$8,200
Newspaper Ads	$1,800	$2,160	$2,592	$3,110	$3,800
Newsletter/Postcard	$6,450	$7,700	$9,200	$11,150	$13,400
Printed Promotional Materials	$960	$1,150	$1,380	$1,660	$2,000
Web Marketing/Support	$1,500	$1,950	$2,535	$3,295	$4,300
Public Relations	$240	$345	$415	$500	$600
Promotional Events	$1,700	$1,950	$2,300	$2,800	$3,400
Website Expenses	$2,400	$2,600	$2,800	$3,000	$3,000
Other	$400	$480	$575	$700	$850
Total Sales and Marketing Expenses	$19,350	$22,935	$27,417	$32,955	$39,550
Percentage of Sales	5.67%	5.56%	5.48%	5.42%	5.34%
Contribution Margin	$135,994	$164,896	$204,858	$249,562	$311,472
Contribution Margin / Sales	39.86%	39.99%	40.98%	41.07%	42.02%

Contribution Margin Monthly

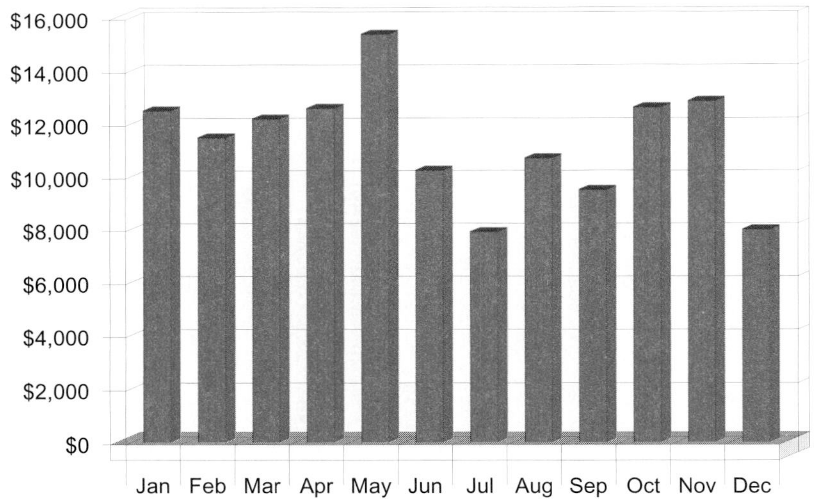

6.0 Controls

The following will enable us to keep on track. If we fail in any of these areas, we will need to reevaluate our business model:

- Gross margins at or above 45%.
- Month-to-month annual comparisons indicate an increase of 20% or greater.
- Do not depend on the credit line to meet cash requirements.
- Continue to pay down the credit line at a minimum of $24,000 per year.

6.1 Implementation

We will manage implementation by having a weekly milestones meeting with the entire staff to make sure that we are on track with our milestones and re-adjust our goals as we gather new data.

Once a quarter, we will review this marketing plan to ensure that we stay focused on our marketing strategy and that we are not distracted by opportunities simply because they are different than what we are currently pursuing.

Table: ROI Calculator

Return on Investment (ROI)				
Campaign Details	**Television**	**Events**	**Online Advertising**	**Radio**
Total Impressions	200,000	300	6,000	75,000
Total Program Cost	$15,000.00	$800.00	$3,250.00	$4,000.00
Response Rate	0.75%	15%	5%	1%
Conversion Rate	30%	40%	3%	20%
Average Customer Purchase	$85.00	$124.00	$800.00	$65.00
Response				
Total Responders	1,500	45	300	750
Total Buyers	450	18	9	150
Revenue Generated	$38,250.00	$2,232.00	$7,200.00	$9,750.00
Costs				
Cost per Response	$10.00	$17.78	$10.83	$5.33
Cost per Sale	$33.33	$44.44	$361.11	$26.67
Total Campaign Profit	$23,250.00	$1,432.00	$3,950.00	$5,750.00
Marketing ROI	155%	179%	121.54%	143.75%

Table: Customer Lifetime Value

Customer Lifetime Value		
Customer Purchase Forecast:		
Average Customer Lifetime (years):		5
Average number of purchases per year:		2
Average purchase value:		$100.00
Average Gross Margin %:	70%	
Gross Margin per purchase		$70.00
Total Customer Purchases:		$700.00
Customer Acquisition Costs:		
Cost of marketing to a potential customer:		$5.00
Average conversion rate:	4%	
Subtotal cost of attracting customer:		$125.00
Other one-off costs for first-time customers:		$0.00
Total Customer Acquisition Costs:		$125.00
Unadjusted Customer Lifetime Value:		$575.00
Adjusted Customer Lifetime Value:		
Discount Rate:	8%	
Net Present Value of Customer Lifetime Value:		$391.34

6.2 Keys to Success

- Maintain gross margins in excess of 45%.
- Retain customers to generate repeat purchases and referrals.
- Generate average sales in excess of $1,000 per business day.

6.3 Market Research

- Initial Question Results — The staff notes customer responses to the "How did you hear about us?" question. We attempt to correlate that with our advertising and promotional activities and referral-generation programs.
- Store Suggestions — The store suggestion box is another method to gain additional information from customers. Some of the most productive questions are:
  - What suggestion do you have to improve the store?
  - Why did you visit the store today?
  - What other products or services would you like to have available in the store?
  - Competitive Shopping — We continually shop other stores.

We visit each store in our market at least once each quarter for competitive information, we also visit stores in the nearby Seattle and Portland markets for merchandising and buying insight, and we subscribe to every catalog we know that has decorator fabrics as any part of their product line.

6.4 Contingency Planning

Difficulties and Risks

- Slow sales resulting in less-than-projected cash flow.
- Unexpected and excessive cost increases compared to the forecasted sales.
- Overly aggressive and debilitating actions by competitors.
- A parallel entry by a new competitor.

Worst case risks might include:

- Determining the business cannot support itself on an ongoing basis.
- Having to liquidate the inventory to pay back the bank loan.
- Locating a tenant to occupy the leased space for the duration of the five year lease.
- Losing the assets of the investors used for collateral.
- Dealing with the financial, business, and personal devastation of the store's failure.

6.5 CRM Plans

Our best sales in the future will come from our current customer base. In order to build this customer base, we need to provide exceptional customer service when they visit the store, have regular follow-up correspondence to thank them for their business (as well as to notify them of special promotions, etc.), and provide personal shopper support so that each visit to the store meets their needs.

In order to keep track of these activities, we will need to create a spreadsheet showing follow-up correspondence with customers and what, if any, feedback we have received from them. At least quarterly, we will plan to meet and discuss if we are, in fact, retaining our current customers and whether that base has grown, or what changes may need to be made.

Appendix Table: Sales Forecast

Sales Forecast	Jan	Feb	Mar	Apr	May	Jun	Jul	Aug	Sep	Oct	Nov	Dec
Sales												
Direct Sales	$33,000	$25,000	$28,000	$30,000	$34,000	$23,000	$20,000	$23,000	$24,000	$32,000	$30,000	$20,000
Web Sales	$1,000	$800	$1,000	$1,200	$1,200	$1,000	$900	$900	$1,000	$1,200	$1,300	$1,000
Consignment Sales	$100	$100	$110	$120	$110	$100	$100	$100	$120	$130	$140	$130
Sub-Lease Revenue	$405	$405	$525	$405	$405	$525	$405	$405	$525	$405	$405	$525
Total Sales	$34,505	$26,305	$29,635	$31,725	$35,715	$24,625	$21,405	$24,405	$25,645	$33,735	$31,845	$21,655
Direct Cost of Sales												
Direct Sales	$18,250	$13,500	$16,400	$16,600	$18,800	$12,750	$11,100	$12,750	$13,300	$17,700	$16,600	$11,100
Web Sales	$550	$440	$550	$660	$660	$550	$495	$495	$550	$660	$715	$550
Consignment Sales	$5	$5	$6	$6	$6	$5	$5	$5	$6	$7	$8	$7
Sub-Lease Revenue	$5	$5	$5	$5	$5	$5	$5	$5	$5	$5	$5	$5
Subtotal Direct Cost of Sales	$18,810	$13,950	$16,961	$17,271	$19,471	$13,310	$11,605	$13,255	$13,861	$18,372	$17,328	$11,662

Appendix Table: Sales Breakdown by Manager

Sales by: Manager	Jan	Feb	Mar	Apr	May	Jun	Jul	Aug	Sep	Oct	Nov	Dec
Sales												
Drapery Weight	$4,638	$4,209	$4,722	$5,076	$5,714	$3,921	$3,425	$3,905	$4,084	$5,398	$5,095	$3,446
Upholstery Weight	$2,319	$2,104	$2,361	$2,538	$2,857	$1,960	$1,712	$1,952	$2,042	$2,699	$2,548	$1,723
Mixed	$8,696	$7,892	$8,855	$9,518	$10,715	$7,352	$6,422	$7,322	$7,658	$10,121	$9,554	$6,461
Special Order	$5,797	$5,261	$5,903	$6,345	$7,143	$4,901	$4,281	$4,881	$5,105	$6,747	$6,369	$4,307
Other	$13,055	$6,839	$7,794	$8,248	$9,286	$6,491	$5,565	$6,345	$6,756	$8,770	$8,279	$5,718
Total	$34,505	$26,305	$29,635	$31,725	$35,715	$24,625	$21,405	$24,405	$25,645	$33,735	$31,845	$21,655
Average	$6,901	$5,261	$5,927	$6,345	$7,143	$4,925	$4,281	$4,881	$5,129	$6,747	$6,369	$4,331

Appendix Table: Sales Breakdown by Segment

Sales by: Segment	Jan	Feb	Mar	Apr	May	Jun	Jul	Aug	Sep	Oct	Nov	Dec
Sales												
"The Window Seat"	$1,014	$921	$1,033	$1,110	$1,250	$858	$749	$854	$893	$1,181	$1,115	$754
Antiques	$2,319	$2,104	$2,361	$2,538	$2,857	$1,960	$1,712	$1,952	$2,042	$2,699	$2,548	$1,723
Other	$31,172	$23,280	$26,241	$28,077	$31,608	$21,807	$18,944	$21,599	$22,710	$29,855	$28,182	$19,178
Total	$34,505	$26,305	$29,635	$31,725	$35,715	$24,625	$21,405	$24,405	$25,645	$33,735	$31,845	$21,655
Average	$11,502	$8,768	$9,878	$10,575	$11,905	$8,208	$7,135	$8,135	$8,548	$11,245	$10,615	$7,218

Appendix Table: Sales Breakdown by Region

Sales by: Region	Jan	Feb	Mar	Apr	May	Jun	Jul	Aug	Sep	Oct	Nov	Dec
Sales												
The Antique Bureau	$360	$360	$360	$360	$360	$360	$360	$360	$360	$360	$360	$360
Event/Sale Revenue	$45	$45	$120	$45	$45	$120	$45	$45	$120	$45	$45	$120
Other	$34,100	$25,900	$29,155	$31,320	$35,310	$24,145	$21,000	$24,000	$25,165	$33,330	$31,440	$21,175
Total	$34,505	$26,305	$29,635	$31,725	$35,715	$24,625	$21,405	$24,405	$25,645	$33,735	$31,845	$21,655
Average	$11,502	$8,768	$9,878	$10,575	$11,905	$8,208	$7,135	$8,135	$8,548	$11,245	$10,615	$7,218

Appendix Table: Marketing Expense Budget

Marketing Expense Budget

Budget	Jan	Feb	Mar	Apr	May	Jun	Jul	Aug	Sep	Oct	Nov	Dec
Television Ads	$780	$0	$0	$0	$0	$0	$0	$0	$780	$780	$780	$780
Newspaper Ads	$600	$0	$0	$0	$0	$600	$0	$0	$600	$0	$0	$0
Newsletter/Postcard	$1,350	$0	$0	$1,400	$0	$0	$1,450	$0	$0	$1,500	$0	$750
Printed Promotional Materials	$80	$80	$80	$80	$80	$80	$80	$80	$80	$80	$80	$80
Web Marketing/Support	$125	$125	$125	$125	$125	$125	$125	$125	$125	$125	$125	$125
Public Relations	$20	$20	$20	$20	$20	$20	$20	$20	$20	$20	$20	$20
Promotional Events	$0	$425	$0	$0	$425	$0	$0	$0	$425	$0	$425	$0
Website Expenses	$200	$200	$200	$200	$200	$200	$200	$200	$200	$200	$200	$200
Other	$25	$25	$50	$25	$25	$50	$25	$25	$50	$25	$25	$50
Total Sales and Marketing Expenses	$3,180	$875	$475	$1,850	$875	$1,075	$1,900	$450	$2,280	$2,730	$1,655	$2,005
Percentage of Sales	9.22%	3.33%	1.60%	5.83%	2.45%	4.37%	8.88%	1.84%	8.89%	8.09%	5.20%	9.26%

Appendix Table: Expense Breakdown by Manager

Expenses by Manager

Expenses	Jan	Feb	Mar	Apr	May	Jun	Jul	Aug	Sep	Oct	Nov	Dec
Drapery Weight	$232	$210	$136	$254	$286	$196	$171	$160	$204	$270	$255	$172
Upholstery Weight	$116	$105	$50	$127	$143	$98	$86	$90	$102	$135	$127	$86
Mixed	$235	$195	$50	$100	$150	$165	$220	$50	$220	$300	$325	$220
Other	$2,597	$365	$239	$1,369	$296	$616	$1,423	$150	$1,754	$2,025	$948	$1,527
Total	$3,180	$875	$475	$1,850	$875	$1,075	$1,900	$450	$2,280	$2,730	$1,655	$2,005
Average	$795	$219	$119	$463	$219	$ 69	$475	$113	$570	$683	$414	$501

Appendix Table: Expense Breakdown by Segment

Expenses by Segment

Expenses	Jan	Feb	Mar	Apr	May	Jun	Jul	Aug	Sep	Oct	Nov	Dec
Fabric Racks	$0	$0	$0	$0	$0	$0	$1,200	$ 0	$0	$0	$0	$0
Office Furniture	$0	$0	$250	$0	$0	$0	$0	$0	$350	$0	$0	$0
Leasehold Improvements	$250	$0	$0	$250	$0	$0	$250	$0	$0	$250	$0	$0
Other	$2,930	$875	$225	$1,600	$875	$1,075	$450	$450	$1,930	$2,480	$1,655	$2,005
Total	$3,180	$875	$475	$1,850	$875	$1,075	$1,900	$450	$2,280	$2,730	$1,655	$2,005
Average	$795	$219	$119	$463	$219	$269	$475	$113	$570	$683	$414	$501

Appendix Table: Expense Breakdown by Region

Expenses by Region

Expenses	Jan	Feb	Mar	Apr	May	Jun	Jul	Aug	Sep	Oct	Nov	Dec
Office Supplies	$35	$35	$35	$35	$35	$35	$35	$35	$35	$35	$35	$35
Fabrication Supplies	$75	$0	$0	$75	$0	$0	$75	$0	$0	$75	$0	$0
Other	$3,070	$840	$440	$1,740	$840	$1,040	$1,790	$415	$2,245	$2,620	$1,620	$1,970
Total	$3,180	$875	$475	$1,850	$875	$1,075	$1,900	$450	$2,280	$2,730	$1,655	$2,005
Average	$1,060	$292	$158	$617	$292	$358	$633	$150	$760	$910	$552	$668

Appendix Table: Contribution Margin

Contribution Margin

	Jan	Feb	Mar	Apr	May	Jun	Jul	Aug	Sep	Oct	Nov	Dec
Sales	$34,505	$26,305	$29,635	$31,725	$35,715	$24,625	$21,405	$24,405	$25,645	$33,735	$31,845	$21,655
Direct Costs of Goods	$18,810	$13,950	$16,961	$17,271	$19,471	$13,310	$11,605	$13,255	$13,861	$18,372	$17,328	$11,662
Cost of Goods Sold	$18,810	$13,950	$16,961	$17,271	$19,471	$13,310	$11,605	$13,255	$13,861	$18,372	$17,328	$11,662
Gross Margin	$15,695	$12,355	$12,674	$14,454	$16,244	$11,315	$9,800	$11,150	$11,784	$15,363	$14,517	$9,993
Gross Margin %	45.49%	46.97%	42.77%	45.56%	45.48%	45.95%	45.78%	45.69%	45.95%	45.54%	45.59%	46.15%
Marketing Expense Budget												
Television Ads	$780	$0	$0	$0	$0	$0	$0	$0	$780	$780	$780	$780
Newspaper Ads	$600	$0	$0	$0	$0	$600	$0	$0	$600	$0	$0	$0
Newsletter/Postcard	$1,350	$0	$0	$1,400	$0	$0	$1,450	$0	$0	$1,500	$0	$750
Printed Promotional Materials	$80	$80	$80	$80	$80	$80	$80	$80	$80	$80	$80	$80
Web Marketing/Support	$125	$125	$125	$125	$125	$125	$125	$125	$125	$125	$125	$125
Public Relations	$20	$20	$20	$20	$20	$20	$20	$20	$20	$20	$20	$20
Promotional Events	$0	$425	$0	$0	$425	$0	$0	$0	$425	$0	$425	$0
Website Expenses	$200	$200	$200	$200	$200	$200	$200	$200	$200	$200	$200	$200
Other	$25	$25	$50	$25	$25	$50	$25	$25	$50	$25	$25	$50
Total Sales and Marketing Expenses	$3,180	$875	$475	$1,850	$875	$1,075	$1,900	$450	$2,280	$2,730	$1,655	$2,005
Percentage of Sales	9.22%	3.33%	1.60%	5.83%	2.45%	4.37%	8.88%	1.84%	8.89%	8.09%	5.20%	9.26%
Contribution Margin	$12,515	$11,480	$12,199	$12,604	$15,369	$10,240	$7,900	$10,700	$9,504	$12,633	$12,862	$7,988
Contribution Margin / Sales	36.27%	43.64%	41.16%	39.73%	43.03%	41.58%	36.91%	43.84%	37.06%	37.45%	40.39%	36.89%

Endnotes

CHAPTER 1

1. www.marketingpower.com (accessed May 2, 2010); www.the-cma.org (accessed May 1, 2010).
2. "Social Marketing Do's and Don'ts," *Adweek*, October 8, 2007; www.facebook.com (accessed May 2, 2010).
3. www.reuters.com/article/pressRelease/idUS156332+09-Jun-2008+MW20080609 (accessed May 1, 2010).
4. www.llbean.com/customerService/aboutLLBean/background.html?nav=ln (accessed May 1, 2010).
5. www.reuters.com/article/pressRelease/idUS122196+27-Feb-2008+BW20080227 (accessed April 16, 2010); M. McCarthy, "Vegas Goes Back to Naughty Roots," *USA Today*, April 11, 2005, www.usatoday.com (accessed April 18, 2010).
6. http://adage.com/century/timeline/index.html (accessed April 20, 2010).
7. Ibid.
8. Ibid.
9. R. Jaroslovsky, review of *Birth of a Salesman*, by Walter A. Friedman, *Wall Street Journal*, "More Than a Shoeshine and a Smile," June 8, 2004.
10. Ibid.
11. "Consumer Interest in Socially Responsible Companies Rising, Survey Finds," July 16, 2007, http://www.GreenBiz.com/news/2007/07/15/consumer-interest-socially-responsible-companies-rising-survey-finds (accessed April 18, 2010).
12. www.firstgencom.com/blog/pepsi-20m-social-campaign/, www.refresheverything.com/ (accessed May 12, 2010)
13. P. F. Drucker, *Innovation and Entrepreneurship: Practice and Principle* (New York, HarperBusiness, 1985).

CHAPTER 2

1. www.marketingpower.com (accessed May 1, 2010).
2. M. Porter, *Competitive Strategy* (The Free Press: New York, 1980).
3. http://dpc.senate.gov/healthreformbill/healthbill63.pdf (accessed May 1, 2010); J. Jackson and J. Nolen, "Health Care Reform Bill Summary: A Look At What's in the Bill," *Political Hotsheet*, March 21, 2010, www.cbsnews.com/8301-503544_162-20000846-503544.html (accessed May 2, 2010).
4. www.onstar.com/us_english/jsp/index.jsp (accessed May 12, 2010).
5. J. Verdon, "Government Regulation Creates New Business Niche for Motor-Oil Company," *The Record*, May 2, 2010.
6. www.irs.gov/newsroom/article/0,,id=206869,00.html (accessed May 2, 2010).
7. www.dominos.com/home/tracker/pizzatracker.jsp (accessed May 2, 2010).
8. www.marketingpower.com (accessed May 1, 2010).
9. www.selig.uga.edu/forecast/GBEC/GBEC0703Q.pdf (accessed August 5, 2008).
10. Ibid.
11. www.marketingpower.com (accessed May 2, 2010).
12. Ibid.
13. Ibid.
14. P. Robinson, C. Faris, and Y. Wind, *Industrial Buying and Creative Marketing* (Boston: Allyn & Bacon, 1967).
15. Y. Wind, "The Boundaries of Buying Decision Centers," *Journal of Purchasing and Materials Management*, 14, Summer (1978): 23–29; Frederick E. Webster, Jr. and Yoram Wind, *Organizational Buying Behavior* (New York: Prentice-Hall, Inc., 1972)
16. P. Robinson, C. Faris, and Y. Wind, *Industrial Buying and Creative Marketing* (Boston: Allyn & Bacon, 1967).
17. www.cat.com/ (accessed May 1, 2010).

CHAPTER 3

1. www.wholefoods.com (accessed May 2, 2010).
2. www.marketingpower.com (accessed May 2, 2010).
3. G. T. Doran, "There's a S.M.A.R.T. Way to Write a Management's Goals and Objectives," *Management Review*, 70, no. 11 (1981): 35–36.
4. www.teva.com (accessed May 1, 2010).
5. R. S. Kaplan and D. P. Norton, "The Balanced Scorecard—Measures That Drive Performance," *Harvard Business Review* (January/February 1992): 71–79.
6. www.balancedscorecard.org/BSCResources/AbouttheBalancedScorecard/tabid/55/Default.aspx (accessed August 21, 2008).
7. E. Wilson, "Swimsuit for the Olympics Is a New Skin for the Big Dip," *New York Times*, February 13, 2008, www.nytimes.com (accessed August 15, 2008); www.speedousa.com/shop/index.jsp?categoryId=3819798 (accessed May 3, 2010).
8. www.marketingpower.com (accessed May 2, 2010).

CHAPTER 4

1. Organization for Economic Cooperation and Development, *OECD Factbook 2009* (Paris: OECD, 2009), miranda.sourceoecd.org/pdf/factbook2009/302008011e-02-01-01.pdf (accessed May 3, 2010).
2. www.californiagreensolutions.com/cgi-bin/gt/tpl.h,content=703 (accessed May 5, 2010).
3. M. Earls, "Advertising to the Herd: How Understanding Our True Nature Challenges the Ways We Think about Advertising and Market Research," *International Journal of Market Research* 45, no. 3 (2003): 313; accountplanning.net/Central/Downloads/Earls_Herd.pdf (accessed September 2, 2008).
4. G. Teague, *Culture Smart!—USA* (Great Britain: Kuperard, 2004).
5. P. Levy, "Keeping It Interesting," *Marketing News* 13, no. 17 (October 30, 2009): 8.
6. www.emarketer.com/Article.aspx?R=1007625 (accessed May 4, 2010).
7. P. Kotler and G. Armstrong, *Principles of Marketing* (Upper Saddle River: Prentice Hall, 2007).
8. R. Markin, "Consumerism: Militant Consumer Behavior," *Business and Society* 12, no. 1 (Fall 1971): 5.
9. "Industry Flayed on Safety Attitude," *Automotive News* 75, no. 5891 (August 28, 2000): 56.
10. "Eight Basic Consumer Rights," *Choice.com.au*, www.choice.com.au/viewArticle.aspx?id=100736&catId=100528&tid=100008 (accessed August 30, 2008).
11. R. Markin, "Consumerism: Militant Consumer Behavior," *Business and Society* 12, no. 1 (Fall 1971): 5,
12. R. Innes, "A Theory of Consumer Boycotts under Symmetric Information and Imperfect Competition," *Economic Journal* 116 (2): 511; www.res.org.uk/society/mediabriefings/pdfs/2006/apr06/innes.asp (accessed September 1, 2008).
13. K. Peattie, "Rethinking Marketing," in *Greener Marketing* (1999), 2nd ed., M. Charter and M. J. Polonsky (eds), Greenleaf Publishing, p. 57–71.
14. J. A. Ottman, E. R. Stafford, and C. L. Hartman, "How to Avoid Green Marketing Myopia—Marketing Green Products to Deliver Consumer Value," *Environment* 48, no. 5 (2006): 22–36.
15. A. Prakash, Green Marketing, Public Policy and Managerial Strategies, 2002, www.greeneconomics.net/GreenMarketing.pdf (accessed May 4, 2010).
16. L. Miller, "Products to Break the Chemical Habit and Get Eco-Friendly," *New York Times*, July 19, 2007, www.nytimes.com/2007/07/19/business/media/19adco.html (accessed September 2, 2008); Hoovers, "Method Products Company Description," 2008, www.hoovers.com/method-products/—ID_155282—/free-co-profile.xhtml (accessed September 2, 2008); Method Products, "Company Information—What We're For," www.methodhome.com (accessed September 2, 2008); www.environmentalleader.com/2010/03/10/method-green-household-cleaners-try-to-take-market-share-from-clorox/ (accessed May 4, 2010).
17. The LOHAS Consumer Trends Database™, Natural Marketing Institute, 2007, www.nmisolutions.com/lohasd_segment.html (accessed September 2, 2008).

18. http://consciousventures.com/tag/lohas-venturing/ (accessed May 4, 2010).
19. "US: Consumers Buying Green Despite Economic Woes," *Just-Food.com*, April 30, 2008, www.just-food.com/article.aspx?id=102186&lk=s (accessed August 30, 2008).
20. B. Cummings, "Despite Economic Dip, Organic Food Sales Soar," *Brandweek*, June 9, 2008, 6.
21. J. Edwards, "Accountability in the Consumer Movement," *Consumer Policy Review* 16, no. 1 (Jan/Feb 2006): 20.
22. M. Solomon, G. Marshall, and E. Stuart, *Marketing* (Upper Saddle River: Prentice Hall, 2008).
23. Ibid.
24. "Advertising Practices—Frequently Asked Questions," Federal Trade Commission, 2001, www.ftc.gov/bcp/edu/pubs/business/adv/bus35.pdf (accessed September 2, 2008).
25. www.themarketer.co.uk/articles/trends/hotspot/ (accessed May 4, 2010).
26. "Settlement on Deceptive Drug Ads," *U.S. News & World Report*, August 18, 2008 (1180); B. Janoff, "Airborne, FTC Reach Settlement," *Adweek*, August 14, 2008, www.adweek.com/aw/content_display/news/client/e3i1fefd617b0921810037928c6c779cb69 (accessed October 1, 2008).
27. "Statement of Ethics," American Marketing Association, 2008, www.marketingpower.com/AboutAMA/Pages/Statement%20of%20Ethics.aspx (accessed September 2, 2008).
28. C. Hawkes, "Regulating Food Marketing to Young People Worldwide: Trends and Policy Drivers," *American Journal of Public Health* 97, no. 11 (November 2007): 1962.
29. E. Creyer and W. Ross, Jr., "The Influence of Firm Behavior on Purchase Intention: Do Consumers Really Care about Business Ethics?" *Journal of Consumer Marketing* 14, no. 6 (Nov/Dec 1997): 421.
30. Corporate Citizenship Report, Wells Fargo Bank, 2008, www.wellsfargo.com/downloads/pdf/about/csr/reports/wf2008corporate_citizenship.pdf (accessed May 4, 2010).

CHAPTER 5

1. M. Salzman and I. Matathia, *Next Now* (New York: Palgrave Macmillan, 2006).
2. www.2goldmansachs.com/ideas/brics/brics-decade-doc.pdf (accessed June 23, 2010).
3. http://news.opb.org/article/6775-chinese-sportswear-company-chooses-portland-first-international-shop/ (accessed May 7, 2010); www.oregonlive.com/business/index.ssf/2009/12/chinese_shoe_maker_slips_into.html (accessed May 7, 2010).
4. K. Vijayraghavan and S. Vyas, "MNC Fast Food Chains Rework Menu for India," *Economic Times*, July 18, 2006, http://economictimes.indiatimes.com/articleshowarchive.cms?msid=1768877 (accessed October 1, 2008).
5. C. Norris, "Going Glocal: Managing a Brand's Global Social Profiles on Facebook," April 13, 2010, http://searchengineland.com/going-glocalmanaging-a-brands-global-social-profiles-on-facebook-39500 (accessed May 7, 2010).
6. http://news.mongabay.com/2007/0220-roundtable.html (accessed May 7, 2010).
7. Ibid.
8. http://nextbigfuture.com/2009/04/china-to-be-worlds-largest-economy-in.html (accessed May 7, 2010).
9. http://europa.eu/abc/panorama/index_en.htm (accessed May 7, 2010).
10. www.ustr.gov/trade-agreements/free-trade-agreements/north-american-free-trade-agreement-nafta (accessed May 7, 2010).
11. www.ustr.gov/trade-agreements/free-trade-agreements/cafta-dr-dominican-republic-central-america-fta (accessed May 7, 2010).
12. www.wto.org/ (accessed May 7, 2010).
13. www.economist.com/markets/indicators/displaystory.cfm?story_id=15549079/ (accessed May 7, 2010).
14. www.bea.gov/newsreleases/international/transactions/transnewsrelease.htm (accessed May 7, 2010).
15. http://news.xinhuanet.com/english/2010-01/07/content_12768908.htm (accessed May 7, 2010).
16. P. Conway, "Trade Policy in Developing Countries; Book Review" [Review of the book *Trade Policy in Developing Countries*], *Southern Economic Journal* 3, no. 68 (2002): 742.
17. www.imf.org/external/about/overview.htm (accessed May 7, 2010).
18. https://www.cia.gov/library/publications/the-world-factbook/fields/2128.html (accessed May 7, 2010).
19. www.abc.net.au/news/stories/2010/05/27/2911562.htm (accessed June 24, 2010); www.guardian.co.uk/world/2010/may/26/pakistan-lifts-youtube-ban (accessed June 24, 2010).
20. www.justice.gov/criminal/fraud/fcpa/ (accessed May 7, 2010).
21. www.apca.net/articles/getarticles.asp?id=1 (accessed May 7, 2010).
22. N. Balu and Norfadilah, "Counter Trade: The Malaysian Experience," *Oil Palm Industry Economic Journal* 2, no. 1 (2002), http://palmoilis.mpob.gov.my/publications/opiejv2n1-6.pdf (accessed May 7, 2010).
23. G. Hofstede, *Culture's Consequences: Comparing Values, Behaviors, Institutions and Organizations Across Nations*, 2nd ed. (Thousand Oaks: Sage Publications, Inc., 2001).
24. D. Ackerman and G. Tellis, "Can Culture Affect Prices? A Cross-Cultural Study of Shopping and Retail Prices," *Journal of Retailing* 1, no. 77 (2001): 57.
25. K. Zhou, C. Su, and Y. Bao, "A Paradox of Price-Quality and Market Efficiency: A Comparative Study of the US and China Markets," *International Journal of Research in Marketing* (December 2002).
26. D. Ackerman and G. Tellis, "Can Culture Affect Prices? A Cross-Cultural Study of Shopping and Retail Prices," *Journal of Retailing* 1, no. 77 (2001): 57.
27. L. Dong and M. Helms, "Brand Name Translation Model: A Case Analysis of US Brands in China," *Journal of Brand Management* 9, no. 2 (2001): 99–115.
28. J. Weinstein, *Social and Cultural Change: Social Science for a Dynamic World* (Needham Heights, MA: Allyn & Bacon, 1997).
29. 2007 Annual Review, The Coca-Cola Company, www.thecoca-colacompany.com/investors/annual_review_2007.html (accessed September 2, 2008).
30. N. Pacek and D. Thorniley, *Emerging Markets* (London: Profile Books, 2007).
31. https://www.cia.gov/library/publications/the-world-factbook/rankorder/2003rank.html (accessed May 9, 2010).
32. M. Corstjens and J. Merrihue, "Optimal Marketing," *Harvard Business Review* (October 2003).
33. P. Kotler and G. Armstrong, *Principles of Marketing* (Upper Saddle River: Prentice Hall, 2008).
34. V. Kumar, "Segmenting Global Markets: Look Before You Leap," *Marketing Research* 13, no. 1 (2001): 8–13.
35. B. Oviatt and P. P. McDougall, "Toward a Theory of International New Ventures," *Journal of International Business Studies* 25 (1994): 45–64.
36. J. Mathews, *Dragon Multinational: A New Model for Global Growth* (Oxford, U.K.: Oxford University Press, 2002).
37. www.export.gov/articles/eg_main_021610.asp (accessed June 25, 2010); www.export.gov/articles/successstories/eg_main_020763.asp; www.vellus.com/ (accessed June 25, 2010).

CHAPTER 6

1. www.oswegocountybusiness.com/index.php?a=2675 (accessed July 13, 2010).
2. M. Williams, "Timeline: iTunes Store at 10 Billion," *Computerworld* (February 24 2010) www.computerworld.com/s/article/9162018/Timeline_iTunes_Store_at_10_billion (accessed July 13, 2010); www.apple.com/itunes/what-is/ (accessed July 13, 2010).
3. R. T. Rust and A. J. Zahorik, "Customer Satisfaction, Customer Retention and Market Share," *Journal of Retailing* 69 (Summer 1993) 193–215; Chris Denove and James D. Power IV, *Satisfaction: How Every Great Company Listens to the Voice of the Customer* (New York, NY: Portfolio, 2006).
4. www.southwest.com/about_swa/press/factsheet.html#Recognitions (accessed May 10, 2010).
5. *Sprint Hangs Up on High-Maintenance Customers*, Reuters News Service (July 9, 2007).
6. V. Kumar, J. A. Petersen, and R. P. Leone, "How Valuable Is Word of Mouth?" *Harvard Business Review* (October 1, 2007).
7. Purdue University Center for Customer Driven Quality, www.ccdq.com (accessed October 10, 2008).
8. www.wheresyours.com (accessed November 2, 2008).

9. F. Reichheld, *The Loyalty Effect* (Boston: Harvard Business School Press, 1996).
10. www.patronsocialclub.com (accessed November 2, 2008); www.brandweek.com (accessed November 2, 2008).
11. D. Peppers, M. Rogers, and B. Dorf, "Is Your Company Ready for One-to-One Marketing?" *Harvard Business Review* (January–February 1999).
12. www.marketwire.com/press-release/eMusic-Unveils-New-A-R-Access-Rewards-Benefits-Program-at-SXSW-1134342.htm (accessed June 8, 2010).
13. www.prlog.org/10145504-why-do-most-crm-projects-fail.html (accessed May 10, 2010).

CHAPTER 7

1. www.marketingpower.com (accessed September 12, 2008).
2. I. Ajzen, "The Theory of Planned Behavior," *Organizational Behavior and Human Decision Processes* 50 (1991): 179–211.
3. Ibid.
4. I. Brace, L. Edwards, and C. Nancarrow, "I Hear You Knocking . . . Can Advertising Reach Everybody in the Target Audience?" *International Journal of Market Research* 2, no. 44 (2002): 193.
5. J. Chebat, M. Charlebois, and C. Chebat, "What Makes Open Versus Closed Conclusion Advertisements More Persuasive? The Moderating Role of Prior Knowledge and Involvement," *Journal of Business Research* 53, no. 2 (2001).
6. I. Brace, L. Edwards, and C. Nancarrow, "I Hear You Knocking . . . Can Advertising Reach Everybody in the Target Audience?" *International Journal of Market Research* 2, no. 44 (2002): 193.
7. C. McDonald, "The Hidden Power of Advertising: How Low Involvement Processing Influences the Way in Which We Choose Brands," review of *The Hidden Power of Advertising*, by Robert Heath, *International Journal of Market Research* 1, no. 44 (2002): 121.
8. S. Youn, T. Sun, W. D. Wells, and X. Zhao, "Commercial Liking and Memory: Moderating Effects of Product Categories," *Journal of Advertising Research* 41, no. 3 (2001): 7–13.
9. Ibid.
10. Ibid.
11. J. Smith, D. Terry, A. Manstead, W. Louis, D. Kotterman, and J. Wolfs, "The Attitude-Behavior Relationship in Consumer Conduct: The Role of Norms, Past Behavior, and Self-Identity," *Journal of Social Psychology* 148, no. 3 (2008): 311–333.
12. C. S. Carver and M. F. Scheier, *Perspectives on Personality*, 4th ed. (Boston: Allyn & Bacon, 2000).
13. K. V. Henderson, R. E. Goldsmith, and L. R. Flynn, "Demographic Characteristics of Subjective Age," *Journal of Social Psychology* 135 (1995): 447–457.
14. Zena S. Blaun, "Changes in Status and Age Identification," *American Sociological Review* 21 (April 1965): 198–203.
15. M. Levens, "Lifestyle Bundles: A Between-Category Product Evaluation Study of Affluent Consumer Behavior," *Journal of Applied Marketing Theory* 1, no. 1 (2010): 45–66.
16. B. Dubois and C. Paternault, "Understanding the World of International Luxury Brands: The 'Dream Formula,'" *Journal of Advertising Research* 35, no. 4 (1995): 69–76.
17. www.marketingpower.com (accessed August 3, 2008).
18. D. Caracci, "The Plan Behind Plan-O-Grams," June 1, 2006, www.aftermarketnews.com (accessed November 2, 2008).
19. G. Cui and P. Choudhury, "Marketplace Diversity and Cost-Effective Marketing Strategies," *Journal of Consumer Marketing* 19, no. 1 (2002): 54–73.
20. Ibid.
21. A. Schneider, "A Changing America Has Changing Tastes," *Kiplinger Business Forecasts* 1227 (December 23, 2002).
22. J. Hood, "Targeting a Multicultural Audience Takes More Than a Dictionary: It Takes Tact, Understanding, and Relevance," *PR Week* 13 (August 18, 2003).
23. G. Cui and P. Choudhury, "Marketplace Diversity and Cost-Effective Marketing Strategies," *Journal of Consumer Marketing* 19, no. 1 (2002): 54–73.
24. Ibid.
25. C. Arnold, "Coloring Outside the Lines," *Marketing News* 4 (November 25, 2002).
26. Ibid.
27. Ibid.
28. www.mavinfoundation.org (accessed August 20, 2008).
29. G. Khermouch, "Didja C That Kewl Ad?" *BusinessWeek* (August 26, 2002): 158.
30. YouthPulse, *Harris Interactive Preview* (2003).
31. Ibid.
32. "Diversity Is Key to Marketing to Today's Youth," *Marketing to the Emerging Majorities* 6, no. 14 (2002): 6.
33. Ibid.
34. www.aflcio.org (accessed June 20, 2010).
35. www.hp.com/hpinfo/globalcitizenship/environment/productdesign/ecohighlights-label.html (accessed September 21, 2008).

CHAPTER 8

1. www.merriam-webster.com (accessed August 11, 2008).
2. www.marketingpower.com (accessed August 10, 2008).
3. http://en-us.nielsen.com/content/nielsen/en_us/about.html (accessed June 29, 2010); J. Honomichl, "Company Profiles," *Marketing News* 44, no. 8 (2010): 23.
4. Ibid.
5. L. C. Lockley, "Notes on the History of Marketing Research," *Journal of Marketing* 14, no. 5 (April 1950): 733–736.
6. www.aaf.org (accessed August 15, 2008).
7. www.merriam-webster.com (accessed August 11, 2008).
8. www.marketingpower.com (accessed August 10, 2008).
9. L. Oppenheim and M. Sherr, "Gathering Customer Perceptions Over the Internet," *Medical Marketing & Media* 34, no. 2 (1999): 50–58.
10. www.jdpower.com (accessed September 12, 2008).
11. www.marketingpower.com (accessed August 10, 2008).
12. www.onsiteresearch.com (accessed September 15, 2008).
13. D. Bradford, "Ten Years After: Online Qualitative Research Has Come a Long Way in Its First Decade," *Quirk's Marketing Research Review* 17, no. 7 (2003): 44–47.
14. N. Ray and S. Tabor, "Cybersurveys Come of Age," *Management and Applications* 15, no. 1 (2003): 33.
15. S. Rogers and K. Sheldon, "An Improved Way to Characterize Internet Users," *Journal of Advertising Research* 5, no. 42 (2002): 85.
16. C. Maginnis, "Online Sample—Can You Trust It?" *Quirk's Marketing Research Review* 17, no. 7 (2003): 40–43.
17. www.e-rewards.com (accessed September 29, 2008).
18. D. Bradford, "Ten Years After: Online Qualitative Research Has Come a Long Way in Its First Decade," *Quirk's Marketing Research Review* 17, no. 7 (2003): 44–47.
19. P. Willems and P. Oosterveld, "The Best of Both Worlds; Combining Phone and Internet Research Creates More Targeted Results," *Management & Applications* 15, no. 1 (2003): 23.
20. www.marketingpower.com (accessed August 10, 2008).
21. Ibid.
22. Ibid.
23. Ibid.
24. Ibid.
25. Ibid.
26. P. Kotler, "A Design for the Firm's Marketing Nerve Center," in *Readings in Marketing Information Systems: A New Era in Marketing Research*, ed. S. Smith, R. Brien, and J. Stafford (Boston: Houghton-Mifflin, 1966).
27. www.marketingpower.com (accessed August 10, 2008).

CHAPTER 9

1. H. Arnold, "Brand Aid," *Financial Management* (November 2001): 33–34.
2. P. Temporal, *Advanced Brand Management—From Vision to Valuation* (Singapore: John Wiley & Sons, 2002).
3. "Ethnic Consumers More Receptive Than Peers to Marketing, But Most Believe Messaging Lacks Relevancy, According to New Yankelovich Study," www.hiphoppress.com/2007/09/ethnic-consumer.html (accessed July 30, 2008).
4. Ibid.
5. D. Abrahams and E. Granof, "Respecting Brand Risk," *Risk Management* 4, no. 49 (2002): 40.
6. S. Broniarczyk and A. Gershoff, "The Reciprocal Effects of Brand Equity and Trivial Attributes," *Journal of Marketing Research* (May 2003): 161.

7. S. Hoeffler and K. Keller, "Building Brand Equity Through Corporate Societal Marketing," *Journal of Public Policy and Marketing* 21, no. 1 (2002): 78–89.
8. L. Williams, "What Price a Good Name?" *Business*, May 5, 2002, 23.
9. D. Abrahams and E. Granof, "Respecting Brand Risk," *Risk Management* 4, no. 49 (2002): 40.
10. Ibid.
11. www.businessweek.com/interactive_reports/best_global_brands_2009.html (accessed May 22, 2010).
12. A. Abela, "Additive Versus Inclusive Approaches to Measuring Brand Equity: Practical and Ethical Implications," *Journal of Brand Management* 10, no. 4/5 (2003): 342.
13. A. Chaudhuri and M. Holbrook, "The Chain of Effects from Brand Trust and Brand Effect to Brand Performance: The Role of Brand Loyalty," *Journal of Marketing* 65, no. 2 (2001): 81–93.
14. S. Hoeffler and K. Keller, "Building Brand Equity Through Corporate Societal Marketing," *Journal of Public Policy and Marketing* 21, no. 1 (2002): 78–89.
15. Ibid.
16. www.prnewswire.com/news-releases/victorias-secret-pink-and-major-league-baseball-properties-announce-new-co-branded-collection-87663702.html (accessed May 23, 2010).
17. V. Kumar, "Segmenting Global Markets: Look Before You Leap," *Marketing Research* 13, no. 1 (2001): 8–13.
18. www.ikea.com/us/en (accessed July 30, 2008).
19. D. D'Alessandro and M. Owens, *Brand Warfare: 10 Rules for the Killer Brand* (New York: McGraw-Hill, 2002).
20. Ibid.
21. J. Mass, "Pharmaceutical Brands: Do They Really Exist?" *International Journal of Medical Marketing* 2, no. 1 (2001): 23–32.
22. NPR, "The Fall of Enron," www.npr.org/news/specials/enron/ (accessed August 25, 2008).
23. A. Rattray, "Measure for Measure: Brand Value May Be Relative But It Is Measurable, Either from a Company or a Consumer Point of View," *Financial Times*, July 9, 2002, 12.
24. S. Davis, *Brand Asset Management: Driving Profitable Growth Through Your Brands*, 2nd ed. (San Francisco: John Wiley & Sons, 2002).
25. www.traderjoes.com (accessed May 23, 2010).
26. www.southerncomfort.com (accessed May 23, 2010); www.kemps.com (accessed May 15, 2010).
27. www.eddiebauer.com/custserv/custserv.jsp?sectionId=601 and www.fordvehicles.com/suvs/expedition/trim/?trim=eddiebauer&showCategoryTab=viewAll (accessed July 11, 2010).
28. D. Arnold, *The Handbook of Brand Management* (London: Century Business, 1992).
29. www.crayola.com (accessed July 14, 2008).
30. M. Yadav, "How Buyers Evaluate Product Bundles: A Model of Anchoring and Adjustment," *Journal of Consumer Research* 21, no. 2 (1994): 342.
31. T. Leopold, "Advertising Builds Character," *CNN.com*, www.cnn.com/2004/SHOWBIZ/08/18/eye.ent.advertising/index.html (accessed August 2, 2008).
32. T. Amobi, "Disney: Mouse on the Move," *BusinessWeek*, May 7, 2007, www.businessweek.com/investor/content/may2007/pi20070507_602321.htm (accessed July 26, 2008).
33. P. Svensson, "Cut Rate Prepaid Plans Shake Up Wireless Industry," *Knoxville News*, April 20, 2009, www.knoxnews.com/news/2009/apr/20/cut-rate-prepaid-plans-shake-wireless-industry/ (accessed May 23, 2010).
34. 2007 CMO Study, www.spencerstuart.com (accessed July 25, 2008).
35. A. Medgisen, "Did eBay Start a Counterfeit Crackdown?" http://freakonomics.blogs.nytimes.com/2008/07/18/did-ebay-start-a-counterfeit-crackdown/ (accessed May 23, 2010).

CHAPTER 10

1. A. Bianco, "The Vanishing Mass Market," *BusinessWeek*, July 12, 2004, www.businessweek.com/magazine/content/04_28/b3891001_mz001.htm (accessed August 13, 2008).
2. Ibid.
3. W. DeSarbo, "Market Segmentation Practices Are Totally Inadequate," *AScribe Newsline*, June 15, 2001.
4. A. Dexter, "Egoists, Idealists, and Corporate Animals—Segmenting Business Markets," *International Journal of Market Research* 1, no. 44 (2002): 31.
5. www.glaceau.com (accessed July 11, 2010).
6. www.curves.com (accessed May 23, 2010); "Fitness Club Is Fastest-Growing U.S. Franchise," *Voice of America*, January 27, 2006, www.voanews.com/english/archive/2006-01/2006-01-27-voa18.cfm (accessed August 5, 2008).
7. www.moosejaw.com (accessed May 23, 2010).
8. W. Kamakura and T. Novak, "Value-System Segmentation: Exploring the Meaning of LOV," *Journal of Consumer Research* 19, no. 1 (June 1992): 119–132.
9. www.chase.com (accessed May 23, 2010).
10. K. O'Brien, "Nokia Deal Aimed at Opening Up Mobile Software," *International Herald Tribune*, June 24, 2008, www.iht.com/articles/2008/06/24/business/symbian.php (accessed July 21, 2008); M. Ahmad, "Nokia Middle East and Africa Marks the Holy Month with the Launch of Ramadan Applications for Mobile Users Worldwide," *Business Intelligence Middle East*, July 13, 2008, www.bi-me.com/main.php?id=23493&t=1&c=129&cg=4&mset=1021 (accessed July 23, 2008); www.nokia.com (accessed May 23, 2010).
11. S. Dibb and L. Simkin, "Market Segmentation: Diagnosing and Treating the Barriers," *International Marketing Management* 30, no. 8 (2001): 21–39.
12. D. Rowell, "All About Satellite Phone Service," *Travel Insider*, April 22, 2008, www.thetravelinsider.info/phones/aboutsatellitephoneservice.htm (accessed August 21, 2008); www.iridium.com (accessed July 24, 2008).
13. www.ford.com (accessed May 23, 2010).
14. www.mcdonalds.com (accessed July 22, 2008).
15. www.movado.com (accessed July 23, 2008).
16. S. Dibb and L. Simkin, "Market Segmentation: Diagnosing and Treating the Barriers," *International Marketing Management* 30, no. 8 (2001): 21–39.
17. www.apple.com (accessed May 23, 2010); D. Coursey, "The Un-Vision: What Steve Jobs Won't Do at Apple," *ZDNet*, February 7, 2002, http://review.zdnet.com/4520-6033_16-4206922.html (accessed July 24, 2008); R. Hof, "100 Million iPods Sold, But How Many Are Still in Use?" *BusinessWeek*, April 9, 2007, www.businessweek.com/the_thread/techbeat/archives/2007/04/100_million_ipo.html (accessed July 23, 2008).
18. "Gas-Saving Sedans," *Consumer Reports*, July 2008; www.greencarcongress.com/2010/04/hybrids-20100405.html (accessed May 23, 2010).
19. B. Calder and S. Reagan, "Brand Design," in *Kellogg on Marketing*, ed. D. Iacobucci (New York: John Wiley & Sons, 2001), 61.
20. www.focushope.com (accessed May 23, 2010).

CHAPTER 11

1. www.london2012.com (accessed May 23, 2010).
2. www.petfinder.com (accessed May 23, 2010).
3. www.reuters.com/article/pressRelease/idUS126101+08-May-2008+PRN20080508 (accessed September 10, 2008).

CHAPTER 12

1. http://www.cia.gov/library/publications/the-world-factbook/geos/us.html (accessed May 24, 2010).
2. P. Kotler and G. Armstrong, *Principles of Marketing* (Upper Saddle River, NJ: Prentice Hall, 2008), 239–240.
3. "The Big Ideas Behind Nintendo's Wii," *BusinessWeek*, November 16, 2006, www.businessweek.com/technology/content/nov2006/tc20061116_750580.htm (accessed August 22, 2008); B. Bremner, "Will Nintendo's Wii Strategy Score?" *BusinessWeek*, September 20, 2006, www.businessweek.com/globalbiz/content/sep2006/gb20060920_163780.htm (accessed August 22, 2008); "Press Release: Nintendo Wii Is Market Leader in Home Console Business," VGChartz.com, August 22, 2007, http://news.vgchartz.com/news.php?id=508 (accessed October 1, 2008); www.nintendo.com (accessed May 24, 2010).
4. M. Solomon, G. Marshall, and E. Stuart, *Marketing* (Upper Saddle River, NJ: Prentice Hall, 2008), 238–241.
5. www.dell.com/home/laptops?∼ck=mn (accessed August 21, 2008).
6. P. Kotler and G. Armstrong, *Principles of Marketing* (Upper Saddle River, NJ: Prentice Hall, 2008), 220–221.

7. M. Solomon, G. Marshall, and E. Stuart, *Marketing* (Upper Saddle River, NJ: Prentice Hall, 2008), 244–245.
8. Wrigley Company, *2007 Annual Report*, http://library.corporateir.net/library/92/927/92701/items/278516/Wrigley2007AR.pdf (accessed August 21, 2008).
9. Computer Sciences Corporation (CSC), "Improving Product Success through Effective, Focused Speed to Market," www.csc.com/solutions/managementconsulting/knowledgelibrary/2115.shtml (accessed August 20, 2008).
10. P. Kotler and G. Armstrong, *Principles of Marketing* (Upper Saddle River, NJ: Prentice Hall, 2008), 254–263.
11. J. Quelch, *Cases in Product Management* (Burr Ridge, IL: Richard D. Irwin, Inc., 1995), 3–42.
12. P. Fisk, *Marketing Genius* (West Sussex: Capstone, 2006), 214–215.
13. DuPont Company, Winners of the 19th DuPont awards for packaging innovation, www.dupont.com/Packaging/en_US/news_events/19th_ dupont_packaging_award_winners.html (accessed August 20, 2008).
14. Target Company, ClearRx, http://sites.target.com/site/en/health/page.jsp?contentId=PRD03-003977 (accessed August 21, 2008).
15. P. Kotler and G. Armstrong, *Principles of Marketing* (Upper Saddle River, NJ: Prentice Hall, 2008), 229–231.
16. The Hershey Company, *2007 Annual Report to Stockholders/Form 10-K*, February 19, 2008, 1–4.
17. J. Useem, "Internet Defense Strategy: Cannibalize Yourself," *Fortune*, September 6, 1999, http://money.cnn.com/magazines/fortune/fortune_archive/1999/09/06/265284/index.htm (accessed August 20, 2008).
18. M. Solomon, G. Marshall, and E. Stuart, *Marketing* (Upper Saddle River, NJ: Prentice Hall, 2008), 260–261.
19. K. Clancy and P. Krieg, "Product Life Cycle: A Dangerous Idea," *BrandWeek*, March 1, 2004, www.copernicusmarketing.com/about/product_life_cycle.shtml (accessed August 20, 2008).

CHAPTER 13

1. R. Heinlein, *The Moon Is a Harsh Mistress* (New York: G.P. Putnam's Sons, 1966).
2. www.apple.com (accessed November 1, 2008); C. Sorrel, "Apple's iPod Strategy: Aggressive Prices, Overwhelming Feature," *Wired Magazine*, September 6, 2007, www.wired.com/gadgets/portablemusic/news/2007/09/ipod_follow (accessed September 10, 2008); E. Hesseldahl, "Are There Problems with iPod Sales?" *BusinessWeek*, February 22, 2008, www.businessweek.com/technology/ByteOfTheApple/blog/archives/2008/02/is_there_troubl.html (accessed September 10, 2008); www.apple.com/itunes/ (accessed May 24, 2010).
3. Air Transport Association, *Quarterly Cost Index: U.S. Passenger Airlines*, September 9, 2008, www.airlines.org/economics/finance/Cost+Index.htm (accessed September 9, 2008).
4. P. Farris, N. Bendle, P. Pfeifer, and D. Reibsten, *Marketing Metrics* (Philadelphia: Wharton School Publishing, 2006).
5. S. Maxwell, *The Price Is Wrong* (Hoboken, NJ: John Wiley & Sons, 2008), 41–44.
6. J. Manning, *Got Milk? Marketing by Association* (American Society of Association Executives, July 2006).
7. M. Sodhi and N. Sodhi, *Six Sigma Pricing* (Upper Saddle River, NJ: FT Press, 2007).
8. R. Baker, *Pricing on Purpose* (Hoboken, NJ: John Wiley & Sons, 2006).
9. "Hasbro Fined for Price Fixing," *CNN.com*, www.edition.cnn.com/2002/BUSINESS/11/29/uk.hasbro.fine/index.html (accessed September 10, 2008).
10. www.applebees.com (accessed November 1, 2008); www.danielnyc.com/dbbistro (accessed November 1, 2008).
11. www.amazon.com (accessed September 17, 2008).
12. R. Baker, *Pricing on Purpose* (Hoboken, NJ: John Wiley & Sons, 2006).
13. J. Cooper, "Prices and Price Dispersion in Online and Offline Markets for Contact Lenses" (working paper, Bureau of Economics, April 2006).
14. I. Sinha, "Cost Transparency: The Net's Real Threat to Prices and Brands," *Harvard Business Review* (March–April 2008).
15. I. Peel, *The Rough Guide to eBay* (London: Penguin, 2006); *2007 eBay Annual Report*, 2008, www.eBay.com (accessed September, 10, 2008); www.shareholder.com/visitors/dynamicdoc/document.cfm?CompanyID=ebay&DocumentID=2286&PIN=&Page=4&Zoom=1x (accessed September 10, 2008).
16. S. Coomes, "The Big Cheese," *Nation's Restaurant News* 34 (January 28, 2008).

CHAPTER 14

1. H. Italie, "Potter, At the Speed of Light," *Washington Post*, July 26, 2007, www.washingtonpost.com/wp-dyn/content/article/2007/07/26/AR2007072601339_pf.html (accessed August 25, 2008); J. Trachtenberg and J. De Avila, "Mischief Unmanaged," *Wall Street Journal*, July 19, 2007; D. Foust, "Harry Potter and the Logistical Nightmare," *BusinessWeek*, August 6, 2007.
2. M. Hugos and C. Thomas, *Supply Chain Management in the Retail Industry* (Hoboken, NJ: John Wiley & Sons, 2006).
3. Ibid.
4. M. Solomon, G. Marshall, and E. Stuart, *Marketing* (Upper Saddle River, NJ: Prentice Hall, 2008).
5. Ibid.
6. P. Kotler and G. Armstrong, *Principles of Marketing*, 12th ed. (Upper Saddle River, NJ: Prentice Hall, 2008).
7. A. O'Connell, "Improve Your Return on Returns," *Harvard Business Review* (November 2007).
8. D. Blanchard, *Supply Chain Management—Best Practices* (Hoboken, NJ: John Wiley & Sons, 2007).
9. M. Hugos, *Essentials of Supply Chain Management*, 2nd ed. (Hoboken, NJ: John Wiley & Sons, 2006), 18–20.
10. D. Blanchard, *Supply Chain Management—Best Practices* (Hoboken, NJ: John Wiley & Sons, 2007).
11. US Department of Transportation, Maritime Administration. 2008 U.S. Water Transportation—Statistical Snapshot, July 2009, www.marad.dot.gov/documents/US_Water_Transportation_Statistical_snapshot.pdf (accessed June 27, 2010).
12. www.alyeska-pipe.com/pipelinefacts.html (accessed June 27, 2010).
13. D. Blanchard, *Supply Chain Management—Best Practices* (Hoboken, NJ: John Wiley & Sons, 2007).
14. American Marketing Association, *Resource Library—Dictionary*, www.marketingpower.com/_layouts/Dictionary.aspx?dLetter=W (accessed September 5, 2008).
15. M. Solomon, G. Marshall, and E. Stuart, *Marketing* (Upper Saddle River, NJ: Prentice Hall, 2008).
16. D. Blanchard, *Supply Chain Management—Best Practices* (Hoboken, NJ: John Wiley & Sons, 2007).
17. Ibid.
18. Ibid.

CHAPTER 15

1. U.S. Census Bureau, Annual Retail Trade Report, 2008, www.census.gov/retail/ (accessed July 12, 2010).
2. U.S. Census Bureau, 2010 Statistical Abstract, www.census.gov/compendia/statab/cats/income_expenditures_poverty_wealth/gross_domestic_product_gdp.html (accessed July 12, 2010).
3. Bureau of Labor Statistics, US Expenditures, 2008.
4. D. Schulz, "Dispensing with Limitations," *Stores Magazine* (June 2010).
5. Forrester Research, "US eCommerce Forecast, 2008–2013."
6. Pew Research, Pew Internet & American Life Project, January 2009.
7. Forrester Research, www.forrester.com/ER/Press/Release/0,1769,1033,00.html (accessed July 17, 2010).
8. Internet Retailer, Top 500 Guide, www.internetretailer.com/top500/ (accessed July 17, 2010).
9. O. Kharif, "M-Commerce's Big Moment," *Business Week*, October 11, 2009.
10. The Importance of Store Atmospherics, http://blog.dmx.com/latest/44 (accessed July 17, 2010).
11. *LVMH 2007 Annual Report*, www.sephora.com (accessed November 1, 2008), 49–50; J. Naughton, "It's Bath Time for Sephora," *WWD*, October 19, 2007, 6; M. Prior, "Sephora Details 10-year Growth into Superstore," *WWD*, April 6, 2007, 193; M. Prior, "Specialty Chains: Rising Architects of Beauty," *WWD*, July 7, 2006, 192; *LVMH Annual Report 2010*, www.worldpressonline.com/

en/150523620545/LVMH%202009%20annual%20results (accessed July 17, 2010).

12. U.S. Census Bureau, *2002 Census of Wholesale Trade* and *2008 Annual Wholesale Trade Report*.
13. Bureau of Labor Statistics, *Wholesale Trade—Employment Statistics*, 2000, http://stats.bls.gov/oco/cg/pdf/cgs026.pdf (accessed September 9, 2008).
14. M. Solomon, G. Marshall, and E. Stuart, *Marketing* (Upper Saddle River, NJ: Prentice Hall, 2008).

CHAPTER 16

1. www.captivate.com (accessed November 1, 2008).
2. C. Gibbs, "Athletic Shoe Makers Discover Mobile Advertising a Good Fit," *RCR Wireless News*, July 21, 2008; T. Lemke, "Adidas Teams Up in Ad Campaign," *Washington Times*, February 5, 2008.
3. "This Year, Next Year," GroupM, www.groupm.com/ (accessed July 21, 2010).
4. "U.S. Ad Spending Down Nine Percent in 2009, Nielsen Says," http://blog.nielsen.com/nielsenwire/wp-content/uploads/2010/02/2009-Year-End-Ad-Spend-Press-Release.pdf (accessed July 22, 2010).
5. J. Neff, "Will P&G Use Canada as Testing Ground?" *Advertising Age*, May 19, 2008, 41.
6. "Heinz Names Winner of Consumer Generated Ad Contest," *Promo*, April 30, 2008, http://promomagazine.com/contests/news/heinz_names_winner_consumer_generated_ad_contest_0430; E. A. Sullivan, "H. J. Heinz Company," *Marketing News*, February 1, 2008, 10.
7. D. Dilworth, "Arby's Coupons Going Mobile," *DM News*, August 25, 2008, www.dmnews.com/Arbys-coupons-going-mobile/article/115847 (accessed July 22, 2010).
8. M. Chen, "Guidelines May Curb Drug Companies' Freebies," *Herald-Sun*, July 23, 2008; M. Healy, "Sold on Drugs: Under the Influence: Savvy Marketing Whets Our Appetite for Prescriptions," *Los Angeles Times*, August 6, 2007.
9. D. Hajewski, "Mattel Leader Aims to Keep Trust," *Milwaukee Journal Sentinel*, October 26, 2007, www.jsonline.com/story/index.aspx?id=679105 (accessed September 13, 2008); J. Haberkorn, "Mattel Admits Fault in Recall," *Washington Times*, September 13, 2007.
10. "Sponsorship Form: The Value of Sport to Other Kinds of Business," *Economist*, July 31, 2008, www.economist.com/specialreports/displaystory.cfm?story_id=11825607 (accessed September 13, 2008).
11. M. Littman, "Creating a Buzz," *Chain Leader*, April 2008, 18–19.
12. L. de Moraes, "Super Bowl's Big Score: 97.5 Million Viewers," *Washington Post*, February 5, 2008; J. Kirk, "New Deal Keeps Budweiser Name Before Eyes of Wrigley Visitors," *Chicago Tribune*, July 4, 2008.

CHAPTER 17

1. *Making the Sale* (Boston: Harvard Business School Press, 2008).
2. A. Sacco, "Inside Pitney Bowes Choice for a Mobile CRM/ERP Solution," April 28, 2008, www.cio.com (accessed September 15, 2008).
3. M. Solomon, G. Marshall, and E. Stuart, *Marketing: Real People, Real Choices* (Upper Saddle River, NJ: Prentice Hall, 2006).
4. A. Barrett, "Manage Your Sales Reps Better," *BusinessWeek*, June 20, 2008, www.businessweek.com (accessed September 14, 2008).
5. www.the-dma.org (accessed September 12, 2008).
6. Ibid.
7. Direct Marketing Association.
8. Internet World Stats, June 30, 2008, www.internetworldstats.com (accessed September 12, 2008).
9. City of Chicago, www.cityofchicago.org (accessed September 12, 2008).
10. "History of the Sears Catalog," www.searsarchives.com (accessed September 12, 2008).
11. www.dictionary.com (accessed September 12, 2008).
12. L. Lee, "Catalogs, Catalogs Everywhere," *BusinessWeek*, December 4, 2006, www.businessweek.com (accessed September 15, 2008).
13. C. Krol, "E-mail, Fastest Growing Direct Marketing Segment, Expands Double Digits," *DMNews*, August 4, 2009.
14. F. Defino Jr., "Creating the Best Personalized Landing Page," September 3, 2008, www.salesandmarketing.com (accessed September 13, 2008).
15. www.the-dma.org (accessed September 12, 2008).
16. www.ftc.gov (accessed September 12, 2008).

CHAPTER 18

1. M. Wnek, "In Praise of Modern Complexity: Forgoing Simplicity, Geico Doesn't Play to the Lowest Common Denominator," *Adweek*, March 31, 2008, 18; E. Newman, "Insurers No Longer Paying Premium for Advertising," *Brandweek*, April 21, 2008, 7.
2. "Dove to Introduce 'Real Beauty' Web TV Channel," *Marketing*, April 16, 2008, 3; J. Neff, "Soft Soap: In Its Campaign for Real Beauty, Dove Tells Women That They Are Beautiful as They Are," *Advertising Age*, September 24, 2007, 1; "Digital Branding: Utilising User-Generated Content," *New Media Age*, May 3, 2007.
3. N. O'Leary and T. Wasserman, "Old Spice Campaign Smells Like a Sales Success, Too," July 25, 2010, www.brandweek.com/bw/content_display/news-and-features/direct/e3i45f1c709df0501927f56568a2acd5c7b?pn=2 (accessed September 1, 2010).
4. "Media Use Statistics," Media Literacy Clearinghouse, www.frankwbaker.com/mediause.htm (accessed July 30, 2010).
5. S. Berg, "Advertising in the World of New Media," in *Kellogg on Advertising & Media*, ed. B. Calder (Hoboken, NJ: John Wiley & Sons, 2008).
6. P. Kotler and G. Armstrong, *Principles of Marketing* (Upper Saddle River, NJ: Prentice Hall, 2008), 436.
7. *The Nielsen Company Issues Top Ten U.S. Lists for 2007,* Nielsen Media Research, December 11, 2007, www.nielsen.com (accessed September 14, 2008).
8. P. Farris, N. Bendle, P. Pfeifer, and D. Reibstein, *Marketing Metrics: 50+ Metrics Every Executive Should Master* (Upper Saddle River, NJ: Wharton School Publishing, 2007), 275.
9. S. Berg, "Advertising in the World of New Media," in *Kellogg on Advertising & Media*, ed. B. Calder (Hoboken, NJ: John Wiley & Sons, 2008).
10. L. Moses, "Best Use of Print," *Adweek*, June 16, 2008.
11. The Pew Research Center for the People & the Press, "Key News Audiences Now Blend Online and Traditional Sources," August 17, 2008, http://people-press.org/report/444/news-media (accessed September 15, 2008).
12. D. Oulette, "Unfit to Print," September 24, 2007, www.mediaweek.com (accessed November 1, 2008).
13. J. Sissors and R. Baron, *Advertising Media Planning*, 6th ed. (New York: McGraw-Hill, 2002), 342–343.
14. L. Miles, "Out of Sight," September 24, 2007, www.mediaweek.com (accessed November 1, 2008).
15. S. Berg, "Advertising in the World of New Media," in *Kellogg on Advertising & Media*, ed. B. Calder (Hoboken, NJ: John Wiley & Sons, 2008).
16. IAB, "Internet Ad Revenues Reach Record Quarterly High of $6.3 Billion in Q4 '09," www.iab.net/about_the_iab/recent_press_releases/press_release_archive/press_release/pr-040710 (accessed July 30, 2010).
17. M. Shields, "Digital Destiny," September 24, 2007, www.mediaweek.com (accessed November 1, 2008).
18. M. Shields, "Best Use of Mobile," *Adweek,* June 16, 2008.
19. J. M. Lehu, *Branded Entertainment* (London: Kogan, 2006), 254.
20. Ibid., 142–143.
21. J. Sissors and R. Baron, *Advertising Media Planning*, 6th ed. (New York: McGraw-Hill, 2006), 215.
22. R. Lane, K. King, and J. Rusell, *Kleppner's Advertising Procedure* (Upper Saddle River, NJ: Prentice Hall, 2008), 254.
23. R. Briggs and G. Stuart, *What Sticks* (Chicago: Kaplan, 2006), 201–208.

CHAPTER 19

1. N. Borden, "A Note on the Concept of the Marketing Mix," in *Managerial Marketing: Perspectives and Viewpoints*, ed. Eugene J. Kelly and William Lazer (Homewood, IL: Richard D. Irwin, 1958), 272–275.
2. E. J. McCarthy, *Basic Marketing: A Managerial Approach* (Homewood, IL: Richard D. Irwin, 1960).
3. S. Baker, "Why Twitter Matters," May 15, 2008, www.businessweek.com/technology/content/may2008/tc20080514_269697.htm (accessed August 16, 2008); www.hrblock.com/company/index.html (accessed July 28, 2010).
4. www.cadillac.com (accessed July 28, 2010).

5. www.fiskateers.com (accessed September 10, 2008); www.fiskars.com (accessed July 28, 2010).
6. "Unilever's Axe Deodorant, Rheingold Beer, and Walt Disney's Buena Vista Pictures Win Business 2.0 Sweet Spot Awards™," *Business Wire*, May 22, 2003.
7. B. Viveiros, "Gold Standard: Godiva Revamps Its Marketing Strategy to Attract a Younger Audience," http://chiefmarketer.com/cm_plus/godiva_marketing_strategy/ (accessed September 15, 2008); D. Zammit, "Chocolate Meets Fashion in New Godiva Effort," *Adweek*, September 13, 2004; www.godiva.com/mobile (accessed July 28, 2010).
8. I. Eckman, "Lego Braces for Big Changes," www.nytimes.com/2005/07/01/business/worldbusiness/01iht-wblego.html?_r=1&pagewanted=2 (accessed July 28, 2010); www.lego.com/eng/info/ (accessed July 28, 2010).
9. www.usfigureskating.org (accessed September 3, 2010); www.icenetwork.com (accessed September 3, 2010).
10. J. English, "The Four 'Ps' of Marketing Are Dead," *Marketing Health Services* 20, no. 2 (2000): 20–22; N. Coviello and R. Brodie, "Contemporary Marketing Practices of Consumer and Business-to-Business Firms: How Different Are They?" *Journal of Business & Industrial Marketing* 16, no. 5 (2001): 382–400.
11. G. Runciman, "Marketing Ingredients," *Supply Management* 4, no. 20 (1999): 47.
12. B.H. Booms and M.J. Bitner, "Marketing Strategies and Organization Structures for Service Firms," ed. J.H. Donnelly and W.R. George, *Marketing of Services* (Chicago, IL: American Marketing Association), 47–51.
13. G. Runciman, "Marketing Ingredients," *Supply Management* 4, no. 20 (1999): 47.
14. Ibid.
15. N. Coviello, R. Brodie, and P. Danaher, "How Firms Relate to Their Markets: An Empirical Examination of Contemporary Marketing Practices," *Journal of Marketing* 66, no. 3 (2002): 33–46.
16. Ibid.
17. D. Wehmeyer, "Testing . . . Testing . . . 1,2,3, . . . ," *Marketing News* 36, no. 23 (2002): 14, 16.
18. G. Ambach, "Measuring Long-term Effects in Marketing," *Marketing Research* 12, no. 2 (2000): 20–27.
19. D. Wehmeyer, "Testing . . . Testing . . . 1,2,3, . . . ," *Marketing News* 36, no. 23 (2002): 14, 16.
20. "It's PR Time for Miller," *TelevisionWeek* 23, no. 48 (2003): 15.

CHAPTER 20

1. www.marketingpower.org (accessed April 26, 2010).
2. www.ad-id.org (accessed April 10, 2010).
3. www.homedepot.com (accessed April 27, 2010).
4. D. Hayman and D. Schultz, "Measuring Returns on Marketing and Communications Investments," *Strategy & Leadership* 3, No. 27 (1999): 26.
5. Ibid.
6. E. Ephron and G. Pollack, "The Idea That Advertising Doesn't Pay May Be More About Packaged-Goods Than It Is About Advertising," www.ephrononmedia.com/article_archive/articleViewerPublic.asp?articleID=118 (accessed April 27, 2010).
7. "Loyalty Highest for Pet Food Shoppers," *Quirk's Marketing Research Review* 16, No. 11 (2002): 72–73.
8. www.millwardbrown.com/Sites/MillwardBrown/Content/Services/Link360.aspx (accessed April 2, 2010).
9. www.nytimes.com/2009/02/23/business/media/23adcol.html?_r=1 (accessed March 15, 2010).

Glossary

4 Cs are a classification of a marketing mix that includes customer value, cost, convenience, and communication. **(p. 278)**

4 Ps are the most common classification of a marketing mix and consist of product, price, place, and promotion. **(pp. 9, 273)**

7 Ps are a classification of a marketing mix that includes product, price, place, promotion, people, physical evidence, and process. **(p. 278)**

A

Actual product is the combination of tangible and intangible attributes that delivers the core benefits of the product. **(p. 164)**

Ad trafficking is the procedure for delivering finished ads to the correct media firms for placement. **(p. 264)**

Advertising is the paid, nonpersonal communication of a marketing message by an identified sponsor through mass media. **(p. 228)**

Advertising appeal is the reason to purchase a product or service. **(p. 229)**

Advertising measurement is collecting and evaluating advertising metrics to determine the effectiveness of an advertisement or advertising campaign in fulfilling customer, organizational, and marketing objectives. **(p. 289)**

Agents and brokers are independent businesses that may take possession of products but never take title. **(p. 219)**

Alternative close is a sales closing technique that seeks to have the prospect make a choice between product features or options. **(p. 242)**

Antidumping laws are laws designed to prevent predatory pricing. **(p. 186)**

Antitrust law is a catchall phrase for federal legislation meant to prohibit anticompetitive actions on the part of manufacturers, wholesalers, or resellers. **(p. 184)**

Applied research attempts to answer questions related to practical problems. **(p. 99)**

Assumptive close is a sales closing technique that involves direct and specific questions. **(p. 242)**

Atmospherics are the layout, furnishings, color scheme, and music that establish the image customers have of a retailer. **(p. 215)**

Attitude is a state of readiness, based on experience that influences a response to something. **(p. 87)**

Attributes are the unique characteristics of each product, including product features and options, product design, brand name, quality, logos, identifiers, packaging, and warranty. **(p. 163)**

Auctions are markets in which buyers and sellers engage in a process of offer and counteroffer until a price acceptable to both parties is reached. **(p. 189)**

Augmented product is the additional services or benefits that enhance the ownership of the actual product. **(p. 164)**

B

Bait-and-switch pricing occurs when a firm advertises a low price on a desirable product but, in an attempt to trade customers up to more expensive items, it does not make a good faith effort to carry sufficient quantities of that product. **(p. 185)**

Balance of trade is the difference between the monetary value of exports and imports of output in an economy over a specific period. **(p. 56)**

Balanced scorecard is a management system that relates a business's vision and mission to individual business activities. **(p. 31)**

Banner advertising is the placement of advertisements (called banners) onto various Web sites that link to the sponsor's Web page. **(p. 261)**

Bar codes (or **barcodes**) are unique product identification codes used to monitor inventory. **(p. 205)**

Behavioral segmentation allocates consumers into groups based on their uses or responses to a product or service. **(p. 134)**

Behavioral targeting optimizes the online advertising potential for brands. **(p. 136)**

Belief is a sense of truth about something. **(p. 87)**

Benefits, realized through product attributes, define the utility (or usefulness) of a product for the customer. **(p. 163)**

Born global is a business that, from its inception, intends to derive significant competitive advantage from the application of resources and commercial transactions in multiple countries. **(p. 63)**

Boycotts happen when consumers refuse to do business with a company or nation in order to signal their disapproval of its actions and encourage change. **(p. 41)**

Brand is a promise to deliver specific benefits associated with products or services to consumers. **(pp. 3, 115)**

Brand activation is the process of bringing a brand to life by creating an experience that reflects the values of a brand. **(p. 234)**

Brand alliance is a relationship, short of a merger, that is formed by two or more businesses to create market opportunities that would not have existed without the alliance **(p. 122)**

Brand architecture is the naming and organizing of brands within a broader portfolio. **(p. 121)**

Brand equity is the power of a brand, through creation of a distinct image, to influence customer behavior. **(p. 117)**

Brand extension takes an existing brand into a new category. **(p. 123)**

Brand health is the collective consumer perceptions, attitudes, and expectations for a brand resulting from historical and current brand experiences. **(p. 291)**

Brand knowledge is the set of associations that consumers hold in memory regarding the brand's features, benefits, users, perceived quality, and overall attitude as a result of prior brand marketing activities. **(p. 117)**

Brand loyalty is the extent to which a consumer repeatedly purchases a given brand. **(p. 118)**

Brand management is the overall coordination of a brand's equities to create long-term brand growth through overseeing marketing mix strategies. **(p. 125)**

Brand manager is the person responsible for managing the marketing activities associated with a brand. **(p. 125)**

Brand personality consists of characteristics that make a brand unique, much like human personality. **(p. 121)**

Brand positioning is the location that a brand occupies in the marketplace relative to competitors. **(p. 120)**

Brand position statement is a summary of what a brand offers to the market. **(p. 140)**

Brand protection involves securing the brand's inherent value, including its intellectual property. **(p. 125)**

Brand strategy is the process where the offer is positioned in the consumer's mind to produce a perception of advantage. **(p. 122)**

Brand stretching is extending a brand to new products, services, or markets. **(p. 117)**

Brand valuation is the process of quantifying the financial benefit that results from owning a brand. **(p. 117)**

Branded entertainment is the integration of brands or brand messages into entertainment media, for example, films, television, novels, and songs. **(p. 258)**

Break-even point is the volume or price at which a company's revenue for a product exactly equals its fixed cost. **(p. 181)**

Breaking bulk refers to the process of reducing large product shipments into smaller ones that are more suitable for individual retailers or companies. **(p. 205)**

Bribery is the practice of offering something of financial value to someone in a position of authority to alter behavior and gain an illicit advantage. **(p. 58)**

Broadcast media include network television, cable television, and radio. **(p. 258)**

Bundling refers to the practice of marketing two or more products and/or services in a single package. **(p. 123)**

Business analysis is the process of validating that the new product will meet all sales and profit objectives. **(p. 166)**

Business markets include individuals and organizations that are potential or actual buyers of goods and services that are used in, or in support of, the production of other products or services that are supplied to others. **(p. 20)**

Business mission is a statement that identifies the purpose of a business and what makes that business different from others. **(p. 29)**

Business objective is something that a business attempts to achieve in support of an overarching strategy. **(p. 29)**

Business plan is a written document that defines the operational and financial objectives of a business over a particular time, and how the business plans to accomplish those objectives. **(pp. 27, 147)**

Business planning is a decision process for people and businesses to manage systems to achieve an objective. **(p. 27)**

Business-to-business, also referred to as **B2B**, involves the sales of products and services from one business to another. **(p. 20)**

Business vision is a statement in a strategic plan that identifies an idealized picture of a future state a business is aiming to achieve. **(p. 29)**

Buyclasses are major classifications of business buying situations. **(p. 20)**

Buying center is the collection of individuals that perform specific roles in the procurement process. **(p. 20)**

C

Cable television refers to television broadcasts using cables or satellite dishes. **(p. 259)**

Call to action is the response that a marketer wants a consumer to take as a result of receiving a direct-mail communication. **(p. 249)**

CAN-SPAM Act of 2003 (Controlling the Assault of Non-Solicited Pornography and Marketing Act) is the law that requires e-mail marketers to abide by certain requirements when e-mailing consumers. **(p. 250)**

Cannibalization is the loss of sales of an existing product within a portfolio to a new product in the same portfolio. **(p. 123)**

Carrier is the entity that physically transports goods from shipper to consignee. **(p. 204)**

Cash-and-carry wholesalers provide few services but offer low prices on the limited number of goods they carry. **(p. 218)**

Cash Cows are products or services with high market share and low growth opportunities. **(p. 30)**

Cash discount is a percentage or fixed amount off the quoted price of an item, and is given when a customer pays in cash. **(p. 190)**

Catalog is a printed direct-mail piece that showcases an assortment of products or services offered by a company. **(p. 248)**

Category killers are retailers that offer a wide selection of merchandise in a narrow product category. **(p. 211)**

Category management involves the management of multiple brands in a product line. **(p. 125)**

Category manager is the person responsible for managing a product line that may contain one or more brands. **(p. 125)**

Census is a survey that collects responses for each member of the population. **(p. 105)**

Channel is a system with few or many steps in which products flow from businesses to consumers while payments flow from consumers to businesses. **(p. 117)**

Channel conflict occurs when two or more channel members disagree. **(p. 201)**

Channel leader is a firm with sufficient power over other channel members to take a leadership role in the channel. **(p. 201)**

Channel strategy describes the levels, organization, and distribution intensity of a marketing channel. **(p. 199)**

Channel switching is creating new product distribution or moving the distribution flow of products from one distribution channel to another. **(p. 117)**

Circulation is the number of published and distributed copies of a magazine. **(p. 260)**

Classified advertising is the online version of traditional classified ads. **(p. 261)**

Clickthrough fees are the amount one online entity charges another online entity for passing along a Web user who clicks an ad or link. **(p. 189)**

Close the sale refers to the part of the selling process in which the salesperson asks for an order. **(p. 242)**

Closed-ended question is a question that has specific survey answer choices available to respondents. **(p. 104)**

Co-branding is the collaboration of multiple brands in the marketing of one specific product. **(p. 122)**

Coding is the numbering of the answer choices for each survey question. **(p. 105)**

Cognitive age, also referred to as subjective age, is the age that a person feels. **(p. 86)**

Commercialization is the process of launching a new product in the marketplace. **(p. 166)**

Commission is the part or all of a salesperson's income that is based on the amount of sales or profit delivered in a given time frame. **(p. 245)**

Commission merchants are brokers who take physical possession of products but do not take title and subtract an agreed-upon commission from the buyer's payment to the seller. **(p. 219)**

Communications mix is the various elements companies can use to communicate with the target market, including advertising, public relations, sales promotion, and personal selling. **(p. 256)**

Competitive bidding involves suppliers in a bid process that receive identical RFQs and then return quotes in secret to the buyer. **(p. 186)**

Competitive budget method is a method of setting the advertising budget where the budget is set to match, dollar for dollar, that of an important competitor. **(p. 229)**

Competitive environment includes those factors that relate to the nature, quantity, and potential actions of competitors. **(p. 17)**

Competitive intelligence involves the systematic tracking of competitive actions and plans and is a significant activity within a business. **(p. 107)**

Components are finished products companies employ to manufacture their own products, for example, microchips or engines. **(p. 165)**

Concept change is an advanced, breakthrough innovation that changes everything. **(p. 167)**

Concept development is the process of concretely defining the features and benefits of the new product. **(p. 165)**

Concept testing is developing prototypes of the product for product testing. **(p. 166)**

Consignee is the receiver of goods being distributed. **(p. 204)**

Consultative selling is when the salesperson is focused more on solving the problems of the prospect rather than trying to sell a product. **(p. 242)**

Consumer behavior is the dynamic interaction of affect and cognition, behavior, and the environment in which human beings conduct the exchange aspects of their lives. **(p. 83)**

Consumer decision-making process is the steps that consumers take to identify and evaluate choice options. **(p. 84)**

Consumer insight is perceived meanings of data collected from the study of consumer behavior. **(p. 97)**

Consumer market insight is an in-depth understanding of customer behavior that is more qualitative than quantitative. **(p. 97)**

Consumer markets include individuals and households that are potential or actual buyers of goods and services that assist in further production only indirectly or incidentally, if at all. **(p. 19)**

Consumer orientation reflects a business focus on satisfying unmet consumer needs and wants. **(p. 6)**

Consumer problem solving is how someone comes to a conclusion about a situation. This is determined by what kind of a decision a consumer is facing. **(p. 91)**

Consumer products are products that directly fulfill the desires of consumers and are not intended to assist in the manufacture of other products. **(pp. 19, 164)**

Consumer promotions are designed to motivate consumers to try a product or buy it again by offering an economic incentive such as coupons. **(p. 231)**

Consumerism is the organized efforts on the part of consumer groups or governments to improve the rights and power of buyers in relation to sellers. **(p. 41)**

Consumer's surplus occurs when a consumer purchases a product or service at a price less than the utility of the product or service. **(p. 19)**

Contact efficiency is the efficiency gained in terms of a reduction in the number of contacts required through the use of channel intermediaries. **(p. 197)**

Context change is when an existing product or service is taken into a new context or market. **(p. 167)**

Contract manufacturer is an entry strategy in which a company directly hires a company in the host nation to manufacture products on its behalf. **(p. 62)**

Contribution margin is the difference between a product's price and its variable cost. **(p. 181)**

Convenience products are products that are purchased frequently with little or no shopping effort, for example, grocery staples, paper products, and candy. **(p. 164)**

Convenience stores are small, self-service retailers that offer few product choices outside their primary offerings of beer, soft drinks, and snacks. **(p. 213)**

Cookies are small files containing certain personal information that are sent from Web servers to a consumer's computer to be accessed the next time a consumer visits a particular Web site. **(p. 107)**

Copy testing is a survey-based process that can assist in measuring advertising and campaign effectiveness. **(p. 289)**

Core benefits are the fundamental product benefits the customer receives from a product. **(p. 164)**

Corporate public relations is how management evaluates and shapes or reshapes long-term public opinion of the company. **(p. 233)**

Corporate social responsibility (CSR) is a philosophy that encourages decision makers to take into account the social consequences of their business actions. **(p. 46)**

Cosmetic change is an evolutionary change to an existing product or service. **(p. 167)**

Cost-based pricing establishes a price based on the cost to manufacture a product or deliver a service. **(p. 181)**

Cost-plus pricing adds a fixed amount to the cost of each product or service sufficient to earn a desired profit. **(p. 181)**

Cost transparency is the ability of consumers to understand a product's actual cost. **(p. 189)**

Counterfeiting is the unauthorized copying of products, packaging, or other intellectual property of a registered brand. **(pp. 58, 125)**

Countertrade is a legal agreement where goods are paid for in a form other than cash. **(p. 58)**

CPM (or **cost per thousand**) is a metric that calculates the cost for any media vehicle to deliver one thousand impressions among a group of target customers. **(p. 259)**

Creating assortments is the process of collecting an assortment of products into a single shipment to a destination. **(p. 205)**

Cross-docking is a warehousing technique that minimizes holding costs by unloading products at a warehouse or distribution center and then reloading them almost immediately for transport. **(p. 205)**

Cue is an environmental stimulus that influences a particular action. **(p. 87)**

Culture refers to the shared values, beliefs, and preferences of a particular society. **(pp. 40, 59, 88)**

Currency exchange rates are variable rates that specify the price of one currency in terms of the price of another. **(p. 186)**

Customer-based brand equity is the differential effect that brand knowledge has on the customer response to marketing efforts. **(p. 118)**

Customer lifetime value (CLV) is the present value of all profits expected to be earned from a customer over the lifetime of his or her relationship with a company. **(pp. 5, 73)**

Customer loyalty is the degree to which a customer will select a particular brand when a purchase from that product category is being considered. **(p. 72)**

Customer relationship management (CRM) is the activities that are used to establish, develop, and maintain customer relationships. **(pp. 5, 75)**

Customer relationships are created when businesses and consumers interact through a sales transaction of a product or service and continue based on ongoing interaction between the business and the consumer. **(p. 5)**

Customer satisfaction is the degree to which a product meets or exceeds customer expectations. **(p. 71)**

Customer value is the difference between the benefits a customer receives and the total cost incurred from acquiring, using, and disposing of a product. **(p. 69)**

D

Data analytics is an inference-based process to transform data into useful information. **(p. 285)**

Data mining is the statistical analysis of large databases seeking to discover hidden pieces of information. This technique can be used with both primary and secondary data. **(pp. 76, 101)**

Deceptive pricing occurs when a price is meant to intentionally mislead or deceive customers. **(p. 185)**

Decline stage is the stage at which the demand for a product falls due to changes in customer preferences. Sales and profits eventually fall to zero. **(p. 171)**

Demand is the financial capacity to buy what one wants. **(p. 3)**

Demand curve (or **demand schedule**) charts the projected sales for a product or service for any price customers are willing to pay. **(p. 182)**

Democracy is a form of government in which the supreme power is retained by the people, but which is usually exercised indirectly through a system of representation and delegated authority periodically renewed. **(p. 58)**

Demographic segmentation divides the market into groups, based on variables such as age, gender, family size, family life cycle, income, occupation, education, religion, ethnicity, generation, nationality, and sexual orientation. **(p. 133)**

Demographics are characteristics of human population used to identify markets. **(p. 17)**

Department stores carry a wide selection of products organized by departments, such as housewares, men's and women's apparel, appliances, and luggage. **(p. 211)**

Derived demand is the demand for a product or service that results from the demand for another product or service. **(p. 20)**

Descriptive research is a marketing research design that is used to describe marketing variables by answering who, what, when, where, and how questions. **(p. 101)**

Differentiated marketing separates and targets several different market segments with a different product or service geared to each segment. **(p. 137)**

Diffusion of innovations is a theory concerning how populations adopt innovations over time. **(p. 172)**

Digital brand strategy is a set of marketing activities that uses digital mediums to connect consumers to brands. **(p. 115)**

Digital media includes electronic media such as e-mail, Web advertising, and Web sites. **(p. 258)**

Direct exporting is a form of exporting in which a firm establishes its own overseas sales branches. **(p. 62)**

Direct investment is an entry strategy in which a company establishes foreign-based manufacturing facilities. **(p. 62)**

Direct mail is a printed advertisement in the form of a postcard, letter, brochure, or product sample that is sent to consumers who are on a targeted mailing list. **(p. 248)**

Direct marketing is any communication addressed to a consumer that is designed to generate a response. **(p. 247)**

Direct marketing channel is a single channel member that produces and distributes a product or service. **(p. 199)**

Direct-response advertising is a direct marketing approach that includes a specific offer and call to action for the consumer to immediately contact the marketer to purchase or inquire about the product. **(p. 249)**

Discontinuous innovations are new product ideas that change our everyday lives in dramatic ways. **(p. 167)**

Discount stores are a type of department store focused on turning over products more quickly than traditional department stores by offering lower prices. **(p. 211)**

Distribution is the process of delivering products and services to customers. **(p. 197)**

Distribution center is a large warehouse used to store a company's products. **(p. 205)**

Distribution intensity determines the number of outlets or locations where a product will be sold. **(p. 200)**

Divesting is the process of discontinuing the production and sale of a product. **(p. 172)**

Do Not Call Registry is a list of consumers who do not want to receive phone calls from telemarketers. Consumers can contact the Federal Trade Commission to be added to the Do Not Call Registry. **(p. 249)**

Do Not Mail List is the list of consumers who do not want to receive direct mail. Consumers can contact the Direct Marketing Association to be added to the Do Not Mail List. **(p. 250)**

Dogs are products or services with low relative market share in a low growth sector. **(p. 30)**

Dominican Republic-Central America-United States Free Trade Agreement (CAFTA-DR) is a trading partnership among the United States, the Dominican Republic, Costa Rica, El Salvador, Guatemala, Honduras, and Nicaragua that represents the first free trade agreement between the *United States* and a group of smaller developing economies. **(p. 56)**

Drive is an internal stimulus that encourages action. **(p. 87)**

Drop shippers are wholesalers who take title to products but never take possession of them. **(p. 219)**

DRTV (direct-response TV) is any kind of television commercial or home shopping television show that advertises a product or service and allows the viewer to purchase it directly. **(p. 249)**

Dumping is the practice of selling a product in a foreign country for a price less than either the cost to make the product or the price in the home country. **(p. 56)**

Durable goods are products that are expected to last for three or more years. **(p. 211)**

Dynamic imaging is the process of systematically populating individual e-mails with products targeted specifically to each consumer, based on behavior patterns and inventory. **(p. 250)**

Dynamic pricing (or **"smart" pricing**) is the practice of varying prices based on marketplace conditions. **(p. 189)**

E

Early adopters are consumers who are more socially aware than innovators and consider the prestige or social implications of being seen using a new product. **(p. 173)**

Early majority are middle-class consumers who do not want to be the first, or the last, to try a new product. They look to the early adopters for direction about product innovations. **(p. 173)**

Economic communities are groups of countries that agree to take certain actions to manage resources of goods and services by lowering tariff barriers and promoting trade among members. **(p. 55)**

Economic environment includes those factors that influence consumer purchase ability and buying behavior. **(p. 17)**

Elastic refers to the situation in which price elasticity is greater than one or when demand is highly responsive to a change in price. **(p. 183)**

Elevator pitch is a brief description of a product or service designed to gain attention of desired parties and to generate interest in achieving a desired outcome. **(p. 28)**

Environmental sustainability is achieving financial objectives while promoting the long-term well-being of the earth. **(p. 42)**

Environmentalism is an organized movement of citizens, businesses, and government agencies to protect and improve our living environment. **(p. 42)**

Equipment is a group of products used in the everyday operation of a business, for example, factories and copy machines. **(p. 165)**

Ethics are a system of moral principles and values, as well as moral duties or obligations. **(p. 46)**

Ethnographic research is a type of observational research where trained researchers immerse themselves in a specific consumer environment. **(p. 102)**

European Union (EU) is an economic and political partnership among 27 European countries. **(p. 56)**

Exaggerated claims are extravagant statements made in advertising, either explicitly or implicitly, that have no substantiation or reasonable basis in truth. **(p. 45)**

Exchange controls are types of controls that governments put in place to ban or restrict the amount of a specific currency that is permitted to be traded or purchased. **(p. 56)**

Exchange functions are activities that promote and enable transfer of ownership. **(p. 9)**

Exclusive distribution refers to the distribution of products in only a few locations. **(p. 200)**

Experience curve is an economic model that presumes costs will decline as production volume increases. **(p. 188)**

Experiential positioning is based on characteristics of the brands that stimulate sensory or emotional connections with customers. **(p. 139)**

Explanatory research is a marketing research design used to understand the relationship between independent and dependent variables. **(p. 101)**

Exploratory research is a marketing research design used to generate ideas in a new area of inquiry. **(p. 101)**

Exporting is a common form of market entry that occurs when a company produces in its home market and then transports its products to other nations for sale. **(p. 62)**

External environment of a business involves all those activities that occur outside the organizational functions of a business. **(p. 15)**

External marketing is the implementation of marketing practices directed outside the business to create value and to form productive customer relationships. **(p. 15)**

Extraterritoriality holds certain individuals such as diplomats accountable to the laws of their home country while exempting them from the jurisdiction of a foreign country in which they may be operating. **(p. 58)**

F

Facilitating functions are activities that assist in the execution of exchange and physical functions. **(p. 9)**

Fair prices are those consumers perceive as offering good value and meeting personal and social norms. **(p. 179)**

Fair value zone is the area on a value map where customers' perceived benefits equal the customers' perceived cost. **(p. 69)**

Fixed costs (or **overhead**) are costs that are incurred regardless of any production or sales. **(p. 180)**

Flanker brand is created to expand an organization's portfolio into a new segment of an existing market category while retaining relevance with current customers. **(p. 123)**

Focus groups are collections of a small number of individuals recruited by specific criteria with the purpose to discuss predetermined topics with qualified moderators. **(p. 101)**

Foreign Corrupt Practices Act is an act passed in 1977 that makes it "unlawful for certain classes of persons and entities to make payments to foreign government officials to assist in obtaining or retaining business." **(p. 58)**

Forward auction is a market in which a buyer states what he or she is seeking to purchase and sellers respond in kind with bids (or prices). **(p. 189)**

Franchising is an entry strategy in which a local company purchases the right to use the processes and brand of another company. **(p. 62)**

Frequency is the number of times an individual is exposed to an advertising message by a media vehicle. **(pp. 229, 261)**

Full-line product strategy is offering a wide range of product lines within a product portfolio. **(p. 169)**

Full-service retailers are typically high-end specialty or department stores where sales personnel provide assistance to customers during and after their visit to the store. **(p. 214)**

Full-service wholesalers typically assume supply chain responsibilities that would otherwise be performed by manufacturers. **(p. 218)**

Functional positioning is based on the attributes of products or services and their corresponding benefits and is intended to communicate how customers can solve problems or fulfill needs. **(p. 139)**

G

General merchandise wholesalers carry a wide assortment of merchandise in a broad product category, such as pharmaceuticals or groceries. **(p. 218)**

Global companies are companies that maintain assets and operations in more than one country and concentrate on penetrating multiple countries with a minimally customized marketing mix. **(p. 55)**

Global marketing includes all marketing activities conducted at an international level by individuals or businesses. **(p. 53)**

Global marketing environment describes the environment in different sovereign countries, with characteristics distinct to the home environment of an organization, influencing decisions on marketing activities. **(p. 55)**

Global marketing processes are a series of strategic marketing decisions including deciding to go global, determining which markets to enter, deciding how to enter the markets, and selecting the global marketing program. **(p. 61)**

Globalization is the outcome of cultures intermingling, sharing experiences, news, and commerce. **(p. 53)**

Glocal describes a company that acts either globally, locally, or both, as needed. **(p. 54)**

Green marketing refers to marketing efforts to product more environmentally responsible products and services. **(p. 42)**

Grocery stores/supermarkets are self-service retailers that carry food and nonfood items. **(p. 212)**

Gross Domestic Product (GDP) measures the total dollar value of goods and services a country produces within a given year. **(pp. 39, 55)**

Gross Rating Points (GRPs) are a way for planners to approximate the impact of media decisions and are the product of reach multiplied by frequency. **(p. 264)**

Growth stage is the stage at which a product is rapidly adopted in the marketplace. Sales grow rapidly and profits peak. **(p. 171)**

Guarantees are promises made by media companies that estimated audience numbers will be achieved, or part of the cost of advertising will be retuned to the advertiser. **(p. 266)**

H

Harvesting is the process of continuing to sell a product in spite of declining sales. **(p. 172)**

Horizontal conflict occurs between channel members at the same level in a channel (e.g., two retailers). **(p. 201)**

House file is a proprietary database of customer information collected from transactions, inquiries, or surveys from the company. **(p. 247)**

Hurdle rate is the minimum amount of financial return that an organization requires before making a financial investment. **(p. 293)**

I

Idea generation is the process of formulating an idea for a new product or service. **(p. 165)**

Idea screening is the process of reviewing a product idea to ensure that it meets customer wants and company goals. **(p. 165)**

Impression refers to the single delivery of an advertising message by a media vehicle. **(p. 259)**

Inbound logistics controls the flow of products or services from suppliers to manufacturers or service providers. **(p. 202)**

Income distribution is the way in which income and wealth are divided among the members of an economy. **(p. 57)**

Income levels are average consumer earnings used to approximate national earnings. **(p. 17)**

Incremental cost is the additional cost to produce or sell one more product or service. **(p. 189)**

Indirect exporting is a form of exporting in which a firm sells its products through intermediaries. **(p. 62)**

Indirect marketing channel is a channel involving one or more intermediaries between producer and customer. **(p. 199)**

Industrial economies are countries with robust manufacturing, service, and financial sectors that are actively engaged in international trade. **(p. 57)**

Industrial products are products sold to business customers for their direct use or as inputs to the manufacture of other products. Classifications of industrial products include equipment, MRO products, raw materials, processed materials and services, and components. **(p. 165)**

Industrializing economies are countries where the manufacturing sector accounts for a small but growing share of the total economy and an increasing number of imported raw materials are required to support manufacturing. **(p. 57)**

Inelastic refers to the situation in which price elasticity is less than one or when demand is relatively nonresponsive to a change in price. **(p. 183)**

Inflation is an increase in the price of a collection of goods that represent the overall economy. **(p. 17)**

Infomercial is a television show that is a combination of an information session and a commercial. **(p. 249)**

Informative advertising provides consumers with information on the product or service. **(p. 228)**

Innovators are consumers who are the most willing to adopt innovations. They tend to be younger, better educated, and more financially secure. **(p. 172)**

Inseparability recognizes that a service cannot be separated from its means or manner of production. **(p. 163)**

Inside sales are members of the sales team who reside inside the office or company location and rarely, if ever, have face-to-face contact with customers or prospects. **(p. 243)**

Insight is the act or result of apprehending the inner nature of things, or of seeing intuitively. **(p. 97)**

Instability is the condition of being erratic or unpredictable. **(p. 57)**

Intangibility recognizes that a service cannot be perceived by the five senses (sight, hearing, touch, smell, or taste) before it is produced and consumed. **(p. 163)**

Integrated marketing communications is the coordination of advertising, sales promotion, public relations, and personal selling to ensure that all marketing communications are consistent and relevant to the target market. **(p. 255)**

Intellectual property is a collection of non-physical assets owned by an individual or company that are the result of innovation and are legally protected from being copied or used by unauthorized parties. **(p. 125)**

Intensive distribution refers to the distribution of products in a relatively large number of locations. **(p. 200)**

Intermodal distribution systems is a distribution strategy that uses more than one kind of transportation mode. **(p. 205)**

Internal environment of a business involves all those activities that occur within the organizational functions in a business. **(p. 15)**

Internal marketing is the implementation of marketing practices within an organization to communicate organizational policies and practices to employees and internal stakeholders. **(p. 15)**

International companies are companies that have no investment outside their home country other than the direct purchase of products or services and are, essentially, importers and exporters. **(p. 55)**

International law is a body of rules and customs by which countries are guided in their relations with other countries and recognized international organizations. **(p. 58)**

Internet research panel is a collection of individuals who agree, for some predetermined incentive, to participate in questionnaires on a variety of topics as determined by the owner and manager of the panel. **(p. 102)**

Internet retailers offer a wide range of products that are sold online. **(p. 213)**

Interval scale is a measurement in which the numbers assigned to the characteristics of the objects or groups of objects legitimately allow a comparison of the size of the differences among and between objects. **(p. 104)**

Introduction stage is the stage at which a new product is introduced to the marketplace. Sales begin to build, but profits remain low (or even negative). **(p. 171)**

Inventory is a store of goods awaiting transport or shipping. **(p. 204)**

J

Jobbers are wholesalers that operate on a relatively small scale and sell and provide services primarily to retailers. **(p. 219)**

Joint ownership is an entry strategy in which a company joins with a foreign investor to build its own local business. **(p. 62)**

Joint venture is an entry strategy in which a company teams with a host company in the particular market they are entering. **(p. 62)**

Jurisdiction is the power or right of a legal or political entity to exercise its authority over a specific geographic area. **(p. 58)**

Just-in-time (JIT) is an inventory management technique in which goods are delivered within a predefined time "window" that corresponds to exactly when the goods are needed. **(p. 203)**

K

Key performance indicators (KPIs) are measurements that assist an organization in quantifying progress toward achievement of marketing objectives. **(p. 287)**

L

Laggards are consumers who are heavily bound by tradition and are the last to adopt an innovation. **(p. 173)**

Late majority are older and conservative consumers who avoid products they consider to be too risky. They will purchase something only if they consider it to be a necessity or when they are under some form of social pressure. **(p. 173)**

Laws are rules of conduct or action prescribed by an authority, or the binding customs or practices of a community. **(p. 44)**

Lead time is the amount of preparation time a media type requires before an advertisement can be run. **(p. 260)**

Learning is knowledge that is acquired through experiences. **(p. 87)**

Legal environment includes those factors that provide rules, and penalties for violations, designed to protect society and consumers from unfair business practices and to protect businesses from unfair competitive practices. **(p. 18)**

Level of service is the service offered to customers on the continuum between full- and self-service. **(p. 214)**

Levels of a product consist of three classifications: core benefits, actual product, and augmented product—and each additional level has the potential to add greater value for the consumer. **(p. 164)**

Licensing is the practice of a company receiving fees or royalties from partner firms for the right to use a brand, manufacturing process, or patent. **(pp. 62, 122)**

Life cycle marketing is a series of targeted messages to customers and prospects based on their experience during a sequence of events that takes place during a specific stage in life. **(p. 250)**

Life stages are similar life events experienced by groups of individuals of varying chronological and cognitive ages. **(p. 86)**

Lifestyle is a way of life that individuals express through choosing how to spend their time and personal resources. **(p. 85)**

Limited-line product strategy is focusing on one or a few product lines within a product portfolio. **(p. 169)**

Limited problem solving occurs when a consumer is prepared to exert a certain amount of effort to make a purchase decision. **(p. 91)**

Limited-service retailers provide assistance to customers upon request. **(p. 214)**

Limited-service wholesalers perform fewer services for manufacturers but may be the best or only way to reach the markets they serve. **(p. 218)**

Line expansions are the addition of entirely new product lines to a product mix. **(p. 169)**

Line extension is an addition to an existing product line that retains the currently utilized brand name. **(pp. 122, 169)**

Logistics is the coordination of all activities related to the transportation or delivery of products and services that occur within the boundaries of a single business or organization. **(p. 202)**

Logistics manager is a person responsible for coordinating the activities of all members of a company's distribution channel. **(p. 202)**

Loss-leader pricing involves the sale of items below cost to drive floor traffic. **(p. 185)**

M

Macroenvironment includes societal forces that are essentially uncontrollable and influence the microenvironment of a business. **(p. 16)**

Make-good ads are given by media companies as replacements for any media that did not run as scheduled. **(p. 266)**

Mail order is the term that describes the business of selling merchandise through the mail. **(p. 248)**

Mail order wholesalers employ catalogs or the Internet as their sales force. **(p. 218)**

Manufacturer brand is a brand owned by a manufacturer. **(p. 121)**

Manufacturer-owned intermediaries are wholesaling or similar entities owned by the manufacturer as a way of controlling the inventory and sale processes and increasing profit margins. **(p. 219)**

Manufacturers' agents are independent agents used in place of a manufacturer's sales team. **(p. 219)**

Manufacturer's showroom is a facility where a firm's products are permanently on display for customers to view. **(p. 219)**

Market is a place, either physical or virtual, where buyers and sellers come together to exchange goods and services. **(p. 61)**

Market structure refers to the type of marketplace situation the company faces: monopoly, oligopoly, monopolistic competition, or pure competition. **(p. 180)**

Marketing is an organizational function and a collection of processes designed to plan for, create, communicate, and deliver value to customers and to build effective customer relationships in ways that benefit the organization and its stakeholders. **(p. 3)**

Marketing accountability is the management of resources and processes to achieve measurable increases in both return on marketing investment and efficiency while increasing the value of the organization in compliance with all legal requirements. **(p. 285)**

Marketing audit is the comprehensive review and assessment of a business's marketing environment. **(p. 32)**

Marketing channel is the network of parties involved in moving products from the producer to consumers or business customers. **(p. 197)**

Marketing communications are the messages sent from organizations to members of a target market in order to influence how they think, feel, and act toward a brand or market offering. **(p. 225)**

Marketing concept is an organizational philosophy dedicated to understanding and fulfilling consumer needs through the creation of value. **(p. 5)**

Marketing decision support system (MDSS) is the software and associated infrastructure that connects the marketing activity to company databases. **(p. 107)**

Marketing environment is a set of forces, some controllable and some uncontrollable, that influence the ability of a business to create value and attract and serve customers. **(p. 15)**

Marketing ethics are rules for evaluating marketing decisions and actions based on marketers' duties or obligations to society. **(p. 46)**

Marketing functions are activities performed both by consumers and by businesses involved in value creation for specific products or services. **(p. 9)**

Marketing information system (MIS) is a series of steps that include collection, analysis, and presentation of information for use in making marketing decisions. **(p. 107)**

Marketing intelligence system is a system that gathers, processes, assesses, and makes available marketing information in a format that allows the marketing activity to function more effectively. **(p. 107)**

Marketing measurement is collecting and evaluating marketing metrics to determine the effectiveness of marketing activities in fulfilling customer, organizational, and marketing objectives. **(p. 287)**

Marketing metrics are units of measure that allow for assessment of the effectiveness of marketing activities. **(p. 285)**

Marketing mix is a group of marketing variables that a business controls with the intent of implementing a marketing strategy directed at a specific target market. **(pp. 33, 273)**

Marketing-mix models evaluate the contribution that each component of a marketing program makes to changes in market performance. **(p. 279)**

Marketing-mix optimization involves assigning portions of the marketing budget to each marketing-mix element so as to maximize revenues or profits. **(p. 279)**

Marketing-mix strategy is the logic that guides the selection of a particular marketing mix to achieve marketing objectives. **(p. 275)**

Marketing objective is something that a marketing function is attempting to achieve in support of a strategic business plan. **(p. 32)**

Marketing plan is a document that includes an assessment of the marketing situation, marketing objectives, marketing strategy, and marketing initiatives. **(pp. 33, 149)**

Marketing planning is the part of business planning devoted to connecting a business to the environments in which that business functions in order to accomplish the business's goals. **(p. 32)**

Marketing program is a consolidated plan of all individual marketing plans. **(p. 149)**

Marketing public relations is how marketers seek to achieve specific marketing objectives by targeting consumers with product-focused messages. **(p. 233)**

Marketing research is the acquisition and analysis of information used to identify and define marketing opportunities that connect consumers to marketers. **(p. 99)**

Marketing research system is a collection of the results of marketing research studies conducted by a company. **(p. 107)**

Marketing strategy is a statement of how a business intends to achieve its marketing objectives. **(pp. 32, 166)**

Markup is a percentage or fixed amount added to the cost of a product or service. **(p. 181)**

Mass marketing is communicating a product or service message to as broad a group of people as possible with the purpose of positively influencing sales. **(p. 131)**

Maturity stage is the stage at which the product has been purchased by most potential buyers and future sales are largely replacement purchases. Sales plateau and profits begin to fall. **(p. 171)**

M-Commerce is a form of nonstore retailing conducted through the use of mobile devices such as smart phones. **(p. 213)**

Measurement is the process of quantifying how much of a variable's set of features or characteristics are possessed in another variable. **(p. 103)**

Media audits measure how well each selected media vehicle performs in terms of its estimated audience delivery and cost. **(p. 266)**

Media budgets specify the total amount a firm will spend on all types of advertising media. **(p. 263)**

Media buyers negotiate and purchase media properties according to the media plan. **(p. 264)**

Media buying is the negotiation and purchase of media. **(p. 264)**

Media efficiency measures how inexpensively a media vehicle is able to communicate with a particular customer segment. **(p. 258)**

Media engagement evaluates how attentively audiences read, watch, or listen to a particular media vehicle. **(p. 258)**

Media flowcharts (or **media footprints**) are visual representations of the media plan. **(p. 264)**

Media impact is a qualitative assessment as to the value of a message exposed in a particular medium. **(p. 258)**

Media objectives are clear, unambiguous statements as to what media selection and implementation will achieve. **(p. 263)**

Media optimization is the adjustment of media plans to maximize their performance. **(p. 266)**

Media planners create media plans based on their extensive knowledge about media vehicles and expertise. **(p. 264)**

Media planning involves the creation of a media plan, which is a document that describes how an advertiser plans to spend its media budget to reach its objectives. **(p. 264)**

Media plans specify the types and amounts of media to be used, the timing of media, and the geographic concentration (national, regional, or local). **(p. 264)**

Media selection refers to the process of choosing which media types to use and when, where, and for what duration in order to execute a media plan. **(p. 263)**

Media type (or **media vehicle**) refers to a form of media used for marketing communications, including types such as broadcast, print, digital, branded entertainment, and social networks. **(p. 258)**

Merchandise assortment is the breadth and depth of product lines a store carries, as well as the amount of each product the store stocks. **(p. 214)**

Merchandise brokers are brokers that specialize in linking buyers and sellers together and are generally well known in their area of specialization. **(p. 219)**

Merchant wholesalers are a broad group of wholesalers that take title to the products that are purchased from manufacturers. **(p. 217)**

Message execution is how the message is delivered. **(p. 229)**

Microenvironment includes those forces close to a company, yet outside its internal environment, that influence the ability of a business to serve its customers. **(p. 15)**

Mobile advertising refers to advertisements delivered over portable communication devices. **(p. 261)**

Modeling is a tool that many large advertisers use to guide their media planning and plan optimization. **(p. 266)**

Monarchy is a form of government in which the supreme power is held by a monarch who reigns over a state or territory, usually for life and by hereditary right; the monarch may be either a sole absolute ruler or a sovereign—such as a king, queen, or prince—with constitutionally limited authority. **(p. 58)**

Monopolistic competition refers to a market composed of firms with somewhat differentiated products and limited pricing power sufficient to influence the price of their own products to a degree. **(p. 180)**

Monopoly refers to a market composed of a single firm with pricing power sufficient to set the marketplace price for all products or services. **(p. 180)**

Motivation is the set of conditions that creates a drive toward a particular action to fulfill a need or want. **(p. 87)**

MRO products are products used in the maintenance, repair, and operation of a business, for example, nails, oil, or paint. **(p. 165)**

Multichannel conflict refers to conflict between different types of channels. **(p. 201)**

Multichannel distribution channel is a system where the consumer has multiple locations to purchase the product. **(p. 200)**

Multinational companies are companies that maintain assets and operations in more than one country and concentrate on adapting products and services to the specific needs of each country. **(p. 55)**

N

Nationalization is the transfer of control or ownership of private property to the government. **(p. 57)**

Need is a necessity to meet an urgent requirement. **(p. 3)**

Needs segmentation allocates consumers into groups, based on their product or service needs. **(p. 134)**

Negotiated price is the result of a back-and-forth discussion between a buyer and seller regarding the final price of a product or service. **(p. 186)**

Network television refers to the broadcast of programming and paid advertising through a nationwide series of affiliate TV stations. **(p. 259)**

New product development is the process of creating, planning, testing, and commercializing products. **(p. 165)**

Niche marketing is serving a small but well-defined consumer segment. **(p. 137)**

Noise is anything that might distort, block, or otherwise prevent the message from being properly encoded, sent, decoded, received, and/or comprehended. **(p. 225)**

Nominal scale is a measurement in which numbers are assigned to characteristics of objects or groups of objects solely for identifying the objects. **(p. 103)**

Nongovernmental organizations (NGOs) are groups of private individuals that monitor the behavior of marketers or governments. **(p. 39)**

Nonprobability sample is a procedure where each member of a population does not have an equal chance, or, in some cases, any chance, of being selected to a sample. **(p. 105)**

Nonsampling error is any bias that emerges in the study for any reason other than sampling error. **(p. 105)**

Nonstore retailing involves the sale of products through the use of vending machines, self-serve kiosks, the Internet, and smart phone applications. **(p. 213)**

Non-tariff barriers (NTBs) are restrictions on imports that are not in the usual form of a tariff. **(p. 56)**

Norms are standards of behaviors imparted to members of a particular group that define membership. **(p. 89)**

North American Free Trade Agreement (NAFTA) is a trading partnership among the United States, Canada, and Mexico. **(p. 56)**

North American Industrial Classification System (NAICS) classifies businesses operating in the United States, Canada, and Mexico into groups based on their activities. **(p. 20)**

O

Odd-even pricing is a practice that sets prices at fractional numbers, instead of whole ones. **(p. 184)**

Off-price retailers sell name-brand products at prices 20% to 50% less than specialty or department stores by acquiring closeout merchandise, production overruns, or factory seconds. **(p. 212)**

Offshoring is a type of outsourcing in which business activities are completed in another country. **(p. 55)**

Oligopoly refers to a market composed of a small group of firms that share pricing power sufficient to set the marketplace price for their products or services. **(p. 180)**

Online pricing is the process of setting prices for products or services sold over the Internet or through an electronic medium. **(p. 189)**

Open-ended question is a question that allows for unrestricted survey responses. **(p. 105)**

Opinion leaders are those individuals who have the greatest influence on the attitudes and behaviors of a particular group. **(p. 89)**

Ordinal scale is a measurement in which numbers are assigned to characteristics of objects or groups of objects to reflect the order of the objects. **(p. 103)**

Organic foods are foods grown naturally without the use of pesticides or synthetic fertilizers. **(p. 43)**

Out-of-home (OOH), or display, advertising includes media types that are encountered outside the home, such as billboards, signs, and posters. **(p. 258)**

Outbound logistics controls the movement of products from points of production (factories or service delivery points) to consumers. **(p. 202)**

Outdoor boards are large ad display panels, usually near highways or other heavily trafficked locations. **(p. 260)**

Outside lists consist of consumer information compiled by an outside company and rented to a marketer. **(p. 247)**

Outside sales are salespeople who meet face-to-face with customers and prospects. **(p. 243)**

Outsourcing is procuring certain services from third-party suppliers to decrease labor costs, access human capital not readily available within the business, or implement specific strategies. **(pp. 55, 117)**

P

Parliamentary democracy is a political system in which the legislature (parliament) selects the government—a prime minister, premier, or chancellor along with the cabinet ministers—according to party strength as expressed in elections; by this system, the government acquires a dual responsibility to the people as well as to the parliament. **(p. 58)**

Pay-for-performance compensation strategy is the compensation system in which salespeople are paid based on the amount of sales or profits they deliver to the company. **(p. 245)**

Penetration price is a price that is set low to maximize volume and market share. **(p. 188)**

Penetration strategy is the process of offering a product at a low price to maximize sales volume and market share. **(p. 172)**

Percentage of sales method is a method of setting the advertising budget where the size of the budget is based on a percentage of sales. **(p. 229)**

Perception is a cognitive impression of incoming stimuli that influences the individual's actions and behavior. **(p. 87)**

Perceptual map defines the market, based on consumer perceptions of attributes of competing products. **(p. 140)**

Perishability recognizes that a service cannot be stored for later use and must be consumed upon delivery. **(p. 163)**

Personal selling is when a representative of a company interacts directly with a customer to inform and persuade him or her to make a purchase decision about a product or service. **(p. 239)**

Personal selling process is a set of activities that salespeople follow in acquiring new customers. **(p. 241)**

Personality involves a sense of consistency, internal causality, and personal distinctiveness. **(p. 85)**

Persuasive advertising entices consumers to increase brand preference by communicating unique product or service benefits. **(p. 228)**

Physical distribution is the process of moving finished goods to customers through various transportation modes. **(p. 204)**

Physical functions are activities that enable the flow of goods from manufacturer to consumer. **(p. 9)**

Pipeline is a transportation mode used for liquids such as oil or natural gas. **(p. 205)**

Place strategy identifies where, how, and when products and services are made available to target consumers. **(p. 33)**

Placement is the implementation of the media plan via the purchased media vehicles. **(p. 264)**

Planning process is the series of steps businesses take to determine how they will achieve their goals. **(p. 27)**

Political environment includes factors that select national leadership, create laws, and provide a process for discourse on a wide range of issues. **(p. 18)**

Population is the total group of individuals who meet the criteria that is being studied. **(p. 105)**

Portfolio analysis is the process a business uses to evaluate the different combinations of products and services that the business offers based on its objectives. **(p. 29)**

Portfolio management comprises all of the decisions a company makes regarding its portfolio of current and future products. It involves deciding which products to add, keep, and remove from the overall product portfolio. **(p. 169)**

Positioning is the placement of a product or service offering in the minds of consumer targets. **(p. 139)**

Post-industrial economies are countries where the manufacturing sector diminishes while service and information sectors become the primary sources of economic growth. **(p. 57)**

Posters are smaller than outdoor boards and are frequently used at bus or train stops. **(p. 260)**

Predatory pricing occurs when a firm sells its products at a low price to drive competitors out of the market. **(p. 185)**

Price is the exchange value of a product or service in the marketplace. **(p. 179)**

Price bundling occurs when two or more items are priced at a single, combined price instead of individually. **(p. 184)**

Price ceiling is the price all products in a product line must be priced below. **(p. 190)**

Price discrimination occurs when a firm injures competition by charging different prices to different members of its distribution channel. **(p. 185)**

Price elasticity is the measure of a percentage change in quantity demanded for a product, relative to a percentage change in its price. **(p. 183)**

Price fixing occurs when two or more companies discuss prices in an effort to raise the market price for their products. **(p. 185)**

Price floor is the price above which all products in a product line must be priced. **(p. 190)**

Price lining (or **tiered pricing, versioning**) is a strategy used to create different prices for different, but related, products or services. **(p. 189)**

Price–quality ratio is the ratio between the price of a product and its perceived quality. **(p. 180)**

Price war occurs when businesses cut prices to take sales from competitors. **(pp. 117, 191)**

Pricing objectives are goals that keep marketing actions in alignment with overall business objectives. **(p. 187)**

Pricing power is the ability of a firm to establish a higher price than its competitors without losing significant market share. **(p. 180)**

Pricing practices are considerations (such as legal requirements or bidding practices) that must be taken into account when establishing a price for a product or service. **(p. 184)**

Pricing strategy identifies what a business will charge for its products or services. **(pp. 33, 187)**

Primary data is information that is collected to address a current research question. **(p. 100)**

Print media include newspapers, magazines, and direct mail. **(p. 258)**

Privacy policy is a company's practice as it relates to renting customer information to other companies. **(p. 250)**

Private label brand is a brand owned by a reseller or retailer. **(p. 121)**

Private label products are store brand items that offer higher profit margins for retailers than name brand products. **(p. 214)**

Privatization is the transfer of government functions to the private sector that creates new business opportunities. **(p. 57)**

Probability sample is a procedure where each member of a population has a known and nonzero chance of possibly being selected to a sample. **(p. 105)**

Processed materials and services are products or services used in the production of finished products or services, for example, lumber, steel, or market research. **(p. 165)**

Product design is a product's style, tactile appeal, and usability. **(p. 167)**

Product life cycle (PLC) is the model that describes the evolution of a product's sales and profits throughout its lifetime. The stages of the product life cycle are as follows: Introduction, Growth, Maturity, and Decline. **(p. 171)**

Product line is a group of closely related products. **(p. 169)**

Product mix depth is the number of versions of products within a product line. **(p. 169)**

Product mix length is the total number of products a company offers. **(p. 169)**

Product mix width is the number of product lines a company offers. **(p. 169)**

Product placement is an arrangement in which the company has its brand or product appear in a movie or other entertainment vehicle. **(p. 233)**

Product portfolio (also called a **product mix**) is the collection of all products and services offered by a company. **(p. 169)**

Product strategy identifies the product and service portfolio, including packaging, branding, and warranty for its target market. **(p. 33)**

Product style is the visual and aesthetic appearance of a product. **(p. 167)**

Production orientation reflects a business focus on efficient production and distribution with little emphasis on any marketing strategy. **(p. 6)**

Products are items used or consumed for personal or business use. **(p. 163)**

Profit margin is the difference between the price of a product and its total cost per unit. **(p. 181)**

Promotion strategy identifies how a business communicates product or service benefits and value to its target market. **(p. 33)**

Promotional pricing is the strategy of using price as a promotional tool to drive customer awareness and sales. **(p. 185)**

Prospecting is the process of researching multiple sources to find potential customers or prospects. **(p. 241)**

Psychographic segmentation assigns buyers into different groups, based on lifestyle, class, or personality characteristics. **(p. 133)**

Psychology involves the study of the mind. **(p. 83)**

Public relations is two-way communication to improve mutual understanding and positively influence relationships between the marketer and its internal and external publics. **(p. 233)**

Publicity is generating unpaid, positive media coverage about a company or its products. **(p. 233)**

Publics are the target audiences of public relations; the people inside or outside the company who have a "stake" in what it does. **(p. 233)**

Puffery refers to claims of product superiority that cannot be proven as true or false. **(p. 45)**

Pull strategy promotes products directly to consumers, who then request the product from retailers. Retailers in turn request the product from the wholesaler, who orders it from the manufacturer. **(p. 256)**

Purchase funnel is a sequential consumer decision-making model encompassing awareness to loyalty. **(p. 291)**

Purchasing power parity (PPP) is the model of exchange rate determination stating that the price of a good or service in one country should equal the price of the same good or service in another country, exchanged at the current rate. **(p. 55)**

Pure competition refers to a market composed of a large number of firms that together lack sufficient pricing power to influence the market price for their products. **(p. 180)**

Pure research attempts to expand understanding of the unknown. **(p. 99)**

Push strategy targets wholesalers and retailers and encourages them to order the product, thus pushing it through the channel to consumers. **(p. 256)**

Q

Qualitative research is a collection of techniques designed to identify and interpret information obtained through the observation of people. **(p. 101)**

Quantitative research is a process to collect a large number of responses using a standardized questionnaire where the results can be summarized into numbers for statistical analysis. **(p. 101)**

Quantity discount is a discount per item purchased that is given to customers buying a larger quantity of a product. **(p. 190)**

Question Marks are products or services with low relative market share in a sector with high growth. **(p. 30)**

Questionnaire is an organized set of questions that a researcher desires that respondents answer. **(p. 104)**

Quotas are limits on the amount of product that can be imported into a country. **(pp. 56, 186)**

Quotation is a supplier's response to an RFQ from a potential customer. **(p. 186)**

R

Rate cards are officially published prices for different types of media. **(p. 264)**

Ratings are the percentage of the total available audience watching a TV show or tuned in to a radio program. **(p. 259)**

Ratio scale is a measurement in which the numbers assigned to the characteristics of the objects have an identifiable absolute zero. **(p. 104)**

Raw materials are unfinished products that are processed for use in the manufacture of a finished product, for example, wood, wheat, or iron ore. **(p. 165)**

Raw materials exporting economies are countries that are plentiful in a particular raw material, yet deficient in other resources, and rely on the export of that raw material for the majority of revenue. **(p. 57)**

Reach is a measure of the number of people who could potentially receive an ad through a particular media vehicle. **(pp. 229, 259)**

Rebate is a cash payment made back to a customer who has purchased his or her products at full price. **(p. 191)**

Reference group consists of people who directly or indirectly influence how an individual feels about a particular topic. **(p. 89)**

Regulations are rules or orders issued by an official government agency with proper authority and which carry the force of law. **(p. 44)**

Reinforcement is a reduction in drive resulting from a positive response experience. **(p. 87)**

Relationship marketing is the process of developing and enhancing long-term relationships with profitable customers. **(p. 74)**

Relationship orientation reflects a business focus on creating value-added relationships with suppliers and consumers. **(p. 6)**

Reliability is the level of consistency of a measurement. **(p. 105)**

Reminder advertising keeps a known product or service in the mind of consumers. **(p. 228)**

Request for quote (RFQ) is a document a buyer sends to a potential supplier that outlines the criteria for the goods or services to be purchased. **(p. 186)**

Research is the studious inquiry or examination; especially: investigation or experimentation aimed at the discovery and interpretation of facts, revision of accepted theories or laws in the light of new facts, or practical application of such new or revised theories or laws. **(p. 99)**

Research design is a framework or plan for a study that guides the collection and analysis of the data. **(p. 101)**

Research question is the question the research is designed to answer. **(p. 100)**

Response is a consumer's reaction to his or her drive and cues. **(p. 87)**

Retail margin is the difference between a product's retail selling price and its wholesale cost. **(p. 214)**

Retail marketing mix consists of the product, price, place, and promotion of merchandise by a retailer. **(p. 214)**

Retail strategies are the decisions to be made regarding the establishment and ongoing operations of a retailer. **(p. 214)**

Retailers are businesses whose primary source of revenue is generated through retailing. **(p. 211)**

Retailing is the activities involved in the sale of products to consumers for their personal, nonbusiness use. **(p. 211)**

Return on marketing investment (ROMI) is the impact on business performance resulting from executing specific marketing activities. **(pp. 33, 293)**

Reverse auction is a market in which a buyer states what he or she is seeking to purchase, as well as the price he or she is willing to pay. **(p. 189)**

Reverse logistics addresses the methods consumers use to send products backward through a channel for return or repair. **(p. 202)**

RFID (radio frequency identification) is an electronic chip and an antenna that can identify the precise physical location of a product. **(p. 205)**

Risk is the potential for loss of investment. **(p. 57)**

Roles are specific actions expected from someone in a group as a member or from a particular position held. **(p. 89)**

Routine response problem solving occurs when a consumer has a well-developed process associated with fulfilling a need or want. **(p. 91)**

S

Sales branches maintain inventory for companies in different geographic areas. **(p. 219)**

Sales management is the process of planning, implementing, and controlling the personal selling function. **(p. 243)**

Sales management process is a comprehensive approach used by sales managers to determine how the sales force is organized and managed and how they will hire, recruit, manage, motivate, and evaluate the performance of the individual salespeople. **(p. 244)**

Sales offices carry no inventory but provide selling services for specific geographic areas. **(p. 219)**

Sales orientation reflects a business focus on advertising and personal selling to create demand and move product inventory. **(p. 6)**

Sales presentation is the formal meeting between a salesperson and a sales prospect. **(p. 242)**

Sales promotion is marketer-controlled communication to stimulate immediate audience response by enhancing the value of an offering for a limited time. **(p. 231)**

Sample is a specific part of the population that is selected to represent the population. **(p. 105)**

Sample error refers to any differences between the sample results and the actual results that would emerge from a census of the population. **(p. 105)**

Sample plan identifies who will be sampled, how many people will be sampled, and the procedure that will be used for sampling. **(p. 105)**

Sampling procedure involves selecting either a probability sample or a nonprobability sample as part of your sample plan. **(p. 105)**

Sarbanes-Oxley Act is a law passed in 2002 mandating organizational leaders from publicly traded companies take responsibility for their business practices. **(p. 285)**

Scatter buys are ads that are not purchased in advance via an upfront market, but are secured on a quarterly basis. **(p. 264)**

Search engine optimization is the process of enhancing Web site traffic through either organic or compensated means. **(p. 140)**

Search marketing is the optimization of Web site keywords and marketing agreements with search engines to drive traffic to Web sites. **(p. 261)**

Secondary data is information that has been previously collected for another purpose. **(p. 100)**

Segmentation (also referred to as **market segmentation**) is the division of consumer markets into meaningful and distinct customer groups. **(p. 131)**

Segmentation base is a group of characteristics that is used to assign segment members. **(p. 133)**

Selective distribution refers to the distribution of products in relatively few locations. **(p. 200)**

Self-identity is the understanding by an individual that he or she is unique. **(p. 85)**

Self-service retailers provide a minimal level of service and contact between customers and employees. **(p. 214)**

Selling agents are independent agents who take responsibility for a wide range of marketing activities in addition to sales functions. **(p. 219)**

Services are activities that deliver benefits to consumers or businesses. **(p. 163)**

Shipper is the owner of goods being distributed. **(p. 204)**

Shopping products are products that are purchased with a moderate amount of shopping effort, for example, clothing, linens, housewares. **(p. 164)**

Significant problem solving occurs when a consumer is prepared to commit considerable effort to make a purchase decision. **(p. 91)**

Skimming price is a price that is set high in order to maximize revenue and profit. **(p. 188)**

Skimming strategy is the process of offering a product at a high price to maximize return. **(p. 172)**

Social and cultural environment includes factors that relate marketing to the needs and wants of society and culture. **(p. 17)**

Social classes are characteristics that distinguish certain members of a society from others, based on a variety of factors, including wealth, vocation, education, power, place of residence, and ancestry. **(p. 90)**

Social marketing concept asserts that marketing techniques may be employed for more than selling things and making a profit. **(p. 46)**

Social networks, such as Facebook and MySpace, connect people with common interests and those who are looking to make friends online. **(p. 261)**

Social psychology is the process to understand social phenomena and their influence on social behavior. **(p. 83)**

Social responsibility refers to a concern for how a person's (or company's) actions might affect the interests of others. **(p. 46)**

Society refers to a community, nation, or group that shares common traditions, institutions, activities, and interests. **(p. 39)**

Specialty line wholesalers focus on a single product line, such as health food, and may cover a wide geographic area. **(p. 218)**

Specialty products are products with unique characteristics that are purchased with a high degree of shopping effort, for example, luxury items, vacations, and homes. **(p. 164)**

Specialty stores concentrate on satisfying the specific needs of a select group of customers. **(p. 211)**

Spill-in occurs when ads from outside a test market "spill into" the test market area. **(p. 266)**

Spill-out happens whenever ads meant for a test market "spill out" and touch people in adjacent markets. **(p. 266)**

Sponsorship is a way of publicly associating a brand with an event or activity that the company supports financially. **(p. 234)**

Stars represent products or services with high growth and high market share. **(p. 30)**

Status is the relative position of one individual relative to others. **(p. 89)**

Sticker price (MSRP [manufacturer's suggested retail price]) is the quoted or official price for a product. **(p. 186)**

Stock-keeping unit (SKU) is a unique identification number used to track and organize products. **(p. 205)**

Storefront pricing (also called **offline pricing**) refers to prices established for products or services sold through traditional sales channels like grocery stores, mass merchandisers, or other "brick and mortar" businesses. **(p. 189)**

Strategic planning determines the overall goals of the business and the steps the business will take to achieve those goals. **(p. 29)**

Strong brand occupies a distinct position in consumers' minds based on relevant benefits and creates an emotional connection between businesses and consumers. **(p. 120)**

Structured interviews are a series of discussions held between a trained interviewer and individuals, on a one-on-one basis, recruited by specific criteria, with the purpose to discuss predetermined topics. **(p. 102)**

Subcultures are groups of people, within a broader society, who share similar behaviors and values. **(p. 88)**

Subliminal perception is the processing of stimuli by a recipient who is not aware of the stimuli being received. **(p. 87)**

Subsistence economies are agrarian societies where enough is grown, hunted, and crafted to provide for the essential needs of the people and any surplus is bartered for basic goods and services. **(p. 57)**

Superstores are the combination of a discount store and a grocery store. **(p. 213)**

Supply chain management is the management of all firms or organizations, both inside and outside a company, that impact the distribution process. **(p. 202)**

Sustainability is a term used to describe practices that combine economic growth with careful stewardship of our natural resources and the environment. **(p. 46)**

SWOT analysis is a tool that helps identify business strengths, weaknesses, opportunities, and threats. **(p. 33)**

Symbolic positioning is based on characteristics of the brand that enhance the self-esteem of customers. **(p. 139)**

Syndicated research is information collected on a regular basis using standardized procedures and sold to multiple customers from a related industry. **(p. 101)**

Systems are groups of interacting related parts that perform a specific function. **(p. 27)**

T

Tactical planning is the process of developing actions for various functions within a business to support implementing a business's strategic plan. **(p. 29)**

Taking title refers to the practice of a wholesaler taking ownership of the products it purchases. **(p. 217)**

Target market is a group of consumers that a business determines to be the most viable for its products or services. **(p. 33)**

Targeting (also referred to as **market targeting**) is the process of evaluating and selecting the most viable market segment to enter. **(p. 136)**

Tariff is a schedule of duties (or fees) applied to goods and services from foreign countries. **(pp. 56, 186)**

Task-and-objective is an approach to media budgeting that allocates dollars sufficient to attain media objectives. **(p. 263)**

Technological environment includes factors that influence marketing, based on scientific actions and innovation. **(p. 18)**

Telemarketing is a phone call placed to a specific consumer to offer products or services for sale. **(p. 249)**

Third-party logistics company (3PL) manages all or part of another company's supply chain logistics. **(p. 202)**

Time-shifting is the practice of recording a television program at one time to replay it at another. **(p. 259)**

Total cost is the sum of fixed and variable costs. **(p. 180)**

Totalitarianism is a form of government that seeks to subordinate the individual to the state by controlling not only all political and economic matters, but also the attitudes, values, and beliefs of its population. **(p. 58)**

Trade agreements are treaties between countries to create a free trade area where business can be conducted without tariffs or other barriers. **(p. 56)**

Trade deficits occur when the value of imports exceeds the value of exports. **(p. 56)**

Trade-in is the cash value given to a customer when he or she offers his or her own product in trade toward a new purchase. **(p. 190)**

Trade promotions are incentives offered to retailers and wholesalers that take the form of discounts or allowances. **(p. 231)**

Trade surpluses occur when the value of exports exceeds the value of imports. **(p. 56)**

Transit advertising appears on and inside buses, in air terminals, in taxis, and wherever people are being transported from one place to another. **(p. 260)**

Transportation management systems (TMS) are software programs used to automate the shipping process. **(p. 205)**

Trial close is a sales closing technique to gauge a prospect's interest in buying. **(p. 242)**

Turnover rate is the percentage of the sales force that leaves a company per year **(p. 239)**

U

Undifferentiated marketing is when a company treats the market as a whole, focusing on what is common to the needs of customers rather than on what is different. **(p. 137)**

Unemployment levels are the number of unemployed persons divided by the aggregate labor force. **(p. 17)**

Unique selling proposition (USP) is an expression of the uniqueness of a brand. **(p. 139)**

United States Patent and Trademark Office (USPTO) is a federal agency responsible for assigning rights for limited times to individuals or companies to use innovations. **(p. 125)**

Universal Product Code (or **UPC**) is the standard format for retail bar codes. **(p. 205)**

Unsought products are products that consumers do not usually search for without an immediate problem or prompting, for example, life insurance, funerals, or legal services. **(p. 164)**

Upfront markets are long-lead marketplaces where TV networks and advertisers negotiate media prices for the fourth quarter of the current year plus the first three quarters of the following year. **(p. 264)**

User-generated content such as social networks (for example, Facebook or MySpace), user blogs, and filesharing (for example, Flickr and Snapfish) are sources of word-of-mouth communications and advertising. **(p. 261)**

Utility is the satisfaction received from owning or consuming a product or service. **(p. 3)**

V

Validity is the strength of a conclusion. **(p. 105)**

Value is the benefits that exceed the cost of products, services, or other items. **(p. 3)**

Value map is a graphical representation of the ratio between customers' perceived benefits and the perceived total cost of a product. **(p. 69)**

Values segmentation considers what customers prefer and what motivates customer response to marketing activities. **(p. 134)**

Variability recognizes that service quality may vary from experience to experience. **(p. 163)**

Variable costs are costs directly attributable to the production of a product or the delivery of a service. **(p. 180)**

Vending machines sell a wide range of products including soft drinks, snacks, hot and cold meals, gumballs, and toys. **(p. 213)**

Vertical conflict refers to conflict between channel members at different levels in a channel (e.g., a wholesaler and a retailer). **(p. 201)**

Vertical Marketing System (VMS) is a channel that is vertically integrated based on acquisition or formal agreement, or by a firm developing its own distribution capabilities. **(p. 200)**

Viral marketing is activities that encourage consumers to share a company's marketing message with friends. **(p. 227)**

W

Want is a desire for something that is not essential. **(p. 3)**

Warehouse is a physical facility used primarily for the storage of goods held in anticipation of sale or transfer within the marketing channel. **(p. 205)**

Warehouse clubs carry a limited selection of merchandise in large quantities that deliver higher value for customers and greater unit volume for manufacturers. **(p. 212)**

Wholesalers are firms that purchase products from manufacturers and resell them to retailers and industry buyers. **(p. 217)**

Wholesaling is the sorting, storing, and reselling of products to retailers or businesses. **(p. 217)**

Word of mouth is communication between consumers about a brand, marketing offer, or marketing message. **(p. 226)**

World Trade Organization (WTO) was established in 1995 as the preeminent organization dealing with the rules of trade at a global or near-global level. **(p. 56)**

Z

Zero-sum game is when one or more parties benefit to the same degree as one or more other parties lose. **(p. 60)**

Index

COMPANY INDEX

NAME INDEX

SUBJECT INDEX

Page numbers with *f* indicate figures; those with *t* indicate tables.